MW01113739

A History of Phuket
And The Surrounding Region

A History of Phuket

And The Surrounding Region

Colin Robert Mackay

White Lotus

First edition published in 2012 by

White Lotus Co Ltd.
G. P. O. Box 1141
Bangkok 10501
Thailand

Sale: 081-558-3234
Tel: (66) 0-38239-883-4
Fax: (66) 0-38239-885
Email: ande@loxinfo.co.th
www.whitelotuspress.com

www.HISTORYOFPHUKET.COM

Printed in Thailand by:
Amarin Printing & Publishing Public Company Limited
376 Chaiyaphruk Road, Taling Chan, Bangkok 10170
Tel: 0-2882-1010, 0-2422-9000   Fax: 0-2433-2742, 0-2434-1385

ISBN 978 974 480 195 1   White Lotus Co Ltd.; Bangkok
iv

Preface

When I embarked on writing this book on Phuket's history one skeptical local quipped, "That'll be a short book." This attitude is fairly common among Phuket's visitors and residents, most of whom are blissfully unaware of the long, ancient and colorful history of Phuket Island and its surrounding region.

At times this history may seem as though it is told from the poop deck of a foreign ship rather than from the vantage point of a local. This is mainly because comparatively few old Thai historical records were kept and even fewer have survived. Therefore it was the European, Chinese, Indian and Middle Eastern visitors over the centuries who have left the most, and in many periods the only, historical records about Phuket and the central peninsula region.

The philosopher Immanuel Kant lamented that "From the crooked timbers of humanity no straight thing shall come." I hold a similarly sardonic view of human nature but I have tried to be balanced in showing the flaws of everyone involved in this story, Thais, Malays and foreigners alike. I personally have no axe to grind against the Thais, but many of the foreign records do have an anti-Thai bias to them. In using such quotes and writings directly I'm simply trying to re-tell this story as the various visitors, commentators and diarists recorded it at the time.

I do take a fairly broad-brush approach to the subject matter as I feel that one can't just look at events on Phuket in isolation but should be aware of the larger historical context they occurred in. Also in many earlier periods there are so few records about Phuket itself that one can only use information from nearby areas to try to flesh out our knowledge about what may have been going on in Phuket.

I recommend the reader not to cherry-pick amongst the various chapters but to start at the beginning and read to the end as in each chapter I presume the reader is already aware of the names, facts and information given in previous chapters. I stand most ready and anxious to have my facts challenged or improved upon where possible, as such dialogue will create further awareness of and a better resource for Phuket's history and hopefully this can become a forum for more discovery and dissemination of a bigger and better pool of local historical knowledge.

My thanks go to several people for their assistance with this book: the inimitable Pranee Sakulpipatana ('Ajarn Pranee') for her enthusiasm and support. The late Rachan Karn-chanawanit and Sakul Na Nakorn for their local wisdom and knowledge. Susan Faircloth the editor whose editorial professionalism kept me relentlessly on the straight and narrow. St John Mackay for his endless assistance and book layout; Alasdair Forbes for the first edit; the librarians at the Siam Society library, Bangkok. Lastly, thanks to my wife for putting up with me taking many research trips over the years and shutting myself in my study leaving her to bear the brunt of the demands of our two spirited young daughters.

Photographs: for assistance with the photographs I would especially like to thank Pranee Sakulpipatana for allowing me access to her wonderful private collection and also to Capt. Boonyarit Chaisuwan of the fine arts department. My thanks to St John Mackay for his photo editing and also to Jeroen Deknatel, Martyn Rolton, Wally Sudik, Robin Plant, Andy Dowden and Heath Norris for their photos and proof reading.

Front cover picture: The cover picture is from a painting done in 1983 by the Thai artist Nab Tichinpong of Nakorn Sri Thammarat. It is one of a collection of four paintings about Thao Thepkasatri, (Lady Chan). It was commissioned by governor Manit Walyapetch, the only local Phuketian to serve as governor of Phuket since Thailand was formed in 1939. The other governors have been posted to Phuket from other provinces. The four paintings are on display at the Sala Prachakom opposite the Governors house in Phuket. The Sala Prachakom was built with a donation from the Vanich Family and I extend my thanks to Ajarn Pranee and Anchalee Vanich and the staff of Sala Prachakom for allowing me to use this picture on the cover.

Colin Robert Mackay M.A.
Phuket, 2012

Contents

Part 5: The 18th Century

Part 6: The 19th Century

Part 7: The 20th Century

Time Line

Events Around Phuket		World Events
Negroes displaced by Mongoloids (Hoabinhians)	30K BC - 1 AD	Civilizations start and develop
Small Indianized kingdoms arise, Funan is overlord	1 AD - 650	Zenith of the Roman Empire
Srivijaya dominates the peninsula, then invasion and...	700	Islam and Christianity spread
... rule by Chola Tamils, Sri Lankans and Burmese	1100	The Viking and Norman era
Tambralinga rules Phuket and invades Sri Lanka	1250s	The Medieval and Crusades era
Thais conquer and dominate the central peninsula	1300s	The Mongols rule in China
Islam arrives, Ayutthaya and Malacca wars	1450s	European Renaissance starts
The Portuguese arrive in the peninsula and Phuket	1511	Spain colonizes the Americas
English and Dutch fight over peninsular trade	1600s	Ottoman Empire era
Dutch try to control Phuket, local resistance strong	1640s	The English Civil War
The governing Tamils are massacred	1678	Piracy is rife in Caribbean
Phuket is run by French governors	1680s	Russia becomes powerful
French military expedition against Phuket fails	1688	Mughal Empire unifies India
Ayutthaya destroyed, Sultan of Keddah takes Phuket	1765	Cook starts exploring the Pacific
King Tak Sin brings Phuket back under Siam	1774	American War of Independence
Light and Scott try to make Phuket a British colony	1780s	The Industrial Revolution starts
Burmese invade Phuket, the heroine sisters defend it	1785	The French Revolution era starts
Burmese conquer Phuket, the island is deserted	1810	The Napoleonic Wars in Europe
Britain takes Tenasserim, Phuket becomes safer	1820	US Asia trade starts (clippers)
Tin mining and heavy Chinese immigration begins	1830s	British Victorian era
Violent Chinese miners rebellion in Phuket	1870	The American Civil War era
Phraya Rassada is governor. Phuket town develops	1900	Germany is a new power in Europe
Rubber trees, mining dredgers are introduced	1904	Japan becomes a Pacific power
The 1932 revolution, then Phibun forms Thailand	1932	Hitler takes power in Germany
Japan invades and ocuppies Phuket	1942	US enters the Pacific War
Tin mining declines and tourism industry grows	1970s	Global tourism becomes mass market

PART I

From Ancient Times until 1500

Geology and Early Men

The Geology of Phuket and Phang Nga

For millions of years India has been drifting northeast at a healthy jaunt of around 10 centimeters per year. About 40 million years ago it bumped into Asia causing it to crumple upwards in a huge semicircle around the impact point, forcing Nepal, Tibet and the Himalayas high into the air where they remain today. To the east the impact folded the land into the high mountains of Yunnan and Burma, which gradually taper down southwards through Thailand to form the verdant and now heavily jungled hills of the Malay Peninsula and Phuket.

Tin, which, as we shall see, was the main lifeblood of Phuket's economy for centuries, is contained inside the granite that folded up out of the sea after the collision with India, which created Phuket's central hills. As these giant granite slabs have gradually eroded away over millions of years, the heavier tin has been washed out of the decomposing granite and settled in large deposits in the streams, valley floors, lowlands and parts of the shallow coastal seabed around Phuket.

Phang Nga Bay and Krabi have a different geology. They owe their majestic scenery to a vast and ancient coral reef that grew up some 200 million years ago when the sea level was over 300 meters higher than today. This gargantuan reef, the biggest the world has ever known, ran all the way from Sumatra up the Malay Peninsula, across central Thailand, Laos and Vietnam to as far north as Guilin in China. As the world's sea levels subsequently fell, this huge coral reef was left projecting high and dry in the air. When coral dies it forms limestone which is easily eroded by rainwater, so this great reef is now eroding and large chunks remain standing starkly upright, jutting so strikingly out of the surrounding sea and green forests of Phang Nga Bay and Krabi.

The Indian tectonic plate is still moving northeast, now grinding and subsiding underneath Sundaland (which is the tectonic plate that holds Southeast Asia). This fault line between the Sundaland and Indian plates runs up just west of Sumatra, past the Andaman Islands and on to Burma. It was yet another small adjustment along this fault line that caused the huge tsunami waves on December 26, 2004 that killed an estimated 250,000 people around the Indian Ocean region and left well over 750 dead or missing on Phuket.

The First Humans

The consensus of opinion is that around 100,000 years ago troops of muzzle-faced, hairy-ish, black-skinned humans started walking out of Africa into Arabia. Over the next 50,000 years, moving with a lolloping gait, small bands of these hairy black humans spread all over Asia as far as Japan, Fiji and Australia. They probably first took up residence in some of the commodious and inviting limestone caves of Phang Nga and Krabi provinces some 60,000 years ago.

As these black humans spread around Asia they suffered from what scientists call "small population syndrome", that is, they were spread out so thinly they interbred and started to evolve differently. One group, in the Caucasus Mountains of Iran, evolved into the Caucasian people, also known as the Aryan peoples (as in "from Iran"). Some of them later moved north into the freezing climes of Europe and turned white and blond like other Arctic animals. Other Aryans moved south to populate the Indian subcontinent, keeping their black hair and dark skins but with Aryan looks.

In Mongolia, probably as a result of being cut off by a freezing period of glaciation, the humans there also developed milky white skin, thinner eyes and smaller noses against the freezing air and became the Mongoloid peoples. They have since spread out around most of Asia and into the Americas.

Negroids and Negritos

The original black-skinned humans who stayed in the tropical zones kept their Negroid features such as wider nostrils for better cooling airflow and their black skin as protection against the burning tropical sun, but they also diversified somewhat to suit their terrain. Some – such as the Fijians or Papuans – grew big while others grew smaller to adapt to living in the tangled tropical jungles. While the larger Papuan-type Negroes have now disappeared from the Malay Peninsula, the smaller Negroes, known today as Negritos, still remain in the peninsula and in the Philippines, In-

1.1. A Negrito family group: Tribes of Negrito and Negro hunter-gatherers like these were the first inhabitants of Phuket and the whole Malay Peninsula.

donesia and the Andaman and Nicobar Islands west of Phuket. Reclusive in their diminishing forest or mountain domains, they are presumed to be the peninsula's oldest existing inhabitants.

The nearest remaining Negrito tribe to Phuket today are the Mani people, who live just a few hours' drive away in the forests of Trang, Satun and Phattalung. While the Negritos' small size made them adept at moving through the tangled forests, it also made them less good at fighting other, larger, humans. Therefore the Negritos have always shied away from contact with outsiders.

The most potent defense devised by these little Negritos, who stand only around 1.4 meters tall, came from their discovery of the poison in the sap of the Ipoh tree with which they tipped their spears and blowpipe darts. In Thailand, these trees are called

Yangyong or Nong trees. Their latex contains a strong cardiac glycoside called Antiarin, which enters the bloodstream and stops the heart. To this day there is no known antidote. This weapon provided enough incentive for other humans to keep their distance from these reclusive forest-dwelling Negritos, probably accounting for their continued existence where these trees still grow.

The Hoabinian Period: From Negroids to Mongoloids

Over the last 50,000 years several different ice ages caused great ice sheets to spread over much of China and sometimes as far south as northern Thailand, forcing some of the Mongoloid tribes and peoples to migrate down into Southeast Asia. They filtered south in many waves, a process which is still continuing today. By around 2000 BC they appear to have displaced the Papuan Negroes, who moved away, were exterminated or were absorbed by interbreeding, which, along with the powerful sun, changed the pure white mongoloids of northeast Asia into the duskier-skinned southern Mongoloids such as the Khmers, Mons, Thais and Malays of today. This Mongoloid displacement of the Negroes in the central peninsula occurred from around 30,000 to 5,000 years ago, during what is now called the Hoabinian period.

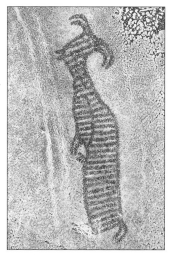

1.2. An ancient cave painting in Phi Hua Toa Cave in Au Luk, Krabi province, but what is it?

Early archaeologists excavating prehistoric cave sites in Southeast Asia in the 1920s noticed a commonality in the chipped stone and bone tools they were finding and decided to call the early humans who had been doing this chipping Hoabinians, after Hoa Binh province in Vietnam where such tools were first discovered. Hoabinian sites have since been found extensively all over Southeast Asia and in most likely looking cave sites in the Malay Peninsula. The oldest known cave dwelling in Southeast Asia to date is the Lang Rongrien cave, just north of Krabi city. This cave, 90 feet up a limestone rock face, was excavated in 1983 and is now a badly kept national park. Artifacts from the burial pits found there have been carbon-dated to 37,000 years BC. Most other likely looking caves in Phang Nga and Krabi have produced Hoabinian artifacts, skeletons and some quite funky cave paintings.

These Hoabinians appear to have started out as large Papuan-type Negroes and ended up as southern Mongoloids. One British Malayan archaeologist tells us, in his 1927 study on skeletons excavated from early dated Hoabinian sites,

> "They seem to have been of commanding stature, six feet or so tall, heavy boned with large skulls and massive jaws and marked brow ridges. Anthropologists who have examined skeletons of these folks have remarked on their similarity to present day Melanesians, such people as those of New Caledonia and the Loyalty islands. "[1]

Yet in later dated Hoabinian site excavations, their skeletons were smaller, teeth structures were reduced and they had become far more similar to those of present-day Mongoloid peoples. By around 4000 BC, or some 6,000 years ago, more sophisticated Hoabinian pottery was being manufactured on the peninsula, such as cooking pots with built-in tripods for placing over the fire. Such pottery, easy to break and difficult to transport, suggests that these Hoabinians were probably no longer wandering hunter-gatherer nomadic bands like the Negritos but had begun settling in one place. This in turn implies that they had domesticated animals, practiced agriculture and had begun trading with each other.

Phuket Island, being granite, has few decent caves. Also, much of the prehistoric evidence on the island has disappeared as, over the past 2,000 years, the valley floors have been extensively churned over by tin miners. Another reason for the dearth of artifacts in Phuket today is that ancient axe heads and other such artifacts were known to the locals as "kwan fa" or "sky axes" and were regarded as mystical items created wherever lightning or rainbows hit the earth. These "kwan fa" were, and in some cases still are, ground down by the locals into a powder and consumed as medicines. Pomchai Sujit noted in a paper he presented at a seminar on Thalang (in Phuket) history in 1985 that the local villagers called these prehistoric items "kwan fa" because "they said they had found the axe heads in areas where they had seen lightning strike and believed they came from the sky. Many such axe heads were found in Kamala, Kathu district".[2]

Walter Burke, a British mining engineer working in Phuket in 1903, also mentioned finding several of these "kwan fa" artifacts and noted, "They are considered to be a most valuable medicine and are powdered and taken as a specific in various ailments. It is therefore difficult to obtain specimens."[3] Yet despite their apparent medicinal and therefore financial value, some Hoabinian pottery and stone axes have remained uneaten and are displayed in the Thalang History Museum today.

The Southern Mongoloids

The early Mongoloid peoples who migrated south can be classed into two main groups: the Malays and the Mon-Khmers. The Malays, it seems, migrated first to the southeastern China coast where they invented the outrigger sailing canoe and lapita farming and embarked on the ancient world's greatest-ever seaborne expansion.

The Malays

Starting some 5,000 years ago, moving eastwards, they crossed the ocean and settled the Philippines and the Pacific Islands as far as Easter Island, some say even as far as Peru. To the west these amazing seafarers settled most of Indonesia and the southern Malay Peninsula and also crossed the Indian Ocean to settle in Madagascar. These Malays, with their superior weapons, farming and fishing techniques, displaced the existing Hoabinians or Papuan Negroes in most places they settled in the region. It is only some isolated islands they missed, such as New Guinea, New Caledonia, Fiji and Australia, which have maintained their larger Papuan-type Negroid populations.

The little Negritos on the Malay Peninsula however, faced with these aggressive new Malay coastal settlers, survived by moving deeper inland into the almost inaccessible interior jungles, where the Malays rarely ventured. The Malays called these Negritos the "Sakai" people, meaning "savage" or "slave" and apparently hunted them to use as slaves or for the sport of it, just as later European settlers hunted the black aborigines of Tasmania into extinction for sport.

The Mon-Khmers

The Mon-Khmer peoples apparently also migrated south from China, but came mainly overland, spreading down through Laos, Thailand, Burma and Cambodia. They devised wet rice farming, creating a staple food supply; their agriculture and domestication of other plants and animals saw their populations swell so they also gradually displaced the Negroes where they settled. These Mon tribes moving down the Malay Peninsula probably reached Phuket by around 5000 BC. Some would have settled in the flat, swampy Thalang area in the middle of the island where they could cultivate wet rice. Some became proficient at fishing and boat building and started traveling by sea, as this was easier and safer than moving through the dense, almost impenetrable ancient jungles, which abounded with nasty animals, reptiles, insects and evil spirits.

These seagoing Mons slept and lived on their boats for security. The numerous offshore islands and bays around Phuket offered plentiful food and shelter from storms, predatory animals and other predatory humans. These different tribes of "boat people" or "Sea Gypsies" moved up and down the peninsular west coast trading with other land and riverine settlements, bartering their sea products for rice, animals and tools or raiding them. These itinerant Sea Gypsies were called the "Selang" or "Selate" (meaning Straits) people by the Malays and are still known in south Burma by these terms today. They are presumed to be the most ancient inhabitants still living on Phuket Island today. One 17th-century visiting European sailor wrote of them,

> "They dwell on the water in boats covered with mats, they are not disturbed by their brutal solitude, the ill air or the dreadfulness of the neighboring woods. They are ingenious at fishing, which they live on … they are so mistrustful but upon any slight strike their spear in any man's body."[4]

The Naming of Phuket

The Malay seafarers and settlers who reached the western peninsular coast probably first encountered these Mon "Selang" or Selat boat people around Phuket. At that time Phuket was most likely still joined to the mainland, forming a mountainous promontory. In 1598 the English geographer Richard Haklyut, using sailors' reports, wrote of "the mainland of Junkceylon".[5] In 1784 Thomas Forrest, a Scottish sea captain who came to Phuket, noted that the island was still only divided from the mainland by "a narrow isthmus of sand … about half a mile in breadth, which is covered only at high water" and could be crossed on foot or by elephant at low tide.[6] The word for a promontory or cape in Malay is "Ujang" or "Tanjung" so it is conjectured that the Malays named this cape (Phuket) "Ujang Salang" or "Tanjung Salang", meaning "Cape of the Salang people". This local Malay name for Phuket was later corrupted by visiting European sailors into various names such as "Ionsalan" and "Junkceylon". These more numerous and warlike Malays began to settle round the coasts and bays of Phuket and also moved into the rice-producing flatlands of Thalang – a name probably also derived from the word "Salang" – where they would have chased out or merged with the existing Mons.

The Malay word for a hill is "Bukit" and the Malays probably referred to the jungle-clad, hilly central and southern parts of Phuket as the "Bukit" part of the island. In the mid-19th century, when large tin deposits were found in Kathu district in this "Bukit" part of the island, Kathu soon became the most heavily populated area and a new port town grew to service the Kathu mines. The town became known as "Bukit", or as now, "Phuket" town. Under Siamese government reorganizations in the later 19th century, control of the entire island, which had previously been under either the rajah (a Malay lord) or Okya (a Siamese lord) in Thalang, was put under a Bangkok Siamese-appointed governor in Phuket town, which by then had become the largest town on the island. The whole island and the surrounding province then became known as Phuket during the later 19th and the early 20th century tin-mining era.

The name Phang Nga is a Thai name whose origin is debatable, but which probably comes from the translation of "broken tusk" in Thai, testifying to the large number of wild elephants that abounded there in former times.

The Bronze Age and the First Demand for Tin

Tin and copper, by themselves, are soft metals, but at least 5,000 years ago it was discovered that if the two were smelted together, the result was a metal that was malleable when hot, yet cooled to become much harder than either of its two components alone. This was bronze, the discovery of which spread and allowed humans to form a huge new range of tools and weapons. Societies all over the world learned to stop scratching around with chipped flints, animal bones and sticks and started using this new metal to make much more efficient tools for agriculture, technological progress and of course weapons.

To make this all-important bronze, however, people needed tin, which Phuket had in abundance, often just sitting on the surface of the ground or lying in the bottom of its streams. Therefore people began to come to Phuket to collect, pan for and dig for this tin, while others came to raid or trade for it. Hence Thalang on Phuket and its early river port settlement of Tharua (which means harbor in Thai), and which is the town by the Heroines Monument today, began to be known to seafarers and raiders all around the Bay of Bengal and the Malay Peninsula as a place to obtain tin and a place of regional trade and commerce.

2

Early Foreign Contacts

500 BC TO AD 300

The annual monsoon winds in Asia take their name from the Arabic word "mausim", meaning seasonal. They are caused by the heating up and rising of the air over the hot central Asian landmass in the summer. This sucks in the cooler moisture-laden air from the Indian Ocean, deluging the south and east of the continent in rain. Asia's subsequent cooling in winter then causes the process to reverse so the drier cooler air is sucked back to the southwest as the warmer Indian Ocean air then rises faster. These winds have blown for six months northeasterly then six months southwesterly since time immemorial.

Early Indian Influences

Indian and particularly Malay mariners learned the rhythm of these monsoon winds at least four thousand years ago. They realized they could hoist their sails and ride these winds either eastwards or westwards across the Bay of Bengal in two or three weeks' sailing. They could then trade on these faraway coasts, wait until the monsoon winds changed and then make the same trip in reverse. These predictable monsoon winds allowed trade and communication to develop between India and the Malay Peninsula as early as 2000 BC or before. Both Malay and Indian sailors began making this cross-ing eastwards carrying goods such as textiles and cottons, and westwards with goods such as tin, aromatic woods or other forrest products. The earliest Hindu text, the Rig Veda, written around 700 BC, alludes to such voyages, stating: "Merchants, under the influence of greed, send out ships to foreign countries … merchants go everywhere in pursuit of gain and frequent every part of the sea."[7]

Other Indians crossed to the more sparsely populated Malay Peninsula to hunt or to live as aesthetic hermits in the remote caves and forests. After 500 BC, during what is now called the "Early Kingdoms Period", India was ravaged by frequent and brutal wars between the smaller kingdoms developing there and some Indian lords and their followers fled their enemies or defeat by crossing over to the Peninsula to set up new fiefdoms there.

An Early Indian Settler

The "Serajah Keddah", the historical annals of the northwestern Malaysian state of Keddah, to the south of Phuket, gives an account of one such Hindu warrior prince, Marong Mahawangsa, who it claims founded the early kingdom known as Langkasuka

Map 1
Ancient Maritime Trade Routes Asia to The Mediterranean

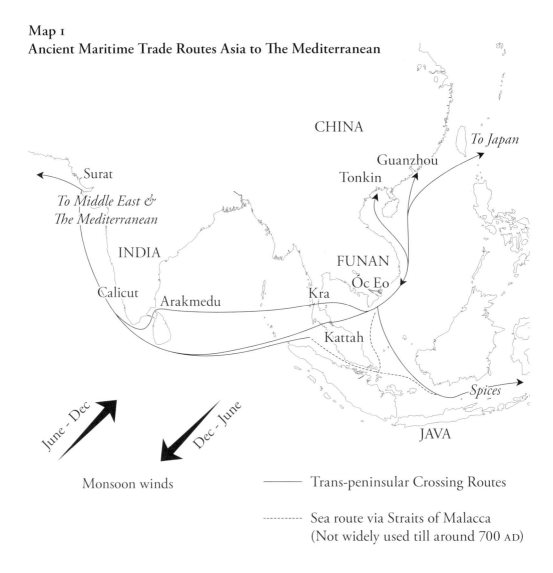

Monsoon winds

———— Trans-peninsular Crossing Routes

---------- Sea route via Straits of Malacca
(Not widely used till around 700 AD)

in the central peninsula region in the first century AD. These rather mythical annals (depending upon which translation one uses – I am here using both Khan and Logan)[8] tell us that in between fighting off a giant bird attempting to steal his ships in its claws and shooting off huge flaming arrows and the like, Marong crossed the Bay of Bengal and "The ships came in sight of Salang Island [Phuket] in the sea called Tappan" (now Andaman), where he anchored off the island and sent a party onshore "to ask permission of the raja to wood and water."[9]

Marong Mahawangsa's fleet then left Phuket and sailed southeast for another "day and a night" until they were caught in a bad storm off "Pulau Lada" (probably Ko Lanta) which wrecked several ships. They eventually landed further south on an island they called "Lankapuri" (Lankawi?):

"the coastline was hilly and jungled. The bays had an abundance of fishes. Berries and fruits could be picked easily and jungle fowl were plenty. No people were seen. Shelters were built … and stockades fixed to keep out prowling wild animals. At nights the vessel and the camp were lit up. These lights drew the Girgassi [local tribal] pirates and they pressed on the camp to loot, but their savage mode of approach could not prevail against organized fighters. Marong Mahawangsa gave battle with his bows, axes, lances and slings and routed them. Thereupon the Girgassis submitted and invited him to be their chief."[10]

2.1. These ancient Hindu stone statues, found in Takuapa overgrown by trees in 1900, date to the 9th century and confirm the ancient spread of Indian culture in the region.

Marong accepted their offer and became the monarch of all the forested lands that lay before him. He named the island "Lankasuka" (Island of Health), "a fitting name, as there prevailed from dawn to dusk a cool breeze that was found vivifying and suitable for human health. He took possession of all the pirate haunts and so removed piracy. Indian and Chinese traders thereafter came and went without fear. He built Hindu shrines and returned to India and brought craftsmen, priests and teachers with him and encouraged trade."[11]

This folkloric tale gives us some idea of how early Indian strongmen founded kingdoms on the peninsula. In Sanskrit, the Malay Peninsula and Sumatra came to be known as "Suvarnabhumi" or "Land of Gold" – a sort of eastern "El Dorado". For many ambitious traders or dispossessed Indian lords it became a case of "Go east, young man". One ancient Sanskrit script warned that if a young man travels east to Suvarnabhumi he will find such riches and distractions he shall be unlikely to return, another – "The Raghumvamsa" – tells us that the breezes from Suvarnabhumi wafted the intoxicating scent of cloves as far west over the seas as India.[12] The 11th-century Indian book "Katah Sarit Sagara", a collection of legends, refers to the Suvarnabhumi as "the home of all felicities",[13] and recites several colorful tales of unrequited love transcending the Bay of Bengal.

Phuket's Hindu Period

In these small river-mouth communities on the peninsular west coast, Indian (mainly Tamil) and then later Arab and Persian mariners and traders developed trade connections and friendships with the local communities and rulers. These traders would often return to the same communities year after year and often stayed for months to trade and waiting for the monsoon winds to turn. They would be allocated a home and a wife for their stay and they begat mixed-race children and just as with foreigners today, many decided to stay on and live there permanently. These Indian traders also brought with them their holy men who spread Hindu, Buddhist and Brahmanist beliefs which – handily for the local leaders – included the Indian concept of a "Deva-raja" (a god-king). This promoted the idea that kings owed their power not only to strength of arms or being born to the right father, but also to divine providence.

These local Malay, Mon and Tamil leaders gained both economically and in prestige and power from associating with these foreign traders and their holy men. In this way, the Indian religions, or at least modified versions of them, merged with the existing animistic beliefs of the locals, were adopted in much of the peninsula from around 500 BC onwards. The Indian historian Professor D.P. Singhal summarizes this process: "Indians came into contact with Southeast Asia principally for commercial reasons, but they [also] settled and introduced their culture and civilization. In turn they were influenced by the indigenous culture, laying the foundation of a new culture in the region."[14]

Hinduism appears to have been dominant in and around Phuket for over a thousand years between about 500 BC and around AD 700. In the foyer of the Phuket History Museum in Thalang stands a large and ancient (possibly ninth-century) stone statue of the Hindu god Vishnu. It was found in 1900 in thick forest overgrowth on the Phang Nga coast and confirms the early presence of Hinduism in the area. Several other ancient Hindu stone carvings and temple remains have been recovered from sites surrounding Phuket – Takuapa, Chaiya, Surathani, Krabi and Keddah. Analysis of the stone in these statues shows that some were carved in India and transported over while others were sculpted on the peninsula. Few, if any, stone buildings were built in Phuket before the 19th century, most ancient buildings or temples were made of wood and so would have disintegrated long ago in the tropical climate or will have since been built over by later Buddhist sites.

Evidence of this ancient Hindu heritage can, however, be seen in the important place Sanskrit and Pali words occupy in the Siamese language, also in the many Indian names still used by Thais and more commonly in the Thai greeting "Sawasdee ka", which probably derives from the Sanskrit word "swastika", meaning "well-being". The swastika is a revered ancient symbol brought to India by its Aryan conquerors, which only fell into disrepute (at least in the Western world) in the 20th century when Adolf Hitler adopted it as a slick marketing logo for his German Nazi party and their Aryan ideals. Additionally, the traditional bowed head and wai hands greeting of Thais is said to have originally been a greeting between Hindu warrior lords to show mutual respect (and that they had no weapon in their hands ready to kill one another).

Chinese Influences

Since their earliest written history there have been Chinese records of trade with the "Nan Yang" (South Sea) and also "Kun Lun" as the Malay Peninsula appears to have been known to the ancient Chinese. They also called the region "The Kingdom of the Naked".

By 500 BC the ideas of the Chinese philosopher Confucius had gained prevalence in the Han imperial court. Confucius was opposed to trade and commerce, seeing them as exploitative and corrupt: "The mind of the superior man dwells on righteousness, the mind of the little man dwells on profit." He was also very pro-family and decried overseas travel, stating that "While his parents are alive, the son may not take a distant voyage abroad." The Han emperors created a raft of Confucian imperial laws banning overseas travel and unauthorized foreign trade. As a result, the few Chinese who did write about the Ma-

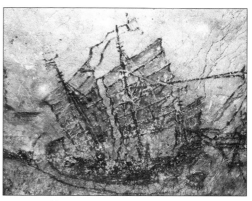

2.2 An old cave painting of a Chinese junk on Ko Phi Phi Island is more evidence that Chinese ships have been visiting Phuket and Phang Nga Bay since ancient times

lay Peninsula in ancient times were mainly official emissaries or sanctioned religious pilgrims on their way to India or Sri Lanka. They kept good records, which today form some of the only remaining written sources of early peninsular history. The problem is that scholars today are confused as to which ancient Chinese place names refer to which actual modern places.

The Chinese chronicle "Liang Shu", or the "Book of Liang", presumed to have been written in the first century AD, gives us one of the earliest Chinese reports of the "Nan Yang":

> "Precious things come from the sea this way ... thousands of varieties, all of which are coveted. Therefore the ships come in a continuous stream and merchants and envoys jostle with each other ... All countries of the world came for purposes of trade as she projects into the sea more than 1,000 li. [A li was about 450 meters, so roughly 450 kilometers.] At this market east and west met together so that daily there were more than 10,000 people and precious goods and rare merchandise. There was nothing which was not there."[15]

The sheer impossibility of effectively policing China's vast and remote southern coastline and the entrepreneurial nature of the Chinese meant that illegal trade and emigration to the "Nan Yang" did continue in a limited way despite the draconian imperial laws against it. Independent Chinese traders and emigrants headed south to trade or find their fortunes in the "Nan Yang" and some, faced with severe punishment including beheading if they returned, stayed on and settled in the region. Tchou Ta Kuan (Zhou Daguan), a Chinese emissary to Cambodia in the 13th century, made a report that still holds much truth for foreign visitors to the region and to Phuket today.

> "Chinese sailors note with pleasure that it is not necessary to wear many clothes and, since rice is easily had, women easily persuaded, houses easily run, furniture easily come by and trade easily carried on, a great many sailors desert to take up permanent residence."[16]

Were the Greeks or Romans in Phuket or the Peninsula?

"The beautiful vessels, the masterpieces of the Greeks, stir white foam on the Periyar River ... arriving with gold and departing with pepper."[17] These lines from an ancient Tamil poem "The Lay of the Anklet", believed to have been written around AD 200, tell of Greek triremes and trade ships arriving and departing from the rivers of south India. However it remains tantalizingly uncertain today whether these same Greek or Roman trade ships ever came that bit further west to trade directly with the west coast ports of the Malay Peninsula. Certainly there is evidence the Greeks were well aware of the existence of the Malay Peninsula. The first known Greek reference to the peninsula is around 100 BC, when it is referred to as "the Golden Khersonese", which was a direct translation of "Suvarnabhumi" (Golden Island), the Indian name for the peninsula at the time.

There is ample archaeological and chronicled evidence that both the Greek and Roman empires traded directly with India and China. Early in the first century AD it is recorded that a Greco-Egyptian sea captain, Hippalus, learned from Indian sailors how to use the monsoon winds to sail directly from the Red Sea across to India. Thereafter trade with the East boomed. The Greek geographer Strabo, writing around 20 BC, tells us that most years a huge Greek trade fleet, numbering up to 120 ships, set off from the Red Sea to make the year-long trip to the Indies and because of this great trade, Strabo noted, "These regions have become better known to us today".[18] The Greeks and the Romans established a series of permanent trade colonies in India. One was at Arikamedu on India's Coromandel (southeastern) coast just a couple of weeks' sail across the Bay of Bengal from Phuket and was probably also regularly visited by Malay trading prows crossing over from the peninsula.

Indeed Malay sailors may also have directly visited Greek and Roman ports such as Berenike on the Red Sea. The Romans used the word "Seres" for Chinese or Asians from further east than India. A report from the Roman historian Julius Flores as early as the reign of the first Roman emperor Augustus (27 BC – AD 14) describes some "Seres" visiting the city of Rome itself: "Even the nations of the world not subject to the imperial sway were sensible of its grandeur … Thus the Scythians sent envoys … nay the Seres came likewise, and the Indians, bringing with them presents of pearls and elephants."[19] However, according to the Chinese annals, the first Chinese man ever to reach the West was Gan Ying and this was in AD 97, over a century after Flores's account. So who were these earlier Seres in Rome with their "gifts of pearls and elephants"? (Both were common export items from the Malay Peninsula.) They may well have been Malays from the western peninsula – the nearest part of eastern Asia to Rome.

Around AD 140 the Greco-Egyptian geographer Claudius Ptolemy wrote his compendium Geographia, which was essentially a travel guide for Greek sailors heading east to trade. In the Geographia some of the physical features of the western Malay peninsular coast are described (although all with the wrong longitudes and latitudes). Ptolemy was a scholar not a sailor and most probably gathered his information in Egypt from returning Arab and Greek or possibly visiting Asian sailors. Ptolemy did note that the main trade emporium on the western Malay peninsular coast was a port called "Takola". Takola is presumed by many scholars today to have been Takuapa, in Phang Nga province, just north of Phuket, though others believe it could have been Trang. Ptolemy mentions a large promontory near this port of "Takola" which may well have been the headland (Ujang) of Phuket before the sea created the channel now separating Phuket from the mainland. Ptolemy also makes mention of an island on the west of the peninsula called "Saline" which may have derived from

2.3 A Roman gold embossed cape clip dating to the 2nd century AD which was dug up in Klong Thom, Krabi, along with many Mediterranean style beads – but is this sufficient evidence Romans visited the region? Or were they just ancient trade items?

Phuket's old name of "Salang" or "Salon". He noted that "In this Island there are a large number of shellfish and the inhabitants are always naked."[20]

The Romans were certainly huge consumers of eastern spices and luxuries and it was the maritime trade with Asia, not the better known overland "silk road", via which the bulk of this trade was carried. Chinese silk, for example, was so popular in Rome it was at times worth more than its weight in gold. In AD 78 the Emperor Vespasian even had to make an edict prohibiting the export of gold to the East for this trade as it was bankrupting the empire. The Roman noble Pliny the Elder complained that, "by the lowest reckoning Indians, Seres and Arabs take from our empire millions of sesterces every year … that is how much our luxuries and women cost us".[21] His son Pliny the Younger also noted that "India is brought near to us by [the Roman traders'] lust for gain." It is therefore quite possible that, to try to cut out the probably voracious Indian middlemen, these profit-seeking Greco-Arab and Roman ship captains would have sailed their ships a couple of weeks further east from India to try to reach the markets of the Malay Peninsula directly.

As early as AD 520, when Cosmos Indicopluestes, a Nestorian Christian trader from Egypt, traveled to India, he wrote that Christian communities already existed in Burma and the Malay Peninsula further east. It therefore remains likely, but still frustratingly unproven, whether Greek or Roman triremes or galleons ever appeared in Tharua, Patong or Phang Nga bays or indeed in any other ports on the west coast of the Malay Peninsula.

No Roman items are recorded as having been found on Phuket Island to date, although, as a form of "kwan fa" they may have been found and eaten long ago. Ancient glass beads of Mediterranean design, however, were unearthed from mounds on Ko Kaew Island in Phang Nga Bay just off Phuket. Also in Klong Thom, south of Krabi, presumed to be an ancient river port, large quantities of glass beads of Roman and Mediterranean design have also been dug up along with three gold Roman carnelian seals dating from the second century AD. These invaluable golden seals were on public show at the sleepy local museum in Wat Klong Thom until late 2007 when an enterprising thief broke through the wat's flimsy corrugated asbestos roof one night and stole the lot.

These glass bead mounds unearthed at Klong Thom and Ko Kaew however may just be evidence of an overseas Indian manufacturing trade base, rather like a modern export trade zone. The nearby Indian port (and Roman colony) of Arikamedu was known to be a major bead manufacturing and trade center at the time. In the old riverbed at Klong Thom near these bead mounds two ancient wooden ship hulls dating to around the second century AD and presumed to be of Indian origin, have also been dug up. Further official excavation needs to be done at this site where the locals still dig up beads and possibly other artifacts, often apparently unrecorded, to sell to the few visitors who stop off at this important but little-known historical site.

Roman artifacts however, have been found in other parts of Thailand such as Kanchanburi. These include a metal lamp, a Roman ivory comb and a German coin minted in Cologne from the time of emperor Victorinus (AD 268–70). Roman coins from the time of Antonius Pius and Marcus Aurelius (AD 138–80) have also been unearthed further east in Vietnam. But such Greco-Roman artifact discoveries in Thailand are paltry compared to those from India where over 6,000 Roman coins have been found. It is also possible that these Roman items arrived in the peninsula only as trade "carry". That is, they may have been brought over by Indian, Arab and Persian middlemen to trade. In sum, Manfred Raschke, a leading scholar on Roman commerce in Asia, best summarizes this enigmatic issue of whether the Greeks or Romans ever appeared in the Malay Peninsula by stating that, "Much is asserted, but little is yet proven."[22]

3

Tradewinds and Portages

2000 BC TO AD 1700

Ancient Trade

One hot day in 1975 some sweaty French and American archaeologists were excavating a site in Tell-Ashara in Syria, an ancient trading town sitting between Mesopotamia and the Mediterranean. Having dug down through various levels of houses built on other houses over the millennia, they eventually reached the remains of one ancient house that had been destroyed by a fire.

The Mesopotamians used to write on soft clay tablets which then hardened. Some of these tablets were discovered in this burnt-out house, baked hard by the fire. When deciphered, these tablets revealed that the house had belonged to a wealthy local trader called Puzrum and they dated the fire to around 1761 BC, almost 4,000 years ago. In the historical scheme of things this fire was of very little consequence – except of course to Mr. Puzrum – but in his pantry, in the compacted dirt in the bottom of a charred ceramic pot, these archaeologists discovered some very dehydrated cloves.

Cloves have long been used in Europe and Asia for their medicinal, aromatic, magical and culinary uses. Today clove trees are found in India, Zanzibar, Madagascar and Sri Lanka, but these were all transplanted there during the European colonial era. Originally, clove trees grew naturally only on five small islands in eastern Indonesia known today as the Moluccas but better known in history as the Spice Islands. These ancient cloves in this charred pot in Syria therefore provide tangible proof that long-distance global trade, reaching from eastern Indonesia probably to the western Mediterranean, was under way at least 4,000 years ago, long before the Greek and Roman empires even existed.

The Trans-Peninsular Portage Routes

A major obstacle for these ancient seafarers, trying to sail with the monsoon winds from these eastern Spice Islands to Arabia and back, must have been the long, green jungled arm of the Malay Peninsula and Sumatra extending far, far down to the south and blocking their way. The equatorial regions south of the peninsula were, and still are, known to mariners as "the lands below the winds", where the predictable monsoon winds petered out. Until around the sixth century AD, the only sea route through this obstacle, via the Straits of Malacca, appears to have been little used. This was partly because ship and sail technology was not sufficiently sophisticated but mainly because frightful pirates bedeviled these Straits. In AD 424 the Chinese monk Fa Hsien noted, while passing through the Malacca Straits on his way home from India, "The seas here are infested with pirates, to meet whom is death."[23]

These pirates were the local "Orang Laut" (sea people) – Malays and Sea Gypsies – who paddled or sailed out from their hidden lairs amongst the islands, mangroves and estuaries in the narrow straits to prey on passing ships. The eighth-century Arab writer Al Masudi described these Orang Laut pirates as having "black wavy hair, strange figures and wearing metal collars."[24] They were described as excellent seamen and fierce fighters who used blowpipes to fire poisoned darts as Al Masudi tells us, "In their small boats they wander round any ships which visit them and shoot a curious type of poison dart."[25]

This sea route through the Malacca Straits was therefore rarely used. Instead, traders sailed directly west or east with the monsoon winds by the shortest routes until they hit the narrow central peninsula. There, these western traders (Indian, Arab and Persian) either sold their cargoes, or offloaded them to agents to be portaged overland to the other coast by elephants, slaves, buffalo-drawn carts and flat-bottomed river boats. On the eastern coast these goods were then purchased and loaded on to boats by traders from the eastern seas (Chinese, Malay, Javanese and Indochinese), to continue their journey with the same monsoon winds further east to Vietnam, China and Japan, or southeast to Indonesia and the Spice Islands. Eastern products, spices, silks and porcelains heading west, followed the same portage journey in reverse.

The narrow isthmian region of the central peninsula was known to the ancient mariners as the land of "Kra". (Hence regional names today such as Kra-bi and Kra-buri.) As early as the first century AD "The Erytheian Pereplus", an early book of Greek navigation instructions for the Indian Ocean, specifically describes the Isthmus of Kra as "the place where boats were hauled". There is sufficient evidence from excavations done in the region by archaeologists from Cambridge University and elsewhere, to speculate that around the 10th century an ancient waterway system may even have been dug across much of the peninsula from near Satun on the west coast to the great Thale Luang Lake and Songkhla port on the east coast (see Map 1). Further research and archaeological work needs to be done in this area.

The central peninsular had long abounded with herds of wild elephants and buffalo, which over time created trails through the thick jungles and swamps. Humans on the coasts used these trails to head inland to hunt, to trade in forest products or open up new areas for settlement. Humans eventually learned to traverse the peninsula from coast to coast using such trails and boats on the local rivers. These became the routes by which the ancient traders portaged cargoes between the Indian Ocean and the South China Sea and vice versa. This would account, for example, for the Mediterranean-style bead-making factory and ancient Indian ship hulls found at Klong Thom, which was probably a western river port on one of these trans-peninsular trade routes.

These trans-peninsular portages are mentioned as early as the first century AD in the Chinese Annals of the former Han Dynasty which cover a period from 206 BC onwards. They mention a trip taken by some Chinese emissaries to India. Midway through their nine-month voyage the emissaries had to undertake an overland portage for ten days. This was probably the early route from the Bay of Bandon to Takuapa or Phang Nga, which took around ten days. So for at least 2,000 years these trans-peninsular routes placed Phuket, Phang Nga Bay and a few other central peninsular ports at the arterial throat of the world's main maritime trade route between the Eastern and Western worlds.

The routes were made safer by local leaders sending settlers inland to establish villages and garrisons to keep the routes clear of bandits and the ever-encroaching jungle. As late as 1822, for instance, an edict by the governor of Phang Nga ordered many villagers from Thalang in Phuket, who had fled to Phang Nga after a Burmese invasion of Phuket, to be resettled along the old Phang Nga to Chaiya trade route to make it safer.[26] These settlers could make a living on these trade routes providing merchants and their retinues with food and lodging or working as guides, guards, porters and prostitutes.

Some Early European Accounts of Trans-Peninsular Crossings

We can get some idea of the conditions on these ancient trans-peninsular crossings from the accounts of some of the earliest Europeans who traveled them. In 1687, for instance, Claude Ceberet Du Boullay, a director of the French East Indies Company, followed the trans-peninsular route from Ayutthaya to Mergui (in Burma today). Du Boullay initially traveled on an elephant whose howdah was "decorated with a gilded seat … carpets and cushions … covered with a kind of dome serving as an umbrella." His luggage was carried on "forty carts each drawn by two buffalo … so narrow in the rear that none of the bales nor chests wider than a foot and a half can go in."[27] These were presumably so designed to negotiate the narrow elephant trails. Ten elephants, "thirty men walking in file" and 50 soldiers accompanying them for protection carried his other goods.

Another Frenchman, Jacques de Bourges, who had made the crossing twenty years earlier, in 1666, complained bitterly of these very same small carts, noting, "We almost always had to walk on foot, the carts being designed to torment travellers rather than relieve them. They seemed more like coffins than carriages, at their widest point they were no more than three feet wide … we had to fit ourselves in these."[28]

Where there were villages, Du Boullay's party stayed in them overnight, but out in the forests the nights were more risky:

> "There were so many tigers that it was necessary to mount a guard throughout the night, to light fires and fire muskets from time to time … to frighten these animals which come in the night to surprise men and beasts … the Siamese who had been placed on guard during the night had to abandon their post because the tigers came to attack them in bands". [29]

The Main Trans-Peninsular Portage Routes

1 **Mergui via Tenasserim River to Prachup Kiri Khan:** This was the most popular trade route used during the Ayutthaya period (1450-1750), when Mergui became the Kingdom of Ayutthaya's main western port.

2 **The Isthmus of Kra:** between Ranong and Chumporn the peninsula is at its narrowest, just over 50 kilometers wide, but a bit hilly. This whole crossing could take only two or three days. It was noted in the 18th century that dispatch runners could cross the peninsula there in just a few hours.

3 **Takuapa-Chaiya:** From Takuapa goods were transported upriver to the Khao Sok Pass (by the Rajaprapat Dam) then loaded on boats and taken downstream to Chaiya on the Bay of Bandon, north of Surathani. This was one of the most well used routes in ancient times and many ancient Hindu, Persian and Chinese artifacts dating from the first to the 10th centuries AD have been found near this route.

4 **Phang Nga to Chaiya:** From Phang Nga, or more specifically the most unremarkable town of Thap Put about 30 kilometers past Phang Nga on the road to Krabi (which was previously known as Marui or Marid City), goods were taken upriver or transported to the Khao Sok Pass (near Rajaprapat Dam today), then down the Tapi River to the Bay of Bandon and Chaiya.

5 **Krabi to Ligor (Nakorn Sri Thammarat):** From Klong Thom goods went upriver and were then portaged across to Ligor, the ruling city and major east coast port in the central peninsula region for many centuries.

6 **Trang to Songkla:** This route ran up the Trang River over the hills to the huge Thale Luang Lake. From there goods were taken overland or by boat on canals north to Ligor (Nakorn) or across the lake to the east coast at Songkla.

7 **An ancient canal from Satun to Songkla:** A series of digs by the Cambridge University archaeology department in Sattingpra (north of Songkla) in the 1990s suggests that trade canals were extensively dug in the region and may even have run most of the way across the low-lying peninsula from Songkla in the east to somewhere near Satun in the west. It is also particularly strange that all the earliest maps of the peninsula, up until around 1640, mysteriously show a river dissecting the central peninsula. No mention of this canal has been found in any existing sources.[35]

8 **Keddah to Patani:** Patani and Keddah were both important port cities surrounded by large areas for growing rice to supply visiting ships. As ancient walled cities today they have some of the best stone archaeological remains on the peninsula. They were connected by a slightly longer overland route and by riverboat and haulage.

Map 2
The Trans-peninsular Trade Routes

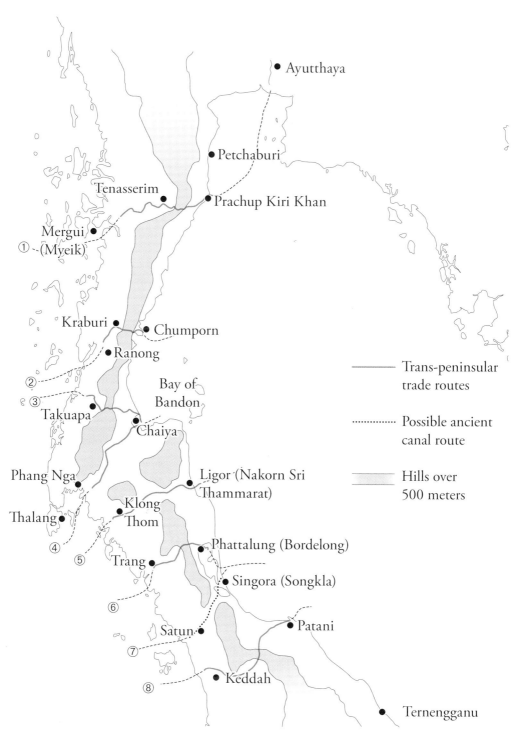

Ayutthaya

Petchaburi

Tenasserim

Prachup Kiri Khan

Mergui
(Myeik)
①

Kraburi

Chumporn

Ranong

②

③

Bay of
Bandon

Takuapa

Chaiya

Phang Nga

Ligor (Nakorn Sri
Thammarat)

Klong
Thom

Thalang

④

Phattalung (Bordelong)

⑤

Trang

Singora (Songkla)

⑥

Satun

Patani

⑦

Keddah

⑧

Ternengganu

——— Trans-peninsular
trade routes

············· Possible ancient
canal route

Hills over
500 meters

One even earlier Jesuit writer, Monsieur Pierre Du Jaric, mentions one unfortunate missionary who had made the crossing in 1608 and had to watch his traveling companion being ripped to pieces by a tiger at night. [30] Mgr. Lambert, a French priest who made the crossing in 1662, also recounts having such tiger troubles at night during his crossing:

"To defend ourselves we built each evening a fortress composed of carts in a circle, the cattle which towed them and our baggage in the middle. We had to fortify our camp with hedges of thorns … [on account of] … the cruel tigers prowling around … we had our arquebuses fired off and made fires all night to keep them away."[31]

Jacques de Bourges also tells us, though perhaps somewhat fancifully, that,

"During the daytime also we were not exempt from the war against the animals. Elephants are frequently met and … these beasts are afraid of nothing. When one meets one, one must not oppose it nor try to escape, one stays quiet out of respect due to this noble animal, which often, taking no notice of persons, continues on its way. If one comes straight at you, the custom is to offer it something like a hat, a cloak or some linen, which it seizes with its trunk, plays with and as though content with this apparent homage offered, it continues on its way. If it is still aroused, the only thing to do is to go at once behind it on the left side as it never normally turns to that side, but to the right … If all else fails one holds onto its tail and turns with it until it tires and allows you the means to escape."[32]

3.1 Elephants transporting goods in Tenasserim province Burma which was one of the major trans-peninsular routes of the Ayutthayan Kingdom.

After many hard days' travel, Claude Du Boullay recounts reaching the summit of the Tenasserim range, "We left[,] crossed the mountain from which one can see both seas, that of Siam on the east and that of Bengal on the west." Heading down through the heavy forests on the even wilder western side of the hills "in almost insupportable heat" he reached the low swampy Tenasserim river basin where "the air of the place was so unhealthy that no European or Siamese could live there. Only the people who were born there would stay there … many of my men fell ill the same day and had much difficulty in overcoming their weakness."[33]

Du Boullay mentions that the mosquitoes "bit voraciously" but malaria, now known to be spread by mosquitoes, was until the late 19th century thought to come from bad swampy air, hence its Latin name which translates as "bad air disease". On this wilder, thickly jungled west side of the peninsula travel was by the Tenasserim River. The French priest Mgr. Lambert in 1682 describes how they were poled along in large canoes "made out of huge trees hollowed out by fire which are a good twenty feet long and covered with a canopy of Palm leaves … One has to prepare one's food and sleep in these boats, it being too dangerous to step on land which comprises only uninterrupted forests full of lions, boars, tigers and other carnivorous beasts."[34]

3.2 An early European painting of Chinese, Indians and Malays meeting to trade in the peninsula.

A List of Ancient Trade Products from Phuket and the Surrounding Region

In addition to being a major through-trade emporium, Phuket and its surrounding region also produced many indigenous products in demand in the markets of China, India and the Arab and the Mediterranean worlds. The following is a list of the island's and the region's main indigenous trade products.

- **Tin:** Has been a major export from Phuket for over 3,000 years. It was panned, mined, smelted and exported from Phuket since the Bronze Age up until the 1980s.

- **Elephants:** Wild elephants abounded in Phuket. Ivory was in demand in all markets east and west and Phuket and the surrounding region carried on a healthy trade exporting live elephants by sea to India to be used by armies or as draft animals.

- **Pepper:** Was harvested all over the central peninsula, mainly in Keddah, Ligor, Songkla and Patani. It was one of the primary early exports of the peninsula, but became less important after the 17th century.

- **Ambergris:** A secretion from the digestive tract of sperm whales. It floats on the surface of the sea, ending up at the high-water mark where it coagulates into a smelly, dull grey film. Before mass whaling in the 19th century ambergris washed up on all the western beaches of Phuket and was collected. As ambergris dries, it gives off a sweet earthy odor and was used as a fixative for perfumes. Chinese palace eunuchs wore a lump round their neck as perfume. Ambergris was used in rich households to fuel oil lamps.

- **Birds' nests:** Cave swiftlets build nests from gummy strands of saliva, which harden to a rubbery consistency. The nests are rich in nutrients and today are still one of the most expensive animal products in the world. The swiftlets make their nests in caves in the limestone cliffs of the islands off Phuket and these nests are still collected for export today.

- **Sappanwood:** This local redwood tree was used to produce a red dye for cotton and as fuel for funeral pyres. In China it was used as an anti-inflammatory medicine.

- **Lac:** A deep crimson or black resin secreted by an insect that inhabits the raintrees of southern Thailand; lac was used primarily as a dye for silks and cottons and for female body painting and cosmetics in India.

- **Aromatic wood:** When burnt, Lakawood, Muskwood and others produce pleasant scents that were popular in the homes of the rich and were burnt for ceremonial purposes.

- **Other woods:** Growing near the sea, the huge, straight trees gave Phuket a reputation among European sailors as an excellent place to acquire timber for ships' masts and spars.

- **Beeswax:** In times gone by, beeswax was used as waterproofing, as the surface for writing tablets, as polish, as a modeling material for casting metal and in many other ways. The gutsy locals would smoke the bees out and steal their nests for the wax – and the honey.

- **Deerskins:** There were large numbers of deer living in the local forests (they still abound today in Ko Phangan where they are protected as they belong to the king). Their hides were a major export to China and Japan.

- **Rattan ware:** People in Phuket were skilled at using the rattan vine to make rope, mats, baskets, hats, shields and even clothes.

- **Areca nuts:** The seeds of a local palm tree, these were chewed with betel leaves to induce a mild high and were believed to have medicinal properties.

- **Cardamom:** A spice for cooking, particularly in Indian cuisine.

- **Camphor:** Tree oil used for treating toothache and inflammation.

- **Pearls:** Phuket's waters abounded with pearl oysters that were collected by the Sea

Gypsies, who were expert divers.

- **Exotic birds and feathers**: Colorful local birds were exported. The aquamarine feathers of the local kingfisher were prized for ornamentation and hair styling.

- **Rhinoceros horn**: Phuket Island and the region abounded with Sumatran rhinoceroses. They were hunted for their meat and skin and their horns were prized in China, India and the West as a remedy for impotence.

- **Shark fins**: Still highly prized as the signature ingredient in Chinese shark fin soup.

- **Tiger and panther skins**: Were in strong demand as a fashion accessory, particularly for bedding.

- **Shark silk**: This mysterious product is mentioned in Chinese records as a highly valuable export of the peninsula. But scholars are not quite sure what it was; probably it was what is called Sea silk today or Byssus, the small gluey hairs that mussels excrete to attach themselves to rocks.

- **Coconuts and nipa wine**: Several Chinese and Indian writers noted that the local people made good, strong nipa wine from their coconuts.

- **Civet oil**: A musky substance secreted from the glands of the civet cat, civet oil was used in China in perfumes and medicine. The animals' pelts were also valuable. Phuket has several species of civet cat some of which may still be glimpsed in the island's rapidly disappearing forests today.

- **Kapok**: Since Phuket was reforested with rubber trees this tree is now rare. It was also known as the silk cotton tree. Kapok trees produce pods filled with a white cotton-like material. This was used to fill pillows and mattresses and, being water-resistant, was also good for caulking ships' planking.

- **Negrito slaves**: Black people were sought after by Malays and particularly the Chinese in China as a trendy accessory, and were often employed as doormen. Some ancient Chinese reports refer specifically to Negrito or Sea Gypsy slaves from the peninsula – or "Kun-lun slaves" as they called them, mentioning that they were expert swimmers who could keep their eyes open underwater and were particularly good at caulking leaky ships below the water line.

- **Other slaves**: Slave raiding and trading were rampant for many years and there was widespread demand for slaves both within in the region and overseas. People at sea, living near the coast, or even straying a bit far from their villages, were always at risk of being carried away. The further from their place of origin female slaves were taken the more exotic and expensive they became.

- **Bears**: Sun bears were popular for performance shows, while Chinese made medicine from their paws and bile (some still do today). Today a few sun bears still live wild in the diminishing jungles of the peninsula.

- **Sea slugs**: Known more politely as Bêche de Mer these are still exported as a delicacy to China. Several 17th- and 18th-century accounts tell us that Ko Maphrao, just off Phuket, was a main collection, drying and trading center.

- **Turtle shell**: The ornamental covering layer was taken off the shell of the massive hawksbill turtles that abounded off Phuket. The shells, reaching up to two meters in size, were carved into a wide variety of ornaments and jewelry. Only a few smaller turtles return to the island's beaches today.

- **Crocodile skins**: Saltwater crocodiles, the largest of all living reptiles, were called "water lizards" or "dragons" by early Chinese chroniclers and abounded in Phuket's mangroves, estuaries and the surrounding seas.

- **Medicinal plants**: There was a wide range of forest plants and mushrooms used for many medicinal and other purposes in Chinese, Indian, Persian and local medicines.

- **Coral**: Coral was used in medicines, most particularly as a prophylactic for women to prevent pregnancy. Cut and polished it was also considered a precious stone. The Romans believed that wearing a piece of coral could avert danger.

- **Giant clams**: Their undulating shells looked like the waves depicted in Chinese and Japanese art, making these clams, and also conch shells, highly sought after in Northeast Asia.

4

The Rise of Kingdoms

AD 1 TO 800

By the first century AD several of the main trade entrepôts in the central peninsula had grown in wealth and power and, infused with imported Indian concepts of divine and theater kingship, their leaders expanded their power over their surrounding areas, creating small Indianized kingdoms. It is believed that scribes in these early kingdoms wrote on cloth then rolled and bound the cloth in banana leaves, like a spring roll, to be stored. These rotted away long ago and no known ancient local written records exist. The only remaining sources are some Chinese, Indian and Arab writings, plus a few local steles (inscribed stones) and archaeological evidence. Trying to piece together the early history of the central peninsula is therefore like trying to complete a large jigsaw with only a handful of pieces.

Funan: The First Great Southeast Asian Empire

It appears that these smaller kingdoms developing in the central peninsula came to be dominated by the Kingdom of Funan from the first to the seventh centuries AD. Funan, probably the first great Southeast Asian empire, apparently started out as a simple pirate base at Óc Eo, strategically situated on the southwest coast of Vietnam today between the Mekong delta and the main east–west maritime trade routes. An early Chinese account tells us that the Funanese were a "dark and curly haired people who went naked."[36]

According to Indian legend, Funan became a more civilized place when an Indian leader of high birth sailed east, married a Funanese princess and became king. He persuaded the Funanese that supplying and trading with passing ships would be more profitable in the longer term than attacking and plundering them. Óc Eo then developed as the main trading port in the Gulf of Thailand region, a central emporium for goods and traders from China, the Malay world and the Indian Ocean. Archaeological excavations at Óc Eo have unearthed objects there from as far away as Rome, India, China and Japan. Kangtai and Zhuying, two third-century Chinese emissaries to Funan, noted the wealth of the Funanese and tell us, "They live in walled villages, palaces and houses … [the people] go about naked and barefoot. Their nature is simple and they are not inclined towards thievery … they undertake agriculture … Customs and taxes are paid in gold, silver, pearls and perfumes … there are books and depositories of archives and other things."[37]

Funan developed a powerful navy and army and attempted to control all trade around the Gulf of Thailand including the important trans-peninsular portage routes in the

Map 3
Early Peninsular Kingdoms 1st to 10th Century AD

DVARAVATI

CHENLA
(Previously Funan)

TEN LUI MEI

• Mergui

◉ Tenasserim

Óc Eo ◉

• Chumporn

Kraburi •

PAN PAN

◉ Chaiya

Takuapa •

• Phang Nga   ◉ Ligor

TAMBRALINGA

Tharua/
Ban Manik
(Phuket) •

• Trang

• Songkla

LANGASUKA ◉ Patani

KALAH/KATTHA

◉ Kattha (Keddah)

◉ Presumed seat of local kings

Note: It appears that prior
to the 6th century the
Chinese called the whole
peninsula "Tun Sun",
when it was under the
Kingdom of Funan

------ Earlier approximate limit
of Funanese control 1st to
7th centuries

Malay Peninsula. A third-century Chinese report tells of a powerful Funanese king called Fan Chu Man who, "by the might of his arms, attacked and subdued neighboring kingdoms and all admitted themselves his vassals … He had great ships constructed in which he crossed over the sea [Gulf of Thailand] and attacked and subdued more than ten kingdoms and expanded his kingdom in all directions for some 6,000 li"[38] (roughly 3,000 kilometers: Phuket Island is only some 1,000 kilometers from Óc Eo).

By AD 503, the imperial court of China officially recognized the king of Funan as the leader of all the "Nang Yang" (South Seas) and conferred upon him the title "General of the Pacified south". By the late seventh century, however, Funan was attacked and overrun by the Kingdom of Chenla, a large Khmer agricultural kingdom to its north. Chenla was a more agricultural and less maritime kingdom and it was ultimately unable to maintain the control that Funan had maintained over the trans-peninsular trade routes and the local kingdoms that

4.1. A drawing of an 8th century temple carving of an ancient Southeast Asian ship with outriggers, Malay seamen sailed to China, Africa and the Middle East in such ships.

had grown up around them. A few existing Chinese and Arab writings leave us fleeting descriptions of these smaller central Malay Peninsula kingdoms during this period of Funanese domination from roughly the first to the end of the seventh century.

Tun Sun

Tun Sun seems to have been the early Chinese name for the whole central Malay Peninsula under Funanese control. It was mentioned that this kingdom was centered on the Tapi River which empties into the sea at Surathani and that it controlled several of the main central trans-peninsular trade routes. One third-century Chinese script tells us that Tun Sun was "An ocean stepping stone, situated on a precipitous coast 3,000 li south of Funan … it has five kings, all vassals of Funan … On the east, the kingdom was in communication with Tongking (South China), on the west, with India and Parthia (Persia)."[39]

Another third-century Chinese source, the "Tai Ping Yu Lan" chronicle notes, "Tun Sun was originally an independent kingdom but King Fan Man [of Funan] subdued it." A fifth-century Chinese chronicle, the "Fu-Nan Chi" tells us:

> "Ton-sun is a dependency of Funan. In the country there are five hundred families of 'Hun' [merchants?] from India, two hundred 'fo-te' [Buddhists?] and more than a thousand Indian Brahmins. The people of Tun sun practice their doctrine and give them their daughters in marriage; consequently many of the Brahmins do not leave the place. They do nothing but study the sacred canon, bathe themselves with scent and flowers and practice piety by day and night."[40]

Clearly these Brahmins, who in India would have been celibate, were enjoying the comparatively more relaxed mores and lifestyle in Suvarnabhumi, which also calls into question their authenticity. The same chronicle also states: "Tun sun is situated across the Gulf of Siam 3,000 li southwards of Funan. Among the inhabitants are many with white complexions."[41] It is unclear whether this means Malays, Persians, Romans or simply rich traders who did not have to work in the fields or on ships.

The kingdom of Tun Sun is, rather strangely, never mentioned in Chinese writings after the eighth century, probably because Chinese travelers and officials got to know the peninsula better and began to identify the individual kingdoms there after they had become independent of Funan's overlordship and several of them began to send their own embassies and trade missions north to China.

Pan Pan – Probably Phuket's Early Overlord (Third to Seventh Century)

The early kingdom of Pan Pan was most likely based in the ancient city of Chaiya, on the Bay of Bandon, north of Surathani. Excavations at Chaiya have produced some of the most impressive ancient architecture, statues and temples on the peninsula. Pan Pan is first recorded by the Chinese as an independent kingdom when it sent tribute missions there as early as between AD 424 and 453. It is also recorded as rebelling against Funanese rule. A main source of wealth for Pan Pan would have been its control of the important trans-peninsular route from Takuapa to Chaiya and it may have also controlled the Phang Nga route. One later 13th-century Chinese historian, Ma Tuan Lin, described Pan Pan thus:

> "Most of the people live on the shores of the sea. These barbarians do not know how to build defensive walls; they are content to set up palisades. The king reclines on a golden couch shaped like a dragon. The important persons of his entourage go on their knees before him. At his court one sees many Brahmins who have come from India to profit from his munificence and are very much in favour with him. In this country there are ten monasteries for monks and nuns who study the sacred books of Buddhism and who eat meat but do not drink wine."[42]

Tambralinga – Phuket's Later Overlord (Seventh to 13th Century)

Tambralinga appears to have bordered Pan Pan to the south and to have been based in the fortified port town of Ligor, now known as Nakorn Sri Thammarat. Tambralinga gradually grew stronger than Pan Pan and probably began to claim the rajah of Thalang as a vassal from around the eighth to the 13th century. In return for the king of Tambralinga's protection, the rajah of Thalang would have had to send him gifts and taxes and to support him with men, elephants, boats and food for his wars. He would probably have also had to give him some family members in marriage – a sort of obedience insurance policy.

By the eighth century Tambralinga had apparently either conquered, or maybe merged with, Pan Pan, and the lord of Ligor appears to have been overlord of most of the central peninsula around Phuket, Takuapa, Chaiya and Ligor. The 13th-century Chinese diarist Chao Ju-Kua, a customs official in Guangdong, wrote of the city of Ligor, the capital of Tambralinga:

> "Around the city there is a wooden palisade six or seven feet thick and over twenty feet high which can be used as a platform for fighting. The inhabitants of the country ride buffaloes, knot their hair behind and go barefooted. For their houses officials use wood while the common people build bamboo huts with leaf partitions. Foreign merchants traffic in pongee (silk) parasols, umbrellas, rice wine, salt, sugar, porcelain and earthenware vessels … The inhabitants are economical in their manner of life. The climate is pleasantly warm. Men and women tie their hair in a knot. Their dress is a white shirt with a black cotton sarong. In their marriage arrangements they use satins, brocades or a measure of tin."[43]

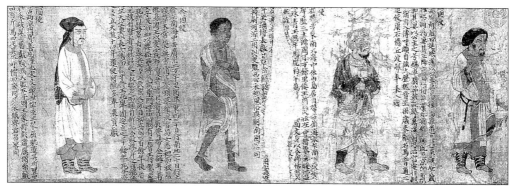

4.2. A Chinese record from around 530 AD depicting an emissary from the kingdom of Langkasuka in the central Malay peninsula. (Note: he's the second emissary from the left).

Langkasuka

Langkasuka was another of the stronger and more important early kingdoms in the central peninsula. It appears to have sat to the south of Tambralinga. Its capital may, as the Keddah annals say, originally have been Kuala Keddah, but more likely it was either the old site of Satingpra (near Songkla) – where the cross-peninsular canal may have run. Later, however, the kingdom appears to have been based in the ancient port city of Patani and the Langkasuka kings and queens probably controlled the important Patani–Keddah trade route. Langkasuka was also apparently conquered by Tambralinga around the 13th century. However, after the demise of Tambralinga (see Chapter 6), during the 15th to 19th centuries Langkasuka evolved into the strong regional Malay and Muslim trade kingdom of Patani. Siam later brutally defeated and then incorporated this ancient state as just another Thai-run province. But many locals still continue to fight today to try to regain their independence from Thailand.

Ten Lui Mei

Ten Lui Mei is today presumed to be the Chinese name for Tenasserim province. The name Tenasserim is believed, like Phuket, to originally be a Malay name derived from "Tanah- sari" or "land of the Fragrant Aloe woods". Tenasserim is today shown on maps as part of southern Burma, but historically it included the whole deserted but thickly forested northwestern peninsular coast from roughly Phuket up to Tavoy in Burma today. Strong leaders in Tenasserim at several times claimed the island as part of their dominions. The Chinese customs inspector and diarist Chau Ju-Kua in 1226 noted the relative backwardness of Ten Lui Mei in comparison to the richer entrepôt cities on the central peninsular east coast: "Its ruler wears flowers in his hair, which is gathered into a topknot. Over his shoulders he wears a red garment covered with white. On audience days he ascends an open dais, for the country is wholly without palace buildings of any kind. Palm leaves are used as dishes in eating and drinking; neither spoons nor chopsticks are used, which is done with the fingers."[44]

Another 12th-century Chinese account of Ten Lui Mei specifically sings the praises of the quality of the region's scented woods, particularly its Gharuwood: "Its trees are a thousand years old … it is like something belonging to the immortals. Light one stick and the whole house is filled with a fragrant mist … it is priceless and rarely to be seen in this world."[45]

Keddah, Katthah, Kedaram, Kalah or Kattigara

This large ancient entrepôt has been referred to by Arab, Persian and Indian chroniclers over the centuries by these various names: Kalah, Katthah, Kedaram or Kattigara. These names are today generally presumed to refer to the port of Kuala Keddah in northwest Malaysia. Some historians however believe that these different names may have referred to separate peninsular ports on the west coast such as Mergui or Takuapa. Or possibly these various names were simply a generic moniker used by these Indian and Middle Eastern chroniclers to refer to the whole peninsular west coast and all its entrepôts.

4.3 The stone base of a temple in Keddah, Malaysia, believed to be around 2000 years old. Most ancient structures in the region were made of wood and have disappeared long ago in the tropical climate.

From the extensive ancient stone ruins found in the Bujang valley at the foot of the great Gunrun Jerai mountain on the Keddah coast today, it is clear that an important ancient entrepôt, a Hindu-Buddhist trade kingdom, was based there from around the first century AD, making it one of the earliest centers of civilization, trade and power in the peninsula. It may even be the kingdom established by the mythical Indian seaman Marong Mahawangsa (see Chapter 2). In later years the sultan of Keddah with his large fleet of war prows and his able and combative Orang Laut (Sea Gypsy) captains, claimed, and sometimes controlled, all the west coast islands up to and north of Phuket, mainly for their yields of birds' nests, tin and the ambergris found on their beaches. These Middle Eastern sailors and travelers have left a large body of writings about Keddah (or a similarly named entrepôt), noting that it was the main port of call for Arab merchants traveling from Oman to China. Al Mas'udi, a 10th-century Arab geographer and visitor from Baghdad, wrote, "The town is the general rendezvous for the Muslim ships of Siraf [the Persian Gulf] and Oman where they meet the ships from eastwards."[46]

Abu al-Fida, a Kurdish geographer, tells us that Keddah was "a fertile land [where] merchant vessels replenished their water casks from the city wells." The seventh-century Sanskrit stage drama "Kaumudi Mahotsava" mentions the city of Katahanga as famous "for its gay life." In 916 Abu Zayed, a trader from Oman, wrote that "Kalah is the centre for commerce for aloewood, camphor, sandalwood, ivory, tin, ebony, spices of all kind and a host of other objects too numerous to mention."[47] Abu Dulaf, an Arab traveler from Uzbekistan, came to Keddah in 943 and wrote, "When I arrived at Kalah I found it very great with strong walls, numerous gardens and abundant springs … I found there a tin mine … in the entire world there do not exist such tin mines as the ones in Kalah."[48] Another early Arab writer, the Moroccan Muhammad Al Idrisi, also speaks of the high quality of the local tin – "the metal was pure and bright" – though he adds, in a more human vein, "After its extraction the local merchants adulterated it before exporting it."[49]

Sinbad the Sailor's Stomping Ground?

These Persian and Arab mariners returned home to their barren and dry homelands with fantastic stories of the exotic jungled lands they had seen on the other side of the Indian Ocean and they soon became the setting for fabulous sailors' legends such as the tales of Sinbad the Sailor in *The Thousand and One Nights*. These fables describe the region as comprising "densely wooded lands … where ships arrived daily from different quarters of the world carrying aloes, sandal, camphor, pepper and ginger."[50] The fables tell us that in these ambrosial lands ambergris flowed in the rivers, itinerant pepper-gatherers sailed between the islands, people consumed madness-inducing marijuana and "frightful savages" practiced piracy and cannibalism on passing traders. The ominous interiors of these islands held lost jungle valleys where rhinoceroses roamed and gigantic man-eating pythons "as long as palm-trees" and other sinister creatures prowled with "eyes like coals of fire".

Such fabulous seafarer tales told of the Malay Peninsula were often actually based on facts. An ancient Chinese account noted that the peninsula was home to a large bird which has the claws of an eagle and speaks in the human tongue. This awesome-sounding bird, on closer inspection, turned out to be none other than the most commonplace mynah bird which does have talons almost like those of an eagle, though much smaller, and which – when captive – can be taught, parrot-like, to repeat a few human words. Greek writers also recorded earnestly that real Satyrs lived in the forests in the Malay Peninsula. (Satyrs are the shy half-men, half-animal gods with tails who prance around in Greek theatre playing flutes, etc.) This yarn no doubt came from tales told by returning sailors of the "Orang-utans", or "Men-of the jungle", shy and with long tails, which lived in the interior jungles.

In The Thousand and One Nights, Sinbad is an Arab sailor from Basra in Iraq, then part of the Abbasid Caliphate (750-1258). In one tale he arrives on one island in the East that produced – (just as Phuket did at the time) – "tin from its mines, Indian canes (rattan) and excellent Camphor."[51] There, Sinbad frequented the society of the learned Indians who had gathered as courtiers and traders around the local rajah. (The rajah of Thalang, as we have seen, would probably have had such Indian Brahmin courtiers at the time.) Sinbad was so enchanted with this Elysian isle he decided to forsake the stress and travails of his busy life back home in Basra and remain on the island where, like many other visitors to Phuket over the millennia, and still today, he recounts how he "married a beautiful lady … bought slaves and fine lands and built me a great house. And thus settled myself … to enjoy the pleasures of life … and employed myself wholly in enjoying the society of my friends and making merry with them".[52]

5

Srivijaya and its Rivals

AD 700 TO 1300

The Mysterious Srivijayan Empire

Today, Palembang, a rather forgettable city in Sumatra, shows little evidence of having once been the center of a great, but rather mysterious, maritime empire that arose during the seventh century and appears to have to become, after Funan, the next great Southeast Asian empire and the overlord of the central peninsular kingdoms and Phuket Island.

Palembang probably started life as another also-ran Malay riverine settlement scraping a living from agriculture, trade and piracy. After about AD 400, as ship and sail technology improved, the east to west merchant and trade ships began to pass through the Straits of Malacca. As we have seen, the main threat on this route was from the pirates in these narrow straits. One Chinese record from 776 calls these peninsular pirates "eaters of men ... who feed upon things more horrible than corpses ... frightful to look at, unnaturally dark and lean, terrible and as cruel as death."[53] Another early Chinese captain who passed through the straits at the time wrote, "When junks sail to the Western Ocean ... of a certainty two or three hundred prahus will put out to attack them for several days. Sometimes the junks are fortunate enough to escape ... otherwise the crews are butchered and the merchandise made off with in quick time."[54]

The rajah of Palembang, strategically situated near this growing new trade route, must have come to the same realization as the Funanese had five centuries earlier – that it was more fruitful to protect and trade with passing ships rather than just raid them. He therefore enrolled the poachers as his gamekeepers by convincing the Orang Laut (Malay Sea Gypsy) pirates in his area to patrol the straits against other pirates and raiders and to force passing boats to call in at Palembang to victual, trade and pay a security tax, the proceeds of which he shared with these Sea Gypsy captains and crews. As the Chinese diarist Chau Ju-Kua reported, "When a trading vessel passes by San-fo-tsi [Srivijaya] without making it a port of call, the country's ships would come out and kill the sailors to the last man, with those who man them being ready to die. It is for this reason that the country has become an important maritime center."[55] By 600, with Palembang and its Sea Gypsy fleets exerting power over the straits and the lesser rajahs on either side of it, the rajah of Palembang became known as a maharaja ("Great Rajah") and called his new kingdom "Srivijaya" meaning "Sacred Victory". In 670, Sri Jayanasa, the maharaja of Srivijaya, sent an embassy to the emperor of China to receive his recognition of his empire. In 671 when the 37-year-old Chinese Buddhist monk and scholar I-Ching [I Tsing] traveled from China to India, he sailed first to Srivijaya and wrote:

> "At the time when the monsoon began to blow, we set sail for the south … the five-tiered sail carried us away from the somber north. For long we voyaged over the illimitable deep, where the sea was intersected by mountainous waves and, slanting across the mighty ocean, enormous swells reached cloud-like to the sky. In less than 20 days we reached … the city of Srivijaya."[56]

I-Ching spent six months there and stated that it had high culture and learning: "In the kingdom, there are more than a thousand Buddhist priests who are devoted to study in every possible subject, exactly as is done in the Middle Kingdom and in India."[57]

The Srivijayan Empire in the Malay Peninsula

A local stele (standing stone) inscription records that in 683 Maharaja Sri Jayanasa left Palembang with a 50-ship fleet and an army of 20,000 men with which "he conferred upon Srivijaya victory power and riches." This may have been when he first subjugated Phuket Island and the rajah of Thalang. However another inscribed stele dated 775 found near the city of Ligor (Nakorn Sri Thammarat today) – and one of the earliest steles found in the Malay Peninsula – commemorates the founding there of new Buddhist monuments by order of the maharajah of Srivijaya. So by the end of the eighth century the central peninsular kingdoms appear to also have become vassals of Srivijaya. Paul Wheatley, a leading scholar of this period, is confident that the maharajahs of Palembang "exerted a monopoly of authority and jurisdiction over the Malacca straits at least as far northwards as Phuket Island."[58] This is further confirmed by a contemporary report by a Chinese inspector of trade at Fukien, who wrote of Srivijaya, "This country lies on the ocean and is the mistress of the straits through which foreign traffic by sea in whichever direction must pass. Her dependencies are amongst others: Teng-ya-nong [Terengganu], Ling-ys-seu-kia [Langkasuka], Ki-lantan [Kelantan], Fo-l-an [Phatalung], Je-loting [?], Tamaling [Tambralinga], Kia-lia [Chaiya], Si-lan, [Ujang Selang – Phuket?] and Lanwouli [Lamuri in Sumatra?]."[59]

The precise political structure of the Srivijayan Empire remains a mystery, but it seems to have been a thalassocracy, or confederation of seafaring communities on the edge of the forests working together to keep the seaways safe in order to attract trade. The maharajah, we are told in one stele inscription, declared that "wherever [merchants] may find themselves in his kingdom, there be in that place no thieves, no ruffians and no adulterers."[60]

Srivijayan dominance and control in the Malacca Straits did seem to restrain the previous rampant piracy there so that more and more ships started using this sea route. By the late eighth century it had become more popular than the more cumbersome trans-peninsular trade routes. It also appears that the peoples of the Srivijayan Empire were lightly burdened by forced-labor corvée, as Srivijaya did not build such huge religious monuments as did the Javanese Sailendra Dynasty and the Khmer kings at the time.

There are, however, some large temples in Chaiya, just north of Surathani, presumed to be from the Srivijayan period. Chaiya is believed to have been an important Srivijayan regional administrative center and some historians have even argued it was a later capital of the empire.

By 851 Sulayman, an Arab geographer, wrote of Srivijaya (which the Arabs called Zabag),"The maharajah of Zabag is the sovereign of a large number of islands which extend for 1,000 parasangs [roughly 800 kilometers] or even more in distance. The maharajah of Zabag exercises his authority over these islands and coasts."[61] In 996, while Europe was wallowing deep in its grim Dark Ages, the Arab geographer Masudi was writing of the glories of Srivijaya, "This empire of the maharajah has an

5.1 The remains of a Srivijayan temple in Chaiya near Surathani, probably the major Srivijayan center in the region.

enormous population and innumerable armies. No one can within two years, with a ship of the utmost speed, go over all these isles, each of which is inhabited. Their king is in possession of more varieties of perfumes and aromatics than any other king. His territory produces camphor, aloes, cloves, sandalwood, nutmeg, cardamom and cubebs, ivory and tin."[62] The Persian trader Ibn al Faqih, explaining the cosmopolitan nature of this empire, more colorfully tells us in 902 that there were so many different nationalities of traders in Palembang that even the local parrots "could speak Arabic, Hindi, Persian and Greek."[63]

Challenges to Srivijayan Dominance, 900-1300

By the 10th century Srivijaya, whose empire now straddled the two most lucrative arteries of east-west commerce, the Malacca Straits and the trans-peninsular routes, was the envy of most other ambitious leaders in the region. Over the next two centuries powerful competitors attacked its domains from various sides. As early as 900 one Khmer inscription tells us that a large Kambojan naval expedition invaded the Srivijayan central peninsular sub-kingdoms of Pan Pan and Tambralinga and "subjected" them "as far as the Bay of Bengal", probably meaning across to the west coast ports such as Takuapa, Phang Nga and Tharua in Phuket. Another inscription believed to be from 994 also tells us that one expansionist Javanese king raised a great war fleet and audaciously directly raided and sacked the Srivijayan capital of Palembang itself.

The Chola Challenge

While Srivijaya was recovering from these attacks from the east, the powerful Chola kingdom then attacked from the west. Chola was an ancient Tamil merchant kingdom on India's southeastern Coromandel Coast (a name derived from "Chola Mandala" meaning Chola Kingdom). Since the earliest periods of Indian-Malay relations, these

Tamil Cholas had been dominant in the Bay of Bengal trade. During the Srivijayan Empire period many of the most influential Indian traders and rulers who had settled in west coast peninsular ports such as Phuket were Cholas.

In 1026, the powerful Chola King Rajendra dispatched a great war fleet under his officer Rajah Shulan to attack Srivijaya. This was probably due to a squabble over access rights through the Malacca Straits and the trans-peninsular trade routes. However, a Tamil inscription on a temple wall in Thanjavur in south India explains, without the political correctness of today, that the attack was simply because "Rajendra Chola was a mighty Rajah … whose purpose was held to reduce all the cities both in the east and west to his subjection."

The Thai historian Srisak Walliporn in 1984 argued that this great Chola invasion fleet of 1026 probably made the base for its peninsular campaign in Phang Nga Bay and Phuket, because there was already a large Chola presence in the area and the local rajahs, such as the rajah of Thalang (Phuket) and their retainer armies may also have been Cholas. One inscription in Pali (Tamil) found on the stone lid of a ninth-century water tank discovered near Takuapa reads, "This is the Avani-maranam water tank, excavated at the command of the Manigramam [a mercantile corporation of Tamil traders] and guarded by the members of Manikpuram garrison and the residents of the military camp."[64] This "Manikpuram" (meaning "Glass Town" or "Jewel Town" in Pali) and its garrison are mentioned in another Indian record as a major Tamil trading center on the Malay Peninsula.

5.2 This stone, inscribed in Pali, dated to around the 9th century tells of a nearby Indian Tamil trader guild and military garrison possibly based in Manik village in Phuket.

In 1963 Yiamyong Surakitbanhan, a Thai historian specializing in southern Thai archaeology, noted that the only place in the whole central peninsula whose current name includes "Manik" is Ban Manik in Phuket.[65] Yiamyong also mentions that several ancient artifacts have been found near Ban Manik. It is indeed possible that Ban Manik in Thalang, which sits on Srisoonthorn Road between the Heroines Monument and Cherngtalay, was the site of this ancient Tamil town which specialized in making glass or jewelry for trade, like the bead-making factory at Klong Tom in Krabi. Ban Manik may well have been the earliest seat of the rajah and Phuket's first main town, as it sits on flat land in the very center of the island far enough inland to be hidden and more safe against surprise raids by pirates or invaders, yet it also lies further up the very same river as Tharua, Phuket's main port in ancient times.

We are told by ancient inscriptions that this great Chola invasion fleet and marine army of 1026 (which was possibly based in Phang Nga Bay) raided and captured the main Srivijayan central peninsular port cities of Keddah, Takuapa, Ligor and Chaiya before heading south into the heartland of the Srivijayan Empire. To meet this Chola force a huge Srivijayan Malay army under the leadership of a Rajah Chula headed north. The two armies met near the ancient fort of Ganga Negara near the mountainous pass just south of Ipoh in Malaysia. The story of this battle is told by an 11th-century Pali inscription on a temple wall in India. It is written with all the normal histrionic and vainglorious clichés of early Indian inscriptions, which related history in much the same style as Bollywood movies do today. However it is still worth recording here, both for its historical value and because it's a dramatic read. The inscription, for example, describes the great Chola army moving south as, "so vast was the army on the march that boundless tracts of forest became treeless plains and mighty rivers were drunk dry."[66] The Srivijayan Malay army facing it was so big it was "as a sea at full tide, the elephants and the horses were like islands in this vast sea, the banners and pendants were like a forest, the weapons serried row upon row."

5.3 A 13th century Kambojan temple bas-relief of a Southeast Asian army on the move.

In the early morning heat near Ipoh the great battle began:

"The very skies were rent by the beating of drums and the blowing of conch shells and then the armies fell upon each other with a mighty roar, so that even if it had thundered in the heavens, the sound would not have been heard for the battle cries of the valiant warriors and the clash of weapon upon weapon. So thick was the dust of conflict that the light of day was darkened as by an eclipse of the sun and such was the confusion that friend could not be told from foe. Attackers were themselves attacked and men even stabbed their own friends. Through the long day the struggle swayed back and forth ... Towards the evening the Malays began to force the men of Kalinga [the Cholas] back towards the sea. Seeing his dreams of a glorious victory celebration and his historical epilogue that he wanted to endure for a thousand years, fading before a vision in front of him of mutilated corpses piled high like a dunghill, Rajah Shulan (the Chola leader) rushed into the fray, hurling a challenge at Rajah Chula (the Malay leader) who was mounted on an elephant of prodigious size. But the elephant of Rajah Shulan was no coward and the two elephants met with a huge crash like that of a thunderbolt splitting a hill, the clash of tusk on tusk sounded like peal on peal of thunderous lightening. Neither elephant would own defeat. Then Rajah Chula stood up on his elephant, poising his spear, which he hurled at Rajah Shulan and it passed clean through the howdah, projecting a finger span on the far side of it. Rajah Shulan shot an arrow which transfixed Rajah Chula through the chest so that he stumbled and fell from his elephant and died. When the men of Rajah Chula saw that he had been killed, they, all of them, broke and fled, hotly pursued by the men of Kalinga who slew any that delayed or fell onto their hands and knees. The men of Kalinga entered the fort of Glenggiu and sacked it, gaining more booty than a man could count. Rajah Chula had a very beautiful daughter called Onang Kiu. She was offered to Raja Shulan, who took her as his consort. Finally Rajah Shulan sailed home to Kalinga taking home as his bride this beautiful orphaned daughter of his former adversary."[67]

This Chola attack of 1026 eventually turned out to be only an extended raid and the Tamil army and fleet returned home with their booty and no doubt with a better deal arranged on taxes for their trade ships and goods passing through the Malacca Straits and over the trans-peninsular trade routes. In 1068, another Chola king, Vira Rajedra, again attacked and captured "Kedaram" (Keddah) and we are told they also raided all the surrounding coasts. However, they also ultimately returned home believing that the Malay Peninsula was "too far beyond the sounding seas" to hold permanently.

By the late 11th century these successive raids appear to have weakened Srivijayan imperial control over the central peninsula sufficiently for the next regional invader to conquer and take hegemony over Phuket and the surrounding regions – this was the joint Mon/Burmese kingdom of Pagan.

The Burmese and Mon Challenge

We first hear of the Burmese as wild tribes-people in eastern Tibet around the third century BC. The Chinese recorded hunting them down to use in their human sacrifice rituals. Not surprisingly, the Burmese decided to clear off further to the south. By the 10th century AD these warlike Burmese tribes began appearing in the Irrawaddy River delta, where they came up against the ancient Mon kingdom of Dvaravati.

The Dvaravati kingdom was an ancient confederation of large walled cities with a highly developed culture; it is believed to have been the first Southeast Asian kingdom to have adopted Indian Theravada Buddhism and subsequently spread it around the region. The marijuana-using Mons of Dvaravati were far more cultured and artistic than the more martial Burmese. They converted these aggressive intruders to Buddhism and united with them to use them to fight against the Kambojan Empire that was then pressuring the Mon cities of Dvaravati by expanding westwards into the Chao Phraya River basin. By 1050 this new, combined Burmese and Mon kingdom was taken over by a bellicose young Burmese warlord from the city of Pagan who crowned himself King Ainruddah (or Anoaratha) of Pagan.

After the Chola raids, Srivijaya's influence in the central peninsula was tenuous and, seeing little opposition in the area, King Ainruddah of Pagan campaigned southwards down the peninsular west coast and by 1058 the Burmese chronicles tell us that he and the Pagan fleets had conquered all of Tenasserim, including Takuapa and "Salankre" as they called Ujang Salang (Phuket). Ainruddah reportedly gave Phuket to one of his loyal warlords as a private fiefdom. A contemporary Sri Lankan chronicle also confirms this Burmese occupation of Tenasserim, specifically mentioning their control of the ports of Takuapa and Salang (Phuket). The rather nationalistic, chest-thumping Burmese "Glass Palace Chronicles", which were commissioned in 1829 by a later Burmese king, claim that the Burmese kings of Pagan even gained suzerainty over the whole Malay Peninsula as far as Singapore, but this is debatable. Based on his studies of Buddhist votive tablets and scripts, G. H. Luce, a leading scholar of this abstruse and little recorded period in the peninsula, believed that the kingdom of Pagan did remain the overlord of Phuket Island for some 160 years, from around 1060 till 1210.[68] However, other leading scholars of the period disagree, such as David Wyatt who believed that by 1130 the kingdom of Tambralinga and its vassal Phuket had actually fallen under the hegemony of the king of Sri Lanka through a marriage between their two Theravada Buddhist royal families. [69]

The Sri Lankan Challenge

The Sinhalese Sri Lankans, like the Tamil Cholas, were another important naval and trading power in the Bay of Bengal since the earliest times. Sri Lankan merchants seem to have particularly predominated on the trans-peninsular trade route from Trang to Ligor in the kingdom of Tambralinga. These powerful kings of Sri Lanka and Pagan apparently fell into conflict over control of these lucrative central peninsular trade routes.

5.4 Sunset over Pagan, Burma, which was the capital of a kingdom which probably ruled over Phuket during much of the 11th and 12th centuries.

The Sri Lankan Chronicle, "The Culavamsa", records that in 1160 the king of Pagan refused Sri Lankan traders the use of any elephants on the northern trans-peninsular routes he controlled. Then in 1162 he decreed that all the Sri Lankans in Tenasserim be arrested, including a high-born Sri Lankan princess who was passing through Mergui with her entourage on her way to wed a Kambodjan prince. This was apparently all too much for the Sri Lankan king and his merchant princes. In 1165 they sent an armed fleet of over 100 warships which raided and sacked the southern ports of the kingdom of Pagan, probably including Tharua in Phuket. The Burmese chronicles themselves note that in this period the king of Pagan's southern provinces fell into a state of "anarchy and rebellion." But after some twenty years of conflict, in 1186, the Pagan and Sri Lankan kings eventually came to a settlement, probably forced on them by the frustrated merchant princes from both their courts. An inscription in one Pagan temple states that by 1196 the king of Pagan again counted Tavoy, Tenasserim, Takuapa and Salankre (Phuket) among his vassal states, whilst Sri Lanka apparently maintained its influence over the more southern trans-peninsular trade routes such as that from Trang to Ligor.

The Demise of the Peninsular Empires of Pagan and Srivijaya

By 1256 a most arrogant king called Narathihapate took over the throne of Pagan. For example, stone inscriptions, which he had made in his own honor, called him "the supreme commander of an army of 37 million men" (which was pure nonsense given the tiny populations then) and "the swallower of 300 dishes of curry daily."[70] He also had an inscription made boasting that he owned, and regularly serviced, over 3,000 concubines. Whilst King Narathihapate was busy indulging in this debauchery of hedonism, far to his north the fierce Mongol horseback warriors under Kublai Khan swept in from the barren western steppes and took over China. In 1270 Kublai Khan then sent emissaries south to demand the subjection of those kingdoms on China's southern borders. Sitting on his decorated throne in Pagan, this supercilious King Narathihapate met with these Mongol emissaries who had the audacity to demand his subjection. With a wave of his bejeweled hand he ordered these insolent visitors to be taken from his sight and killed. This rather intemperate act provoked Kublai Khan to send 12,000 of his best Tartar cavalry south in response. They defeated the Pagan army and sacked and destroyed Pagan city and King Narathihapate fled south where his own son ultimately killed him. The kingdom of Pagan, probably the overlord of Phuket for much of the 12th and 13th centuries, then disintegrated and for the next 250 years Burma degenerated into little more than a pit of infighting between snarling local Shan, Mon and Burmese warlords.

By the 12th century, Srivijayan supremacy in the central peninsula had more or less dissolved under the numerous raids and attacks from outside contenders. In 1170 a Chinese customs officer recorded that Persia and Java, no longer Srivijaya, were now the richest nations trading with China. By 1178 the Chinese emperor even decreed that embassies sent from Srivijaya were no longer important enough to even enter the Chinese court and had to remain on the Fujian coast.

The former Srivijayan capital of Palembang was ultimately taken over in a revolt by some 2,000 Chinese émigrés who lived there. They gained control of the city and governed it themselves as one of the first Chinese-run cities in Southeast Asia. These renegade Chinese turned back to piracy. The former Srivijayan lands of western Borneo, southern Sumatra and the southern Malay Peninsula were taken over by the increasingly powerful new Hindu Majahapit Empire of Java.

So by the later 13th century, the great empires of both Srivijaya and Pagan and the authority they seem to have held for several centuries over the central peninsula and the rajah of Thalang on Phuket, faded away. This gave Tambralinga, the local kingdom based in the fortified city of Ligor (Nakorn Sri Thammarat), the opportunity to rise up and become the new independent power in the region and to exercise its hegemony over Phuket.

6

The Kingdom of Tambralinga and Chandrabanu

1200 TO 1250

During the 12th and 13th centuries, despite all the regional fighting, trade continued to burgeon and flourish in the Malay Peninsula. Sung dynasty Chinese records, for example, show that in 1053 annual imports into China of products from the "Nan Yang" such as elephant tusks, rhinoceros horns, strings of pearls, aromatics and incense totaled 53,000 (Chinese measured) units. By 1175, only a century later however, Chinese records show the volume of imports had grown almost tenfold to 500,000 units.[71] In Ligor (Nakorn Sri Thammarat) a central hub in the trans-peninsular trade and the capital of the now Buddhist kingdom of Tambralinga, the local lords, nobles and traders grew increasingly wealthy and powerful.

In 1196 the Chinese chronicle, the "Daoyizazhi", tells us that the kingdom of Tambralinga became sufficiently strong and independent to start sending its own emissaries and tribute missions to the Chinese court. Later Thai chronicles also tell us that by the start of the 13th century, Ligor had become the strongest city in the peninsula under a forceful king they called Sri Tammasok, who is most probably the same leader known to the Malays, Sri Lankans and Indians as Chandrabanu.

Little is known of the early life of this King Chandrabanu (it is also possible that there were two kings with the same honorific title). It seems he was born sometime around 1200 and rose to become king of Tambralinga in his early twenties. An inscription on a stele found near Chaiya dated to 1230 states that it was erected to honor "Dhanmarat Chandrabanu Sri Thammarat, King of Tambralinga." This stele indicates that Tambralinga was probably already independent of any Srivijayan hegemony by this time, as there is no reference to the latter. It also indicates that Tambralinga had by then probably subdued Chaiya, formerly the capital of the kingdom of Pan Pan. One of the earliest Thai chronicles tells us that Chandrabanu and his armies expanded Ligor's rule as far north as Prachuap Kiri Khan and as far south as Keddah and Patani and that Ligor included amongst its vassals "Sa-ulan" – which was probably Salang, or Phuket.

Tambralinga's, or Ligor's, claim over Phuket is also supported by a contemporary seal dug up in Nakorn Sri Thammarat showing a design with a constellation of the 12 "naksat" (subordinate) states ruled by Ligor. One is them is called "Takuathalang", or "Tin Town of Thalang" (Phuket). Each naksat state was assigned one of the animals in the Chinese zodiac; Thalang was given the dog as its emblem and the official seal of the subordinate rajah of Thalang later featured the image of a dog. Indeed the name Kamala, or Kamra as it used to be called, is said by one local Phuket historian to derive from "Ban Kra maa" or "dog seal village" though others assert that it comes from the old Malay word "Gamara", meaning beautiful lady. Thalang is also referred to in another Ligor script as "Dog City". Lt. Low, a British East India Company emissary who visited Phuket in 1824, wrote that, "On the east side of the island at the point called Laem Phra Chau there is a rock on which the Siamese affirm there is a sculptured figure of a dog with a crow by his side ... Their worship of the dog can be traced to remote antiquity. The last remnant of this idolatrous worship ... was a statue of a dog situated near Tarooa. It was conveyed off the island only two years ago by some Malays."[72] The base of this statue may be the still-revered stump of the "Lak Muang" (city post) which stands in the middle of Tharua town today still colorfully bound in Buddhist ribbons and garlands.

Chandrabanu's Sri Lankan Invasions

During the mid-13th century, as the kingdom of Tambralinga grew in wealth and power and straddled several of the trans-peninsular trade routes, it, with its large navy, became one of the region's more powerful trading states. The only remaining outside power with any real influence in Tambralinga was Sri Lanka. In 1233, therefore, the ever-ambitious King Chandrabanu declared war on Sri Lanka. According to the Thai chronicles, this was done to obtain the two great relics of the Buddha – his left canine tooth and his alms bowl, which were held in the Sri Lankan city of Kandy. Obtaining such relics would of course greatly enhance King Chandrabanu's spiritual eminence and credibility. However, local leaders and their spin-doctors – the monks – often used the quest for Buddha relics as a righteous reason to raise an army and for their men to give up their lives in battle.

6.1 A statue of the over-ambitious King Chandrabanu of Tambralinga.

There were probably more practical reasons for Chandrabanu's decision. Sri Lankan traders probably still controlled much of Tambralinga's trade. The Theravada monks of Sri Lanka, who had possession of the Buddha relics, held much spiritual kudos among the local people of Tambralinga and Ligor is estimated at the time to have had the biggest population of Sri Lankan Brahmins and monks in the peninsula. [73] They were both politically and economically influential, as their monasteries controlled much land and many slaves that fell outside King Chandrabanu's earthly remit. The spiritual ascendancy of Sri Lanka in this era is testified to by the common myth from that period of the hallowed Lady White Blood. There are many versions of this myth today, mainly Buddhist but even some Muslim versions. Essentially they tell of a devout daughter from the central peninsula who made a pilgrimage to the Buddha relics in Sri Lanka. She returned sanctified and undertook a virtuous life and built temples around the region including, so they say, the one in Phuket in Thalang town beside the main Thalang traffic lights on Thepkasatri Road today.

In 1233, undaunted by such spiritual muscle, the ambitious King Chandrabanu ordered a huge war fleet to sail against Sri Lanka to be assembled in the Trang River. The fleet probably consisted of upwards of 100 war prows carrying anywhere between 20 and 70 men each. The rajah of Thalang, as a vassal of Chandrabanu, would have been obliged to supply men, boats and war provisions for this expedition. This invasion is historically notable as it is the only known time that a Southeast Asian nation has invaded another country or kingdom outside of Southeast Asia.

6.2. An early Malay war boat with its warriors shooting poisoned darts from blowpipes. Phuket men would have been called upon to join King Chandrabanu's invasions of Sri Lanka.

"The Culavamsa", a Sri Lankan chronicle, tells us that in 1234, "under the treacherous pretext that they were also followers of Buddha … a king of the Javakas [Malays] known by the name of Chandrabanu, landed with a terrible army and Lanka, which had just been harassed by Magha (a Chola leader), was ravaged anew by these Javakas … The wicked Javaka soldiers invaded every landing place and, with their poisoned arrows, like terrible snakes, without cease, harassed whomever they caught sight of and, raging their fury, laid waste to all Lanka."[74] The Sea Gypsies, as we know, used poisoned arrows and poisoned darts, which they had probably learned about from the Negritos and no doubt Chandrabanu used these able Sea Gypsies to captain and man his war fleet. Place names and archaeology also back up this ancient chronicle's accounts; for example several krisses – the distinctive snake-like, wavy-bladed Malay knife, often poison tipped – have been excavated in Sri Lanka and dated to the period. Chandrabanu and his Malay army appear to have been soundly defeated when they moved inland to attempt to take the Sri Lankan capital of Kandy.

Undaunted, the ever-ambitious Chandrabanu and his fleet returned to Tambralinga and set about preparing a second invasion fleet. This time he persuaded a Tamil Chola prince from southern India to join him and in 1247 a second Malay fleet sailed west from Phang Nga Bay and Trang and again landed in the Jaffna Peninsula and again advanced on Kandy – and was again defeated, this time by a joint Sri Lankan and Tamil Pandyan army which apparently came south from India to support the Sri Lankan king. The Culavamsa notes that Chandrabanu, "The Lord of Men, was sent flying defenseless by the Pandyan general."[75]

Tambralinga Disappears

Chandrabanu's Malay and Tamil army again retreated to its bases and ships on the Jaffna Peninsula. Chandrabanu then proclaimed Jaffna a vassal state of Tambralinga and gave it to one of his sons who ruled over Jaffna with his Malay troops for some 30 more years until his death. It is argued by some historians that King Chandrabanu died during this second Sri Lankan expedition; this is unclear. Certainly Chandrabanu is never heard of again. Nor is the ancient kingdom of Tambralinga, which had probably been the overlord of Phuket for several centuries. One has to deduce that the covetous Chandrabanu's grandiose Sri Lankan expeditions, and his attempts to make Tambralinga a central player in the lucrative trans-peninsular and Bay of Bengal trade, must have severely weakened the kingdom and facilitated its annexation and subjugation by the next warlike people to move south into the central peninsula – the Thais.

7

The Coming of the Thais and Islam

AD 600 TO 1400

The T'ai people probably originated, like other Mongoloids, in the frozen wastes of Mongolia, and like many other Mongoloid tribes they gradually headed south to warmer and more hospitable climes.

T'ai people means "free people". The Thais appear to have always lived just outside the jurisdiction of the Chinese Empire. As imperial China expanded south, the T'ai peoples kept migrating south just ahead of it in small clans and tribes. Today these different groups of T'ai peoples have spread out very widely in Southeast Asia and include the Thais, the Laos, the Shans of Burma and the Ahom people in Assam, India. By 650, the Thai peoples had formed a large, independent, highly militarized and relatively civilized kingdom called "Nan Chao", in what is now Yunnan province, China.

By the eighth century other Thai clans, still heading south, began emerging from the mountains into the river valleys of what is northern Thailand today. Being a martial people and good horsemen, these Thai warrior clans tended to dominate and rule over the Mon and Khmer agriculturalists they encountered in northern Thailand, moving over them, yet keeping their own Thai culture like, it has been said, oil on water. By the 10th century, these Thai tribes and warlords reached central Thailand and, like the Burmese, came up against the walled cities of the more Indianized and civilized Dvaravati and Khmer kingdoms. It was most probably from contact with the Mons of Dvaravati that the Thais gave up their earlier more animist and Chinese culture and adopted Indian Theravada Buddhism as their religion and Indian names, Buddhist art and architectural styles.

The Khmers of the kingdom of Angkor called these hardy Thai newcomers from the north the "Syam" people meaning "savage". The first references to the "Syam" people appear in early 11th century Chinese chronicles. These "Syamese" men worked as mercenaries or farmers or moved into the Mon and Khmer towns and worked as craftsmen while their industrious womenfolk worked as market traders or craftswomen. Zhou Daguan, a Chinese emissary visiting Angkor in 1296, wrote that, "The Siamese women sew and mend and when the fabrics worn by the Cambodians become worn, Siamese are called in to repair the damage."[76]

The Rise of Sukhothai

The Khmer kingdom of Angkor, which ruled over what is north and central Thailand today, was weak at the time and unable to exert real military control over its far-off northern provinces. In 1238 the Thai chronicles tell us that one Thai warlord, Sri In-draditya, and his henchmen took control of an important Kambojan walled city and its surrounding feudal area in the central Thai plain. He renamed the city "Sukhothai" meaning "Happy Thai" and defeated a Khmer force sent north to try to subdue and discipline him.

Soon after the establishment of Sukothai, in 1253, Mongol China attacked and overran the 600-year-old Thai state of Nan Chao in Yunnan, forcing the Thais there to migrate further south in greater numbers. Under various chieftains and strongmen, these Thai and Lao warlords began to control more and more towns in the region of present-day northern Thailand and Laos. The Khmer kings in Angkor eventually declared war on these ever-encroaching Thai warlords and tribes. These brutal wars went on for over nine years. Zhou Daguan, the visiting Chinese emissary to Angkor in 1296, recorded at the time that, "In the war with the Syamese, all the population was called upon to fight … countryside and villages were completely destroyed."[77]

7.1 A 12th century temple mural depicting market women in Kamboja.

Ramkamheng was the son of Sri Indraditya, the first king of Sukhothai. He was a tall, strong boy who, by the age of 19 had already proved himself in battle. He ascended the Sukhothai throne in 1279 in his early twenties. He formed alliances with the other powerful Thai warlords such as King Mengrai in his kingdom of Lanna at Chiangmai and the T'ai Lao leader in Vieng Chiang. This left Ramkamheng free to fight the Kam-bojans and expand his rule southwards. Ramkamheng turned Sukhothai into a highly militaristic state and spent his first 15 years as king almost permanently on military campaigns in which he beat the Khmers and Mons back and conquered most of the city-states in the central Thai plain. He then moved his armies southwards into the Ma-lay Peninsula. Maybe Ramkamheng, hearing that Tambralinga had been badly weak-ened from its Sri Lankan escapades, made its capital, the holy Buddhist city of Ligor, his next target. The rather disjointed Thai chronicles of Ligor mention a great epidemic in that period which wiped out much of the population of Ligor, possibly facilitating Ramkamheng's conquest of the city. It is unclear today when the first Thai peoples and tribes began to migrate into the central peninsula region. Prof. Charnavit Kasetsiri of Chulalongkorn University, in his book on Ayutthayan peninsular expansion in the

14th and 15th centuries, wrote that there are "numerous indications that … groups of Thais were already living in the … Nakorn Sri Thammarat [Ligor] area before the rise of Sukhothai, (in the mid 13th century) thus assisting the general spread of Sukhothai influence into the area."[78]

What is recorded in some early Thai chronicles, and supported by some Chinese writings, tells us that by 1260 a Thai lord named Phra Panom Wang, the son of the Thai ruler of the powerful city of Petchaburi, had started ruling in Ligor. This new Thai lord reportedly exercised his control over his new Malay, Khmer and Tamil populated dominions by sending out "nine ships to take control of a number of Malayan cities … [and] … sent Malays to establish control over the twelve naksat states traditionally subordinate to Nakorn"[79] (these subordinate "naksat" states of Ligor as we have seen included the rajahdom of Thalang or Phuket Island).

In 1293, according to a Thai stone inscription, which is today suspected of being fictitious, Ramkamheng is reputed to have sent his Sukhothai armies and navies as far down the peninsula as Singapore and through a combination of brute force and marriage alliances, he impressed Sukhothai's power and dominion over many of the Malay rajahs in the peninsula and brought them under the hegemony of Sukhothai. But just over a decade later, in 1307 Ramkamheng drowned whilst swimming in a river in the rainy season. Sukhothai's power was based mainly on his personal stature and prowess. His son, a more scholarly and less martial boy, was unable to hold this far-flung kingdom together. In the far-off peninsula the Malay rajahs and

7.2 The Thai leader King Ramkamhaeng of the Sukhothai Kingdom was probably the first to extend Thai dominion over the Malays in the central peninsula and Phuket in the later 13th century.

the Thai lords in Ligor rebelled and broke away from Sukhothai hegemony and the Thai lords in Ligor probably tried to rule independently over the rajahs and sultans in its subordinate naksat states in the central peninsula.

The Rise of Ayutthaya

As Sukhothai's power faded after Ramkamheng's death, the Syamese plain (central Thailand) disintegrated into a patchwork of small, warring, mainly Thai dominated city-states. The Royal Chronicles of Ayutthaya then tell of the rise to power in the late 14th century of a man called U-tong, who was born to a wealthy Chinese merchant father and a Thai mother in Petchaburi in 1351. U-tong and some followers set up a new settlement on an island in the Chao Praya River and called it Ayutthaya after the holy

Indian city of Ayodhya in the Ramayana. U-tong named himself King Ramathibodi. Ayutthaya became a fortified river port in the lower delta; with a rich agricultural hinterland and the financial backing of his father's Chinese merchant friends the new city prospered and grew. Both neighboring Kamboja and Burma were weak at the time, so King Ramathibodi, by force of arms, commerce and marriage alliances was gradually able to expand Ayutthaya's control over Sukhothai and the patchwork of other Mon, Thai and Khmer city-states in the lower Chao Praya River basin and the northern Malay peninsula. We are told in the Thai chronicles that it was through royal marriages that the city of Ligor and its naksat states next became vassals of Ayutthaya.

As Ayutthayan power grew, its armies, like Sukhothai's beforehand, also pressed down the peninsula and forced most of the Malay rajahs and sultans there to become its vassals. Ayutthaya actually demanded comparatively little from its Malay vassals. They were obliged, once a year, to show their fealty by sending a "Bunga Mas", a small tree made of gold and silver leaves and some gifts, to the king in Ayutthaya. Their rulers were also required to come to Ayutthaya at least once every three years to pay homage, drink the waters of allegiance, give and receive gifts and engage in inter-marriages. In times of war, they were expected to provide provisions and men as the king of Ayutthaya or his viceroy in the peninsula at Ligor demanded. In return, as long as they were obedient, these local sultans and rajahs received the protection of the king in Ayutthaya and his viceroy in Nakorn and were generally left alone as lords of their people and lands. Under this loose system, the peninsula remained a generally wild and lawless place governed and misgoverned by often despotic and piratical local lords.

The Rise of Malacca

Some 40 years after the founding of Ayutthaya, Parameswara, a young Malay lord from Sumatra, "a very warlike young man", rebelled against his Hindu Javanese Majapahit overlords. But his rebellion was defeated and Parameswara was forced to flee with a few followers to the Malay Peninsula. They settled on Temasek Island (Singapore) and lived by piracy and fishing until they were chased out by a fleet from Patani under orders of the Ayutthayan king. In 1402 Parameswara and his followers moved and settled in a bay near the narrowest point of the Straits of Malacca, a logical spot for a pirate and trade base. Many other Malays, wanting to be free of their Majapahit overlords, soon moved to join Parameswara in his new independent Malay settlement and within four months, it is said, 100 Malay families had settled there. Parameswara and his Malay fleet, like the Srivijayans and Funanese before them, decided they could better use their prime position on this central sea route, not just to plunder, but also to trade with and service the Indian, Arab, Chinese and other trading ships passing through the straits. As a result, the place became a convenient trade port and was named Malacca, believed to be derived from the Arabic word "Malakat", meaning market. Malacca soon became a convenient trade entrepôt for other Malay settlements up the west coast of the peninsula such as Phuket.

Map 5
The Peninsula in Ayutthayan Times 14th to 18th Centuries

Tavoy

Ayutthaya

Bangkok

Mergui

Phetchaburi

Tenasserim

Prachup Kiri Khan

Kraburi

Chumporn

Takuapa

Chaiya

Phang Nga

Bangkhli

Ligor (Nakorn Sri Thammarat)

Thalang

Bordelung (Phattalung)

Trang

Singora (Songkla)

Patani

Keddah

Trengannu

Aceh

Perlak

Perak

Pahang

Siak

Malacca

Johore

Temasek
(Singapore)

Cheng Ho and the Great Chinese Fleets

In 1368, a few decades before the establishment of Malacca, the Chinese Ming warlords had expelled the Mongols from China. The new Ming Chinese emperor decided to make an international show of his new power and between 1405 and 1433 he sent out nine huge official Chinese fleets designed to project Ming authority over the "South Seas" and the "Western Ocean" (Indian Ocean). These vast junk fleets were put under the command of the hardy Admiral Cheng Ho, a 35-year-old Chinese Muslim eunuch whose skin, we are told, was "rough like the surface of an orange." There were up to 20,000 men on each of some 50 to 60 huge junks, some over 100 meters long and painted white with two huge eyes on the front.

These fleets sailed as far as India, the Middle East and East Africa from where they brought back gifts for the emperor such as "camel birds" (ostriches) and a giraffe which, we are informed, "gave the emperor great 'wei' [a pleasurable sense of danger]" when it was released in front of him. They also enforced China's political will in the whole region, attacking and dethroning the king of Sri Lanka for having been disrespectful to the Chinese emperor and eliminating the remaining nest of émigré Chinese pirates still operating from Palembang, the old Srivijayan capital. It is recorded that more than 5,000 pirates were captured and executed there by Cheng Ho and his marines.

As Malacca became richer and more successful as a trade port, it remained under threat from both the covetous Ayutthayan and Majahapit kings to their north and south. The Chinese Ming chronicles tell us, "The country was under the rule of Siam and yearly it paid five thousand ounces of gold as tribute. Should it fail to do so, the Siamese would attack it."[80] Parameswara was therefore quick to offer Malacca's submission to Cheng Ho and to request Chinese protection and over the next 20 years Malacca's rapid growth as a trade port was protected and also promoted by China. Malacca became China's de facto offshore trade colony for the South Seas and her naval base and gateway port to the Western Ocean. Cheng Ho established a fortified warehouse in Malacca where goods were brought to be stored and picked up on the voyage home. A large Chinese population established itself and Cheng Ho even brought Chinese women to settle in the city. With such overt Chinese protection and support and a brisk trade, more and more Chinese, Malays, Javanese and Indians came to trade and settle in Malacca. By 1430, in just 30 years, Malacca had grown to become the preeminent peninsular trade centre for cargoes moving from east to west and back, making it one of the biggest and most bustling ports in the world – much to the jealousy and chagrin of the kings of Ayutthaya.

The Coming of Islam

In the early 7th century Mohammed, a former camel caravan manager, took some time off from his camel driving to go and sit in a cave in the silent desert hills outside Mecca and meditate. There in 610 he claims he received his first messages and revelations from Allah which started the new religion of Islam. His inspired Arab followers swept out from their single-story desert mud huts and astonishingly, within a century, had conquered most of the great and civilized empires of North Africa, the Middle East, Persia and even North India, which included the main ports at the western end of the Indian Ocean maritime trade with the Malay Peninsula.

Some Indian chronicles tell of Muslim traders and teachers first appearing on the Malay Peninsula in the 7th century, long before Ayutthaya and Malacca ever existed. In the year 774 two Muslim Arabs, Khurtas Bey and Sulaiman, wrote that they had left the teachings of Islam in Keddah. The earliest archaeological evidence of Islam found in the peninsula to date is a half-dirham Abbasid coin unearthed in Keddah and dated 848.

By the 11th century, as the Muslim Mogul Empire conquered much of North India, more and more Indians converted to Islam. These Muslim Arab, Persian and Indian traders tended to make their eastern trade bases nearest to India in the northern Sumatran ports such as Aceh and Pasai where they had already converted some local Malay lords in the region to Islam, in the same way that their Hindu and Buddhist predecessors had also made converts. By 1136 permanent Islamic communities existed in both Keddah and Trang. Islamic traders would probably have regularly visited Phuket around this time and may have begun making converts there. Marco Polo when he sailed north through the Malacca Straits in 1292 wrote, "The people of Perlak (a port in north Sumatra opposite Phuket) used to all be idolaters, but owing to contact with the Saracen merchants who continually resort here in their ships, they have all been converted to the law of Mahomet."[81]

7.3 An early photo of some Phuket Muslims.

It was mainly through the informal proselytization of these Islamic traders and the preachers and clerics they sometimes brought with them that predominantly Sunni Islam began to spread amongst the Malays in the peninsula. Increasingly, the Malays of Phuket and Phang Nga, despite having Thai overlords in Ligor, would have begun to trade with Malacca and make it their central mart, as it was Malay and much nearer by sea than Ayutthaya or Ligor.

By 1433, due to the great cost of the naval expeditions of Cheng Ho, the Ming court stopped sending out these huge treasure fleets and Parameswara, still the leader of Malacca, was shorn of his Chinese protection. He now urgently needed a new trade and defensive allegiance against the Buddhist Ayutthayans to the north and the Hindu

Javanese to his south. He therefore turned to the growing community of wealthy and increasingly powerful Muslim traders established in the northern Sumatran ports, a coalition of whom was already at war with the Majapahit Empire over terms of access through the straits.

In 1441 Parmeswara converted himself to Islam to gain admission to the Umah or Dar el Islam (the community of Islam) and to obtain these wealthy Muslims as his new trading partners and allies. At the age of 72, he was circumcised, took the new name of Ishkander Shah and made sweeping commercial concessions to all Muslims. The Muslim traders sealed the deal by giving him a beautiful teenage Muslim princess from Sumatra as a wife. Many of these wealthy Persian, Arab and Indian eastern traders then moved from the Sumatran and other surrounding ports, often with an entourage of thousands of servants, wives, slaves and retainers, to set up shop in Malacca. They also brought with them their mullahs and teachers and built mosques; with Parameswara's conversion to Islam, most Malays in Malacca and the city's trading partners in the surrounding ports and river settlements up and down the straits were quick to convert to Islam. This of course also earned them trade connections and tax and political benefits. For example the ruler of the powerful Malay state of Keddah converted to Islam, as did the sultans of Patani, Pahang, Terengganu and Kelantan soon after. It was around this time that Islam would have started to spread among the Malay communities settled around the coasts of Phang Nga Bay and Phuket. These people increasingly began to look to Malacca for Malay leadership, trade and business and to try to avoid the often very harsh local Siamese rule exercised by the Ayutthayan king and his appointed regional viceroy in Ligor.

Ayutthaya and Malacca Compete for Supremacy in the Peninsula

Islam gave the Malay leaders of the peninsula some cohesion against the rule of Buddhist Ayutthaya, and Parmeswara gathered more and more peninsular sultans and rajahs to his side in defiance of Ayutthayan claims of sovereignty over the region. By 1452 he must have felt strong enough to refuse to keep sending his annual tribute of gold to the Ayutthayan king. In response King Trailokanat in Ayutthaya ordered his viceroy in Ligor, Okya Chakri, to raise an army and go south to remove and punish the rebellious Parmeswara and the southern Malay lords who supported him. Tome Pires, a Portuguese who lived in Malacca only some 60 years later, noted however that this conflict between Malacca and Ayutthaya was also about who could control the lucrative tin deposits of the peninsular west coast in places like Phuket. As he noted, "the tin districts … which are on the Keddah side and which were originally under Keddah [which was under Ayutthaya] were taken over by Malacca and they quarreled for this reason, but chiefly it was the [Malay] revolt against subjection". [82]

The rajah and men of Phuket were most likely called upon to join this Ayutthayan/Ligor army that was ordered to head south in 1455 and attack Malacca. The Ayutthayan army encountered the Malaccan army coming north to meet them near Muar in Pahang district in Malaya. As is sometimes the case in central peninsular history, the story of the war is told quite differently by Thai and Malay historical sources. A Thai chronicle, believed to have been written in 1680, over 200 years later, tells us, "The king suppressed the contending factions and went to Prabpak [Pahang] and made his camp at Pathai Kasem and after having taken 120,000 prisoners of war, the royal army returned."[83] However, the Malay Annals, the Sejarah Melayu, written even later, state: "The forces of Siam came and fought against those of Malacca. After a long struggle many of the king of Siam's troops were killed, but Malacca was not defeated. The Siamese retreated … After the Siamese had retreated the defence force dispersed."[84]

7.4 An early Photo of some Malay warriors.

Most likely the result of the battle was inconclusive, so Parmeswara in effect won, as he was able to remain un-subdued and continued to defy Ayutthayan dominion and expand his power over the Malay sultans in the southern peninsula. The next year, 1456, Ayutthaya attacked Malacca again, this time sending a large naval force south. The Thai chronicles this time mention only that, "In 817, the year of the Pig, the king prepared and sent an army to conquer Malacca."[85] The Sejarah Melayu, on the other hand, gives us a much more chimeric version:

> "Sri Bijadira [a Malaccan leader] had a son named Tun Omar, who was very brave. He was also very reckless ('gila gila basa'). Tun Omar was sent out to scout … when he came upon the Siamese fleet he forthwith attacked and two of the Siamese vessels were worsted. He sailed right through their fleet and attacked more of their vessels and again worsted two of them. Then Tun Omar returned. After it got dark

Okya Tejo [the Thai leader] advanced. The bendahara [Malay leader] Paduka Rajah then attached burning torches to the mangroves and other seashore trees. When the Siamese saw these innumerable fires their captains said, 'The Malays have so many war vessels you cannot count them. If they attack, what is it going to be like for us? We didn't even defeat that one boat of theirs this afternoon. ' So Okya Tejo said, 'yes, its just as you say, we had better retire. ' So the Siamese retreated."[86]

At the time Ayutthaya was occupied with much more critical and important wars in the north and Malacca also needed rice supplies from Ayutthayan-controlled peninsular provinces such as Keddah to feed its growing population and visiting trade ships; the two leaders therefore came to a settlement. Malacca apparently agreed to pay tribute again to Ayutthaya, but continued to act independently and consolidate its leadership amongst the surrounding smaller Malay sultanates.

Thus by the end of the 16th century, after so many centuries of movements of different peoples, religions and armies, the Malay Peninsula was beginning to take the shape we know today, with a strong Thai Buddhist kingdom ruling over the northern peninsula and a community of smaller Islamic Malay states in the south. The predominantly Malay-populated island of Phuket and Phang Nga sat on the border between these two worlds – mainly Malay in culture but subjects of the Thai kings of Siam.

Part 2

The Fabric of Island Life,
1400 to 1900

8

The Social Fabric

1400 TO 1900

Everyday life in Phuket appears to have changed relatively little from the time the island fell under the dominion of the Siamese kings in the 14th century until the reforms of Kings Rama IV and V and the massive influx of Chinese on to the island in the later 19th century. By using various observations from Phuket and the surrounding region during this 500-year period (and not in any specific chronological order), this chapter aims to give an impression of the general fabric of life in Phuket and the region.

The People

The people in Phuket during this era appear to have been predominantly Malays mainly ruled over by Thais, with some Mons, Chinese, Tamils, Bengalis, Arabs, Persians and Europeans living amongst them. The relative acceptance of foreigners, the religious freedom and the relaxed sexual mores in Phuket – as in the peninsula in general – meant that these different groups interbred reasonably freely, and as today, many Phuket locals had the mixed blood of two or more of these different peoples. It was really not until the 1930s that the concept of a homogeneous nation state of "Thailand" was forged out of the heterogeneous kingdom of Siam.

The Political System

When Sir John Bowring, a British ambassador sent to Siam in 1855, met with the Thai King Mongkut in Bangkok, the king explained that although Siam had a fertile soil he lamented that "A soil without a people is but a wilderness."[87] This was indeed the case in the under-populated central peninsula where small islands of people settled essentially along the shores of a huge ocean of forest. One 17th century French visitor described southern Siam as "little more than a vast desert, for as you advance within the land you will find nothing but forest and wild beasts."[88]

Without people, the boundless tracts of untouched and almost impenetrable forested lands blanketing most of the peninsula were fairly worthless to local leaders. It is notable that as late as 1875 the sultans of Terengganu and the rajah of Kelantan told Sir William Jervois, then the British governor of the Straits Settlements, that they knew nothing of the interior boundaries of their states. Without decent maps they did not even know which other states they adjoined. [89] So for any self-respecting rajah or lord, owning people was as important as owning land or more so. Power lay with the number of people, not the amount of land a lord controlled. The local kings and lords (sultans and rajahs) therefore claimed direct ownership over both the people and the land in their area (hence they were often called "lords of men"). These lords then allocated control of these people (as vassals and slaves) and their land as they saw fit to try to make their sub-lords and henchmen beholden to them. As late as 1850, Henry Burney, a British envoy in southern Siam, noted that in the region, "One of the essentials of statecraft was the maintenance of population" and that the local lords in the central peninsula "dreaded any diminution of population in the states they ruled."[90]

The common peasant however probably saw life much less strategically. The Thai historian Kobuka Suwannnathat-Pian tells us that, for them, "The village was the main focal term of reference in the life of a man; his safety and the safety of his family [were] under the jurisdiction of the village, his obligations were always to the chieftain of the village."[91]

8.1 *The village was the focal point of life on Phuket. The Thais lived predominantly as agriculturalists in the center of the island where they were safer from sea-raiders and pirates. The Malays lived nearer the coast and engaged in the sea-raiding and piracy.*

In Phuket the population until the mid-19th century fluctuated between about 1,000 and 15,000 people. Most lived in the more secure, rice-producing flatlands of Thalang district in four main villages: Ban Don, Ban Takkien, Ban Lipon and also the river port settlement of Tharua. The often interrelated families from these villages usually provided the local rajahs of Thalang and later the Siamese-appointed governors and their ruling councils. On some occasions, these different families and towns fought amongst themselves for ascendancy.

The island's ruler (rajah) exerted his immediate control over the local village chiefs and people through a retinue of some 100 to 500 armed retainers and mercenaries beholden to him. He also of course had the potential backing of his overlords in Ligor, Mergui, Keddah or the Ayutthayan king to support him. Thomas Forrest, a Scottish sea captain who visited the island in 1784, mentions that the Phuket governor had three assistants in government, each of whom had "about sixty followers, a kind of retainer, who in great measure live on the community, for receiving little pay, they oppress the inhabitants. Their arms are a musket and bayonet, sword and dagger."[92] Chen Lun-Chiung, a 17th century Chinese visitor in southern Siam, noted, "The land is thinly populated … and the people are cruel by nature … the king and officials are naked [above the waist] and bare-footed just like the rest of the inhabitants. When they go out they are accompanied and protected by several score of brave men, each one of whom carries a spear."[93]

These local lords in the central peninsula had a great freedom to oppress the subjects under them. The typical peasant had little reason to work hard for extra wealth, as the lord's thuggish henchmen would most likely just take it from him. Henri Mahout, the French naturalist who visited Siam in the mid-19th century, noted, "numerous taxes, slavery and never ending forced labour are imposed on the people by the ruling class, which coupled with the corruption and dishonesty of the mandarins, engulf and ruin whole families and render all work fruitless."[94]

The extent of this oppression of the local peasants is illustrated by Pierre Poivre, the later governor of French Mauritius, who spent several months on the peninsular west coast of Siam in 1745,

> "The labourer does not dare to cultivate his field because he is sure that someone will come and take away his harvest … if nature, which is more productive in this country than elsewhere, produces by chance a fruit tree on one's piece of ground, the owner has no choice but to cut it down quickly because if someone discovers that he has such a tree then as soon as the fruits are setting [the lord's] soldiers come to count them on behalf of the king or some official. From that time on the owner is no more than a trustee and he is responsible for all the pieces of fruit that are missing at the time of maturity – whether they fall by themselves or are eaten by birds and insects or are stolen by the neighbours or by the very soldiers who counted them. The poor wretch alone is responsible in such a way that whatever care he takes to watch over them night and day he is always sure of being most ill treated for his efforts or to be ruined by arbitrary and exorbitant fees."[95]

Many of the common people were the lords' direct slaves (around 20-30 percent) and the remaining semi-freemen were vassals who still had to spend about half their time doing corvée – forced or compulsory – labor for the lord and they had to fight whenever he wanted to raise an army. The local lords or the king's agent also took around 25 percent tax from the buyer and 50 percent from the seller on almost all trade transactions. Those caught trading illegally were beaten, flogged, tortured or enslaved. The common people's daughters, sisters and even wives could be taken off for sex at any time by the local lord or his retainers. A lord could also create his own local laws and judicial decisions, which often favored himself. This meant bribery and corruption became inherently rife. The only real way the local people had to resist such excessive despotism was usually by violent rebellion. The early visiting Arab traveler, Abu Dilaf Masari, in Keddah recorded such when he wrote of the region in the 15th century, "the people put themselves in a state of defence against the rajahs when they wish him to respect their wishes."[96] So the political system of Phuket and indeed most of southern Siam during this era, at least until the late 19th century social reforms of King Mongkut, might be summarized as a "dictatorship tempered by assassination."

Fortifications

In Phuket, the people lived predominantly in what are still known to older locals as "the beautiful rice fields" of Thalang, the swampy flatlands cultivated for rice that turned bright green against the surrounding dark green jungle with each crop of the year. Surrounding these wetlands were plantations of various fruit trees and vegetables and some locals also undertook the husbandry of animals, water buffaloes, chickens, ducks and the like. By living in Thalang in the center of the island, the locals were better hidden from the sea and harder to find by seaborne pirates or raiders, plus they had more time to flee into the hills and jungles if such ominous boats or men were seen approaching the coast or coming up the island's rivers.

Nearer the coast or in other valleys such as Patong, Kamala and Chalong, there would also have been some small Malay thatch-roofed villages surrounded by coconut and fruit trees, possibly some rice fields and animals and the locals would have also gone fishing. These villages would have had but a few people, who could easily flee into the local jungles if raiders or pirates were spied. Cornelius Van Nijenrode, a Dutch East India Company official who lived for five years in the central peninsula from 1612 to 1617, noted that the place was "well supplied with all manner of livestock and animals … vegetables, fruit and a thousand other products of the soil abound, sufficing for a man's subsistence … so that in time of necessity he can always supply his needs, indeed lavishly so."[97] There was no winter as in the northern world, causing people to stockpile food and fortify places to protect it. Houses were easy to build, so usually flight into the forest was always the easiest form of defense for locals.

Lt. James Low, a Scottish visitor to Phuket, in 1824 noted the carefree way the locals took their torches of wrapped bark dipped in oil into their palm thatch huts at night and "fearlessly" kindled large fires beside the flammable walls "which are composed of matted rushes of plaited leaves." He felt the reason for this careless attitude was that the local people "build their houses very cheap and care little about what becomes of them. They never use brick and mortar. Everyone is his own carpenter and, the whole of lower Siam abounding in forests, the materials are always available."[98] This all accounts for why, despite the violent history of the region, there were so few walled cities or castles.

The most commonly used form of fortification was the Malay Kubu or temporary stockade, often made with bamboo, which could be both erected and dismantled quickly. Fernao Mendez Pinto, a Portuguese who traveled the peninsula in the 16th century, tells us "most towns have no fortifications or walls … other than wooden palisades, thus making it easy to whomever attacked them to make themselves master of them."[99] It was more effective simply to flee and hide in the forest, live off the bounty of nature there and wait for an enemy to move on, which, with no people around, they would usually do.

One Frenchman, Simon De La Loubère, who visited Siam in 1687, wrote that the Siamese explained to him that "if they built great forts and lost them to an enemy, they would just have great trouble to retake them."[100] In 1615 Jan Pieterszoon Coen, the head of the Dutch East India Company, was told by the local Malays, "We fear no Portuguese, Spanish, Hollanders or Englishmen … the mountains are sufficient for us; they cannot follow us there with their ships."[101] Only the very biggest central peninsular trading ports of Ligor, Chaiya, Keddah, Patani and Takuapa were walled, as their harbors and warehouses of trade goods made them worth defending. Furthermore most of these towns were also regional seats of sultans and viceroys and so they had to project a semblance of power and strength as the center of the "mandala" (an Asian lord's fiefdom or kingdom).

Warfare

When battles needed to be fought, it was usually the peasants and fishermen themselves and their boats and food supplies that the overlord would call upon to form and to feed an army. George Earl, a British officer who visited Siam in the 19th century, noted, "Every man is obliged to serve as a soldier when called for and to bring with him provisions for his own subsistence sufficient for his supply for several months. Wars therefore entail little expense on the government which may account for the readiness with which they are undertaken."[102] Ibrahim, a Persian trader who visited the peninsula and Phuket in 1688, wrote: "The peasantry and the army are one and the same and if the army suffers, the country itself falls into ruin. Consequently, when the natives wage war … the struggle is wholly contained to trickery and deception. They have no intention of killing each other or inflicting great slaughter because the general … would be shedding his own blood, so to speak."[103]

The point of warfare was mainly to gain more subjects as prisoners, not waste them in bloody pitched battles. The ancient Indian book of statesmanship, Kautilya's Arthashastra, which the historian D.G.E. Hall tells us was normally studied at Southeast Asian courts, prescribed that "wars were fought for the acquisition of people rather than territory and were accompanied by large scale deportations of Captives."[104] The historian Mabbet explains that "the successful king is not the one who wipes out all the others, he is the one who gets them to acknowledge him as overlord and give him tribute."[105] The Europeans, who were accustomed to much greater ruthlessness and death on the battlefield, were often struck by the "local reluctance to press on with battle."[106] This probably accounts for the fact that small numbers of Portuguese invaders were able to inflict victories over much larger armies and why Portuguese, Japanese, Turkish and other foreigners, due to their dedication to war, and actual killing in particular, were such sought-after mercenaries in the region. The French visitor Simon de La Loubère wrote in 1691 that he felt this constant pursuit of captives was the reason the local armies were not very effective fighting forces: "They busy themselves only in making slaves. If the Peguans [Burmese] on one side, invade the lands of Siam, the Siamese will at another place enter the lands of Pegu and both parties will carry away whole villages."[107]

In 1607 a Malay leader explained to the Dutch Admiral Cornelius Matelief that he was unwilling to commit men to battle because he was "not like the Admiral who gave his men upkeep and wages so that they had to do whatever he said. Here each [Malay nobleman] had to bring a certain number of people and feared to loose his slaves, which are their only wealth."[108] Battles, therefore, usually meant assembling large armies with decorated elephants, fancy pendants and maneuvering and demonstrating martial skills for show. The opposing forces would erect temporary stockades within hailing distance and engage in abuse and challenges. As late as 1826 one British administrator from Penang wrote of the Malay and Siamese battles he witnessed, "There is a great deal of bravado but not much fighting."[109] Battles were often won or lost on the basis of superior posturing or supernatural occurrences, such as a lightning storm appearing or an eagle taking a bird in midair, which were interpreted as omens by the simple peasant soldiers.

Often, local champions fought it out in individual duels. Peninsular history abounds in stories of heroic single combat of a few in front of two posturing armies. In the Malay world it was the "amoks" who had this role. Tome Pires, in 1515, tells us, "The Amocos are knights among men who resolve to die and who go ahead with this resolution to die."[110] These local champions, he noted, were often completely whacked out on opium, cannabis or other drugs "to inspire them to defy death"; their crazed actions have given rise to the English phrase "to run amok".

Cannons appear to have been first introduced into the region during the early 15th century by the Chinese, Ottoman Turks and Gujaratis from India. These were initially short bronze culverins, often highly ornamented and given ominous supernatural names to scare the locals. After the arrival of Europeans in the 16th century European cannons and muskets were most sought after by regional lords and kings and quite widely used.

Slavery

Since labor was such a scarce resource, slavery remained legal in Siam until 1905 and was integral to peninsular society. Hwang Chung, a visiting Chinese trader in the 16th century, reported that on the peninsular west coast the people said, "it is better to have slaves than to have land because [the labor of] slaves [is] a protection to their masters."[111] In 1809 Antonio de Morga, a Spaniard, writing of the rampant slavery in the Malay world noted that "slaves constitute the main capital and wealth of the natives …Thus they are sold exchanged and traded just like any other article of merchandise."[112] In 1855 the British ambassador visiting Bangkok, Sir John Bowring, noted, "there are distinctly much more than a third of all Siamese who are slaves."[113] As late as 1890 Mr. Alabaster, a British adviser to the Siamese king, went so far as to say, "nine tenths of the non-Chinese inhabitants of Bangkok were slaves."[114] There are no such precise figures given for Phuket, but a sizable proportion of the island's population, at times over 50 percent, would have been slaves.

There were generally five ways whereby one became a slave in Siam.

1   Peasants selling themselves or their family into bondage in exchange for cash, food or upkeep; these would probably have been the most numerous in Phuket.

2   Failure to meet one's debts; the debtor was often his own collateral.

3   Being sold off by an overlord as a punishment for not paying fines or for committing crimes. (The idea of prisons as developed in Europe would have seemed like a ridiculous waste of manpower and money.)

4   Being captured in war or in frequent slave raids; these captives were the lowest class of slave.

5   Being born a slave through inheriting the bondage or debts of one's parents. War slaves in Siam, especially foreign war slaves, were, by all accounts much more harshly treated than debt slaves.

Debt slavery, which was often voluntary, was usually the most common form of slavery. In 1664 the scribe to a Persian ambassador to Siam wrote,

> "The pawning of men or women is one of the most common practices in Siam. For a certain sum the Siamese will pawn themselves or their sons and daughters. An attractive girl will go for ten to fifteen thousand dinars. Whoever is doing the pawning keeps the money … and when he has attained his end with the capital and regained his dignity, he pays back the loan in full … while they cannot pay back the loan they work for the pawnee as if they were his slave … they may remain in their master's chains until the true proprietor, God, claims the cash of their existence and forecloses on the loan of their life."[115]

The Dutchman Dieter Wilkens says that gambling debts, especially on cock fighting, were a common cause of bondage and men would go to cock fights with a special rope as a sign that their bodies were surety for their debts. The Portuguese Galvão (Galvano) in 1544 noted, "Whoever does not avow his debt is … punished by death."[116]

Slaves were used in all sorts of work: as domestic helpers, laborers, soldiers, agricultural workers, market traders, fishermen, musicians, concubines, craftsmen and even surgeons. Debt slavery in the peninsula seems to have been more like serfdom, or like domestic servants in Europe. Slaves were often able to buy their own freedom by working outside and saving their pay. Bowring in 1857 felt that, "Masters cannot ill treat their slaves for they have always the remedy of paying the money they represent and he must be a very worthless character who cannot get somebody to advance the sum … in fact whenever they are emancipated they always sell themselves again."[117] Carl Bock, a 19th century traveler in Siam, agreed, noting that a debt slave "very rarely succeeded in working off [his] indebtedness … and lives in a permanent state of semi bondage with which his indolent nature fully harmonizes, I have seldom seen a slave debtor discontented with his lot."[118]

Debt slavery appears to have been relatively benign because it was relatively easy for a slave to run away. In 1798 the Dutchman Johan Stavorinus explained that exasperated slaves often ran away from their masters, who thereby lost a valuable property. To counteract this, it was common law that another member of the slave's family would be bound to return the runaway, or take his/her place. Such runaways might be killed if the master so wished, thus let's not paint too rosy a picture; it was still slavery, which allows for massive abuse and a slave owner could essentially do what he liked with his debt slaves. If for example he chose to kill them to discipline them few people of importance would object as anyone else of position and power had slaves too.

The rajah of Thalang would have acquired most his slaves by advancing credit to people unable to pay it back, sometimes at interest rates of up to 30 percent a year. The 19th century French vicar apostolic Jean Baptiste Pallegoix tells us, "a family in need is obliged to [take a] loan at usurious rates and since it usually does not find anything to pay the interest and the debt doubles or triples in a short time, the creditor, by virtue of law, may take his wife and children as slaves."[119]

Marriage between slaves and freemen was common, as was owners using slaves for sex. One Siamese rajah's slave woman on the peninsula explained her work thus:

8.2 Phuket women panning for tin using the "du-lang" method. A lack of population in the Malay Peninsula meant women had more rights, freedom and power than in more populous parts of the world. They traditionally did much of the trade, work and breadwinning, as is still the case today.

> "Our chief works are cooking, nursing and carrying water, splitting firewood, pounding rice and at nights we are to prostitute ourselves, giving half of this earning to the rajah and half to supply ourselves with clothing and provisions for the sultan's house and other slaves. If we fail to get money from prostitution we are punished with thick rattans. We are prevented from marrying anyone who wishes to [make an offer for] us in marriage."[120]

A raft of laws existed concerning the position of children of liaisons between freemen and slaves and between a slave owner and a slave woman: were they his slaves or his (free) children? These laws applied only to unmarried slaves; it was both illegal and immoral under Siamese law to interfere with a married slave. A female follower who became a concubine of her master and bore him a child could be entitled to her freedom. Rajahs or

68

powerful men often kept a retinue of female slaves, to satisfy their own sexual appetites and more importantly those of their young retainers, both to attract more henchmen and to prevent them from making forays among the ruler's peasant subjects to seduce or abduct the women for sex as common law allowed them to do in most places.

The Influential Position of Women

The comparatively small population in the central peninsula meant women were more highly valued than in more populous India and China and therefore had more rights, autonomy and economic independence. One 19th century French visitor, Henri Mouhot, wrote that in Siam "women enjoy greater liberty than in almost any other oriental land ... in the bazaars and markets nearly all the buying and selling is done by them."[121] Antonio Galvão, a Portuguese visiting the region in 1544, noted, "the more daughters a man has the richer he is."[122] Family lines were often matrilineal. At weddings, as is still the case today, the bridegroom paid money to the bride's parents, the reverse of the custom in most other parts of the world. Tome Pires, the Portuguese commentator, explained in 1515, "the man must give the women ten tahil and six mas of gold as dowry, which must always be actually in her power."[123]

Divorce was easy, as the 16th century commentator Antonia de Morga noted: "Husband and wife may part again at pleasure, dealing their goods and children without further circumstance and may remarry if they think good without fear of shame or punishment."[124] In 1462 the rather shocked Arab navigator, Ahmad Ibn Majid, noted that Malays "do not treat divorce as a religious act."[125] Even under the later influences of male-dominated Confucianism, Hinduism, Buddhism and Islam, this indigenous trait still remains strong in the peninsula. In Muslim Malaysia for example, divorce rates are still well above the norm for Islamic societies.

Siamese and Malay women traditionally ran the household and the financial affairs. Ma Huan, the scribe to Admiral Cheng Ho, wrote in the 15th century,

> "It is the Siamese custom that all affairs are managed by their wives. Both of the lords and the common people, if they have matters which require thought and deliberation – punishments light and heavy, all trading transactions great and small – they follow the decisions of their wives, for the mental capacity of their wives certainly exceeds that of the men."[126]

George Earl, the British military officer who visited Siam in the early 19th century, concurs with Cheng Ho's earlier statement,

> "The women indeed may be said to compose the most important portion of the community. They transact the greater part of the mercantile business and are the principal cultivators of the soil, cheerfully undertaking the most laborious employments in the support of their families ... The males affect to consider the women in the light of an inferior order of beings, but these lordly personages seldom enter upon any undertaking without first consulting their wives."[127]

The Scottish trader Alexander Hamilton, who visited Phuket in 1727, also agreed, "The women of Siam are the only merchants in buying goods and some of them trade very considerably."[128] The famous English buccaneer William Dampier in 1699 noted that in Siam all the moneychangers were women. In 1699 one Chinese visitor to peninsular Siam recorded that, "The women are very good at trade so the traders who come here all tend to marry a woman to help them trade."[129] Chou Ta Kuan (Zhou Daguan), another Chinese visitor to the region as early as the 13th century, said the very same, "It is the women who are skilful in commerce. Thus a Chinese who arrives down there and takes a wife profits in addition by her commercial aptitude."[130]

This is all rather remarkable, given that women were never educated formally. Jeremias Van Vliet, the 17th century Dutch East India Company's Ayutthaya station chief, tells us that Siamese boys were sent to the wat (Buddhist temple) at about seven years of age to learn basic literacy and numeracy, but "girls seldom learn to read or write." Nevertheless, women often held high positions in the peninsula. Kings in Ayutthaya, for example, kept a female guard in their palace, as they were trusted more than men not to murder their ruler in the night. Sultan Al Mukammil, the 17th century ruler of Aceh, put a woman in charge of his large navy "for he would trust no other." Women were often sent out as negotiators in wars and political affairs. The Portuguese Fernao Mendes Pinto in the 16th century tells us, "The reason they give us is that … God has given more gentleness and inclination to courtesie, yea and more authority, to women than men, who are more severe."[131] The kingdom of Patani, through its most powerful period in the 16th and 17th centuries, was led by powerful queens and in Phuket it was the two heroine sisters, Chan and Muk, who famously led the defense of the island in 1785. Still today in Phuket, over half of all registered businesses are owned and run by women and Thailand also has the highest percentage of female CEOs running public companies in the world.

Sex

This dominance by women extended to sex and relationships. Stamford Raffles in 1815 explained that, among Malays, "If a man was absent for the space of seven months on shore, or one year at sea, without sending any subsistence … the woman could dissolve the marriage and move in with whomever she chooses without any further process."[132] Women were usually free to choose their partners. The Sejarah Melayu (Malay Annals) mention one local fighter, Hang Tuah, who was so handsome that "if Hang Tuah passed, married women tore themselves from the embraces of their husbands so that they could go out to him."[133] Duarte Barbosa, a sailor on Magellan's world expedition, thought that Malays were "fond of music and given to love."[134] Edmund Scott, an early British spice merchant who traveled to the East in 1604, described the Siamese as "very lasciviously given, both men and women."[135]

The Austrian visitor in 1623, Christoph Carl Fernberger, though he only visited Ayutthaya in Siam, where commercial prostitutes worked near the docks, felt the Siamese women were "excessively lewd … they are always approaching the men and urging them to go with them into their houses and have sex with them."[136] He also visited Muslim Patani and mentioned that the women there also "enjoyed many liberties." Hans Morgenthaler, another Austrian, a geologist who came to work in southern Siam's tin mines in the late 19th century, recalls "suddenly becoming the hero of all womankind whereas I was formerly only one of the crowd … this sympathy which every brown woman betrays in such an unmistakable manner is at first surprising then agreeable."[137]

This sexually open culture for women stems primarily from the Indian heritage in the peninsula where, since the earliest times, Hindu sculptures publicly depicted overt and often taboo sexual acts, even on temple walls. Indian texts such as the Kamasutra also promoted a more lascivious sexuality in which sex could be enjoyed by both sexes for its own sake. Alexander Hamilton, a Scottish captain who visited Phuket several times in the 18th century, encountered an Indian sex training school for ladies in Bengal, which he called "a seminary of female lewdness where girls are trained up for the destruction of unwary youths."[138]

This power of women may account for the willingness of men in the peninsula and Phuket to undertake the painful insertion of penis balls and bells. Ma Huan, a Chinese visitor in 1434, explains:

> "When a man has attained his twentieth year, they take the skin which surrounds the membrum virile and with a fine Knife … they open it up and insert tin beads inside the skin and heal it with medicinal herbs … the beads look like a cluster of grapes … if it is a great chief or a wealthy man, they use gold and make hollow beads inside which a grain of sand is placed, making a tinkling sound and this is regarded as beautiful."[139]

In 1604 the Dutch explorer Jacob Van Neck, a little confused by this custom, was told it was because "the women obtain inexpressible pleasure from it."[140] The early English trader Ralph Fitch agreed, "women do desire them." In 1515 the Portuguese diarist Tome Pires tells us that men from Pegu (Burma) would have up to nine penis balls made into bells with different notes, "beautiful treble, contralto and tenor ones … Malay women rejoice greatly when Pegu men come to their country and are very fond of them. The reason for this must be their sweet harmony."[141] Baronet Sir Thomas Herbert, however, a 17th century English traveler – who appears to have been a homosexual himself – claims that this bell-wearing tradition in Siam had originated not to pleasure the women, but to deter the rampant homosexuality amongst the Siamese men who "have beene wicked sodomites [in foregoing times] … and to deterre these calamities … all male children should have a bell … put through the prepuse, which in small time not only became not contemptible, but in a way of ornament and for musik sake, few are now without three or four."[142]

Men and women endured another painful form of cosmetic enhancement – having their teeth blackened. Nicolas Gervaise, a Frenchman, noted in 1685, "The Siamese women cannot bear to see our white teeth for they believe the devil has white teeth and it is shameful for a man to have teeth like those of beasts."[143] Both girls and boys aged around 15 had to endure a painful three-day tooth-blackening ceremony using lemon juice and burnt coconut. After the process, "The teeth are so weakened … they would fall out if the owner risked eating anything solid … so the patient lives on cold broths only … until the hardening of the gums and the stopping of the swelling of the mouth."[144]

Unlike today however, many visiting foreign men were quite un-enchanted by these black-toothed Siamese ladies who wore more or less the same clothes and hairstyles as men. Fred Arthur Neale, a 19th century British doctor who worked in the Siamese king's medical service, felt that:

> "Siamese ladies may, without the smallest fear of competition, proclaim themselves to be the ugliest race of females upon the face of the globe. With their hair worn in the same fashion as the men (a porcupine cut or top knot) the same features and the same clothing, the man must be a gay Lothario indeed who would be captivated by their leering glances. But as though nature had not formed them sufficiently ugly … [they] dye their teeth and lips of a jet black colour … and in order that their gums be of a brilliant red … they resort to chewing betel from morning to night … and as they never swallow the juice, the results are very detrimental to the cleanliness of the floors of their houses and of themselves generally."[145]

Edmund Roberts, an American ambassador to Siam in 1832, held a similar opinion, saying Siamese ladies were "excessively ugly; and when they open their mouths, truly hideous; resembling the inside of a black painted sepulcher."[146]

Many European observers commented on how young children were when they became sexually active and got married or bore children – usually in their early teens. (This however, was not much different from Europe; in Britain, for example, 12 was the age of consent until 1885.) The Frenchman Pallegoix felt that "This is very wise because if one delays too long, young girls let themselves be debauched by young men and flee far from the paternal nest with their lovers … these flights of their daughters with their lovers are a very common thing."[147] Premarital sex was regarded indulgently and virginity at marriage was not expected of either party. However, if a pregnancy came of it, the couple was expected to marry.

Virginal blood was in fact seen as unclean and we are told there were men whose official job was to ritually deflower young virgins. One wonders whether they were paid for this, or did the job out of the goodness of their hearts. There are reports of foreigners in the peninsula being asked to perform this service. The early Bolognese traveler Ludovico de Varthema, while passing through Tenasserim province, north of Phuket, tells us that his partner was requested by a local merchant to deflower his virgin bride, "but we were afraid it was a mockery." The merchant however assured them, "'do not be dispirited for all the country follows this custom' … My companion said to the merchant he would be willing to undergo this fatigue … he did himself well, as he told me later, and had wished that the one night would have lasted a month. She was a pretty brown child of sixteen years. But after this night if found with her again he would have forfeited his life."[148]

According to the English sea captain Daniel Beckman, who came to the region in 1718, married women appear to have been chaste, honorable and "were very constant when married but very loose when single."[149] In 1544 a visiting Portuguese, Antonio Galvão, noted how chaste Malay and Siamese wives were, "Although they always go round among the men nearly naked ... [they] do not fail to be very chaste and good which seems to be quite impossible amongst such a debauched people."[150] In 1865 John Cameron, who took over as editor of the Singapore Free Press newspaper, notes that Malay marriages were affectionate due to the ease of divorce. Generally marriage was monogamous, though richer men often had several wives. The Frenchman Gervaise felt that in Siam the wives of polygamous men and nobles:

> "are accomplished and full of sense. It is rare to find among them flirts and un-faithful ones, either because adultery does not go unpunished, or because they are of a temperament altogether different from that of European women. ... They would have me believe that the common people were chaste and virtuous because polygamy was not effectively very common, but I have myself always believed they were not so ... and did not have several wives as they wished to save them-selves the expense of keeping so many."[151]

Prostitution

The availability of slave women for sale meant that prostitution was never a thriving business in Phuket until later in the 19th century, when thousands of single Chinese male "coolies" arrived to work in the tin mines. Before that, concubinage served the purpose for any horny foreign sailors visiting the island. The Dutchman Admiral Van Neck, who visited Patani in 1604, explained the system there:

> "When foreigners come there from other lands ... men come and ask them whether they do not desire a woman. These young women and girls themselves also come and present themselves, from whom they may choose the one most agreeable to them, provided they agree what he shall pay for certain months. Once they agree about the money (which does not amount to much for so great a convenience) she comes to his house and serves him by day as his maidser-vant and by night as his wedded wife. He is then not able to consort with other women or he will be in the gravest trouble with his wife. She is, similarly, wholly forbidden to converse with other men, but the marriage lasts only as long as he keeps his residence there, in good peace and unity. When he wants to depart he gives her whatever is promised and so they leave each other in friendship and she may then look for another man as she wishes, in all propriety, without scandal."[152]

In the 18th century, Portuguese sailors in the peninsular west coast ports also tell of women paddling out to their ships in boats to offer their temporary services. Alternatively, a visitor could buy and use a slave woman then simply sell her on when he left. Edmund Roberts, the American ambassador in the 1830s, noted, "Temporary marriages are so notorious, that to sell a daughter wholly to a stranger, or for a stipulated term of time, is as common among the middling and lower classes of people, as to sell any common commodity to be found in a bazaar."[153]

One British officer, Col. Garnett Wolseley, wrote triumphantly back to his brother in England that in the East he had acquired a woman who "fulfilled all the purposes of a wife without giving any of the bother."[154] Captain Edmund Scott, in 1606, tells us the Chinese used this method, buying "women slaves … by whom they have manye children, when they return to their owne countrey … they sell their women but the children they carrie with them."[155]

Straight prostitution in Siam was usually organized via a "farm" – a license for a monopoly purchased from the local lord or king. In 1680, for example, the king in Ayutthaya sold the prostitution farm rights for the city to one Chinese official, who used a stable of 600 enslaved women. [156] The Frenchman De La Loubère, in 1688, however, felt that "the Siamese are naturally too proud easily to give themselves to foreigners or at least to invite them." He thought that Mon, not Siamese women, "do more highly esteem of foreigners", and without their blackened teeth, were generally "of a more amorous complexion than Siamese."[157]

Mixed-Race Children

Ibn Majid, in 1462, was taken by the relaxed mores of the peninsula: "The infidel marries Muslim women while Muslims take pagans to wife."[158] It was also official Portuguese colonial policy to encourage interbreeding and by the 17th century significant Portuguese Catholic mestizo communities existed in Tharua in Phuket and Takuatung in Phang Nga. Most of the local women the Portuguese took as wives and their children were converted to Christianity. However as increasing numbers of European and Chinese arrived wanting women, often on a temporary basis, a sense of the impropriety of temporary marriages with foreigners grew among the Siamese. In the 17th century, King Prasat Thong forbade Siamese women to marry foreigners, and, always in need of manpower, strictly forbade the removal of any mixed-race offspring from the kingdom.

Medicine

There was the normal range of diseases in Phuket as anywhere else, the worst being fevers, malaria, dengue, cholera, leprosy, smallpox, measles, tuberculosis, cholera, polio and of course sexually transmitted diseases, all of which could kill. Medicine was not very advanced, remedies were usually herbal and spiritual. The 17th century Persian envoy Al Ibrahim reported, "In general the science of spells and incantations is practiced to a great extent in Siam."[159] At the same time the French envoy Simon de la Loubère was particularly depreciative, stating that "medicine cannot merit the name of Science amongst the Siameses … they are utterly ignorant of Anatomy … they know nothing of surgery."[160]

Monks and doctors studied remedies written in books or passed down orally. One 19th century traveler in Siam tells us that, if patients were not cured, it was not thought to be the fault of the remedy, but due "to the want of sufficient goodness in the life and character of the doctor or the patient." He also explained, "if a sick man dies, the doctor gets no remuneration for his services."[161] The locals invested a great deal of faith in spells, incantations and talismans. Alfonso de Albuquerque, the Portuguese leader in the siege of Malacca in 1511, tells us of one Malay fighter who did not bleed from the many sword wounds they had inflicted on him, until a sacred bone amulet was removed from his arm. "When they took this off all his blood flowed away and he expired."[162]

Childbirth

Commentators and historical evidence show that Malay and Siamese women tended to start giving birth earlier, had fewer babies and finished sooner than elsewhere in the world. Pallegoix tells us in the 19th century that, by tradition, Siamese "women do not suckle their children for six months … but for two and even three years, even while giving them rice and bananas to eat."[163] The Sejarah Melayu notes that abortion was not uncommon, being accomplished by herbs and massages. The prevalence of abortions may have had something to do with the extremely unpleasant ordeal of "roasting" pregnant mothers; one 18th century missionary in 1818 said that this frequently caused the women to emerge "scorched and blackened … [with] … severe blistering of the skin … it is difficult to explain this singular custom in a country where it is so hot. Nevertheless everybody is convinced that it is indispensable and that one must go through it."[164] Dr. Bradley, an American missionary doctor in 19th century Siam, similarly writes of witnessing one of these "cruelties of Siamese midwifery … fiery ordeals … the poor woman was doomed to lie before a hot fire a full month on a narrow wooden bench without a cushion … exposed to a fire about eighteen inches distant. The fire … was sufficiently hot to have roasted a spare rib at half the distance … she complained much of soreness."[165] In this case, as in many, the child died. Dr. Bradley was unable to persuade the midwives – "conceited and headstrong old women" – to change their ways.

Many Siamese children died within a year or so of childbirth. The French missionary Nicolas Gervaise in 1683 tells us, "As soon as the child comes into the world they go and wash it in the river, after which, without a single swaddling cloth, it is placed in a little bed where it remains until it is six months old … many children cannot get accustomed, at so early age, to this Spartan code of life and die within a few days or months after their birth. It is by great luck, that of every ten or twelve born, two or three are saved."[166]

Law and Order, Punishment and Torture

Generally, in each village, as is still often the case today, the village headman would arbitrate in lesser disagreements, but larger problems would be taken to the rajah, whose decisions usually favored himself. The Thai code of law until the late 19th century was based on the Buddhist Laws of Manu or the Dharmasastra, much of which depended on magic and the intervention of the supernatural. The missionary Father Sangermano tells us that under Siamese law the two parties plead their case to the local rajah, starting with formidable oaths such as:

> "May all such as do not speak the truth die of inflammatory diseases, pains of the stomach and bloody vomit … may their bodies be broken in pieces, may they lose all their goods. May they suffer putrid and ulcerous diseases, may their bodies be covered by pustules and buboes … and as soon as dead may they be precipitated into the eight great hells … and after they have suffered in these hells every species of torment, may they be changed into animals, swine, dogs, etc."[167]

If, after such formidable oaths, the principals still maintained contrary versions and the rajah and his advisers could still not decide who was right, both sides were put to trial by ordeal. One form of ordeal consisted of the parties holding their heads under water, the first to come up for breath, or the first to pass out, being clearly the party in the wrong. Other solutions to disputes included combat using various weapons, seeing who could stand on hot coals the longest, or the choice of whatever ordeal the defendant, not the plaintiff, chose.

De La Loubère tells us in 1691 of one Frenchman in Phuket who accused a Siamese of stealing some tin from him. The defendant decided the ordeal would be who could hold his hand in molten tin the longest. The Frenchman went first, putting his hand in the molten tin: "He drew it out almost consumed. The Siamese being more cunning, extricated himself, I know not how, without burning, and was sent away absolved, and yet six months after, in another suit, he was convicted of robbery … but a thousand such like events persuade not the Siamese to change their form."[168]

An 18th century Chinese traveler mentions similar ordeals,

> "using a few words the lord decides the case and nobody dares to disobey … if the case is difficult the king orders ordeal by water. There is another more severe test, the ordeal of thrusting the hand in boiling oil … Even if he initially argues his case with force, [the accused] always admits guilt in front of the boiling oil cauldron. As the country has such tests, disputants are never very stubborn."[169]

The visiting Frenchman Pierre Poivre noted in 1745 that rulings could often be prearranged or overturned and influenced by the use of old-fashioned bribery and corruption. "After their affair is judged, the condemned party appeals to the courts where they obtain the blackest injustices by means of presents to officials."[170]

Once a decision had been arrived at, judgment was handed down. This might be a fine payable to the lord that, if not paid, enslaved the guilty to him. The lord could then either sell the criminal to get the money, or use him as a slave. This was another handy, cheap way for a lord to obtain more slaves under his direct control.

Criminals were also paraded through the streets and beaten. Sir Francis Light, a British resident on Phuket in the 18th century, wrote, "Fines and stripes constitute the chief punishments in Siam for all offences and the latter can be very generally applied. Corporal punishment, however, is so very frequent that the infliction of it is hardly considered as an affront."[171] De Choisey, a French visitor in 1685, also wrote that, "Flogging is a common form of punishment in Siam. The offender, stripped to the waist, is suspended by both hands above his head while his bare back is thrashed, the implement being a rattan tightly bound around with string … sufficient cuts are usually given to strip the skin from the offender's back completely."[172]

The Frenchman Commodore De Beaulieu in 1620 tells us of one Malay "peeping tom" being sentenced to 30 strokes of the cane after being caught secretly watching his neighbor's wife as she bathed.

"The executioner being ready to begin … lifted his arm high. The condemned man then began to negotiate and made an offer of six mas [gold coins]. The executioner demanded forty. As the culprit was slow in agreeing to this sum, he suffered such a rough blow that a deal was quickly concluded at twenty mas, which he paid in cash. And on that consideration it was necessary to give only twenty nine blows of the rattan on his clothes … this deal was struck in the presence of all and in full view of the judge."[173]

The penalties for more severe crimes included amputation or death. Adultery with the wife of an upper class Malay resulted in execution by being stabbed in the heart. Other sure-fire death sentences amongst Siamese law were for treason, rebellion and murder of anyone of high class, theft from a monastery, profaning a lord, or any theft from a rajah or the king. Normally this was done by a relatively simple beheading with a sword, but several early European commentators, despite coming from the barbarity of inquisition Europe, were shocked by some of the fiendish methods of torturous death applied in Siam. Jacques de Coutre, for example, a gem merchant from Bruges who lived in Siam in 1596, later wrote of some of the savage tortures he saw there in a book he called "Of the cruelties and other things I have seen in Siam" in which he tells us at the end, "I have seen in Siam such cruelties that they stunned me by their improbability. This is the reason I have not mentioned most of them."[174] He however does tell us one example, of "a little girl aged eight serving the queen" who had stolen a small piece of gold. The queen's husband, the warrior King Naresuan, condemned the child along with 27 of her child companions – young girls serving the queen – who were guilty only of not knowing that she was the culprit, or at least of not denouncing her, to a slow and most atrocious death. "They had one of their eyes removed, then the skin from their hands was detached and their nails were torn out. After a certain time a piece of their flesh was cut from their backs and stuffed in their mouths. And so that they should suffer slowly they were roasted over a very low fire, each in her own pan, until they died."[175]

King Naresuan's queen had the mouths of her ladies-in-waiting sewed shut if they chattered too much so that they starved to death. In 1666, William Ackworth, a British trader stationed in Ayutthaya, tells that his "cooly" (Chinese) servant set off a gun by mistake. As the noise had disturbed the king his punishment was to have "all his bones broken and sharp pinns run under the nails of his fingers and toes … he will never recover from it his fingers are rotting off."[176] One Chinese-Portuguese visitor called Joao

Pay in 1610 reported that he saw criminals "put entirely naked in big dry copper cauldrons over a fire and were slowly roasted in them." He also saw 40 other men "placed seated likewise completely naked between two great fires, who died in great torment."[177] The French envoy Marcel le Blanc in 1688 mentioned other such torments, including frying men in vats of boiling oil by very briefly plunging them in it from time to time to make the death longer and more unpleasant. [178] Other reported methods of execution were: being bound and impaled anally on a long cone-shaped stake and left to slowly slide down it and be torn open; exposure for days with broken legs and arms in excruciatingly painful positions; being skinned alive and dipped in lime and salt; having your flesh pinched off with red hot irons; being made to swallow molten metal; having bits of your own flesh cut off, grilled, often in spicy sauces and fed to you over several days until your demise; being tied upside down and sawn in half from the groin to the head; being skewered and slowly and publicly spit roasted; and being publicly tied to or locked in a cage with a hungry wild tiger as an edifying spectacle for the local crowd. In one case, a criminal was staked to the ground naked and in public and then devoured bit by bit by two starving tigers, each one held by a rope which the executioner gradually let out and then pulled back in over a period of days.

An Execution Observed

P.A. Thompson, an American painter who traveled in southern Siam in the early 19th century, gives us this graphic account of one provincial beheading he witnessed, along with a crowd of some 100 people:

> "When the condemned man arrived he was handed over to the monks who spent the morning in preaching to him, but he appeared to derive little comfort from their words. When this was over he was allowed to ask for anything that he wanted but he only desired a little rice. It is said condemned men are often given opium, but this man had none … they had planted a bamboo with a cross piece about two feet from the ground. To this the condemned man was led. He sat cross-legged on the ground with his back to the bamboo and his arms, closely pressed against his sides, were tied at the elbows to the cross-piece … Then one of the executioners kneeling beside him, filled his ears with clay and gave him lighted joss sticks to hold. At times, also, he appeared to stroke the condemned man's face almost as though he were trying to mesmerize him, but if such were his object it was of no avail for the joss sticks fell unheeded to the ground. Now the second executioner came out, dressed in red with a red band round his forehead and carrying a sword. He advanced until the condemned man could see him out of the tail of his eye, and there, some twenty yards away on the man's right hand, he sat upon his heels and appeared to await the moment when he should strike. Thereafter the condemned man kept his head turned towards him, looking over his right shoulder. Meanwhile the first executioner had run back and donned the red dress. He now entered the wide ring of spectators directly behind the condemned man, during his stealthy advance he kept always on his

left-hand side … and then raising his hands to heaven he took his sword – a long slightly curved blade broadening towards the point with a thick heavy back and edge keen as a razor. He danced out with half a dozen prancing steps on tiptoe and stopped with one foot in the air. His sword was held above his head, one hand grasping the handle and the other fingering the point, so in a series of little rushes varied by extraordinary posturing and twirling his sword, he crept nearer and nearer to his unsuspecting victim, amidst a silence that was painful. At the end his movements were so rapid that we could scarcely follow them. He was well out of striking distance when there came a quick rush, a circle of light in the air and a sudden jet of crimson. He had not paused for the fraction of a second to take aim, but the head was severed with that single blow … then the body was laid in a grave already dug near by while the head was stuck upon a pole and left as a warning to other evil doers."[179]

8.3. A condemned man beheaded by sword in a traditional Siamese execution.

Food

The French naturalist Henri Mouhot in 1864 tells us, "The hovels of the common peasants are bare and comfortless, the furniture a few coarse vessels of earthenware or wicker work and a mat or two on the floor."[180] The main foods for most residents of Phuket would have been coarsely milled rice and seafood with a variety of local vegetables, tree shoots, eggs and fruit. They also kept ducks, chickens, goats and water buffaloes and hunted the plentiful fowl and wildlife abounding in the jungles. The locals also ate most things – deer, crocodiles, snakes (boa constrictor being a specialty), gibbons, frogs, worms, turtles, bats, birds, lizards, dung beetles, other insects and ant eggs. The 17th century Frenchman Gervaise stated, "the curries are very good … but sometimes abominable things are in their vessels, as when they make a curry of rats, bats or animals that have died of disease."[181] Another 17th century Persian visitor noted, "The natives are inclined to roast lizards and snakes and this is quite a common practice in Siam. In all the market places you see these repulsive animals on sale instead of partridge and lamb."[182] Generally, the plenty of nature on Phuket and the surrounding sea meant obtaining enough to eat was relatively easy, but still the 17th century French diplomat De La Loubère stated simply, "The table of the Siamese is not sumptuous."

Recreation, Home Life, Alcohol and Drugs

Several foreign observers commented that there was little intellectual life in the remote west coast ports of Siam such as Phuket. The Frenchman Pierre Poivre, who stayed in Tenasserim in 1745, believed this was because "the pursuit of Knowledge has become impractical because no use can be made of it for a livelihood. All the arts have been neglected because as soon as an individual achieves a little success at one of them he is obliged to work solely for the lord or king – who usually rewards him with beatings."[183]

Recreations on Phuket included lower-brow affairs such as boat races, fishing, kite flying, boxing, puppet shows and, of course, gambling. One 19th century visitor to Siam mentions that the Siamese "are born gamblers and to make a bet is the delight of everyone, from prince to peasant. They will bet on the results of cock fights, boxing matches, a fight between crickets or combat between their pugilistic fishes."[184] In the 1820s the French vicar apostolic in Siam, Jean Baptiste Pallegoix, tells us, "The Thai possess a passion for cock fights despite the king's prohibition … they bet … and the game often ends up in quarrels, so that after having seen the cocks fight, they end up seeing fighting between men."[185]

Buffalo, tiger or elephant fights, though rarely staged, were also very much appreciated. Sir Frank Swettenham, a late 19th century governor of the British Straits Settlements, recalls watching a fight staged between a buffalo and a tiger. It was "a rather sorry affair … an ordinary water buffalo taken from the shafts of a cart, walked quietly to the centre of the enclosure and stood there." The tiger was then released into the area and "the two beasts

8.4. Gambling on a buffalo fight in southern Siam in the early 20th century.

stared at each other and the hairs on the buffalo's neck stood up." The tiger, "surrounded by moving shouting people … sought only to get away and started to run round the area keeping close to the fence." The buffalo then attacked and "judging his enemy's pace with accuracy, he rushed head down at the tiger, transfixed him with his horns and smashed his body against the palisade." The "grievously damaged tiger" was prodded by the spectators "with sticks and umbrellas in an attempt to get him moving again. He was however past that, or any other effort and never moved again." The buffalo however escaped with only an "unimportant scratch on his nose."[186]

The Frenchman De La Loubère in the 17th century noted that, "The home life of the Siamese is filled with leisure. Aside from his public duties [corvée labor or military service for the lord] he hardly works at all, he seldom goes out and hunts and is usually to be seen on his back or on his hunkers eating, smoking or sleeping. … The time between meals is occupied with siesta, gaming and gossip. It is women who do the work in the fields as well as buying and selling."[187]

Many locals, both male and female, cultivated and constantly chewed areca nut with betel leaves and lime, turning their gums, lips and black teeth bright red. However, for a stronger escape from the hardships of life, some turned to coconut nipa wine or a strong alcoholic drink of fermented rice, brewed by the Chinese and called "arrack" by Europeans. This wicked liquor, according to many reports, rapidly led to the drinkers' ruin; they would sell off their wife and children, go into debt slavery and very often die from "a profound drunkenness." They also smoked dope as the Frenchman Pallegoix in the 1850s tells us, "The Thai plant hemp, pick the leaves of it and smoke them … because it excites and causes fantastic dreams."[188] Opium became the main drug in use by the locals after the 17th century and consumption increased dramatically with the arrival of the thousands of Chinese tin miners in the region and particularly on Phuket Island in the 19th century.

Character

Nicolas Gervaise, a French resident in Siam in 1688, says of the Siamese character:

> "They make no scruples about being a little [dissembling] and those to whom they sometimes show the greatest politeness and respect are those for whom in their heart they have often contempt and antipathy … usually they trouble themselves with nothing that concerns anyone but themselves, and the indolence in which they are born leads them to prefer the obscurity of an easy and quiet life to all the pleasures, honours and wealth they could acquire if they did any work."[189]

Pierre Poivre, an 18th century French visitor to the peninsular west coast, noted:

> "the land is good and would produce a lot if the less lazy individuals among the inhabitants would make an effort to cultivate it. But the land still lies fallow, there is nothing any where but forest. I do not know whether the land has ever been cultivated since the biblical flood. No one either clears or cultivates it except in proportion to the extent of what is needed. No one foresees in one year the mishaps that may occur in another … the year I was there, the country was threatened with famine and rice had begun to be quite scarce."[190]

The French Bishop Pallegoix however, was more admiring. "The Thai receive foreigners with kindness ... the Thai have a gentle, light, unthinking, timid and gay character. They do not like quarrels or anything that feels like anger or impatience ... they have a charitable nature and never let a poor person leave without giving some rice or fruit ... Old age is very much honoured by them. This nation is remarkable for its gentleness and humanity."[191] This view was shared by De Bourges, who felt that for most Siamese, "a gentle poverty is better than an abundance of goods accompanied by worries."[192]

One 19th century British traveler also notes the laid-back character of the local Malays. "On the whole the Malays do as little work as possible. They some own small gardens with fruit trees, others are sailors and have seagoing prahus, raise large families and wait lazily for such subsistence as the bounty of nature may provide. The male Malay in his own country is a sort of gentleman who keeps aloof from trade whose pride is in his ever ready Kriss."[193] Hans Morgenthaler, the Austrian geologist who worked in southern Siam, defends this languid ease, believing it made for a better life than the poor had in early industrializing Europe. "In the west it seems to me all achievement is the result of a grim and sullen despair arising from the impossibility of escaping from frenzied work, ... here in Asia things are different. Life gives everyone all that is most essential for living, a loincloth, a stomach full of rice and fruit, a wife and his betel quid. They are not tortured by any consuming and unattainable desires."[194]

During the same 1855 discussions mentioned at the beginning of this chapter in his ornate palace in Bangkok with the British envoy Sir John Bowring, King Mongkut of Siam attempted to explain the laid-back character of the Siamese. "We have no wants, we have a hot sun. A gentlemen here only requires a waistcoat or so, but with you, [the British] how many wants?" To this Sir John Bowring motioned around the king's fancy palace, whose elegant walls were festooned with many new-fangled western contraptions, clocks, telescopes and other imported ornaments and replied, "But you do have wants, or why all these clocks, looking glasses, ornaments and a hundred things?"[195]

Spiritual Life

Thai dominance over the local population from the 15th century onwards meant Theravada Buddhism was imposed over, or at times merged with, the islanders' previously more animistic beliefs which held in veneration spirits of the forest, trees, sea and sky, etc. The pluralistic and tolerant nature of Buddhism, however, meant the Malays and Muslims on the island were free to continue to embrace Islam.

Almost every village had a small Buddhist monastery (wat), often just a rude bamboo building with a dormitory for the monks, with teaching going on under some large tree (preferably a Banyan, being the same kind the Buddha sat under when he achieved enlightenment). The wat and the monks were usually sponsored by the rajah or the local élite who donated land, slaves and money and the common people gave them food. In return, the wats, repositories of learning, provided education to many of the males in the area and gave them moral instruction along with rudimentary reading, writing and numeracy. This education system in monasteries was often co-opted by the élite supporting them. Monks usually taught the people not to come up with original ideas and to acquiesce to the rapacious lord. The more radical Thai historian, Somsamai Srisudravarna, states that the Buddhist monasteries tended "to delude the peasants into believing that human beings could not thwart destiny … [they] decreed life was subject to merit, karma and fate."[196]

But monks also tried at times to hold the moral high ground and occasionally played the part of ombudsman for the serfs (phrai) and slaves. Monks could deliver petitions to the overlord in Ligor and they were also avenues for inter-community and village discussion and arbitrated in disputes. By emphasizing the principle of a "Dhamma-raja" (a leader who is acclaimed the peoples' choice through his knowledge and "virtues"), they were able to provide some moral opposition to the excesses of the despotic local lords in that they could mobilize public opinion.

Pierre Poivre, the rather cynical Frenchman who visited the area in the 18th century, noted that:

> "Buddhist monks are held in extraordinary veneration in this country … If an offender or wrongdoer is able to take refuge in their temples he finds there an assured asylum against all pursuits of justice … one finds amongst them some orderly men. They are zealous, at least in appearance, for the purity of principles and panegyrists of virtues … if such persons are really what they seem to be, one cannot deny them the greatest praise for maintaining such virtue in the midst of the greatest corruption."[197]

There were draconian moral and particularly earthly punishments for anyone stealing from a wat, such as amputations or being slowly roasted to death over a small fire lit intermittently to delay death. A wat also served as the repository for wealth in a society without banks. People often hid their gold in Buddha statues they donated to the monastery for safekeeping, or they buried their wealth in monastery lands. The local Malay Muslim communities, usually based nearer the coast, also built mosques (often wooden and rudimentary), which served much the same spiritual and social purposes as the wats did for Buddhists. The numerous Chinese temples now on Phuket did not appear in any numbers until the mass influx of Chinese émigrés in the later 19th century.

Wildlife

Until the late 19th century, a thick cloak of jungle, often quite impenetrable, almost universally covered Phuket and the whole region. It was teeming with wildlife – elephants, various deer, tigers, clouded leopards, black panthers, tapirs, black and sun bears, pangolins, banteng (huge buffaloes), rhinoceros, dugongs, water buffaloes, koupreys (wild oxen), huge hawksbill turtles, gazelles, binturongs (Asian bear cats), great monitor lizards, crocodiles, wild pigs, peafowl, porcupines, civet cats, martens, gibbons, antelopes, sea eagles, numerous breeds of monkeys and thousands of species of reptiles, snakes, birds and marine and insect life. Pierre Poivre, the 18th century French horticulturist, noted that "there are very fine forests and hunters find all sorts of game there in abundance ... harts, wild boar, gazelles, antelopes, porcupines and roe deer. But the hunt is often interrupted by frequent encounters with elephants, tigers and bears."[198] Despite some forest clearing by locals for fruit farms, it was not until the onset of large-scale tin mining in the 1850s and particularly the development of rubber plantations in the early 20th century, that most of Phuket's forests were cut down and most of its previously abundant wildlife was killed and eaten.

Dr. Jean Gerrard Koenig was a Danish botanist who spent three months on Phuket Island on a botanical expedition in 1779. He mentions his visit from Tharua town to a place called "Cockreau". He went there by a road "which was very muddy ... passing through a very dark wood often traversed by the rhinoceros."[199] The locals killed the rhinos for their valuable horns and ate the meat. Koenig mentions that one morning, "At breakfast I was treated to some rhinoceros hide." Elephants were also plentiful as Koenig mentions, "while botanising away from town ... I met a wild elephant from which I had to escape ... the bamboo and sugar cane which grows to almost a man's height, make this island a favourite resort for elephants, therefore as soon as one comes into the jungle one finds many paths made by the elephants."[200] These wild elephants were captured by the locals using a variety of methods, such as driving them into a large compound where they were then left for a while to starve and weaken. Then tame elephants were sent in to dominate them.

Elephants were one of Phuket's main exports to India where they were used as work machines or in armies. Sir Francis Light, a long-term Phuket resident in the 18th century, tells us that the main elephant loading pier was in Pak Pra (near the Yacht Haven today). It consisted of a long jetty along which elephants could be led and loaded on to the boats. He mentioned that each elephant required 60 or 70 banana trees per animal to eat on the trip to India. These elephants, which could easily smash apart the hull of a ship if they became excited or scared at sea, were usually drugged for the journey by being fed local marijuana bushes.

Tigers, leopards and black panthers also prowled the island. Thomas Bowrey, an English visitor to Phuket in the 1670s, tells us of one black panther caught near Ban Lipon in Thalang, "Once when I was up at Luppone, several of the natives went out and set a trap for a Tyger that often resorted to the place where the Radjahs Goats were kept. They took one of the smallest goats and placed him for baite to trap the Tyger and caught him by the leggs which done they seized fast his mouth as also his paws."[201] They had in fact caught not a tiger but a black panther, as Bowrey explains, "his colour was cole [coal] black and although his body was but of an ordinary size, much lesse than some Tygers I have seen in Bengala (Bengal), yet his teeth and claws were the largest that I ever saw, ... the Radjah ordered one of his soldiers to knock out the teeth and claws and gave them to me which I thankfully received as a great rarity."[202]

Dr. Koenig, the same visiting Danish botanist, tells us that even in the island's main port town of Tharua at the time, "A tiger visited our house but was satisfied with only one goose for this time, which he carried away with him to his hiding place about 200 yards from our house in a dense … wood at the back of the house."[203] We are also told of one man-eating tiger in the 18th century which attacked and ate four people in one village. When the villagers went to hunt and kill the tiger, the local monks advised them against this un-Buddhist act and persuaded them to leave it in peace. A few days later however, the ungrateful tiger attacked and ate one of the monks that had saved him, perhaps indicating that the Buddhist karmic wheel of fortune is not always completely round.

Increasing Thai Influence and Domination and the Sakdi Na System

It appears that the first Thai settlers arrived in Phuket and Phang Nga around the 12th century to work as craftsmen, farmers or tin-panners in the local streams. The first Thai troops to come to the island and exert their will would probably have been the black and gold helmeted cavalry from the army of Sukhothai during Ramkamheng's campaigns in the south. Either the Thai commander may have fought and deposed the local Malay rajah and granted the governorship to one of his Thai officers, sub-lords or someone more loyal. Or he may have simply shown his strength and accepted the submission of the local Malay rajah, who would have had to drink the waters of allegiance, and give gifts and probably some of his kin or daughters as concubines (hostages) to the new Thai overlord. The offspring of these concubines would then have contributed to the complex interrelationships between those who held power locally. Much lordly power in peninsular communities was held together, as it still is today, by elaborate kinship connections. The new Thai overlords would also have demanded, on pain of severe retribution, that the local rajah send men and supplies when they were needed for the Thai overlords' armies and wars in the region.

After the city of Ligor fell under Sukhothai's and then later under Ayutthayan suzerainty, more and more Thai influence would have been exercised over its subsidiary state of Phuket. But the looseness of Siamese control at such peripheral points in the kingdom as Phuket probably allowed the local rulers, normally still from the hereditary local families on the island, to continue to exercise a very high degree of autonomy and despotism. Phuket would have remained a remote and independent community, continuing in its ways of desultory tin mining, fishing, trade and piracy.

The locals were mainly Malay but after about the mid-16th century the Thai language would increasingly have been used by the island's leaders and the monks and slowly would have become dominant. In 1784, the British sea captain Thomas Forrest, who stayed a while on Phuket, wrote that, "The people of Jansylan [Junk Ceylon/Phuket], though they generally understand the Malay tongue from their intercourse with that people (greater formerly than now), speak the Siamese language. They resemble in feature the Malays with a good deal of the Chinese look."[204]

Phuket might be said to have first joined the "Muang Thai" (Thai world) around the time of King Trailok (1448-1488) of Ayutthaya. He launched several peninsular military campaigns and strengthened his grip over Ligor and all its naksat states in the area by implementing the "sakdi na" system, meaning "power in controlling rice fields". Sakdi na was a method of classifying everyone in the kingdom and bringing them directly under the king's power through the prescribed issue of land to everybody at the king's pleasure. Sakdi na specified the different classes of people and the amount of land that could be assigned to a person of each class. A great prince of high rank, a chao phraya, for example, could receive 20,000 rai; a phraya or lesser lord such as the governor of Phuket could receive 4,000 rai, while a common freeman received only 10 rai. These were not hereditary grants; only the king or his nominated viceroys, lords or governors issued sakdi na land. If a provincial governor or any lesser subject was disobedient or irritated the king or his lord he could have his land allocation revoked and be punished. For example, article 75 of the Ayutthayan Palatine Law of sakdi na stated, "those who possess sakdi na from 10,000 to 1,600 rai (lords), if found in the company of one another in their homes or any quiet corner or in a conspiring manner … will be punished by execution and their properties confiscated."[205] In this way the governor of Phuket, in theory at least, had control over his subjects, just as his overlord in Ligor and the king in Ayutthaya had over him. The sakdi na system also facilitated opportunities for lordly abuses, as one Thai historian tells it: "From the very beginning the sakdi na system saw the exaction of conscripted labour, taxes in kind and various levies, along with usury. This arose because the peasants were squeezed to the point where they could not get enough to eat and were forced to borrow, which led into enslavement."[206]

The Ayutthayan rulers also attempted to enforce the loyalty of their peninsular sub-lords by sending advisers (usually spies) and military commissioners with troops to oversee them. They demanded that the peninsular sultans and rajahs showed their subservience by sending the king an annual "Bunga Mas" (an ornate and ritualistic gold and silver tree) and other presents signifying the lesser lord's fealty. It was also an institution that a rather petulant Malay sultan of Terengganu once likened to "a parasite living at the top of a tree."[207] In the late 15th century King Ramathibodi in Ayutthaya also introduced compulsory military service or corvée labor whereby all men in the kingdom had to be registered and had to do at least two years' service and often longer, either as soldiers or as royal servants on construction or irrigation projects. This resulted in men from remote communities such as Phuket traveling to other parts of the kingdom and beginning to get a knowledge and sense of the kingdom of Siam.

Kings Trailok and Ramathibodi II, who came after him, both also encouraged the adopted Brahmanic concept of a "Deva-raja", or God-king from India. This made them divine, untouchable, all-powerful rulers. As a result, by the time the first Europeans arrived in Phuket in the 16th century, the Malays, Siamese, Mons, Tamils and other locals may already have had a burgeoning sense of being not just under the power of, or often the actual property of, their immediate rajah in Thalang, but also of living under the more transcendent control of an omnipotent god-king in faraway Ayutthaya and therefore of being part of the Ayutthayan kingdom of Siam.

PART 3

The 16th Century

9

Spices, Zealots and Adventurers

1450 TO 1600

The Spice Trade

The Latin root-word "species", meaning a type or kind, has bred a family of words in English: "specific", "special" and the word "spices", which first appeared during the fifth century AD in Roman Egypt when the "Alexandria Manifest" was compiled. The Alexandria Manifest listed 54 "species" of high-value, taxable Eastern goods entering the Roman Empire from the Indian Ocean. Many products found in the Malay Peninsula are listed in this manifest: ginger, pepper, cardamoms, aloe woods, ivory, even "Indian hair" which was apparently highly prized for making wigs. It was the potential fat profits to be had from trading in these "spices" that first drew the Europeans to the Malay Peninsula.

Spices were not just a luxury in Europe in the late middle ages, but a necessity, as the distinguished historian J. H. Parry explains, "Europe suffered from a chronic shortage of winter feed, so large numbers of beasts had to be slaughtered every autumn and their meat preserved for winter by being salted or pickled … apart from salt, the preservative spices were all produced in tropical countries: pepper, cinnamon, nutmeg and the most valuable preservative of all, cloves."[208] The 14th century French poet Eustache Deschamps puts it more pithily, telling us that spices "expel the stench and smell of rotting meats" as well as "rectifying" it, and that without spices to preserve meats, "many would be in grave peril and at risk of death."[209]

Since Roman times European nobility were most discerning at the table. John de Hauteville wrote in 1190, "Nobility is judged by the costliness of the table and the taste gratified by the greater expense."[210] So if European noblemen were to impress their guests and consume at least semi-appetizing meat through the winter, spices became practically de rigueur. However, to reach these noble pantries in the forlorn wintry zones of northern Europe, these spices had to make an epic journey. Across the Moluccan seas in Malay prahus, carried overland through the jungles of the central peninsula, loaded in Indian and Arab dhows to reach the Levantine souks, crossing the Byzantine Mediterranean in Muslim, Venetian or Genoese merchant caravels, pack-horsed over the Alps or shipped around via the stormy Atlantic to the bleak wintry lands of the north. Prices were of course marked up at every stage of the journey until reaching astronomical levels in Western Europe. In England in 1284, for instance, a mere pound of mace (the flesh of the nutmeg fruit), picked free in the

Moluccan islands, cost four shillings and seven pence, which was more than three sheep, or enough to keep a whole peasant family for a year.

These spices were used by the well heeled for cooking, to preserve wines, as medicines and as perfumes to mask the smell of unwashed bodies and breath. They were also used in the bedroom – Al-Tifashi, a 13th century Cairo physician, recommended "cinnamon, cloves, ginger and cardamom … [for] … strength for coition."[211] The wealthy Catholic Church also used aromatic spices in ceremonies "with the aim of numbing the rational faculties and provoking a state of ecstasy."[212] Pepper seeds became so valuable they even were used as currency, hence the phrase, "a peppercorn rent." Yet despite their high cost, as early as 973, Ibn Jaqub, a Jewish merchant from Andalusia, recorded that he was flabbergasted at the vast quantities of Indian spices for sale in the German town of Mainz. All over Europe guilds of spicers and pepperers plied their trade, daily promoting a large and high-value market that promised great riches to those who could supply it.

Finding the Spice Route

When the armies of Islam burst out of Arabia and took control of the Middle Eastern ports handling this spice trade, the Muslims started making vast profits from the Christian end users – they and the Italian city states of Venice, Genoa and Florence, which had dominated the carrying trade of spices from the Levantine ports to Europe ever since they started ferrying the Crusaders to the Holy Lands in 1095.

In the far Atlantic west of Europe by the mid-15th century, the kings of Spain and Portugal, in their own Iberian Crusades, had pushed the Muslims out of Iberia. Now fired with great confidence and Christianizing zeal and an envious eye on the wealth of the Italian city states, these Iberian lords pondered the possibility that the world might be round and that they could maybe sail west, or south round Africa, to reach the jackpot of the spice-growing lands of the Indies.

In 1492 Christopher Columbus, sponsored by the Spanish throne, sailed an expedition west, reached the Caribbean and America and erroneously claimed it was the Indies – or at least the West Indies. Meanwhile, the visionary Portuguese prince, Henry the Navigator, was beavering away in the town of Sagres in the Algarve. He had established a navigational school and raised funding for Portuguese naval expeditions to try to go east by sailing southwards round Africa. Several Portuguese expeditions gradually reached further south down Africa's west coast, then in 1487 a fleet under Bartholomew Dias eventually rounded the Cape of Good Hope but soon had to turn back. When another Portuguese expeditionary fleet heading south was blown off course and bumped into eastern Brazil by chance, the Catholic kings of Portugal and Spain, instead of fighting over who should own these new worlds they were discovering, applied to the Pope to make a ruling on the matter. In 1494, in what is probably one of the world's most arrogant, if not ambitious, treaties ever made, Pope Alexander VI – for a handsome fee of course – took a world map and drew a line down the Atlantic Ocean. He then very kindly made a papal bull that gave all new lands discovered to the west of the line to Spain and everything to the east of it to Portugal. He then further dictated that no sailors from any other countries were allowed to sail to these new lands.

In 1497 another Portuguese fleet of three naus (carracks) was dispatched to sail southeast round Africa under the 37-year-old navigator and naval commander Vasco da Gama. Da Gama had earned a tough-guy reputation captaining a patrol ship off the Algarve against French pirate corsairs. By Christmas 1497 Da Gama had rounded the Cape of Good Hope and headed northeast up the East African coast. In Malindi in Kenya, he found a Hindu pilot who guided them across to the south Indian port of Calicut, which at that time was the central cog in the whole Indian Ocean pepper trade. The zamorin (rajah) of Calicut let the Portuguese trade for two months and they loaded up with pepper. Returning to Portugal against the winds, however, was much less easy. Half of Da Gama's crew died of scurvy on the way, "their feet and hands swelling and their gums growing over their teeth so they could not eat."[213] Two ships of his fleet eventually limped back to Portugal with only 55 of the original 170 men still alive. However, the profit they made on the pepper they had bought in India was more than 4,000 percent.

The Portuguese Head East

Enthused by this huge profit, the Portuguese court conceived a grand plan to commandeer and divert the whole Indian Ocean spice trade via Portugal. In Portugal the financiers rubbed their hands and King Manuel of Portugal excitedly wrote to King Ferdinand of Spain: "The great trade which now enriches the Moors of those parts … shall in consequence of our regulations be diverted to the natives and ships of our own kingdom so that henceforward all Christendom shall be provided with spices."[214] The Florentine financier Guido Do Detti, hearing this news, gloated that if their rivals the Venetians were deprived of this most lucrative Levantine spice business, they "will soon have to go back to fishing."[215]

Brute Force

In 1500, a second Portuguese fleet under Pedro Cabral reached Calicut to attempt to establish a trade treaty and a permanent trade factory there. The zamorin of Calicut, however, was under intense pressure from the port's existing traders, mainly Arab Muslims who "could ill digest"[216] this new Christian competition. The zamorin was persuaded to attack the Portuguese and started by killing some 50 Portuguese who were ashore building their new trade factory. In retaliation Cabral bombarded the city for days before eventually returning to Portugal.

Two years later Vasco Da Gama returned to India, this time with a full war fleet of some 20 ships, plus around 1,500 men and the ambitious intention of "subjugating all India." He would do this by using sheer brute force against the normally cannon-less Indian Ocean Muslim trading ships and generally poorly defended Indian ports. Sheer brute force proved a most convincing tool. He started by taking vengeance on Calicut itself. His fleet sat off the city and soon encountered a large Muslim ship returning to

Calicut from Cairo carrying hundreds of Muslim pilgrims returning from Mecca. Da Gama attacked and captured this ship and set fire to it with all aboard until it sank and its "survivors were left swimming." The Portuguese then launched two longboats and "plied about killing them with lances ... Out of eight hundred none were spared."[217]

9.1 A European depiction of the Portuguese fleet attacking the pepper port of Cochin to dominate the Indian Ocean spice trade by brute force.

Next, a similarly innocent and ill-fated fleet of some 20 Muslim trading dhows appeared from the Coromandel Coast loaded with rice, ghee, spices and piece goods. The Portuguese attacked and captured these trading dhows. Then in full sight of the people onshore, the hapless Indian crewmen were strung up by their feet from the masts and spars and used for crossbow practice by archers from the Portuguese ships. We are told they shot at them for several hours "until they tired of that sport."[218] These captured Indian ships were pillaged of their goods. Then, still decorated with the arrow-riddled corpses hanging from the rigging, they were set on fire and sent floating towards Calicut. The rest of the numerous captive Indian crewmen were then bound together and loaded into two of the largest dhows and, as Gaspar Correa, the scribe with Da Gama's expedition, records:

> "The Admiral commanded [his men] to cut off the hands, noses and ears of all the crews and to put all that [the severed body parts] into one of the small vessels into which he ordered them to put the friar, [a peace emissary who had been sent out by the Calicut zamorin] also without his ears or nose or hands ... a necklace made of these amputated body parts was ordered to be strung around his neck with a palm leaf for the zamorin on which he told him to have a curry made of what his friar had brought him [a potential peace offer treaty]. When all these Indians had been thus mutilated he ordered their feet to be tied together, as having no hands, they could not untie them. In order that they could not untie them

with their teeth, he ordered his men to strike upon their teeth with staves and they knocked them down their throats."[219]

These unfortunate Indian sailors were bound together in the two dhows, their sails set for the shore, then the two ships were set alight and left to drift slowly in the balmy tropical afternoon breeze towards the coconut-fringed shoreline with their mutilated passengers screaming frightfully as they roasted alive for all the Muslims of Calicut port to see and hear.

Using such brutish methods, the Portuguese soon won the submission of most Indian ports and were able to enforce their terms of trade over much of the Indian pepper ports. As the French writer Voltaire later wrote, "After the year 1500 there was no pepper to be had at Calicut that was not dyed red with blood."[220] These few daring and aggressive Portuguese fleets and adventurers, in some great sea battles, also defeated several huge Muslim Ottoman, Persian and Arab retaliatory fleets sent out into the Indian Ocean against them. Their sheer barbarity won the day. Ludovico di Varthema, a Bolognese diarist who was in the East at the time of this violent Portuguese expansion, noted, "The king of Portugal has killed, and everyday kills great numbers" to exert his diktat, which was, as Vasco Da Gama made most clear to all the defeated Indian port lords he dealt with: "All the rivers and ports which have got shipping have to obey him [the Portuguese king] and pay tribute … and this they must do in order that their ports may be free and that they may carry on their trade in security, neither trading in pepper, nor bringing in Turks … because for any of these things, the ships found to have offended will be burned with as many as may be captured in them."[221]

Farangs Arrive on the Peninsula

In India, the Portuguese soon learned that several of the most valuable spices actually came from further east, from a Muslim port called Malacca. The Italian adventurer di Varthama, who had visited Malacca in 1506, before the Portuguese arrived there, had noted that:

> "The city has about twenty thousand dwellings …This is the principle port on the Ocean and truly I believe that more ships arrive here then in any other port of the world. Here are brought all kinds of spices in great quantities …a great quantity of sandalwood is here as well as mines producing tin. [This would have been brought to Malacca from surrounding peninsular ports such as Phuket.] They trade as middlemen in spices and silkenware. The people are of brown colour and have long hair, they dress in similar fashion as in Cairo … They are an evil race… nobody dares walk about at night because they strangle and kill each other like dogs. All merchants who arrive there sleep at night on their boats."[222]

The Portuguese also learned that to the north of Malacca there was a large kingdom of non-Muslims called "Sorneau" (Siam), which was at war with Malacca. Ayutthaya's last attack on un-compliant Malacca had been in 1500, just six years previously. Also, being unaware of Buddhism, they assumed the people of "Sorneau" were probably Christians, or if not, might at least be enrolled as an ally against their foes the Muslims. The Portuguese captain Diego Lopez De Sequeira was dispatched with a squadron of five carracks to make contact with Malacca.

His small fleet arrived off the Malay Peninsula in September 1509. Ever since the early Crusades, which were led by the Franks (French), Arabs had referred to all Christians as Franks, "farangks" or "ferengi". Muslim traders then spread this name east to the Malay and Siamese ports. When this "ferengi" squadron arrived in Malacca's bustling harbor, it must have vexed Malacca's leader, Sultan Mahmud Shah, Parmeswara's grandson. He surely knew of the likelihood of a savage response if he were to refuse their demands, but he was also being aggressively prevailed upon by the powerful resident Muslim merchants to have nothing to do with these dangerous new arrivals.

The first Portuguese longboat from De Sequeira's ship was ceremoniously rowed ashore in the hot morning sun, with one of his officers standing dressed in full regalia and with the Portuguese flag and other pendants fluttering in the hot breeze. The oarsmen, dressed in white cotton, rowed in unison and, on a call from the officer, pulled up their oars in order as the longboat glided in and landed on the beach. The Europeans had arrived on the peninsula. The Sejarah Melayu (Malay Annals) records this scene:

> "The people crowded round to see what these ferengi looked like. They were all surprised at their appearance. The Malay people said, 'These are white Bengalis.' Dozens of Malay people surrounded each ferengi. Some twisted his beard, some knocked his head, some took off his hat and some grasped his hand. The captain of the ship then presented himself to the bendhara [chief minister]. The bendhara … gave him honorific cloths. The ferengi captain then presented the bendhara with a golden chain studded with jewels, which he himself put around the neck of the bendhara. At that everybody became angry at the ferengi captain [one was not allowed to touch a bendhara], but they were stopped by the bendhara who said, 'don't get carried away, for these are people who know nothing of manners'."[223]

The term "white Bengalis" ("Bengali puteh") was a bit of a pun. It probably referred to their lighter skin, Aryan features and beards, but a "Bengali" at this time was also a derogatory Malay term for a rapacious and avaricious merchant.

The Portuguese requested the right to trade in Malacca and set up a factory. The bendhara agreed, but the main Muslim traders were not so happy and pressed Sultan Mahmud, seeing how few Portuguese there were, to attack them now, take their ships and cannons and be done with them. "They go about destroying and blotting out the name of our holy prophet, let them all die."[224] Sultan Mahmud was eventually convinced, and when some 50 Portuguese had gone ashore, the sultan, like the ill-fated zamorin of Calicut, ordered his attack. Over half these Portuguese were killed and some 20 captured. The squadron commander, De Sequeira, with his five small ships now in danger from the many Muslim vessels moored all around him, was unable to secure the release of the captive hostages. Wishing to spare their lives, he did not attempt a bombardment of Malacca or other retribution, but hoisted sail and returned to Goa. These Portuguese captives were to remain imprisoned in Malacca for nearly two years.

The Portuguese Capture Malacca

Back in Goa, the aggressive new governor of the Portuguese "Estado da India" (State of India), Alfonso d'Albuquerque, was incensed. He set about raising a war fleet of 18 ships, manned by 500 Portuguese and some 2,500 Malabar Hindu mercenaries and set sail for Malacca to exact revenge. When he reached Malacca, d'Albuquerque immediately attacked all the Muslim ships in the port, taking care, however, not to attack those ships belonging to Hindus, nor five Chinese trade junks which may have been in the service of the king of Siam. The Chinese junks offered d'Albuquerque their services if he required them and reportedly informed him that Malacca could muster an army of nearly 20,000 men, including Javanese, Persian, Turkish and Arab mercenaries, war elephants and many cannons.

The Portuguese launched their attack on Malacca city early on St James's Day in July 1511. The day was hot and the battle brutal. At one point the Portuguese repelled a Malay counter-charge of 3,000 men led by mounted, armored elephants by piercing the elephants' eyes with their lances so the huge beasts turned and ran back amongst the attacking Malays. It was notably the Malay poisoned darts that were most lethal, killing over 70 Portuguese and Hindu attackers. Of all those struck by such darts only one survived, a Portuguese soldier, Gomez de Lemos, who promptly cauterized himself deeply with a red-hot iron where the dart entered him. All the others hit were dead by nightfall. By the early afternoon, fighting in the scorching heat all day with little water, the Portuguese were too thirsty and spent to continue their attack on the fortified city. They set fire to the mosque and all homes and suburbs outside the fort and retreated to their ships.

9.2 Alfonso d'Albuquerque the Portuguese leader who conquered Malacca and tried to befriend the non-Muslim king of Siam as an ally and trade partner.

The Portuguese fleet then stood for nearly a month just out of range of the smaller Malay cannons in the fort and bombarded it to weaken the walls before launching their second attack. This time the Portuguese attackers wrapped sailcloth around any exposed skin to fend off the poisoned darts. The Portuguese Captain Antonio d'Abreu, who led this second attack, was shot in the mouth by a matchlock ball which "carried away many teeth, his cheek and tongue", but he fought on gallantly until carried away by his men, "more by force than by his own wish."[225] The battle continued through the day and into the night and as dawn approached the Portuguese, "fighting demoniacally," broke into the fortified city and once again showed their policy of brute force by setting about a massive orgy of killing, rape, butchery and theft. Correa, the Portuguese chronicler at the scene, tells us, "Moorish women and children there died by the sword in an infinite number for no quarter was given to any of them … the streets were lined with the dead."[226] Over the next few days a vast amount of plunder was accumulated – "bars of gold, jars of gold dust, jewels, priceless silks, rare perfumes and scented woods."[227]

D'Albuquerque loaded his flagship, the Flor de la Mar, with one of the greatest hauls of treasure ever recorded, including two huge gold elephants from the sultan's throne room, his golden throne and four bronze lions with huge red rubies inset as their eyes, plus many of Malacca's most skilled artisans. But a few days' sail northwest of Malacca the overloaded ship hit a reef at night and the hull cracked. Before it could be unloaded, the waves split the broken ship into two parts and the bulk of it fell off the reef into deeper water, too deep for the Portuguese divers to reach, even using the local pearl diving women and the primitive diving bells of the day. This priceless treasure has never been salvaged (officially, anyway) and still sits a few hundred kilometers southwest of Phuket off the Sumatran coast on the ocean floor in only some 35 meters of water and is by now covered with mud. It is estimated to be one of the world's most valuable shipwrecks. Its cargo would probably be worth well over a billion US dollars today. It remains un-salvaged today, as d'Albuquerque purposely made errors in recording the site of the sinking as he intended to return and salvage it himself, but died from a fever soon after his return to Goa.

The Portuguese Reach Siam

Duarte Fernandes was a "novo Cristao" or new Christian, a former Jewish tailor and one of many who had converted to Catholicism to escape the inquisition in Portugal. He was one of the twenty-odd Portuguese who had been held captive in Malacca for two years, during which time he had learned Malay. When d'Albuquerque heard that the Chinese junks which had joined his attack on Malacca were leaving for Sorneau (Siam), he sent Fernandez with them to negotiate a trade agreement or alliance with this mysterious kingdom to the north.

Almost a month later, in Ayutthaya, King Ramathibodi, wearing an ornate sarong and naked above the waist, was seated in his airy palace overlooking the boats on the serene, muddy brown Chao Praya River when a breathless royal messenger entered his chamber and prostrated himself on the floor, unable to set eyes on this god-king. He informed him that a horseman from the fort at Paknam at the mouth of the Chao Praya River had just arrived bearing news that an ambassador from the farangs was already heading up the river on one of the king's junks from Malacca. The Siamese king had probably already heard about these new arrivals in the Western Ocean, both of their brutality and of their fancy weapons. He may even have already heard that they had attacked irksome

Malacca, the thorn in his southern foot. He ordered 200 river barges in full regalia to receive this envoy and escort him to Ayutthaya.

Hundreds of people gathered in Ayutthaya to see this strange foreigner, a skinny former Jewish tailor, thin from his imprisonment and with a beard bigger and thicker than most had ever seen. Ramathibodi met Fernandes in his palace in his best finery, seated on a gilded chair on a raised platform surrounded by his many wives and children. Fernandes presented the king with a gift of a sword whose hilt was studded with jewels and a letter from d'Albuquerque. The Portuguese chronicler Galvano (Galvão) tells us that that the king "showed great courtesy"[228] and expressed his satisfaction at the defeat of his "rebellious vassal", the sultan of Malacca. He was probably happy to have these aggressive Muslim-bashing Portuguese in Malacca as a foil against the nettlesome rajahs and sultans in the southern peninsula and no doubt he also wanted to get his hands on their fancy new weapons so he consented to friendship and trade between Malacca and Siam.

Fernandes returned to Malacca by crossing the trans-peninsular route from Ayutthaya to Tenasserim, "where they imbarked themselves in two ships" and sailed down the western peninsular coast past Junkceylon to Malacca, "leaving it all discovered (so much as it can be by sailing along a coast)."[229] On his trip Fernandes saw a "vast abundance of animals, especially elephants." He noted that the people on the peninsula would eat "all kinds of beastes or vermine or fish." Fernandes was also most curious about the "the bells within the skin of their privy members" and felt that compared to "all other people of those parts they be most virtuous and honest" and, notwithstanding the "strange practice" of their penis bells, "pride themselves on their chastity and povertie."[230]

Later that same year a second, more noble Portuguese ambassador went to Ayutthaya and signed a treaty of peace and trade, the terms of which were essentially that the Portuguese would sell weapons, mercenaries and slaves to Siam in exchange for rice for Malacca and pepper from the central peninsula. Tome Pires, an early chronicler in Malacca however, later noted that "the chief merchandise they take from Malacca to Siam is male and female slaves which they take in great quantities."[231] By 1515 Portuguese muskets and cannons were in use in Ayutthaya's army and several Portuguese mercenaries joined the Siamese army as musket and artillery instructors and fought for Ayutthaya in their interminable wars with the other Thai leaders, internal rebels and the Burmese, Laotians and Cambodians. In return, the Siamese king allowed the Portuguese to build a trade factory on the river south of Ayutthaya and granted them religious freedom and the right to build churches and even to preach Christianity in his kingdom.

The Portuguese in the Peninsula and Phuket

The Portuguese capture of Malacca in 1511 dislocated the existing peninsular trade patterns. Patani immediately became the new hub for the Chinese and Japanese trade. Previously, minor ports such as Thalang would have had Malay, Indian, Arab or Chinese visiting from Malacca to trade, or the local traders would have sent cargoes to Malacca themselves. However, as the Portuguese and their armed ships attempted to impose their new "carteza" – licensing and monopoly rights – these Indian and Muslim traders moved north. They started frequenting lesser ports further up the west coast such as Tharua to avoid the Portuguese patrol ships in the Malacca Straits by using the older trans-peninsular trade routes. The early 16th century therefore probably saw a significant increase in the number of Malays and Muslims moving north to Phuket, Phang Nga Bay and Krabi.

Tome Pires, a Portuguese apothecary (chemist) and diarist from Lisbon who lived in Malacca from 1512 to 1515 just after its conquest by the Portuguese, noted that "Juncalan [Phuket] was one of the seaports where trade fell on account of the Portuguese scourings along the coast."[232] Whether "scourings" meant Portuguese trade, or their attacking and pillaging of Muslim settlements further south and therefore driving Muslim trade further north, is unclear.

Most of the Portuguese in the East were primarily a hardy bunch of lower-class adventurers. Due to the high risk of sailing to the East (over one quarter of the Portuguese ships making the trip were lost at sea and many on the ships that made it died from diseases), many were half-breed Negroes and Indians picked up as crew en route from the Portuguese colonies in Brazil, Angola, Mozambique and India. Nuno da Cunha, the governor of the "Estado da India" from 1529 to 1538 for example, had to pass an edict that all men in the East should muster for daily target practice and their weapons should be checked to make sure they were clean and the men were "not to pawn them for drink."[233] It was mainly such boorish ruffians who set about expanding Portuguese influence around the peninsula.

After taking Malacca the Portuguese visited Patani, at the time the main east-coast peninsular port for pepper and Chinese and Japanese trade. The queen of Patani allowed the Portuguese to settle to trade and to build a trade factory and by 1518 Pinto tells us there were over 300 Portuguese living in Patani. [234] Portuguese vessels would also have been seen around Phuket with increasing frequency after 1520, visiting the west-coast ports to trade, to police the carteza or raid for slaves. Duarte Barbosa, the Portuguese factor of Cannanore in Kerala, India from 1500 to 1516, recorded that the west-coast port of Tenasserim in Siam exported many elephants and sandalwood, the port of Keddah specialized in pepper and Selangor and Phuket in tin. In return he says the local "Moors" bought copper, quicksilver, vermilion, saffron, velvets and Cambrai cloths. [235]

Tome Pires, the Portuguese diarist in Malacca from 1512 to 1515, tells us that, "On the Tenasserim side [of the peninsula] Siam trades with Pase, Pedir, with Keddah, with Pegu, with Bengal and the Gujaratees come to its ports every year, they trade richly outside and liberally inside the country."[236] He observed that the port towns in the central peninsula belonged to Siam, but "All have lords like kings … every one of these ports is a chief port and they have a great deal of trade and many of them rebel against Siam."[237] His overall impression of this Siamese rule over the Malays in the peninsula, however, was that "they are great Tyrants." He tells us that the viceroy of Ligor was the overall ruler of the peninsula after the Siamese king, "the second is the viceroy of Lakon [Ligor] … he is governor from Pahang to Odia [Ayutthaya]." Pires also wrote, though perhaps erroneously, that it was the viceroy of Tenasserim, based in Mergui, who ran Phuket and the other Siamese-controlled ports down the peninsular west coast. "He is the chief person, he has jurisdiction over them all; he is the lord of many people and a land plenteous in foodstuffs."[238]

Portuguese ships probably started trading with Phuket in the late 1520s or early 1530s, though it is not clear when exactly the first Portuguese began their settlement on the island. The Portuguese writer and a relative of the governor of Malacca, Fernão Mendes Pinto, reports that in the 1540s he was sent north from Malacca to search for Portuguese living in the smaller west-coast peninsular ports such as Phuket to order them to come back to Malacca, as they were needed for the defense of the city against the frequent Muslim counter-attacks. He records however that he "passed by Tenasserim, Mergui, Juncay [Junk Ceylon] … without finding any trace of the one hundred Portuguese I was looking for in those parts."[239] By the late 1560s the Portuguese had built a wooden-fortified trade factory in Tharua and by 1571 there must have been sufficient Portuguese and their offspring living in Tharua to justify the Jesuits building a wooden Catholic mission building there. In 1585 the Portuguese also apparently opened their own tin mining operation near Cherngtalay in Phuket.

The Portuguese chronicler Manuel Teixera tells us of another band of Portuguese renegades who established a pirate colony on some islands just north of Phuket, probably the Surin Islands, and from there they preyed on Muslim shipping. These Portuguese raiders also preyed on the locals and ran a handsome business capturing slaves from the surrounding areas and shipping them off to India and Europe. Fernão Mendes Pinto noted that this pirate band's depredations "led to a sharp decline in the customs revenues of the ports of Junk Ceylon [Phuket] and Mergui so that the people in those places were forced to report it to the Emperor of Sornau [king of Siam] … and asked him to remedy this evil."[240] One Indian ballad also tells of these peninsular Portuguese pirates threatening the Muslim Indian traders involved in the Bay of Bengal trade: "The dreaded Portuguese Pirates … were constantly watching the ships, stealthily following them through the nooks of the coast and islands. They plundered the ships and assassinated their crews and the sailors and captains trembled in fear."[241] In 1544, to get rid of these Portuguese pirate colonies on the west coast, the Thai king sent a fleet of 15 ships under the command of one of his toughest mercenary captains, an Ottoman Turk named Heredim Mohamed. The king, we are told, promised him the "Duchy of Bancha" (Bang Saphan?) if he would bring back the heads of the four Portuguese pirate captains. The Turk and his Siamese fleet met the Portuguese raiders' fleet in a sea battle and Fernão Pinto records that the Portuguese pirates "achieved a total victory on 29 September 1544."[242]

A strong Muslim and Malay backlash in the region against these aggressive anti-Islamic Portuguese was soon led by the deposed sultan of Malacca and the powerful sultans of Aceh and Johore, sometimes backed by Ottoman mercenaries, fleets and cannon. In the

16th century they attacked the Portuguese in Malacca fort 12 times but never managed to retake the stone fortress the Portuguese had rebuilt there using, amongst other materials, the destroyed great mosque and headstones from the city's Muslim cemetery. But battle lines were not always clear-cut, as many local Muslim leaders also went into allegiance with the Portuguese to fight against other stronger Muslim rivals in the region. The stronger Muslim and Malay powers also fought back by raiding Portuguese ships in the region, as well as the vulnerable small Portuguese trade bases on the peninsular west coast. In the 1540s for example, one Portuguese account tells of a Portuguese trading post being established at "Tilau", which was "off the coast of Juncalan on the south west coast near to the kingdom of Quedah, a hundred and forty leagues from Malacca."[243] Tilau was most probably Trang. In 1547 the sultan of Aceh attacked and took over this Portuguese base, slaughtering the inhabitants and then raiding the surrounding coasts for slaves. In response, in 1550 a Portuguese war fleet from Malacca came up to Trang and defeated the Acehnese force there in a naval battle and then fortified and re-held Trang port themselves.

In 1568 Ayutthaya city was for the first time conquered and occupied by the Burmese. For the next 20 years Ayutthayan control over the rajahs and sultans in the central peninsula dissolved. These local leaders attempted to become independent, a move which soon led to in-fighting amongst themselves. Starting in 1584 the famous Thai King Naresuan led a Thai uprising which managed to recapture Ayutthaya and expel the Burmese army from Siam. He then spent a further decade until his death in 1605 campaigning to re-establish Ayutthayan control over Tenasserim and the central peninsula. As Peter Floris, the Dutch VOC factor in Patani recorded in 1612, Portuguese mercenaries and cannoneers fought for both the Siamese and Burmese kings and indeed, for anyone else willing to pay them during this particularly turbulent and war-torn period in the region. In 1605, for example, the Portuguese Captain Diego De Medoca Furtado used his fleet to help the new Siamese lord of Tenasserim defeat a Burmese fleet just north of Phuket. This so delighted King Naresuan's successor in Ayutthaya, his brother King Ekathotsarot, that he gave Furtado a Siamese lordly title and an allowance. Then in 1611 King Ekathotsarot sent Furtado to attack the rebellious sultan of Keddah who, amongst other things, had laid claim to Phuket and its surrounding islands and the lucrative tin and birds' nests on them.

During this anarchic period of the first Ayutthayan Burmese wars, some more ambitious Portuguese mercenaries even established their own independent fiefdoms in the region. A most notable one was the adventurer Philip De Brito, a former cabin boy-turned-soldier who had worked as a mercenary leader for the king of Arakan. In 1599 he and his followers took over the city-states of Martaban and Syriam in the war-torn region of northern Tenasserim and ran them for 13 years as his own private kingdom. The Burmese king eventually defeated De Brito's mercenary force in 1613 and had De Brito publicly crucified "in the Burmese Fashion" which, it seems, meant being rectally impaled on a conical spike set in the ground. The ambitious De Brito reportedly died after three days in agony, sliding down the skewer and being ripped open. Then, for good measure, his head was cut off and stuck on a pole outside the city and left to rot as a warning to others.

Portuguese Interbreeding

In his book, Empire and Sexuality, Ronald Hyam notes that "European expansion into Asia was not only a matter of Christianity and commerce" but also of "copulation and concubinage."[244] Women were barred from going on Portuguese ships due to the sailors' superstition that it was unlucky. All Portuguese men therefore came East as single men and were quick to take local native girls on the peninsula for sex or breeding, as mistresses or wives – a policy encouraged by their early leader in the East, Alfonso d'Albuquerque, as a way to increase the numbers of Portuguese descendants (and therefore Christians), in his new "Estado de India." D'Albuquerque himself was a major womanizer who took so many local wives after the capture of Goa that one Portuguese writer commented that "not even Mohammet had it so good."[245] D'Albuquerque felt that, compared to the Africans and Indians further west, the local Malay and Siamese girls were far preferable for interbreeding, as their skin was almost the same color as that of the Portuguese. The king of Portugal even granted freeman status and exemption from crown taxes to Portuguese men who married and interbred with local women overseas. By 1604 some 200 mixed marriages were recorded in Malacca and more interbreeding took place in other west-coast Portuguese settlements like Tharua on Phuket where the Portuguese men were exhorted – by their priests and leaders – to even greater sexual reproductive efforts for the sake of Christianity, God and their king.

Bigots, Chilies and Tobacco

Behind the soldiers and traders arrived the priests and missionaries, who came east to save the poor Siamese souls from their "deceitful and false doctrines" and the "lies and snares with which the devil had filled their minds."[246] The first to arrive in Siam were two Dominican friars in the 1540s, who were very shortly set upon by a Muslim mob who killed one and badly injured the other. Despite the ferocious bigotry of these Catholic missionaries emerging from the mental confines of Inquisition Europe, they were often impressed by the piousness of the Buddhist Siamese. One early Jesuit priest, despite condemning the Siamese for being "under the influence of a false faith," saw them as a model for Christians, stating that he "was edified by seeing … so many pious acts and so much charity such as the giving of alms, payment of debts and the provision of free tables bearing every kind of food … bestowed for the love of God on whatever people might come to share them, irrespective of class. Such

9.3 An early Dominican friar – these blinkered Catholic missionaries were shocked by the religious freedom they found in Siam.

acts are indeed more to be expected of Christians than infidels, but in them they surpass many Christians."[247] The Jesuit father Manrique in 1609 commented that Buddhist priests, somewhat remarkably to him,

> "do not only preach renunciation, but really practice it. The Raulins [Buddhist monks] are so moderate and forbearing as regards ambition and the insatiable desire for the acquisition of riches, that they not only council it, but also teach it by example, knowing how much greater is the effect of actually doing what one preaches, rather than merely preaching what one does not do, as do so many persons who follow the Catholic faith."[248]

These Catholic missionaries however were generally casting their seed on barren ground and very few achieved many conversions or baptisms other than of some wives, children and slaves of the Portuguese. Much more fertile than the barren seeds of Catholicism were the seeds of the small red and green chili peppers the Portuguese had brought with them from Brazil. These peppers were used on Portuguese ships to prevent spoilage and to cover the foul taste of rancid food. The Thais learned to use these chilies in cooking and took to them with gusto and they remain a defining hallmark of much Thai and peninsular cuisine today. The Portuguese and Spanish also introduced to the region several other new foods and drugs from the new world of the Americas such as potatoes, tomatoes, pineapples, papayas, corn and cassava plus of course in 1575 the new cure-all drug of the time, tobacco, which was widely smoked or chewed by visiting sailors as well as being used as an antiseptic on wounds. By the early 17th century smoking cheroots of tobacco had become very popular amongst both men and women in Siam. Smoking tobacco was strongly recommended by visiting European physicians at the time as a sure remedy against all tropical sicknesses, jungle fevers, scurvy, syphilis and other more serious afflictions like lung cancer.

10

The Amazing Adventures of Mr. Pinto

1540 TO 1550

Colorful Tales from a 16th Century Portuguese Adventurer

Fernão Mendes Pinto was born in 1509 into a minor country family in Portugal but among his relatives was an uncle, Pero de Faria, who became Governor of Malacca. Fernão Pinto headed east in 1539 to join him, arriving in Malacca 28 years after the Portuguese had seized the city from the Malays. He decided to try trading with Sumatra and up the western peninsular coast with places such as Phuket. His accounts, gathered in a book called Peregrinação (Travels), are criticized by commentators for being somewhere between slightly fanciful and pure yarns. But they do give us a rare historical snapshot of life in the region in the mid 16th century by someone who was actually there. In one story Fernão Pinto tells us of a stop he made at Keddah on his way north to trade in Phuket.[249]

An Incestuous Affair

"Steering a course for the port of Junkceylon, we ran under fair winds for two and a half days and came to anchor in the Perlis River in the kingdom of Keddah, where we stayed for five days. While we were there, on the advice of some local merchants, the Moor [Khoja Ali, his Muslim Malay business partner and traveling companion] and I went to pay our respects to the king, bringing him a gift of a few articles of sufficient value to serve our purpose and he gave us a good reception. At the time we arrived in Keddah the king was in the midst of conducting elaborate funeral services for his father, whom he had stabbed to death in order to marry his mother, who was pregnant with his – the king's – child. There was music making, dancing, shouting, screaming and free meals for the poor who flocked there in great number. In order to stamp out the public indignation that was aroused by this horrendous and utterly abominable crime, the king had issued a proclamation to the effect that anyone heard gossiping about what had happened would be ruthlessly put to death. And from what we were told, he had already carried out this threat by executing, in an exceptionally brutal manner, some of the most important people in the kingdom, as well as a considerable number of merchants whose property he had confiscated, thus enriching his treasury. At the time I arrived, all the people were already so frightened that no one dared breathe a word. Khoja Ali was by nature a very loose-tongued fellow, who was in the habit of speaking his mind when he felt like it. He thought that, as a foreigner, especially one who was known to be acting as agent for the Captain [Governor] of Malacca, he would be freer to [talk] than the natives. One day he was invited to dinner by a relative of his – another Moor, a merchant of Patani. From what I was told later, when they had already had too much to eat and drink they began talking about the affair quite openly; this was reported to the king by the many spies he had posted around for that purpose. The king had the house surrounded and all seventeen members of the dinner party were taken into custody and brought before him, bound hand and foot. Without any semblance of justice, without making the slightest attempt to determine their guilt or innocence, he had them all executed by an extraordinarily cruel method they call 'gregoge', which consists of slowly sawing a live man to death, starting with the feet, then the hands and the chest all the way down the back to the bottom of the spine, which is the way I saw them afterwards.

"That same night, out of fear that the Captain [Governor of Malacca], might take offence at his having executed an agent of his and use that as a pretext to seize some merchandise he had already shipped to Malacca, the king sent his men to fetch me from the Jurupango [Pinto's ship] when I was fast asleep and had not the faintest idea what was going on … By the time I reached the outer courtyard of the palace it was already past midnight and the first thing I noticed were the many guards posted about, armed to the teeth with lances, swords and shields and I began to get nervous … I wanted to leave immediately but the men there would not let me go, telling me not to be afraid of what I had seen and that the armed men present were merely a police patrol the king was sending out to catch a thief. I must confess, their explanation did not satisfy me in the least. By this time I was stammering so badly that nothing I said made any sense. I managed to ask them if they would let me return to the Jurupango to look for some keys I had forgotten and I offered to pay them all forty cruzados in gold immediately if they let me go. To which they retorted 'Not for all the gold in Malacca … It's not worth the risk of having our own heads sawn off. ' … About this time another fifteen or twenty guards joined them and together they formed a ring around me and kept me confined in that way till dawn."

The next morning Pinto was brought before the king.

"God only knows what state I was in by that time – poor me – I was more dead than alive. I found the king mounted on an elephant with more than a hundred armed men around him. Observing the deplorable condition I was in, he tried to reassure me. 'Jangao Tacor,' he said, repeating it twice. 'Don't be afraid. Come over here and I will tell you why I have sent for you. ' At a sign from him ten or twelve people moved back and he motioned me to look at something. I saw a heap of sawn-up bodies lying on the floor in a pool of blood and among them I recognised the remains of Khoja Ali … At the sight of him lying there I became so panic-stricken that without knowing what I was doing I threw myself at the feet of the elephant. 'I beg you, sir,' I cried, unable to control my tears, 'Please take me for your slave instead of having me killed like the others, for I swear by my faith as a Christian, that I have done nothing to deserve it, and don't forget that I am the nephew of the Captain of Malacca, who will gladly pay any amount of money to ransom me, and then there's Jurupango in the harbour with all its valuable cargo which is yours for the taking whenever you please. ' 'Good God, man!' exclaimed the king, 'Do you think I'm as bad as all that? Calm yourself. You have nothing to fear. Just sit down and rest a while, for I can see you are a little upset. After you have regained your composure I will explain why I ordered the execution of that Moor you brought with you. ' Then he brought me a pan of water from which I drank long and thirstily and he made me feel more comfortable by having them fan me."

The king then explained to Pinto that he had been forced to kill his own father, who was plotting to kill him because some "evil men" had told the father that the king had impregnated his own mother, which he swore was not true:

"'God knows I hated to do it [said the king] as I had always been a good son to him and since I did not want my mother to remain poor and defenceless, which is the fate of many widows, I have married her. As a result I have had to refuse other good offers of marriage I had been considering, to women from Patani, Berdio, Tenasserim, Siak and Jambi. That Moor of yours is lying there in pieces because last night in the company of other dogs like him who had had too much to drink, he said so many disrespectful things about me that I am ashamed to repeat them to you … and that my mother was a bitch in heat … Therefore, I beg you, do not think unkindly of me for what I have done [only sawing his business partner into pieces]. And if by chance you think I was looking for a pretext to confiscate the cargo belonging to the Captain of Malacca, believe me that such a thought never crossed my mind, for I have always been a good friend of the Portuguese …'

"Though I was still far from calm … I told him that his Glorious Highness had performed a great act of friendship for his brother, the Captain of Malacca, by killing the Moor, because he had been robbing him shamelessly … and he had tried to poison me twice so I would not tell the Captain about his tricks and that he was an evil dog who was always getting drunk and saying whatever he had in his mind, like a dog barking at every passerby. This crude answer of mine … satisfied the king completely and made him happy. 'You are indeed a good friend of mine,' [he said]. 'That's why the things I did do not seem as bad to you as they did to those dirty dogs lying there. ' Then he took a gold embossed kriss and handed it to me, along with a letter for Pero de Faria [the Malacca governor] containing some lame excuses for what he had done. I took my leave of him as best I could, telling him I would remain there for another ten days, but I embarked immediately. Just as soon as I set foot on the Jurupango, without a moment's delay, I cut the cables and clapped on full sail, though I was unable to shake off the sensation that the entire country was coming after me, an illusion created by the harrowing experience I had been through just a few hours before."

Pinto relates that he continued south towards Malacca until he reached an island he called "Pulao Sembilan", where he "found three Portuguese naos [trade ships], two of them inbound from Bengal and the other from Pegu … [which] … escorted me safely all the way to Malacca."

Another Most Unpleasant Experience

On another trip between Phuket and northern Sumatra, Pinto tells us of being caught in a storm: "The wind whipped us to pieces, sails, poles and all leaving the lanchara [a small sloop] dismasted." They then floated at the mercy of the storm for many hours before their boat finally sank. They clung to parts of the wreckage and they drifted for three more days. "Out of the twenty eight people on board twenty three drowned."[250]

10.1 A Depiction of Pinto's "lanchara" sinking in the Malacca Straits.

The five survivors eventually reached land on the Sumatran coastline. "The entire shore was a swampland covered by jungle growth so thick that not even the smallest bird could have flown between the thorns on the tightly laced branches of the mangrove swamp." They battled along the shoreline, "sinking waist deep into the slime, until just before sunset when we reached the mouth of a river." There they spent the night thirsty and "tortured by sand flies and mosquitoes that came swarming out of the jungle."

The next morning one of the five, a Moor, "expired because of the weak condition he was in, for in the storm his head had been split wide open and the gray matter was all crushed and exposed and oozing pus." Pinto was also weak, too, "from sheer dizziness and loss of blood from the lacerations on my back." The four survivors decided to cross the wide river:

"to spend the next night in some trees that were visible on the other side, as a precaution against the tigers and rhinoceroses roaming in the area, to say nothing of the different kinds of poisonous animals lurking around, hooded cobras and another kind of green and black speckled snake, which are venomous enough to kill you with a whiff of their breath … I urged two of them to go ahead and the other to stay with me and help me because by then I was extremely weak. [The first two went ahead], calling out to me to follow and not to be afraid, but just when they had gone a little past the middle of the river, two huge lizards [crocodiles] lunged at them, cutting each of them into four pieces in no time at all, reddening the river with their blood and dragging them down to the bottom. At the time it happened I had already waded chest deep into the river with the other black who was holding me by the hand. I was so frightened out of my wits that I couldn't even scream. Nor do I have any recollection how I escaped with my life … I was in a state of shock for over three hours … finally the other sailor and I returned to the sea and remained there in the surf till morning.

"[Later that same day] we caught sight of a coastal barge that was heading for the mouth of the river. As soon as it came alongside we emerged from the water in all our nakedness and threw ourselves down on our knees and with arms uplifted pleaded with them to take us on board. The occupants of the boat stopped rowing when they saw us and after taking in our situation for a moment – for they could tell from the pitiful state we were in that we had been cast up by the sea – they moved in closer and asked us what we wanted. We told them we were Christians from Malacca and that we had been shipwrecked nine days before and begged them for the love of God to take us with them wherever they were going. 'From the looks of you you're not even worth feeding,' said one of them, 'But if you have any money hidden on you, hand it over first and then maybe we will be moved to pity by your tears … otherwise you're out of luck.' And so saying, they made as if to move off, but once again we pleaded with them, in tears, to take us along as captives and sell us for ransom wherever they felt like, making a point that they could get a good price for me, since I was Portuguese and a close relative of the Captain of Malacca. 'That's different,' they replied. 'But we warn you, if it doesn't turn out the way you say, we'll thrash you and throw you overboard – alive, tied hand and foot.' Four of them jumped ashore and helped us into the boat because we were in such bad shape we could hardly move.

"Once they had us on board they seemed to think that by threatening and beating us they could make us confess where we had some money hidden away … they tied us to the foot of the mast and with two rattan canes folded in half they flogged us until the blood flowed. Since I was already half dead by that time, they did not make me drink the foul stuff they forced down the throat of my unfortunate companion, which was some kind of lime mixed with urine that made him throw up his guts, as a result of which he died an hour later. Because they did not find any gold in his vomit as they thought they would, that was why, as it pleased God, they spared me the same treatment. Instead, they applied the same concoction to my lash wounds to make sure I wouldn't die of them, but the pain was so excruciating, it nearly killed me … We anchored the following day at Vespers in front of a large village of thatched huts, where they kept me for twenty seven days during which time – God be praised – I recovered from the flogging. But when the seven partners who owned me came to realize they could find no use for me in their occupation, which always kept them out on the river fishing, they put me up for auction three times, each time without success, for no one was willing to bid for me. As a result, having given up hope of ever finding a buyer for me, they threw me out so as not to have to feed me, for I was of absolutely no use to them."

Pinto claims he then spent 36 days in what he later discovered was the town of Siak in Sumatra, being "left to shift for myself like a sorry old nag put out to pasture, begging from door to door for a bite to eat, which I seldom received, for the people of that country are all extremely poor." Some of them, he says, "supported themselves solely by killing lizards and making poison from their livers in which to dip the arrows they fight with."

Eventually, he met "a visiting Moor from Palembang [who] had been to Malacca several times where he had come to know the Portuguese." Pinto convinced the merchant to buy him and take him to Malacca where he would get a profitable ransom from his uncle, the governor. The Moor bought him and took him back to Malacca along with his stinking cargo of "the roe of the shad fish." In Malacca, Pinto's uncle, the governor, paid the Moor "sixty cruzados and two bolts of Chinese damask" and additionally waived the customs duty on the cargo of fish eggs.

It should be noted that, in 1614, after the posthumous publication in Portugal of his book Peregrinação about his travels in the East, the Portuguese literati made a play on the author's name, changing it from Fernão Mendes Pinto to Fernão Mentes Pinto, which translates as Fernão "Liar" Pinto.

II

The Pugnacious Protestants

1580 TO 1640

By 1550 pepper bought in the Orient was selling in Europe for a profit of over 4,000 percent. Portugal's revenues from the spice trade were equivalent to four times the kingdom's total tax income. Naturally, the Portuguese tried hard to keep their navigational information about the route to the Indies secret, but the cat was soon to escape the bag.

A Forgotten Malay Is the First Man to Circumnavigate the World

Fernão de Magalhaes, better known in English as Ferdinand Magellan, was one of the 20 Portuguese who had been imprisoned in Malacca for two years. He survived the Portuguese conquest of the city and eventually returned home. He took with him a Malay slave whom he had bought in Malacca and had named Enrique. It is not known where exactly on the peninsula Enrique came from, it may even have been Phuket. Back in Europe in 1519, Magellan, due to his knowledge of the East, was offered a commission from the king of Spain to lead a fleet to attempt to reach the lucrative spice ports of Asia by sailing westwards through the Spanish half of the world. Magellan agreed and took Enrique with him to act as an interpreter when he reached the Indies.

His small fleet found a route round the bottom of South America and then crossed the Pacific westwards. By 1521 he reached the Philippines, where he was shot by poisoned arrows and then speared and clubbed to death by the rather xenophobic natives of Mactan Island off Cebu. Sebastian Elcano took his place as fleet commander. He reached the Moluccan Spice Islands then headed west to reach home. On the way they called in at Malacca, and when they did, Magellan's Malay slave, Enrique, became the first known person to circumnavigate the world. However, as he was brown-skinned and Asian, this fact was completely disregarded by the Christian chroniclers of the time, who credited Sebastian Elcano with this honor when he eventually made it back to Seville in 1522.

The Protestant Challenge for the Spice Trade

By the late 16th century the increasingly venal Catholic Church and papacy were losing their moral monopoly over hearts and minds in Europe. Northern Europeans began protesting against the massive corruption in the Church and demanded reform. By the 1570s this "Reformation" movement and the new "Protestant" religion it spawned pitted the northern European Protestants in wars against the Catholic powers. The papal edict barring other nations from the lucrative new worlds was challenged by the now irreverent and anti-Papist Protestant maritime states of England, Holland and the Baltic.

Holland, or the Spanish Netherlands as it had been, was previously part of the Hapsburg Spanish Empire, but in the late 16th century the Protestant Dutch states had revolted against Spanish Catholic rule and were supported by England. These two countries discovered that privateering – attacking and seizing Spanish ships and cargoes – was a good way both to attack the Papists and to make money at the same time. In 1577 the English Captain Francis Drake was commissioned by Queen Elizabeth I to harass catholic shipping. Off the Azores, he captured a Portuguese carrack with a spice cargo worth 108,000 pounds sterling, a vast fortune at the time, alerting the English to the huge profit potential of these spice cargoes from the East.

In 1583 the English merchant explorer Ralph Fitch, funded by merchants of the Levant Company in London, traveled overland through India and as far east as Siam and Burma. From Pegu he also sailed to Malacca and recorded passing on the way "the islands of Tenaseri [Tenasserim], Junsalon [Phuket] and many others."[251] With this increasing knowledge of the route east and after the English and Dutch defeated the Spanish Armada in 1588, merchants and financiers in both London and Amsterdam became confident enough to attempt to compete directly in the lucrative eastern trade themselves, or at least to hunt and rob the Catholic ships conducting this fruitful trade.

The First English Privateers in Phuket

In 1591 the first English privateering fleet was funded to go to the East for, as its charter stated, "The anoyinge of the Spaniards and Portingalls, (nowe our enemys) as also for the vendinge of oure comodities."[252] The fleet of three warships left Plymouth with 198 men under the command of James Lancaster, a hero of the Armada victory. Off South Africa, one ship had to turn back, as over 50 sailors were sick from "the skurvie". Another ship was wrecked off the Natal coast. Only the flagship, the Edward Bonaventure, with a crew of 33 mainly sick and weak men eventually managed to reach the Malay Peninsula in 1592. They moored off Penang island south of Phuket as, "Our men were very sicke and many fallen … we espied a canoe which came neere to us …

11.1 James Lancaster who based his English privateering expedition in Phuket in 1592.

having in it some sixteen naked Indians, with whom nevertheless, going afterward on land, we had friendly conference and promise of victuals."[253] They rested on Penang, eating vegetables, fruit, fish and oysters to recover and refitted their damaged vessel. They then headed off again "determined to runne into the straits of Malacca" to attack any Portuguese ships which "must needs come from Goa or St. Thome for the Moluccas, China and Japan." They captured three Portuguese ships carrying rice and food to Malacca. Then they were fortunate enough to: "meet with the ship of the Captain (Governor) of Malacca, of seven hundred tunnes, which came from Goa, we shot at her many shot and at last shooting her maineyard through, she came to anker and yielded." She was a rich prize of "sixteene pieces of brass [brass cannons], [carrying] Canarie wine and nipa wine [palm wine] … all kinds of haberdasher ware, velvets, taffetas, Spanish wooles, silks, shoes, hats, playing cards, rice but little treasure," apart from "some False and counterfeit stones which an Italian had brought from Venice to decieve the rude Indians with."[254]

They sailed to Aceh in Sumatra to sell and trade their captured goods. Then setting back to sea, they decided to set up their eastern privateering base on Phuket Island. We are informed of their arrival off Phuket by the pen of Edmund Barker, the scribe on the Edward Bonaventure, who gives us what may be the first still existing European report of anyone going ashore on Phuket. He tells us that they moored in

11.2 Drunken English privateers on a tropical beach enjoying their booty.

> "a baie in the kingdom of Junsalaom [probably Patong Bay] which is between Malacca and Pegu … to seeke for pitch [damar] to trim our ship. Here we sent our soldier (a Portuguese) … because he had the Malayan language, to deal with the people for the pitch, which he did faithfully and procured us some two or three quintals with promise of more and certain of the people came unto us. We sent commodities to their king to barter for Ambergris and for the horns of abath [rhinoceros], whereof the king only has the traffic thereof in his hands. Now this abath is a beast which has one horn only in her forehead and is thought to be the female unicorn and is highly esteemed of all the Moores in those parts as a most souraigne remedie against poison. We had only two or three of these hornes, which are the colour of a brown grey and some reasonable quantity of ambergris. At last the king went about to betray our Portingal with our merchandise, but he, to get aboard us, told the king we had gilt armour, shirtes of maile and halberds, which things they greatly desire, for hope whereof, he let him returne aboard and so he escaped the danger."[255]

After waiting around Phuket for some days, these English caught sight of some distant sails belonging to "three ships, being all of a burthen sixty or seventy tonnes, one of which we made strike with our very boat."[256] One was a Portuguese ship, which they attacked, captured and plundered. The other two were Burmese ships they allowed to go on their way. Then a few weeks later, "upon a Sunday, we espied a saile which was a Portugall ship … and that night we took her, being of 250 tunnes, she was laden with rice for Malacca … In this month also we tooke a great Portugall ship of some hundred tun, laden with victuals, chests of hats, pintados [fish] and other commodities . . . These ships were bound for Malacca with victuals because that victuals there were very scarce."[257]

By 1594, after two years of pirating, mainly based off Phuket, several men had succumbed to tropical diseases. "Our captain being very sicke and more likely to die than to recover … oure men declared unanimously that they would stay no longer in this country and insisted upon directing our course for England; and as they would listen to no persuasions, the captain was under the necessity of giving way to their demand, leaving all hope of the great possibility we had of making some rich prizes."[258] Only 25 sick, scorbutic and starving survivors of the original 198 who set out so ambitiously, managed to get home and without any real profit. Such was the fate of the first Englishmen to attempt to make their fortune in Phuket.

They fared, however, much better than the second English attempt. This time, in 1596, another English privateering fleet of three ships, using information gathered by Lancaster's expedition, also sailed east to base themselves in Phuket. Benjamin Wood, a successful Caribbean privateer, led this expedition. With the exception of one French crewman, who jumped ship in uninhabited Mauritius where he lived like Robinson Crusoe for 20 months, none of these ambitious privateers was ever heard of again.

First, one of the three ships was wrecked off Madagascar; then, after a period of raiding along the Indian coast, the remaining two ships came to Phuket to wait for passing Portuguese vessels. Our knowledge from here on is gleaned only from Portuguese sources, which report two English ships in the area undertaking piracy. They may even have been doing fairly well, until they had the misfortune to encounter a full Portuguese war fleet just west of Phuket. A running battle was fought for eight days until, the Portuguese reported, the two out-gunned and badly damaged English ships went into hiding on the coast of "old Keddah" for repairs. Due to the damage to the ships and the greatly diminished number of crewmen, many having been killed or severely wounded by Portuguese cannon and musket fire, "the Englishmen abandoned their smaller vessel." They all headed out to sea again in their remaining badly damaged ship, which "shortly afterwards foundered in a storm off the island of Buting"[259] (most probably Ko Batang off Tarutao) and there ended the "miserable disastrous success"[260] of the second attempt by the English to make their fortunes in Phuket.

The Dutch Head East

The Dutch fared better than the English. Before their revolt against Spain, they had been the principal maritime distributors around Northern Europe and the Baltic of eastern spices which they had bought in Portugal. After the Dutch Protestant revolt however, this lucrative business was closed to them, so some Dutch merchants decided to attempt to obtain these spices directly from their sources in the East. Between 1594 and 1612, seven Dutch fleets tried to pioneer a northern or Arctic route to the Orient, either northwest around Canada or northeast around Russia. They all failed. Some most miserably.

Several Dutchmen had previously worked on Portuguese ships which had sailed east. One of these was the merchant Jan Van Linschoten who went to Goa in 1583, stayed there eight years and kept copious records which he published as a book in Holland in 1598. Though he apparently never visited the Malay Peninsula himself he knew that it extended south to "the Cape of Singapura… like an arme" and tells us that "all this land in time past was under the power and subjection of the king of Siam." However since the Burmese had defeated Ayutthaya (15 years earlier in 1568) he said, the power of the Siamese king "is much declined, so that many of these kingdoms (the local peninsular sultans and rajahs) that in times past used to pay him tribute, doe nowe refuse to do it and hold their kingdoms of themselves."[261] He calls the northwestern part of the peninsula "the Kingdome of Tanassaria" and tells us that "the most important ports in this kingdom are Myrguim [Mergui] and Jonsalam [Phuket]… [which were good] … for repairing ships, as masts and the woods requisite for building large ships are so cheap there."[262] He also records that "there is found much Calaem, which is like tinne, … from Jonsalam lying upon the coast north north west from Queda 30 miles."[263]

Dutch spies in Portugal also conspired to obtain their cherished navigational information on the route east. One of these spies, a suave young merchant, Cornelius De Houtman, managed to acquire navigational charts and sufficient information so that, in 1594, some Dutch merchants were confident enough to back him to lead a fleet of four vessels and 247 sailors to the Moluccas Islands to buy spices. They reached Java having lost many men to disease and scurvy en route. Asian ships at the time often had women on board and the local rajah of Bantam (by Jakarta) was so astonished to learn that these strange, blond and bearded Dutchmen had traveled all that way without any females that he immediately dispatched several women to their ships. After such a cordial start, the Dutch made a trade treaty of friendship with this magnanimous Javanese king. Their welcome off the island of Madura further east, however, was less affable; there they were attacked by a fleet of Malay prahus, which they eventually dispatched with some healthy European broadsides of grapeshot and ball. De Houtman then ordered his men to attack a nearby town in retribution and kill all the men and rape all the women. After the battle, with fewer than a hundred men left alive and many of them very ill, De Houtman decided to turn back. He reached Holland two and a half years later with only 87 of his original crew alive.

The expedition was not a financial success, but investors in Amsterdam were sufficiently encouraged to fund a second fleet in 1598 that reached the Moluccas, loaded up with spices and got back to Amsterdam. It has been calculated that, in modern terms, US$45 worth of nutmeg and cloves bought in the Moluccas at the time sold for US$1,800 back in Lisbon. This second Dutch fleet recorded a profit of well over 1,000 percent, exciting the Dutch merchants so much that within a couple of months three more fleets were promptly funded, by different merchant companies, and sent east. The fifth fleet, sent in 1600, was the first to do business on the Malay Peninsula. From their "general rendezvous" point at Bantam in Java, two ships from this fifth fleet were sent to Patani, which after the fall of Malacca had become the largest Malay port in the peninsula, dealing in pepper and with Chinese and Japanese trade. They arrived in November 1601 and the queen of Patani, despite vehement protests from the Portuguese, Chinese and Muslim traders already in town, agreed to allow the Dutch to buy pepper and other local produce and build a trade factory there. The Dutch ships left Patani in 1602, leaving behind a trade factory built of wood and 26 Dutchmen to run the business.

By 1602, in just two years, the mad rush for spice riches saw more than 65 Dutch ships sail east independently. It was decided that, rather than having several small companies competing and pushing prices higher, it would be better to amalgamate all into one great company with pooled resources. Thus, in 1602, the Vereenigde Oost-Indische Compagnie – the Dutch East India Company, or VOC – was formed with a monopoly over eastern trade. It had many shareholders and large resources and was governed by a board of 17 directors representing the most important trading towns of Holland. This powerful company set about trying to muscle the Portuguese and all other competitors out of this lucrative eastern spice trade.

As early as 1603 the Portuguese viceroy of Goa was writing to complain of Dutch seizures of several Malacca-bound ships in the Andaman Sea off Phuket. In 1604 a VOC ship commanded by the Dutch Admiral Wijbrand Van Warwyck came to Ayutthaya to try to obtain a trade treaty with Siam. King Naresuan, who was still obsessed with his many wars, was happy to accommodate these new Europeans, mainly to try to get his hands on their superior weapons. He also tried to convince the Dutch to bring their powerful ships to fight on his side in his various campaigns, but the VOC, looking mainly for trade and profits, refused to be coerced. After King Naresuan died in 1605, his successor King Ekathotsarot was keener on trade; he also wanted a foil against the increasingly unruly and pushy Portuguese in his kingdom. Despite reportedly bursting out laughing when new Dutch emissaries told him they had no king, he made a treaty, allowing the VOC to build a factory in Ayutthaya near the Portuguese. The Dutch sold King Ekathotsarot guns and cannons and sent him military advisers to assist him in his many wars. They also sent him craftsmen to work as shipwrights, carpenters and enamellers and, with relations generally cordial, the king gave the Dutch permission to open trading factories in the peninsula at Ligor and Songkla to deal in pepper, tin and deer hides, which of course further upset the Portuguese.

Siam's Conflict with Portugal

Portugal and Siam had generally got along well at first, but the Portuguese, especially after they united with the Spanish crown (1580-1640) grew increasingly arrogant and overbearing towards the Siamese kings Ekathotsarot and Songtham. In 1613 for example, a Portuguese fleet on its way from Goa to Ayutthaya attacked and sacked Keddah without the Siamese king's permission. Then in 1617, with Holland and the united Catholic Iberian kingdom at war in Europe, a Portuguese ship in Ayutthaya attacked a Dutch frigate in the Chao Phraya River right in King Songtham's back yard. This was too much for him and the offending Portuguese ship was surrounded by hundreds of Siamese war boats and captured. The Spanish captain, Don Fernando de Silva, was gruesomely executed and his sailors cast into prison.

In retaliation, the Spanish authorities in Manila captured, sacked and burnt a Siamese junk carrying a cargo belonging to King Songtham on its way home from China. The Siamese king then "put an embargo upon all Portuguese ships which were found in the ports of Lygoar and Tannasary [Ligor and Tenasserim]"[264]— that is, in all the peninsular ports such as Phuket. All the Portuguese in Siam, including the Jesuit priest and the few Portuguese tin traders in Phuket, were arrested and imprisoned, "out of which they were not set at liberty till two years later." This Portuguese dispute with King Songtham lasted for 15 years until his death in 1628 and it allowed the Dutch and the Japanese to gain the upper hand over the Portuguese in the Siamese and peninsular trade.

The Dutch Muscle the Portuguese out of Phuket and the Peninsula

The better-armed VOC ships continued to harass and attack any Iberian shipping in the region at every opportunity they had. "The Dutch", venomously noted one Portuguese writer in Malacca, "are only good cannoneers. For everything else they are only worthy of being burnt as reprobate heretics."[265]

As early as 1606 the Dutch allied with the sultan of Johore and jointly attacked the Portuguese stronghold of Malacca, but with its stout walls, the city's fortress was adjudged to be "not a cat to be handled without gloves."[266] The Portuguese withstood the siege, as they had withstood the 14 previous sieges of the city by the Acehnese and Johorese Malays and other Muslims. The Dutch mounted two more unsuccessful attacks on Malacca, in 1608 and 1615.

In 1618 the VOC came under the leadership of its fourth governor general, the ambitious and cruel Jan Pieterszoon Cohen and it became much more aggressive. Over the next 30 years the Dutch brutally evicted the Portuguese from most of their eastern bastions. In 1618 the VOC captured the Portuguese bases in the Moluccan Spice Islands. In 1619 they attacked and captured Jakarta, which they fortified, renamed Batavia, and made their main base in the East. Operating from there, VOC warships raided Portuguese shipping in the Malacca Straits and right up the peninsular west coast. One VOC report in 1620 tells of two Portuguese ships encountered leaving Phuket "heading for Trang," which were attacked just off the island by a VOC patrol ship. "One was wrecked and the other taken."[267]

In 1640 a huge Acehnese fleet of 236 boats and 20,000 men launched yet another attack on Portuguese Malacca which weakened the city's defenses. Then, just a few months later, in January 1641, the VOC, in alliance with some 1,500 Johorese Malays, followed up and attacked the weakened city once again. The attack and siege went on for over a year. Inside the city the defenders starved, the inhabitants being forced to eat cats, dogs, snakes, rats and leather and mothers were even forced to eat their dead babies. [268] Malaria, typhoid and cholera also took a huge toll on both sides. The Dutch siege general reported he had lost half his force, "a little under 1,000 men killed in action and dead through epidemics."[269] He estimated that over 7,000 of the roughly 10,000 people inside the besieged city had died. Eventually the Dutch broke through the fort walls and the Portuguese defenders still fought them street by street, putting up a heroic defense and only surrendering after their commander was killed.

11.3 A Dutch and Portuguese fleet in a sea battle in the Malacca Straits south of Phuket.

The Dutch general, awed at their gallantry, buried the dead Portuguese with full honors and, out of respect, let the defenders leave the city with their possessions and sail off to Goa. This general was later reprimanded for this compassion by VOC shareholders in Holland, who complained that, "The vanquished enemy was quite thoughtlessly allowed full liberty against all customs of war ... In this way they carried off more than 100,000 reals worth of gold and jewelry, besides the most valuable slaves of both sexes ... This foolish act robbed the Company of at least four to five tons of gold."[270]

After 130 years' dominance around the peninsula's coasts, the Portuguese had been overthrown. Malacca was almost completely destroyed after the siege, as one Dutch official in Batavia complained. "From a well built city, cultivated land and more than 20,000 inhabitants, it has been reduced to a heap of ruins, a desert with few inhabitants."[271]

In Phuket, at the same time, in 1641, the Portuguese mestizo community and the Franciscans had just been building a new and bigger mission in Tharua to support their growing colony there, but just after its completion, a Dutch patrol ship and its marines chased out the Portuguese residents. These Portuguese refugees, under Siamese law, were forced to leave their half-breed children and Catholicized wives behind. Most of them continued to live in Tharua near the mission, practicing a strange form of homegrown Catholicism. They and their mestizo Christian descendants became the choice local partners, mistresses and wives for later Christian sailors visiting the island. The male mestizo Portuguese of the island, we are told later, specialized in fishing and obtaining forest products from the interior regions and bringing them to Tharua to trade with foreigners.

The Honorable East India Company in Siam

In late December 1600, as the winter dark fell over the drizzling, grim but bustling streets of London, passers-by may have heard a cheer emanate from the lamp-lit windows of a building in Leadenhall Street. Inside were some of the city's leading lords and merchants who had just agreed to form a joint stock trading company for undertaking eastern trade, the Honorable East India Company or EIC, which was given a monopoly by the king over all eastern trade.

The EIC started by trading in India; in 1612 it dispatched the ship the Globe armed with a gilded letter from King James I of the United Kingdom to try to open trade with Siam and the Malay Peninsula. The Globe first called in at Patani, where they were "met with an honourable reception from the queen and the people, but with some distaste from the Dutch." The clearly enamored English scribe from the Globe described the queen of Patani as "tall of person and full of majestie ... having in all the Indes not scene any lyke her." He reported that Patani was a most flourishing port with some 500 foreigners; Portuguese, Japanese, Chinese and Dutch were already living there and the port was "resorted to by ships from Surat, Goa, the Coromandel coast ... and junks from China and Japan."[272]

The queen of Patani agreed to a trade compact with the English, who noted, "after much running, toyling and giving of gifts, wee got leave to build a pack house hard by the Dutch house." The Globe then sailed on north to Ayutthaya. Peter Floris, a Dutchman who was left in charge of the VOC trade factory in Patani, later reported "the strangest robberye" in their newly built palm-leaf-thatched pack house. "Being all of us in the house above 15 persons sleeping, Mr. Lucas and I in a bedde aparte lying close together, having a great black dogge lying under my cabine, my trunke standing at my feete, being no greater space between the bedde and coffer butt that onely the lidde might shut and open, yet notwithstanding all this and a lamp burning, thieves forced the padlock of the chest and stole [all the cash] and dyvers other things such as appareill, linen and my rapier which had at leaste 25 Rupies in silver upon it."[273] The robbery however may have just been a fiction concocted to cover the EIC employees for having sold the goods themselves to pay for their drinking, gambling and womanizing – not an uncommon occurrence amongst the somewhat dissolute EIC factors in the East.

When the Globe arrived off Paknam fort at the mouth of the Chao Phraya River, the ship's scribe tells us, "the native shabandhar [customs officer] of the port came down ... mainly with an eye to a personal present."[274] These were duly given and the ship was allowed into the Chao Phraya River. After offloading the ship's cannon at the fort of

Bangkok down river from Ayutthaya, as was customary for any visiting ship, the crew sailed and rowed the ship upriver to Ayutthaya. They were given an audience with King Songtham and presented him with the letter from King James I. The Siamese king gave the English permission to build a factory in Ayutthaya plus the right to trade in Siam's peninsular ports. At this point the main trade article the Europeans wanted was pepper and it was Patani, Ligor and Keddah, not Phuket, which were the main pepper ports in the peninsula.

The Anglo-Dutch Naval War in the East

By the early 17th century the English and Dutch were moving towards war in Europe over herring fisheries and there was also much ill feeling between the two communities in the East. In 1615 one Dutchman reported that "the English in … Siam are very ill behaved," describing them as "a rude and ungoverned nation, given to drunkenness and abusing of women, quarrelling, fighting and such like."[275] In 1619 the VOC governor, Jan Pieterszoon Cohen, venomously wrote that the English factors in Siam were so poor "they had to sell their whores"[276] to pay for food. The English in Siam on the other hand reported back that the Hollanders "endeavoured by all possible means to wrong and hurt the English by their vigorous lying scorpion tongues" and that "if we could hear but one true word proceed out of a Dutchman's mouth I would think one amongst a thousand honest."[277]

As Anglo-Dutch relations worsened the VOC, under the combative Cohen, attacked and took over the factories recently established by the English in the Spice Islands and then tortured and killed many of the English prisoners taken there in what is known as the "Amboyna Massacre", In 1618 in retribution for this Dutch "insolence" the EIC declared war on the VOC and in 1619 an EIC fleet attacked Jakarta, chasing out the Dutch fleet. Then off the Malay Peninsula they captured the richly laden VOC trade ship the Black Lion. An EIC captain, John Jourdain, was sent to the Malay Peninsula from India with two warships, the Hound and the Sampson, designed to reinforce the EIC defenses in the region. These two EIC warships arrived and were moored in Patani roads when a full VOC naval division of three large men-o'-war with over 800 men was suddenly sighted approaching the harbor. Jourdain, the English commander, decided not to sail his two smaller ships out to sea and attempt to flee because "he disdained to appear to have run before his enemy, as his doing so might have damaged, in the opinion of the natives, the reputation his nation had established for courage, so he determined therefore to fight them in full view of the town."[278]

In truth the local natives couldn't really tell the difference between the Dutch and the English. In Java, for example, where both the VOC and EIC had trade stations, both companies had to stage frequent parades specifically so that the confused locals could tell who was Dutch and who was British. The natives in Patani were soon treated to five hours of entertainment as the two fleets battled it out in full sight of the enraptured local spectators on shore. True to Jourdain's word, the two English ships never moved from their anchors, conduct which one of Jourdain's contemporaries claimed deserved "favourable censure" for bravery, but which was not great tactics. The bigger Dutch ships simply blew the two smaller English ships apart with broadside after broadside, killing over 50 English sailors and wounding many more. According to Marmaduke Stevenson, an officer from the Hound, when all appeared lost, Jourdain went on deck to attempt to parley, but a sharpshooter in the rigging of one of the Dutch ships gave him a "death wound with a musket ball under the heart."[279] The remaining Englishmen on the two ships thereupon surrendered, were taken prisoner and treated with great brutality. "Men burnt with gunpowder and terribly wounded by splinters ... were most inhumanely forced to put their legs down gratings"[280] to imprison them. When the time came to release them, these gratings had to be sawn apart, so much had the prisoners' legs swollen. The English prisoners were shipped off to Japan by the Dutch and one, the mate of the Hound, later wrote that the Dutch had them "exposed in a cage to the inhabitants of each Japanese town as proof of their superiority over the English."

11.4. European ships fighting, sometimes in full sight of the shore, would have been an awe-inspiring but very entertaining spectacle for the locals on the peninsula.

Dutch Dominance

The VOC was a bigger and much better funded company than the EIC and over the next four years of war between the two companies, the merciless VOC chief, Jan Pieterszoon Cohen – who liked to exhort his men to "ride the locals with a sharp spur" and of whom even one Dutch VOC officer later complained that he conducted his business in the East "in such a criminal and murderous way that the blood of the poor people cries to heaven for vengeance"[281] – continued to relentlessly harass the EIC, killing off its fledgling Japan and China trade. By 1623, losing money and almost broke, the EIC abandoned its Ayutthaya office and its peninsular trade altogether. Instead, the British concentrated on trading in a few stations in India well away from the VOC. Thus the

VOC had ingratiated itself with the Siamese king, disposed of most British and Portuguese competition in the East and by 1641, after capturing Malacca, the Dutch had become the predominant maritime power on the peninsular west coast.

Part 4

The 17th Century

EASY, BRUTISH AND SHORT

12

"Easy, Brutish and Short"

1600 TO 1700

Thomas Bowrey was an English merchant adventurer who traded around the Bay of Bengal between 1669 and 1688. He compiled the first English-Malay dictionary and was the first Englishman to describe the effects of marijuana after he and some mates drank Bangue, a marijuana beer and spent one stoned afternoon "sweatinge profusely" in a hot room. "Four lay on carpets highly complimentinge each other, each man fancyinge himselfe no less than an emperor … [another] terrified with fear, wepte bitterly."[282]

Thomas Bowrey, the First European to Live on and Describe Phuket

Bowrey stayed on Phuket several times during this period and was the first European to leave a fairly comprehensive description of Phuket. He tells us the island was almost completely covered with thick jungle, huge trees and giant bamboos: "a very mountainous and woody country, not one tenth part of it is made use of more than by the wild elephants and tigers … All the fruit this country affordeth is coconut, pantun, samcau and betele, save the wild calabashes that grow in the woods, an excellent food for the wild monkeys … some of them of a very large stature with great teeth."[283]

He noted that Thai inhabitants of Phuket generally spoke Malay "from their intercourse with that people"[284] and the Thais, or "natural Syamers", were friendlier than the Malays. He felt the Thais were "for the most part a very civil good humoured people"[285] who stayed inland in Thalang in the main interior villages of Ban Don and Ban Lippon. The villages were home to the Siamese families who often provided the island's rulers. The coast was inhabited by the Malays, who, he felt, were a more "resolute … roguish, sullen, ill natured people."[286]

Provisions on the island were "not very plenty," although the governor did provide Bowrey and his ship with "henns ducks coconuts plantains etc."; seafood abounded and the rice was excellent, but "scarcely enough to subsist with the whole yeare."[287] Food such as rice, salt, butter and oil from "Gingalee" (Bengal), were imported from Keddah. "The whole island affordeth nothinge save some elephants and tinne that are fit for transportation and tinne they have in abundance and were they industrious they might have tenne times as much."[288]

Bowrey mentions three ports on the island with "very excellent roads" (harbors), but the entrances to their rivers were very shallow "not afording more than seven foot."[289] He mentions one harbor as "Lippone". Ban Lippon at the time was the main town of

Phuket and seems always to have been in the interior of Thalang, so he probably meant Tharua, as this was the main port for Thalang and the villages of Ban Lippon, Ban Don and Ban Takkien. The second port was "Buckett", most likely what is now known as Tongkah Harbor or Phuket Bay – Phuket City's harbor today. The third harbor he called "Banquala", which he describes as being on the southwest coast and a safe, almost landlocked harbor. This can only be Patong and Banquala is probably how the road Soi Bangla got its name. Originally Soi Bangla would have been the path that led from Patong (Palm Forest) village, which sat inland on the klong (canal) near Wat Patong today, down to the sea at Banquala ("Bangla") Bay.

The Salateers and Piracy around Phuket

Bowrey notes that the coasts and islands round Phuket were the haunt of the "Salang", Sea Gypsy pirates referred to by 17th and 18th century Europeans as "Salateers" or "Straits people". He says they were a nomadic people, "great seamen" and "formidable" raiders. "The Salateers are absolute Pirates and are often cruiseinge about Jansalone and the Pulo Sambelon Isles near this shore. They are subject to no manner of government and have many cunninge places to hide themselves and their men of warre prows in upon the maine of the Malay shore."[290] Alexander Hamilton, a Scottish merchant captain who traded in the area in the 1720s, also tells us of these Salateer pirates round Phuket, "Between Mergui and Junkcelon, there are several good harbours for shipping, but the sea coast is very thin of inhabitants because there are a great numbers of freebooters called Saleteers who inhabit the islands along the sea coast. They both rob and take people for slaves and transport them to Aceh and there make sale of them and Junkcelon often feels the weight of their depredations."[291]

One Persian visitor to the region in the late 17th century noted that these Salateers usually avoided the better-armed European trading ships:

> "They have many ships and small boats which they … [have] stationed in certain places for the sake of robbery and capturing helpless travellers. As soon as they catch sight of a ship they pursue it and open fire once they are within range. They will struggle to capture a ship as long as their life's soul remains within them. They will attack any vessel except one which belongs to the Franks [Farangs, or Europeans] as these pirates have already burned themselves several times in the crackling fire of the Franks."[292]

The Malays and others living on Phuket itself, like most other people in the lawless region, also engaged in raiding, piracy or slave-taking whenever the right opportunity to do so presented itself. This was generally seen as just another means of obtaining an income; indeed, the Malays had no word for piracy at all until the Europeans appeared. It was seen more as just a commercial activity, as one early 18th century Chinese visitor to the region noted, "The common people treat life lightly, indulge in killing … From time to time they go out to sea and engage in piracy."[293] Hsieh Ching Kao, a Chinese merchant who also visited the region in the later 18th century wrote,

"From Songkla to Phang Nga the people are Malay. They are mostly fierce by nature and when going about they always carry a dagger."[294]

Lawlessness, Violence and Fear on Phuket

There are many Dutch reports of the unstable and lawless conditions on and around Phuket in the 17th century. In 1643, for example, Dutch VOC records mention a raid carried out by some "Johorese Salateers" who carried off 24 people from Phuket and "not a few" from neighboring Bangkhli village in Phang Nga, which was then the main port of west Phang Nga and a primary base for Chola and Indian Muslim merchants whose descendants can still be seen living there today; now, however, they are known as "Thai Muslims". [295]

In 1679 the VOC also recorded that King Narai warned them that he was preparing a force in Ligor to come to Phuket's aid after several attacks by Malay raiders who had carried off many of Phuket's pearl fishermen. Another VOC report in 1691 relates that the people of Phuket were readying themselves for a rumored attack by Panglima Kulup, a renowned local sea pirate.

The Acehnese from Sumatra were also feared predators in the region. Richard Rowe, the English sailor who discovered Christmas Island, noted in 1615 that Sultan Iskandar Muda of Aceh "has a fleet of three hundred sails of junks, galleys frigates and prows pretending to carry over the straits near a hundred thousand men."[296] The Portuguese less affably wrote that he had the "power of a prince to play the pirate."[297] In 1619 the Acehnese attacked and occupied Keddah, their big rival in pepper trading, and uprooted and destroyed Keddah's entire pepper crop. In 1617 Acehnese raiders carried off over 1,000 slaves in a raid on Pahang. They apparently also frequently raided round Phang Nga and Phuket for slaves or booty.

In the 1630s a spat also broke out between the Siamese king in Ayutthaya, Prasat Thong, and his normal ally on the other side of Burma, the king of Arakan (now a coastal state on the west side of Burma). The king of Arakan had refused to recognize the Siamese king, as he had usurped the throne, and in retaliation the new Thai king, Prasat Thong, ordered all Arakanese ships in Siam's ports to be seized. The rajah of Arakan then sent his war fleets to sack Siam's west-coast ports, such as Phuket, to cut off trade and make the river mouths and ports unsafe "to prevent the moors (Muslims) from the coast of Coromandel from coming to trade." This constant threat of raids, piracy or slavers effectively prevented any real development or economic progress in mining, agriculture or fisheries in Phuket, and any significant population growth during the whole 17th century. Francis Light, a British captain who lived in Phuket in the 18th century, said of the coast around Phuket: "The country, as far north as Mergui … is uninhabited, there are many good rivers and the coast abounds with tin ore … many attempts have been made to settle this by the Siamese, Malays and Tannoes from the great facility with which they can procure tin there … [but]… the few people who have gone there have been plundered and carried away."[298]

Map 6
Main Towns and Villages of Phuket Before 1850

Takua Tung ◉

◉ Bangkhli

● Kok Kloi

Pakpra
Channel

Ban Sahkoo ●　　● Ban Muang Mai

　　　　　　　　　● Bang Rong

　　　　◉ Ban Takien

　　　　　◉ Ban Lippon

Cherng Talay ●　◉ Ban Don

　　　　　　　● Yamoo

　　　　　● Ban　◉
　　　Manik　Tharua　Tharua Roads

Kamala ●

Banquala
(Patong) ●

　　　　● Buket

　　● Chalong

Kata ●

● Villages

◉ Main Towns

▨ Hills

Dacoitery and Monkeys

Inland things were no safer. The jungles abounded with dangerous and scary things: mosquitoes, fevers, tigers, snakes, rhinoceroses, elephants, crocodiles, ghosts and particularly predatory humans. Captain Light also noted that most of the country around Phuket "is covered only with impenetrable forest in which there are a great number of wild elephants."[299]

A visiting Chinese trader similarly wrote that inland in the peninsula,

> "The land is thinly populated, there are high mountains with thick forests and many old trees … The land has many epidemics … The people living in the mountains either farm or gather wood and they are very poor … they only wrap bark peeled from large trees around the lower part of their bodies. They have no houses but live in caves in the wilderness or in small plank huts in the trees. All the natives are expert at throwing spears. These spears can kill a man from a distance of several scores of paces. In going about the natives always have their spears with them and kill and rob people arbitrarily… In temperament the people are cruel and evil and their customs are strange … [If there was a dispute] … they are both willing to use spears and die without regret. Their king will permit the ordeal by spear, [and] orders the one he thinks is in the right to throw first. If he hits and kills the other then the dead man's family takes the corpse away. But if he fails to hit then the other side can throw back. Hence, these people seldom miss."[300]

One French missionary, who worked in the Catholic mission in Tharua on Phuket from 1671 to 1674, noted that he believed it impossible to go on foot more than half a league from Junk Ceylon without life and property being endangered by bandits and "consequently everyone travelled by convoy for protection." This dearth of people in the interior jungles of the peninsula is more colorfully related in the 18th century story told of a visiting Indian prince from the smaller maritime trading state of Golconda in southeast India who was sent as an ambassador to Siam. He landed at Mergui and "crossed the immense wilderness which lies between that place and Ayutthaya." In the capital "one of the Siamese ministers railed him about the small extent of his master's dominions in comparison to those of the Great king of Siam." The Golconda ambassador ruefully replied that though small, his master's dominions were at least "inhabited by human beings, whereas the territories of his Siamese majesty were for the most part peopled only by monkeys."[301]

Government and Trade

When Thomas Bowrey first arrived in the 1670s, he stated that Phuket "wholey belongeth to the kinge of Syam and he hath a governor here whom the natives entitle Radja, as indeed he is a vice kinge to the great kinge of Syam."[302] Ayutthayan authority over distant Phuket (and the whole peninsula) was weak and normally exercised by his main viceroy in Ligor. In 1605, when King Ekathotsarot (1605-1610) took the Siamese throne, he increased taxes on all trade and imposed royal monopolies on the most valuable peninsular export items. The succeeding kings, Songtham, Prasat Thong and Narai, who ruled for most of the 17th century, expanded these royal monopolies to cover most things of any value. So the kings became officially the only traders with the right to export or import in Siam. They developed their own royal trade fleets and appointed trade agents and port officers in the main ports to conduct the business of trading and to collect taxes on their behalf. Of course, in ports as remote as Phuket, there was much smuggling, illegal trade and of course corruption amongst the local officials. The king's trade department was under the overall control of the phra klang (head of the royal trade department) and in the local ports under a shabandar – a port and trade officer.

Most of the traders visiting the west-coast peninsular ports, such as Phuket, were from the great Muslim empires bordering the Indian Ocean – the Sassanid Persians, the Ottoman Turks, the Indian Moghuls, the Chulia Tamils and the Arabs. Siamese and Malay men traditionally never dealt in an activity as low-class as trade – which involved such demeaning things as market haggling; therefore it was mainly these foreigners, Indians, Persians and also Chinese, who were employed by the Siamese king to run his trade and treasury departments and whose friends and relatives were appointed as shabandars (port officers) in Siam's west-coast ports. This practice of using foreigners reached a high point under King Narai (1656-1688) in the second half of the 17th century. Persians and Indians ran his western trade department; Europeans both built and captained the ships of his western trade fleet (dealing with India and the West). The Chinese built and operated the junk fleet and trade of his eastern trade department (dealing with India, Japan and the East). One Persian visitor in the 1680s wrote, perhaps rather presumptuously, that he felt the real reason King Narai used so many foreigners in his government was that "The Siamese are devoid of intelligence and any practical abilities. They are unable to undertake a simple task with any hope for success. Thus the king is cautious and never confides to any great extent in the natives."[303]

A Short Period of Japanese Rule over the Central Peninsula and Phuket

In 1629 when King Songtham of Ayutthaya died, his cousin, Okya Kalahom (minister of defense), and his supporters effectively usurped the throne by killing King Songtham's designated heir and placing King Songtham's six-year-old son on the throne as King Chetha, with Okya Kalahom as his overseeing regent, which gave the ambitious defense minister real power over the kingdom. Okya Kalahom would have preferred to have also killed King Songtham's son and just taken the throne himself. But King Songtham had kept a private palace guard of some 600 Japanese mercenaries whose commander, a tough and loyal warrior called Yamada Nagamasa (his Siamese lordly title was Okya Senaphimuk), had given his oath to King Songtham that he would protect his son after his death.

The Japanese were feared all over the East as a fierce and martial people at the time. Many had migrated to Siam as traders, mercenaries and pirates and were known as a "people so desperate and daring that they are feared in all places." Most peninsular ports for example, had a policy that no Japanese could come ashore unless they first disarmed. So, with loyal Yamada and his Japanese praetorian guard in and around the palace, plus an estimated 3,000 other Japanese supporters living in Ayutthaya, Okya Kalahom's hands were somewhat tied by Yamada's "authority and the consideration in which the Japanese were held"[304] – but not for long.

The cunning Okya Kalahom soon demanded that all the provincial Siamese lords must now come to Ayutthaya to pay homage to the new boy king. He anticipated that the viceroy of Ligor, the king's first lord in the central peninsula, would refuse because he had been loyal to the old King Songtham and did not like the usurpation and "on account of the state of his province, which was threatened with war by the people of Patani and because the inhabitants were on the point of Taking up arms" (in rebellion). [305]

12.1. Yamada Nagamasa and his band of unruly Japanese mercenaries ruled over Southern Siam briefly in the early 1630s.

When the viceroy of Ligor did not come to pay homage, Okya Kalahom proposed to Yamada that as the boy-king's guardian, he should take his Japanese warriors south to arrest and kill the disobedient viceroy. If successful, he flatteringly proposed, Yamada, as a great man himself, could become the next viceroy of Ligor and the entire peninsula. Van Vliet, the Dutch VOC factor in Ayutthaya at the time, tells us that Okya Kalahom "represented [to Yamada] that the government of Ligor was the most important of the whole kingdom, partly by reason of its provinces which have several seaports … and partly by reason of the disobedience of the southern inhabitants who required a vigorous man to inspire their enemies with terror and its subjects with respect."[306]

Suitably flattered, Yamada left Ayutthaya with his Japanese mercenaries and another 1,500 or so of Ayutthaya's Japanese, who expected to benefit from the establishment of this new Japanese-run fiefdom in the central peninsula. Van Vliet also notes, "This greatly pleased everybody, everyone being glad to see the court cleared of this rabble" and that the subsequent arrival of Yamada in Ligor "inspired everyone with such great dread that he dispatched the whole rebellion at once."[307] Yamaha's Japanese troops soon defeated and captured the rebellious viceroy of Ligor and his naksat sub-lords in the central peninsula, probably including the rajah of Thalang, and had them "put to death and punished … and in a short space of time, he swept all the provinces … and established his authority."[308]

The properties of the Ligor viceroy were re-allocated to Yamada and his Japanese officers and he may well have replaced the rajah of Thalang with a Japanese overlord and henchmen, although this cannot be confirmed from other sources. Van Vliet tells us that Yamada "began to take all measures, to distribute considerable presents to his favourites, to make okyas and operas (provincial sub-lords) and to appoint mandarins."[309] To celebrate his success, Okya Kalahom in Ayutthaya sent more flattering letters and many presents to Yamada including high-born concubines, one of whom was a beautiful Siamese virgin of royal blood. He ordered Yamada to continue on with his great successes and to subdue the rebellious kingdom of Patani, and thereby enlarge further his great new fiefdom. The malleable Yamada took his forces further south to attack Patani.

The artful Okya Kalahom used this occasion to complete his coup in Ayutthaya. The young boy-king was arrested, put in a velvet bag and clubbed to death with sandalwood clubs. This was the traditional, and most polite, method for dispatching a member of royalty in Siam. Okya Kalahom then took the throne as King Prasat Thong (1630-1655) and embarked on a reign of great terror and cruelty. He started by having some 3,000 lords who had opposed him, and their families, attacked, arrested and killed off with the greatest barbarity. Their heads and severed limbs were displayed around the towns and country for all to see. Their slaves and properties were redistributed to the new king's henchmen and supporters and Van Vliet tells us that "The great cruelty shown in these executions closed the mouths of all the others."[310]

Meanwhile, in the peninsula, Yamada's forces subdued Patani, but Yamada was badly wounded in the leg. He returned to Ligor as the new master of the central peninsula and decided to crown his glory with a combined ceremony of his coronation as viceroy of the south and his wedding to the beautiful royal Siamese virgin King Prasat Thong had sent him. However, Yamada's doctor in Ligor was either a supporter of the previous viceroy, or in the pay of King Prasat Thong. Whilst tending to Yamada's wounded leg, Van Vliet tells us that, "Just when [Yamada] believed he was going to enjoy the fruit of his love ... at the height of the rejoicings of his wedding ... Apra Marit [the doctor] applied a poisoned plaster to his leg which caused him to die in a few hours."[311]

With Yamada's death, some of the Japanese troops wanted Yamada's son to take over, but another faction wanted his main general. This schism resulted in internecine fighting between these two Japanese factions who "did not cease to contend continually for the government, the result was that the Japanese were diminished everyday in these continual encounters."[312] With the Japanese now far away, leaderless and infighting, the new King Prasat Thong made his final move to clear out the remaining Japanese from Ayutthaya. In 1632 his troops "set fire to the Japanese quarter in the night ... he had cannon fired into their houses with such fury that they were compelled to throw themselves into their junks ... [to escape down the river] ... fighting all the time as they retreated ... Japanese who dwelt in other quarters of the town were then diligently searched for and were put cruelly to death."[313]

In Ligor, King Prasat Thong's agents encouraged the locals to rebel against their new Japanese overlords and a large Ayutthayan army was dispatched to assist them. "Seeing how little advantage they were getting from their stay,"[314] the Japanese in Ligor left on boats for Cambodia. Soon after this episode the Japanese shogun Tokugawa expelled all the Christians in Japan, closed Japan's doors to the outside world and decreed that Japanese were no longer allowed go overseas, on pain of death. Japanese soldiers would not be seen again in Phuket and the central peninsula for another 300 years.

The South in Rebellion

In the central peninsula, Van Vliet tells us that the local people and their chiefs, "finding themselves delivered from the Japanese, also wished to shake off the yoke of Siamese domination … accordingly they took up arms and refused to recognise the new usurper king (Prasat Thong) as their sovereign lord, their purpose being, to separate themselves from the crown and to make an independent state."[315] In response to this rebellion, King Prasat Thong dispatched to the south an army of some 10,000 men with many elephants and cavalry who defeated the rebels and captured Ligor and the southern rebel provinces. The rebellious southern lords were reportedly sent in irons to Ayutthaya where "without any trial, sheets of red hot iron were applied to their feet, they were bound with heavy chains and buried in the ground up to their shoulders."[316]

King Prasat Thong's newly appointed viceroy of Ligor then put his own men in charge of the southern naksat fiefdoms to try to "bring them back into the fold of obeisance," but for much of the rest of the 17th century the peninsula remained a rebellious, lawless and violent place. In 1634, the Dutch factor in Ligor complained that, "The wars between these kingdoms and Ayutthaya [have] destroyed the pepper growing areas,"[317] and these constant wars of rebellion eventually forced the VOC to close its Ligor office for several years in the late 1630s and 1640s.

12.2 A Siamese painting showing a battle scene in the late 16th century

Patani remained in rebellion against Ayutthayan rule. In 1638 King Prasat Thong sent a big army which besieged the fortified city of Patani for over a month and was also supported by some Dutch warships. But this Siamese force made little headway so eventually the sultan of Keddah brokered a peace. Javanese Muslims governed the cities of Songkla and Phattalung in the southeast at the time. They also rebelled and held off a succession of Siamese armies sent against them. It was not until 1674, a full 30 years later, in the era of the next king, that Songkla and Phattalung were finally defeated and that area brought back under Ayutthayan domination.

Then in 1645, King Prasat Thong's own appointed viceroy in Ligor and his naksat sublords also rebelled. King Prasat Thong had to dispatch yet another huge army of 60,000 men and elephants to the south, which again defeated the Ligor rebels. The rajah and people of Phuket were most probably part of this rebellion. Dutch VOC documents filed in Batavia in October 1645 inform us that shortly after this southern rebellion the "Rajah of Ujong Salang [Phuket] was arrested and brought to Ligor"[318] – where he no doubt met some very ghastly fate. We are also informed that King Prasat Thong's newly appointed viceroy in Ligor then abused and "vexed the subjects of Trangh [Trang], Bangarei [Bangkhli], Salangh [Phuket] so harshly that many departed elsewhere."[319]

Forty years later, in 1686, Ligor and its naksat states rebelled again and yet another huge Siamese army had to be sent south to defeat the southern mutineers.

Diseases Sweep Phuket

In addition to the frequent rebellions and wars, plus the piracy and lawlessness in Phuket and the region, 17th century French records from India also note a series of natural disasters and deadly epidemics on Phuket Island. In 1681, they reported that a smallpox epidemic broke out in Phuket which "carried off many of the inhabitants and the trading ... formerly carried [on], had to be abandoned by many."[320] In 1685 they recorded that "the pepper vines in the region were ruined because of severe flooding."[321] In 1696, they reported another smallpox plague that spread over Phuket, killing many.

In his book Leviathan, Thomas Hobbes described life in the European Dark Ages as "nasty, brutish and short". Seventeenth century Phuket still had its languid sun-kissed days, balmy nights and ample food and fruit, but it was so bedeviled by wars, lawlessness, piracy and disease that life on the island at that time might be characterized as "easy, brutish and short".

13

"Yea We Are Deadly Hated by All"

1640 TO 1700

By the mid-17th century, although the Dutch VOC had battled to become the strongest naval force in the region the lion's share of trade in the peninsular west-coast ports such as Phuket still remained in the hands of Muslim traders. These were mainly Indians from the Moghul Empire, including Bengal, Tamil Nadu, Golkonda and Gujerat and Arabs and Persians, all of whom were simply called "Moors" by the Europeans in the region. With a lower cost structure and longer and better local trade connections, the Indian Muslim traders could offer goods more cheaply and pay more for local produce. In 1674 the VOC governor in Malacca, Balthazar Bort, noted, "The English, Portuguese, French and Danes previously frequented Keddah, whereas since the moors are there they mostly stay away, knowing that as regards the trade in cloth in competition with them, they have no chance."[322]

The 17th century Siamese kings Songtham (1620-28), Prasat Thong (1630-55) and Narai (1656-88) had, as we have seen, appointed many such trusted Muslim traders as their governors and shabandars in their important west-coast ports, including Phuket. Around 1610 a Persian Muslim, Sheikh Ahmad Qomi, had been appointed phra klang (minister of treasury and trade). This Sheik Ahmad and his relatives and associates had run the western trade part of this department for many years and gave preferential treatment to kin and other Muslim traders. Sheikh Ahmad's family eventually became the lordly Siamese Bunnag family, which still today remains one of the most politically and economically powerful families in the kingdom, numbering over 40,000 family members.

The Dutch had improved their standing in Siam after 1630 by promptly recognizing and allying with the usurper King Prasat Thong. Prince Henry of the Netherlands had sent him a fancy letter of congratulation and the VOC agreed to pay him a royalty of 5,000 florins annually for the right to trade in Siam. In return the VOC became his main supplier of arms and instructors and in some cases, such as in Patani in 1638, it even deployed ships to fight with him. King Prasat Thong gave the VOC a buying monopoly on several peninsular items such as deer hides and pepper. During King Prasat Thong's reign VOC trade flourished and between 1633 and 1663 some 276 VOC ships are recorded as visiting Siam – an average of nine trade ships a year. [323]

The Dutch Claim Phuket Island and Attempt to Control its Trade

The Dutch had originally come to the peninsula to buy pepper. But as the market in Europe for porcelain, tea and silk began to boom they concentrated more on their trade with China and Japan. The problem was that Holland, in fact Europe, had few products that China needed. But China did always want tin, which was widely used in religious ceremonies and for making bronze (rust-proof) cannons. So the VOC started to focus on obtaining tin in the Malay Peninsula for its China trade. For this it began to turn to the tin mines of southwestern Siam around Phuket. The official VOC "Dagregistrar" (records book) records that the first Dutch tin-buying expedition to Phuket had been in 1639 under Captain Orlando Thibault. However two years later, after conquering Malacca in 1641, the Dutch moved more aggressively to expand their tin-buying activities up the surrounding peninsular west coast.

13.1. Dutch Malacca in the 17th century: The Dutch claimed that Malacca's traditional "dominion" over Phuket had devolved on them "by right of conquest".

King Prasat Thong must have felt that having the powerful Dutch as semi-allies to cover the cantankerous and rebellious Malay lords in the peninsula was an attractive alternative to sending and having to pay for his own less formidable warships. He therefore gave the Dutch permission to open fortified factories in several peninsular ports and the right to make exclusive trade contracts with the local lords there. In 1642 the Dutch established a factory in Keddah. In 1643, trade contracts were signed and factories built in both Phuket and Songkla and two years later at Bangkhli (a town in Phang Nga province just north of the bridge between Kokloi and Thai Muang today), which was then the main tin port of western Phang Nga province.

In 1644 the VOC then built a fortified trade factory in Phuket, probably just east of the big Chinese temple opposite the wat by Thepkasatri road in Tharua today. It was most likely constructed of a mortar of lime and stone, plastered, then whitewashed, with a nipa palm thatched roof and surrounded by a defensive earth rampart and wooden palisade about two meters high. Here the VOC agents lived (for security) and stored all the trade goods they were buying or selling.

VOC correspondence during the 17th century shows that the Dutch considered that the traditional Malaccan, not Ayutthayan, jurisdiction over Phuket Island and the west-coast tin centers still applied. For example, Governor Balthasar Bort, the VOC head in Malacca, wrote that Malacca's "dominion and jurisdiction in this strait have always extended to the said island [Phuket] … tolls and licenses … instituted by the Portuguese for the maintenance of the rights of Malacca have now devolved on us by right of conquest."[324] The Siamese court in Ayutthaya of course did not interpret this situation in the same way.

The VOC adopted the former Portuguese monopolistic licensing system from Malacca. The company started trying to force all non-Dutch ships trading in Phuket and other surrounding ports to get a license from it. In this way, the VOC believed local trade could be diverted through Malacca, which apart from allowing it to secure more tin at cheaper prices, was also a means to get rid of the pesky and more efficient Muslim traders. As Commissioner Schouten in Malacca clearly stated, "It would be a good thing if the company's territory could be cleared of Moors [Muslim Indians] and Gentyos [Hindu Indians] because not only would more tin be secured but also large quantities of cloth could be marketed."[325]

This VOC licensing blockade of the southwestern Siamese ports was enforced by armed Dutch blockade ships policing the region and forcing any unlicensed ships to go to Malacca to apply for expensive licenses. These were meant to oblige everyone to come to trade in Malacca at controlled prices favorable to the Dutch. The Dutch blockade captains were instructed that all non-VOC vessels must be "politely and not rashly examined" and merchandise from unlicensed ships should be confiscated and "half the tin taken out and the owners paid 40 reals a bahar for it [below market price]."[326] The English however described the activity of these Dutch blockade ships in less rosy terms. The English private trader William Dampier, for example, summarized this policy as: "Where there is any trade to be had, yet not sufficient to maintain a factory, so as to secure the whole trade for themselves, [the Dutch] send their guard ships which lying at the mouths of rivers deter strangers from coming thither and keep the petty princes in awe of them. They commonly make a show as if they did this out of kindness to the people, yet most of them know otherwise."[327]

Captain Francis Light, an Englishman who lived and traded on Phuket in the 18th century wrote of the Dutch blockade ships, "These vessels ill paid and commanded by the lowest people became pirates and smugglers as it suited their conveniency, Their custom is to order the Naqueda (Muslim trade captain) on board to examine his pass which they frequently take from him and plunder his vessel, and they sometimes meet with resistance, their barbarity proceeds so far as to destroy the whole crew."[328]

Local leaders soon realized that the VOC was insisting on paying unrealistically low prices for the tin by backing up its trading dictates with force. The local and Moorish traders attempted successfully to dodge their tall blockade ships. One VOC report at the time grumbled that, despite their trade agreements with the local rajahs, the Moors "still crept past the Dutch cruisers." In response, the VOC increased the number of patrols and the harshness of its searches and confiscations, taking a further step down the slippery slope towards conflict.

Local Resistance to the Dutch Naval Blockade

Resistance to the Dutch blockade and monopoly soon started in these contumacious west-coast ports. In 1645, a VOC report tells us that in "Bangarai" (Bangkhli in Phang Nga) Obbe Heeres, a blockade captain, tortured and killed three Malays, suspecting they had attempted to poison him and his men. Then in 1651 all 27 Dutchmen manning the VOC factory in Perak (in Malaysia) were attacked and killed and the Dutch factory there burnt. In Keddah, in spite of their pre-agreed monopolistic trade contract with the sultan there the VOC grumbled that he now ignored it and sent "great quantities of tin to Coromandel and Java" and also allowed Muslim merchants to carry cloth overland "to Patani, Ligor and Pahang." In 1652 Johan Truijtman, the VOC envoy in Keddah, was killed, souring relations further. Then in 1658 the Keddahnese attacked the VOC factory there and slaughtered all the Dutch. They then boarded the Dutch blockade ship the Hourn, which sat off Keddah, and killed nine of its crew. The

12.2 A "Moor": This generic name was given by the European traders to all the Indian, Persian and Arab Muslim traders who carried on the lions share of trade in Siam's western peninsular ports in the 17th century. This man is more specifically a Tamil "Chola", from Southwest India who were frequently the dominant traders and financiers in Phuket and the Phang Nga ports.

Dutch tried to seek recompense from the sultan of Keddah or the Siamese king but received little other than some gifts and abstruse responses.

Tin production in Phuket in the period ranged between about 500 and 1,500 bahars per year. (A bahar was about 180 kilograms – so about 90-270 metric tons.) In 1644, in the VOC's first year of trade, the VOC factor in the trade station in Phuket informed Batavia that he had received far less tin than expected and that part of his consignment of textiles, worth over 726 guilders, had been eaten by ants and had to be burnt – or did he just privately sell it? In any case, the cloth did not sell well, as the inhabitants of Phuket were generally so exploited by their overlords that few had anything to trade in return. Thomas Bowrey, the English trader based in Phuket a few decades later, estimated that 20 bales of Indian chintz and calicoes would cover Phuket's demand for six months.

Soon after the establishment of the VOC factory in Tharua on Phuket, trouble started. One Dutch employee was stabbed to death in the town in a fight with a "Tamabangh" (which probably means a Chola Indian trader). The governor of Malacca wrote to Okya Phet, the Phuket governor, demanding that the guilty man be put to death. Okya Phet replied that this was "not in his power", meaning either that the accused was not a subject of his, or that he was simply obfuscating. Okya Phet however, did send some tin, ambergris and a rhinoceros horn to the VOC governor as a gift. The VOC sent him back a musket and a Japanese writing desk. Yet despite this attempt at kiss-and-make-up, problems remained. Due to the cheaper purchase prices demanded by the VOC, most Phuketians sold their tin elsewhere. In 1652 the VOC factory in Tharua was able to buy less than 100 bahars of tin. In 1654 the VOC annual records sum up the Phuket factory's business as being of "little significance"[329] with only 125 bahars of tin bought that year. This was not even enough to cover the cost of the factory, never mind the blockade ships.

Corruption and Drunkenness

The other problem for the VOC was rampant corruption and private trading by its own agents in their remote outposts. In 1656, for example, the head VOC factor in Phuket, Jan Van Groeningen, was recalled due to his alleged extensive private trading and his poor receipts of tin of less than 200 bahars. When a new Dutch factor replaced him in Tharua the next year, he was able to buy 1,000 bahars of tin which was picked up by the ship Cleen Batavia. [330] Then later that year he purchased an additional 451 bahars. This was a 700 percent increase on the previous year under Van Groeningen, probably showing the extent of his private trading for his own account, or his drunkenness, which was also a common problem in these remote trade outposts. In 1672, for example, the VOC governor of Malacca wrote to the head of the VOC in Ayutthaya, stating that "drunkenness, carelessness and private trading" by VOC agents in the peninsular ports were "not seldom" the cause of the company's poor trade there.

These young Dutchmen in the VOC in their isolated stations in Asia, just like their British EIC counterparts, often turned to drink and debauchery. William Hickey, the 18th century British libertine rake, was amazed by one EIC officers' dinner he attended, calling it "the most sustained debauch I had ever seen in my life."[331] Alcohol, like tobacco at the time, was believed to be good for the health and to kill the germs that caused "jungle fevers". This theory backfired however, as the historian C. M. Boxer notes, "Most Dutch or English males who died in the tropics died of drinking, even making allowances for the heavy toll taken by malaria and dysentery."[332] For example, in 1716 the Madras directors rebuked the EIC's sleepy trade factory in Bencoolen, Sumatra over the size of its drinks bill. In the month of July 1716 alone, the handful of British employees there had drunk: 888 bottles of wine, 288 bottles of beer, 42 gallons of Madeira wine, 6 flasks of shiraz, 274 bottles of toddy (fermented palm sap), 3 barrels of arrack and 164 gallons of Goa toddy. [333] This would probably hospitalize even the most hard-drinking modern expat today. It is also noticeable that they drank the largest amounts of the nastiest liquors, no doubt immobilizing them with some ghastly hangovers the following hot, sweaty and un-air conditioned day.

King Narai's Conflict with the Dutch

In 1655 when King Prasat Thong died, the VOC lost its biggest ally in Siam. King Narai, another usurper, then took the throne. By this time the VOC was increasingly frustrated in its dealings in Siam and felt it was constantly being cheated and gouged on its agreements and trades and had received little compensation. The VOC was becoming more forceful in its demands and several on the VOC board of directors were pushing for war and a full colonization of Siam, or at least of some of its peninsular sub-states such as tin-rich Phuket Island and Keddah. The VOC had recently attacked and taken Java and several kingdoms in Sumatra opposite Phuket and the new King Narai probably now feared the same for Siam. To mitigate the situation he agreed to allow the powerful Dutch to continue their advantageous trade deals in Siam but soon set about seeking another strong European ally to offset and counteract the now overbearing Dutch.

When he heard that the English had sort of defeated the Dutch in the first of their several naval wars in Europe, King Narai wrote to the British EIC head office in India in 1660 and invited the company to return to Siam and reopen its offices. As an inducement and an attempt to kill two birds with one stone, he offered to cede to the EIC the kingdom of Patani which was, as usual, in a state of rebellion. The EIC was unwilling to take on the expense of trying to control cantankerous Patani and declined this offer, but it did agree to reopen the small office in Ayutthaya. The

13.2 A contemporary etching of Dutch marines going ashore to attack a Malay village in the 17th century.

EIC also opened a factory in Keddah, but this proved completely unsuccessful and was soon closed.

The generally self-serving Muslims that King Narai employed as his royal trade agents, also wanted the Dutch out so they could impose the king's own monopolistic rights over the tin in the peninsula and thereby make more profit themselves. To do this they increasingly conspired against the Dutch – as Coolhas, the VOC factor in Ligor, complained, "The mandarins try to misuse their power towards the foreigners [and quite often get the best of it] and make us feel their greed."[334] Another VOC report complained that, despite the official contracts made with the king and the local lords, there was continual "cheating" going on and "the Okya Berckelang [the trade minister] has been named as the foremost cheat."[335]

By 1664, with the VOC owed a great deal of money by Siam and losing patience, it sent a squadron of four warships to blockade the Chao Phraya River entrance. With these ships, along with their blockade ships already in place in Siam's western ports of Mergui, Phuket and Keddah, the VOC effectively closed off most of the Siamese king's profitable external trade. The Siamese war fleet was incapable of taking on the powerful VOC warships brimming with cannon and King Narai was forced to sign an even more unequal trade treaty giving the VOC monopoly rights over buying several peninsular items such as deer hides in Ligor and tin in Phuket. This treaty was a real humiliation for King Narai. However, as one Thai historian notes, "At first the treaty worked to Dutch satisfaction, but soon the wily king, by controlling prices, managed to rob the Dutch of all their newly won advantages."[336]

Blockade Running and Dutch Troubles in Phuket

During the 1660s the VOC-Siam relationship soured further as the price of tin rose, but the VOC still insisted on paying 30-35 reals per bahar. De Rooj, the Dutch factor in Ayutthaya, reported that Bengali and Coromandel Indians were willing to pay 54 reals per bahar and wrote that the VOC tin monopoly on Phuket, which he called that "distant and desolate land,"[337] would never work as long as the Dutch paid so little for their tin. This proved to be true. The more harshly the VOC gunboats tried to enforce their monopoly over Phuket's tin trade, the more resentful the locals became. Apart from the lower price they paid for tin, the exclusion of Malay and Indian merchants also meant Phuket was not receiving the normal daily provisions they required, such as salt, sugar and rice, which the "Moors" traditionally carried to the island from Keddah, Aceh or Bengal.

Things came to a head in 1656 when an armed mob attacked the VOC factory in Tharua and killed several of the Dutch employees based there. The VOC factor was severely wounded but managed to escape on a boat with some others down the Tharua stream to the Dutch patrol ship Dolphin which was sitting in Tharua harbor (near the Boat Lagoon entrance channel today). That night the Phuketians took to their canoes, snuck up on, boarded and attacked the Dolphin, killing several crew. A later VOC report on the event states that "some foreigners [Malays or Indians] … among whom were three Makasarese hadjis" (Indonesian Muslims on pilgrimage to Mecca) pillaged and burnt down the VOC factory as well as killing several employees and the total losses from "items robbed and burnt amounted to 22,327 guilders."[338]

The VOC suspected the Phuket governor, Okya Phet, was behind the attack as he allowed the ringleaders to flee unharmed to Keddah; the VOC complained to King Narai who eventually agreed to send investigators to Phuket. Four years later, in 1660, one VOC report notes, "The commissaries sent to make enquiries into the murder of the Dutchmen committed in Oudiang Salangh [Junk Ceylon – Phuket] returned to Siam in June last, after an absence of nearly a year, bringing with them Opra Peth, Governor of Salang and also three Malays who were held to be guilty."[339] Okya Phet was found not guilty, but Van Rijk, the VOC factor in Ayutthaya, noted that he had simply bribed himself out of trouble. "The uparat [governor] of Oedjangh Salang having been summoned to Ligor to redeem the murder committed on our people … managed to maintain his credibility and esteem [probably by gifts and presents] and thus our complaints about him appear to be considered as of little."[340] The remaining three Malays, who had less money to pay bribes, were said by the Siamese to be guilty and were handed over to the VOC, who took them back to Batavia to receive punishment. We do not know their fate, but it was surely most unpleasant. Okra Phet however was allowed to return to Phuket as governor.

After the 1656 attack the VOC never reopened its factory in Phuket. Anyway, in most of the 13 years of its existence it had only lost money and it was now felt to be too risky for Dutchmen to stay ashore on Phuket. The VOC, however, still believed that Malacca held time-honored "dominion and jurisdiction" over the island and so VOC trade ships continued to call into Phuket to try to buy tin and VOC blockade ships continued to patrol round Phuket. The Englishman Thomas Bowrey, who was in Phuket at this time, wrote that the Dutch "did continually keep a ship of 16 or 20 guns and two or three sloops to cruise about this island."[341] This was done, he claims, to "deprive [the locals] of the extensive importation of Moorish cloth, to have the people buy from their company." But blockade running remained rife and the disheartened VOC governor in Malacca lamented that Junk Ceylon was simply too close to India and too favored by the monsoon winds for a few ships to prevent a flourishing trade in tin and elephants with the Muslims and even other European merchants.

In response to this increased blockade running, the Dutch stepped up the severity of their blockade and banned all Indian Muslim trade ships from Phuket. But still they kept slipping past the Dutch blockade ships. In 1663 the frustrated crew of the VOC patrol ship the Exeter saw one Moorish blockade-running prow sneaking away from Phuket. They caught up with and boarded the prow and then massacred everyone aboard. The Dutch sailors also reportedly raped the Muslim women on board then threw them overboard with sacks of rice tied around their necks. One terrified young girl leapt off the Muslim prow and swam to the Dutch ship and climbed aboard, pleading for her life. A Dutch sailor reportedly seized her by the ankles and dashed her head against the ship's side splitting her skull and killing her. This atrocity caused uproar amongst the Phuket locals and the VOC in Malacca. The four Dutch leaders of the massacre were arrested when the Exeter returned to Malacca. Their right hands were chopped off, then they were crucified on cartwheels where their arms and legs were broken. Later they were beheaded. Five more members of the Exeter crew were also hanged. [342]

In Phuket, the locals, who presumably did not know about the harsh justice handed down in Malacca, felt even more aggrieved. In 1672, the two Dutch patrol boats in Phuket were attacked while at anchor off Phuket and all but two of the Dutch aboard were brutally killed. Governor Bort again accused the Phuket governor, Okya Phet, of being behind the attacks. Again Ayutthaya sent commissioners to the island, but again little justice was seen to be done. In response, in early 1673 there is a VOC report that Stephan Claarbout, a Dutch blockade ship captain, went ashore at the port of Bangkhli in Phang Nga (just north of Phuket) to punish a local Malay called "Intgie Lilla" for a crime committed against the Dutch that had gone unpunished by Siam; this was probably the attack on the two Dutch boats the year before. Captain Claarbout imposed the punishment himself as he reported that neither the Phuket nor Bangkhli governors would do so. He set fire to the village houses and took all their tin. There was a tense stand-off between the Bangkhli governor, his armed retainers and the locals and the Dutch marines. Claarbout accused the local Muslim governor of "seeming to love [the Dutch] with his tongue but the Keddahnese with his heart."[343]

The 1675 Battle of Patong

The Englishman Thomas Bowrey was on Phuket as the island's trouble with the Dutch escalated. He tells us that the main base for the Dutch patrol ships was "Banquala" Bay (Patong), where they were based to intercept boats coming east from India. Bowrey relates that in 1675 "a great prowe of about 40 tunns,"[344] from Aceh, funded by an Englishman, Willian Jersey, "an eminent Merchant at Fort St George [Madras] … had got in [to Banquala (Patong)] privately and traded for tinne."[345] To hide itself the blockade-running prow had entered the creek that today empties into the south of Patong Bay. (This creek was bigger and much less silted up than it is today.) She was pulled up the creek towards old Patong village where she was concealed and unloaded. The next morning a Dutch gunboat appeared in Patong Bay and dispatched some Dutch marines ashore to seize the Aceh prow in the creek. Bowrey then tells us:

> "The merchants and inhabitants of Banquala did (in a very civil way) desire the Dutch not to molest them any, especially to make prise of them, soe longe as they were under the Radja of Jansalone's protection and in theire river. But the Dutch, swelled up with ambition, told them plainely that all Roads and Rivers of Jansalone were theirs and therefore the prowe and her goods were theire lawful prize. Whereupon the Malay inhabitants, a very resolute people stood up for the achiners and took the prow and her goods by violence out of the hands of the Dutch."[346]

During this fight a Dutch marine fired a blunderbuss into the locals, killing two and dispersing the rest of the crowd. The Dutch gunship itself then also entered Patong creek and came up to "where the river was very narrow,"[347] presumably to take on the prow's confiscated cargo.

Bowrey tells us that some while later an armed mob of around 200 locals soon reappeared near the captured Aceh prow. He also tells us that further down the creek other locals

> "cut downe 20 or 30 great trees, that fell athwart it and blocked it up so that not any passage back was left for sloop or boat. The Dutch finding … the country too hot for them, betooke themselves to their sloop to be gone out into the roade [Patong Bay] but … when they came downe to this stoppage they could neither

go down nor come up againe. Then they had nothing to trust to but their fire-arms which could not helpe them very longe, for the Malayars overpowered them and cut off every man and pulled their sloop in pieces."[348]

With the British again in Siam and with the powerful French also courting him to gain acccss to Siam and Phuket's tin, King Narai now felt sufficiently confident to resist the consequent VOC demands for compensation for the Patong incident. In 1677, two years later, a frustrated Governor Bort of the VOC in Malacca complained,

"up to the present, not the smallest vengeance has been taken nor punishment inflicted for this murder and damage, nor has any satisfaction been given, where-fore the governors in that state have been encouraged and have become more insolent and petulant and have treated our people with so much less esteem and regard. They have even taken the whole of the trade from us and handed it over to other foreigners coming from abroad."[349]

To make matters worse, that year (1677) the Phuketians attacked and pillaged yet another Dutch blockade ship. After this assault and still no recompense, the VOC directors seriously discussed invading and colonizing Phuket. When King Narai was informed of this planned Dutch invasion he immediately sent orders to Phuket that each of the island's three seaports should build two large war prows big enough to carry ten guns. Bowrey informs us that King Narai's instructions were that these war prows "should keep two and two to-gether and if they should meet a single Dutch ship they should fight her and give her no quarter. If they met with a fleet they should runne in and give intelligence for the countrey to be up in arms and not suffer any sloops to come up their rivers or land, neither should they observe any

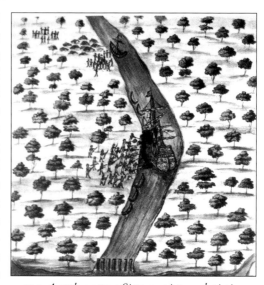

13.3. A 17th century Siamese picture depicting stakes and trees being used to block a European ship in a river before attacking it – a technique the locals of Patong Bay used successfully against a Dutch patrol ship in 1675.

flagge of truce or have the least converse with them."[350] Moreover, if any Phuket officials failed to comply immediately, the king would have them executed. The Phuket governor immediately sent out his officers to "presse all the carpenters and set them to work." El-ephants were employed to "carry down the guns, firearms, shot and powder, thereby to have all things in readiness"[351] and the armed war prows were ready in just over a month.

Ultimately, however, the VOC directors decided they had had enough. They did not want a war with Siam nor the cost of building forts and defending Phuket, which they anyway felt was just "a poor and under populated area with an unhealthy climate."[352]

Even maintaining the blockade of Phuket, for a trade so meager and troublesome, made little financial sense. The VOC at the time already employed over 3,500 sailors and 18,000 slaves on its patrol ships in the East at great expense. Plus the tin price had recently fallen in China and the VOC was only making a 21 percent mark-up on the tin it bought in Phuket whilst items from other peninsular ports made much more, for example deer hides from Ligor sold in China at 189 percent profit and Sappanwood made over 300 percent. [353]

The VOC did continue to try to get King Narai to honor its tin-buying monopoly contract in Phuket that he had signed, but King Narai evaded the issue by telling the Dutch that the lawlessness on the island made it too dangerous a place for them. In 1679, for instance, he wrote to Batavia to inform them that some Keddah Malays and pirates had attacked and taken Phuket and he was sending a force from Ligor and Tenasserim to chase out the intruders. In the meantime however, the wily king was busy getting into bed with his new "best friends" – the French – to whom he also gave tin-buying rights on Phuket. Then in 1682 he appointed a Frenchman as governor of Phuket and the frustrated VOC factor in Ayutthaya soon wrote back to Batavia lamenting that a Moor had told him that Phuket was now selling over 1,000 bahars of tin per year to the French, which was being taken "principally to Tenasserim, Aceh, Bengal and Pondicherry."

Bowrey tells us that the stubborn, violent resistance by the Phuketians had eventually "so squashed the Dutch designs over this place that they went away with theire ships and other sloops and never molested Jansalone any more."[354] Bowrey, an Englishman was clearly no great fan of the Dutch and felt that "by their too much presumption and encroachinge (as their usual way is in every place they do get footing in) they utterly lost it."[355] Today there is almost no trace at all on Phuket of the half century that the Dutch claimed dominion over the island. The only evidence seems to be the two VOC iron cannons dating from 1620 on display in Phuket City Hall. These cannon may have been sold to Siam, stolen from the VOC factory at Tharua or maybe taken from one of the captured VOC patrol ships. Further research needs to be done on these two cannons.

Diminishing Dutch Dominion

By the 18th century the Malays and Muslims in the region began to establish their own new clandestine trade centers away from the VOC's prowling gunboats. One English sea captain who traded at these covert Muslim trade meets explained that the Malay traders were so harassed by the Dutch patrol ships that they "had no certain places to frequent, but wandered from place to place in search of purchasers and meeting in un-inhabited places like thieves, gathered together to divide their spoil. The Malay chiefs, equally disposed to trade or plunder, performed either, as circumstances permitted."[356] All over the East Indies the local Malays grew to despise the overbearing Dutch and their brutal attempts to monopolize all trade. The Malay pilot on one later British naval ship off Keddah told his British captain, "The Hollanders have been the bane of the Malay race, no one knows the amount of villainy, the bloody cruelty of their system towards us. They drive us into our prahus to escape their taxes and their laws and then declare us pirates and put us to death. There are natives in our crew … ask them why they hate the Dutchmen [and] why they would readily kill a Dutchman?"[357] Onshore on the peninsula the Dutch were never safe and there are numerous accounts of lone or drunken Dutchmen being secretly dispatched by the poisoned krisses of Malays.

13.4. The Dutch VOC cannons outside Phuket City hall dating to around 1660 are one of the only remnants left from the violent Dutch era in Phuket.

The end of the 17th century was the zenith of Dutch power and trade in the region. In Europe the French and British navies grew bigger than the Dutch and pressured them in the Atlantic and the rest of the world. In the peninsula a growing disdain for Dutch power arose amongst the locals, particularly after the arrival and settlement on the peninsular west coast of the Bugis in the early 18th century. The Bugis were fierce Malay pirates and traders from Sulawesi in Indonesia who began to build larger prahus, acquire cannons and muskets and started directly engaging and sometimes defeating and capturing these VOC blockade and trade ships. By 1756 the Bugis became confident enough to launch a full-scale attack against the Dutch city of Malacca itself.

The other European nations in the region no doubt watched the gradual demise in Dutch naval supremacy with considerable gratification. The head of the French trade station in Pondicherry for example gloatingly referred to Dutch Malacca as "a place of little trade … a ghost of its former self which could not even control the second rate local powers of the straits."[358] Rijklof Van Goens, later to become the governor general of the Dutch East Indies, was probably quite realistic when he wrote in 1680 that "There is nobody who wishes us well in all the Indes, yea, we are deadly hated by all nations."[359]

14

The Massacre of the Cholas

1676 TO 1679

In 1676 when he was warned that the VOC was planning to invade Phuket to make it a colony, King Narai had ordered the removal of Okya Phet, the anti-Dutch governor as a sop to the vexed VOC. Okya Phet petitioned heavily in Ligor and Ayutthaya to try to retain his lucrative governorship. Thomas Bowrey tells us he gave away 100 catties (six kilograms) of silver and other gifts to "various Grandees"[360] to save his position. But despite these bribes he was still accused of maladministration, stripped of his lordly title and banished to a godforsaken part of Siam where it was expected he would succumb to the "pestiale" climate.

Phuket under Indian Governorship

In his place Aqa Mohammed, the leading Persian official in King Narai's court, appointed two fellow "Moors", Mohammed and Ishmael Beg, to be the new governor and shabandar (port officer) of Phuket. The Beg brothers were Cholas – Tamil Muslims from India's Coromandel Coast. As we have seen, these Cholas, or "Chulias" as they were later called by the British – had been trading and living in Phuket for some 1,000 years. And they comprised one of the major trading communities in the local port towns of Tharua, Bangkhli and Takuapa.

Bowrey tells us that the Cholas in Phuket "were of the Mahometan sect but not very great observers of many of his laws." He describes Mohammed Beg, the new Chola governor as "an austere man, one that had been bred a Warrior." Bowrey clearly did not care much for the Cholas, describing them as "a subtle and roguish people … a very great hindrance … for wherever these rascals be wee cannot sell any goods to a native of the countrey but they creep in alonge with them and tell them in private what our goods cost upon the coast in Surat, Bengala or elsewhere, which doth many a Christian a great prejudice."

Within a year of their appointment, the Beg brothers brought in almost 100 more "Moor" (Muslim Indian) assistants and retainers to help them control the island and its trade. Bowrey tells us that "This caused much local discontent," most particularly amongst the Siamese and Malays from the traditional leading families of Ban Takien, Ban Don and Ban Lipon, called by Bowrey "the councillors, secretaries, shabandares, bandarees etc, men of ancient standing and choice men of all the countrey." These people normally constituted the ruling élite on the island. By 1677 Bowrey wrote that "the most eminent men, both Syamers and Malayars" began grumbling about being "tyranised over" by these Indians and "the hard measure they received from this present Radja and his counsel, men altogether of another nation." Bowrey notes that Mohamed Beg, the new Chola governor, forced the members of these élite families to

> "labour hard in cuttinge downe the woods, buildinge houses under the pretence that they were by order of and for the use of, the king of Syam, which were no sooner built but were given to one Cholar or other, the Radjas favourites, and to burne and beat lime for the building of a stone fort, which things seemed tedious to them that were not allowed soe much as theire victuals for their paines, soe that they soon began to slight the work."

The locals' reluctance to work on Mohammed Beg's development projects – such as a badly needed fort on the island, angered and frustrated the new governor to the point that he threatened that, in order to keep up with his schedule, he would even force the islanders' wives to work. This, says Bowrey, represented "a most severe and haynous punishment to the Malayars, which are in general Mahometans."

Worse still, these new Indian administrators had started creaming off much of the tin trade profits, away from the local élite families, by shipping most of the metal up to Mergui and selling it at low prices to other "Moorish" associates of Aqa Mohammed, the Beg brothers and their Muslim cronies. These Moors would then resell the tin for much greater profits to traders or ship it overseas.

The Locals Revolt and Murder the Indians

This despotism by these Indians governing Phuket soon became too much for the island's truculent locals, who probably numbered some 9,000 at the time. The Siamese troops or retainers, who were theoretically there to protect and obey the Beg brothers (as royal appointed agents), were probably neutralized by some cunning diplomatic work by the locals, no doubt particularly by the women. Bowrey tells us that the locals then mutinied:

> "The Malayars and Syamers rose up in arms (with joynt consent) and on a sudden beset the Radjas house and killed him with his brother Ishmael and all his household, save the women and children and all the Moors and Chulyars upon the island, save two that made theire escape to Bangaree (Bangkhli) and thence to Queda ... I judge they killed in this insurrection seventy five moors and Chulyars, none resistinge save the Radja and his brother whoe, although surprised in the house, yet killed six of the most resolute Malayars. For which cause the whole countrey being in such a confusion I went awaye into the roade and sailed for Queda."

15

The Failed French Attempts to Colonize Phuket

1670 TO 1688

The White Brothers

In England in 1670, George White, a ship's navigator from Somerset, was offered a job on one of the brigs of King Narai's western trade fleet based in Mergui. He sailed to the East on the ship Hopewell, accompanied by his wife and his handsome younger brother Sam. On the voyage to Madras, young Sam met a spirited young widow, Mrs. Povey, on her way out to marry an officer in the EIC army based in Madras. In those sultry nights on the Indian Ocean, young Sam and Mrs. Povey fell in love and on her arrival in Madras, Mrs. Povey returned the gifts previously sent to her by her intended and called off the engagement. A French priest then married her to Sam White in Madras because the EIC chaplain refused to have any part in such a shocking scandal.

Besieged by gossip, the couple soon left Madras and sailed across the Bay of Bengal to Mergui with Sam's brother George, where Sam also acquired a job on one of the ships of the king of Siam's western trade fleet. These ships were Western-designed brigs, built in Siam by Dutch, Portuguese or English shipwrights and sailing under the Siamese flag. They carried cargoes, mainly elephants, aloe wood, ambergris and tin, from the western Siamese ports of Mergui, Phuket, Keddah, Trang and Takuapa predominantly to India to trade for textiles and arms. Sam and his new wife set up house in Mergui and were happy there for several months until his wife, like so many other Europeans in the East, soon succumbed to "jungle fever" and died while Sam was away at sea on his second voyage.

Constant Falcon and Mr. Burnaby

Nine years previously, King Narai had invited the British EIC back to Siam and the EIC had reopened its Ayutthaya office in 1661. It was staffed by two Englishmen and some slave workers and was again losing money. In 1674, the factory clerk died of disease and the chief EIC factor, a hopeless alcoholic, shortly thereafter committed suicide. The EIC then dispatched a Mr. Edward Burnaby from its Java factory to take over the Ayutthaya office. Burnaby brought with him from Java a promising 27-year-old Greek subordinate called Constantinos Gerakis. Constantinos had been born on the Greek island of Kefalonia. His father, an inn-keeper, had fallen on hard times and when he was young his mother had given him over to a British ship to work as a cabin boy. After some years in the Royal Navy he had signed up to head east as assistant gunner on the brig Hopewell. Gerakis is Greek for "falcon", so Constantinos had Anglicized his name to Constant Falcon. In India he had joined the EIC and was posted to Java. He was a natural linguist and in just two years in Java he had become proficient in Malay and Portuguese, the main commercial languages in the East at the time.

Whilst he had been traveling east to India from Europe on the ship Hopewell, Constant Falcon had met the White brothers who were travelling on the same ship. Coincidentally they turned out to be old friends of his new EIC boss Mr. Burnaby, who was also from Somerset. On arriving in Ayutthaya, Burnaby and Falcon set about their affairs and made contact with their mutual friends the White brothers in Mergui. Within a year Falcon had learned Siamese proficiently and Burnaby recommended him to the Ayutthaya barcelon (trade minister) to serve in the much-needed role of interpreter. Burnaby even agreed to pay Falcon's salary from EIC funds, believing that it was only by having someone inside this notoriously corrupt department that the EIC could ever hope to obtain the sort of trade advantages enjoyed in Siam by the entrenched Muslims and the importuning Dutch.

The ploy worked. Falcon's diligence, linguistic abilities and friendship with the Persians who controlled the department meant he was soon taken along as interpreter on a Siamese commercial embassy to Persia. On his return from Persia, Falcon met King Narai, who took a shine to him, particularly when Falcon explained to him, privately, how the Muslims in his trade department were stealthily swindling and defrauding him and had been doing so for years. This was, of course, a most dangerous game for the ambitious Falcon to play against the powerful Muslims. But it paid off and within a few years King Narai appointed Falcon as his private royal servant. Falcon then managed to persuade King Narai to remove the perfidious Muslims in charge of his royal trade in Siam's main western port of Mergui and instead to give this position to Falcon's equally nefarious British colleagues, Burnaby and the White brothers. And King Narai agreed.

Burnaby was made the governor of Mergui and George and Sam White the shabandars (harbor masters). Burnaby and the Whites then replaced most of the Muslims in the king's service in Mergui with mainly British adventurers, particularly as captains of the king's trade fleet there. Falcon, Burnaby and the White brothers, all now in cahoots, started to profit nicely, using their positions to undertake surreptitious private trade deals using the royal ships and trade infrastructure for their own ends – just as the ousted Muslims had before done.

The EIC office in Ayutthaya, meanwhile, continued to lose money. Some whispered that this was because of embezzlement by its new factor, a Mr. Samuel Potts; he, however, officially blamed the monopolistic and unfair trade practices of Siam. The EIC head office in Madras eventually gave an ultimatum to King Narai: either grant the EIC better terms of trade, or the company would have to close up and leave. In reality King Narai actually had little need of the EIC's imported woolens, hats and overpriced

148

cottons, much of which he bought simply to keep the English happy. What King Narai really wanted was a strong ally against the increasingly menacing Dutch. King Narai, however, had become rather disconcerted by the EIC's tepid enthusiasm for Siam and had become more impressed by the French, who seemed much more zealous in their desire to ally with him. King Narai therefore refused better terms to the EIC. So in 1684, after a fire in its factory in Ayutthaya, the EIC closed its operations and again left Siam. King Narai then instructed his now favored private secretary Falcon, who also spoke French, to try to bring the French into Siam in a bigger way to counter the domineering Dutch.

The French and Siam

The first French contacts with Southeast Asia came as early as 1529, when the flamboyant Parmentier brothers of Dieppe raised funding for a two-ship expedition to try to reach the lucrative Spice Islands directly. Their luck ran out when they reached the malarial west coast of Sumatra, where both brothers and many crewmen promptly died from "tropical fevers". The remainder of the crew elected to turn back to France and the expedition was an utter financial failure.

Undaunted, between 1602 and 1630, several more French trading fleets, privately funded by merchants mainly from St. Malo and Dieppe, headed east to try to buy pepper and spices. Some even attempted to establish small trade factories in the region, but few were successful. Dutch naval supremacy, sickness and the complications of trading in the Malay world made life too difficult. Eventually, like the English, the French decided it was easier to avoid the powerful and aggressive Dutch in the Far East and limited their trade factories to India.

By 1664 several of these private French trading companies elected, like the Dutch and English before them, to combine forces to form their own royal-backed monopolistic cartel for eastern trade – the French East India Company or Compagnie Française des Indes Orientales (CFIO). The CFIO set up several factories in India in the later 17th century and from its main factory in Pondicherry in southeast India, CFIO ships intermittently traded with some western peninsular ports, including Phuket. This was usually in joint venture with Indian merchants who preferred to send their cargoes in French bottoms as a way to foil the Dutch embargo, the salateers and other pirates. Nicolas Gervaise, a Frenchman who lived in Siam in the 17th century, noted that in this French trade, "the most important ports in the kingdom are Mygri [Mergui] and Jonsalem [Junk Ceylon]."[361] Therefore when Falcon wrote to the CFIO in 1680 on behalf of King Narai and invited it to open a factory in Ayutthaya, it accepted enthusiastically.

Handily, the conquest of markets and of souls required much the same infrastructure, some of which was already in place in Siam due to earlier French Catholic missionary involvement in Siam. By the mid-17th century, with Spain and Portugal in decline, Bourbon France had become the dominant Catholic power in Europe and King Louis IV had taken the lead in supporting overseas Catholic missionary endeavors. In 1659 the

Société des Missions Etrangères de Paris had been established to build on the previous work of the Jesuits. In 1681 two French Société missionaries arrived in Siam and were astonished at the religious freedom they found there, as one wrote, "I do not believe there is any country in the world where there are more religions and where their practice is more (freely) permitted than in Siam."[362] This religious freedom and Siam's central position in the region had determined the Société to choose Ayutthaya as its eastern headquarters. To encourage fund-raising, the missionaries sent glowing, if not always true, reports back to France of the possibility of mass conversions in both Siam and China such as, "We are dealing with … an empire which surpasses Europe in grandeur, which we are told contains in its extent more than two hundred million souls."[363]

Seeing France, which he knew had just defeated the Dutch in a war in Europe, as his new potential ally, King Narai was most accommodating to these French Catholic missionaries. In this accommodation these hopeful French missionaries saw the potential for his conversion. For these blinkered French Catholics there was only one truth, relentlessly believed to the exclusion of all others and they were unable to grasp the Buddhist mind-set that allows multiple truths. One of these missionaries, Jacques de Bourges, noted that one Buddhist monk explained to him, "The various religions are like the five fingers of one hand … Heaven is a great place to which several paths lead, some are shorter, some more frequented, some more difficult but all in the end arrive at the place of bliss which men seek."[364] The Catholic de Bourges, however, felt this was a "pernicious opinion".

15.1. French envoys in Ayutthaya presenting a letter from King Louis XIV to King Narai. The Greek Constant Falcon is pictured kowtowing on his hands and knees.

King Narai allowed the French to build missions around the country and in 1670 a Société branch mission was established to take over the old Jesuit mission in Tharua on Phuket. A Portuguese priest, M. Perez, was sent to minister to the small community of mainly mestizo Portuguese Christians. He did not fare well, reporting that few conversions were made. Another later French priest in Phuket dejectedly reported that the local Catholic Tharua mission achieved little but "some baptisms of young children, the dying and a few conversions of adults."[365] Falcon, a Catholic himself and always ambitious, had even started writing promotional letters to the Pope about the progress of these Catholic outposts in Siam. In one letter in the late 1680s he wrote of the new mission in Phuket.

"There used to be a father of the French Mission there but for some reasons unknown to me he left his flock unprovided with the sacraments and it is now six months since he returned there. I was very surprised to see him here [in Ayutthaya] and asked him to what man he had handed over his charge. 'To no one,' he replied without a blush – and he hoped his superiors would not take his departure ill since he had remained there long enough without relief."[366]

Phuket under French Governorship

These French missionaries established schools for technical training and hospital work with the sick. One of these hospitaler missionaries who had come to Siam in 1677 was Brother René Charbonneau from the St. Lazurus mission in Paris, who, "by his industry knew how to let blood and give remedy to a sick person."[367] He had been helping the priest at the mission hospital at Ban Plaet in Ayutthaya. Dutch reports at the time referred to him as "a former employee of the Siamese king in the capacity of physician."[368] He was by all reports a good man who had learned fluent Siamese, married a Siamese Christian wife and had children by her. As well as a good blood-letter, it appears he was also a bit of a dab hand at building forts and had previously been sent to the Burmese border, on loan to the Siamese king, to assist in building a military fort there.

From its main base in Pondicherry the French CFIO began sending more ships to Phuket to trade for tin. After the murder of the Chola Beg brothers on the island, when King Narai still feared that the Dutch might invade and take over Phuket in compensation for the destruction of their ships, he elected to appoint Brother René Charbonneau as the new governor of Phuket. This was both a snub to the Dutch and a sweetener to his new confidants, the French. Charbonneau may also have been chosen because of his medical skills, as many epidemics had been sweeping through Phuket and Keddah, particularly a virulent smallpox outbreak that killed off a great many of Phuket's people.

René Charbonneau became governor of Phuket in 1680. He seems to have been liked by the locals and during his period as governor many more French ships began visiting the island to buy tin. In early 1680, the CFIO record that one of its ships went to Phuket and bought a full cargo of tin. In August 1680, François Martin, the French station head at the main French eastern base of Pondicherry, reported sending a second ship under a Captain Germaine to trade with "Jonceland" (Phuket). Germaine returned in February the following year and Martin noted:

"The voyage had been quite profitable by reason of the tin brought from this island and which it had formerly supplied in quantity when it was peopled. Small pox, which broke out there a few years back and is like the plague on these shores, carried off many of the inhabitants and the trading that the people … formerly carried on had to be abandoned by many. There were four elephants on board which the governor [M. Charbonneau] requested me to sell on his behalf."[369]

The next French ship to arrive from Pondicherry with the early summer easterlies managed to get no tin at all, probably due to the depleted population. According to Martin this ship "returned, but the journey had not been profitable," as instead of tin the ship had loaded with "elephants teeth [ivory], benzoin [a tree resin] and Sappanwood."[370]

In 1683 the Dutch, as compensation for their losses in Phuket and now angered at the favors given to the French there, yet again applied pressure on King Narai to cede Phuket to them and they threatened to blockade Ayutthaya if he did not. King Narai ordered Falcon to advise the CFIO chief in the company's Ayutthaya factory, Deslandes, to also immediately apply for Phuket to be ceded to the French because, as Martin in Pondicherry later reported: "On the advice that Sieur Deslandes received that the head of the Dutch factory had requested the island of Junk Ceylon, he also sought it for the [French] company, in order to spite the Dutch. The result was as he expected, the king of Siam declined to cede the island to one or the other in order not to cause any jealousy."[371] The French missionary Nicolas Gervaise, however, gloated that with the appointment of a French governor, Phuket had become pretty much theirs anyway. "The king has entrusted its governorship to a Frenchman who is well placed there and has no intention of granting the Dutch entry in the near future."[372]

King Narai appointed another Frenchman, Monsieur Rewane, as the governor of the Bangkhli and Takuatung tin ports in Phang Nga, just north of Phuket; then in 1685, to the further chagrin of the Dutch, he granted to the French "the monopoly of the commerce of tin in the isle of Junkceylon and permission to build a factory there."[373] A new French priest, Father Martineau, was also sent down to care for the Christian flock in Phuket and he noted how scattered the Christians were, living in settlements on Phuket, Takuatung and Bangkhli. He bemoaned the local Christians' ignorance of matters religious, the strange hymns they sang and the fact that despite his high ambitions he too made few conversions.

The French Build a Fort at Thalang

It was during the tenure of the French governor René Charbonneau that the Thalang fort was built. This was the fort used some 80 years later by Phuket's famous heroine sisters in their defense of Phuket against a Burmese invasion. The fort was built somewhere between Ban Don and Ban Lippon, but, quite remarkably, no one on Phuket today seems able to point authoritatively to where exactly this fort stood. Contemporary reports tell us it was made of thick planking with an earth-and-wood embankment on the inside forming a platform from which muskets and cannon could be fired; there may even have been a moat around it. It was square in shape and some 400 meters long on each side with raised wooden watchtowers at the four corners sheltered by nipa palm roofs. Inside the fort were store-rooms and buildings made of adobe and wood, also with nipa palm roofs.

It is not clear if the fort was built directly by Charbonneau or possibly by the French engineer Monsieur La Mare, who had earlier been sent to the south by King Narai to rebuild the city walls of Ligor. De La Loubère tells us that, "By the king of Siam's order he [La Mare] went to Ligor to take a draught thereof. The governor would not permit him to go round it [the city wall, for an inspection] in under two days, though he could have done it in less than an hour."[374] Poor Monsieur La Mare had to sleep outside the walls overnight, voraciously besieged by mosquitoes. After constructing the new city walls of Ligor, he may afterwards have come to Phuket to assist in building the fort there.

By 1684 Charbonneau, who had been the governor of lawless and sickness-ridden Phuket for four years, wanted to go back to Ayutthaya because, as Martin in Pondicherry noted: "He was governor of Junk Ceylon by commission and with great approbation because he desired to return to the city of Siam (Ayutthaya) to his wife's relations which are Portuguese. Monseigneur Billi, the master of Ambassador De Chaumont's palace, succeeded him in this employment in Jonsalem."[375]

With the appointment of this second French governor by King Narai, François Martin and the CFIO chiefs in Pondicherry must have been optimistic enough about their prospects in Phuket that, in 1687, they felt able to send the aforementioned Captain Germaine, a CFIO employee, back to Phuket to prepare a report on the island's suitability to be taken and turned into a fully-fledged French colony. Germaine made his report as follows:

"Jongcelan is a small island 35 miles in length … there are but a few inhabitants on the island, perhaps six thousand persons adult and child and the surrounding areas are even more sparsely populated. There is nothing beautiful, good, rare nor curious in this place. One sees on all sides only impregnable jungle full of tigers, wild elephants and rhinoceros, which we eat sometimes in place of beef, not to mention several other ferocious beasts … There is no town, only some hamlets and villages scattered here and there in the corners of the woods. Nevertheless, the most considerable of the villages is called a town. A small wooden fortress surrounded by four towers was built when M. René Charbonneau ruled. People in this place are still wild men and do not know how to act like good mannered people, or to put it in a better way, less polite than those in other areas of this kingdom of Syam … They apply themselves to nothing that is curious, they cultivate neither science nor art, their occupation consists solely in cutting wood, sowing rice and digging the ground in order to find the entrails of tin which is the greatest wealth of the country …The island has a bad climate and foreigners cannot stand this kind of climate. Jungcelon has four colonies and one of these smaller colonies (Bangkhli) is also governed by a Frenchman M. Rewane."[376]

The Problems Start

Falcon became King Narai's preferred minister in his court and was promoted to phra klang (trade and foreign relations minister). King Narai was becoming old and very ill with dropsy and his open door, pro-foreigner policies were increasingly frowned upon by the more conservative Siamese khunnang (the most noble lords). They disapproved of his obsession with foreigners and believed he had outstripped all the normal limits of reserve expected of Siamese royalty. They felt he lacked respect for the Sangkha (the Buddhist monks' high council) and most particularly they were jealous of the private wealth he was amassing from his hugely increased royal trading monopoly. This trade income and having the French as his new allies meant he was no longer so beholden to these khunnang lords for his power, men and income. The khunnang felt their traditional power slipping away and many wanted King Narai and particularly his controversial private secretary Falcon replaced. King Narai had sensed their displeasure and had moved out of Ayutthaya to a fancy, well-guarded new palace he had built at Lopburi some 50 kilometers away. This was ostensibly for his health and his hunting and, it was also said, partly to emulate the great King Louis IV's palace at Versailles. No doubt it was also because he felt safer in Lopburi than in conspiratorial Ayutthaya city.

In 1684 King Louis IV invited King Narai to send a Siamese embassy to Paris to bring the two kingdoms closer. He accepted, and the Siamese ambassadors traveled to France on board a French ship and arrived to a magnificent reception. The hype and pageantry of their visit made all of France enthusiastic for trade with – and the proposed religious conversion of – Siam. Louis IV then sent a French embassy back to Siam in 1685, which arranged a formal alliance between the two kings. In return for beneficial trade rights and the right to proselytize, the French agreed that they would send to Siam an expedition of six warships and a contingent of some 1,000 troops and "technical advisers" (mainly missionaries in disguise).

King Narai wanted this French force in Siam now not only to foil Dutch pretensions but also as a bulwark against the increasing threat of a coup against him from his own disaffected khunnang lords and the displaced Muslim trade fraternity. He offered the French military contingent a base at arm's length in the mutinous peninsular town of Songkla which had just been re-conquered by Siam. The French, however, wanted somewhere more strategic and less troublesome. They requested the Bangkok fort, which controlled river access to Ayutthaya, or a western port such as Mergui or Phuket, with trade and naval base opportunities and lucrative tin mines. The French ambassadors received no formal agreement from Narai or Falcon on this issue before they sailed back to France to arrange the French expeditionary force to come to Siam.

By 1686 this great French expeditionary fleet to Siam was ready. It set off from France with great pomp and ceremony, full of grand hopes of converting Siam to Catholicism and then possibly colonizing the place. The expedition consisted of six men-of-war and 1,361 people. These included 300 advisers and clerics and 636 troops under the command of the aged French General Desfarges. It was a difficult trip according to the Abbé de Choisey, an effete, occasional cross-dressing Parisian socialite who was one of the expedition's lesser ambassadors. Apart from the many deaths from disease amongst the men, he recounts in his diary being caught in a local storm off Phuket while entering the Straits of Malacca. "Oh what a terrible, frightening day! … Thunder, rain, lightning, night in the middle of the day, the sea half the height of the mast, the rolling … the waves slamming into our vessel like the battering rams of Agamemnon breaking the walls of Troy."[377] Nearly one-third (154) of the French troops died of sickness and scurvy on this journey out, leaving fewer than 450 soldiers, many very ill, to disembark in Siam.

Immediately upon the French arrival at Paknam at the mouth of Chao Phraya River the problems started. The French sent word to Falcon in Ayutthaya that King Louis of France insisted that he wanted his troops stationed at the Bangkok fort, not at Songkla and that although the French did not want "to have to apply pressure openly, since it would gravely prejudice the cause of Christianity"[378] (that is their hoped-for conversion of the country) if they were refused, force would be used as "His Majesty Louis IV is determined to force an entry into Bangkok." This was a most awkward situation for Falcon and King Narai. They knew the disgruntled khunnang – and the Siamese people – would not readily accept French troops stationed within striking distance of Ayutthaya. On the other hand, if they refused, the French would either force their way in or simply depart, leaving King Narai and Falcon without protection against the Dutch or, now more ominously, the looming domestic political forces arrayed against them. Falcon therefore made a compromise, agreeing that the French troops could stay in the Bangkok fort if they swore allegiance to King Narai and fell under Falcon's orders.

The 1687 War between the British East India Company and Siam

Meanwhile, back in Mergui, Burnaby and the White brothers were prospering from their nefarious trade activities. George White, the elder brother, had already returned to England wealthy enough to retire as a landed nabob (the old name for someone who made his fortune – often ill-gotten – in the East). Burnaby and Sam White now had over 100 Europeans, mainly British, in their employ, operating the Siamese royal trade fleet in direct competition with both the Muslims in the Bay of Bengal and the British EIC, earning these "interlopers" (as the EIC in Madras called private traders) opprobrium from both parties.

This western Siamese fleet was now being operated by Sam White and Burnaby almost independently of the ailing King Narai and even their supposed partner Falcon. They had taken over much of the Siam trade previously carried on by the Muslims, often by means foul rather than fair. Many of these victimized Muslim traders were Indians from Masulipatnam in Golconda (Machilipatnam today) on the Coromandel Coast. In 1681 one of these royal Siamese trade ships, carrying a cargo belonging to King Narai (and White and Burnaby) was wrecked in rough weather in Masulipatnam as the port officer there refused to sell the Siamese ship more cables in retaliation for the mistreatment his merchant ships had received in Mergui. Burnaby, as governor of Mergui, got King Narai to demand retribution. When this was refused, François Martin, the French factor in Pondicherry, tells us, "The monarch [Narai] ordered the governor of Mergui to arm two small vessels and send them to patrol Golconda."[379]

Captain Coche, one of the English captains working in Mergui, was put in charge of this Siamese punitive expedition against Golconda.

"He took with him sixty Europeans from diverse nations and came to Masulipatnam. He went ashore as night fell and seized the customs house. They pillaged what they could take away and set fire to it and some nearby houses before withdrawing. The fire spread … and the whole town was threatened with being engulfed. The king of Siam's vessels set sail and the people on board made other raids in different places on the Chola coast before withdrawing afterwards to Mergui."[380]

This action started a war in the Bay of Bengal between the Golconda fleet on one side and the farang-led fleet of King Narai in Mergui on the other. Over the next few months the Mergui ships seized seven Golconda ships, a Bengali ship plus, more controversially, the New Jerusalem, a ship owned by a wealthy Armenian in India, which was loaded with a valuable private cargo belonging to some EIC directors in Madras. This theft plus the brazen actions of these British "interlopers" from Mergui both angered and embarrassed the "honorable" EIC directors in Madras, who had just recently formed a trade alliance with the king of Golconda. The EIC complained to the Siamese king and in London the influential EIC directors pressured King James II to proclaim it illegal for any Englishmen to work on other nations' ships.

Back in Ayutthaya, even Falcon could no longer sanction the increasingly audacious actions of his associates in Mergui. He ordered White and Burnaby to desist and return to Ayutthaya. In their place, as a way out of his awkward predicament with the French troops now billeted in the Bangkok fort, he invited the French to station their troops in Mergui and nominated a French officer, the Chevalier de Beauregard, to be the new governor of Mergui.

White and Burnaby, unsure of what fate might await them in Ayutthaya, did not return immediately, as Falcon had ordered. Then matters took a turn for the worse. Falcon had previously ordered some Indian jewelry for King Narai from the EIC in Madras and when the EIC ship carrying the jewelry arrived in Mergui, the price for the jewelry had gone up as it now included compensation claimed from the Siamese king for the EIC directors' cargo lost when the New Jerusalem was seized. Falcon refused to pay this bill and sent the overpriced jewelry back. This was the last straw for the EIC, which had already lost much money to what it saw as unfair and crooked Siamese trading. Siamese ships, manned by semi-piratical English interlopers, were embarrassing the EIC in front of its Indian trade partners and now, worse still, it was hearing rumors that Falcon had agreed to allow the French – the EIC's arch-rivals – to take over the strategic port of Mergui. In 1688, using the unpaid jewelry bill as a pretext, the EIC declared war on Siam and dispatched two warships with marines to capture Mergui port.

These two EIC warships, the Curtana and the smaller James, were under the command of 27-year-old Captain Anthony Welden. He was given instructions to arrest all the English working in Mergui (their presence there now being illegal under British law)

Map 7
European Trade Stations in the Bay of Bengal during the 17th and 18th Centuries

and confiscate all their ill-gotten wealth as compensation for their piracy. In addition, Siam was to be given 60 days to pay for the jewelry. If Siam failed to pay, he should take possession of Mergui port before the French could establish themselves there, and hold it until a main force of EIC Indian army sepoys arrived to occupy Mergui, secure and fortify it and make it a new EIC colony.

White and Burnaby got word of these EIC plans and decided it was time to grab their loot and scarper. They loaded up Sam White's private ship the Dorothy with their ill-gotten goodies and were making final preparations to sail for England when the Cur-tana and James entered Mergui harbor and seized the Dorothy and one of the king of Siam's ships moored there. White and Burnaby, who were onshore at the time, ordered the locals to resist these EIC warships. They started to plant bamboo stakes in the harbor to thwart a landing. The English Captain Welden put paid to this action by firing two broadsides of grapeshot into the luckless workers building the shore defense who "suffered most severely."[381] He then sent his sepoys ashore and after a brief skirmish they captured the town and arrested Burnaby and White and the other British "interlopers" there. Following his instructions, Captain Welden then re-sent the jewelry bill to Ayutthaya and settled in to wait 60 days for the payment ultimatum.

The Massacre of the Farangs in Mergui

It so happened that Captain Welden, like Burnaby and White, was from Somerset and apparently he also enjoyed boozing and womanizing. During his wait in Mergui, the charismatic Sam White soon tempted the younger Welden with local girls and lavish drinking sessions. In the meantime, Siamese troops began to appear on the outskirts of town and the Mergui locals, seeing the partying between the British invaders and the British locals, whispered rumors (fueled by Siamese agents infiltrating the town) that the British intended to band together, take the town and kill all the Muslims. The locals, a motley port-smorgasbord of Indians, Siamese, Chinese, Malays, Burmese and Muslims backed by the Siamese troops outside town, secretly readied themselves to fight.

On the night of July 15, 1688, White had again invited Welden and some officers to dine at his house on shore. After dinner, as they were partaking of their usual post-prandial boozing, the Siamese troops and locals made their move. Many quietly surrounded White's house, while others silently set upon and killed the Indian sepoy shore battery guards. They then opened fire with the shore cannons on the British ships in the harbor.

The sound of the cannons was the signal and the massed locals and Siamese troops rushed White's house. The outnumbered and inebriated Englishmen grabbed their weapons and made a fighting run for their longboats on the beach. Edward Burnaby was caught by the mob and hacked to pieces. Captain Welden received a sword stroke that cut deep into his right arm, but reached the river. Sam White with a few others "forced their way past the body of Siamese who opposed them"[382] and made it to his small boat at the base of his garden. They pushed out to sea, fighting off the attackers. While fleeing, Sam White saw the wounded Captain Welden floundering one-armed in the harbor, and despite the fire from the shore cannons and muskets and some Siamese canoes pursuing them, they rescued him and made it to the security of his ship, the Curtana. A cannon ball from the shore battery had hit the smaller EIC ship, the James, at the waterline and she was taking on water and sinking.

The Siamese mob meanwhile, their blood up, continued on to attack all the houses of the resident Europeans in town, massacring them and their families and pillaging their houses. Over 60 European men, women and children were slaughtered that night. In a later French report on the incident, it is stated that amongst the "principal personages" killed in Mergui that night were "Burnaby, the governor of Mergui, Captain Lesley a Scottish captain of one of the king of Siam's vessels … two English Army officers and Don Joseph, a Spaniard known to all the traders on that coast."[383] White and Welden, once on the Curtana, sent some men across by boat who managed to capture the Siamese trade frigate, the Revenge, which was moored near them. Both ships with as many men aboard as had made it, then headed out to the open sea. On the way, they passed "the bodies of five Englishmen which the tide had carried out to sea. They had many wounds and were entirely disfigured with blows inflicted after their death. To savage in this way the bodies of their enemies is the nature of most peoples in the Indies but especially the Siamese."[384]

Once at sea, Welden ordered the ships to head back to Madras. Sam White persuaded the wounded Captain Welden, who now owed him his life, to give him and his men command of their Siamese prize ship the Revenge and he promised he would follow Welden and the Curtana back to Madras to face any charges. But a few moonless nights later, Sam White and the Revenge disappeared in the night and sailed back to England, leaving the young Captain Welden to return to Madras to announce his failure alone. Sam White eventually made it back to Somerset, to live as he had dreamed of in Siam, as a prosperous nabob living off his eastern riches. However, as life would have it, he died of illness only six months later.

For letting the English steal his ship and possibly for abetting the massacre of the king's European employees (though some say King Narai himself had ordered the attack), the governor of Tenasserim was recalled to Ayutthaya and was reportedly sentenced to death by having his "flesh pinched off with red-hot irons."

The Revolt against King Narai and the French

Back in the fort at Bangkok, the French general, Desfarges, had accepted Falcon's offer to move a detachment of troops to occupy Mergui. By the time of the massacre of the English there he had already dispatched the new governor De Beauregard and 120 men on the one-month march over the Tenasserim hills. Two of the four remaining French warships were also dispatched to head west into the Bay of Bengal to reinforce the new French garrison in Mergui. These ships, however, would arrive too late to save this isolated column of sweaty Gallic soldiers marching westwards through Kanchanaburi in the intense Siamese summer heat.

King Narai meanwhile had fallen gravely ill from his dropsy and had retired full-time to his palace in Lopburi where he lay bedridden. In March 1688 his health took yet another turn for the worse and it became clear he would soon die. Falcon, back in Ayutthaya and still cloaked in the king's patronage, was increasingly running Siam's foreign policy.

The nationalist khunnang lords meanwhile, hearing of King Narai's imminent death, started planning and maneuvering a coup. Lord Petracha, a close royal relative and adviser to King Narai, led these conspirators. Petracha was supported by his rather odious and violent royal son, Luang Sorasak, who loathed Falcon and a few years earlier had punched him in the face in a palace argument, knocking out two of his teeth. This group of disaffected Siamese lords also had support from the disaffected Muslims plus the disaffected Dutch and talk of a revolution was in the air. The Frenchman Abbé Artus de

Lionne who was in Siam that April in 1688 wrote, "The whole country was arming. The road from Lopburi [the king's palace] to Ayutthaya was thronged with armed men and even the boatmen and the very dregs of the population carried weapons … insinuations of a nature to increase their unpopularity were in circulation against the French … that they were plotting to conquer the country … and convert everyone to Catholicism."[385]

Lord Petracha launched his coup by ordering some of his lordly followers in Lopburi to enter the palace to "guard" King Narai on his deathbed. Then thousands of the khunnang lords' armed troops and militias converged around Ayutthaya and the small French force in Bangkok fort. Soon after this, King Narai reportedly died (or was murdered?) in his palace at Lopburi. Lord Petracha immediately ordered men to arrest Falcon in Ayutthaya. He was caught and dragged around the streets of Ayutthaya for public derision. He was then tortured for several days to find the whereabouts of the great wealth he was believed to have embezzled and hidden. Then Lord Petracha's son, Luang Sorasak, took him into the country and reportedly cut him into small pieces. Luang Sorasak next murdered King Narai's two sons, his natural heirs, and any other relatives who could have any claim to be potential heirs. Petracha then ordered the capture and imprisonment of all the French civilians and clerics in Siam and an attack on the French garrisons in Bangkok and Mergui. Bangkok fort was surrounded by Siamese troops, some say as many as 40,000, backed by 100 cannon. Unfortunately for the 200 or so French troops defending it, the remaining two French warships, their only means of escape, had recently left to go on patrol out to sea. The Frenchmen repulsed several massed night attacks and spent their days under a hail of missiles, fireballs and cannonballs being fired into the fort.

In the besieged fort General Desfarges sent one young officer, Sieur de Saint-Cry, with 12 men to try and escape down the river on the fort's large yawl to try to reach the sea and locate the French warships in the Gulf of Thailand. That night the yawl was spotted leaving the fort and was soon surrounded by Siamese war canoes filled with hundreds of men. The Frenchmen carried on a running fight downriver until a cannon ball hit a stock of brandy stored on the yawl. The French soldiers on board, not wanting the brandy to go to waste, reportedly started drinking it until some became too drunk to continue to fight. Realizing they would be overrun, Sieur de Saint-Cry determined to die honorably. He loaded all the yawl's gunpowder, grenades and grapeshot in a pile on the deck. As their boat was boarded and filling with Siamese attackers, Saint-Cry ignited the gunpowder. There was an almighty explosion which blew apart Saint-Cry, the drunken French troops, many of the Siamese war boats grappling her and reportedly over a hundred Siamese attackers. Martin in Pondicherry later wrote, "the losses on the Siamese side were considerable," but showed the Siamese "the intrepidity and resolution of the French … so in the future they were more guarded in their attacks."[386]

The vastly outnumbered Frenchmen in the fort held out for over three months until they ran out of all provisions and gunpowder. The warships, their only hope, were still nowhere to be seen. After four months General Desfarges was forced to discuss terms of surrender with Petracha, who had now crowned himself king of Siam. An agreement was struck that if the French handed over their weapons, they would be allowed to leave on Siamese ships, for which, humiliatingly, they would also have to pre-pay the charter fees. The French civilian and missionary captives in Ayutthaya however would remain imprisoned as hostages against any later potential retaliation.

The Revolt in the Peninsula: Mergui and Phuket

When word of the revolution and coup in Ayutthaya reached Phuket and Phang Nga, the two French governors Monsieurs Billi and Jean Rival (who had replaced Rewane as the new governor of Bangkhli and Takutung), also the new priest at the Jesuit mission and the few other French residents on the island who had come to build the new CFIO factory in Tharua were arrested, transported to Ayutthaya and imprisoned. Monsieur Billi, the governor of Phuket, died there; however it is not known if he was executed, as were some of the French civilian prisoners, or like most the others, died from disease in the insanitary and exacting circumstances of their imprisonment. For example, many of the French civilian captives in Ayutthaya were chained 10 in a row with large wooden yokes on their shoulders and made to perform hard manual labor all day. They were underfed and at night they had cangues fixed round their necks – these were thick wooden collars with large spokes like a cartwheel, which made movement difficult and lying down impossible. Monsieur Martin in Pondicherry tells us, "thus they suffered a succession of afflictions to which [they] had been reduced by such treatment and many died."[387]

The only exceptions, thanks to the high regard in which the Siamese held them, were René Charbonneau, the first governor of Phuket, and one other Frenchman, who were left free to find food and to minister to the other French prisoners. One group of French captives, including General Desfarge's two sons, attempted to escape. But they were caught, tied behind horses and dragged around Ayutthaya "with people following with rattan sticks forcing them to run at the same pace as the animals. One died from this form of torture."[388]

Meanwhile, in Mergui, the French garrison troops had arrived shortly after the massacre of the British. They busied themselves constructing a star-shaped fort of wood and earth on a hill near the harbor shore and were allocated 3,000 local workers to assist them. They were unaware of the coup when it took place in Ayutthaya, but Martin in Pondicherry tells of creeping complications:

> "The workmen [for the fort] were at first provided by the local mandarins according to the numbers requested. Some time after, a slowdown was observed in the work and only some of the workmen came, then none at all. An explanation was sought from the mandarins with whom a very chilly relationship was evident for some time. They gave reasons which were mere excuses (they went to plant rice) but which showed that they had received secret orders to act thus."[389]

De Beauregard, the new governor, and De Bruant, the commander of the 120 French troops in Mergui, who suspected the death of King Narai or that a revolution had occurred, sent a messenger to Ayutthaya but he was soon turned back by Siamese soldiers. Meanwhile we are told that "Victuals began to run low and the garrison was refused supplies. The French were badly treated and learned that the inhabitants were assembling with arms."[390] The fort's water well also mysteriously collapsed one night and De Bruant, now fearing the worst, tried to strengthen the unfinished fort "by constructing a palisade of stakes and other obstacles." At this point, however, "The mandarins, recognizing by this conduct [that] the French were perhaps informed of their intentions, declared themselves openly. The Siamese troops assembled around Mergui, numbering several thousands, appeared in a body but were a rabble … without discipline."[391] "Thus war was declared on the French in Mergui before they knew about its cause."[392]

The Siamese troops then attacked and, according to one of the French survivors:

> "The talpolins [monks] gave them symbols which they thought made them invulnerable and opium which makes them bold and they left their pagoda with barbaric cries for the attack. But these Siamese were not Makassars [fearless Malay fighters] and the French cannons soon dispersed them without difficulty … Over the following few days the Siamese attempted several assaults on the fort which were repulsed. The cannon and musket fire kept them in disorder and at a distance."[393]

The battle turned into another siege and a long-distance hilltop cannon duel between the French battery and a Siamese battery on a nearby hill. Marcel Le Blanc, a French missionary in Mergui at the time reported, "They fired a great deal from there which caused much trouble … our cannon were better than theirs, we killed their cannoneer, a Portuguese, disabled their battery and after that they remained disinclined to fire or come to attack."[394]

As the siege dragged on one of the French reported that, with "victuals and water lacking … no expedient was found but to withdraw."[395] There were two ships in the harbor of Mergui at the time, a small visiting English ship and the Mergui, a Siamese trade frigate. One rainy night De Bruant made his move; using the monsoon rain that night as cover he sent a secret raiding party to capture the Mergui. This was successfully achieved and the two ships were made ready to depart and brought closer to shore and their longboats were prepared to pick up the French troops. The remaining 80 or so French troops then left the fort openly and in formation in the now pouring rain, some carrying the heavy gold coin trunks of their treasury and they all advanced, making for the longboats. Marcel Le Blanc, a missionary who was with them, records:

> "The enemy thought that this retreat was an attack on them and fled away allowing our men to reach the sea unhindered. But as they came down from the eminence [the fort] on a steep wet and slippery slope some soldiers broke ranks and fell on the others. Most of them were carrying heavy loads of arms, money and munitions and could not withstand this initial disorder and some of the troops in front also broke rank. The enemy saw this disorder in our troops and thought they were afraid. The fear and disorder amongst our soldiers made them

[the massed Siamese besiegers] bold and they came and attacked with sabres and spears."[396]

The outnumbered Frenchmen then started to run for the longboats and "thought only of getting on board, tumbling over each other and abandoning their baggage." Between 15 (a French report) and 60 (Francisco Nogeuira, a Portuguese Jesuit in Macau) were killed during this running melee. "We lost in the retreat Commissioner Chambiche and some soldiers who were trapped in the shore mud because they were transporting heavy loads of coin, the Sieur Hiton, a brave officer was drowned and with him some of his company in a longboat which sank to the bottom."[397] The Siamese shore cannons now fired on the fleeing French troops, who were both swimming and in the longboats, "killing another ten or twelve men … a great number of Siamese galleys appeared in pursuit … but they did not dare approach the ships."[398] Only some 50 of the 80 Frenchmen men managed to reach the ship. The Mergui, which was not in good condition, weighed anchor and, against the wind, set sail from the harbor and away from the cannon shot. "In this way the French retreated from Mergui poorly equipped and with few victuals."

Outside the harbor, however, they saw two ships bearing down on them: these were "Siamese vessels in full rig which the governor of Tenasserim had hastily armed … manned by some Dutchmen with a Siamese and Moorish crew."[399] De Bruant and the French on the Mergui, we are informed, "showed a bold front" and challenged this Siamese ship to a fight. But the Siamese ship withdrew, not wanting to tangle with these "desperate and embittered" Frenchmen. The French tried to sail due west to Pondicherry in India but it was the wrong season and they were beating right into the southwest monsoons. The Mergui, we are told, was "badly equipped, with few victuals and sorry local sails at an unfavourable time of the year."[400] The French therefore attempted to navigate round the north coast of the Bay of Bengal.

This trip took several months. Thirsty and starving, the French fugitives sought water and food where they could. Some men under De Bruant became so desperate that they elected to take a longboat and head up a river in Burma to find victuals and they were never heard of again. The remainder, starving and near death, were eventually captured by an English warship near the mouth of the River Ganges. They were held as prisoners, as England had gone to war with France again in Europe. Eventually, six months later, on January 15, 1689 some 30 survivors of the Mergui occupation force of about 120 were returned from prison in Madras to Pondicherry aboard a British frigate. Two weeks later the three Siamese ships with the French troops from the Bangkok fort also arrived in Pondicherry carrying General Desfarges and fewer than 350 survivors of the 636 French troops who had left France so gloriously in the expedition to Siam.

The French Invade Phuket

General Desfarges, ashamed at his failure, had no desire to return to France without some victory to restore his name. Despite the many French civilian hostages the Siamese were still holding in Ayutthaya, he resolved to make a show of force to attempt to get some redress. A CFIO war council was called and Desfarges proposed that the CFIO should invade and occupy Phuket Island, as this might free the hostages in Ayutthaya or at least win France Phuket Island, which in their eyes was a valuable asset – "the centre of the tin trade." Several men in the war council were against the expedition and advised against "the scant utility to be drawn from this enterprise,"[401] but Desfarges got his way.

15.2. The French East India Company headquarters in Pondicherry from where they launched their ill-fated invasion of Phuket in 1688.

In April 1689, 322 French troops boarded three French frigates, Oriflame, Siam and Luovo, which were also loaded with "trade goods lacking in those parts" to barter for provisions en route. The French soldiers showed little enthusiasm to return to Siam and had to be surrounded by other CFIO French troops in Pondicherry to prevent desertions while they were herded and forced aboard. Also aboard were two returning Royal Siamese ambassadors whom the French had taken prisoner in Pondicherry, thinking they might be used as bargaining chips. This rather quixotic expeditionary force left Pondicherry on April 10, 1689.

When the French force arrived off the Malay Peninsula their first problem was that no one on board had been to Phuket before, so no one knew which of the many jungly and deserted islands on the west coast was actually Phuket. The fleet reportedly stopped at some islands to ask directions to ensure that they invaded the right one. The locals on Phuket, who had probably by now got word of their approach, had no doubt adopted their normal defense plan – clearing off to hide in the jungles and hills or fleeing to Phang Nga – and then waiting for the French to go away and stop bothering them.

When the three French warships did eventually reach Phuket, it was June, the rainy season was upon them and it was hot, humid and uncomfortable. Flying the tricolor, the fleet (probably) entered Tharua harbor and sent an armed expedition ashore to Thalang. But Martin in Pondicherry reports, "They found the whole place flooded, without habitation, and saw no one."[402] However, several officers reportedly still disagreed that the island they were invading was actually Phuket as they did not recognize it from their maps.

General Desfarges then sent an emissary, one Siamese hostage and a letter north to Ayutthaya to offer a deal; he would leave Phuket alone and free his other Siamese hostages if the French prisoners in Ayutthaya were freed and peace declared. When this letter reached Ayutthaya, King Petracha rejected the offer and "renewed the severities against the French prisoners there and more of them were killed including the French Bishop of Ayutthaya."[403] He then sent word back to Desfarges that more would be killed if he continued his aggression, "and fear for their safety deterred him from taking any drastic action at Phuket." Moreover, King Petracha said he would only start to discuss the matter if Desfarges first released all his Siamese hostages. Desfarges, now a man clutching at straws, must have looked around at the forested and deserted lands surrounding him in Phang Nga Bay and Phuket and resolved to release his Thai hostages. After this, it is reported that the French hostages in Ayutthaya were treated better.

While Desfarges deliberated rather hopelessly on what to do next, the French fleet lay at anchor just off Phuket by (probably) Ko Rang in Sapam Bay (Tharua roads). (Some people say, however, that the French ships sat off Ko Pheh further north.) Either way, Ko Rang later became known as "French Island." Dr. Koening, a Danish botanist and diarist who visited Phuket in 1783, some 80 years later, wrote of passing "French Island" as he sailed into Sapam Bay. Indeed, it is speculated that the name Ko Rang today is just a shortened version of "Ko Farang" or "Ko Farangcaise". (The local Phuket dialect is famous for shortening words.)

From Pondicherry, the ketch Saint Joseph was sent after the invasion fleet with more supplies – "wine and other refreshments." But this crew was also unsure about which island was Phuket. They appear to have arrived in Patong Bay – on the opposite side of the island from the French fleet– and they also found the island to be deserted. They "fired cannon shots as a signal to our people who might be there"[404] and sent men ashore to hunt for any locals to ask them, first, if the island was actually "Jonsalam" (Phuket) and second, whether they might possibly have seen a French invasion fleet anywhere recently. Reportedly they "found a local man who assured them that nothing had been seen of them [the three ships probably in Phang Nga Bay].[405] They then cruised around the islands looking for their compatriots and firing off their cannons but never found the three other French warships probably moored and hidden behind either Ko Pheh or Ko Rang, so "Finally, meeting no one, they decided to return."

The now dispirited French troops sat on their hot, dank ships through the rainy season with no one to attack. They were probably watched covertly by the Phuket locals as they sat eating mangoes, durian and roasted monkeys in their jungle hideouts in the surrounding hills. To kill time the French officers "sought refreshment by hunting on neighboring islands where there was plenty of game and fish were also caught … It was noted that this island had very fine trees for making masts suitable for the biggest ships in use in Europe."[406] Martin in Pondicherry however tells us, "People were sick of the whole enterprise … those who had so passionately advanced this voyage had nothing to say."[407]

A Most Ignominious French Retreat

After some six months the French force met a Portuguese ship and one Chinese junk with some Europeans on board who informed them that a new war had broken out in Europe and that France was now at war with both the English and the Dutch. With their sails starting to rot and their vessels in no shape to fight a British or Dutch brig if they passed by, even General Desfarges "recognized that it was not prudent to stay longer in those parts." In December 1689, "with nothing gained but the knowledge that his invasion had merely increased the term of suffering of the French prisoners,"[408] Desfarges decided to return to Pondicherry. To add insult to ignomiy, his sorry fleet was chased much of the way back across the Bay of Bengal by a lone Dutch ship.

After leaving Pondicherry to head back to France in 1690, one of the expedition's two remaining ships was captured by the Dutch. General Desfarges died from sickness on the way, possibly haunted by the prospect of the humiliation he would face in France. The last remaining expedition ship, the Oriflame, got within sight of France when she encountered an Atlantic storm that wrecked her on the Brittany coast. Everyone drowned with the exception of two young officers, who struggled through the cold surf to crawl ashore waterlogged and half dead, the last remnants of the great French expedition to colonize Siam and convert Southeast Asia to Catholicism.

In 1693, almost five years later, the remaining 70 or so French prisoners still alive in Ayutthaya were eventually set free. All immediately chose to leave Siam except René Charbonneau, the former Phuket governor, who stayed on in Ayutthaya with his family until his death at the age of 80. In Phuket the new French mission in Tharua remained without any pastor until the mid-1690s when a Spanish missionary, Nicholas Toentino, was sent there by the Vicar Apostolic. He was just as unsuccessful at making any conversions as any of his predecessors.

The war that had broken out in Europe was the War of the Spanish Succession. This pitted France against England, Holland and Spain and prevented both France and England from taking any real revenge on Siam. France was too vulnerable to send any ships to the East until the war finished 14 years later. The EIC decided against any retribution against Siam because it felt it just wasn't worth the bother, as the EIC directors in London wrote to Madras in 1691, "Syam never did, nor will bring, two pence advantage to the company but many thousands of pounds loss."[409] The EIC never dropped its claim for the 67,000 pounds compensation from the Siamese crown for King Narai's jewelry. But with King Narai and Falcon now dead, the dispute faded away over time and within a decade we hear of some EIC ships starting to trade again with Siam and Phuket.

Part 5

The 18th Century

16

The "Ban Plu Luang" Period

1688 TO 1766

The new usurper king, Petracha (1688-1705) applied his rule with an iron fist. One of his first acts in addition to imprisoning all the French was to arrest 48 Royal Siamese lords who were against him. He then tortured and killed their whole families in front of them and gave their slaves and lands to his own followers. As his tyrannical pièce de résistance, he ordered that chunks of flesh be cut off these captive lords each day and cooked in different spicy sauces and the hapless lords were then forced to feed on themselves for 12 days before finally "being impaled and disemboweled."[410]

Despite such cruelty against his enemies, in the peninsula the mainly Malay rajahs and sultans used King Petracha's usurpation as yet another excuse to attempt to throw off the onerous yoke of Ayutthayan domination. The viceroy of Tenasserim province north of Phuket was the first to rebel. A French observer in India wrote that King Petracha responded by sending an army "of twelve to fifteen thousand men" against this Tenasserim army under the command of a general who "had the adroitness to win over the chief conspirators … the rest were dissipated. The guilty were punished with the usual tortures applied in that nation."[411]

The rajah of Patani then joined forces in rebellion with the viceroy of Ligor and his naksat lords, including the rajah of Phuket. King Petracha sent an army of over 10,000 men overland along with a fleet of 100 warships by sea with another 5,000 men against the mutinous south. He ordered his generals that these rebel leaders from the south of the kingdom should be "captured and cut into Fragments so small that the crows would have no difficulty swallowing their pieces."[412] This royal army forced the rebels back into Ligor city, but was unable to breach the new French-built city walls. The Annals of Nakorn tell us that Ligor was then put under siege for almost three years before it eventually fell. The Annals do not, however, record if the crows ever received their meal. The "Pongsawadan Mu'ang Thalang" – the Thai Annals of Thalang – state curtly that at this time the governor of Thalang was arrested and killed. One can only imagine in what ghastly way he might have passed his final hours.

Eventually, King Petracha enforced his tyrannical sovereignty over Siam so ruthlessly that relative stability was restored in the kingdom and he established a new dynasty which is now known as the Ban Plu Luang Dynasty. This dynasty lasted almost 80 years – from the Revolution of 1688 until the Burmese destruction of Ayutthaya in 1766. This Ban Plu Luang era is now considered as Ayutthaya's golden era – a time of high culture, art and architecture. Ayutthaya's power was strengthened in the peninsula by Petracha's Siamese successors and their viceroys in Ligor, the holders of which post became known in this period as "the second king of Siam."

Phuket in the Ban Plu Luang Period

According to foreign accounts, during the early 18th century Phuket remained a remote, unruly and lawless place plagued by piracy. However, the Thai Annals of Thalang, written over a hundred years later in 1840, paint a much more rose-colored picture. They state that two large interrelated local families ruled "harmoniously" in Phuket during this period. One was the family of Ban Takkien village and the other was from Ban Don village. The Annals tell us: "Of the noblemen of Thalang … perfect harmony reigned between the two families of Bandon and Ban Takkien, both acquired distinction and their descendants ruled the territory in succession."[413] The people of Ban Lippon village, the third main village on Phuket, were clearly not so happy about this cozy relationship. The Annals tell us that they revolted and their leader, a local nobleman called Chom Jay Surindr, "mischievously plotted setting up as supreme chief." Fighting ensued between these Thalang villages and "a warrant was issued from the capital to arrest and execute Jay Surindr and his henchmen." The viceroy of Ligor sent his troops to assist his kinsman, the governor of Ban Takkien village, "who killed off the Ban Liphon leaders of the revolt … thus the race of good men [in that village] came to an end."[414]

King Petracha and his successors were more feudal and anti-trade than King Narai had been. Therefore Siam and Phuket became much more closed to the outside world during the early 18th century Ban Plu Luang era. All trade was taken over by the kings and had to go through their agents, making them more monopolistic, corrupt and difficult than before. Pierre Poivre, a Frenchman who came to Mergui in 1745, noted that:

> "The trade of Siam is not considerable, the king who is the sole trader in his domain causes so many difficulties for and injustices to foreigners who go there to trade that he has discouraged most, except the Moslems, Chinese and Dutch … The French, English and Portuguese came to Siam in former times [to trade] but these nations … were discouraged by trading that they could not do honourably and without being exposed to constantly renewed injustices."[415]

The French, British and Dutch East India companies, having all had their fingers burnt in their often-unprofitable trade in the small, lawless Siamese west-coast ports, began to leave trade there mainly to their independent private merchants – "freeburgers", as the Dutch, or "country traders" or "interlopers" as the British called them. The Danish and Swedish East India companies however, which had traded with Siam since 1621, increased their trade with Siam and Phuket in this period, as did the Chinese.

The Chinese and Tin

In the early 18th century, a rise in demand for tin in China drove up the price in Canton. Tin bought in the peninsula could be sold at a 200 percent profit in China, so more and more of these ever-entrepreneurial Chinese, drawn like moths to a flame, began to appear in the southwest Siamese ports to trade for tin. As this independent trade was still illegal in China, these hardy individual Chinese traders received no support or protection from China against piracy or exploitation. As a result, they often suffered greatly, as Sir Francis Light, the founder of British Penang, later said of them: "The Chinese traders are oppressed by the petty rajahs and the Dutch with whom they trade, are plundered by pirates and unsupported by their own government which prohibits all trade to the peninsula."[416]

16.1. An Chinese tin smelter still using the primitive and wasteful charcoal-fired method.

Some of these Chinese began settling to trade or to open small open-pit tin mining or smelting operations, usually in collaboration with the local rajah or strongman. As late as 1764, when an increase in the tin supply from the peninsula meant the tin price had halved in Canton, Captain Jackson of the British frigate Pitt, who also traded tin between Phuket and China, wrote, "Tin is always fixed at 30-33 dollars per bahar but the less you contract with the king [through his monopoly agent], the better, as what you can buy off the private local people will cost you no more than 20-24 dollars per bahar, which, even at the very low price tin is now at in Canton, is near 100% profit."[417]

The Chinese already controlled much of the trade in the capital Ayutthaya and in Siam's east-coast ports. During this Ban Plu Luang era they also began to compete with the traditional Indian and Muslim control over trade in the west-coast ports. Pierre Poivre, the Frenchman in Siam in 1745, noted, "Among the Chinese who go to Siam many have become familiar with the country and have now established themselves there. Today they form a considerable community. They are the ones who carry on the retail trade throughout the kingdom where they have spread out and established themselves … These foreigners now number more than 6,000 in Siam … which increases every year."[418]

Some of these Chinese traders and miners in southwest Siam applied to the local lords to purchase positions as tax farmers, or in some cases as regional governors. This usually entailed them agreeing to pay the local rajahs, the viceroy in Ligor or the king (or all of them) a fixed fee and they then had the right, with the leader's support, to tax and exploit the locals as much as they could to make a profit on their investment outlay and efforts.

Captain Alexander Hamilton, a Scottish "Interloper"

Alexander Hamilton was one of the few independent British sea captains who visited Phuket and Siam during this period. He was a Scotsman who traded on his own account around the Bay of Bengal between 1700 and 1719. He wrote of Phuket (then called Junk Ceylon) during the early 18th century:

> "The north end of Junk Ceylon lies within a mile of the continent ... between the island and the continent is a good harbour for shipping in the south west monsoons [Tharua] and on the west side of the island Puton [Patong] bay is a safe harbour in the north east winds. The island affords good masts for shipping and an abundance of tin, but few people to dig for it by reason of the aforementioned outlaws and the governors, being generally Chinese who buy their places at the court of Siam and to reimburse themselves, oppress the people in so much that riches would be but a plague to them and their poverty makes them live an easy, indolent life. Yet the villages ... drive a small trade with shipping that comes from the Coromandel coast and Bengal but both the buyer and seller trade by retail so that a ship's cargo is a long time in selling and the product of the country is as long in purchasing."[419]

An Adventure in the Nicobar Islands

On his first visit to Phuket, in Tharua port, Hamilton encountered some stranded British sailors whose ship had foundered on the Nicobar Islands, as he explains:

> "One Captain Owen lost his ship in 1708 but the men reached an uninhabited island in the Nicobar group ... finding no inhabitants, they made fires in the night and the next day there came five or six canoes from Ning and Goury, about four leagues to the westward of their desert island. Very courteously they carried the shipwrecked men to their islands with what little things they had saved of their apparel and other necessities ... The captain had saved a broken knife about four inches long in the blade and having laid it carelessly by, one of the natives made bold to take it. The captain, seeing his knife in the poor native's hands took it from him and bestowed some kicks and blows on him for his ill manners which was very ill taken ...The shipwrecked men could observe contentions arising between those who were their benefactors in bringing them to their island and others who were not concerned in it ... The next day, as the captain was sitting under a tree at dinner ... a dozen natives saluted him on every side with a shower of darts made of heavy wood with the points hardened in the fire

so he expired in a moment ... The benefactors kept guard about [the Englishmen's] house till the next day and then presented them with two canoes ... put some water in pots, some coconuts and dried fish and pointed to them to be immediately gone, which they did, being sixteen in company. They divided equally and steered their course for Junkceylon, but on the way one of the boats lost her outrigger and drowned all her crew. The rest arrived safe and I carried them afterwards to Masilputlam."[420]

These fellows were luckier than another Scottish "interloper" friend of Hamilton's, Captain John Fergusson, a man listed in the Madras records as a "seafaring man, not a constant inhabitant of Madras." Hamilton tells us that while sailing from Madras to Malacca and passing the Andaman Islands, Fergusson was "driven by a strong current onto some rocks and the ship was lost, the other ship with him was driven through a channel ... and was not able to assist the shipwrecked men. Fergusson nor any of his people were ever more heard of again, which gave to conjecture that they were all devoured by those savage cannibals."[421]

16.2 A fisherman on the Nicobar Islands.

The Seizing of a British Frigate off Tharua

Hamilton tells us of the lawlessness in these remote peninsular west-coast ports. "The country produces more tin than any in India, but the inhabitants are so treacherous, faithless and bloody that no European nation can keep factories there with safety."[422] In 1756, for example, a row broke out in Phuket over a tin trade between the captain of a visiting EIC trade ship, the Northumberland, and the governor of Thalang. The Northumberland, a small, lightly armed trade frigate, was moored by the river mouth in Tharua roads (near the entrance to the Boat Lagoon Marina today). One night the ship was stealthily approached by some armed locals, who boarded it, killed all the sleeping crew and seized the ship and its cargo. Despite their protests, the EIC, like the Dutch before them, received no satisfaction because the rajah of Thalang blamed the sultan of Keddah for the incident. The sultan of Keddah blamed the people of Phuket and each in turn adamantly denied the other's accusations.

Pierre Poivre

Pierre Poivre, a 27-year-old French horticulturist, visited the Siamese west coast in 1745. He was later to become the governor of the French colony of Isle de France (Mauritius). Poivre had been returning from China on a fleet of three French trade ships during another Franco-British war, when his ship was attacked and captured in the Malacca Straits by a British warship. During the encounter a cannonball smashed Pierre Poivre's wrist and a surgeon on the British ship had to amputate part of his right arm to prevent the spread of gangrene. The captured Frenchmen were imprisoned in Dutch Batavia (Jakarta) for several months until 60 of them, including Poivre, were set free and given another captured French ship, unarmed and in poor condition. They wanted to sail to Pondicherry, but

16.3 Pierre Poivre, the later governor of Mauritius, who left an acerbic account of the corruption, greed and abuse in Siam's western ports in 1745.

it was August and the wrong season to sail west against the monsoons, so they sailed up the peninsular west coast to Mergui, a port which was still occasionally visited by French ships.

On their way north, having just passed Phuket, their ship was again attacked, this time by a pirate ship sailed by "twenty four deserter villains of English nationality."[423] These renegade English pirates stole all of the Frenchmen's weapons, money and other belongings, but let them go. Poivre and his destitute crew eventually reached Mergui, where they spent several months waiting for the monsoon winds to turn. Poivre gives us a snapshot of life in a Siamese west-coast port in this period.

> "It is inhabited by Burmese, Muslims, Portuguese mestizos, Siamese and Chinese … these poor wretches are extremely harassed by the Siamese officials who steal from them with impunity … The inhabitants are extremely poor, since they eat little and wear hardly anything at all, they need little to live … there is nothing so false as what has been published in accounts … touching upon the excess of riches of Siam … a traveller who knows Siam cannot prevent himself from laughing when reading our accounts about the efforts of France in seeking the friendship of this East Indies king."[424]

Poivre then relates with some bitterness that,

> "We found a Muslim governor there who treated us well … the same was not true of the (Siamese) viceroy of the province. He issued orders to all the inhabit-

ants forbidding them to supply us with any food. The reason derived from our not having any substantial presents to offer him as having been pillaged by the English we scarcely had any clothes to wear … as we were seized with hunger … we gathered together some handkerchiefs, two or three old mirrors, a gun (which was our sole weapon on board) together with a little areca nut … After a long dispute with the officers of the viceroy, who were not at all satisfied with the smallness of its value, it was finally accepted … we were not let off the hook by this present alone, it was also necessary to give one to the rajah, to the second Phra Klang, whom the king had sent to this province to examine the conduct of the viceroy. There was no one down to the scribes of the officials who did not also want to receive a present … is there anything in the world so crude and shameful as this greed … to demand a present from foreigners in order for them just to obtain permission to buy food."[425]

With little money, the Frenchmen were forced to sell off everything from their ship to buy food to survive, "and to do that on a retail basis as there are no traders in the country rich enough to take on, in a single purchase, a considerable part of the goods … The trade of Siam is not considerable …Tin alone is a subject that is worthy of attention … there is a profit in taking it to the Coromandel Coast [he estimated about 150 percent-200 percent]. The tin found in Mergui comes from Tavoy…Additional tin comes from the island of Janselon [Phuket] which can supply 300 bars of it."[426]

Poivre felt the only other trade products worth buying were elephants of which "ordinary vessels can carry 14 or 15 of them, the king sells them for 1,600 livres and the Muslims resell them (in India) at 6,000 to 6,500 livres (or swapped them for horses to resell in Siam) but one runs the risk of loosing everything because if the crossing to the Coromandel coast is a bit long all of them die. The Mughal lords … train them for war."[427] Thirty years later, in 1773, James Scott, another independent Scottish trader who lived for several years in Phuket, wrote of obtaining similar fat mark-ups of over 1,000 percent by buying elephants in Phuket to sell in India: "the island price was 50 dollars, the export price (in India) from 4-800 dollars."[428] The elephant loading jetty in Phuket was in Pak Pra where we are told in an 1832 report on Phuket that "planks were laid out for the transit of the animals" from shore to ship or back and that this elephant loading jetty was frequented by "vessels from the Coromandel coast."[429]

Poivre and the stranded Frenchmen in Mergui tried to earn the local viceroy's favor by volunteering to join the crew of a vessel of the Siamese king based in Mergui to hunt down the same English renegade pirate ship that had attacked them and was still reportedly prowling the nearby coasts, attacking shipping and towns. Poivre notes that this royal Siamese warship was normally manned by "a mixed company of lascars, Siamese and local Portuguese – all of them incapable and useless."[430] The Frenchmen joined the ship and searched for eight days without locating the English pirates. Poivre felt the ship was probably only sent out by the local viceroy "in order to make his master the king believe he was zealous in his service … and [for the viceroy] to have the opportunity, under the fine pretext of service to the king, to demand exorbitant contributions from the local people for his personal gain and to then show to the king imaginary expenses which he was certain of getting repaid as though they were real."[431]

Captain Thomas Forrest

Captain Thomas Forrest was another Scottish "interloper" captain who traded in Phuket on behalf of a private syndicate of Calcutta merchants. A fluent Malay speaker, he visited Phuket in 1784 and mentions that the people there "resemble in feature the Malays and were familiar with the Malay language."[432] He also grumbled about the greedy local rajah and the king's trade agents: "as soon as goods are landed, the king's merchant sells them for an advance of 25 per cent [which Forrest thought was] a selfish policy which starves the subjects … and … encourages smuggling … I have been told the export of tin from the island is about 500 tons yearly, formerly it was much more."[433]

Forrest noted that the local tin miners had to give 12 percent of their tin to the Chinese tin smelter in Tharua "who farms this privilege from the governor." Dr. Koening, a Danish botanist who visited Phuket the year before Forrest (in 1783), recorded that the people actually had to give 20 percent of their tin to the smelter. Forrest then tells us that before this tin or any other export could be sold, the rajah or king's merchant then took a further 25 percent cut. Forrest disagreed with such heavy tax, "as in consequence, the trade of the place has dwindled much." He also lamented a recent Siamese law forbidding the use of opium, which hampered his business in Phuket. "The vend for [trade in] opium was thirty or forty years ago very great as this was a free port. The opium came from Bengal generally in English country ships and was bought up by Malay and Bugis prows, who after having sold a mixed cargo by retail to the natives in exchange for tin, then exchanged their tin with the Bengal vessels for opium, which they carried to other Malay lands."[434]

A Colorful Court Case

Captain Alexander Hamilton also leaves us a most colorful account of the working of a Siamese law court of the time. He first tells us the official punishment for rebellion in Siam at the time. "Criminals are ripped up alive and their guts and entrails taken out and their carcasses then woven up in a twig-case and tied up to a stake for vultures and other voracious fowls or dogs to feed on. I saw eighteen one morning going to be so executed for mutiny."[435] Whereas, for those found guilty of treasonable talk:

> "An elephant is the executioner. The condemned person is made fast to a stake driven into the ground for the purpose, the elephant is brought to view him and goes twice or thrice round him. When the elephant keeper speaks to the monstrous executioner, he twines his trunk round the person and stake and pulling the stake from the ground with great violence, tosses the man and the stake into the air and in coming down receives him on his teeth [tusks] and shaking him off again puts one foot on the carcass and squeezes it flat."[436]

In 1718 while visiting Ayutthaya, Hamilton found himself accused of treason and facing a Siamese court. If it did not go well, he knew he would also end up facing a "Pachyderm executioner".

Although the EIC had not reopened a factory since its spat with Siam in the 1680s, it had appointed a commercial representative in Siam, an Englishman, Mr. Collet. Hamilton tells us Collet had an assistant, "a Persian by birth who had come to Siam with his father when very young, and had remained about forty years in Siam." This Persian held the Siamese title of Okya Sennarat and was probably part of the Bunnang family. Mr. Collet and Okya Sennarat did not like non-EIC "interlopers" trading in Siam and he claims they frequently obstructed the EIC's ability to trade freely. Hamilton disparagingly called Okya Sennarat a "remora" (a smaller fish which attaches itself to sharks and feeds off the shark's debris) and said of him, "He was as complete a rascal as Collet could have found for his villainous purposes, for by false information to the king he had brought many honest men into trouble and some treasure into the king's coffers ...

16.4 An execution by elephant.

This Persian and I were discoursing one day of my affairs in the Hindustan language which is the established language spoken in the Moguls' large dominions [in India]."[437]

Having been refused the right to trade, Hamilton stated he had a mind to see the king and offered Okya Sennarat 1,000 dollars "if he could find means to introduce me. He answered that 'the English had not good manners enough to be admitted into the presence of so great a king and therefore I ought not to expect to appear before him' ... About a week after, I had a summons to appear before a tribunal to answer an indictment of speaking treason of the king."[438]

Hamilton was most surprised and understandably more than a tad apprehensive about maybe being found guilty. He then discovered that it was the Persian Okya Sennarat himself who had brought the indictment. However, as Captain Hamilton explains:

> "I knew myself innocent and appeared at the time appointed ... the court was held in a large square oblong hall open on all sides. About nine the judge came with some thousands of attendants and as he passed by me to take his place he viewed me very narrowly, as I did him with much attention. He was a man of middle stature about fifty years of age of a pleasant but grave countenance and had a quick sparkling eye. He spoke to my interpreter and bid me have a care of my tongue lest I should prejudice myself in answering intricate questions. I thanked him for his admonition ... he then ordered my indictment to be read. ... My impeachment was grounded only on my saying that 'the king had been imposed upon' and by the by, I found that saying the king of Siam was capable of being imposed on is

rank treason … Had I been cast in my process my head would be a sacrifice to my adversaries' resentment and my ship and cargo [would go] to the much injured king and all my ship's company would become the king's slaves …

"The judge chose out of the assembly two procurators for each of us … the judge put Okya Sennarat to prove what I was accused of and he produced two of his servants, who had stood at some distance when we were discoursing of my affairs. My advocates then challenged the laws of Siam for their insufficiency, for that law admits not of a servant's testimony, either for or against his master. Then he proffered to bring an undeniable witness against me, who was the only person with us when we discoursed and that was Mr. Collet. The judge then interrogated him if he had heard me say in my discourse that the king had been imposed on. He affirmed he had, on which I perceived a cloud overspread the judge's countenance and many others who had come to hear the trial seemed sorrowful … After a little pause, the judge by the interpreter, asked me what I had to say to Collet's evidence. I answered that he might be an honest man or otherwise as his interest led him. All continued mute for a little space and I broke the silence by desiring the judge to ask Collet in what language I held that discourse with Okya Sennerat, which the judge did, and was answered that he believed it was in the Hindustan language. I begged the judge to ask him if he understood that language and he did so. Collet, after some pause, answered "No," … at which the whole crowd gave an Huzza! And clapped their hands and seemed joyful. The judge reprimanded Okya Sennerat for putting him and the court to so much trouble and complimented me on my safe delivery and so departed seemingly well satisfied."[439]

17

Pirates and Slavery

1600 TO 1850

Since the very earliest written records about the Malay Peninsula the chroniclers have decried the blight of piracy around its coasts. Piracy, pillaging and slave raiding were constant daily threats to all the sailors, fishermen and coastal and riverine communities down the peninsular west coast. Even today, the Malacca Straits remains one of the last few haunts of shipping piracy. These pirates were most commonly the local Malays and Orang Laut (Sea Gypsies), for whom sea-raiding in the area was a major part of their commercial life. However people from many other nations – Europeans, Indians, Chinese and other Asians – also undertook piracy down the peninsular west coast under various guises. One renowned English pirate who operated in the Andaman Sea in the 1630s was David Jones, a mate on a corsair licensed by King Charles I to go privateering in the East "from the Cape to China." David Jones became famous for scuttling any ships he captured and people now say he is the reason the undersea world became known to mariners as "Davey Jones' locker."

A 17th Century Fight between an English Ship and Japanese Pirates

Many pirates and raiders from Japan and the Ryukyu Islands came south to raid in the Malacca Straits from the 15th to the 17th century. On December 27, 1605, the scribe on the English ship Tiger, the flagship of the fourth East India Company (EIC) fleet ever to go east, recorded an encounter with a Japanese pirate ship just southwest of Phuket. The Tiger was heading south under a fair wind, when it sighted a strange ship on the horizon. As it approached, they made out "more than eighty strange squat slant-eyed fellows on board."[440] The English dispatched a boat to investigate if their vessel was a prize worth taking. They discovered it was "a Junke of Japons." The Japanese greeted them in a friendly manner and informed them, most happily, that they were pirates and asked if they could come aboard the Tiger. Strangely, Sir Edward Michelbourne, the captain of the Tiger, agreed and, even more strangely, did not have them disarmed before letting them come aboard as was customary. The two groups started fraternizing and drinking when suddenly, on a cry from their leader, the Japanese drew their swords and attacked the English sailors on deck. John Davis, the navigator on the Tiger and a famous Armada hero and Arctic explorer, was probably the first Englishman ever killed by a Japanese. He was stabbed with "six or seven mortal wounds" and bled to death on the deck.

Captain Michelbourne acted quickly by passing out pikes to his men. The English sailors then rushed the Japanese, whose swords and knives were outreached by the

English pikes, and skewered many, "killing three or four of their leaders." They cornered 22 Japanese, who managed to escape below and locked themselves in the main cabin. None of the English wanted to go in after them, so instead, they kept guard at the door while others manhandled two demi-culverins into the narrow passage outside the cabin. They loaded the guns with bar and case shot and fired two deafening blasts right through the wooden cabin wall at point-blank range. Screams were heard and as the smoke cleared, the English sailors cautiously entered the devastated cabin with swords drawn, only to find debris, corpses and shredded body parts and blood littering the cabin walls and floor. The case shot, we are told, had "violently marred them with boards and splinters … their legs arms and bodies were so torne, it was strange to see how the shot had massacred them."[441]

The English ship then pursued the fleeing Japanese junk. Being the faster, the Tiger drew parallel and poured several broadsides into her at close range until the junk began to take on water and sank. One Japanese survivor swam to the English boat. He was hauled aboard and when asked why they had attacked, he explained in sign language that they "meant to take our ship and cut all our throats". He then requested to "be cut in pieces."[442] Instead, the English elected to give him a slower death by hanging him by the neck from the yardarm on a thin rope. But after he had been dangling for just a short while, the rope broke and he dropped into the sea; as the coast was not far away, the narrator of this story felt the fortuitous fellow might even have escaped with his life.

The Salateers

The most common and most feared pirates in the region were the local Malays and Orang Laut themselves. Notably around Phuket there were the renowned "Salateers" who operated from lairs in the many offshore islands and estuaries around Phuket and frequently they inhabited the remote bays of Phuket Island itself. One of the only ways for Phuket's local agriculturalists and tin miners to avoid their depredations was simply not to live anywhere near the coast. The British Captain Thomas Forrest in the 18th century wrote that Phuket's residents "keep purposely the skirts of the island in a state of nature, I suppose to prevent invasion. Their vessels consist only of a few prows about the size of an Indiaman's long boat and small canoes that find their way up these creeks to the well cultivated plains abounding with rice fields in the middle of the island."[443]

Most people on Phuket lived inland, in Thalang, where it was harder for raiders to reach or surprise them. Captain Francis Light, a British trader who lived in Phuket, described the coastline north of Phuket in 1774. "The continent opposite Salang from Popra [Pak Pra] to Tacorpa [Takuapa], is very thinly inhabited by Siamese and has only five or six villages situated three or four miles from the sea shore. Between the villages and the sea is thick jungle left to prevent the Malay pirates from making incursions to their habitations."[444] Thomas Bowery, in the 17th century, explained that on Phuket "the Syamers" lived inland and the Malays on the coast because the Malays were liable to turn their hand to piracy when any opportunity arose. Lt. James Low, a Scotsman who visited

Phang Nga in 1824, tells us the same, that the Siamese and Chinese lived in the inland towns while "several hundred Malays are interspersed in the creeks about the mouth of the river as the Siamese do not let them stay near the town."[445]

Dr. Koening, the Danish botanist who visited Phuket in 1774, recounts that while traveling on his ship's longboat from Tharua Harbor to a nearby island, probably Ko Naka, where he went to do some botanizing, "My researches were soon interrupted by the arrival of seven or eight Malay prahus, whose neighbourhood is always dangerous for all Europeans ... Our ship lay in the harbour, but we had much trouble to reach it on account of the many trees floating in the water cast there by recent storms."[446]

The local rajahs in the region often worked in league with these pirates. One 19th century British administrator in Penang summed up the Malay communities on the peninsular west coast as "kings and pirates are in most of the islands near synonymous."[447] Ibn Battuta, an Arab traveler, also noted that when he visited Keddah, south of Phuket, "A number of boats [were] preparing to make piratical raids and to deal with any ships that might attempt to resist their exactions, for they impose a tribute on each passing ship."[448] In 1675, for example, Thomas Bowrey tells of an incident illustrating this collusion between the local rajahs and pirates.

> "A small Vessel belonginge to the English ... laden with very fine goods was met with the Pyrats ...They sett upon her and killed Sammuel Ware, the master and two more of his men and tooke the vessel, they sent away the other seamen in a prow bound for Achin [presumably for sale in the slave market there] and then came boldy to Quedah [Keddah] and sold the goods to Sarajah Cawn, a Chuliar [Tamil Indian] and chiefe shabandar of Queddah, ... This rogue, by reason he bought them very cheape, made no question how they came by the goods, although he saw English marks and number upon each baile."[449]

The Bugis

During the 17th and 18th centuries, piracy in the region became even more rampant with the arrival of two new groups of fierce Malay peoples – the Bugis and the Illanun. The Bugis were in many ways the Vikings of Southeast Asia, sea raiders and traders who dressed themselves for battle in chain mail and Norman-style steel helmets with protective steel nosepieces. Fiercely militaristic, they were also fine seamen who traveled out from their homeland on Sulawesi (Celebes) to raid and trade. As one 18th century British sea captain described them, "Their bearing was haughty and reserved and they seemed quite ready to be friends or foes as best suited their purpose ... In battle they were fearless ... and gave little quarter to anyone other than those whom they felt were of value as slaves."[450]

The Bugis carried off thousands of people from the peninsula to sell in the slave markets of Celebes, Sulu, Java, Aceh or other ports in the Malay Peninsula. The British Captain Francis Light, who lived in Phuket in the 18th century, said of them: "The Buggesses come from Wadjoo, a country on the south side of the island Celebes, they are totally free and independent … their prows are from 15-25 tons and carry 40-50 men, the greatest part of whom are fighters … [each year] over seventy sail of these prows visit the straits of Malacca."[451] By the later 17th century, some Bugis groups also began settling in the thinly populated, under-governed peninsular west coast and Sumatra. They preyed on shipping and raided the surrounding communities for slaves. Their commercial and navigational skills also became sought after by local leaders, as their far-flung trade connections stretched from the Spice Islands in eastern Indonesia to Bengal. Local Malay rulers started to use the Bugis instead of the Orang Laut as ships' navigators, traders and mercenary warriors. Even the Dutch East India Company (VOC) at times employed them as mercenaries and sailors.

These Bugis as well as all the other pirates also raided or frequently settled for a while on or round the coasts of Phuket. Sometimes they came in fleets of up to 30 war prows containing over 1,000 fearsome, iron-helmeted, chain-mailed raiders. This was usually a much stronger force than the governor or people of Phuket could raise; therefore in the face of such raiders the locals' only real defense was vigilance and flight into the jungled hills or across to the mainland until the raiders moved on.

The Illanun

The Bugis were followed in the 18th century by an even more menacing group of pirate raiders from the Sulu Sea region – the Illanun. Unlike the Bugis, the Illanun did little trade, concentrating almost exclusively on piracy and slave raiding, sometimes going on raiding tours that lasted as long as five years and taking their unfortunate prisoners from the peninsula back to the Moluccas or Borneo. The Scotsman James Brooke, who later became the white rajah of Sarawak and fought against these Illanun in the 19th century, leaves us this description of an Illanun raiding party of 18 prows.

"The Illanuns are fine athletic men with a strong resemblance in appearance to the Bugis … all these pirates are addicted to the excessive use of opium, but the effects of it are by no means so deleterious or so strongly marked as has been represented and it must likewise be remembered that they are in other respects dissolute and debauched … they lead a wandering piratical life. …The smallest of the boats carried 30 men, the largest (and they are mostly large) upwards of a hundred, … these large prahus are too heavy to pull well, though they carry thirty, forty or fifty oars. Their armaments are one or two six-pounders in the bow, one four-pounder stern chaser and a number of swivels, besides musketry, spears and swords … the boat is fortified with strong planks … the women and children are crammed down below, where the unhappy prisoners are likewise stowed away during an action. They are indifferent to blood, fond of plunder, but fondest of slaves. They despise trade … and look upon this [piracy] as their calling and the noblest occupation of chiefs and freemen. Their swords they show with boasts as having belonged to their ancestors who were pirates renowned and terrible … but still deem the wielding of it the highest of earthly existences. That it [piracy] is in reality the most accursed, there can be no doubt, for its chief support are slaves they capture on all the different coasts. If they attack an island all the women and children and as many of the young men as they require, are carried off ... and when they have a full cargo they quit that coast or region and visit another in order to dispose of their human spoil to the best advantage ... the devastation and misery they inflict on the whole Malay archipelago is well known."[452]

In 1789 a large force of Illanun pirates, under a leader called Syak Ali, captured the city of Songkla and he then sent his men inland to prey on the trans-peninsular crossing traffic, closing down many trade routes for several years. When these pirates eventually left Songkla after some years, we are told they "carried off a large number of people and two Chinese junks."[453]

In 1791 the sultan of Keddah, who wanted the British out of Penang, offered 20,000 Spanish dollars to a large squadron of Illanun to attack Penang at night and murder all the British on the island. They appeared in Keddah waters with 18 prows with heavy artillery – six and 12-pounders – and 30 other ships with over 1,000 men. The plan, however, fell through, as the British had been tipped off and had been able to ready their defenses.

17.1 An Illanun pirate.

The Siamese, Malay and Indian trading ships of the west coast ports, usually without any decent cannon and manned by 20 or so crew or fewer, were sitting ducks. As one British sea captain explained, "Every boat they take furnishes its quota of slaves ... considerable damage to native trade takes place."[454] The hardy Illanun also attacked European ships. One 18th century British merchant captain wrote of their mode of attack. "Their principal plan is boarding a vessel and carrying her by numbers and certainly if a merchantman fired ill, she would inevitably be taken, but with grape and canister fairly directed the slaughter would be so great that they would be glad to sheer off before they neared a vessel. This of course is supposing a calm."[455] In calm waters all merchantmen were at great risk, as the Bugis and Illanun war prows had many oars, were sometimes double-tiered and manned by slaves like Roman galleys. Attached to each raiding fleet were a number of light, fast spy boats for scouring the nearby seas in search of prizes, or capable of rapidly approaching a becalmed ship from the stern. The stern was usually covered at best by only by a small swivel gun and by getting under it and jamming the ship's rudder they could disable the vessel. They could then attempt a mass boarding at their will later.

17.2 Fast Illanun pirate boats driven by oars could outrun most foreign sailing ships in light winds: note the bow cannon.

The Lizzie Webber: An Heroic Defense against Malay Pirates

We are left one epic account of just such a calm weather attack by an Illanun pirate squadron against a lone British ship in 1863. The ship was the Singapore-based coastal trading brig, the Lizzie Webber; she carried 12 six-pounder cannon for her defense and was captained by John Ross Northwood assisted by the chief officer Mr. Simpson and a local Malay crew. On one of his trading trips to Borneo, Captain Northwood had taken his English wife and four-year-old son with him on the ship. In Borneo he loaded passengers and, amongst other cargo, a large box of gold and silver coins from some local merchants to take back to bank for them in Singapore. Word of this valuable cargo must have got out, as one day in port a Malay "trader" came aboard the Lizzie Webber, but "never came down to business"; instead he seemed suspiciously curious about the ship's cannons. Kassim, Northwood's faithful Malay first mate, later heard that the visitor had actually been Si Rahman, a renowned Illanun pirate chief.

The Lizzie Webber set sail that evening but by the next morning she found herself becalmed in a listless sea near Labuan Island. Then eight Illanun war prows were spotted approaching in the far distance, their oars pacing swiftly through the bright morning sea.

> "He [Captain Northwood] knew he had no chance of running from the pirates so he must fight his ship … the men beat to quarters, the cannons were run out and rifles and cutlasses served to the crew. Captain Northwood hurried below to find his wife. She knew as well as he the fate that would await her if the pirates carried the ship, he handed her a revolver telling her to shoot both her son and herself if the pirates carried the ship … The pirate squadron swept down on their prey, each prahu pulling some forty oars or more. The pirates were several hundred strong and had they gone straight to work, the fate of the Lizzie Webber would have been settled within half an hour. That fortunately is not the native way of doing things … instead the leading pirate prahu came within easy hailing distance."[456]

Amidship on the lead prahu was a raised platform. Si Rahman, the pirate chief, stood up on it, resplendent in a scarlet coat. He shouted across that they needed some tobacco and asked if they could come aboard. Captain Northwood shouted back that he knew pirates when he saw them and, if the prahus did not "sheer off", he would open fire. Si Rahman advised Northwood to give up his ship without a useless fight, as he himself was "kabal" (one who had undergone magic) and wore a magic charm which rendered him invulnerable to shot or steel. At this point, without being ordered, Northwood's Malay first mate, Kassim, fired his gun at Si Rahman.

"And thus commenced the action…The crew kept up a rapid fire which greatly disconcerted the pirates. … her twelve pounders were each loaded with round shot and a canvas bag of bullets rammed home on top of it which made a very effective charge at short range … The pirates who mounted a number of light guns, replied vigorously … The roar of the guns and the constant rattle of the musketry made a terrific din, above which rose the yell of the pirates."

"Within a few minutes after the action commenced, Mr. Simpson (the chief officer) was carried below badly wounded with three native sailors in the same condition. In the absence of any surgeon, Mrs. Northwood had to attend as best she could to the wounded. Poor Lady! She had trouble enough on her hands. Her son Johnnie, who so far from being frightened by the din of battle, made frantic attempts to escape to the upper deck to see what "papa was doing". He had finally to be carried off by his mother kicking and screaming with rage, to be locked up in a spare cabin."

"In the meantime Captain Northwood fought his ship for all he was worth. His great object was to bring down Si Rahman, who exhibited the most extraordinary daring – possessed as he was of the idea that his magic charm would preserve him from all danger. He stood on his platform, like a scarlet demon, directing the attack and constantly exposed to a rattling fire and somehow nothing could touch him … scores of shots were directed at Si Rahman without hurting [him]. The man was perfectly aware of the unavailing attempts to bring him down and openly rejoiced in the strength of his magic charm. It really seemed as if the charm was working to some purpose. Kassim especially tried the united effects of roundshot and bags of bullets on his hated enemy, but while they took full effect on the crew of his prahu, nothing could touch the scarlet Si Rahman."

"After three hours of desperate struggle there came a lull. At a signal from Si Rahman all firing from the pirate squadron ceased and they pulled away from the Lizzie Webber … Captain Northwood went round his decks and saw that the heated 12 pounders were sponged out and ready for further service and the small arms reloaded. Barely had he completed his round when the pirate vessels swept down upon them again under the full pressure of their swift oars. Si Rahman's plan of battle was now evident … what he should have done some hours before, that is throwing his hundreds of men on the deck of the Lizzie Webber and leave cold steel to do the rest. The eight prahus made a dash for the starboard side of the brig, leaving her port battery idle. Northwood saw the coming on-rush with the blackest despair. How could he hope with his scanty crew to withstand the onslaught of some hundreds of desperate Illanun pirates? He had half a mind to rush below and after dispatching his wife and child to blow up the magazine … he watched the shots from his starboard guns flying harmlessly over the approaching prahus which lay so low in the water that it was impossible to depress the muzzles of the cannon sufficiently to hit them. Si Rahman's own prahu, by far the best manned, drew rapidly ahead of the rest and was almost alongside the brig when Northwood saw Kassim about to fire his twelve pounder again … Northwood shouted "don't fire over the prahu", but Kassim showed that he had driven the wedge beneath the cannon's breech as far as it would go and could depress the gun muzzle no further. Looking round with hunted desperation in his eyes, Northwood saw a mast spar lying on the deck. Bending down he put forth the whole of his great strength and lifting the gun carriage bodily, he got Kassim and another sailor to roll the spar beneath it. Then taking a hasty look along the sights, he fired. … dire yells arose from the pirate prahu while shouts of joy rang from the deck of the Lizzie Webber. What Northwood saw when he looked over his bulwarks was a pile of wreckage in place of the famous platform on which Si Rahman had so recklessly displayed his scarlet coat. As for Si Rahman himself, a scarlet patch in the water swirling around the sinking prahu sufficiently accounted for the fiery Illanun Chief. His magic charm had failed him at the critical moment."

"The other pirate prahus attempted to rescue as many as they could from the sinking boat under a hot fire from the Lizzie Webber and then pulled away … A gentle breeze had sprang up and the Lizzie Webber was beginning to get some way on her. Captain Northwood availed himself of this respite to put his ship in fighting trim yet again. The guns and small arms were reloaded and the tired crew given their first meal during this terrible day. The pirate fleet still hung around the brig, their boats could pull much faster than she could sail and it was clear that the foe was only waiting for darkness to deliver his final attack. It was a grim and hopeless prospect, but the breeze was freshening all the time."

"As the Lizzie Webber began to slip though the water, the pirates, thirsting for revenge and plunder, closed on her again under the rays of the evening sun. Once more the firing raged hotly on both sides … Then Mrs. Northwood appeared to tell her husband there were only six more kegs of gunpowder … This would just allow her guns to fire one more round apiece, with some to spare for the muskets … suddenly he [Northwood] altered his tactics … down went his helm, he spilled his sails and before the pirates could comprehend his move, he was sailing through their fleet firing his last broadsides. One of the prahus was caught at a disadvantage and springing to the wheel Northwood altered the Lizzie Webber's course again … next minute there was tremendous crash as the keel of the brig rode over the wreck of the prahu. Some of the pirates were shot as they swam away, others with the usual agility of natives managed to climb up the ship's chains in an endeavor to reach the deck but were promptly cut down. Then came the sudden darkness of the tropics and in its welcome obscurity the Lizzie Webber's sails filled and bore her to safety."[457]

The author of this stirring passage was John Dillon Ross, the four-year-old "Johnny" in this story. He followed in his father's footsteps in becoming a Singapore trader captain and later made several trips up the peninsular west coast carrying coolies, mining equipment and other such cargo to Phuket, Penang and some other local ports.

17.3 A Sketch of a pirate prahu attacking the "Lizzie Webber".

The Sorry Lot of Captives and Slaves

Professor James Warren, who specializes in Southeast Asian history, has conducted extensive historical research on the first-hand testimonies of captives and slaves taken by Illanun and other Malay sea raiders and pirates.

One Siamese woman captured in the central peninsula in 1838 and taken back to Indonesia testified that "about half a month since, myself, eight other women and a man named Boy Kay How were collecting shellfish on the beach when a number of pirates landed from three sampans and seized the whole party. Boy Kay How was killed by the pirates and the females were put on board six large prahus."[458]

Women and children were more highly valued as slaves than men, as they were usually less troublesome. Women were useful for agriculture, conducting business and for sex and breeding more slaves. Children, whether captured or bred, could be also trained by their new owners. One child captive in 1834 recalled, "Myself, my father … and my younger brother … went out to fish in a small boat and when a considerable distance from the land we were attacked and captured by four Illanun pirates. My father was shot through the head and killed."[459] Another child captive said in testimony after escaping years later, "sometime ago … myself and my father named Labby, were fishing close to the beach when we were seized … my father resisted and attempted to escape and in the struggle he was killed by the pirates."[460]

Any sea traveler, trader, fishermen, or anyone cutting mangrove wood, making salt, collecting pearls or simply living too near a river mouth or the coast was constantly at risk. Dr. Koening, the Austrian botanist who visited Phuket in 1792, tells us about the large island of Ko Yao Yai (Pulau Panjung in Malay) off the east of Phuket remaining deserted for years for just this reason. "The tin in Pullau Panjung had formerly been collected … as they do here. There was enough tin there to furnish many people with an occupation, but Malay pirate ships had often killed and robbed the people so that in the end they had all fled."[461]

To attack villages and river mouth settlements, the pirates would bring their main pra-hus nearby but keep them well out of sight. They would then board their smaller raiding canoes that could fit 20 men, usually at night, and hide in the mangroves nearby. At dawn or at night, they would approach a village, with most of the men lying on the floor of the canoe so that from a distance it appeared to carry only one or two fishermen, until it was too late to flee. "When the pirates made a raid, those offering resistance would be killed. Women and children were taken in preference to men. They would be knocked down by a cudgel. If they resisted strenuously they were killed."[462]

Captives would be bound and taken back to the bigger prahus of the main fleet. Friends, acquaintances and relatives would be separated to lessen the chance of resistance. They would be stripped naked and bound with rattan, often by a ring tight round their neck, and secured to the ship. One captive later explained, "On reaching the piratical prahu (prow) … my hands were put into a ring or stocks and a rattan collar around my neck."[463] C.Z. Peters, a Dutchman taken by Illanun pirates in the 19th century, says he was knocked out while being captured. "When I came to, I found that I was stripped naked and bound in a Prahu … tied up by the hands, feet and neck. The rope by which captives are tied by the neck is taken off in the daytime. At six o'clock in the evening, whether they are inclined to sleep or not, captives must lie down and are bound by the feet hands and neck to the deck of the prahu."[464]

Captives were sometimes tied up for weeks, or months on longer journeys. In order to stop them trying to jump overboard and swim to shore, the more robust ones were deliberately caned with heavy bamboo on the elbows and knees and on the leg and arm muscles so they could hardly use them. Also, "to deter captives from leaping overboard … the pirates had a supply of long barbed bamboo spears ready to throw on an instant's notice … captives hit by one were easily recaptured."[465]

Ebenezer Edwards, a British sailor also taken by Illanun raiders, wrote: "Our food con-sisted of only a little rice and water and the rice was generally spoiled and the rations so small that we never had enough."[466] Another captive said the worst thing was the thirst and pain caused by the salt water they were forced to drink. "They never gave us fresh, but mixed three parts of fresh water with four of salt."[467] Another freed captive reported: "Water and rice were given us very sparingly. Some died from hunger, some from being handcuffed, some from grief. They untied me after about a month. If prisoners were so sick they could not pull an oar they were thrown overboard."[468]

One daring British spy, Admiral Hunter, who accompanied the Illanun on a cruise dis-guised as a Malay, noted that on his 95 foot-long war prow, the double-tier banks of 90 oars "were rowed by captives who were treated with great cruelty. They were fed on rot-ten rice and bad water and when worn out were thrown overboard. They were forced to row for hours at a time and when they became exhausted the Illanuns kept them awake by rubbing cayenne pepper in their eyes."[469] Warren tells us that "the victims were packed together for weeks and even months on end amongst the cramped provisions… or on deck rowing with no shelter from the tropical heat and the rain squalls, … a number died on the voyages from malnutrition, hard labour rowing and fecal borne diseases."[470]

On reaching the slave markets, the prisoners would be sold. In many cases the people who had been captured were already slaves and were usually no less badly treated by their new owners. One Spanish captive lived 15 years with his master who "treated him very well." His only reason for escaping was "an unconquerable yearning to behold my native country once again."

Piracy around Phuket

By the 18th century, all trade ships and settlements in the region were potential prey and even European warships were being attacked. As one EIC report noted, "Among that long series of islands formed by the Malay Peninsula and Sumatra … the pirates now attack and take the Dutch cruisers, plunder the islands … and in great measure stop all trade. The numberless islands, shoals, rocks, creeks, rivers etc. , which are formed by the islands there give them secure retreat in case of attack and from thence they issue and appear before their prey."[471]

In 1771, the Selangor Bugis' rajah, Daeng Merwah Theyan, came from Rhiau to attack Keddah. We are told that he and his followers first landed on Phuket and reportedly occupied the island for some months as a base to mount their attack on Keddah. The Siamese navy was never usually strong enough in the southwest to control such pirates, though its ships did show up when their depredations became excessive. In 1824, for instance, the EIC emissary Lt. James Low visited Trang just after it had suffered several recent pirate attacks. He asked the local headman where the pirates who infest that coast generally lived.

"He said that their chief resorts were about the Lancavy [Langkawi] islands and that it was conjectured they had about forty boats and that they were seldom seen all at once. He added that some months back some Siamese prows chased several of them beyond the 'Boontings' [islands near Ko Taratao] … The river Marbo [near Trang] is also a noted nest for these pirates … they generally attack small Malay boats or Siamese prows. They are afraid of the Chinese who are resolute in defending their vessels."[472]

The Chinese trading junks in the region also turned to piracy when it suited them. By the early 19th century, these Chinese junks were large – up to 200 tons – and their crews often included renegade European sailors who worked as gunners and navigators. These large junks attacked European vessels as well as local shipping. The following record, by the EIC envoy Lt. James Low, illustrates how inter-knit piracy was around Phuket in 1824. On one visit to Phang Nga town Lt. Low heard of a nest of Macao Chinese pirates there, who it seems worked for the Phang Nga governor, doubling as tin miners and farmers when not raiding:

"In the course of one evening one of my sepoys [an Indian soldier] happened to be conversing with a native of Hindustan who … had been here [Phang Nga] for a year or two. Some Siamese officers came up, seized the Hindustany and having beaten him, conveyed him to prison, observing that he was betraying the secrets of the place. This man had informed my sepoy that a piracy had been committed at the place where our brig then lay (the Phang Nga River) about twelve days previous to our arrival, by twelve Chinamen and five Malays. They had attacked a Coromandel Chulia [Tamil Indian] vessel and murdered all her crew and passengers amounting to sixty people and had afterwards plundered and burned her. He added that most of these Chinese were then still in Phang Nga … My endeavours to ascertain what credit ought to be attached to this account proved fruitless."[473]

Lt Low did not pursue the matter further as he was on more important official EIC business connected with the first Anglo-Burmese war. He also felt the locals "valued their lives too much to risk exposing him [the governor]." Lt. Low did, however, bring the subject up with the governor later, just before departing.

"The chief observed that the lad [the Indian] was silly and had been shut up until we went away to prevent his getting into scrapes. … I was apprehensive that the poor fellow would lose his head and indeed it is most probable that when conveyed away from the bazaar he was quietly dispatched. … I observed to him that pirates were in the habit of infesting the coast from Penang up to Junkceylon … and that the Siamese must be aware that it would be in their true interest to suppress them. I requested further that he prohibit all suspicious persons seeking refuge in his river and drive away any who should appear to be in league with the pirates … I impressed upon the mind of the chief that the British government [held] those who afforded an asylum to piratical vessels as equally culpable and could not but deem them public enemies."[474]

19th Century British Navy Steamships Suppress Piracy in the Region

After occupying Penang in 1785, the British described the piracy in the area as "a great and blighting curse … a very formidable and frightful system … and so evil and so extensive it can be out done by the strong hand alone."[475] British warships started patrolling the Malacca Straits and up the peninsular west coast against these pirates, but it was hard. The British frigates' "great height and towering masts made them visible long before they sighted the long low Malay galleys and sent every pirate for miles scurrying for shelter amongst the islands and swamps."[476] Also, in calm weather, the British gunships had no oars and had to be pulled by their longboats. The pirates, whose war prahus were lighter, could escape a British ship in all but the strongest winds. There are even records of pirates rowing out and attacking ships in full view of becalmed British and Dutch patrol ships.

The beginning of the end of the excessive piracy around Phuket only came in the later 1820s, after Britain won the first Burmese War and took Tenasserim, adding to its colonies in Penang, Singapore and Malacca and thereby effectively controlling most of the peninsular west coast. The British then began to take a more concerted and aggressive stand against piracy during the 1830s. They kept two ships of the line and five gunboats on full-time anti-piracy patrol in the region; these ships relentlessly harassed and destroyed the local pirate nests and vessels. The gunboat HMS Neride, for example, attacked several pirate lairs in the islands between Penang and Phuket and reported sinking more than 100 pirate war prahus.

The more colorful HMS Wolfe, which patrolled off Penang and Phuket from 1836 to 1838, inflicted heavy losses on the pirates by sailing in disguise, pretending to be a trading ship carrying tropical animals. To quote one of her officers: "Baboons flew playfully at your legs, a loathsome orangutang crawled up to shake hands … pigs, peccaries, fowls, a honey bear and a black panther made her a perfect floating menagerie."[477]

17.4 A 19th century illustration of British Royal Navy steamships pursuing Malay pirates into a river mouth.

One EIC official suggested that the pirates must be made to feel that "Piracy is like sitting on a barrel of gunpowder with a lighted match in the hand. Then, and then only, will they discontinue it, and until piracy is completely suppressed there must be no relaxation."[478] The Dutch adopted similarly aggressive tactics along the Sumatran coastline, preventing any refuge on the east of the Malacca Straits. Siam also joined the fight against piracy. In 1873, for instance, Bangkok instructed Phraya Zaiburi (the governor of Siamese Keddah), along with the governors of Phuket and Phattalung, to send a force to assist British efforts in suppressing pirates round Langkawi. [479]

What really confounded and ultimately defeated the local pirates was the arrival of steamships in the region in 1833. These ships were low in the water and traveled fast, whatever the wind. The first steamship to patrol the waters off Penang and Phuket was HMS Diana, a British Royal Navy steamer of 168 tons, which did five knots and carried two nine-pounders and a crew of 25. Her captain, Sherrard Osborne, tells of his first encounter with Illanun pirates. The pirates, never having seen a steamship, decided from her smoke that she must be a sailing ship on fire, whose masts had burned down and was therefore a prime target. They approached, anticipating an easy capture. "To their horror the Diana came up to them against the wind and then, stopping opposite each prahu, poured in her broadsides at pistol shot range. One prahu was sunk, 90 Illanuns were killed, 150 wounded and 30 taken." The other five galleys escaped in a shattered condition "and baling out apparently nothing but blood and scarce a man at the oars … three of them foundered before they reached home."[480]

After some 15 years of relentless British naval steamship pursuit and attacks on their ships and lairs, the local pirates must indeed have felt as if they were sitting on that "keg of gunpowder with a match." By the late 1850s, according to local records of the Straits Settlements and Phuket and from the logs of local captains, piracy around Phuket had become much more limited and inconsequential, but never fully disappeared.

18

The Dauntless Mr. Sin

1763 TO 1785

Ayutthaya Is Destroyed

In late November 1763 in the city of Ava in Burma, the Burmese throne was taken over by a most hawkish 27-year-old who called himself King Hsinbyushin. He had ambitions to become the "Cakkravattin" – the supreme monarch of the Buddhist world. To this end, in 1764 he crossed the Tenasserim Mountains to the east and invaded Siam. By 1767 his huge army had surrounded and besieged the thick walls of Ayutthaya. King Hsinbyushin's intention was not, as the Burmese had done in the 16th century, to capture and rule over Ayutthaya as a vassal state, but to totally destroy both the city and kingdom of Ayutthaya so that it would never trouble Burma again.

At the time, Ayutthaya was one of the biggest cities in the world and King Hsinbyushin's army besieged the great walled city for over a year. On April 7, 1767 the Burmese besiegers managed to break through the city walls and embarked on one of history's more notable orgies of destruction, theft, rape and butchery. Monseigneur Turpin the French Vicar of Siam at the time tells us that the Burmese "raped their weeping daughters before their eyes" and put so many men, women, children and priests to the sword that "The countryside as well as the temples were strewn with corpses and the river was choked with bodies of the dead, the stench of which attracted swarms of flies causing much annoyance."[481]

Almost all the art and records of Siamese culture up to that date were smashed and burnt. The Siamese King Ekatat was killed and his royal palaces, temples and most of the city was destroyed and burnt and the surrounding countryside was laid to waste. Fortunately for the Siamese, shortly after Ayutthaya fell, a Chinese army attacked Burma from the north and the Burmese had to refrain from further destruction and return in haste to defend their own capital of Ava. They took with them around 30,000 Siamese as slaves and thousands died of exhaustion and sickness on this horrific death march back to Burma. A Burmese garrison of around 3,000 troops was left near Ayutthaya to control the now destroyed and depopulated central region of Siam. Father Corre, a French priest working in Siam wrote that a year after the Burmese invasion:

> "the inhabitants who had escaped the fury of the Burmese were reduced to a state of extreme misery … they were [so] thin their bodies wasting away, they found only the leaves of trees and grass to eat …Thieves and criminals are to be found

everywhere … people cannot risk to travel without arms … The capital had become almost deserted and the retreat of tigers and savage animals."[482]

With its head smashed in and its heart ripped out, the kingdom of Ayutthaya disintegrated - just as King Hsinbyushin had intended, but new claimants to the leadership of Siam soon arose in the ensuing power vacuum. In Korat one royal heir set up court, in Phitsanulok one governor of high birth declared himself the new Siamese king and wars between competing lords and strongmen broke out all over.

In the south Phraya Palat Nu – the viceroy of Ligor, still controlled the largest swathe of the ex-kingdom of Ayutthaya which was untouched by the Burmese conquest and destruction. He declared Ligor and its vassal states, such as Phuket, as a new independent kingdom in the central peninsula, crowned himself King Musika of Ligor and set about trying to exert his control over his newly claimed kingdom of Ligor.

The Rise of Tak Sin

Another contender for the leadership of fractured Siam was a 33-year-old Sino-Thai called Sin. He had been born to a Siamese mother and a rich Teochow Chinese father – a gambling "farmer" – in Ayutthaya. As a young lad, Sin was adopted by a Thai royal minister in Ayutthaya and was given a good lordly upbringing and a temple education. At the age of 31 he was appointed governor of Tak province and was given the lordly title of Phaya Tak Sin.

When the Burmese army had invaded, Tak Sin went to Ayutthaya to help in the defense of the city and proved to be a charismatic leader. But, like many others, he soon became disillusioned with the weak and ineffectual leadership of King Ekatat and eight months into the siege, as things were beginning to look hopeless, Tak Sin gathered some 500 followers and made a daring nighttime breakout through the Burmese lines and escaped to the Southeast to Rayong, near Pattaya. There, Tak Sin called his father's wealthy Teochow Chinese trading associates to provide him with financing and arms. In return he promised them their rewards later and not to molest them. Tak Sin was still in Rayong gathering his army when Ayutthaya eventually fell.

Tak Sin soon subdued the entire southeastern seaboard region and was soon joined by his two adoptive brothers, the also Sino-Thai sons of his noble adoptive father. Duang, the older of these brothers, with the title of Lord Chakri, became Tak Sin's leading general and most trusted associate. Tak Sin then moved his army north to occupy the old fort at Bangkok to control the main Chao Praya River access to central Siam and he made his base in the village of Thonburi on the opposite bank from the fort. He mustered more followers and attacked and defeated the Burmese garrison in central Siam and crowned himself the new king of Siam in late 1767.

Over the next three years, King Tak Sin and Lord Chakri held off several large Burmese counter-attacks sent against them and also defeated the forces of the other pretenders to the throne of Siam. Then in 1770, looking south, King Tak Sin moved to reincorporate the Malay Peninsula into his new kingdom of Siam as it had been under Ayutthaya. He dispatched Lord Chakri with an army of 15,000 men against the newly proclaimed Kingdom of Ligor. The Ligor army held off this Bangkok army and forced them to retreat north to Chaiya and wait there until King Tak Sin himself came south with an even bigger army and in two battles near Chaiya he defeated King Musica and his peninsular forces and entered Ligor city and carried King Musica, (who now became plain old Palat Nu again) back to Thonburi as his prisoner. King Tak Sin was not too harsh with Palat Nu as he needed supporters and allies not more enemies. After he had proved himself loyal for six years King Tak Sin even re-appointed Phraya Palat Nu once again as viceroy of Ligor.

Phuket During the Interregnum

E.H.S. Simmons, one of the leading scholars of southern Siamese history during this period between the fall of the kingdom of Ayutthaya and the rise of the kingdom of Bangkok, writes, "The history of Thalang at this period is not well documented, especially on the Siamese side."[483] There are a few Malay accounts and some contemporary reports and letters by visiting foreign traders. The most prolific of whom was Captain Francis Light, an English trading captain who lived on Phuket just after this period. But even he seems to have been confused as to who actually controlled Phuket during the interregnum period. In one report to the EIC directors in India Captain Light stated: "Before the destruction of Siam by the Burmahs, the island belonged to the Ligore department and was governed by three officers appointed by the king of Ligore … [but during the interregnum] … The government has been changing so often it is difficult to fix on any one period for a description."[484]

The Thai Annals of Thalang, written much later, tell us that when Ayutthaya fell, a certain Chom Rang of the Ban Takkien family had ruled as the governor of Thalang. He was a relative of Phraya Palat Nu, the viceroy of Ligor and another relative, Chom Thau of Ban Don was the vice governor. These two Phuket leaders were also half-brothers from the same father.[485]

In 1767, after the fall of Ayutthaya, the sultan of Keddah took advantage of the ensuing power vacuum and sent a war fleet north which captured Trang, Phang Nga and Phuket. He laid claim to these ports and their surrounding offshore islands with their valuable crop of birds' nests. In 1768 in response, Phraya Palat Nu (now the newly self-proclaimed King Musika of Ligor), sent an army west to try to repel the Keddahnese but was unsuccessful and the sultan of Keddah was able to control Phuket for the next four years. Captain Light tells us "After the loss of Siam the Malays got possession of the island and the sultan of Keddah maintained an absolute authority treating the Siamese as his slaves."[486] Francis Light also tells us how it was eventually the Phuketians themselves, not Ligor troops, who eventually chased these Malay invaders off the island.

> "The islanders were inspired with the idea of liberating themselves, which they performed one night, at an annual assembly which the Siamese celebrated in

honour of their Prophet. One of the islanders, unarmed, fought with a Malay armed with his creese or dagger. The islander conquered in spite of the creese and beat the Malay to a mummy. The chief of the Siamese represented to his people how shameful it was for them to behold themselves in subjection by people so much weaker than themselves. As it was necessary to be secret, only seventy chosen men were assembled in the dead of night. They attacked the Malayan town with fire and sword. The Laxamana [leader of the Malays], conceiving the whole island was raised against him, fled with his people in their prows. In the morning not a Malay was to be seen, they left their guns, tin, money and merchandise to the islanders and never dared to return."[487]

The Thai Annals of Thalang recount the same, telling us that "A Malay from Keddah came to rule [Phuket] for a while, but the islanders rose in arms against the Malays, built stockades at Mai Khau and Pak Sakhu and erected dykes [probably to stop Malay war prows moving inland by river], thus becoming masters of the situation."[488] The Annals then tell us that, shortly afterwards, "Governor At was shot dead by dacoits."[489] This however may be reference to an invasion of Phuket at the time, reported in other sources, by a Selangor Bugis war fleet under Daeng Rajah Merwah Theyan from the Riau Islands. This Bugis force apparently used Phuket for a few months as a base to attack Keddah in retribution for a payment the Keddah sultan owed the Bugis rajah but had refused to pay.

Siamese Authority Re-imposed

In early 1770, the next governor of Thalang after this Bugis raid, (and its not clear who this was), appears to have taken his Thalang militia to fight alongside King Musika of Ligor against King Tak Sin's Thonburi army when he came south to re-conquer the central peninsula. After he captured Ligor, King Tak Sin appears to have sent a force west to coerce the west coast rajahs and sultans there to also submit to his hegemony. We hear indirectly that he probably deposed and punished the rebellious leader in Phuket because in 1772, Edward Monkton, an EIC employee in Madras, noted that Francis Light had written to him from Phuket saying, "The new king of Siam [Tak Sin] had lately sent a man over to depose the old governor and that they [the governor and his retainers] were shut up in a small compound and were without arms and ammunition. They were surrounded by one or two thousand Siamese troops and would very shortly fall sacrifice to them."[490]

A Malay written record preserved in the Penang State Museum also states that after King Tak Sin's Siamese troops recaptured rebellious Phuket, "the island was devastated by the Siamese soldiery who treated the inhabitants with ferocious cruelty"[491] and "large numbers of the islands population" were disposed of by "tying them together and having them trampled to death by elephants", which as we have seen, was the normal Siamese method of execution for acts of mutiny or treason.[492]

The Annals of Thalang also tell us that this rebellious Thalang governor – who is called a "khaek", indicating he was either Indian or Malay – was replaced by a new governor.

"At Thalang, Khang-Seng, a citizen from the capital, was sent out as governor."[493] Khang-Seng's name suggests he was Chinese. This would make sense as King Tak Sin installed several Chinese as governors in many of the southern peninsular ports after he re-conquered them. These gifts of governorships were probably one of King Tak Sin's ways of repaying his early Teochow benefactors, or perhaps, being half-Chinese himself maybe he felt the Chinese were more likely to be loyal to him than the local Siamese or Malays.

King Tak Sin ensured his control over the newly re-conquered southwest provinces by establishing Siamese military commissioners with power over all the local governors. The military commissioner and his troops for the Southwest were based at "Pakpra" (probably meaning Kokkloi, in Phang Nga). This would make sense, as Kokkloi was then located strategically at the crossroads between the main regional tin mining centers and ports of Thalang, Takuatung, Bangkhli, Phang Nga and Takuapa. King Tak Sin soon also forced the Sultan of Keddah to re-submit to Siamese authority and resume sending his annual Bunga Mas tribute to Him. So, by 1774, seven years after the destruction of Ayutthaya, Phuket and the other former southwestern provinces of Ayutthaya were now reincorporated into King Tak Sin's new Siamese kingdom based in Thonburi.

In 1776 when King Tak Sin re-appointed Phraya Palat Nu as Viceroy of Ligor he in turn appointed one of his previous trusted followers, Phaya Pimon, the former governor of Phattalung, to become his new governor of Thalang (Phuket). This was probably because Phaya Pimon had just recently married a Phuket woman from an influential local family – who would soon earn her fame as the elder of Phuket's two heroine sisters.

King Tak Sin Goes Mad

Through his brilliant military leadership King Tak Sin reunited broken Siam against overwhelming odds. But he had spent much of his life at war and in his early forties he developed an affliction that today would probably be labeled "Post Traumatic Stress Disorder". He became paranoid, withdrawn, eccentric and violent and was convinced that he was a "Sotopanna" (a reincarnation of Buddha) and that he could fly. He began to "pass all his time in prayer, fasting and meditation in order to be better able to fly through the air"[494] and had several priests brutally flogged, tortured and killed for insinuating that maybe he couldn't really fly.

Next he ordered that all Christians in Siam should be expelled from the country or executed. This led to most of the quite numerous Christian community of Phuket and Phang Nga moving south to Keddah and soon on to the newly established British colony on Penang Island.

We hear of one particularly nasty example of King Tak Sins violent paranoia when one jealous concubine told him that his two favorite wives, the Princesses Ubol and Chim - one of them several months pregnant with his own child, had had sex with two Portuguese palace guards who had gone into their room to catch a rat that had been eating the hem of their curtains. In a sudden fit of jealously Tak Sin ordered the two wives executed by being flogged all over until their skin was torn open, then having salt and lime put into the open wounds. When the wives failed to die from this agonizing process Tak Sin lost his temper, grabbed a sword and "cut through their breasts and hacked off their feet and hands."[495] This did the trick nicely and they soon bled to death. When Tak Sin calmed down from his rage he became so remorseful he attempted to kill himself and had to be physically restrained.

This increasingly cruel and unhinged behavior made him unpopular with both the people and his Chinese backers, as Father Descouvriers, a missionary in Siam in 1782, related:

> "For some years the king of Siam has tremendously vexed his subjects and the foreigners who come to trade in the country. Last year the Chinese, who are accustomed to trade here, were obliged to give it up almost entirely. This year the vagaries of this king, who is more than half mad, were even more frequent and cruel. He has had imprisoned, tortured and flogged, according to his strange whims, his wife, his sons, even the heir presumptive and many of his highest officials, trying to force them to admit to crimes they were innocent of … All this has made the king hated by his people and his own officers."[496]

By now, Lord Chakri, Tak Sin's adoptive brother was effectively running the army and the government. In 1785 when Lord Chakri left Thonburi with an army to campaign against Cambodia, a group of anguished Thai nobles attacked King Tak Sin's palace at night, overcame his guards and, according to the Thai Chronicles of the first reign, beheaded the king. Others, however, secretly whispered that due to their respect for Tak Sin for having reunited Siam after Ayutthaya fell, his executioners actually put a servant into a royal velvet sack in Tak Sin's place before beating the unfortunate person in the sack to death with the ritual sandalwood clubs. King Tak Sin, they continue to whisper, was secretly whisked off to a monastery in the south near Phrom Kiri in the forest near Ligor where he lived until 1825, spending his days sitting cross-legged, meditating and flying happily through the air towards the divine light of Buddha.

The New Kingdom of Bangkok

When Lord Chakri was informed of the coup against King Tak Sin, he returned immediately with his army to Thonburi where he captured and executed the rebel lords and declared himself the new king of Siam. Fearing a new Burmese attack would probably come before he could properly impose his rule, Lord Chakri immediately moved his royal court from Thonburi on the west bank of the Chao Phraya River, to the fort of Bangkok on Rattanakosin Island on the much more defensible east bank. In 1785, aged 46, Lord Chakri was formally crowned king of the new Siamese Kingdom of Bangkok. Today Lord Chakri is better known as King Rama I, the founder of the Chakri dynasty, which still reigns in Thailand today.

19

The Heroine Sisters

1780 TO 1788

"The Nine Armies War": Burma Invades

As the new king, Rama I (Lord Chakri), had expected, just after his coronation in 1785 the Burmese did again invade. This time they mustered a huge force estimated at some 144,000 men, split into nine armies. Seven armies attacked north and west Siam and for the first time, two armies attacked south into the peninsula. The first of these two southern forces, comprising some 6,000 men, crossed over the Tenasserim hills and captured Prachup Kiri Khan; they then headed south, capturing Chumporn and Chaiya before attacking Ligor. They were joined in this attack by yet another Malay rebel army from Pattani, Terengganu and Kelantan. The isolated and outnumbered viceroy of Ligor and most of the people in Ligor city fled to hide in the forests and are said to have established the town that today is Tha Sala. The Burmese and the Malay rebels captured Ligor, Phattalung and Songkla and carried off many prisoners as slaves and much loot.

The second southern force was a seaborne fleet of some 5,000 men under the Burmese General Yiwun, which sailed down the peninsular west coast from Burma. Tenasserim and the main western Siamese port of Mergui had fallen to the Burmese in 1767 when they had defeated Ayutthaya; this attack down the west coast therefore was probably aimed at stopping the flow of weapons from the west reaching Bangkok through Siam's only remaining west coast ports of Takuapa, Phuket and Trang and also at opening a supply line to the Burmese army in Ligor. This Burmese fleet captured Ranong in December 1785, then moved south and took Takuapa. In those days, Takuapa sat further up the river than the more modern Thai administrative town that exists today. It was protected by a stone fort that still stands. But the people of Takuapa had adopted their normal defensive plan and fled into the jungle. The Burmese fleet then sailed on south to attack Bangkhli and Phuket.

The two Siamese military commissioners in Kokkloi, Phraya Thammatrailok and Phraya Phiphithokhai, had only a small regular force of Siamese troops at their disposal and urgently ordered a militia draft of men from surrounding Phuket, Takuatung and Phang Nga. They decided to make a stand at Kokkloi junction where the jungle trails split, going north to Bangkhli, south to Phuket and east to Takuatung and Phang Nga. The Burmese fleet, with some 3,500 men, landed on Kokkloi beach, advanced inland and attacked the Siamese force fortified behind their bamboo stockades. The Siamese

Map 8
Exisiting and Proposed Fortifications in Northern Phuket

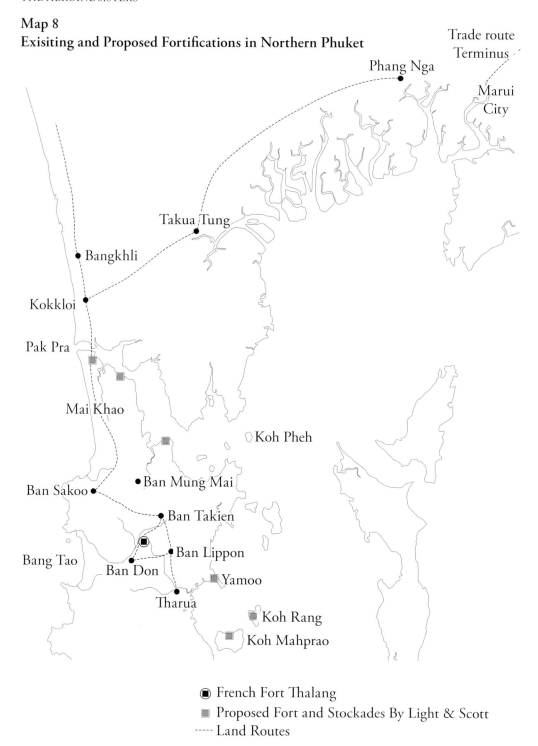

Trade route
Terminus

Phang Nga

Marui
City

Takua Tung

Bangkhli

Kokkloi

Pak Pra

Mai Khao

Koh Pheh

Ban Sakoo

● Ban Mung Mai

Ban Takien

Bang Tao

Ban Lippon

Ban Don

Yamoo

Tharua

Koh Rang

Koh Mahprao

◉ French Fort Thalang
◼ Proposed Fort and Stockades By Light & Scott
---- Land Routes

were routed and fled. Phraya Thammatrailok was probably killed in the engagement and Phraya Phiphithokhai, the remaining military commissioner, retreated with what was left of his force inland to the Kao Sok pass (near the Rajaprapat Dam) – presumably to try and hold this main pass to the east coast. This move, however, left Phuket and Phang Nga completely exposed and the Burmese victors moved south against Phuket. Captain Francis Light, the English merchant captain living in Phuket at the time, recorded that this invasion force consisted of "3,000 of the Burmar army in 80 large prows."[497] He noted this as he left Phuket on his trade ship for India. James Scott, a Scottish trader who also lived on Phuket at this time and also fled Phuket on his ship noted in his ship's log for February 8, 1786, as he sailed away, that he sighted the van of this Burmese war fleet approaching Phuket.

Lady Chan and Phaya Pimon

On Phuket the people were leaderless as the governor of the island, Phaya Pimon, had died just a month earlier and no successor had yet been appointed. His widow, Lady Chan, was about 45 years old. She had been born around 1740 to Chom Rang, head of the hereditary family of Ban Takien and a former governor of Thalang. Her mother Mah-sia, we are told, was a well-to-do Muslim from Keddah who had come to Phuket in disgust after she was widowed and her younger brother had then stolen her estate. Chom Rang and Mah-sia had five children together on Phuket – two boys and three girls – all of whom, it is presumed, were Muslims. Lady Chan was the eldest daughter and was followed by her sister Mook.

Early in her youth Lady Chan had married Mom Si Phakdi, an official from Takua-tung in Phang Nga. She had one daughter with him who had died of disease as a child in 1762. She had also had a son named Thian. When Lady Chan was around 30 years old, she divorced and then married Phaya Pimon, who at the time was governor of Chumporn. Around 1775, about ten years before the Burmese attack on Phuket, Phaya Pimon had been appointed as governor of Thalang under King Taksin's new rule. Phaya Phimon was an outsider in Phuket but his marriage to Lady Chan had brought him local credibility and connections on the island. James Scott, a Scottish resident on Phuket at the time, noted, "Pia Pimon derives his local influence from his wife's family."[498] In those days, the husband usually moved into the wife's family house on marrying. In this case Phaya Pimon resided in Ban Takien with Lady Chan's family. This in effect made Lady Chan the first lady of Phuket.

As governor, we are told, Phaya Pimon had kept a house for business in Tharua port, probably by the old governor's house that stands in ruins in the Phuket History Park in Thalang today. However the couple reportedly used Lady Chan's country house in Ban Takien as their main residence. In 1784, the year before the Burmese invasion, the visiting Scottish sea captain Thomas Forrest had visited the governor's country house "on some commercial business." He was accompanied by a fellow Scot, the Tharua resident James Scott. Captain Forrest recorded that from Tharua to Ban Takien (just east of

Thalang town today), the two men and their guards traveled "on an elephant through a path worn like a gutter … by the elephants feet and so narrow as not to be above an inch or two wider than his hoof. I wondered how the huge animal got along. About two miles from Tharua we got into open country again full of rice fields, well watered yet not swampy. In about three hours we reached the governors house which is more commodious than the one at Tarua."[499]

Capt. Forrest tells us that Lady Chan's country house was:

> "built as all their houses are, of timber and covered with palm leaves, an universal covering in Malay countries. In his garden we found limes oranges and pummel noses [pomelos]. The governor gave us a very good dinner but did not eat with us. He did not speak Malay but had a linguist who spoke Portuguese. After dinner we were entertained with three musicians who played on such string instruments as the Chinese play on at Canton. Having drank teas we took our leave."[500]

Phaya Phimon, already in his seventies, fell very ill shortly after this visit and died in December 1785, just before the Burmese invasion of the island so the Phuket locals now looked to his wife, Lady Chan, for leadership.

Lady Chan Resolves to Fight

The Thai Annals of Thalang report that Lady Chan was in Kokkloi with the Siamese military commissioners when the Burmese attacked there. Maybe she had gone there with the Thalang militia the commissioners had requested, however Phuket lore, according to the local re-enactment theatre they put on each year, says she had just been arrested by the military governors as she and her husband had been late with tax payments due to the crown.[501] After the Thai defeat in Kokkloi Lady Chan fled back to Thalang with the remnants of the Phuket militia. She later wrote to Captain Francis Light: "When the Burmese came, Phaya Thammatrailok [the commissioner] summoned me to Pak Pra. I returned home when they captured Pak Pra. Those who guarded the place had gone away and left it and everything had been looted … when the Burmese defeated the [Siamese] at Pak Pra, (Kokkloi) the people became scared and fled into the jungle leaving their homes and properties which were later seized."[502]

When Lady Chan returned to Thalang the people of Phuket may have heard that Ligor had fallen to the Burmese and also the rumor, spread by the Burmese, that Bangkok had also fallen to them. The people on Phuket therefore had no idea if any Siamese force might be coming to their rescue. A meeting was called to decide whether they should all attempt to flee to Phang Nga and the jungle or attempt to make a stand at the fort at Ban Don built by René Charbonneau almost a hundred years earlier. At this time, Captain Light estimated that Phuket had a population of around 14,000 souls, of whom only around 2,000 were able fighting men and of these, only a few hundred were professional fighters. Most of these were the former retainers of Phaya Phimon, who now followed Lady Chan. She apparently took good care of them so as to keep them loyal, as we see from another letter she sent to Captain Light in Keddah. "The men sent to guard the town and the fort are short of opium. Please have Captain Sakat [Scott] bring up nine or ten Thaen [a measure of opium]."[503] The rest of Phuket's militia were a motley mix of traders, fishermen, farmers and miners.

So whilst deciding to stand and fight was not a great option, fleeing was also hard, as the Burmese were already on the mainland opposite and their war prows were scouting all around the island to intercept fleeing boats or swimmers (to keep or sell as slaves). Supported by her younger sister Mook, Lady Chan took the brave decision to make a stand at the Thalang fort. Since the Burmese had captured Mergui almost 20 years before, Phuket had become Siam's main western port for arms importation from India and the West. So, in her favor, Lady Chan knew the fort had many cannons and the island was well stocked with powder, grapeshot and muskets. Victuals, arms and valuables were hurriedly taken to the fort and any remaining food sources outside the fort were destroyed to prevent the Burmese from getting them. We are told that about 600 Phuketians, men women and children, crowded into the fort.

19.1. A painting of Lady Chan and her sister exhorting the people of Thalang not to flee but to take a stand and fight the Burmese invaders.

The Thalang Fort Holds Out

The Burmese fleet landed at Nai Yang beach in northwest Phuket and captured Ban Sakhu, the town just south of the airport. Others paddled their war prows inland to Thalang up the klong (river) that flows down from Thalang and empties into the sea at Layan beach north of Bang Tao, and to this day this klong is still known by many locals as "Burmese soldier Klong." The deserted villages of Ban Sakhu, Ban Takien, Ban

Lippon and Tharua were sacked and then burnt by the Burmese invaders who then converged on the Thalang fort, which stood somewhere between Thalang and Ban Don.

The Burmese troops on Phuket probably numbered fewer than 3,000 men. They had no large siege cannons, just the small-caliber demi-culverins and swivel cannons they took from some of their war prows and remounted on wooden platforms. These were not sufficient to bring down the earthen and wooden walls of the Thalang fort. Nor could they outrange the bigger Danish and British field cannon in the fort. Some of the Burmese troops had muskets and bayonets but most would have carried only spears and swords. The Burmese army surrounded the Thalang fort, but stayed out of range of the fort's cannons. There they dug trenches and built stockades in preparation for a siege of the fort.

Lady Chan apparently attempted to bluff the Burmese as to the strength of her forces by having the women in the fort made up to look like soldiers. This was not difficult at that time as Siamese men and women, as we have seen, wore similar clothes and hairstyles. Some 50 years after the siege of Thalang John Anderson, an EIC government official in Penang, recorded (though perhaps rather simplistically) how Lady Chan had done this:

> "The wife of Pia Pimone, the former Siamese governor of the island, was in the habit of relating to her visitors, with particular satisfaction, a strategem for intimidating the Burmahs … when they had effected a landing and attempted a night attack. A small fort had been constructed, with a door in front and one in the rear. Having but few muskets, the old lady caused the leaves of coconuts [palm fronds] to be stripped and cut to the length of a musket and made all her attendants throw one across each shoulder. They then paraded round and round the fort, entering at one door and going out the other, thus giving the appearance of a large assemblage of troops entering the fort, as if they had come from a distance. The Burmahs, seeing so many men parading about became alarmed … and took off to their vessels."[504]

The Thai Annals give us a more heroic version of the siege, telling us that the Phuketians

> "assembled men and built two large stockades wherewith to protect the town. The Dowager governess [Lady Chan] and her maiden sister displayed great bravery and fearlessly faced the enemy. They urged the officials and the people both males and females to fire the ordinance and muskets and led them day after day in sorties out of the stockades to fight the Burmese. So the latter were unable to reduce the town and after a month's vain attempts, provisions failing them, they had to withdraw."[505]

The Burmese siege of the Thalang fort lasted 25 days and involved some heavy day and night fighting. The new governor of Thalang appointed shortly after the Burmese invasion recorded that "The Burmese suffered between 300 and 400 casualties, killed and wounded. They then broke off the action and retired."[506]

Phuket historical lore today likes to tell us that the Burmese in Phuket left because of the indomitable leadership of Lady Chan, her sister Mook and the stout defense by the Phuketians. This may well be so, but a more cogent reason was probably the inspirational and decisive generalship of Rama I. In the north, he had rapidly defeated the main Burmese military thrust at Bangkok. He then equally rapidly dispatched an army down the peninsula to relieve the south. This army defeated the Burmese and Malay rebel force in Ligor and the eastern peninsula at a big battle just north of Chaiya. They then pursued the fleeing Burmese force back across the Tenasserim hills into Burma. The Burmese force in Phuket, on hearing about this defeat, probably realized that their main raison d'être – creating and holding a supply line to their eastern peninsular army – had disappeared. Therefore staying on Phuket served little purpose. They were hungry, outgunned by the cannons in the fort and had already sacked and burnt all the rest of Phuket. They had pillaged anything of any value and had captured hundreds of locals who were carried back to Burma as slaves. So there was little point in staying and on March 13, 1786, five weeks after they had first invaded Phuket the Burmese reportedly returned to their war prows and sailed back north up the coast to Burma.

By any standards, Rama I, one of Siam's greatest generals, had won a brilliant victory. For her forthright leadership in the south, Rama I later awarded Lady Chan the title of Thao Thepkrassatri. Being a woman, she was unable to take over from her husband as governor; however, later on one of her sons became governor of Phuket. Her younger sister Mook was given the title Thao Srisoonthorn and Rama I requested one of her daughters as a concubine in his royal palace in Bangkok; she later bore him a child. In 1967 the Heroines Monument was built at Tharua on Phuket and the two main roads that meet there were named after the sisters, Thepkrassatri Road from Phuket Town and Srisoonthorn Road from Kamala.

A Bitter Victory

Today the so-called heroine sisters' defense of Phuket is hailed as a great victory by the locals, but it most surely would not have seemed like that at the time. Although the Burmese had gone and some of the locals had kept their few valuables and avoided being killed or dragged off as slaves, that is about all the good that can be said of it. For a month the Burmese had occupied and utterly devastated the entire island outside the small confines of the walls of the wooden Thalang fort. No figures are known, but hundreds of locals probably died in the fighting and from food shortages and disease or drowning when trying to flee to the mainland. Probably several hundred if not a few thousand more were captured and carried back to Burma to become slaves. Most others had fled to the mainland and the island was depleted of people. All the villages, temples, homes, boats and crops had been pillaged, burnt, uprooted and destroyed by the Burmese scorched-earth tactics before they left and the real suffering and hardships – and many more deaths by starvation – were still to come. There was a shortage of food and people to work the fields or to dig for tin. Captain Light kept many of the letters written to him by the people of Phuket during this difficult period. They are now in a collection in London and give us a sense of the hardships following the Burmese invasion.

Lady Chan, for example, wrote to him shortly after the siege, "Now I am destitute without anything … because of the Burmese attacks on Thalang, the district is in confusion … we are in great dearth of food … the people of Thalang are starving from want of rice."[307] T'ha Prom, a nephew of Lady Chan, also wrote to Light, "This is to let you know that I am undergoing the most extreme degree of hardship and difficulty … In the Burmese attack on Thalang many of my friends were lost to me, killed in the fighting."[308] Lady Chan again wrote to Light some months later, appealing for him to send up rice urgently from Keddah:

> "At present the people of Takuathung and Bangkhli are scattered because of the destruction of their villages. The whole region here is in disorder. The Burmese burnt much rice and it is in very short supply; there is insufficient to provide for the people until rice is again available from the fields. Please think of [us] and have your captain bring up a trading ship with merchandise and rice so that the officials may be able to distribute enough for the people to go on cultivating their fields. … I have organised the digging of tin in the forest and have obtained some which has been used to purchase all the rice available at a high price."[309]

The newly appointed governor of Thalang after the Burmese invasion also wrote to Light pleading for him to send food. "The people at Thalang are starving for want of rice. Out of your goodness have Captain Scott bring up two or three thousand gunnies [sacks] of rice for distribution to the people to save them from death."[310] Captain Light himself wrote to the EIC directors in Madras, telling them, "The people of Junksalong, after expelling the Burmese, are distressed by famine and expect another attack this season."[311]

In November 1786, a year after the invasion, Light also wrote to Madras to say that the sultan of Keddah had just been ordered by Rama I to prepare his fleet and army to defend Phuket against an expected new Burmese attack. Smaller-scale Burmese attacks and slave raids also continued up and down the west coast of Siam throughout the following years, keeping the distraught and starving people in the greatest fear.

So, with Phuket depopulated – its towns, business, agriculture and villages ruined and many of the locals dead, dissipated, enslaved, starving and fearful of another Burmese attack at any time – the great victory celebrated by the locals today would have seemed rather specious at the time. But a victory it was, compared with the horrors that Phuket would suffer when the Burmese invaded again 24 years later.

20

The Schemes of Light and Scott

1770 TO 1794

The events covered in this chapter took place simultaneously with the events described in the previous two chapters, 18 and 19, namely: the sultan of Keddah's attempt to capture Phuket; King Tak Sin's reconquest of the region, his deposition and the new king, Rama I, taking power, the Phuket governor Phaya Phimon's marriage to Lady Chan, his subsequent illness and death; the 1785 Burmese invasion of Phuket and Lady Chan's defense of the Thalang fort.

Francis Light and James Scott

Francis Light was born in Dalinghoo, near Woodbridge in Suffolk, England in 1740. He was the illegitimate son of a country gentleman and a local serving girl. After attending a local county school he joined the British Navy and saw action against the French during the Seven Years War. By the age of 22 he had became a lieutenant on the warship HMS Arrogant. Another young officer on the Arrogant at the same time was a 17-year-old Scotsman by the name of James Scott who was born in 1746 in Makerstoun in the Scottish borders. He grew up in Edinburgh, where his father was a liberal lawyer and his cousin was the celebrated Scottish author, Sir Walter Scott. These two men, Francis Light and James Scott, almost succeeded in making Phuket their own private British colony in the

20.1. Sir Francis Light, from his statue in Penang.

late 18th century. British colonialism began to take on a more ordered, conservative and moral character in the Victorian 19th century. Light and Scott can be seen as amongst the last adventurers of the earlier, more swashbuckling era of European colonialism.

When the Seven Years War finished the navy downsized and young Francis Light, now aged 23, was back on land and looking for adventure. He bought himself a passage to Madras, India on the brig Clive. In Madras, he found employment with the firm of Jourdain, Sullivan & De Souza, one of several "country traders" – local private merchant firms ("interlopers") trading with the smaller ports around the Bay of Bengal. Light was given command of one of the company's armed trading sloops and for the next several years he sailed amongst the ports around the Bay of Bengal as a "navigating merchant" trading his company's wares. By 1769, 29-year-old Light, a good linguist, had learned Hindu, Malay and Siamese. He was posted to Aceh in Sumatra to manage his firm's new factory there and he was based in Aceh for about three years. During his time in Aceh he received news that his old navy companion James Scott was also working in the Bay of Bengal as a "navigating merchant" and he was living in Tharua on the Siamese island of Phuket.

Light had made several visits to both Phuket and Keddah selling arms, cotton and opium. He had also become acquainted with Sultan Mohamed Jewa of Keddah, whose troops, during the recent Siamese interregnum, had occupied and just been expelled from Phuket. In 1771, the sultan of Keddah was then shaken by the attack and plundering of Keddah by the Selangor Bugis pirate fleet from Phuket and he now wanted protection, namely an alliance with a European-led force with trained troops, cannon and warships. He proposed to Captain Light, whose firm also ran a business of leasing out British Indian trained sepoy mercenary troops, that if his company would agree to defend and operate his main port of Kuala Keddah, he would give them a fifty-fifty share of his royal trade monopoly there. The directors of Light's firm Jourdain, Sullivan & De Souza turned down this offer, believing it required too much of a commitment for a small and unsure market. Light then offered the same deal to the EIC in Madras.

The EIC Searches for a Suitable Eastern Base

During the 18th century, tea and Chinese porcelain became all the rage in Britain, greatly boosting the number of EIC ships sailing from India to China. But as the Dutch had discovered previously, neither Britain nor India had many products desired by the Chinese. British traders had handily managed to stimulate a market for Indian opium by creating many addicts in China but they also knew that several products from the Malay Peninsula, such as tin, birds' nests, aromatic woods, sea slugs (bêche de mer), ambergris, rhinoceros horn and shark fins were always in demand in China. And, unlike in China, in the Malay Peninsula and Siam there was always a demand for goods from India and the West – mainly weapons, cotton textiles, ironmongery and opium – so a lucrative triangular trade developed between India, the peninsula and China. The EIC was now seeking a base on the peninsula to conduct this trade more efficiently. Ideally, this base should also be close to the shipping bottleneck of the Straits of Malacca to allow EIC ships heading to China a victualing and defensive harbor to counteract Dutch naval power in the region as well as the numerous and increasingly resolute and well armed pirates in the Malacca Straits.

The EIC had previously attempted, unsuccessfully, to establish victualing stations en route to China east of the Dutch-controlled Malacca Straits. The first was established in 1702 on Con Son island off southern Vietnam, but after three years the Indian sepoys mutinied and killed all the British there apart from two, who rather miraculously escaped in a rowing boat and managed to reach Kelantan and then get back to India. The next was on Palawan Island in the Philippines, but this station was overrun and destroyed by Illanun pirates. At Syriam (Thanlyin today) in Burma a trade station and boat repair yard had also been attempted, but malaria had killed off many of the settlers; then the king of Burma attacked it and finished off the rest. So when Light approached the directors in Madras with the possibility of using Keddah as an eastern base, they were interested enough to send one of their officers over to try to negotiate a deal. These negotiations fell through, as the EIC refused to get contractually involved in defending the fickle and self-indulgent sultan in his local wars, and this was also specifically against EIC company policy from London at the time.

Francis Light in Phuket

But Francis Light, at 32 years old, had now conceived his big idea, one he would doggedly pursue to its fruition over the next 20 years. With his local knowledge and languages, he believed that if he could arrange the desired EIC station or colony in the area and become involved in governing it, he would have the opportunity to cream off great wealth and become as fabulously rich as most of the other self-serving, nest-feathering EIC station managers in the East. He could then buy some land and retire to Suffolk as a successful eastern "nabob" himself.

After the Keddah deal fell through, Light considered Phuket as an option for this intended trade station. Possibly this idea was first proposed to him by the sultan of Keddah, who was still sore about having his occupation troops chased off the island by the locals a few years earlier. In 1772 Light wrote to Madras stating "the laksamana (sultan of Keddah) constantly regretted the loss of this island and offered me 8,000 men when it was proposed … to establish a settlement there."[512] To the EIC, this offer must have seemed rather odd, coming from a sultan who had just been trying to obtain protection against enemies in his own backyard so they put the matter on hold. Light had now acquired his own armed trade ship, the Blake, and he left his old firm to trade on his own account; in early 1772 he sailed to Phuket to join his old friend James Scott in Tharua.

In 1765, seven years earlier, the Burmese had captured Siam's main western port of Mergui and still held it. Phuket, Phang Nga and Trang, along with Keddah, were now Siam's most important west coast ports and trade there was growing. In 1779, for example, Dr. Koening, the Danish botanist and diarist, arrived in Tharua Bay in Phuket on Light's ship Blake. He tells us that "two English trading ships, that of Captain Scott and that of Captain Peterson"[513] already stood in "Tharua roads" (harbor) and during his three-month stay he tells us three more European ships arrived to trade, including a Danish ship and "the ship of a Captain Welch which arrived from the coast of Sumatra."[514]

When Light first arrived in Phuket in 1772, the islanders had only recently kicked out the sultan of Keddah's occupying troops, King Tak Sin had not yet come south to coerce the island back into Siamese vassalage and the island was in an independent-minded, refractory and lawless state. The insecurity and danger on the island meant Light initially stayed on his ship in Tharua roads, though some nights he would stay ashore at James Scott's house, built near the Tharua River so that Scott could rapidly flee by his longboat to his ship in the harbor at any hint of trouble. Light soon enrolled James Scott in his new scheme to persuade the EIC to make Phuket its colony.

It is not clear exactly how long James Scott had been living in Tharua before Light's arrival on the island. When he came east Scott apparently never worked for the EIC, nor (unlike Francis Light) for any other notable Indian country trading company. He had somehow set himself up with his own ship and acted as a trader on his own account (possibly with an Indian loan or an Indian business partner).

John Adolphus Pope, on another Bay of Bengal country trade ship at the time tells us in one letter that since James Scott had been in the East he had led "a vagrant life amongst the Malays and adopted the dress and customs of the Malays."[515] Indeed Scott often dressed like a Malay, wearing a sarong, and had an unkempt beard (unusual then). In Tharua he lived with at least one Malay woman and had begotten mixed-blood children with her and he apparently had other native women and children in other ports down the coast. But despite his dress style he was a former Royal Navy officer and constantly faced the menace of the pirates and Dutch in the region so he clearly knew his naval tactics, gunnery and how to fight a ship. His liberal attitudes and Malay lifestyle, however, did not sit so well with the often more conservative and supercilious EIC men in the region. One crusty EIC director in Madras referred to Scott somewhat disparagingly as "a perfect Malay." Major Macdonald, an EIC army officer who later became the superintendent of Penang and frequently quarreled with the free merchants there, complained that he found Scott's Malay "dress, manners and mode of Living … dishonorable and degenerate."[516] Clearly the more dapper Englishman Francis Light carried more credibility with the EIC but James Scott was a tough man who spoke Malay and had a good understanding of local circumstances on Phuket. He seems to have been most happy to assist his old friend Light to establish his business on Phuket and to join him in furthering their potentially lucrative scheme to make the island a British trade colony and naval station.

Light described the island's main port town of "Tharma" or Tharua when he first arrived there in 1772: "The seaport town contains about 400 houses and sits about two miles from the sea. The river which was formerly navigable for sloops is now choked up and boats can only go up at high water."[517] (This is the klong from Tharua that today joins the sea near the entrance to the Boat Lagoon. It is even less navigable today, thanks to massive silting from later tin-mining operations upstream and the advance of the mangroves.) Captain Thomas Forrest, who visited Phuket

20.2. A 19th century traditional European house on Penang Island. Light, Scott and the other European residents of Phuket would have lived in similar style atap roofed houses in Tharua.

in 1785, a few years after Light, noted that, "After having with much difficulty got up this narrow creek where oars cannot be used on the upper part, paddles only and against a strong current, one is much pleased to reach the pleasant rivulet above."[518] Forrest also tells us that Tharua "Consists of about 80 houses, on a plain through which runs a pleasant brook … The town is well situated, there are roads leading to the principal places on the island and to Jamboo [Cape Yamoo]. On the south side of the town is a piece of high ground that commands the whole. All strangers reside here … in pleasant buildings of stone."[519]

As we have seen, in 1772, shortly after Light first arrived, King Tak Sin reincorporated Phuket into Siam. His military superintendents were then posted to Kokkloi with their troops to keep order. Phaya Pimon, the new husband of Lady Chan, was then appointed the new governor of Phuket and Light began to feel safe enough to also take a house in Tharua as Edward Monkton, an EIC employee, mentioned in a letter to the company directors in Madras: "Mr. Light had settled at Junkceylon as a private trader and had been well received by the governor and the principal inhabitants."[520]

Siam, in an almost constant state of war under King Tak Sin, had a great need for weapons. Light and Scott soon established a brisk trade importing arms, cotton wares, opium and sundry goods from India and rice and salt from Keddah. They were paid mainly in tin, though sometimes in elephants, birds' nests and ambergris. One letter in Light's collection mentions that Light delivered, in one shipment alone, 1,826 muskets to Tharua and a further 490 were immediately ordered. The historian E. H. S. Simmons calculated from Light's existing letters in his collection in London alone, that Light sold to Siam at least 8,372 muskets, 50 cannon and a huge volume of cannon balls, priming powder, flints, sulphur and saltpeter for making gunpowder.[521] Scott and Light also supplied the sultan of Keddah with arms, partly for his own use, but also because the sultan reportedly ran a thriving business as a clandestine arms supplier to Burma. As a major provider of weapons to King Tak Sin and one of the few foreigners proficient in speaking and writing Siamese, Light was held in high esteem locally. He was invited to meet Phraya Palat Nu, the reinstated viceroy of Ligor and was not even required to remove his shoes, a sign of great respect. "As chief for the English I sat with my shoes on … and took precedence over the Chinese"[522]

Sometime around 1774, Light took a shipload of muskets up to King Tak Sin's new capital Thonburi and was granted an audience with the king himself. The king must have taken a shine to Light, for he ordered more muskets and gave Light the honorary title of "Kapitan Bangken" and made him the leader of peninsular Siam's foreign community, or "hat wearing people", as the Siamese called them then.

On Phuket, Light made enough money to increase his fleet to three ships. He employed several Britons, such as the Scottish Captain Lindsay, who skippered his schooner Speedwell. Light captained his newest ship, Bristol and another British captain skippered the Blake. There was a Mr. Phillip, the translator; a couple of local Christian clerks; and the "writer" or accountant, who lived in Tharua and ran the business during

Light's frequent absences trading. Light took a piece of land on the island, noting, "I look upon a part of this island to be my property, it was granted to me by their own free will, the ground cleared at my own expense."[523]

Light also took up with a local girl Martina Rozells, a member of the Christian community in Tharua. She appears to have been half-Portuguese and half-Siamese, though some claim she also had some French blood; some also claim she was from a family of one of King Tak Sin's close allies. She used the Thai name Thong Di and initially spoke no English. She and Light never married, but in his will in Penang, he affirmed that he cohabited with her for many years and they raised five children together. The children stayed with them in Tharua and later in Keddah and Penang.

20.3 *William Light, one of Phuket's more colorful sons.*

Light's first son, William, was a quarter Siamese, and became one of Phuket's more notable sons. He was sent off to boarding school in England from a young age. He later joined the British army and distinguished himself as the adjutant to Lord Wellington in the Spanish Peninsular War against Napoleon. He was badly wounded in the army and he spent some years traveling in Europe including spending time in Sicily as a painter. He was then employed by Mohamed Ali Pasha, the founder of modern Egypt, to build a modern Egyptian navy. Following this he spent some years as the captain of a Nile paddle steamer until 1836 when he was hired by the South Australian Company as their surveyor general and he designed the city of Adelaide, the capital of the state of South Australia. He also named the nearby Barossa Valley (now famous for its wine) because it reminded him of the landscape near Cadiz, Spain where he fought the French in the battle of Barossa in 1811.

The Christian community in Tharua was mainly comprised of mestizos of Portuguese ancestry plus some other half-breeds with some European blood, usually the result of liaisons with visiting sailors. As late as 1901, wrote Walter Burke, a British mining engineer living in Phuket, the level market ground in front of today's Thalang History Museum was still called "Talat Farang" or "Foreigners' Market" and, he noted, the Portuguese descendants were still identifiable in Tharua. "They are as a rule fairer than the Siamese … the men have more hair on the face and often large mustachios. They do not profess Buddhism and appear to be without any religion … but they do not work on Sundays … their numbers are now very small."[524]

After the fall and destruction of Ayutthaya in 1767, many Christians had fled south to the mission in Tharua, swelling Phuket's Christian population. Then in 1781, as King Tak Sin started going mad, he issued his edict expelling all Christians from Siam or they would be killed. One record of the Catholic mission in Keddah notes that, in that same year alone, some 80 Christians moved their residence from Phuket to Keddah. The 200-year-old wooden mission building in Tharua, built by the French, was probably torn down by opportunistic local Buddhists and Muslims for cheap building materials. Francis Light wrote in 1784 that after the expulsion of the Christians, "Tacoatany [Takuatung – en route to Phang Nga] is a Christian village, formerly very large, but now so reduced that a priest cannot procure a maintenance."[525]

It was around this time that Light's wife Martina and his children also moved to Keddah. Maybe Martina simply wanted to move with her Catholic peers and friends. However, at the same time, Light, as we shall see, was also beginning to have problems on the island, so maybe he chose to move Martina and the family away for security reasons. Having Martina in Keddah also allowed him to more freely indulge in his apparent proclivity for womanizing on Phuket.

Light the Lothario

Both Light and Scott seem to have enjoyed their bachelor lives in Asia. Despite living with Martina, Light seems to have been quite a philanderer and to have had lovers in other villages on Phuket and in many other ports he visited for trade. James Scott is estimated to have had at least eight children on Phuket Island alone and at least as many more around the region from second wives, bibis, slave girls and other encounters. Both men kept permanent cabins with ladies in other trade ports, such as Selangor in Malaya. When Light moved away from Phuket, first to Keddah then to Penang, he received letters from several Phuket girls (now in his London letter collection) that have a very similar feel to some of the emails sent by the bar girls of Patong today to their departed foreign lovers and clients. For example one lady signing herself as Chao Rat wrote to him:

> "This is to let you know that during your long absence I have been in great distress and I cannot find any happiness. I have been trying to make a living remaining faithful to you and I raise my hands in salutation to you every morning and every night when I lie down to sleep. Now I am like a nestling or a tiny fawn bereft of its mother. I have to hide myself away faithfully waiting for you … I have had to use the articles you gave me to buy food at a high price. I had nothing left except my clothes and a robber stole all these."[526]

Another, Bun Chan, wrote to him soon after he left Thalang:

> "Formerly you used to come to Thalang frequently and [word illegible in letter] me then. You left some trade goods with me, five bolts of cloth, seventy cowries and three sacks of milled rice. Some of the money has been used to get the fields ploughed, some has been exchanged for other goods and the cloth has been bartered for rice to eat."[527]

Bun Chan also wrote again:

> "I am thinking of you very much. I have not forgotten you. Although Captain Scott's ship has been twice to Thalang I have received no news of you. If you are still unable to come to Thalang all well and good, but please send some things that are needed here. Please – two bolts of cloth white and black and opium as well."[528]

Another Thalang woman, called Bun Kaeo, wrote to him,

> "It is my sad fate not to be connected with you anymore. It is not like when we used to gather flowers together. I am short of money these days. I have no clothes to wear, nor rice to eat. Please look after me and do not let me die."[529]

Chao Chipat, the wife of a clerk in his company who had died while Light was in Phuket, also wrote to him appealing for help and gifts. These last two letters, it should be recalled, were sent in the aftermath of the 1785 Burmese invasion of Phuket, when the islanders were desperate and starving to death.

After Martina moved with the family to Keddah, Light also bought himself a new wife in Thalang in Siamese style. Her name was Amdaeng Rat. She was the wife of Khun Thalakang, a minor government official who had pledged his wife as security to a Chinese moneylender called Wong for a debt. Such debt bondage was common practice. Siamese records with the Thalang Treasury Seal show that Light paid off the debt to Wong (six and half bahars of tin), giving him rights to Amdaeng Rat and she became his new wife on Phuket and they lived together whenever he was back in Thalang.

Light's letters in London show he had become a friend of the Governor Phaya Pimon and also apparently of Lady Chan and her daughters. This close friendship continued even after the death of her husband the governor Phaya Pimon. Mae Prang, one of Lady Chan's daughters, was obviously quite taken with Light, as she wrote to him, "I think unceasingly of you … I think of you day and night for nobody troubles about me and my affairs … I need two pieces of good quality flowered chintz and a bottle of rose water. I ask you for this out of your generosity."[530] Light at some point must have lent her some money as she also wrote him a letter stating: "I am very worried about the money that I have owed you for some time … I was going to send you some things but the Farang Nylip [possibly Mr. Phillip, his interpreter] was in a great hurry and I could not get them ready in time. I have got ten melons for you."[531]

The Plot to Take Phuket and Make it a British Station

During the whole period he was in Phuket, Light, believing Phuket to be a fine spot for a colony, persevered in trying to obtain his coveted trading station. He wrote several reports to the EIC directors in India promoting the island. Addressing the need for a harbor, he claimed that Pak Pra and Tharua harbors were "the best harbours and naval port in all India,"[532] but conceded that due to a large mudbank stretching from Cape Yamoo to Ma Phrao Island, "ships [in Tharua Harbor], though defended from all weathers would be exposed to an enemy attack."[533] However, he felt that the harbor could be well defended by building forts on "Maprau Island and a main fort at Cape Yamoo, which could be easily defended … on its north side no ship can come within gunshot."[534]

Phuket, he reported, had "plenty of wood and water," was good for a shipyard and repairs and "produced rice sufficient for its inhabitants" in two crops a year, "one from the high ground and hills in September and the other from the plains in January." The island's main asset was its tin deposits, which he felt could quickly "earn enough revenue to pay the costs" of defending the place. [535] He also mentions the large amounts of ambergris collected on the west coast beaches, particularly at "Tantalay" (Cherngtalay, or Bang Tao beach), which is:

> "A fine bay with a large sandy beach on which is found much ambergris during the N. E. monsoons: here is excellent fishing too. … The pasture of Salang is excellent, the buffaloe is very large, its meat more sweet and tender than [in] other parts of India. Beef, sheep and goats thrive well here, but the inhabitants can possess no property, therefore nothing is cultivated nor even poultry reared. In the woods are elephants, rhinoceros, tigers, elk, deer, bears, hogs and a great variety of feathered species, whose plumage is highly valued by the Chinese. The lakes abound with wild fowl and the sea with fish … Birds nests are found among the islands from Salang to Mergui … The collecting of these employ every year 1,000 prows and 4,500 people. The king … grants a licence for collecting the birds nests and sea slugs to some officers, for which he receives 12 to 15,000 Spanish dollars per annum."[536]

This was a huge amount of money in 1780, when a well-to-do European family could get by on 100 dollars a year. Light continued: "It is known from experience the soil is favorable for pepper, cotton, sugar, coffee and that the natives of the Coromandel and Tanjore [Indians] prefer it to their own. From the richness of the soil and climate of this island, nothing is wanted to make the inhabitants happy but a rational government."[537]

A British Colonel Kydd, who was sent to Phuket by the EIC to make a strategic study of Phuket with a view to colonizing it, estimated the population of the island before the 1786 Burmese invasion at around 14,000 people. [538] However, as Light wrote to the EIC, under "the rational government of British rule" and lower taxes, he believed "the number of inhabitants would increase daily … the Chinese who are now reduced to great misery in Keddah will come here, Dutch trade with Batavia would be diverted."[539] Moreover, he claimed the people of Phuket were desperate to have him take the island from their "oppressors", the Siamese, and would fight alongside him for their freedom from Siam.

> "The inhabitants have for many years strongly solicited me to deliver them from the cruel oppression of Siam. As they are capable of defending themselves they most want a chief in whom they can confide and an assurance that they shall enjoy a reasonable portion of that liberty to which all men are by nature and reason entitled … if the company took possession, the population would have a free enjoyment of their goods and chattels and would be at liberty to improve their estates without fear of their being taken away from them."[540]

Establishing a colony and a trading and naval station in Phuket, he concluded, "would immediately pay the expense of its government and would be an admirable situation for a place of arms. This would remain, were even Bengal and the Carnatic to be lost."[541]

Light and Scott felt there were two ways to get their hands on the island. One was to try to make a treaty with the Siamese king. The other was an alliance with the locals to take it from Siam by stealth and force. James Scott, who was also writing to Madras to promote the colony idea, felt that, "could the island be obtained by treaty, or with the unanimous consent of the locals, [i.e. without Siamese consent] … I know of no place of so much value."[542]

Light and Scott worked on both possibilities. Light wrote to Madras that, in his meeting with King Tak Sin in 1774, the king had said he was open to the idea of a British station in Siam. "The king in his conversation expressed a strong desire of cultivating a friendship with the honourable Company [the EIC] and showed great uneasiness at no English vessel having come to his ports. He said his soldiers would go against Mergui this season and if they took it he would give it to the English."[543]

However, the most plausible method to obtain the island did seem to be by working with the locals to take it by force from the Siamese king. Light, Scott and the other foreign traders living on Phuket at the time believed the people of Phuket would support this as they "did not like their Siamese oppressors and wanted to be taken over as a European settlement. All the head people of the island are willing to give the company any terms they may ask in exchange for protection."[544] Light also wrote that the locals

"are obliged to maintain all the [Siamese] officers with their attendants without receiving any other satisfaction than stripes [whippings] – In the three voyages I have made to Siam I have observed every year the people grow more despondent. The Chinese merchants are plundered and all the inhabitants, by a few mercenaries whom (the viceroy of Ligor) lets loose on whoever is suspected. The people have often hinted to me I ought to take the government of Junk Ceylon myself."[545]

To illustrate the local disgruntlement, he mentions a "Hong" – a hidden limestone valley – next to Phang Nga Bay where "the country wears a romantic appearance, steep rocks, caves, high mountains and rugged islands"; here many Thalang people had fled to escape the oppression of their Siamese overlords:

"Near Poongha I am told, is a valley of a circular form to which there is only one entrance under a large rock. At high water the passage is closed and at low water the rapidity of the current, with the shelves and rocks, renders it impossible for the smallest boat to pass. The only time to go out is at half tide. Here 500 people have taken refuge from the tyranny of the Siamese government. I have received this account from Chinese and Malays who have been there."[546]

Captain Thomas Forrest, who was on Phuket at the same time as Light, also mentioned the distaste of the Phuket people for their Siamese overlords.

"The government takes 25% before the tin can be exported. This gives so much dissatisfaction that they [the people of Phuket] wish to throw off their dependence on Siam and it is said that if Pee Piemon [Phaya Pimon, the governor] could get support he would readily do it. How far his having those associates in government might prevent such an attempt I cannot say, possibly their appointment is with that very intention by the despots of Siam."[547]

Under King Tak Sin, there seem to have been three levels of administration over Phuket: the governor, the regional military superintendents – to check on the governors and control the people – and a trade officer to enforce collection of royal trade revenues and send information to the capital.

Cutting a Deal

Light and Scott must have approached the Phuket governor Phaya Pimon with their scheme and he seems to have agreed to conspire with them in undertaking their planned British takeover of the island. As early as 1773 Light and Scott formally agreed terms with governor Pimon for the island to put itself under EIC protection without the consent of the new King Tak Sin in Thonburi. John Anderson, an early British government official in Penang, explained. "Mr. James Scott submitted … an offer from the Native governor of the Island Named Pia Pimone, to transfer the island to the British government upon very advantageous terms."[548] These terms were, as James Scott wrote to the EIC council in 1773, that, "If the English would take on them the sovereignty of the island of Jangsylan and send a force to resist any future attempts from Siam, he [Phaya Pimon] will deliver them the peaceable possession of the island on the following terms."[549] These terms are recorded in a contract in Light's letter collection in London and signed by Phaya Pimon. The main clauses of this takeover agreement were:

1. "That all debts to the king of Siam by the islanders be cancelled forever."

2. "That the slavery of the people arising from their being considered as slaves of the king be abolished and everyone be entitled to the product of his labours."

3. "That private property remain unchanged and debts due from inhabitants be recoverable as before."

4. "That the arrack and gambling farms be, at least for a time, abolished (i.e. no more huge taxes on residents' drinking and gambling habits)."

5. There is also a clause that the EIC would buy tin for 25 percent more than the Siamese king, that is at four dollars a measure instead of the three dollars the king's agents paid at that time and that the EIC would be allowed a 5 percent tax on imports. [550]

Phaya Pimon showed his trust in Light and Scott by signing the agreement that also states "Everything else he [Phaya Pimon] trusts to the wisdom and consideration of the company [the EIC] and hopes they will be speedy in sending him an answer as the existence of himself and family will depend on the protection he may receive from them."[551]

[That is, if he was discovered scheming treason like this by King Tak Sins spies he and his wife Lady Chan and their families would probably be arrested and executed.]

Along with to this letter of agreement from Phaya Pimon, Scott also sent to Madras and Calcutta (in 1772 Calcutta was made the new capital of British India) a profit-and-loss forecast showing the expected cost and revenues of the colony, including the cost of maintaining military protection:

> "There would be wanted to secure this island during the first few years of possession: 500 sepoys [British-trained Indian troops] and 100 Europeans, artillery included, with 6 months provisions, a double proportion of light field pieces and great guns for two small forts, a complete set of artificers, 5,000 gunny bags [for sandbags] should it at any time be requisite to throw up a fort in haste on the lands of Popra … your marine should be two small snows [two-masted merchant vessels], two long boats and two row galleys armed thus: the Snows to carry 10-12 four or three pounder Guns, with one cannonade in the bows for throwing grape and canister. The Long Boat about 10-15 tons, decks fitted for carrying 10 swivels one bow gun and one cannonade with blunderbusses on swivel sticks. The two snows, unless judged necessary to keep up a communication with India, might be dispensed with on the second year if Siam remained quiet."[552]

Scott was convinced the Phuket locals would also fight against Siam. "As the natives of Salang have long groaned under a severe despotism, where flogging is a trade regularly learnt, they would be so fully sensible of their charge that their loyalty might be depended upon."[553] Both Scott and Light also imagined that under British government there would be several trading ships normally based at the island, which could be drafted into Phuket's navy if required. They obviously believed that if, like Great Britain, they controlled the sea, the Siamese could not land troops in any great numbers.

Light and Scott Are Evicted

By late 1779 this seditious plotting by Light and Scott appears to have reached the ears of King Tak Sin's regional military superintendent. When the botanist, Dr. Koening, arrived on Phuket in 1779, he was warned to stay on the boat and not to take a house in Thalang because "the atmosphere on land was rather unsafe for Europeans during the last days on account of some quarrels between some English captains and the king. I was therefore called back to the ship."[554] Light had taken the earlier precaution of sending Martina and their children off to Keddah. In a letter of early 1780, Light, who soon also moved away to Keddah, explained how the Siamese military superintendent had moved against him:

> "I sold them [the people of Thalang] 1,700 bags of rice payable in three months. It was so divided scarce an inhabitant on the island but what had a share. By an unparalleled act of tyranny, he [the military superintendent] forbade the inhabitants to pay me. The people were sensible of the injustice done both to themselves and me, many of them brought payment at hazard of their lives. He then plun-

dered my house … my writer unhappily died last July, 700 peculs of tin were due to him [the writer] from the officers and people, he [the military superintendent] stopped payment … The inhabitants, enraged at his repeated acts of tyranny, called aloud for some power to take the island, Burmans, Malays, Europeans, they cared not whom, as it was impossible their condition could be rendered worse by any enemy. I hinted to them I would endeavour to relieve them and they declared not only their readiness to join me, but they would deliver over themselves and the island to my direction. Some of them waylaid the Chao Pia [military superintendent] and shot at him but he escaped and is now afraid to remain on the island. He has built a house at Papra [Pak Pra on the mainland] and barricaded it with a double row of palisades. Every person is obliged to go there to receive their orders."[555]

In Phuket, Light's land was taken from him by the Siamese military superintendent. He wrote: "though unjustly drove off … I think myself at liberty to resume it when ever I have the power."[556] (His claim of being "unjustly" deprived is rather rich, given that he was plotting the theft of the island and a rebellion in which many Siamese, including the superintendent general, might die.)

Light remained in Keddah, but got some limited vengeance, in a small way, against the military superintendent general. At that time, imported goods could be sold only to the superintendent general, the governor or a king's officer, from whom the people were forced to buy the goods at a fat mark-up. Captain Hamilton, who had visited Phuket earlier in the century, explained that while he was in Phuket, a ship under a British Captain Lloyd arrived from Bengal. The king's merchant was the only one allowed to buy his goods; after bargaining him down, they agreed on a price. As soon as the goods were landed, he sold all of them at a 25 percent mark-up to the people and only then paid Captain Lloyd.

Light sent one of his ships under a Captain Wilson up to Phuket with a shipload of opium, textiles and silver. Wilson sold over half of his load to the superintendent and his officers, then turned round and sold the rest directly to the people at a substantial discount, leaving the superintendent and his officers holding expensive products no one needed. In Keddah, Light soon received a most huffy letter from the superintendent general, complaining of the incident.

"When the captain of a sloop brings merchandise to sell here, according to customary practice, the governor and council agree on prices. They undertake the selling of goods to the people and make a small profit. You were here formerly and you know all about this. You sent Captain Wirasen [Wilson] with opium, silver and cloth to sell at Thalang … Wirasen sold direct to the people at a lower price than that which he had sold to the officials who had bought a large quantity and lost money on the deal. This is contrary to the rule and custom of our state. If you do not control your captain and he does this again there will be a quarrel between Captain [Light] and the council."[557]

The Deed Is Done

Meanwhile, Light and Scott knew that the EIC was not in good shape financially at that time, so, in order to give new impetus to their deal, they proposed that the expenses of the new colony in Phuket could be met by private subscription, mainly from businessmen in British India and therefore the EIC would only need to support the project with logistical and administrative backing, as Light wrote to the directors: "If this plan is approved of by the honourable company, I hope for assistance from the supreme council of men and ammunition, security being given for defraying the charges [from outside subscribers]. I am humbly of the opinion it will be, in but a few years, a very great acquisition."[558]

Across the Bay of Bengal, word went out about this new colony to be established and the fundraising got under way. In India and as far away as London, agents working for a commission solicited subscriptions from wealthy merchants and investors. In Madras, at the EIC headquarters for Asia, Warren Hastings, the new director general of the EIC, met with the board directors to consider this new proposal for a private subscription-funded colony on Phuket under the auspices of the EIC. The plan was approved but permission was still required for such a significant action from the EIC main board in London.

A year later, word eventually reached Light, in Keddah, that both the EIC boards, in Madras and London, had approved the takeover of Phuket. Light and Scott were jubilant. They could finally take Phuket by force from Siam and operate it as their private company, a trade, mining and pepper center and a British naval base under the jurisdiction of the EIC in India. John Anderson, a later EIC administrator, noted, "In 1780 during the administration of director Hastings, a plan was formed by the merchants of Calcutta for a settlement at this island (Phuket), the subscriptions for that purpose were made and the measure received the sanction of the government."[559] As the money for the project rolled in, preparations were made in Madras. However, on the opposite side of the world, a totally unrelated event was just about to drop a large spanner into the works.

A New War with France and America

In December 1773, in Boston Harbor, Massachusetts, a gang of some 200 American-born colonists, dressed as Red Indians, raided an EIC ship and threw its boxes of imported tea into the sea; this "Boston Tea Party" essentially launched the American War of Independence in which Britain was plunged into a war against America, France, Holland and Russia. Britain suddenly needed vast numbers of ships to fight in the Americas, the Atlantic and elsewhere and Asian trade was badly disrupted. Britain had to concentrate its naval forces in the Atlantic and left its Indian colonies relatively unprotected. Then France sent one of its most brilliant naval commanders, Admiral de Suffren, to the Bay of Bengal with a war fleet which greatly disrupted British and EIC shipping. The military preparations for Light and Scott's Phuket colony had to be put on hold, as Anderson explains: "Before the necessary preparations could be completed, a war with France was certain and with the government not being able to grant any supplies, and the merchants unwilling to trust their property on the eve of war, the plan was abandoned for a time."[560]

From Keddah, Light and Scott tried to continue with their trading. In early 1783, Light took his ship Blake, loaded with rice, to India. However, off the Coromandel Coast, one of de Suffren's French naval patrol ships captured him and took his ship and rice. Light was imprisoned in the French base of Trincomalee for over a year until the end of the war. James Scott, attempting to take his ship Prince south to Selangor to sell muskets, was also captured by a Dutch patrol ship and also thrown into a dank prison in Malacca until war's end.

When word that the war was over and peace had been declared reached the Indies in 1784, both Scott and Light returned to Keddah. By 1785, they must have felt it was safe enough to return to Phuket to try to resume their scheme with Phaya Pimon. But now Phaya Pimon was becoming very ill. Lady Chan wrote a letter to Light on his ship in Tharua. "I was going to come down and meet you but the Chao Khun is still very ill so I am sending the chief official of Muang to meet you." Undeterred by Phaya Pimon's health issues, Light and Scott pushed on again and re-proposed their old scheme to the EIC in Madras.

During the recent war, de Suffren's French fleet in the Bay of Bengal had been permitted to use Mergui and Aceh to repair their ships after engagements. However, particularly during the easterly monsoon, Britain had no suitable harbor on the Indian east coast and damaged British ships had to limp right around to Bombay for repairs. This made the EIC now more aware than ever of the urgent need to have a British naval base on the eastern side of the Bay of Bengal. The EIC board in Madras gave the project to colonize Phuket the green light, with one EIC officer waxing lyrical: "that Junk Ceylon possesses every advantage that can be desired as a productive country with a healthy climate for a British settlement, has been fully established by the concurring testimony of all persons who have visited the place or considered the subject."[561]

The Burmese Invasion of Phuket

As subscriptions and preparations for the occupation of the island were resumed, yet another black cloud appeared on the horizon. In 1785, after King Tak Sin was assassinated, Rama I took the throne amid rumors that a Burmese invasion of Siam – and of Phuket – might be imminent. Light and Scott, as opportunist as ever, decided to turn the situation to their advantage. In order to get the Siamese to pay for and build the forts they themselves would require on Phuket for its defense and thereby save on the up-front costs of establishing their colony, Scott laid out their rather Machiavellian scheme in a letter to Lord Cornwallis in India:

> "In order to enable him [Phaya Pimon – the Phuket governor] to put himself into a state of defence without suspicion, I have here improved the rumour of the Burmese war and invasion against which he is now providing. As I have offered my aid to repel this invasion, they mean to give me people to construct a fort [at Yamoo] which shall be sufficiently strong to serve as a place of arms and have lodging for 3-400 men. The Burman invasion [rumor] is to continue the ostensible course of preparations until February, or until our force arrives from Bengal."[562]

In December 1785, to Light and Scott's exasperation, just as the second EIC invasion force for Phuket was being prepared again in Madras, and before Scott could build his discount-price forts on Cape Yamoo and Ko Rang, Phuket was suddenly pitch-forked into war when the Burmese did actually invade the island. Just two years before, the British parliament, pushed by Prime Minister Pitt, had passed an Act to regulate and control the increasingly prodigal EIC. The company was now, by law, no longer allowed to get involved in any local wars without first obtaining British government permission. As there was now a local war on Phuket the EIC directors informed them that, yet again, the taking of Phuket by force must be put on hold.

Local Phuket historical lore today tells of how captains Light and Scott tried to help the people of Phuket, warning them of the approaching Burmese and even offering to assist them in building defenses and to fight. But, as one can see by digging slightly deeper into the facts, any such actions arose only from their selfish and duplicitous motives. As the first Burmese invasion fleet appeared off Phuket, both Light and Scott just cleared off, leaving the islanders to their fate.

Phaya Pimon, the Phuket governor and husband of Lady Chan, had, as we have seen, had just died some days before this invasion. With the Burmese fleet already at Takuapa and about to invade, Lady Chan wrote a plea for help to Francis Light just before he fled. "I have heard news that you are making ready your ship to leave and we have received news that the Burmese are coming to attack Thalang and the Governor is very ill. If the Burmese come I must depend on you as a post to cling to."[563] By the general tone of their correspondence it appears that Light and Lady Chan had become good friends. Nevertheless, when the chips were down, Francis Light took to his ship and simply sailed away leaving Phuket, Lady Chan and her daughters to their fate. James Scott, as we have seen, also left his wife and children on the island as the Burmese fleet approached and sailed his ship away to Tranquebar, the Danish trading station in India,.

Both Light and Scott probably expected Phuket to be overrun and destroyed. Therefore, the speed with which the king, Rama I, repelled the huge Burmese invasion and the fact that Lady Chan and the Phuketians in the Thalang fort held off the Burmese must have surprised them somewhat. Maybe even embarrassed them as, to convince the EIC to back their scheme they had previously been emphasizing to Madras the weakness of the Siamese military. Scott even wrote to Madras inferring that the Burmese retreat was not necessarily due to Siamese military strength and good generalship but possibly to internal issues within the Burmese army. "On a sudden the Burmese army disappeared, but [whether] beat by the Siamese or occasioned by a dissention among their generals is uncertain."[564]

After the invasion, Light did at least send assistance from his own pocket to the starving people on Phuket (which no Siamese lords did), but this of course was not for purely philanthropic reasons, as he wrote to Madras: "I have sent to the people of Junksalong 500 bags of rice in order not to lose entirely the goodwill of the islanders."[565]

It was not only Light and Scott who were surprised by the speed with which the Siamese repelled the Burmese. The sultan of Keddah, it appears, had been lucratively selling weapons to the Burmese king that he had probably been buying from Light and Scott. He may even, as was rumored, have been conspiring with the king of Burma against his Siamese overlords, as were some of the other mutinous Malay states. With the war now over and the Siamese back in control of the central peninsula, the sultan probably felt he urgently needed protection against any potential Siamese retribution for his suspected duplicity, as well as against any further attacks on his kingdom by the Bugis pirates and raiders in the region. The sultan promptly contacted Light and this time made him a new offer – he would cede to the EIC the almost uninhabited offshore island of Penang in return for an annual rent and British military protection.

Why Penang Was Colonized and not Phuket

Now, after 12 years of intrigues, Light and Scott had two islands potentially in their hands – Phuket and Penang – and an EIC in the mood to do something to obtain a base on the east side of the Bay of Bengal. Light, seeing this open offer of a gift of Penang Island as a less troublesome and less expensive way to get his colony established, now changed tack and started extolling the virtues of Penang over Phuket to the EIC. He wrote to tell them it had an even better harbor than Phuket, and it was closer to the Malacca Straits. The two men, however, continued to hedge their bets by proposing that the EIC take both ports – as Scott wrote to the EIC: "In Pulao Penang you acquire the best and most convenient Marine port which the Malay coast affords whether you consider it a retreat for a war fleet or a port of economical commerce. In possessing Salang (Phuket) you enter into the receipt of a certain and rapidly increasing commerce on the premises pointed out."[566] Light even wrote to Madras using an "economy of scale" argument, saying that Penang could be taken and held using the same ships and men that could be used to take and defend Phuket and the two birds could therefore be killed with one stone.

The EIC directors in India called for a report from one of their members, a Mr. Joseph Price. He preferred Penang, as its harbor lay right on the route to China and nearer the Malacca Straits. However, he felt Phuket would be a more viable commercial center and agreed with Light and Scott that the same force could be used to occupy and defend both islands. Madras passed this dual colony scheme for the approval of the main board in London. In 1786, after many months' wait, a ship arrived in Calcutta with a letter from the EIC directors approving that "Possession is to be taken of the ports and islands offered to us by the King of Cudda [Keddah] and especially Junkceylon which is occupied by a separate people to the number of 50,000 who have offered Captain Light the sovereign command amongst them."[567] Clearly, Light's liberal use of statistics (Phuket's population after the first Burmese invasion was around 8,000 at most) had worked. The reason the EIC gave for taking possession of these two islands was: "Not merely for the purpose of excluding the French, (though that is a capital object) but for the expectation of very valuable commercial acquisitions and shipping conveniences … and for extending our commerce amongst the eastern islands and indirectly by their means to China."[568]

Given that Penang was being offered willingly by the sultan of Keddah, and not wanting to damage their trade prospects with Siam by having a war over Phuket, the EIC directors made the decision to take Penang Island first. In late August 1786, Francis Light, supported by an armed EIC frigate and a contingent of Indian army sepoys from Madras, landed and raised the Union Jack on Penang Island, giving the British their first foothold in the central peninsula. A congratulatory letter soon came from the EIC in India, which also advised Light and Scott that, due to the current state of the company's finances, the directors felt it would be more prudent to operate just one colony first and see how it fared. The obdurate Light and Scott, who both preferred the commercial possibilities offered by tin-rich Phuket, refused to give up on their plan for also taking Phuket. Scott tenaciously wrote back to Calcutta urging the EIC to continue the plan to take Phuket, as, he claimed, profits there "were more quickly to be gained and would be enough to defray the expenses of both colonies."[569]

20.4 A re-enactment of the British and Indian troops that occupied Penang. This EIC force was originally also meant to occupy Phuket Island at the same time.

But by early 1787, the next year, conditions changed on Phuket. The new king, Rama I, had taken firm control over the central peninsula and a new Siamese superintendent general with troops was positioned in the south. On Phuket itself, a new governor was put in place. Despite gaining great acclaim for her leadership and heroism against the Burmese and her sister Mook's daughter being one of the king's concubines, Lady Chan was no longer as powerful on the island as when her husband had been the governor. She wrote to Light, "At present the Chao Praya Thalang [new governor] and I are not on good terms. I am sending Nai Phet, Nai Kaoe and Nai Thit Phrom to let you know the details, please send a small gun of good make for my personal use."[570]

Light also clearly had a very low opinion of the new governor, who was probably the one referred to in the Annals of Thalang with the catchy name of Phaya Phetsirisiphji-chaisongkhram. "The present governor styled Chau Praya Salang is one of the greatest villains who has raised himself by ingratitude, deceit, murder and rapine from a low and indigent state. He wrote me a letter expressing great esteem and friendship to which I did not answer."[571] However, despite his obvious distaste for the man, Light – still doggedly in pursuit of his objectives – was not above dealing with him. He wrote a most private letter to this new governor and offered him the same seditious deal to make Phuket British, on terms similar to those Phaya Pimon and Lady Chan had agreed. Light reported back to India on the new governor's quick and positive response, "A few days ago he sent me a messenger to assure me if I would next November send a vessel with some troops, he would deliver the island to the English and only required a small annual allowance for himself."[572] The EIC directors, however, in a cautious mood, still wanted to see how Penang fared first. Scott and Light, now knighted as Sir Francis Light, continued their trade with Phuket. Scott returned to Phuket regularly and apparently started a new family there. Light, however, never did return, being too occupied with governing Penang.

The immediate financial success of Penang, just as Light and Scott had foretold, meant that the EIC directors in India probably felt it was more beneficial to keep Siam as a potential friend and trading partner and not to risk war. Light always regretted not obtaining Phuket, which he later admitted he had always preferred to Penang. He wrote rather frustratedly in his memoirs:

> "Had he [Phaya Pimon] lived, I would have secured possession of the island. His death, which happened in December 1785, altered the certainty of success to a dubious point. His widow, the only person of estimation, would willingly have given up her power. Her sons and nephews beseeched me to take the government of the island. Could I have had the assurance of support from [the British] government I should have embraced the offer and secured both these islands."[573]

Epilogue

One of the last letters Light received from Thalang was in 1793, from the son of Lady Chan, who had now become the governor of Thalang; he wrote, "Please spare a thought for Khun Munda [Lady Chan]. She has aged very much lately and is not in such good health as she used to be. Mae Prang her daughter has died. Please send some white cloth for ceremonial use [mourning]."[574] Light, now aged 53, was also not well. He suffered from recurring bouts of malaria that were progressively sapping his health. He had been knighted and had become rich running his colony, just as he had envisaged. In 1793, he wrote back to his home village in Suffolk to his childhood friend, George Daughty, the guardian of his eldest son William in England. Light had recently sent Daughty a large sum of money for two purposes: to buy William "the best education that money can procure" and also to buy Goldsberry farm right beside Light's own birthplace. "I have a longing desire to become the owner of it, I shall then think of retiring in good earnest."[575]

A year later, stricken with another particularly severe bout of malaria, he wrote his last letter to his old childhood friend Daughty. "I have a sensation that I shall not have the happiness to see you again … Adieu my dear friend. Continue to plough your fields, it is a thousand times preferable to Governing."[576] After freeing most of his slaves the day before, Sir Francis Light died in Penang in 1794, aged 54. He lies buried under some frangipani and raintrees in the old Protestant cemetery in Georgetown behind the grand Eastern and Oriental Hotel.

James Scott went on to become the richest man in Penang, with large property holdings and trading businesses. He had a new family of six children there. One of his sons, William, later became the harbormaster and postmaster in Singapore and another, Robert, settled in Java. After Light's death Scott made a grab for much of Light's estate from his "widow", the mother of his children, Martina Rozells. Martina unsuccessfully fought Scott in the Penang courts and lost much of her wealth and land. She eventually married an Englishman named Mr. Timmer and lived on Penang until her death in 1822.

James Scott appears to have simply abandoned his Siamese wife and children in Phuket. When the Burmese again invaded Phuket in 1810, the victorious Burmese general wrote a letter to the governor of Penang, stating that the Burmese had "found there the wife and children of Captain James Scott a servant of your company [the EIC]."[377] They had told the Burmese that their husband and father, James Scott, who now lived in Penang, was coming to get them. "Captain Scott," continued the Burmese general, "not being a Siamese, nor a subject of the Siamese government, shall receive no hurt from us and is at liberty to come and carry away his wife and

20.5. James Scott's grave in Penang today.

children who await him at any time he pleases."[578] Unbeknownst to his abandoned wife and children in 1810, so anxiously awaiting their father's return to Phuket, James Scott had died in Penang in 1808, some 18 months earlier.

The 19th Century

21

Kathu's New Treasure

1790 TO 1810

Light and Scott were soon proved right. Under their "rational government" of low taxes, free trade, clear laws and relative security, Penang grew in eight short years from a simple nipa hut fishing village in 1786 to a town of over 10,000 people, plus some 2,000 "transients" living on ships, junks and prahus by the time of Sir Francis Light's death in 1794. The economic freedom of Penang began to attract many poorer emigrants from south China, some of whom then headed north to Phuket, where, in the jungles and swamps of Kathu in the late 1790s, large new lodes of surface tin were being discovered.

Phuket Town Develops as Tin Mining Starts in Kathu

Kathu had previously been an area frequented only by hunters chasing flocks of water-fowl in the swamps or rhinoceros, tigers, deer and boar in the forests. In 1870, Dr. D. B. Bradley, publisher of the Bangkok Daily Advertiser, visited Phuket and tells us the history of the early development of these new mines at Kathu.

"The island was, some few years ago, divided into two provinces, called Salang [Tha-lang] and Poket. Before the division, the island consisted of only one province called Salang, the principle inhabitants of which were Malays, with a few Siamese, and they cultivated rice and caught fish sufficient for their own consumption. The Governor of the island was then Phra Phalat [the son of Lady Chan]. He was sent to Poket when it was only a fishing village and being an enterprising sort of man he determined to see what treasures were concealed beneath the soil and was so far successful as to find something which he thought would in a few years amply repay the outlay which he might make ... The Chinese soon flocked in numbers to Phuket and Phra Phalat furnished them with funds to commence work and the place prospered and grew apace."[579]

Access into Kathu at the time was up the crocodile-infested Klong Bang Yai, the stream (now very silted up and in most places encased in concrete as a stormwater culvert in Phuket City) which runs down from Kathu past Sam Kong (by the new Tesco Lotus store) into Phuket City, past the Tavorn Hotel and then enters the sea at Sapan Hin (the bay here was known formerly as "Bukit" or "Tongkah" Harbor). Small flat-bottomed boats poled supplies, equipment and people up this river, through thick jungle, to the primitive Chinese mining camps being set up in clearings (in the area around Get Ho village in Kathu today). By 1800, about a mile up this Klong Bang Yai from the sea, far enough inland to deter pirates, a ramshackle Chinese shanty port town appeared to supply these prospectors and miners with food, equipment, opium and gambling and to smelt their tin ore. This settlement became known as "Bukit", "Poket" or now "Phuket" town.

Bangkok Gets Closer: A New Road across the Peninsula

By the early years of the 19th century, tin production in the region had increased to around 400 tons a year. Some years as much as 40 tons was transported to Bangkok as tax and much of the rest was used to buy weapons and cloth, which also had to be transported to Bangkok. Due to the constant threat of piracy, it was unsafe to ship these valuables via the Straits of Malacca to Bangkok. Instead, they were usually sent by the old trans-peninsular route overland from Marid Town (Thap Phut today) in Phang Nga by river boat upstream, then carried by elephant or ox carts over the Khao Sok Pass (near the Rajaprapat Dam today), then downstream by river to Surathani, where they were loaded on to junks for Bangkok. The route was arduous and slow and many goods were lost en route. For example, one late 18th century Thai document tells us that the governor of Takuatung in Phang Nga, who, as a gift for the king, brought from India a shipload of "piece goods and silver vessels enameled in various colors as used at court … The Governor had all these valuable things conveyed under his personal supervision to Tha Khao Sok."[580] There, they were loaded on boats to go downriver to the Bay of Bandon on the east coast, but "owing to a sudden flood in the river, the Governor's boat sank and all the enameled ware was lost." Many other goods were lost in the crossing, both to the river and to dacoits and bandits, who preyed on these trans-peninsular trade convoys.

In 1804, Phraya Surindr-raja, a respected Thai commissioner for the region, set about building a new and easier route "for the conveyance of Royalties in kind and other dues over the peninsula … as the Khao Sok route was hardly practicable on account of the numerous rapids and [water] falls in the streams, hence crown property had gone many times lost … The king approved of the scheme and granted elephants for the purpose … to cut a track through the jungle from Pak Phanom to Phang Nga."[581] A squabble soon arose with the viceroy of Ligor and Phraya Surindr-raja about who would collect tolls along a section of the road that passed through Ligor's lands, a squabble which Phraya Suridr-raja won. This was a first early sign that Phuket, with its increasing wealth from tin, was beginning to challenge the traditional dominance of the ancient city of Ligor. This newly cleared route reduced the peninsular crossing time to four or five days. It also meant that Bangkok's previous remote and distant rule over Phuket was becoming closer, as the island became more valuable.

(Note: Around the early to mid 19th century visitors and foreigners started to refer to the ancient city of Ligor – today called Nakorn Sri Thammarat in Thai – by its Thai name, so we shall henceforward refer to it in this book as "Nakorn", not Ligor.)

22

The Burmese Conquest of Phuket

1809 TO 1811

King Bodawpaya of Burma (1792-1819), like some of his more audacious predecessors, decided he should be a "Cakkravartin" (the supreme ruler of the Buddhist world). In 1806 he revealed his new messianic military goals to his grand council of lords and court officers. Put simply, they were to "Destroy ... the Siamese, then turn his arms against the emperor of China and make him his tributary, thence he would bend his course towards the west, possess himself of the British colonies, attack the great Mogul in his empire [India] and make himself master of the whole Jambuwipa [the Buddhist area on earth]."582 Unfortunately for the residents of Phuket, their island sat near to the top of this megalomaniac shopping list.

Given the mediocre results of the last two Burmese invasions of Siam, King Bodawpaya resolved on a new strategy. This time he would attack the peninsula first to join forces with the "birds with two heads", which, in contemporary Asian king-speak, meant disaffected sub-lords who could be persuaded to change allegiance, such as the sultans of Keddah or Patani and most other peninsular Malay sultans chafing under Siamese rule. He would then join with them to attack north against Bangkok from there. He legitimized his attack to the south by stating that Burmese trade "has been repeatedly interrupted by the pirates of Tullebong [Ko Libong, off Trang], Pulo Sumawa [Ko Surin?] and Taun Lantar [Ko Lanta]. These places were inhabited by Chinese and Malay robbers who have been stimulated to acts of depredation by the Siamese Chief of Junkceylon ... it pleases him [the Burmese king] to issue the command for the destruction of the kingdom of Siam for thus sheltering thieves and robbers."583

In 1800, hearing from his spies that Siam's brilliant general, Rama I, was now on his deathbed, King Bodawpaya started the preparations for his attack. His atiwun (palace chamberlain) took 10,000 soldiers south to Tavoy and had a war fleet built of 237 war boats. The larger ones held around 50-70 men and were equipped with a bow cannon and a swivel gun. He taxed the area for supplies and raised a further 20,000 conscripts from the region, as, we are told, "if the atiwun was unsuccessful in this campaign against Siam he would be put to death."584

Rama I died in late September 1809 and almost immediately King Bodawpaya ordered his invasion. The Burmese southern army of some 28,000 men was split into an east wing and a west wing. The east wing with around 18,000 men moved against and captured Ranong and then marched across the peninsula and took Chumporn, thereby in theory sealing off the central peninsula from Bangkok. The west wing was the war fleet of around 300 war prows and some 10,000 men. Burmese records list this fleet as carrying 20 bow cannons, 200 swivel guns and 3,500 muskets with bayonets.[585] Most of the Burmese soldiers were armed only with swords and spears. This fleet was to proceed down the west coast to capture Phuket and the other western seaports of Siam.

22.1. A Burmese village headman raising a militia. The Burmese fleet and army that destroyed Phuket in 1809 comprised many such conscripted villagers.

In early October 1809, a force of 70 Burmese war prows and 3,000 men stopped to attack Takuapa and as one captured Burmese officer later testified, "The town did not put up any resistance, the people simply fled. We captured 13 four-inch caliber cannon, two swivel guns and nine muskets with about 2,000 sat of paddy, which was loaded aboard the ships. We also captured two old women."[586] The next day, 100 ships landed 4,000 troops at Na Toi near Thai Muang and Bangkhli. The same officer reported, "There was no resistance; the people fled. We captured 20 cannon, five swivel guns, 13 muskets and 3,000 sat of paddy rice."[587]

Rama I was succeeded as king by his son, Rama II, who at the age of 42 had had plenty of military experience, learned from his father, and was also an astute military leader. To counter the Burmese invasion, he moved his main army to Kanchanaburi to fend off the expected capital assault against Bangkok. He could only spare 5,000 men for the south. He dispatched them under Phraya Chasenyakon, who raised more men by militia levies as he went. They encountered the Burmese east wing army just north of Chumporn and after a victorious battle there, they forced the Burmese to retreat south to try to join with the west wing troops and fleet at Phuket.

The First Burmese Attack on Phuket

Meanwhile in Phuket, the governor ordered siege supplies to be urgently stockpiled in the Thalang fort and built stockades for the defense of Tharua port. But there was little time. The Burmese fleet landed in Phuket near Ban Saku (on Nai Yang beach near the airport) only three days after leaving Ranong. The Burmese commander of the invasion force later reported:

"General Nga-u … ordered me to embark my 3,000 men and told Singkha Turi-ang to take another 3,000 men … the two forces being ordered to meet up at Pak Pra, a thousand men were left to guard the boats. My force crossed over to the village of Sakhu (on Phuket) where it met a Siamese patrol and a brief skirmish ensued before the Siamese withdrew. We pursued them as far as Ban Takkien while the Siamese retreated to their fort at Thalang. We set up camp at Ban Takkien and … proceeded to invest Thalang by setting up fifteen stockades to cut off the town."[588]

Phuket's residents fled on boats, hid in the forests, swamps and hills, or gathered for refuge in the Thalang fort, which had held out during the last Burmese attack 24 years earlier. The fort was armed with 85 cannon and 20 swivel guns, many muskets and large stores of grapeshot that could tear an attacking army to shreds, but stores of material for making gunpowder were short. [589] Almost 2,000 Phuketians, without time to flee, crammed into the wooden fort, which was square in shape and only 400 meters on each side.

Part of the Burmese invasion fleet then sailed around Phuket's coast, raiding and pillaging the outlying settlements and looting and burning the deserted and undefended new Chinese settlements in Kathu. The fleet then converged on Tharua Harbor (Sapam Bay), where the locals had also resolved to make a stand. They had built stockades with cannons on Cape Yamoo to defend against any such naval approach. They had also, as usual, chopped down trees to block the river route up to Tharua and built defensive stockades in Thalang and on land approaches to the port town.

That night, the Burmese landed hundreds of men on the muddy shallows and in the mangrove forest south of Tharua. In addition, around a thousand Burmese troops came south from their main camp in Thalang. At dawn the next day the Burmese attacked. In just a few hours of fighting, they captured both the Yamoo stockades and Tharua town and spent the rest of the day "plundering all the valuables. Next they set fire to the dwellings so that conflagrations broke out in many points of the town. This done, they took with them whatever inhabitants they had succeeded in capturing alive."[590]

After a week, the 3,000 Burmese on Phuket were joined by an additional 1,000 troops, who had finished their plundering in Phang Nga province. On the night of November 18, ten days after they had first landed on Phuket, the Burmese commander launched their first massed night attack on the Thalang fort. It was a vicious and bloody night and the fort's defenders' cannons and grapeshot took a terrible toll; according to one captured Burmese officer's testimony: "We made a night attack on the Thalang defenses but we lost over 500 men killed as a result of Siamese cannon fire, as well as a great number of wounded and we withdrew to our stockades."[591] Shortly after this failed attack, the captured Burmese officer explained that the Phuket force received news that the main Burmese commander of both armies in the south, "General Nga U, had fallen sick and died. We were ordered to break off the siege and withdraw."[592] Burning most of the towns and taking their loot and many captive prisoners with them, the Burmese retreated to their prows and sailed back to Pak Chan, which is the island just

Map 9
1810 – 1812 Burmese Conquest and Siamese Reconquest

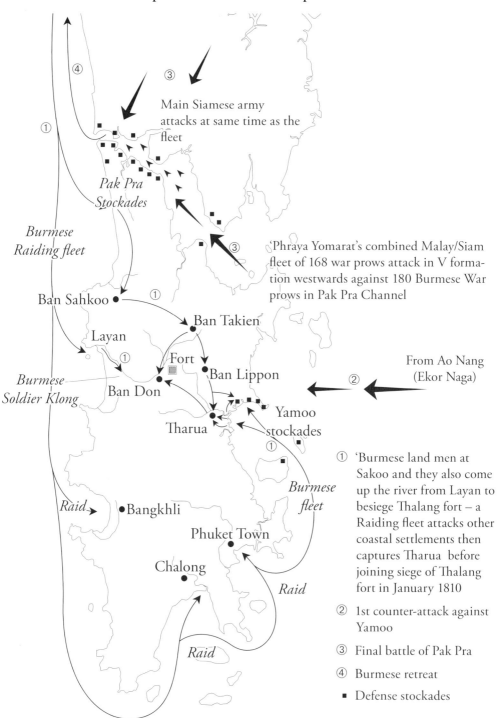

④

③

Main Siamese army attacks at same time as the fleet

①

Pak Pra Stockades

Burmese Raiding fleet

'Phraya Yomarat's combined Malay/Siam fleet of 168 war prows attack in V formation westwards against 180 Burmese War prows in Pak Pra Channel

③

Ban Sahkoo ●

①

Ban Takien

Layan

①

Fort

From Ao Nang (Ekor Naga)

Ban Lippon

②

Burmese Soldier Klong

Ban Don

Tharua

Yamoo stockades

①

Burmese fleet

① 'Burmese land men at Sakoo and they also come up the river from Layan to besiege Thalang fort – a Raiding fleet attacks other coastal settlements then captures Tharua before joining siege of Thalang fort in January 1810

Raid ● Bangkhli

Phuket Town

Raid

Chalong ●

② 1st counter-attack against Yamoo

③ Final battle of Pak Pra

Raid

④ Burmese retreat

■ Defense stockades

234

off Victoria Point and Ranong at the Burmese border today. There they tended to their wounded, divided their booty and shipped off their captives. The Burmese east wing army was still marching in retreat across the peninsula to meet the fleet at Phuket, so, after three weeks, the fleet was ordered to sail back from Pak Chan to capture and hold the Thalang fort and Phuket. The Burmese officers in charge were told very plainly by the overall commander that "If we failed again, we were to be put to death."[593] However, as the same Burmese officer also testified, while waiting at Pak Chan "our force had lost a considerable number of men through sickness, death and desertion and we now had only about 6,000 men left to invest Thalang."

Meanwhile, in Phuket, the elated locals, believing they had driven off the Burmese yet again, just as they had under Lady Chan in 1786, set about burning the dead, scavenging for food and repairing their homes and farms. They were therefore taken by surprise when the huge Burmese war fleet suddenly reappeared and again landed on Nai Yang beach in north Phuket, on the night of December 17.

The Second Burmese Attack

The Burmese left about 1,000 men with the fleet, which then spread out again to raid around Phuket's coast and the islands further south and also to try to capture and enslave any locals attempting to flee from Phuket to Phang Nga by swimming or by canoe. The 5,000 or so Burmese troops landed at Nai Yang rapidly marched from Ban Sakhu to Ban Takien and Ban Don in Thalang. This time Phuket's people had little time to restock the fort with victuals, and gunpowder supplies in particular remained critically short. Many of the people in the outlying villages had no time even to reach the fort, so they fled into the jungles and hills or tried to reach the Phang Nga mainland. "The Burmese attacked with such speed and straight away laid siege to the Thalang fort. ... The people who were able to get into the fort numbered only some six hundred. The besieging Burmese army swarmed around by the thousand."[594]

A later French Bishop, Jean Baptiste Pallegoix, wrote of an unfortunate French missionary named Monsieur Rabeau who had just been sent up from Penang to become the new pastor to the small flock of remaining Christians in the Tharua mission. He had arrived by boat from Penang only the day before this second invasion. In a letter he wrote later he noted, "I had arrived at Junkceylon on Saturday, towards midnight ... The following day I received information that the Burmese were already disembarked ... I fled into the citadel ... the hope and refuge of all the inhabitants of the island and remained there all the time of the siege."[595]

The Burmese army surrounded the Thalang fort again and, staying just out of range of its cannons, constructed stockades around it, five on each side. They then hauled their largest cannons up to the Khao Pratheo mountain in Thalang (the big hill near Ton Sai waterfall), from where we are told they could fire down into the Thalang fort.

Over the ensuing days, hundreds of flaming arrows were fired into the fort to terrorize the inhabitants, to set alight the wooden and nipa shelters and roofs of the buildings inside and to try to set off their gunpowder. Several probing night attacks were made which the Phuketians held off with noisy volleys of cannon, grapeshot and musket. Daytime probing attacks also continued, in order to get the Phuketians to fire off their muskets and cannons and use up their scant gunpowder reserves. The Burmese also set about digging trenches, protected with bamboo redoubts for shelter, which slowly approached the Thalang fort walls. The French Father Rabeau, stuck in the fort, tells us, "I was in perpetual fright but thanks to God I received no injury. I was busy tending to the sick."[596]

The Burmese pillaged and destroyed everything outside the fort – villages, temples, boats, fishing nets, crops, animals and fruit trees. Any people in hiding were hunted down. Those caught were thrown in wooden cages and sent back to Burma as slaves. Burmese war prows also patrolled the north and east coast, intercepting any boats, canoes or swimmers trying to reach the mainland. The bulk of the Burmese fleet remained moored in the Pak Pra channel (between the Yacht Haven marina and the Saracen Bridge today); this was to fend off any attempted Siamese counter-attack from the Phang Nga side of the Pak Pra. The Burmese army occupied the existing Siamese stockades along the south side of the Pak Pra Straits and built more on the mainland Phang Nga side.

These stockades stood about two to three meters high and were made from bamboo stakes, often with sharpened stakes protruding all around the base and with loopholes cut in the bamboo, through which to fire muskets. The stockades were surprisingly resilient. British gunners in the first Anglo-Burmese war, just 14 years later, recorded that cannonballs of up to six inches in diameter did little damage to such stockades, as the bamboo simply flexed and the cannonballs passed right through. Of course, a six-inch cannon ball passing through the stockade would annihilate any soft, juicy humans it hit, splattering meat and blood around the place and no doubt gravely disconcerting any other occupants, but the stockade itself would remain standing. One frustrated British gunner wrote, "A battering which would have dashed masonry to ruin, made a very poor breach in a stockade."[597] The British gunners solved the problem by loading their cannon with a half-weight of gunpowder. The slower-moving cannon balls now did not pass through but instead "prostrated that which they [previously] only wounded in their rapid passage."[598] The Malays and Siamese, it seems, got around the same problem by firing bar shot (for bringing down ships' rigging) at the stockades.

Back at the fort, the covered Burmese trenches slowly approached the Thalang fort. The siege and the trenching had been going on for three weeks when the 8,000 troops of the Burmese east wing army eventually reached Phuket in their retreat from Chumporn. The Burmese now had around 13,000 soldiers on the island and a fleet of over 200 war prows offshore. Around 600 Phuketians were trapped in the besieged fort – without their cannons and grapeshot, they knew they would surely be done for. The worst of it must have been that they had no way of knowing whether any relief was even on its way. It must have been a frightful wait.

The Siamese Relief Forces

After countering the main threat against Bangkok and sending south the first force that defeated the Burmese east wing army at Chumporn, Rama II dispatched a senior lord, Phraya Thai Nam, to Nakorn and Songkla to order all the southern governors to raise a force and go to the immediate relief of Phuket. The king also sent a second force under Phaya Thotsayotha by sea to Chaiya, with orders to levy more men and march to the aid of Thalang. Then, a month later, after finally defeating the Burmese in the north, a large Siamese army under the control of Phaya Burinthra also marched south. These different forces heading for Phuket were put under the combined control of Phraya Yommarat, a senior royal Siamese lord and distinguished general.

When the first envoy, Phraya Thai Nam, arrived at Nakorn bearing the king's orders, Phraya Borirakphubet, the new viceroy of Nakorn at the time, who was more commonly known as Viceroy Noi, immediately dispatched his west coast fleet of 17 ships based at Trang to Phuket. But this small fleet could do little against the huge Burmese fleet, so it loitered ineffectually near Ko Lanta.

The real naval power on the Siamese west coast was Keddah, whose Malay and Orang Laut (Sea Gypsy) captains were the best naval warriors in the region. However, because of suspicions of his earlier collusion with Burma, neither Nakorn nor Bangkok trusted the contumacious sultan of Keddah. The governor of Songkla was therefore dispatched with an army which camped near the sultan of Keddah's palace to oblige him, first to supply the Siamese army with rice, secondly to put a fleet together to assist Phuket and thirdly to make sure that this Keddah fleet did not then join the Burmese side. This overt Siamese action made relations a little tense. One Malay writer reported that the governor of Songkla "ordered supplies of rice to be furnished and sent up to Trang. His behavior was rather extreme. Judging by the way he went about matters, it was as though he suspected that Keddah was in collusion with Burma. It almost came to an open breach. His majesty [the sultan] contemplated a resort to arms."[599]

Bangkok and Nakorn were not wrong in their estimation of the loyalty of the duplicitous sultan of Keddah. In a later interrogation of Zeya Suriya Kyaw, a Burmese commander captured in Phuket, he admitted that at the time he had received a most peeved letter from the sultan of Keddah, stating that "a Siamese force of about 3,000 men had come down to keep an eye on him and therefore any attempt to join the Burmese would meet with opposition. He therefore asked for a Burmese force of 6,000 men to be sent down to attack Keddah and facilitate Keddah joining the Burmese."[600] But the Burmese were too preoccupied in the north to worry about Keddah, so knowing he faced a certain and probably most unpleasant death if he disobeyed the orders from Nakorn or Bangkok, the Keddah sultan duly dispatched 28 war prows from Kuala Keddah, Langkawi and Tarutao. It is from a Malay poet who traveled with this Malay fleet that we get our best account of the whole ensuing battle for Phuket through his lengthy and illuminating poem, "The Sayair Sultan Maulana" ("The Sayair"). The late Australian Professor Cyril Skinner translated this poem into English.

The Keddah Malay fleet sailed north and was joined by seven more prahus from Setul [Satun], 15 boats from Trang and Ko Talibong and the first 17 vessels from the Nakorn squadron, making a fleet of 67 war prahus and approximately 2,500 men. This allied Siamese-Malay fleet arrived in early January 1810, after the Thalang fort had been under siege for three weeks. The bulk of the Burmese war prows were still gathered in the Pak Pra channel in the north, but some were still scouting and raiding for prisoners and booty. The Siamese allied fleet stopped first out of sight of the Burmese patrol ships at Ekor Naga, a headland point between Krabi and the island of Ko Yao Yai. They sent a scouting team under "Captain Elak a man from the Talibong squadron" to Phuket to assess the situation. The author of "The Sayair" tells us that he returned the next day and reported that Thalang

> "was hard pressed by the Burmese who had built a great number of stockades all along the shores. The people of Thalang had put up a stout defence … from inside their defence they fought, keeping up a continuous bombardment from the town, preventing the Burmese from moving about freely, but they [the Burmese] had invested it with stockades which enveloped the town like a mosquito net, so that no matter how large the relieving force, it would be unable to break through. … [Even at Ekor Naga] We could hear quite clearly the thunder of the cannons."[601]

The Battle of Cape Yamoo

This motley Siamese fleet of Malays, Orang Laut and Thais, all under different leaders, held a council of war and decided their best move would be to attack the stockades on Cape Yamoo to test the Burmese strength. The fleet approached close to Cape Yamoo under the cover of night. "The Sayair" poet then tells us:

> "When it was almost light they sailed up to Tanjung Jambu [Cape Yamoo]. As the stockades loomed up before them the oarsmen rowed as fast as they could towards the enemy. The Burmese were lined up within their palisades and were the first to fire off their cannons. The Burmese war boats were there – we counted at least nineteen – they were un-manned as the men had all gathered in the stockades … The fleet came on and reached the shore, shooting at the stockades, which began to splinter. Our cannon were using chain shot [used for bringing down rigging – another means of countering the stockade's permeability] and the Burmese could not carry out observations. The ghurabs [big Malay war prahus] came on one after another; although the Burmese gunfire was intense, pride prevented them from retreating. The young men, anxious not to disgrace themselves, advanced in good order side by side. Acting like true knights, the cream of our young nobility paid no heed to the thunder of the cannons, although it seemed more than the ships could bear … the Burmese had erected their stockades on top of the hill, five in a row. With their cannon and swivel guns they bombarded us until we felt we could take no more. The noise of the gunfire was deafening, the shouting and cheering were indescribable. The noise from our

war drums swelled the din as on every ship the drums were beaten. The Nakorn squadron … seemed very frightened, they did not keep in line but hung back in the rear … the Burmese fired from their trenches and the shots came buzzing past like bees. Most however were too high … falling behind our troops and splattering into the sea with a hissing sound, like a shoal of mullet. The [Malay] commanders ran their vessels up on the beach. They were followed by their men and battle was joined in earnest. The battle swayed to and fro and went on till noon when the Burmese, unable to hold out any longer, broke and fled in confusion. The more vigorous of our troops stormed into the stockades searching for loot and prisoners. They seized all manner of equipment which they carried off … the wounded Burmese were unable to flee, being too weak to move. The Nakorn men came up at a gallop and slaughtered them before they could ask for quarter. The commissioner too leapt ashore, his sword whistling through the air and when he saw some wounded Burmese approach him, he cut three of them down on the spot…The troops looted absolutely everything right down to pieces of sacking and matting … before setting fire to the stockades and the [Burmese] war boats. The Orang Laut were very smart and managed to capture three Burmans whom they at once took down to their kakaps [smaller boats] to be put in irons. The Burmese dead in the stockades totalled at least seventeen men. The reason why the stockades were put to the torch was because we had not sufficient men to garrison them. In the same way all their war boats had resin poured over them and were burnt because we were unable to safeguard them against attack from any Burmese reinforcements that might arrive." [602]

The Phuket people in the Thalang fort may have heard the cannon fire from the battle at Cape Yamoo and now knew that someone was trying to come to their relief. For the Burmese, it meant redoubling their trenching efforts. Some of the Phuketians, who had been hiding in the nearby jungles and also heard the fighting at Yamoo, came out from hiding to reach the Siamese-Malay fleet and troops. "The Sayair" poet tells us:

"They gave us news of Thalang. The Burmese had surrounded the town, the sufferings of the garrison were unbearable and they had almost run out of powder and shot. Supplies of food were completely exhausted and the population was in great distress. If help was delayed, Thalang would fall. When they had told us their news, the squadrons assembled to hold a council of war, but decided if we were to advance overland the enemy force would be much too strong for us …The discussions had not been going on for long when the damned Burmese returned. They came on like wounded animals, with a rush, charging right out in the open. Their commander wore a red coat and waved his sword as he led his men on. In carrying out the charge we bombarded them from our ships and they had to crawl along like animals but still they pressed home their attack … They quickly reoccupied their stockades. It was fortunate that our army had already returned to our ships in good order – if not we would have had some hard knocks and we were lucky to avoid a mauling … Even if we were to attack again and capture the stockades it would be of no avail as we had no one to look after them. The signal gongs were beaten and the entire fleet hoisted anchor and put out to sea. We went back to Pulo Penaga [Ko Yao Yai] … We had four different forces, Siamese and Malay, foreign to each other and they could not agree on a common plan so nothing could be done … We awaited the Bangkok army."[603]

Just after the battle at Cape Yamoo, the EIC ship, the Montrose, under the command of a Captain Peters, sailed into Tharua Harbor, apparently quite unaware of the battle going on in Phuket. The Burmese commander in Phuket sent him back to Penang as a trade. He explained what happened in an attached letter to the British EIC governor of Penang:

"I had a party of observation of 3,000 men at Jumboo [Yamoo] and Turro [Tharua] to watch the motions of the Siamese and Malay boats that came to the relief of that place. It was at this time that Captain Peters arrived … [He] landed in his ships boat and was immediately seized by the advance party who were ignorant whether he was a friend or an enemy. He was brought to my headquarters which were at Sagoo [Ban Sakhoo]. I requested Captain Peters to write to Captain Hay [a passenger on board who had taken over command after Captain's Peters capture] to come round with the vessel to the roads of Sagoo near which the main army now lay encamped … The vessel did come round to Sagoo but went off without giving us any opportunity of sending Captain Peters onboard. I therefore send our Admiral John Bartel [a mercenary working for the Burmese] to carry Captain Peters to Penang and bring back sundry articles."[604]

22.2. A 1768 Danish cannon which now sits outside Phuket's central police station. Before its destruction in 1809 we are told the Thalang fort was defended by around 80 such imported European cannons but not enough gunpowder.

The Fall and Destruction of the Thalang Fort

The Siamese attack on Cape Yamoo had taken place around January 12, 1810, after the Burmese had been besieging the Thalang fort for 26 days. The Burmese leaders, aware that Siamese forces were now approaching, decided to make a final assault on the fort.

Inside the fort, "The Sayair" author tells us:

"The garrison was under strength and powder and shot were very short and they had run out of saltpeter and sulphur [for making more powder] … The Burmese were aware of their weakness and brought all their resources to bear upon them. The Burmese brought their stockades nearer and nearer, working by night and resting by day … the Siamese did not try to escape, they merely stayed there waiting for help to arrive … The Burmese rested a row of logs on the top of their stockades, projecting downwards in the direction of the fort, forming a chute down which they could roll firewood … including logs of considerable size into which they had plugged charges of gunpowder. The firewood was picked up by the Thalang men and put down inside the fort … The Burmese worked night and day to pile on even greater quantities of firewood to a height sufficient to cover a man's head. The Siamese … were at the end of their resources … and were unable to drag it away. The Burmese then set light to the wood and caused it to blaze up. The flames rose above the city inside and the suffering was too great to be borne. They set fire to the fort on three of its sides and waited with their weapons trained on the fourth side. Anyone who tried to dash out faced certain death."[605]

The flames from the fort walls became too big and too hot and the defenders were forced to attempt a breakout. As soon as they opened the gate to flee, the Burmese opened fire and then rushed at the fort and the fleeing Phuketians.

"Great numbers of men were killed and many others wounded or maimed. Some were captured and put in prison cages and only a few were able to escape. Mothers, fathers, sons and wives lost contact with each other in the indescribable confusion, few of them had anywhere to flee to and it was every man for himself. They fought to get out first and several were cut down by their own comrades … women and children were crushed like mushrooms at the gates … the besieging Burmese swarmed around by the thousand and the sufferings of the defenders were unbearable. And so the fortress of Thalang fell on the ninth day of the month of Zulhijjah [the last month of the Islamic lunar calendar – the time of the Hajj pilgrimage]."[606]

Out on Ko Yao Yai that night, the allied fleet of 64 ships, waiting impotently, saw a great orange glow in the sky over Thalang from the fire in the fort. "That night flames were seen from a great fire in the centre of the island which burnt all through the night."[607]

Father Rabeau, the French missionary trapped in the Thalang fort, wrote that as the fortress walls burnt he tried to keep the few Christians in the fort together and united in prayer, but:

"they absolutely wanted to go out of the citadel, I followed them but met the enemy in the middle of the citadel, Burmese with naked swords and spears in hand … I advanced towards them holding a cross in my right hand and the picture of the holy virgin in my left and I said to them, 'I am a priest of the living God. I never do harm to anybody. ' God touched their hearts, they put their hands on my head and on those of the Christians who followed me and they made us sit down, then they tied us up and took my long clothes and my prayer book. Afterwards they untied us and under the protection of one of their chiefs, led us to a camp and put fetters to our feet. I remained in the open air ... they divested me of all my clothes except my pants. ... After a very bloody siege of four weeks, the fortress, the hope and refuge of all the inhabitants of the island, had been burnt and taken by the enemy. Some of the inhabitants have been killed, a great number made prisoners and the majority scattered into the forests. ... After having pillaged everything at Jongselang the Burmese embarked for a place near by."[608]

A captured Burmese officer later reported that, after the fall of the Ban Don fort, "The town was taken and we captured 84 three and four pound cannon, 20 swivel guns, 50 muskets and over 300 families and 3,000 bars of tin, all the weapons and the captives were sent up to Tavoy."[609] Father Rabeau and the Christians were apparently also shipped off the island as captives on a Burmese ship captained by a Frenchman and manned by some Bengali Indian Muslims. According to the later testimony of one of the Christian captives, these Bengali sailors mutinied en route and Father Rabeau tried to prevent them from harming the French captain. The Bengalis however bound him in ropes and "the reverend Father Rabeau was cast into the sea by these Mohamedans and perished."[610]

Any Phuketians who managed to escape the Burmese went into hiding in the forests and tried to flee across to Phang Nga. The next day, "The Sayair" author tells us, the allied fleet on Ko Yao Yai met the first of these refugees, who had rowed a canoe across from Phuket. He confirmed that the fort had fallen and "the Burmese had overran the whole island and were pursuing and hunting down people all over the place."[611]

The allied fleet in Phang Nga Bay, according to "The Sayair" author, could still do little, as they were too few to attack the Burmese on land and were awaiting the arrival of the main Siamese armies. The best they could do was to patrol the east coast of the island and try to assist any islanders trying to flee. "Isolated groups of men coming in, we collect them and ferry them across to the mainland – and if the enemy come after us we will fight. The smaller boats ferried them while the larger boats formed a line of battle ... those hiding in the woods had to fight off the Burmese ... some three thousand people were taken across to the mainland."[612]

The main Burmese fleet of around 180 war prows remained in the Pak Pra channel. They occasionally "came out and threatened to attack and the Malays prepared to do battle ... they would not close with us and remained on guard at the mouth of the straits ... They erected stockades on the promontories on both sides of the narrows."[613] The Malays were confident on the water against the Burmese, of whom they said: "In fighting a naval battle they were only average – they were much better at fighting on land ... although we would have liked to go straight in and attack them, their stockades inspired too much respect ... what action there was [was] limited to cannonades. We remained alert, exchanging shouts and jeers."[614]

The Siamese Reconquest

So after two months, where were the Siamese relief columns? "The Sayair" author (who, as a Malay, was not over-fond of the Siamese) tells us the force under Phaya Thotsayotha had marched down from Chaiya and set up camp in Phang Nga "before the fort was seriously threatened. Messenger after messenger came from the fort urging them not to remain idle at Phang Nga, but they did not advance ... only when the citadel was about to fall did they attempt to strike a blow in Takuatung where the Burmese were reported to be weak and even though the Burmese retreated they still did not pursue them."[615] "The Sayair" poet rather disdainfully tells us that, on hearing that the Thalang fort had fallen, Phraya Thotsayotha and his forces pulled back to Phang Nga town and sat there while "the citadel of Thalang had been burnt to the ground, the people captured and put in cages, the cannon and all that was of value in the city had been carried off ... the Burmese were all over the province rounding up the population and also erected many stockades to check the approaching army."[616]

22.3. A traditional Malay prow. During battles these were fitted with bow cannons and wooden armored planking on their foredeck. Eighty were built in Trang in just over a month for the Siamese re-conquest of Phuket in 1810.

Eventually, the main Siamese army from the north, under Phaya Burithra, joined Phraya Thotsayotha's force and marched towards Pak Pra on the opposite shore from Phuket. Meanwhile, Phraya Yomarat, the overall Siamese commander, had sailed from Bangkok to Nakorn and then crossed to Trang with "an army of thousands of men which included hundreds of experienced fighters, soldiers of proven worth used to fighting against the Burmese."[617] In Trang, however, he discovered there were not enough boats available for his army, so he "set his men on a great boat building scheme … He ordered them to work without cease, with no let up by day or night. The work was completed in only twenty days. Eighty ships were built, big and small, complete with oars and sails."[618] Phraya Yomarat was also joined in Trang by a squadron of 50 more boats and 1,000 men enlisted from Phattalung and Patani. This relief force sailed north to Phuket. Eventually, in early March, over three months after the Burmese had first invaded Phuket, the combined Siamese land and sea forces of around 8,000 men and 180 boats were assembled for the reconquest. Against them, the Burmese army must have numbered some 9,000 men and around 180 war prows.

The Great Naval Battle of Pak Pra

On March 10, 1810, Phraya Yomarat ordered the attack by a combined land and sea assault on the Pak Pra straits to shift the Burmese fleet and clear their stockades, now erected on both sides of the straits. The plan was for the Siamese fleet to advance in a V-shaped formation from Phang Nga bay between the stockades and cannons into the Pak Pra channel and attack the main Burmese fleet, sitting between where the Yacht Haven marina and the Saracen Bridge are today. Simultaneously, the Siamese land army would attack the Burmese stockades on the Phang Nga side of the channel.

The allied fleet positioned the Keddah boats at the point of the V-formation – not just because they were renowned sailors and sea warriors with better and bigger war prahus, but also because the Siamese did not trust them and wanted them in the front where they could be watched. The fleet assembled with "flags and pennants fluttering in the breeze and their cannoneers ready". In the stockades overlooking the channel, the Burmese cannons and marksmen readied themselves. As the Siamese land forces started their attack on the Burmese stockades on the Phang Nga side, the author of "The Sayair" describes the frontal naval attack:

> "Into the straits rowed the fleet borne on the rising tide … The Burmese were drawn up waiting for them in a line that bridged the straits … like a fortress, a truly awesome sight and when they turned their gaze towards the shore, the stockades they saw seemed to foreshadow their doom and their limbs were as heavy as lead. … The Burmese opened a general bombardment and the thunder of their guns was deafening … Hearing the guns boom out, many sat there on their benches like a cat on hot bricks. The Malays too fired off their cannon as they rowed forward to the attack … seeing the stockades blocking their advance and with shots raining down upon them, some of our comrades looked as though they had just drunk of a bitter tasting medicine … Due to the strong current in the Pak Pra channel … there could be no question of retreating … The admiral put himself at the head of the fleet. Determined not to bring disgrace upon himself, he hastened into the attack. The enemy were bombarding us from their stockades, but with the help of Almighty God, none of the shots did any damage. Our can-

non kept up a thunderous bombardment directed at the stockades and the galleys. The Burmese were hard pressed because they were so close together. We could see our shots hitting the mark and hear them strike home as they landed on the boats one after another … The enemy gave every appearance of solidarity and we truly felt it was here we must meet our fate. But, because God made them weak, they were unable to withstand us. Our shots fell thick and fast, some fell on the war boats and others on the Burmese positions ashore and eventually all their boats turned tail. The [land] defenders took to their heels, some leapt into the war boats, while others made for the jungle. Some swarmed into boats too small to hold them all and when the westerly's whipped up the waves, the boats sank and the men struggled to find safety. The [Siamese] army, hot on their heels, overtook them and they were all put to death on the spot. Their war boats made off. Fighting to get through the mouth of the straits in confusion, they were scattered by a storm as they tried to escape the cannon balls that fell amongst them. They thought only of flight and would not wait for their comrades left behind … our fleet did not follow them as it was late in the afternoon. Many of their war boats were abandoned with their cargoes, paddy, rice and so on, jugs of this, jars of that, all looted by our comrades. As for the Siamese civilian prisoners, after the Burmese defeat, some were executed, others were taken away, while some managed to escape … [The victorious attackers] … were overjoyed as though the gates of heaven had opened up before them. This was the day that put an end to the fighting … Only two Keddah men came to grief; one man died with his arm severed and another was severely wounded … They met their doom from their own cannon. There were still some sparks left behind in the barrel when in foolhardy fashion they pushed in the shot, the cannon exploded and the gunners were blown up."[619]

The credit for the victory, claims "The Sayair" author, belonged to "the Keddah admiral and his lieutenant Paduka Seri Raja. He performed with an iron determination; he attacked without the slightest hesitation, if it was possible to set a value upon his bravery, the sight of him in action would have sent his price sky high … In the action you could see how their superior breeding made itself felt, the fame of his illustrious ancestors was increased and enhanced."[620]

The Siamese fleet pursued the Burmese up the coast the next day but did not find them and returned to Phuket. The Keddah fleet remained at Phuket for about another two months before being allowed to return home. The Phuketians who had escaped Phang Nga did not return as the island was now just a devastated wasteland. A contingent of Siamese troops remained on the island in case the Burmese came back again – which they soon did.

The Last Burmese Attack on Phuket

The Burmese war fleet had again stopped at Pak Chan by the Burmese frontier and remained there while it was re-supplied and new troops levied. Then, three months later, in late June 1810, King Bodawpaya ordered the fleet, now with about 6,000 men, to attack Phuket again. But the monsoon winds had now turned and, while heading south, the Burmese fleet ran into a heavy rainy season squall and many of the Burmese war prows, overloaded and low in the water, were swamped or were driven by the wind and waves into the breakers on the coast. Many Burmese soldiers were caught in the surf and rip tides and drowned. One of these captured Burmese officers explained under interrogation that the Burmese war prows:

> "ran into a storm … three boats sunk and over 100 men drowned … when the force reached Takua Pa it rested for three days. The next morning it set out but ran into a southerly gale with torrential rain, 16 more ships were lost and 30 men drowned … the boats returned to Takua Pa with only 44 boats and 3,000 men in the land and sea forces combined. We stopped there for five days … the force then marched south for five days until it reached Pak Pra. We cut down trees and built some rafts and got hold of a boat and we were able to ferry the entire force across in 8 days."[621]

The Burmese had lost nearly half their men in that storm – drowned or shipwrecked. Those who did survive the storm and made it to shore found themselves on the deserted and hostile coast of Phang Nga, clogged by thick jungle. While trying to make their way back northwards to Burma, many stragglers were captured, enslaved or killed by the locals and Siamese troops sent to attack them. The weather remained rough and when the fleet tried again to approach Nai Yang beach (near the airport today), several more boats foundered as the fleet came through the surf. The Siamese troops were ready for them and, "On being appraised of this unexpected good luck, the governor of Phuket swooped with his men on the shipwrecked Burmese, captured their war boats and made numbers of prisoners, including the lieutenant commander Chik-ke himself, whom he sent to Bangkok." However, as more and more Burmese troops reached the shore, the Siamese force broke and retreated by crossing over to the mainland in Phang Nga. The Burmese troops again marched into Thalang, which was now an utterly destroyed and deserted wasteland and they set up camp under instructions to build a new fort at Thalang "to be surrounded by an earth wall and a moat."[622]

But there was now little food to be had and the rain fell, and, rather like the French 120 years earlier, the Burmese realized there is not much one can do with Phuket and its tin mines when everyone has fled. The Burmese soldiers were desperately short of food. "We were reduced to digging up yams and tubers to eat. Sickness set in and a number of the men in the force died of hunger in the forest."[623] Two months later, in early September 1810, almost a year after the first Burmese invasion of that war, Viceroy Noi of Nakorn appeared on the mainland across the Pak Pra straits with a Siamese army of nearly 10,000 men and elephants. The Burmese, ill, disheartened and starving, decided they were too weak to fight and the whole force boarded their war prows and fruitlessly sailed back to Burma.

23

Destruction and Atrocities

1812 TO 1821

Phuket Destroyed and Depopulated

After the Burmese invaders left Phuket for the third time, the author of the poem, "The Sayair", describes the devastated island they left behind:

"The town of Thalang had been turned into a wasteland. The Burmese had really gone to extremes in reducing it to a wilderness. Every district we saw had been left desolated – villages and houses, stockades and forts were no longer visible; they had burnt them to ashes. Elephants and horses had been taken for food. They had felled the coconut trees and areca palms; every village had been leveled to the ground; they had destroyed all the crops – no sign of them remains. They uprooted all the chili plants and betel vines, heaped them together and burnt them. The chickens and ducks had been slaughtered; not one was left. Everything there was to loot the Burmese had looted. They squeezed the district dry … the people of Thalang who were still on the island had fled to the jungle in utter confusion, men and women, old and young. In all, only about a thousand of them came out. Many suffered from dysentery or colic and were reduced to mere skeletons. They had lost all spirit. Many had died in the marshes. Those who took refuge elsewhere did not come back for some time … The Indians, who had escaped and fled into the jungle, pinned their hopes on the treasures they had buried, but even these had disappeared. Many of the Chinese who survived were anxious to get away, frightened of being plundered again by the Siamese troops and some of them lost their lives in less time than it takes to burn cotton."[624]

Of a population of around 12,000-15,000 people on Phuket before the invasion, perhaps 3,000 died in the battles and famine. Some 5,000 people were taken by the Burmese as slaves and some 5,000 fled to Phang Nga and stayed away, fearful of another Burmese attack. Only a few brave or desperate souls remained on Phuket. Burma and Siam remained at war for over a decade after this invasion. There were frequent slave-raiding attacks back and forth across the Tenasserim range and up and down the Andaman coast. Phuket remained deserted and overgrown for almost a decade afterwards and became a base for pirates, who thrived in the lawless environment.

In 1818 the Burmese reportedly attacked and sacked Phuket again, purportedly in retaliation for "Malays from Phuket attacking Chinese and Burmese prows engaged in collecting birds' nests."[625] The sultan of Keddah also complained in a letter to the British in Penang that Siam had ordered him again to send war prahus, men and rice to join a Siamese force assembling in the Trang River, which then moved north to attack this Burmese naval force raiding round Phuket and other centers.

In 1824, six years after this last Burmese conquest of Phuket, Lieutenant James Low, an EIC envoy from Penang, visited Phuket and noted in his diary, "The Burmans … keep the people in perpetual commotion and strike terror into the population from Tannau [Tenasserim] down to Perlis … Captain Forrest in 1784 had rated the population of Salang (Phuket) at 12,000 souls … but since his day things have changed much for the worse … I was informed by the chief of Tharooa … that the island would not afford more than 1,000 men fit for labour."[626] Lt. Low estimated the population of Phuket at the time was less than "6,000 souls". Two years later, in 1826, Henry Burney, another EIC envoy, visited Phuket and estimated the population of the island as only 800 to 1,000 men "and most of their women and children spent the wet monsoon every year at Phang Nga."[627]

The Brutal Keddah War of 1821

The new Sultan Tajuddin of Keddah got on much better than his father had with the British settlement in Penang. In 1798 he also rented them a strip of land on the Keddah mainland opposite Penang, which the British named Province Wellesley. The EIC paid him a rent of ten thousand Spanish dollars a year for it and, much to the chagrin of his Siamese overlords in Nakorn and Ayutthaya, he gave none of this money to them. Siam also suspected that the new sultan of Keddah was, like his father, colluding with the Burmese and selling them arms. Worse still, probably because he now believed the British in Penang would come to his defense if Siam attacked him, Sultan Tajuddin also stopped sending his traditional "Bunga Mas" submission tribute to Bangkok. Such uppity insolence was too much for Bangkok.

In the summer of 1821, the later Thai Annals tell us, Lim Hoi, a Macao Chinese merchant from Phuket, was returning on his armed trade junk from Penang when he spied a Burmese boat heading south. He attacked and captured it and allegedly found a letter on it from the king of Burma to the sultan of Keddah, confirming their collusion in planning a new combined attack on Phuket. Lim Hoi passed this letter to the governor of Thalang who sent it on to Bangkok.[628] This may have been just a set-up, but it certainly gave the Siamese king a convenient excuse to discipline the recalcitrant sultan. As a reward [or pay-off], Lim Hoi was appointed Luang raja – the head of the small but growing Chinese community in Phuket – and to the position of tax farmer (collector) of the king's royalties. He was also awarded the equally lucrative tin smelting monopoly on the island.

The Siamese king ordered an army from Bangkok to head south and "join forces with the local troops from Nakorn, Phattalung, Songkla and Thalang and to go to ravage Keddah to a total ruin … [Malay leaders will find that] … whenever they behave [with] disloyalty they will be brought to destruction."[629] Led by Viceroy Noi of Nakorn, a Siamese army of over 7,000, including a levy of men and war prows from Phuket, marched and sailed south to Keddah to take vengeance. Bangkok wrote to the British in Penang first, explaining the reason for their attack: "the governor of Queddah … thought of connecting himself with these Burmese enemies … we desired him to come to Siam in order that he might receive advice and become good."[630] Sultan Tajuddin of Keddah, who suspected that this "advice" might involve some ghastly tortures, stayed home and desperately requested British protection. Unfortunately for him, such involvement in local wars was against EIC policy at the time and the EIC officers in the Penang colony had been strictly ordered by Madras not to "come to a rupture with Siam,"[631] so the British left the miscalculating sultan and his people to their brutal fate.

There are many Malay accounts about the brutalities committed against them by the Siamese over the centuries in their attempts to keep them obedient vassals, but this Keddah War of 1821 was the first Siamese campaign witnessed by independent onlookers. One British official in Penang reported:

> "There has been a continuous scene of the most brutal rapine, carnage, oppression and devastation that can be imagined … Their religion is violated … Wives and daughters were forcibly dragged from their husbands and fathers and ravished by the Siamese soldiery … aged parents and helpless babies were butchered ruthlessly … and the most wanton murders, perpetrated by means most cruel and painful to the wretched victims are of daily occurrence … the Siamese butchered them in great numbers, putting them to death by means most cruel and revolting to human nature … it is impossible to calculate the number of Malays who perished by the swords of the Siamese."[632]

The captain of one British warship off Keddah just after this war tells of some atrocities described to him by his Keddahnese Malay crew.

> "Many of their cruelties do not bear repetition, but there are two refined modes of torture I will venture to describe … One was cooking a human being alive. A hollow tree … scooped out by manual labour, was left with merely its bare stem standing. Into it the prisoner was put naked, his hands tied behind his back and a large piece of pork fat lashed on his head. The tree was then coated with mud to prevent its ignition or so it might merely smoulder and then a slow steady fire was maintained around it. The unfortunate victim's sufferings being by these means terribly prolonged, his shrieks and exclamations [were] responded to by the exultant shouts of his executioners … Another Siamese torture was choosing a spot in the mud where the sprout of a young plant, a species of Nipa palm, was found shooting upwards which it does at a rate of several inches in twenty four hours; they would construct a platform around it and lash their miserable victim in a sitting posture over the young tree so that its lance like point should enter his body and bring on death – a slow mode of impaling … The climax to this tale of horrors, was the gambling which took place upon the capture of unfortunate

Malay women who happened to be 'enceinte' [pregnant], the stakes depending upon whether the infant was a boy or a girl, the diabolical game concluding with the death of the mother to decide who were the winners [after cutting the child from her belly] … such were the cruelties perpetrated … such have been the miseries which throughout Birmah, Siam and Malaya that first one master and then another practice upon their unhappy subjects."[633]

John Anderson, another British official in Penang, recorded that:

"The rajah of Ligore (Viceroy Noi of Nakorn) next invaded the Langkawi islands, which, independent of possessing between 3 and 4,000 souls, had received a large accession of emigrants from Queddah. Here too, commenced a terrible scene of death and desolation, almost exceeding credibility. All the men were murdered and the women and female children were carried off, while the children were either put to death or left alone to perish. That fine island is now nearly depopulated."[634]

The sultan of Keddah, closely pursued by several Siamese war prows, managed to find a boat and make a break from the mangroves across the straits to reach British protection on Penang. He was pursued and almost caught by some Siamese wars prows. The viceroy of Nakorn then brought his whole war fleet across, stood just off Penang and sent a letter "couched in very haughty and disrespectful terms"[635] ordering the British to hand over the sultan. The Penang residents now wondered whether the real motive of this large Siamese force standing just off their island was actually to recapture Penang and Province Wellesley for Siam. The Penang governor hurriedly ordered the only two armed EIC frigates on Penang to "fend off" the Siamese fleet and the Penang residents prepared for a battle. The two EIC frigates approached the Siamese fleet and, along with the cannons of Fort Cornwallis on land, trained their bronze and steel guns on the Siamese war prows. Faced with this firepower, Viceroy Noi reluctantly moved his fleet back to the Keddah side of the straits.

Bangkok decided to annex Keddah. It would no longer be an independent tributary state under the sultan as before. The Thais renamed it Saiburi province and put it under the direct control of Viceroy Noi in Nakorn and a Siamese Chinese governor and tax collector. Now, with the British Province Wellesley directly bordering Siamese Saiburi, Britain and Siam, two of the world's most arrogant kingdoms at the time, had become neighbors.

24

New Neighbors

1818 TO 1822

In Phuket's evolution from a desolate and lawless tropical backwater to the developed, quasi-jet set island it is today, one of the most significant events in this transformation occurred at a board meeting in London one drizzly afternoon in 1824.

British Power Ascendant

In Europe in 1794, the armies of revolutionary France attacked and occupied Holland. The Dutch quasi-monarch, William of Orange, anxious to avoid the sharp blade of "La Guillotine", fled to London. To prevent his Jacobin revolutionary opponents gaining power over Holland's colonies, he instructed the Dutch governors in their sweaty colonial outposts not to oppose the entry of British troops who were moved in to temporarily take over all the Dutch colonies in Asia. By 1815, when revolutionary France was eventually defeated in the Napoleonic Wars, both France and Holland, traditionally Britain's main competitors in the East, were crippled and Britain's navy had become the most powerful in the world. The British EIC directors could now look at the map of Asia in a new light. Like the great Asian trading empires of Srivijaya and Malacca before them, they realized that to be the top dog in eastern trade, it was of paramount importance to control the Straits of Malacca. So in 1824, Britain came to a lopsided agreement with the Dutch over the return of their colonies. The EIC kept Malacca and Holland agreed that the Malay Peninsula and the Malacca Straits were now a British sphere of interest. In return, the British gave the Dutch their failing, malarial colony of Bencoolen in western Sumatra and gave them back their former Indonesian colonies, agreeing that Indonesia would be a Dutch sphere of influence.

So by 1824, the EIC held Penang at the northern end of the Malacca Straits and Malacca in the middle; five years earlier, in 1819, the EIC employee Stamford Raffles had also established a British colony in Singapore at the southern end of the straits. These three ports were combined to form a new colony called the British Straits Settlements, which fell under the control of the EIC boards in Calcutta, India and London.

The Napoleonic Wars also allowed Britain to pull the rug from under their only other significant European competitors in the Asian trade, the French and the Danes. The Danish East India Company was founded in 1616 and had first come to trade in Siam and Phuket in 1621. At the outbreak of the Napoleonic Wars in the late 18th century, the Danish East India Company and the Swedish East India Company (formed in 1731) were importing more tea from China into Europe than the EIC, most of which they smuggled into Britain and sold at a huge profit. The Danes also competed strongly in selling weapons, clothing and opium from their bases in India such as Tranquebar to Phuket and to the other petty despots on the peninsula. King Tak Sin alone had ordered well over 1,000 cannons from the Danish East India Company, many being delivered via Phuket. The two polished bronze three-pounder Danish field cannons that today sit so magnificently on the lawn of the Central Police Station in Phuket City were possibly part of this shipment. They were cast in 1767 in Frederiksvaerk. During the Napoleonic Wars, Denmark had sided with Napoleon. Admiral Nelson had audaciously attacked Copenhagen harbor and captured, destroyed or stolen almost the entire Danish war fleet there. By 1845, struggling Denmark decided to throw in the colonial towel and sold all its Eastern trade stations, including the Andaman Islands, to the EIC.

The First Anglo-Burmese War

After his failures in attacking eastwards into Siam, the ever-belligerent Burmese King Bodawpaya attacked westwards into Assam and Manipur. On a few occasions, his troops crossed into British Indian territory, which was also expanding east from Bengal. This raised imperial British eyebrows in Calcutta, but more disturbing to Calcutta was the news that King Bodawpaya was cozying up to the French, allowing their warships to repair in Syriam and Mergui and giving them special trading concessions. For the British, having the French making inroads so near to the Straits of Malacca or using Burma as a back door to the China market simply would not do. So, using some rather trumped-up justification, the supreme board of governors of the EIC met one wintry afternoon in 1824 at their headquarters in Leadenhall Street in London and voted to go to war with Burma. It was this decision that was so greatly to assist the future growth and prosperity of Phuket Island.

The EIC expeditionary force completed a comprehensive defeat of the Burmese in less than two years. Under the terms of the subsequent surrender in 1826, the EIC helped itself to chunks of Burma, including the province of Tenasserim, making Britain no longer Siam's neighbor in little Province Wellesley alone, but also right down Siam's western peninsular provinces.

For beleaguered Phuket Island, the British annexation of Tenasserim meant that the constant threat of Burmese attacks and raiding parties was removed, plus, as we have seen, British gunboats soon began to hound the local pirates and slave-raiders in the area into relative insignificance. Phuket was soon no longer a place where people and trade were debilitated by the constant fear of being attacked, butchered or dragged off into slavery. By the late 1820s, for the first time in centuries, Phuket became a place where one could trade or live without excessive risk and in constant fear of one's life.

With the taking of Tenasserim, the EIC now controlled almost all the lands bordering the Bay of Bengal, making it almost a British lake. The EIC were soon ruling from Ceylon, northwards through India and Bengal through Tenasserim and down almost the whole west coast of the Malay Peninsula to Singapore. Indeed, the only part of the Bay of Bengal coastline not controlled by the EIC by the mid-19th century was the 800-kilometer strip of Siamese territory round Phuket from Ranong down to Keddah. The Siamese courts in Bangkok and Nakorn must surely have been getting a little paranoid about this powerful and aggressive new imperial neighbor right on their doorstep.

Siam and Britain Become New Neighbors

In 1822, Britain and Siam knew very little about one another. It seems that no one in the Siamese court spoke English and in Penang only two officials had learned some Siamese. The two countries had only traded slightly in the 150 years since the EIC had been so ignominiously chased out of Siamese Mergui in 1688. In addition, over the last two decades, even British interloper trade with Phuket or British trade from Penang had almost completely stopped due to the Napoleonic Wars, the Burmese destruction of Phuket and the general increase in lawlessness and piracy.

Fortunately, Siam and Britain held very different interests in the central peninsula. For Bangkok, which still officially claimed authority over all the peninsular Malay states, the interest was strategic and diplomatic. The Siamese received very little economic benefit from the area. The few royalties and gifts or Bunga Mas trees, if they ever arrived, or indeed if they were ever sent, did no more – at best – than defray part of the expense of Bangkok constantly having to send armies south to put down rebellions in its thorny and mutinous Malay sub-states. As for the British, the EIC was still just a commercial stockholders' company interested mainly in its bottom-line profit. The purpose of the new Straits Settlements ports was primarily to protect and assist its already profitable trade with China. The EIC directors saw little direct benefit in the small, somewhat sordid markets in the jungled, under-populated peninsula. For the EIC accountants, war and colonization represented only large entries in red ink on the balance sheet. All they really wanted was to trade with a relatively stable partner whose taxes were not too onerous and who could offer sufficient security and protect fair trade. Ideally, this should be furthered by treaty arrangements requiring as few obligations as possible on the part of the EIC. The EIC therefore much preferred to deal with a less-than-independent state that it could bully and exploit, rather than be lumbered with the tiresome and costly business of conquest and administration. EIC policy was to absorb regions solely for strategic reasons – meaning to protect its already profitable businesses.

The only potential exception to this rule in the region, however, appears to have been the small island of Phuket. Many in the Penang commercial and government community had already set their beady little eyes on annexing this island because, as John Crawfurd, Penang's first EIC emissary to Siam, noted in 1820: "The richest mines of Siam exist on the island of Junkceylon." Mr. Clubley, a member of the EIC governing board in India, expressed the view held by many of the British in Penang in the early 1820s:

> "Shortly after the occupation of Penang there was a considerable trade in Tin and other articles and vessels were constantly passing to and from Junk Ceylon.

[But today] …The island [Phuket] is still in possession of a power which does not appear disposed to draw forth its resources and the dread of an attack from the Burmans prevents the inhabitants of the adjoining Coast from settling upon the island … if the valuable island of Junk Ceylon could be added, either by conquest or fair negotiation, to the possessions of the Honourable Company, their revenues would be materially increased. … That Junk Ceylon possesses every advantage that can be desired for a British settlement has been fully established by the concurring testimony of all persons who have visited the place or considered the subject."[636]

Siam's punitive attack on Keddah in 1821 and its rebuff by the EIC warships meant that relations between Siam and Britain as new neighbors had not got off to a good start. The two countries remained in dispute over the sultan of Keddah, who remained under British protection. The Siamese wanted to arrest and presumably execute him, while the British wanted him to be reinstated as, for as long as they had given him rent money, he had been obedient and pliant, whereas the more arrogant Siamese were not. For example, when Siam directly took over ruling Keddah as Saiburi province, the new Chinese governor, a business associate of Viceroy Noi of Nakorn, rented out all the river mouths to Chinese tax farmers who used their monopolies to charge high taxes and made trade expensive and troublesome. The British, who almost religiously believed in Adam Smith's free trade and low taxes, found the feudal, monopolistic, high-tax system in Siam most irksome. One EIC official grumbled that the Siamese ministers enforced trade terms that were "most vexatious … compelling the foreign merchants to sell their cargo at a very low figure and buy Siamese goods at a very high price, by the simple expedient of forbidding all other traders to deal with them … Almost every article of the produce of the country suited to a foreign market is in one shape or another made a subject of monopoly to the crown."[637]

John Crawfurd's Vexing Mission

The EIC wanted to trade with Siam, but with a more advantageous trade treaty and environment. In 1820, just before the Anglo-Burmese War had broken out, Penang sent its first envoy, John Crawfurd, a Scotsman who spoke Malay, to Bangkok to attempt to draw up a treaty and gather more information about this still rather mysterious new neighbor. Crawfurd was instructed to request that the sultan of Keddah be reinstated and to try to obtain a trade treaty "to fix a known scale of taxes and fees to the otherwise arbitrary and exorbitant fees … so as to expose British traders to the least possible vexation,"[638] and lastly he was instructed to try to allay Siamese fears arising from the "violence, imprudence and disregard of national rights which characterized the conduct of all European nations [in] the states of further India."[639]

Crawfurd's negotiations did not go well at all. The Siamese flatly refused to reinstate the sultan of Keddah; they would not agree to any trade privileges; they refused to exempt foreigners from Siamese law and refused to make a treaty. Crawfurd also felt greatly hampered by the Chinese, who were dominant in Siam's trade and commerce as a result of the advantageous terms they had received in Siam since King Tak Sin's rule. They had no wish for new competitors and Crawfurd complained that they were "misrepresenting" him by advising the Siamese ministers, most of whom were their monopolistic business partners, that "The English come now with smooth words, pretending to want to trade only ... and finally they will seize the country as they had done on many similar occasions."[640]

A dominant party of monopoly-holding lords in the Siamese court absolutely opposed any relaxation of the trading system, as it would reduce the large profits that fell to them personally. An irritated John Crawfurd therefore came back from Bangkok with very little except a bad opinion of the Siamese, as evidenced by his post-trip report to the EIC directors.

"The character of the government of Siam was discovered to be unusually sordid, insincere and rapacious ... one of the finest and most favoured countries in the world is oppressed by one of the most mischievous forms of government. To their character of venality and corruption we found superadded a remarkable degree of national vanity, yet with an extraordinary jealousy and distrust of all strangers and especially of Europeans ... Intercourse was courted, but merely as affording an object of extortion to those in power, for whether with regard to foreigners or to their own people, a more reckless undisguised disregard for equity and the public interests cannot well be conceived. With a government thus at once vain, jealous, insincere and corrupt ... it was no easy matter to conduct negotiation at all."[641]

Crawfurd, clearly in a bit of a huff, recommended that, faced with such intransigence, the British should resort to force to achieve their ends, as the Siamese army was "extremely contemptible ... an undisciplined and ill armed mob raised from a cowardly and timid people."[642] He also felt the fortifications of Bangkok were "feebly and unskillfully constructed. Two small gun brigs would destroy them." However, the decision of the more somber EIC board of governors in India, who read Crawfurd's rather intemperate report, was that they really did not want a "costly and unnecessary war" as he recommended.

Crawfurd Passes Phuket in 1818

John Crawfurd passed Phuket in 1818 while traveling down the Tenasserim coast to Penang and made a short report on the island and its surroundings.

"In general the country is a mere wilderness. The best peopled portion of this territory is the island of Salang [Phuket]. The island is under a governor ... subject to his jurisdiction are seven districts on the continent extending all the way to the Burmese frontier. The most considerable place in question is Ponga [Phang Nga – where the Phuket governor was now staying after the Burmese invasions], which contains between three and four thousand inhabitants among whom are said to be from eight hundred to 1,000 Chinese. Tin mines or rather stream works appear to be wrought in the district of Ponga as well as Junkceylon."[643]

This was only seven years after the devastation of the Burmese invasions and Crawfurd illustrates the edginess of the local inhabitants at the time by describing an encounter he had with some local fishermen just off Phuket. He had been sailing south down "the mainland coast north of Phuket", which consisted of:

"nothing but one universal forest of stately trees. The beach is beautiful white sand … we afterwards saw one neat village within a mile of the Popra [Pak Pra] strait. On the shore we observed a few fishermen drying their nets while their canoes lay on the beach … we endeavored to make our wish for an intercourse intelligible by signals … [The men] were most timid seeing our ship … At length we sent a boat ashore and after considerable hesitation two individuals consented to come on board, but not until one of our men was left behind as a hostage for their safety. This extraordinary timidity arises from the situation in which these poor people are placed. They live on territory disputed between the hostile Burmans and Siamese and consequently are in a state of perpetual insecurity and distrust, while they are now rarely visited by European shipping. Our visitors proved to be a Siamese and a Chinese mestizo of Siam … in complexion and features he was no longer distinguishable as a Chinese and could only be recognized as such by the fashion in which he wore his hair [in a pigtail]. We addressed them in Malay but they understood but a few words and we could carry on no conversation with them … The coast abounds in fish and for the value of two rupees we obtained a very large supply of an excellent description."

Crawfurd then sailed south, down the west coast of the island.

"We passed the western opening of the narrow strait which divides Junkceylon from the continent. Sandy points form the mouth of the strait on each side, which is not more than half a mile broad. It was low water and so shallow is it, that the sea was breaking over a reef that crosses it and which at all times renders it un-navigable for large vessels; one can pass only at high water. A severe squall forced us to keep at a respectable distance from the coast of Junkceylon. The shore is bold and precipitate and the coast frequently so indented as to give to many of the headlands at a distance the appearance of islands. The aspect of the country presents a perpetual succession of hills or mountains, apparently so close upon each other that there can be little room for extensive valleys capable of affording room for profitable cultivation. The whole appeared covered with an immense forest and not a single habitation or a single patch of culture was discernible. A view of the eastern, sheltered side of the island would no doubt have presented a somewhat more favorable aspect, but it is sufficiently known that the island is but thinly inhabited and poorly cultivated at present. During all night and today we had a great deal of rain and blowing weather. This prevented us from landing as we intended."[644]

25

Lieutenant Low's Failed Mission

1824

Viceroy Noi of Nakorn, reputedly a son of King Tak Sin, was the last of the power-ful viceroys of Nakorn to exert control over the whole central peninsula. He was also highly miffed that the British were now interfering in what he saw as Nakorn's traditional Malay vassal states in the peninsula. He was indignant at having lost face in his showdown with Penang over the sultan of Keddah and retaliated by putting an embargo on any food going from Keddah to Penang. In 1824, Viceroy Noi then got into a spat with the sultan of Selangor over tin revenues from Perak and resolved to attack Selangor to punish the sultan. He ordered a fleet of 300 war galleys to be built in the Trang River.

A British Gunboat Blockades Trang

On hearing of these war plans, the anti-Siamese Scottish governor of Penang, Robert Fullerton, sent an observer to check on this gathering Siamese war fleet in Trang. The observer reported that it consisted of some 300 war prows "rowed by fifty or sixty men each … few of them have decks. Their guns or swivels are generally unmanageable and the whole equipment very paltry. They might easily be sunk by a single shot from a six pounder … such a fleet would never hazard a meeting with one well armed Brig."[645]

Governor Fullerton wrote to Viceroy Noi, claiming that as Selangor had been subordi-nate for hundreds of years to Malacca and as the Dutch had now transferred Malacca to Britain, Siam did not have the right to attack Selangor without British permission. Viceroy Noi disdainfully brushed off this warning and continued with his war prepara-tions. Fullerton wrote again more forcefully, "I am forced once more to caution your highness not to attempt to attack Selangor … I cannot permit a fleet such as yours to approach this island [Penang] or pass through the straits."[646] To make his point this time, Fullerton dispatched an EIC gunboat to the mouth of the Trang River. British seamen at that time could fire and reload their cannon four times a minute. The Sia-mese fleet captains knew that even with 300 boats, it would be carnage to take on the British gunship's repetitive broadsides of ball, grape, chain and canister shot. Reluctant to face this potential onslaught of British metal the Siamese had to concede that their war fleet was blockaded in the river. Much to his chagrin, Viceroy Noi had to back down again and the EIC had effectively stymied any real Siamese dominion over those Malay sultanates in the southern part of the peninsula.

Lt. Low's Mission

Just after this Trang dispute in 1824, the first Anglo-Burmese War had started the general in charge of the EIC expeditionary force in Burma thought it might be prudent to try to solicit some support from Siam against "their inveterate enemies" the Burmese. To this effect, a Lieutenant James Low was dispatched to meet Viceroy Noi in Nakorn. Lieutenant Low was yet another Scotsman, the son of a gentleman farmer from Kettle in Fifeshire. After studying mathematics and philosophy at Edinburgh University, he had joined the Indian Army and now, aged 33, was adjutant to the Penang governor and was in charge of the Penang local militia. He was adept at languages and was one of only two EIC employees to have learned Malay and Siamese; in 1824 he received a special bonus from the EIC for doing so.

From Keddah, Low knew there was "a path through the forest which conducts to Ligor in four days"[647] but the Siamese governor of Keddah refused Low permission to use it. Low then headed by ship to the Trang River to try to reach Nakorn from there. When his ship arrived at Trang, Low reported that the Siamese chief there was "considerably alarmed, being under an impression that we had come with no friendly intention."[648] The chief, however, later informed him that the locals were scared of any unknown ship as "they were in constant dread of being invaded by the Burmans."[649] Low waited in Trang while a message was sent overland to request a meeting with Viceroy Noi. Meanwhile he "explored the country behind our camp … the place is uncultivated now as pirates infest the river occasionally … while we were all in perfect health, a very bad fever prevailed at several villages on the river higher up and one or two cases of cholera were reported."[650]

Viceroy Noi refused to meet Lt. Low on court etiquette grounds, but in Low's opinion the viceroy's refusal was because "he was suspicious of the views of the British government towards Siam"[651] and did not want Low poking his nose around Nakorn's defenses. However, with Britain now at war with Burma, it may have been that the Siamese were happy to let Britain and Burma, their two greatest potential enemies, fight it out and see who the victor might be before deciding which course to follow. Lt. Low then decided to head north to Phuket and Phang Nga to try to arrange a meeting with the viceroy via the governor there, as he was informed that the people of Phuket "have a greater regard for Europeans than those of other Siamese ports … and most especially the British, with whom they have ever been best acquainted."[652]

En route to Phuket he stopped at Ko Talibong, just below Ko Lanta, where "In one cave we perceived about twelve human skulls lying close beside each other, it was concluded that they had belonged to some people who had been murdered probably by raiding pirates."[653] He tells us the coast south of Phuket was mainly inhabited by Malays who "fear and detest the Siamese and never fail when they can do so with chance of impunity, to retaliate upon them the miseries they have endured, this they effected by the creese."[654] Ko Talibong was uninhabited, though Low tells us it was "formerly inhabited by Malays, but when the Burmans ravaged Salang (Phuket) they also plundered all the inhabitants of this island and their destruction was likewise hastened by the visits of pirates from Rhio and other Malayan ports. There were still to be seen parts of the plank wall defenses that had surrounded the ruined town on Ko Talibong … ten feet in length, eight inches broad and one inch thick."[655] These planks, Low tells us, were the same as those used in the Thalang fort in Phuket. Lt. Low took some of the planks to have furniture made with them in Penang.

> "These may seem but weak materials for defense, but the Burmans brought no cannon with them and when they attacked the stockade of Bandan [Ban Don] in Salang, formed of upright planks, they went through all the tedious formalities of a siege, such as ditching and mining before they made themselves masters of it."[656]

During his exploration of Ko Talibong about lunchtime Low, "observed a party of about fifteen armed men quietly stealing along the coast. The island being uninhabited and it is reported that pirates regularly came here." As he and his party was unarmed, he sent for some of his armed Indian sepoy guards to come ashore from his ship for their protection. The surreptitious men, they later discovered, were not pirates but "the Chief of Trang, who with his attendants … had come to shoot buffaloes."[657]

Lt. Low in Phuket and Phang Nga

Low continued north to Phuket and entered "Tarooa Roads" (Sapam Bay) in the evening. The ship anchored and sent a longboat to try to find someone who might guide them to the right opening in the mangroves of "Tarooa stream," so they could get up to the port town. They found no one. So, early the next morning, they

> "got the longboat out with a party of sepoys … rowed off at six am, but passed the creek or mouth of the Tarooa stream. It is scarcely to be distinguished from the other openings in the mangroves, which here thickly line the beach … [They stopped for breakfast on Ko Maprao, from where they] … perceived a boat under a rock in a cove and made for it to gain intelligence. The people in it, observing us … took alarm and rowed off with all their might … when they saw we had the advantage they pulled on shore. Five or six men, armed with firelocks and sword, leapt onto the beach and prepared to escape into the woods, leaving a priest and some unarmed men in the boat. They were soon relieved of their apprehension. The chaukoo or priest took the helm … they rowed on before and showed us the river. It was soon evident we should have a hard day's labor to reach the town … The stream came down with such force that our heavy boat could scarcely make any way. At length, we were forced to get out a rope, fastened to a tree some distance in advance to pull the boat up by it."[658]

The crew eventually had to strip off and got into the river,

> "sometimes swimming and almost always up to the neck in water. … We reached Tharooa about sunset and I walked to the house of Loung Bamrong the superintendent of the island. He received me with much hospitality and about eight

o'clock his wife, an elderly woman, set before me some well dressed dishes of meat and confection ... We conversed till midnight by the light of dammar [resin] torches ... A great number of people crowded his house to see me, but they behaved with the utmost decorum. Mats were then spread on the floor and they left me to rest."[659]

Low notes that, while Tarooa had contained many houses before the invasions,

"The Burmans ravaged Salang and the adjacent Siamese possessions about twelve and fourteen years ago. This was its death blow ... at present there are only eight houses in the town ... Their houses are built on strong piles although the site of the village is dry ... The people of Salang appear to lead a simple life. They have been placed under the government of Phoonga since the island began to decline. The women took few pains to conceal themselves, they had little or no covering from waist upwards ... this evidently arose from motives of economy and not from any ignorance of what is decorous."[660]

Before he left Penang, Low had been informed that after the expected EIC victory in their current war with Burma, the EIC harbored a plan to take the province of Tenasserim from Burma and give it back to Siam in exchange for Phuket and all the other offshore islands between Penang and Phuket. The EIC felt that "The Siamese covet this possession [Tenasserim] exceedingly and it may not be improbably conjectured that they would readily accept it in exchange for Junkceylon, Pulo Panjang (Ko Yao Yai), and Pulo Tellibong ... Of all the Siamese possessions on the west coast, Salang seems to be of the greatest intrinsic value, but to its present possessors it is little better than a barren waste."[661] This, Low felt, was because of a shortage of people "due to fear" and also due to the "selfish" policies of the king of Siam which

"have a direct tendency to retard the growth ... The Siamese are anxious to encourage population ... but the emperor of Siam follows no law but that of his corrupt will ... he views his subjects in the light of mere instruments by which his pursuits may be forwarded. No rank is hereditary, no property, however arduously acquired, is safe [the sakdi na system]. People are torn from the bosom of their families without regard to ability or future consequences and sent on distant expeditions leaving their wives and children to support themselves ... to fill up the vacuity which such a perverted policy creates, they carry off the population of whole villages from the territory of their neighbours and planting them like exotics in a new soil vainly fancy that they will add strength to the state. The Siamese have lately been successful in this species of man-stealing and have carried many thousands of Burman families into captivity."[662]

Sounding much like Light and Scott forty years before, Lt. Low felt that

"The powers productive of natural wealth now lie dormant under its selfish and avaricious system ... an establishment on Salang by the British would no doubt bring signal aid to the cause of humanity and civilisation by rescuing thousands from their unmerited thraldom, both of mind and body, under which they groan, and of diffusing happiness, the chief end of all good government. The present inhabitants of Salang would rejoice at the change … preferring positive happiness and a rational degree of freedom to slavery and its attendant degradations and miseries under them [the Siamese]."[663]

Low presciently noted that even without a British takeover of Phuket, things would in any case soon improve for the island, as the British army were about to take Tenasserim and in his opinion this would "at once relieve the Siamese from all fear … when a short period will have given change its due effect, Salang will rise in the estimation of the Siamese and they will then, without acknowledgement, reap the fruits of British protection [so that] the internal as well as external advantages it possesses will soon become apparent."[664]

Like Light, Low also felt Phuket would make a fine colony.

"Salang has a very fertile soil and might be made to yield both spices and Pepper with all tropical fruits and European culinary vegetables. The hills are well adapted to the cultivation of coffee … The lowlands are excellently fitted for rice … The eminences nearest to the bay in which the harbour lies had formerly been cleared and planted with fruit trees, but these have now relapsed into their original wilderness. They present airy and salubrious sites for garden houses. The island is well watered … and abounds in deer, but this is rather a disadvantage as they are destructive to crops … The harbour is excellent and might be easily defended."[665]

He proposed that if the island could be swapped for Tenasserim, Cape Yamoo should be fortified and the island's main town should be built on the "advantageous … sloping ground" approaching Yamoo, which, before the Burmese invasion "was in fact formerly occupied by a large village, though now deserted through fear of pirates." Ko Yao Yai, he noted, "is also very rich in tin mines which have scarcely yet been broken on by the natives owing to their fear of Burmans and pirates … Salang holds out a reasonable prospect of yielding an annual revenue more than sufficient to pay for a small establishment on it by a European Power."[666] This revenue, he claims, would come from tin, birds' nests, agriculture and "a very considerable quantity of opium may be yearly disposed of amongst the Siamese of this coast, as although the use of it is forbidden by Bangkok, the Chinese and Siamese in the south pay little attention to the prohibition."[667] In his opinion though, the biggest earner for the island would be trade, but only if it could be "thrown open … subjecting trade to equitable restrictions and not permitting, as at present, it to be clogged with complicated and burdensome restrictions."[668]

Old Phang Nga

The governor of Phuket was based in Phang Nga where most Phuketians were still living since the Burmese destruction of Phuket a decade before. This was mainly for security against ongoing Burmese raids. The Penang official Anderson recorded in 1824 that "Pungah (Phang Nga) is a recent settlement formed by a part of the inhabitants of Junkceylon who fled in 1810 when the Burmese invaded and took possession of the island. The chief is styled Pia Salang or Governor of Junk Ceylon and its dependencies."[669] On his way to Phang Nga, Low reported that "A heavy squall with rain carried us quickly past the pyramids of Phoongna [the karst islands],"[670] and they anchored at the mouth of the Phang Nga River.

The next morning they took a lighter and rowed upriver to Phang Nga town. "The town does not contain more than 70 houses. About 30 of that number belong to Chinese settlers. Their houses are large and convenient and regularly built so as to form a street."[27] Low estimated there were

"6 or 7,000 souls. There were about 600 active Chinese … The females at Phoonga secluded themselves more than those at Salang did, which I attributed to their own modesty … women in this country are allowed much freedom … The house of the chief is a little larger than the rest but has scarcely any exterior decoration and is enclosed by palisades of planks and stakes. On the south of the chief's residence is the Chinese tin smelting house where one furnace is employed. A great portion of the population is employed during half the year at the tin mines, returning during the other months to cultivate rice … The ore which they dig is sold to the Chinese contractor and the profit goes to the chief … Although the Chief of Phoonga takes advantage of the power given him and enriches himself at the expense of his subjects, his government is not so oppressive as that of the rajah of Ligore. His people also are more attached to him, or in other words, do not hate him so violently as the Ligorians hate their prince. The difference showed itself in one instance. In the rajah's country (Nakorn) every article supplied for my table was extorted from his subjects, but at Phoonga the chief bought out of the bazaar all the provisions he sent to me."[671]

The Phuket governor in Phang Nga could also not help Low to obtain a meeting with his overlord in Nakorn and after yet more stonewalling by Viceroy Noi in Nakorn – who still refused him an audience – Low returned to Trang, where Governor Fullerton instructed him to return to Penang and wrote that "Lieutenant Low has been now nearly three months awaiting his highness's determination and has remained upwards of six weeks in that jungly country, without even being favoured by replies to his last two letters."[672] Like the EIC's previous envoy Crawfurd, six years before him, Lt. Low was also unimpressed with the Siamese leaders he met, summing them up by saying, "Cunning and treachery engross a great portion of the Siamese political character. The rulers have little or no regard to justice, while the governed, do not even expect it from them, having drunk of the cup of oppression to the dregs."[673]

Lt. James Low was relieved to get home to the relative security of Penang, where he later compiled the first English-Thai dictionary and had Thai letters specially made up for the Penang printing press.

26

Righteous Burney

1825

Lt. Low's fruitless attempt to meet the Viceroy of Nakorn meant the EIC army fought the Burmese without assistance from Siam. According to Lt. Low however, this was no great loss, as after his visit to Siam he did not hold a high opinion of the Siamese troops: "It is doubtful if a Siamese soldier can stand erect. A slavish submission to their rulers had physically affected the whole of the male population and a slinking slouching gait is their most prominent outward characteristic."[675] The EIC top brass seemed to concur, they now felt that asking for Siamese cooperation would be perceived as a sign of weakness and probably even a liability due to their "most cruel and barbarous mode of warfare".[676] As one EIC military officer noted: "Pillage and plunder are regular parts of Siamese warfare"[677] and this did not sit well with the British concept of an ultra-disciplined force.

Siamese Slave Raids During the Anglo-Burmese War

Despite a difficult start to the campaign in 1824, by 1825, the British were ascendant and were moving against the Burmese capital of Ava. The Burmese king had recalled back most his army back to defend his capital. This left a power vacuum in the outlying regions such as Tenasserim in the south. The Siamese were quick to exploit this vacuum by raiding across the frontier into Burma to plunder and capture slaves.

In the summer of 1825, the governor of Chumporn led a large body of his troops over the Tenasserim Mountains and into the undefended river port town of Tenasserim. They reportedly pulled down the newly hoisted British flag "with insult"[674] plundered the town and carried off many of its inhabitants as captives. A young British officer and a company of EIC Indian sepoys who had been stationed nearby the town on occupation duty got word of this raid. They pursued and attacked this large Siamese force, killing several Siamese troops, taking another 124 prisoner, and freeing most the Burmese captives. The Chumporn governor and the rest of his men fled back over the hills to Siam. By the end of the war the British military estimated that these numerous Siamese slave-catching forays into Tenasserim had carried off around 2-3,000 people, a lot from such a thinly populated region.

The EIC takes Tenasserim: Lt. Burney's mission to Siam

The EIC force finally entered the Burmese capital in late 1825 and in the ensuing peace treaty forced the Burmese king to sign over Tenasserim province. The EIC accountants in India were actually quite unenthusiastic about the prospect of having to bear the cost of administering this vast, backward and under-populated province. This move to take Tenasserim appears to have been motivated largely by pressure from the new Straits Settlements colonies, in particular by the Penang commercial lobby that believed Tenasserim could then be swapped with Siam for Phuket Island where "the richest tin mines of Siam are".[678] More specifically, Penang had proposed to Madras that they should offer Tenasserim (formerly an important Siamese province) back to Siam:

> "in exchange for an engagement to avoid all future interference with the states on the Malayan Peninsula from the latitude of eight degrees forty north, which includes the island of Junk Ceylon, a post which might be turned to great account … if such a scheme were practicable and a settlement formed at Junk Ceylon it would certainly become the emporium of the east and rival the most flourishing of our establishments."[679]

The emissary chosen by the EIC to go to Siam to try to affect this swap was Lt. Henry Burney a 35-year-old Englishman born and raised in Calcutta. He had served as an officer in the EIC Bengal Native Infantry and was later posted to Penang as the military secretary to the Governor. He had fought in the recent Anglo Burmese war and had learned some Siamese. This time Viceroy Noi in Nakorn, seeing the clear victory of the British army in Burma, consented to a meeting. Lt. Burney decided to travel to Nakorn via Phuket to meet the governor there and to review this proposed and hoped-for new prize for the EIC.

However, Just before Burney left for Phuket, new instructions arrived from the EIC directors in Madras quashing Penang's proposed plan for getting their hands on Phuket. They declared that they now

26.1 A newspaper illustration of British expeditionary force troops advancing northwards through Burma.

felt the retention of Tenasserim and its main port of Mergui as a harbor and a tin-producing area "would bring the same benefits as were looked for from Junkceylon … [they also believed that] … the court of Siam was also most unlikely to cede Junkceylon, nor waive its claims to the Malay states to the south."[680] Therefore the directors in Madras felt it would be more advantageous if Lt. Burney could instead try to negotiate a better overall trade and commerce treaty with all of Siam. And secondly that he should try to more clearly define Siamese and British spheres of influence in the Malay Peninsula so as to avoid the risk of any more potentially explosive incidents such as the Trang River Blockade affair or the recent Anglo-Siamese fighting in Tenasserim.

In early 1826 Lt. Burney set off first to Phuket and then on to Phang Nga where the local governor and most Phuketians still lived for more security. Phuket Island still remained largely deserted since the destruction of the Burmese invasions 15 years before. While on Phuket, Burney, however noted optimistically in his diary that "[In the past]… the island has been kept in such a constant state of alarm from the Burmese so as to have entirely prevented the settling of inhabitants there … [however] … The recent successes of the British arms on the Coast of Tenasserim now promise to afford the Chief and inhabitants a degree of security which they have never before enjoyed and the very first consequence of our Burmese war will be to induce the Siamese to turn their views towards improving Junkceylon. The Siamese are fully aware of the value of Junkceylon".[681]

Phuket's War Captives

In Phang Nga Burney met the Phuket governor Phaya Narong Ruangrit Songkram. He still sadly lamented all his missing people "who numbered 5,000"[682] whom had been carried off to Burma during the 1811 Burmese conquest of Phuket. The governor requested Burney's help to see if the British, who had now just taken Tenasserim, might assist in locating and returning any Phuket captives they could find there.

Henry Burney's father was a renowned evangelical humanitarian in India who ran the EIC orphanage at Kidderpore near Calcutta where Burney had been born and raised. Burney had also studied in England in the age of agitation against slavery and the protestant missionary societies. All this humanitarianism zeal had rubbed off on him and he took this slavery issue to heart. He would also have been aware of some of the hardships endured by war slaves in the region. For example, Mr. Gould, a British official working in Siam a few years later, describes seeing some 6,000 or so war captives taken by Siam in Laos being marched to Bangkok for sale:

> "The unfortunate creatures, men, women and children, many of the latter still in arms, were driven in droves through the jungle … great numbers died from sickness. starvation and exhaustion on the road. The sick, when they became too weak to struggle on, were left behind. If no house was at hand which was oftener the case in the wild country they were traversing, the sufferer was simply flung down to die miserably in the jungle. Any companions attempting to assist the poor creatures were driven on with blows."[683]

In Bangkok, Mr. Gould later saw those who had survived the march. "They are nearly all in a state of disease … wretched and thin. Great numbers had every joint swollen up to a great size and numbers more were covered with a foul eruption on the skin often extending over the entire body."[684]

So Burney formulated a humanitarian plan. He agreed to try to find any Phuket prisoners remaining in Tenasserim and, in addition to the 124 Siamese raiders recently taken by the EIC in the skirmish in Tenasserim, he would then try to exchange them for the estimated 2-3,000 Burmese captives that the Siamese had just stolen in their recent Tenasserim raids.

After this meeting with the Phuket Governor Burney crossed overland to Nakorn. Viceroy Noi was now acting much less haughty. He agreed to recognize Britain's right to Penang if Britain recognized Siam's right to Keddah in return, however for doing so he did make the request that the EIC should now pay the fat 10,000 Spanish dollars annual rent for Province Wellesley to himself instead the deposed sultan of Keddah. He also agreed to arrange a meeting for Burney with the king in Bangkok. The year before in 1824, King Rama II had died and was succeeded by his son, King Rama III, a competent 37-year-old soldier, conservative, religious and steeped in the traditions of the Siamese court.

Burney in Bangkok

Burney returned to Penang then sailed to Bangkok via Singapore on a British brig The Hunter. In Bangkok Burney records that he found the Siamese court in a "state of the utmost apprehension" over the fall of Burma. Indeed, he also noted that when his ship came up the Chao Phraya River flying the Union Jack, "the Siamese expected, as I was assured, that the vessel was the first of the English expedition against Siam."[685] Such rumors, complained Burney, only "augmented the spirit of procrastination which characterizes the Siamese at all times."[686]

Burney remained in Bangkok for three months to try and negotiate a trade treaty. King Rama III was most cordial. He even invited Burney's six-year-old son, who was with his father, to their meeting and gave him gifts. Such behavior, says the historian D. G. E. Hall, was "indicative of the greater degree of urbanity shown by the Thais in dealing with representatives of the west than any other South East Asian leaders."[687] This Thai charm often disarmed the Europeans and, along with the Thais' wily diplomatic skills, ultimately played a large part in preserving Siam's, and Phuket's, independence. Despite his apparent cordiality, Rama III's main emotion seems to have been one of extreme suspicion. He later wrote:

> "The British now want to take the land between Penang and Victoria point in southern Burma … waiting for an opportunity to negotiate, so as to make [the peninsula] theirs … If the English could find a situation whereby they could successfully give support to the Malays … with the English as their patrons [the Malays] would soon launch attacks on Muang Thalang (Phuket), Phang Nga, Takuatung and Takuapa. Siam will in these circumstances lose all the western seaboard region."[688]

Burney was unsuccessful in making any meaningful changes to the existing trade terms. And like Crawfurd before him, he complained that he was impeded all the way by the corrupt and selfish "senabodi", the top royal administration department ministers, who gained the most pecuniary advantage from Siam's monopolistic trade system and therefore had the most to lose from giving it up. Burney also felt that "the king was unaware of the amount embezzled by the prakhlang and his officers,"[689] and as righteous as ever, he took it upon himself to give such details to the king, explaining, for example, how foreign traders in Siam "buying rice, paddy or salt, had to pay a tical a day each to 40 clerks to see the articles measured although only one of them turned up … [A foreign] merchant had to wait weeks and weeks to trade, until they either forced him to submit to their terms, or lose the chance of selling his cargo to any advantage."[690]

Not surprisingly, telling such tales to the king further increased the hostility of the "senabodi" towards him. He notes that they gave him "infinite trouble … it was extremely difficult to persuade such a capricious and mistrustful court to disclose its real views."[691] He also complained that at his subsequent meetings with these royal department heads, he was not even provided with a chair, "nor even a cushion as was common," forcing him to sit on a hard floor in a kneeling position with his legs out behind him in a "most irksome position."[692] The righteous Burney also complained that "it was as though indefatigable lying was part of the Siamese statesman's duty"[693] and exasperatingly Burney felt the Siamese presumed the same to be true of the British! Maybe righteous Burney had never heard the Elizabethan diplomat Sir Thomas Smith's pun, that the definition of an English ambassador was an Englishman sent "to lye abroad" on behalf of his country.

In the end, Burney, good soul though he was, obtained little of what the EIC wanted. Trade was not reformed, Phuket Island was not ceded and the sultan of Keddah was not restored. He did, however, get a rather bland agreement defining British and Siamese influence in the peninsula and an agreement that unrestricted (though not free) trade could continue between the Straits Settlements and Siam, as Article 10 of his treaty reads: "The English and Siamese mutually agree that there shall be an unrestricted trade between them in the English countries of Prince of Wales island [Penang], Malacca and Singapore and the Siamese countries of Ligor, Singora, Patani, Junkceylon, Queddah and other Siamese provinces."[694]

An Exchange of Captives

The one area in which Burney did achieve a result was his proposed exchange of prisoners. In Bangkok Burney witnessed the "disgraceful and cruel treatment which the Burmese captives have experienced in Siam."[695] He discovered that most of the Burmese captives had actually been allocated as slaves primarily to the very Siamese "senabodi" ministers he was dealing with, such as the Phra Klang. These Burmese slaves were doing much of the menial work in Bangkok and most had no clothing or living quarters and little food. Indeed, in order to save himself from paying for the slaves' food, Burney noted that the Phra Klang – the biggest slave owner – allowed his slaves to prey upon boats plying the Mekong and "We repeatedly saw two or three Burmese prisoners in a boat chasing and plundering the boat of some old Siamese women."[696] Burney estimated that at least half the Burmese captives – men, women and children – had died through hardship on their march from Tenasserim to Bangkok. On their arrival in Bangkok, they had been separated and sold off. Of course, in their defense, the Siamese reminded Burney that the Burmese were their enemies who had caused so much death and destruction to Siam in their previous invasions, that no pity could be felt for them and that "these horrors of repeated invasions were not to be forgotten."[697]

Despite resistance from the "senabodi", Burney did get the consent of the king, Rama III, to organize the prisoner swap. "The king has ever been desirous of sending back these captives but his ministers and petty servants deprecate the loss of so many laborers and are striving to avoid the execution of his Liberal orders."[698] Burney claims that the "senabodi" then removed many of the captives from Bangkok and told him they had only 800 prisoners instead of the 1,600 he was led to expect by British military intelligence. After much cajoling, Burney eventually got some 585 men, women and children delivered a few at a time to his mission quarters in Bangkok, where he describes the prisoners as "lying about in all directions around my house, many afflicted by smallpox, with no food save what I give them, with scarcely any clothes, with no other shelter other than the trees and a few loose ataps, while the thermometer at nights has been as low as 60 degrees."[699]

Seventeen prisoners died in his garden and 21 were too ill to be moved. Eventually his unremitting zeal broke the ministerial log-jam in Bangkok and he got a pass to send the Tenasserim captives back to Mergui. In return, the British sent back the Siamese who had been captured when undertaking slave raiding in Tenasserim and any of the former Phuket captives they had managed to identify in their newly captured part of Burma. Burney then describes the arrival of the Burmese captives in Tenasserim, no doubt a scene that would have made

26.2. A 19th century picture of British Indian army sepoys with captives in Burma.

his saintly old father in India proud. The prisoners' relatives, noted Burney, "crowded round the mission with presents and tokens of gratitude in the most pleasing and gratifying manner. No instance had ever before occurred of the return of captives … and the arrival of these prisoners … was as astonishing and embarrassing as the return to life of the dead."[700] He uses the word "embarrassing", as some masters appeared and tried to reclaim some of the captives as former slaves. Many husbands and wives had also remarried and had new families and there were in-laws who had taken their relatives' properties. Burney felt this was fair enough, as "upon their abduction … all had undergone alienation according to ancient custom,"[701] but it still must have been embarrassing. The British authorities set up a court to decide on the conflicting claims. There may be some Siamese or even British records of the events surrounding the return of the Phuket captives who had been taken to Burma over 15 years before, but if such records exist, this author has yet to locate them.

27

The Tan Clan

1822 to the Present Day

Phuket Is Freed of Debilitating Fear and Repopulated

After the British took Tenasserim, the constant threat of Burmese raids on Phuket ended and the threat from pirate raids was also dissipating. Phuket people began to come back home from Phang Nga to live on the island again. The capital of Thalang was re-established by the governor Luang Cherm in the north of the island at Ban Muang Mai, which still had boat access into Phang Nga Bay through hidden mangrove waterways. In 1837 the next governor of Thalang, Phaya Thalang Rerk, moved the capital to Ban Bangrong in Paklok, the town near the present-day gibbon sanctuary, again hidden up a mangrove waterway. It was not until 1862 that the Thalang town of today was established on its present site between Ban Don and Ban Takien,[702] but by then the new, predominantly Chinese settlement of Phuket town had become the main economic center on the island.

On his way from Phuket to Phang Nga in 1824, Lt. Low noted that he passed an American brig, the Hope from Boston. Until their independence in 1776, by law, the American colonies could only trade with Britain. After independence, some enterprising New York and New England merchants began to enter the China tea trade. They sailed east around Africa and through the Indian Ocean. However, the only American products that China really wanted were ginseng and guns, so, like the Europeans, US ships began to call in first at the Malay peninsular ports to try to trade for tin, ambergris and other products wanted in China. Low tells us that this Bostonian brig was trying to trade a quantity of clapped-out old muskets to the natives for tin. However, what these Yankees from the other side of the world probably didn't know was that the "natives" in Phuket had a longer history of gunrunning than the Americans and simply refused to buy their "clumsy old artificers … that would be more danger to the persons using them."[703] But at least the presence of the Hope in Phang Nga Bay shows that, by 1824, foreign trade was resuming on Phuket.

Chinese Immigration Increases

Bigger developments were taking place in the new port settlement and mining centers of "Puket" and Kathu where more and more Chinese immigrants were arriving to try to make their fortunes in the recently unearthed tin fields. Lt. Low visited these new mines during his 1824 visit to Phuket and noted that "a Chinese smelter informed me that he could afford to produce tin at a cost of one half, at the utmost, of the market rate … One bahar (of tin) can be prepared for the market at an expense of 20 dollars and it can be sold for 52 and often much more."[704] With such fat profits of 100 percent or more and with Phuket now relatively safe, it was but a matter of time before the indefatigable Chinese would appear in their thousands, like moths to a flame, to start digging at the ground like a swarm of human termites and completely eclipse the small existing Thai and Malay population on the island.

27.1 A local coastal trading junk: many Chinese immigrants arrived in Phuket on such ships.

In the early 19th century, large numbers of southern Chinese were fleeing the overpopulation, economic hardship, famine and wars in south China by emigrating. Many came to the new and economically open British Straits Colonies (later British Straits Settlements), which encouraged the immigration of these enterprising immigrants. Many of these often penniless, lower class Chinese arrivals in Penang and Malacca soon heard about the new tin finds and opportunities in southwest Siam and started coming north to Phuket. Hsieh Ching Kao, a maritime merchant from Guandong province who traded in the region between 1795 and 1815, wrote that "the Fukian and Kwantung people who come here to mine tin and to trade are very numerous." Particularly in Penang, where "the clothing, food and houses are all magnificent … There are Fukian and Kwantung people who come here to trade. They also leave to travel two to three days northwest by land or for more than a day by sea and arrive at Yang-hsi-lang [Junkceylon]. If they go a further three to four days by land or about a day by water they arrive at P'eng–ya [Phang Nga]."[705]

Canny Mr. Tan

In underpopulated Phuket these new Chinese immigrants were welcomed by the governor as a useful means of re-populating the island and obtaining a labor force. Tan Gaik Tam was one of these early Chinese immigrants. A Hokkien reportedly born around

1800 in the town of Lianshan in Tongan county, Fujian province, China, Tan Gaik Tam is now considered to have been the patriarch of the powerful Tan clan in Phuket, whose descendants have dominated much of Phuket's economy and government over the past 150 years.

As a youth in China, Tan Gaik Tam had been a member of the Heaven and Earth Triad, a patriotic organization opposed to the Qing Dynasty. This triad was closed down in 1822 by the Qing police and its members hunted down. To flee the police, Tan and two friends bought a passage on a junk to Penang and arrived at bustling Beach Street Quay, Penang, like most 22-year-olds – full of ambition and hope. They did laboring and other menial work for some years before moving north to Phuket in around 1825, just after the Anglo-Burmese War.

27.2 An early small-scale Chinese tin mine and ore separation plant.

In the new, ramshackle and developing tin-mining settlement and port of Phuket the three men pooled their meager capital and cooperated in raising chickens and setting up a bean-curd factory. Later they started trading in tin. By 1828, Tan Gaik Tam had reportedly won the backing of Lim Hoi, the now wealthy and influential Macao Chinese merchant who had exposed the sultan of Keddah's plotting with Burma eight years before. With Lim's assistance and capital, Tan established his own tin mining and trading company called Hup Hin on virgin land in the Sapam /Rassada area north of Phuket town. As his businesses developed and he became a towkay (a rich Chinese business owner), he sent word back to China for more relatives to come and work in Phuket. He married a local Thai woman and as he grew richer, he took several more wives, both on the island and around the region. Over the next 20 years Tan Gaik Tam, through his business success, his large family and by attracting other Tan kinsmen from Fujian, was instrumental in establishing his Hokkien Tan clan as the largest and most influential Chinese group on Phuket.

As Tan Gaik Tam grew wealthier, he became more philanthropic, funding local social projects and the construction of temples and shrines. He became the head of Phuket's strongest triad, or workers union, the predominantly Hokkien Kian Teck Triad. In the early 1870s he was appointed deputy mayor of Phuket town and joined the island's governor, a son of Viceroy Noi Na Nakorn, in running Phuket's lucrative opium monopoly. In 1867, the Siamese king awarded Tan a Siamese lordly title, Luang Sakhonkapitan and he was recognized as the head of the fast-growing Chinese community on the island, many of whom were his employees and relatives, or both.[706]

As Tan's local-born Sino-Thai children grew up, they and other family members from China helped run Tan's businesses on Phuket and Tan Gaik Tam himself began to spend more time in the safer and more salubrious surroundings of Penang, where he bought a large mansion and invested much of his wealth in the bustling property market and British banks there. He is also listed as one of the early principal contributors to the Tan Kongsi in Penang. (A kongsi is a Chinese family or clan shrine and kin help association.) Tan Gaik Tam sent many of the new Tan kin arrivals in Penang north to work for him in Phuket.

The Tan Clan and Other Towkays in Phuket

When Tan Gaik Tam died around 1876, his eldest son, Tan Jao, took over as the clan patriarch in Phuket and leader of the powerful Kian Teck Triad. He also became a close associate of the Phuket town mayor and governor and was also given a Siamese title. In the 1890s Tan Jao's two tin mining companies in Phuket, with financial assistance from the government, were chosen to pioneer the introduction of new mining machinery and techniques on the island. Tan Jao and his three brothers each had several wives and many children in Phuket and the region, further diversifying the Tan clan and spreading its web-like influence. Tan Jao's younger brother alone, for example, had many wives and reportedly more than 400 grandchildren. Over the ensuing century of rapid growth in Phuket and in southwest Siam's tin-mining industry, these Tan descendants

27.3. Tan-Pack Huad in 1912, a wealty Hokien mining towkay who received the Royal Siamese title Luan Aram Sakornket

were well placed to prosper. The extended Tan clan has now built shrines in Phuket, such as the ornate Saeng Tam shrine on Phang Nga Road, helping to make Phuket the spiritual center for members of this diverse émigré Hokkien clan. Today, the Tan clan consists of many different families related through blood or marriage, as these wealthy Chinese patriarchs usually had multiple wives and children.

These Tan families, like most other Chinese families in Thailand during the 20th century, adopted Thai family names such as Tanthawanit, Tanthai, Tandavesa, Tantiwit and Hongsyok. Today they comprise a majority of the élite Sino-Thai families of Phuket in terms of wealth, landholdings and commercial interests. They still own many of the island's hotels, shophouses, rubber plantations, golf courses, car and alcohol dealerships and hold many of the important political positions on the island today – Phummisak Hongsyok, for example, the great-great-grandson of wily Tan Gaik Tam was mayor of Phuket town for many years and recently served as the island's representative in the Thai national senate.

27.4. A Chinese funeral in Phuket town in 1921.

Other successful early Chinese immigrants became towkays and also established notable local families and clans in Phuket such as the Hokkien Khaw family, now the Na Ranong family, and the Ngan family, who made their fortune in property and mining and have adopted the Thai name Ngantawee. In the early 20th century the immigrant Yap Kim Jian made his fortune in tin mining and the first to start extensive palm oil plantations in the south; the Yap family adopted the Thai name Wanit (or Vanich) and still remain significant economic and political players on the island. Yap Kim Jian's granddaughter, Anchalee Vanich Thepabutra, has been for several years Phuket's representative in the Thai parliament and the secretary to the prime minister of Thailand. In 2007 her husband Tossaporn was also elected as one of Phuket's two MPs.

Within the small confines of Phuket town over the last century and a half, there have been many intermarriages between these wealthy, mainly Hokkien, élite Sino-Thai families who still control and dominate much of the economic and political landscape on the island today, almost two centuries later.

27.5 A Tandavanij family mining towkay with his new car imported from Penang in the 1930s

28

Dangerous Ladies and Dissension

1831 TO 1842

Nai Mi Discovers Phuket's Dangerous Women

There are only a few records of life in Phuket in the mid-19th century; one comes from Nai Mi, a writer of Niras verse, a Thai form of poetry written in a maudlin romantic vein. Nai Mi was a Sino-Thai from northern Siam who entered a Buddhist monastery in Bangkok. After his ordination, he traveled with some friends to Phuket in 1841. He and his friends sailed from Bangkok to Surathani then crossed the peninsula, traveling for five days by boat and pack elephants on the trail cut in 1804. On the jungle path down from Kao Sok to Phang Nga, they slept in a sala for travelers, keeping their fires lit all night because "the neighbourhood is haunted by tigers aplenty." During the night "rhinoceros's roars are heard at various intervals issuing from the gloomy recesses of the jungle."[707]

Eventually arriving at Pak Pra opposite Phuket, Nai Mi recorded that as late as 1841 the Pak Pra Channel could still be forded by elephants at low tide. They then continued south to the new settlement of Phuket town, which was beginning to be a tin boom town.

"The town and its environs pale in comparison with a large city. Hills encompass the town, the country is intersected by high mountain ranges whose towering peaks seem to threaten the clouds and form a charming view. The river flows broad and deep through the midst of the town, junks from all parts of the world come hither to trade and ride at anchor downstream, their sails are seen in unbroken succession. They bring every kind of merchandise with which they keep the place abundantly supplied. The merchant shops and bazaars on shore hustle and encroach upon one another. Tin is bartered for dollars [gold and silver coins] and commodities are hawked all round … in town wellbeing and gaiety are the rule. The islanders of Thalang love to dress tidily and tastefully. Handsomely built damsels are in evidence, but awestruck I dare not glance upon them, for I am deeply afraid of their subtle Philtres and craftily concocted charms that so easily lead to perdition, … The local beauties chatter in the quaint jargon of country people, … Thalang women are in fact exceedingly clever talkers, they excel in the art of charming the ear and netting partners. Once they make love to a lad it is done with him: he is inextricably inveigled. Such is the fate that overtook many youngsters from the central provinces."[708]

During his stay, Nai Mi took a trip to the island's west coast where "it is related an impression of the sacred foot [a Buddha's footprint] exists on a wide sandy beach, but the journey there is rather long."[709] It sounds as though he traveled north first to Tharua, then across to Bang Tao Bay, as he writes:

28.1 *One of the earliest photos taken of Phuket's "Dangerous" ladies in the later 19th century.*

"Taking the track wending towards the west we had to make our way through forests of lofty trees to ford rivulets and cross pools in the forest ... after proceeding for a while we came to a hamlet. It rises on the site of an ancient but now abandoned town left in ruins by the Burmese. It is now a heap of debris shrouded in jungle. Only a few widely scattered habitations peep out of the foliage ... The people cultivate orchards and paddy fields. Beyond the village I came across the seashore and walked along the ... majestic expanse. By the edge of the sea stretch smooth flat banks of pure crystalline sand. On the right hand side runs a fringe of Casurina trees. In these waters ambergris is also to be found. Tossed by the waves it is cast ashore to the top of the broad beach and while drying it exhales a foul carrion-like stench. But when dried and freed from all impurity it acquires an agreeable perfume ... on the left the ocean stretches boundless."[710]

More Rebellions in the South

In the rest of the peninsula things were not so calm and jolly. In 1831, ten years before Nai Mi was fending off Phuket's "handsome" women, 3,000 followers of the deposed sultan of Keddah had rebelled and massacred many of the Siamese troops stationed there. Viceroy Noi of Nakorn ordered the governors of Phuket and the other southwest coastal provinces – almost all of whom were now his sons or relatives – to gather a fleet and an army. This Siamese army of 8,000 men eventually surrounded the Malay rebels in the Keddah fort, where they put up a heroic defense for over four months until the last group of defenders committed mass suicide with their krisses.

It is interesting to read a description of the Siamese troops in Keddah by one British naval officer, as it contrasts with the generally more dismissive accounts of other British observers:

"Great numbers of their soldiery were in the fort and town and struck me as being a fine soldier-like body of men, if measured by an Asiatic standard ... A cloth round their hips falling to the knee and another fashioned like a Malay sarong hanging across the shoulders formed their sole attire ... The power of endurance of these soldiery I had often heard my Malays extol and looking at the spare athletic limbs in which there was more bone than flesh I could easily understand they were capable of making long marches … Beside their arms, these men each carried a slip of bamboo on his shoulder, at either extremity of which was suspended all [his] baggage, cooking gear and several days' rice tied up in a bag with a little salt … The celerity with which an army that thus carried its equipage and commissariat upon the men's shoulders could move from point to point of an extensive empire like Siam must be remarkable. … All those I saw had firearms of some description or other, the majority had flint muskets … Round their waist was secured … the charges of powder and on the same belt a bag was suspended filled with musket balls and pieces of a felt-like vegetable substance for wads."[711]

While Viceroy Noi was quelling this Keddah Malay rebellion, the sultans of Patani, Kelantan and Terengganu also rebelled yet again and marched against Songkla and besieged the city. During 1831 and 1832, four armies were sent down from Bangkok but were unable to defeat this southern Malay rebel army. It wasn't until Viceroy Noi and his southern force had subdued Keddah and joined the Bangkok army that the rebels were defeated. In retaliation the Siamese ravaged Patani and carried away many people as slaves.

Just seven years later, in 1838, the Malays in Keddah and Patani rebelled yet again and were again eventually defeated. However this time, Siam did as it had done in Keddah and dismembered the ancient kingdom of Patani, turning it into several smaller subsidiary provinces directly under Siamese rule. The sultan's palace was burnt down, his family evicted and many Patani men, women and children were shipped back to Bangkok as slaves.

28.2 Malay rebels, note the Portugeuse style blunderbuss muskets

The imperious Viceroy Noi of Nakorn now held direct control over Keddah and Patani and his sons (he had 34), relatives and friends sat as the governors, tax farmers and monopolists in most of Siam's southern provinces. More worryingly for Bangkok was the fact that Viceroy Noi was now getting on well with the British in Penang, whose navy had assisted Siam in its recent wars in Keddah. Bangkok may well have now feared that Viceroy Noi was scheming – as other viceroys of Nakorn had done – to declare the southern peninsular provinces independent from Bangkok's rule and then turn to the neighboring British for protection. Certainly Lt. James Low suspected as much. "It has ever seemed to me that the chao praya or Siamese governor of Ligor … would be glad of an opportunity of shaking off his fetters and asserting independence. The court of Siam tried to guard against such a contingency by retaining about it a number of the chao praya's relatives and by keeping spies, in the shape of councilor's, about his person."[712]

The End of Nakorn Sri Thammarat's Regional Dominance

The king, Rama III, decided to clip Viceroy Noi's wings by promoting Songkla, one of the few southern towns not run by his relatives, to become the second Siamese administrative center in the south. Songkla and its ruling Chinese family were given administrative control over Patani, Kelantan and all southeastern Siam. Viceroy Noi and his family were left to rule only the southwestern provinces. This reorganization may have been made because Rama III was less than impressed with Viceroy Noi's sons as local governors. The Royal Bangkok Annals say of Noi's sons, who were then governors of Phuket, Takuapa and Phang Nga: "The governor of Thalang was a drunkard whose main interest was in fishing; the governor of Takuatung … was a corrupt official who exploited the province for his own gains and the governor of Phang Nga was under house arrest in Bangkok."[713]

Viceroy Noi Na Nakorn died in 1839 around the age of 64. He was the last of the great viceroys of Nakorn. After his death, Bangkok gradually began spreading its administrative power more directly into the southern provinces by creating smaller provinces ("changwat") and directly nominating their governors and administrators instead of having a feudal sub-lord do so, as had been the case previously. Although Viceroy Noi's lordly Na Nakorn family would still remain a most prominent family in southwest Siam, they were to be slowly pushed out of regional power by the increasingly numerous and entrepreneurial Chinese arriving in the region.

With Bangkok intervening to run the south more directly and Phuket and its tin mines taking over as the wealth-generating engine in the south, the historic pre-eminence of Nakorn Sri Thammarat, which had ruled the central peninsula for centuries, began to fade. Today, this ancient and revered Buddhist city is, unfortunately, almost as renowned amongst the Thai youths of today for its hit-men and gangsters as for its great reliquary and ancient provenance.

29

Bending With the Winds

British and American Pressure: Reform or Be Colonized

Despite official antipathy in London and India towards the cost of administering more territory on the peninsula, the commercial lobby and local officials in the new British Straits Settlements colonies of Penang, Malacca and Singapore, a group known as the "Forward Party", still wanted to advance British territorial expansion in the peninsula. They particularly wanted to get control over the lucrative tin mines of Phuket Island and Phang Nga. The EIC directors in India, however, now gorged with Tenasserim, strictly forbade any further increase of EIC territory on the peninsula. "Our basic policy," they trumpeted, "is not to attempt to control, but to keep clear of native disorder" and they ordered the aggressive "Forward Party" to avoid relations with Siam altogether, "lest they should lead to an entirely undesirable war."[714]

But the Straits colonies merchants continued to be frustrated by the "vexatious and unfair" trading system in Siam which stifled their potential profits. Stamford Raffles, the founder of Singapore, explains why:

> "On arrival in a Siamese port the most valuable part of the cargo is immediately presented to the king [or king's agent] who takes as much as he pleases; the remaining part is chiefly consumed in presents to the courtiers and other Mandarins, while the refuse of the cargo is then permitted to be exposed to sale. The part consumed in presents to the Mandarins is entire loss; for that which the king takes he returns a present which is seldom adequate to the value of the goods he has received; but by dint of begging and repeated solicitation this is sometimes increased a little."[715]

The British Straits traders and the commercial community petitioned the EIC to use its military muscle to enforce these more modern and beneficial trade terms on Siam. Apart from wanting lower tariffs and easier rules, these British merchants distrusted Siamese laws and courts, which still solved legal cases by ordeal – dunkings under water, thrusting hands into burning oil and the like. They wanted clear, standard law imposed and preferably the principle of extraterritoriality, which is "the exclusive jurisdiction of British authorities over British subjects" in Siam.

In 1850, under increasing pressure from the Straits commercial lobby, Britain deputed James Brooke, later to become the famous "white rajah" of Borneo, to go to Siam and attempt to "make some arrangements that would effect an improvement in the British commercial relations with that country." However, Brooke and Rama III were both the wrong men for this job.

Twenty-four years before, in 1826, the last EIC delegate, Henry Burney, wrote that he believed the young king, Rama III, was "the most enlightened and moderate man at the court." However, by 1850 when Brooke arrived in Bangkok, the king was 62, in failing health and had become very conservative, almost reactionary. He is now seen as the last of the old-style feudal kings of Siam. For the previous 20 years, for example, he had left his palace grounds only once a year to go to a particular temple on ceremonial duty. Closed off from a changing world and ageing, he still believed that his kingdom was great and powerful and that contact with foreigners should be on Siamese terms, as it usually had been in the past.

James Brooke, on the other hand, was a belligerent Scotsman and an imperial British supremacist who had spent much of his time in Asia fighting Malay pirates off Borneo. He looked down on Asian kingdoms as "imperfectly civilised states." Brooke's forthright and arrogant attitudes left Rama III unimpressed. He rejected all Brooke's arguments. "Why", Rama III asked him, "do we need a new treaty when we already have one?" Affronted by Brooke's attitude, Rama III told him that he had "never encountered anyone else who came to conduct diplomatic negotiations like a professor giving instructions – instructions! – that pour forth like waters flooding forests and fields."[716]

Brooke left Bangkok empty handed, frustrated and bent out of shape and, like his fellow Scot, Crawfurd 30 years before him, he wrote to the EIC in India after his trip that, in his opinion, the best way forward was to declare war on recalcitrant Siam to force her stubborn hand. He proposed that "A more equitable treaty in accordance with the observance of civilised nations" should be presented to the Siamese court and, "should these just demands be refused, a force should be present immediately to enforce them by a rapid destruction of the defences of the river [Chao Phraya] which would place us in possession of the capital."[717]

Local British military opinion at the time held that only two warships would be required to defeat Siam – one to blockade the Chao Phraya River and stop all Bangkok's commerce, the other to advance upriver with a detachment of marines and take the king's palace. This was, in fact, the approach the Dutch had used and the French were to use, rather successfully, some years later. The EIC directors in India, however, believed that a much larger and more expensive occupation force would be required to subdue Siam, a country that had always fought most determinedly to uphold its freedom. The EIC accountants and directors therefore did not take up Brooke's rather bellicose suggestions and instead urged restraint, knowing that Rama III was already very ill and that his younger brother and heir, said to be a much more open-minded and liberal man, would probably soon be on the throne.

The Americans, with growing trade interests in Asia and Siam in the early 19th century, had made their first trade treaty with Siam in 1833, after Burney's treaty. The Siamese welcomed the US trade to counteract overbearing Britain and France. It is telling that while Henry Burney took over seven months in Bangkok and met with "a thousand vexations" to get the British trade treaty ratified, Edmund Roberts, the US envoy in 1833, took only one month to conclude his. He noted in his diary that "the Americans were decidedly preferred to any other foreigners."[718] However, by 1850 the most difficult and capricious trade conditions in Siam meant that most Americans had also stopped trading there. So in 1850, like the British, the Americans also sent an envoy to persuade Siam to open itself to reform and fairer trade. This was Joseph Balestier, an aged and grumpy American merchant from Singapore. He also was severely stonewalled in Bangkok, especially after committing the faux pas of losing his temper and shouting at the Siamese lords during negotiations. He also went away empty handed, frustrated and also belligerently recommended to his government that, "The way to negotiate with the Siamese is to send two or three men-of-war, of not more than sixteen foot draft of water [so they can cross the Chao Phraya River bar], let them … proceed up to Bangkok and fire off their salutes. In such case a treaty would not require more days than I had consumed weeks."[719]

Western imperial pressure was clearly mounting on xenophobic and feudal Siam to open up and reform or to have such reform forced upon it – by being colonized.

King Mongkut's Era

On his deathbed in 1851, King Rama III presciently advised his attendant councilors and lords, "There will be no more wars with Vietnam and Burma. We will have them only with the west. Take care and do not loose any opportunities to them. Anything that they propose should be held up to close scrutiny before accepting it. Do not blindly trust them."[720] One of those at his deathbed was Prince Mongkut, heir to the Siamese throne. He had spent the past 27 years in a monastery studying Western science and economics and had learned to speak English from American missionaries. As one of only a handful of people in Siam who could do so, he had assisted in previous negotiations over treaties and according to the accounts of all the foreigners he met, was a charming, intellectual and comparatively enlightened man. King Mongkut took the throne aged 46, as Rama IV and, understanding that the waters of the modern world were now lapping – if not quite crashing – against Siam's shores, he cautiously began the reforms that probably saved Siam, and Phuket, from being colonized.

In the years 1839-1842, Britain had defeated China in the First Opium War and had imposed the first of its "unequal treaties" because China was too recalcitrant to open up its foreign trade. Next door, the haughty Burmese kings had refused even to deal with foreign emissaries who would not take off their shoes in front of the king. The equally haughty British had refused to do this, so communications had broken down. Partly in consequence, in 1852, the second Anglo-Burmese War broke out and the

British attacked and took most of the country under their jurisdiction. Japan was also being forcibly pressed to open up at the time by American naval muscle and France was busy to the east intimidating Vietnam. The new King Mongkut saw that if Siam did not show flexibility and guile and begin reforming and opening up, it too risked being colonized. Just after King Mongkut took power, in a letter to the EIC, the son of the Siamese Phra Klang (minister of trade and treasury) informed the British, "The new king fully understands … relations [with] foreign nations, any intercourse or consultation may hereafter be conducted in an easier manner than before."[721]

The Bowring Treaty of 1855

With the new King Mongkut in power, the British decided to have another try at securing a treaty more amicably. In 1855 they sent the 63-year-old Sir John Bowring, the governor of Hong Kong (which Britain had recently seized by force from China). Like King Mongkut, Bowring was an intelligent and discerning man who spoke 17 languages and had been a spy and a businessman before joining British government service in the East.

King Mongkut knew that reforming Siam's feudal and monopolistic economic system would be hard, as he relied on the support of the great lords (senabodi) around him for his kingly power, yet it was these very lords who benefited most from the monopolies that so irritated the foreigners. But he

29.1 Sir John Bowring, the Brisish emissary to Siam in 1855. He warned King Mongkut "I have a large fleet at my disposal, but I would rather visit as a friend than bearer of menace."

felt he might sway these lords by arguing that, if they gave up some of their benefits now, they would receive far greater benefits in the future. The British Straits Settlements were indeed shining examples of the success of free markets, but few of Siam's regional lords had ever read Adam Smith or even been outside Siam. So King Mongkut's stronger argument was that failure to reform would probably result in a colonial attack and the loss of not only their most fruitful monopolies – but also their sovereignty.

Fortunately, the Bunnag family (of Persian origin) agreed with King Mongkut. They were the richest and most powerful trading family in the kingdom who, as hereditary Phra Klang lords, held the lion's share of all the juiciest trade monopolies. They saw the dangers and the benefits of King Mongkut's realpolitik and threw their weight behind his campaign for reform. They also realized that they actually needed this threat of the covetous imperialists to assist them, as Chuang Bunnag wrote to Bowring, the British envoy, just before he arrived in Siam:

"The system of taxation at present in the country falls most oppressively on the poor and producing portion of the population ... what renders these taxes more burdensome ... is the manner of collecting them through a farmer ... who of course retains a considerable profit for himself over and above the amount paid by him [to the crown] ... under this system the country grows poorer daily and is losing its commerce through having so little produce to export. What therefore is needed is that the people should be relieved of this burden, their industry encouraged and a market provided for their produce, but who has the power to effect this great change? Dare any of the ministers propose it and brave the clamour that would immediately be awakened by those in high places ... who are all interested in the present pernicious system ... If it be the benefit of the Siamese people that you have at heart, your influence should be exerted to bring about that radical and necessary change which cannot otherwise be accomplished."[722]

Like King Mongkut, Bowring was sagacious and calm, but did not fail to remind the Siamese of his big stick. In his letter to King Mongkut just before his arrival to negotiate the treaty, he reminded him, "I have a large fleet at my disposal, but I would rather visit as a friend than the bearer of menace."[723] He also understood the problems confronting the reformers domestically: "There are two parties – one wishing to maintain the ancient, restrictive system, the other willing to liberalise Siamese policy."[724]

The Thais have a saying which translates: "Big trees fall, while small trees that bend in the direction of the angry storm will survive." King Mongkut and his reformist clique, faced with overwhelming force, like the small tree, bent. Realizing they were unable to contest the power of industrialized Britain, the Siamese even used it to their advantage. They felt their British neighbors were at least a devil somewhat known to them and as one contemporary British Straits official wrote, they "were well aware that we had no wish to extend in the East those dominions under our rule which are already almost too large for our control. This however could not be said of other European nations."[725] Even the rather xenophobic Rama III had said of the British: "England ... has shown herself to possess enough moral obligations and is unlikely to take uncalled-for measures."[726] King Mongkut and his reformists seemed to believe that if they let Britain secure the prime strategic and commercial interest in Siam, in return for recognition of Siam's independence and their protection, this would limit the ability of the other covetous, but less powerful, imperial powers to make greater demands on them. So within a month of Bowring's arrival in Siam, a new treaty was signed. The two sides agreed to perpetual peace and friendship, taxes on foreign trade were reduced and standardized at 3 percent on imports and 5 percent on exports and Siam agreed to the principle of extraterritoriality, with a British consul to be posted to Siam to oversee legal cases involving British citizens.

This treaty caused major structural changes to the way the Siamese economy worked. Bowring called it "The best deed of my political life ... My success involved a total revolution in all the financial machinery of the government ... It uprooted a great number of privileges and monopolies that had not only been long established but were held by the most influential nobles and highest functionaries in Siam."[727] He also recognized that this agreement was due to "the remarkably liberal and enlightened character of its present sovereign and certain liberal ministers."[728] As envisaged by King Mongkut, the Bowring Treaty soon became the model used by other Western nations wanting access to the Siamese market; by 1860 – just five years later – Siam had signed similar treaties with the USA, France, Prussia, the Hanseatic countries, Australia, Spain, Portugal, Sweden, Norway and Belgium. The effect on Siam's trade and business was immediate, according to the French priest Pallegoix, who was living in Bangkok at the time; in 1852 only three European merchant ships had traded in Bangkok, but by 1856, only a year after the Bowring Treaty was signed, more than 200 ships of different nations had traded there. Revenues, even for the former monopolists, soon grew larger than before. In Phuket and the southwestern provinces, trade and commerce also started to blossom. Writing in 1860, Bowring congratulated himself yet again: "The Anglo-Siamese treaty has brought the most beneficial fruits. The number of vessels engaged in foreign trade has been centupled … the productive powers of all the land have increased."[729]

King Mongkut's Further Reforms, 1855-1868

With the success of these trade reforms, King Mongkut now had the wind in his sails and pushed on with further trade reforms, particularly reducing the number of tax farms, so the only remaining monopolies were those on the lucrative vices the government wanted to control – opium, gambling and spirits.

He then set about the more difficult task of trying to reform Siamese society, starting with his divine self. Previously, under the old Indian concept of inaccessible divine kingship, common people could not even set eyes on the Siamese king. When the monarch ventured out of his palace, guards would go before him and everyone had to lock themselves away. Even if a dog barked at the procession, one European visitor explained, "They would have killed the dog and its master in the cruelest fashion in the world."[730] One Thai historian tells us: "Policemen with bows and arrows would precede the king and spot through every hole in the windows whether there were any eyes peeping through the holes. If so, the sharpshooters would shoot their eyeballs out."[731] King Mongkut abolished all this, allowing the common people to see him and even meet him and tender petitions. He declared that his ministers, who previously came to court shirtless and sweaty, should wear clothes in court. He started the first secular schools in the country and passed laws to reduce the most repressive powers of the regional lords. For example, before King Mongkut's reforms a local lord's retainers could still simply drag off any young girls in their land to use for sex. King Mongkut forbade this practice.

Like King Narai two hundred years earlier, King Mongkut also began to employ foreigners as trainers, teachers and advisers. To keep the British sweet and to obtain their protection, he allowed them the choicest commercial contracts in Siam. They got teak concessions in the north and Chinese British citizens from Penang took up most of the tin mining rights in the south and Phuket. British ships were carrying almost 90 percent of Siam's exports and the British banks, the Hong Kong and Shanghai Banking Corporation and Standard Chartered Bank, were allowed to conduct all Siam's national banking. King Mongkut bought most of his new military weapons from Britain and permitted the British to construct a telegraph line to Penang, greatly reducing the time for communications down the peninsula. As one British official in Penang wrote, "He is certainly the best friend we have in the country and I have no doubt that while he continues so everything will go on well."[732] Whilst King Mongkut was friendly to the British he was cautiously so, calling them his "eating friends, but not dying friends."[733] In 1857 he sent a diplomatic delegation to Britain, which also visited Paris, as the wily King Mongkut had figured out that his best defense was again to play the balance-of-power game. While he believed that British protection and friendship could be earned by giving them a satisfactory economic stake, he was, like King Narai before him, astute enough to temper their overbearing imperiousness by playing them off against the other great powers of the time, notably the French, Russians and Americans.

At the outbreak of the Civil War in America, for instance, King Mongkut wrote to Abraham Lincoln, offering his support to the Union Army in the form of two elephants, a male and female which, he suggested, could "multiply their race in the American forests"[734] and could be used in the army and for logging. Lincoln later replied, politely declining his offer, as he feared the American winters would be too cold for the animals to prosper. One wonders whether Lincoln may have been too hasty. Elephants, protected with sheets of armor plating, as they often were in Asian battles, with, say a Gatling gun in a fortified howdah at the head of an advance, might have saved many a Union soldier's life in the mindless infantry death charges of Gettysburg, Antietam or Bull Run.

King Mongkut also encouraged American Christian missionaries to teach English, including training his own children and wives in a palace school. That was until they began to nag him about his "most sinful practice" of polygamy. This, it seems, was one reform too far for King Mongkut. He soon closed the palace school to get rid of these hectoring missionaries.

29.2 King Monkut with his son and heir, the later King Chulalongkorn. Between them these two kings pushed through modernizing reforms that probably saved Siam from being colonized.

When he wrote his memoirs in Hong Kong, Sir John Bowring stated that King Mongkut had 600 wives; this was roughly the number of women he had seen on his visit to the royal palace and had mistakenly assumed they were all the king's wives. King Mongkut was so perturbed by this salacious error that he took up his pen and wrote personally to Bowring, upbraiding him for his statement and pointing out that he had in fact, only 39 wives. [735]

King Chulalongkorn's Reforms, 1868-1910

In 1868 King Mongkut (Rama IV) died of malaria and was succeeded by his son King Chulalongkorn (Rama V). Despite his father's reforms to date, young Rama V still took over a kingdom described by Malcolm Smith, a British physician in royal service in Siam at the time, as having

> "no fixed code of laws, no system of general education, no proper control of revenue and finance, no postal or telegraph service. Debt slavery was not abolished, the opium laws were badly administered, no medical organisation to look after health, no army on modern lines, no navy at all, no railways and almost no roads, a calendar out of step with the world and this list could be extended." [736]

Despite strong initial resistance from conservative lords, the new young king pushed ahead with his father's reforming steps with many more modernizations and during his 42-year reign, presided over a quite remarkable set of reforms which turned Siam from a sprawling, feudal kingdom – run at its extremities by almost-autonomous lords – into a smaller, relatively centralized and modern state.

He ordered people to dress in Western clothing and for men and women to wear different styled clothes and adopt Western hairstyles rather than the traditional top-knot or porcupine styles. He abolished the system of hereditary, semi-autonomous governors in the provinces, who managed affairs from their palaces in self-serving, irregular fashion. In 1896 King Chulalongkorn's brother, Prince Damrong, created the Tessaphiban system, grouping all provinces into 18 monton ("super-provinces"), each under the control of a resident high commissioner appointed by Bangkok to override these semi-hereditary local lords. All new appointments of provincial governors were henceforward made by Bangkok, not by regional lords such as the viceroy of Nakorn. At the local level, he even introduced the first tiny step towards democracy in 1897, when village people were able to elect their Kamnan and Phuyaibaan or district and village chiefs.

He also created many new advisory ministries: for war, finance, culture, public works, mining, the southern provinces, police, foreign affairs, etc. In 1872 he replaced the system of corrupt semi-independent tax collectors and tax farmers and started a central revenue department to collect taxes directly. In 1898 he metricated the Siamese currency, with 100 satang to the baht, and started issuing notes and coins and allowed his brother to establish the first private Siamese-run establishment to undertake banking and trade finance with the local Chinese businessmen. This was later to turn into Siam's first private bank, the Siam Commercial Bank, in 1906.

In 1891 King Chulalongkorn also took away the rights of local lords to make laws and rulings in legal cases and instead centralized the legal system, creating a ministry of justice, founding a law school and building law courts and prisons in the provinces and employing foreign advisers to draft national laws. In 1897 a national police force was set up and run by a Dane, General Gustav Schau, who placed mainly Danish officers in charge of the provincial police forces, including that of Phuket, which was probably when the two 18th century Danish cannons outside the central police station in Phuket town were brought to the island. The astute young king knew that only by demonstrating Siam's ability to deliver justice to international standards could he get the foreign powers to rescind the now humiliating and troublesome extraterritoriality powers thrust upon them in his father's treaty negotiated with Bowring. Extraterritoriality often allowed foreigners to undercut the Siamese with relative impunity. To give one example, let's take the case of booze.

King Chulalongkorn had kept alcohol as one of his few monopolies. This gave him control over its use as well as a healthy royal income. It prevented widespread alcoholism by keeping import tariffs and alcohol prices high. However, under the Bowring Treaty, when import duties on all items fell to 3 percent, foreigners started importing much cheaper, wicked, rot-gut, "samshoo" arrack from Java and China and the local liquor could not compete. When Siam insisted that foreigners needed a license to sell this alcohol, they fell back on the extraterritoriality clause in their treaties and refused, and Siam could not rule on this. Many died from drinking this imported "shamshoo" liquor and drunkenness and crime rose until murders were an almost daily occurrence, particularly in the Chinese areas of Bangkok and also in Phuket, where Penang Chinese imported the cheap hooch under cover of their Penang British citizenship. The American Consul General in Bangkok at the time, a Mr. Partridge and his son, even started privately selling American citizenship to Chinese to allow them to become liquor dealers. The Partridges earned 14 baht per "trading paper" (a certificate of American citizenship), split this with their Chinese agents who solicited buyers for a commission and the buyers also got a free US flag to fly over their boats or shops. The Siamese government eventually prevailed upon the Western powers to allow the tax on alcohol to be raised and General Partridge was replaced by the US State Department for encouraging the trade in this "most infamous traffic in poisonous rums."

One of King Chulalongkorn's more significant reforms was the abolition of slavery and corvée labor. There were several reasons for this reform: these practices gave the semi-autonomous lords too much local power; they were also anathema to most of the foreigners, not just morally, but because they kept almost half of Siam's labor off the free market, making labor rates some of the highest in Asia. King Chulalongkorn started in 1874 by capping the supply of new slaves by introducing a law decreeing that no person could in future be born a slave and that no new slaves could be created. The main causes at that time of people becoming enslaved were taking loans or gambling and using themselves as collateral. He made these practices officially illegal. He decreed that the owners of slaves must credit all existing slaves with four baht a day until their debts were paid off. This process took some 30 years to run its course, by which time most hereditary slaves had died off and most debt slaves had worked off their debts. So, by 1905, there were officially at least, no longer any slaves in Siam.

The remarkable list of King Chulalong-korn's reforms goes on and on. Railways were built; the first state railway was opened in 1896, though the southern line down the peninsula was not completed until 1922. A modern postal system was established and in 1881 the first telephone system. A national school system was set up in the 1890s, a ministry of education established and universities were built. In 1891 King Chulalongkorn made a tour of the southern provinces and visited Phuket, which had by then established itself as the most important economic center in the south. He was so impressed with booming Phuket town that it soon became the head of a new Siamese monton, which included all the southwestern provinces apart from Keddah (Saiburi).

29.3 A postman of the new Siamese postal service set up by King Chulalongkorn.

Monton Phuket however, remained a comparative backwater where central control remained weak because it lay some two weeks' journey away from Bangkok at best. However, the reforms taking place, the growing world tin market and the new freedom of international trade meant Phuket's business trade and wealth were booming. Penang, now just one night's comfortable steamship ride to the south of Phuket, was a much more convenient commercial center for Phuket's more prosperous islanders than was far off Bangkok. Because of this, as well as the island's largely immigrant Chinese population, Phuket's first big growth period at the turn of the century was to be influenced as much, if not more, by the Anglo-Chinese Straits Settlements to the south than by Bangkok or Thai influences from the north.

30

The Boundary Question

1860 TO 1910

Siam (and Phuket), unlike most other states in Southeast Asia, were never colonized. This was largely because Great Britain, the predominant world power in the later colonial era, wanted semi-obedient buffer states between its Indian empire and the colonies of the other great powers. It's no coincidence that all the states bordering the British Indian empire – Persia, Afghanistan, Tibet, Yunnan and Siam – remained un-colonized by any other Western powers. These periphery states were maintained as buffer states under Britain's imperial thumb, which in large measure determined or influenced their policies with latent military threat, not by actually ruling. Credit must of course also be given to the guile, urbanity and diplomatic skills of the Siamese leaders of this era. In particular, the two enlightened and pragmatic monarchs Rama IV and Rama V who used their absolute power to force through reforms that allowed the British to engage more efficiently in trade and exploitation – the main raison d'être of British imperialism. This both forestalled the need for Britain to actually colonize Siam and by default enrolled the British as Siam's de facto guardian against any other ambitious colonial powers.

The Terengganu Affair: British Gunboat Diplomacy

Since 1824, when Penang had blockaded Nakorn's war fleet in the Trang River, Siam had been forced to accept that the southern Malay Peninsula had effectively fallen under British, not Siamese, influence, but it remained unclear where the limit of each other's influence lay. The 1826 Burney agreement left this issue definitively grey, with both sides agreeing not to "obstruct or interrupt commerce" in these Malay states. In 1859 the issue came to a head when, during a succession dispute in Pahang, Siam sent a war fleet south to Terengganu to place a new sultan on the Pahang throne. Members of the British Straits Settlements Forward Party saw this as Siamese interference beyond the tenebrous terms of the Burney agreement.

Major General Sir William Cavenagh, the governor of the Straits Settlements at the time, was an old ex-Indian army warhorse. He had had one foot shot off and the horse under him killed by a cannon ball in the battle of Maharajapore (1843), then an arm partially shot off by another cannon ball in the Sikh wars (1846). He was an ardent imperial Forward Partyist and apparently loved a jolly good war. On hearing of this Siamese political meddling, and with Britain supporting a different candidate as sultan of Pahang, Governor Cavenagh immediately dispatched two British gunboats to Terengganu to request that "the sultan dismiss his intriguing guest"[737] and added firmly that his refusal to do so would be met with force. When Siam's preferred sultan did not depart, the British gunboats bombarded Terengganu fort for three hours, then sent in their marines, who captured the fort, spiked its guns and set fire to all the Siamese warships in the port. This was sufficient inducement for the sultan to bow to the British "request" and the Siamese force, with their preferred sultan, returned to Bangkok. Cavenagh had taken this action without the knowledge of Calcutta or London, who were furious when they heard of it. As they, looking at the larger diplomatic and economic picture, wanted to promote a closer, more amicable relationship with Siam.

30.1 A contingent of Siamese navy marines, one of the main Siamese instruments to control the often querulous and rebellious Malay states in the peninsular. Note the elephant mounted canon.

The Crocodile and the Whale

The French conquered Saigon in 1859. They then turned their covetous colonial eyes towards Cambodia, which, like the Malay states and Laos, was claimed as a vassal state by Siam. When a new king (Noradom) came to power in Cambodia in 1863 and was faced with rebellion, a French gunboat sailed up the Mekong and raised the French flag in Phnom Penh, claiming that the new king had asked for French protection – which he may have done, but he certainly denied this to Bangkok. King Mongkut protested vehemently to Paris but had to accept the reality that there was little that Siam, with its small, poorly equipped army, could do against the French. He had little choice but to rely on Britain to defend him. In 1864 he wrote, rather dejectedly, to Chuang Bunnag, or Phraya Suriyawongse, the Siamese ambassador to Europe in Paris:

> "I think that now is the chance for Britain to put into practice her policy of bringing Siam under her protection, since Siam is being harassed on one side, with the British colony on the other … it is for us to decide what we are going to do, whether to swim up the river to make friends with the crocodile or to swim out to sea and hang on to the whale … supposing we were to discover a gold-mine in our country … enough to pay for the cost of a hundred warships and all the armaments from their countries … they can always stop the sale of them when they feel we are arming ourselves beyond our station. The only weapons that will

be of real use to us in the future will be our mouths and our hearts constituted so as to be full of sense and wisdom for the better protection of ourselves."[738]

As the British "whale" was unwilling to go to war with the French "crocodile" over the issue, King Mongkut was forced to sign away Siam's right to dominate eastern Cambodia. In 1867 King Mongkut wrote acquiescently to his foreign minister, "It is sufficient for us to keep ourselves within our house and home. It may be necessary for us to forgo some of our former power and influence."[739]

King Mongkut died in 1868 and his son King Chulalongkorn (Rama V) took power. He was much more pro-British than his father and Britain took full advantage of the commercial opportunities he made available to it over the next decades. Lord George Curzon, later to become viceroy of India, noted after a visit to Siam in 1892:

> "Of the great ships lying in the river off Bangkok, there is scarcely one that is not owned by British subjects, 88 percent of the entire trade of this port is so carried. Thousands of British subjects, Indians, Burmese, Shans and Chinamen are pursuing their avocations or trade in different parts of the country. They constitute the predominant mercantile interest. The heavy rice crops of the Menam valley are bought by British merchants and exported in British hulls. British engineers and contractors are laying the important railways and British concessionaires hold the most important of the Siamese mines."[740]

He neglected to mention that Britain also supplied Siam with most of its military weapons, trained the army, had over 40 advisers in the Siamese government, ran its finance ministry and British banks held all of Siam's reserves, gold and money and did all its banking.

French Encroachment in Laos

In 1883, France annexed all of Vietnam, then, claiming that Laos was a former vassal of Vietnam, not Siam, sent French military expeditions to push east into the Laos jungles where no maps existed and no borders were delineated. In response, King Chulalongkorn sent two Siamese military columns to try to occupy and defend the region. In 1893, some skirmishes occurred between Siamese and French troops. In one, a popular young French officer called Grosgurin was killed while attacking a Siamese outpost. This incident was seized on by the hawkish Partie Colonial in France, which after inflaming the French public with nationalist and colonial jingoism in the press, demanded outrageous reparations from Siam essentially for having had the audacity to defend itself. France demanded that Siam cede to them all lands east of the Mekong River plus pay a huge sum of money in compensation.

King Chulalongkorn, in disbelief, turned to Britain. London, however, had no interest in going to war with France over what it regarded as the strategically unimportant, under-populated middle Mekong region. As Lord Curzon pointed out in a speech in Parliament,

"French gunboats may parade the tranquil reaches [of the Mekong] but they will unfortunately find no one to overawe. French steamers may transport the wares of the Syndicat du Haut Laos, but they will find no one to whom to sell them … If the French choose to embark upon costly experiments in a region so destitute, other nations are not called upon to inveigh against their folly."[741]

Indeed, Britain, as conniving as ever, actually saw this French move as a jolly good opportunity to appease an expansionist France through what was then known as "the doctrine of compensatory advantage." France would be allowed to take a big chunk of eastern Siam to compensate for Britain having just annexed the rest of Burma after the third Anglo-Burmese war in 1870. With such a theoretical balance achieved, Britain wanted the rest of Siam to become a buffer zone for its Indian em-

30.2 Siamese troops in Laos 1893. Poorly equipped, they could not withstand the well armed disciplined military might of Britain or France

pire (which now included Burma). Britain therefore told King Chulalongkorn that it would not defend him in this case and advised him to settle with the French quickly and not provoke a fight that might result in France gaining even more of Siam. "Siam is too weak to stop France," Britain bluntly advised, so Siam should "agree with your enemy quickly … and save the rest."[742] Chulalongkorn, outraged at this French aggression and the condescending British response, refused to consent to these exorbitant French demands.

French Gunboats in Bangkok

To force the king's hand, the French sent three iron gunboats to Paknam, at the entrance to the Chao Phraya River and Bangkok. The big naval guns at the newly renovated Siamese fort at Paknam, which guarded the river entrance, were commanded by a Danish officer, Andreas de Richelieu, and six other Danes in the employ of the Siamese king. These Danish officers instructed the French that they would resist the French ships' entry into the river. With its ships sitting offshore, Paris leaned heavily on Copenhagen and got the Danish government to telegraph their consul in Bangkok to order these Danes to resign from Siamese military service immediately or be guilty of treason in Denmark. De Richelieu and his officers replied defiantly that they would not resign and indeed were ready to fight to the death for their employer, the Siamese king. For this loyalty, Chulalongkorn later promoted de Richelieu to Admiral and Commander in Chief of the Siamese Navy. (Richelieu Rock, a famous diving site to the northwest of Phuket today, is named after him.)

The three French warships then advanced into the river. De Richelieu and his men opened fire and hit and sank one of the French gunships. The other two ships returned fire and shouldered their way past the fort and upriver to Bangkok, where they anchored in mid-stream directly opposite King Chulalongkorn's palace – broadside on, with their large, shiny guns trained directly at his palace – and sent a message demanding the king sign the compensation treaty.

With the two French warships moored so menacingly opposite the palace, a frigid political calm prevailed over the sultry heat of Bangkok. King Chulalongkorn desperately tried to muster support from Britain, Germany and Russia. The Germans, who since forming as a nation in 1871, had the most rapidly growing commerce with Siam, sent a warship to Bangkok to "observe" the French ships. Britain, which must by now have felt the French were sticking their Gallic gunboats too near to British commercial interests, also dispatched two "observation" warships and sternly informed Paris that "the independence of Siam was a subject of grave importance to the British."[743] At the same time Britain scolded the Siamese for their failure to follow its advice and artfully warned that a further such failure might well "result, at no distant date, in the more or less complete extinction of the Siamese national existence."[744] Whether this would occur at the hands of Britain, France or both was cryptically unspecified. In the end, because might is usually right, Siam lost its tributary lands east of the Mekong and the British were happy little Machiavellians, as Lord Curzon later gloated, "The recent French movements have driven the Siamese, already greatly predisposed towards the English, still more into the latter's hands."[745]

30.3 French bullying: A cartoon from the British Punch magazine of 1893 entitled "The French Wolf and the Siamese Lamb".

The Anglo-French Border Agreement for Siam

Two years later, in 1895, France and Britain just about came to blows again, this time in Mong Sing, an obscure outpost in the remote mountains where French Indochina met British Burma on opposite sides of the Mekong. The French attempted to take a position on the west bank of the upper Mekong, but were met by 130 Gurkha troops and a Union Jack flag. There was again much jingoism in the imperial press of both countries and talk of war. However, with Germany now flexing its considerable muscle in Europe, France and Britain decided they should come to some formal agreement over Siam to avert further disputes (see Map 10).

The British wanted to leave all of Siam as a buffer state. The French proposed that the two divide Siam into equal parts. In 1896 the British and French foreign ministers met in Paris to decide the fate of Siam. It is indicative of the times that the Siamese ambassador in Europe was not even invited to attend these negotiations. The French first proposed that a line be drawn following the Chao Phraya upstream then more or less due north to western Laos; France should have all the territory to the east of that line

Map 10
Siam's Lost Territories, 1867 – 1909

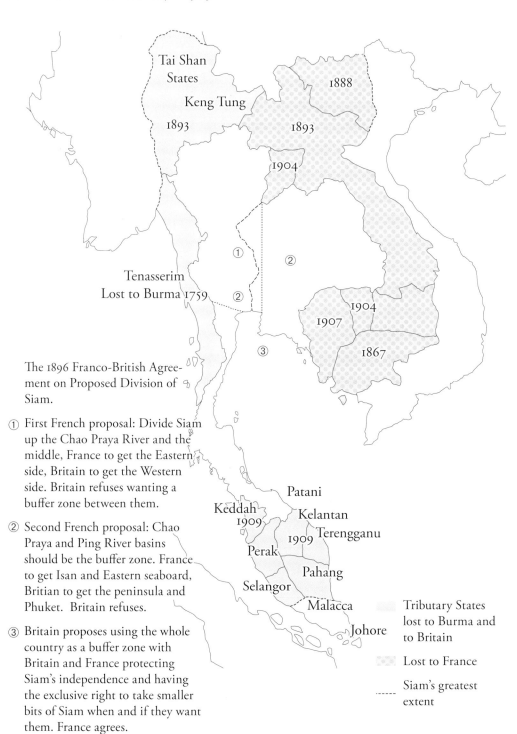

Tai Shan
States

Keng Tung

1893

1888

1893

1904

Tenasserim
Lost to Burma 1759

①

②

②

1904

1907

1867

③

The 1896 Franco-British Agreement on Proposed Division of
Siam.

① First French proposal: Divide Siam
up the Chao Praya River and the
middle, France to get the Eastern
side, Britain to get the Western
side. Britain refuses wanting a
buffer zone between them.

② Second French proposal: Chao
Praya and Ping River basins
should be the buffer zone. France
to get Isan and Eastern seaboard,
Britian to get the peninsula and
Phuket. Britain refuses.

③ Britain proposes using the whole
country as a buffer zone with
Britain and France protecting
Siam's independence and having
the exclusive right to take smaller
bits of Siam when and if they want
them. France agrees.

Patani

Keddah
1909

Kelantan

Terengganu

1909

Perak

Pahang

Selangor

Malacca

Johore

Tributary States
lost to Burma and
to Britain

Lost to France

------ Siam's greatest
extent

and Britain could take everything to the west, including peninsular Siam and Phuket. Britain rejected this deal, seeing it as leaving too much potential for another border incident, plus Britain already had the economic advantage in the central Chao Phraya river basin. France then put forward a second plan that involved leaving the Chao Phraya and Mae Ping river valleys (central and northern Thailand) as the buffer zone, with France taking Isan, the northeast and the eastern seaboard and Britain getting the whole peninsula up to Kanchanaburi so that its Malayan and Burmese colonies would be contiguous.

Meanwhile, Prince Svasti of the Siamese legation in London, no doubt most unsettled at not being invited to this meeting, lobbied to convince the negotiators to consider the Siamese idea, which was that the two imperial powers might perhaps want to use the whole country as a buffer zone. This British favored this policy, as Lord Curzon noted, "We have no desire to imperil our amiable relations [with France] by coming to closer quarters and we particularly desire to avoid them as neighbours."[746] Britain eventually triumphed with this argument, though it did agree to a small caveat allowing each side just a little expansion room if required, so that Britain would not be "debarred from any further extension in the Malay Peninsula."[747] In 1896, with this caveat inserted, France and Britain signed a joint guarantee that together they would "uphold the independence of Siam against any third party," thereby effectively securing Siam's independent status in a world being rapidly colonized.

British Territorial Expansion in the Peninsula

After the Indian Mutiny of 1857-1859, the government of Britain's Asian colonies was taken away from the EIC and put under the British government. Then in 1866, London removed the Straits Settlements colonies from under India's control and made it a separate, self-governing colony based in Singapore.

The strongest lobby for further British territorial expansion in the peninsula came from the Straits Forward Party. The most extreme colonial members of this Forward Party still wanted Britain to annex the entire Malay Peninsula, while the less extreme wanted Britain to annex just Keddah and Monton Phuket (southwest Siam) with its tin mines, up to the Burmese border by Ranong, so that the Straits colonies would be joined by land to Burma and India. The Forward Party's main argument for annexation was essentially that bad Siamese governance in the Malay states was affecting the ability of the Straits Settlements to do business in the central peninsula. An 1896 article in the Malay Daily Chronicle summed up their view by stating that the Siamese peninsular states were

> "egregiously misgoverned. The people are oppressed, agriculture and commerce are pursued under every possible difficulty and communications hardly exist. Siam, as everybody knows, has completely ceased to exercise any decent authority over the remote parts of its kingdom and indeed, in most Malay states its authority has always been repudiated the moment the king's vessel was out of sight."[748]

For example in Phuket, despite official policy previously agreed in the Bowring Treaty that all export taxes would be a maximum of 5 percent, as late as 1896 the Chinese smelters and tax farmers in Phuket were still demanding duties and taxes of 16 percent or more on tin. Phuket Island and indeed the whole south of Siam had neither roads nor railways so that tin miners still had to use elephant tracks and rivers to get their product to the coast from interior mines. Lawlessness and brigandage were also rife. One ardent Siam critic, a Mr. Lillee, wrote an article in 1896 calling for the full annexation of peninsular Siam, arguing that because of the unchecked lawlessness in southern Siam, "The world can see for itself that something is wrong, everything is wrong ... The country is falling to pieces of itself. No country whose condition is even moderately prosperous could possibly show [such] a list of brigandage and robberies as Siam."[749] The Foreign Office in London, which was, as usual, looking at the bigger diplomatic picture, responded to these calls for British annexation by writing that "If we are to copy the French and bully the Siamese, we cannot expect the latter to continue [to be] as friendly as they have hitherto shown themselves."[750]

A compromise was found between London and Singapore by the use of the resident system, whereby the British intervened in the government of several of the southern Malay states without actually annexing or colonizing them. The resident system essentially meant the local sultan was paid a handsome stipend to retire to a nice palace while a British adviser, or "resident", administered the economic life of his kingdom for him. In 1895 several of these British-administered Malay states were grouped together as the Federated Malay States, which were effectively under British administration. They made such swift economic and social advances that the Straits Forward Partyists, such as the pro-Malay, anti-

30.4 British bullying: Death and destruction in Mindhla during the third Burmese war. The Siamese court was well aware that in 1885 when the Burmese king refused British demands a small British expiditionary force took a only ten days to capture the capital, depose the king forever and take over running the country.

Siamese Sir Frank Swettenham – later to become the governor of the Straits Settlements – wanted to do the same with all the Malay states and Phuket Island as well, on the basis that "It does not appear that Siam has ever had either excuse or invitation to justify the extension of her influence and authority over the Malay states ... [which had not] ... benefited at all by their long connection with Siam."[751]

Northern Malay rajahs of states such as Patani, Keddah, Terengganu and Telubin, chafing under Siamese domination, requested Singapore to place their states under British protection and let them become part of the Malay Federation. Sir Frank Swettenham, when he became the governor in Singapore, used these requests to put renewed pressure on London to annex southern Siam. "British intervention has been invited and the results of our intervention and influence in the federated states are sufficient reason to extend it."[752] But London still refused to be drawn into doing something that might irritate Bangkok and drive her into the arms of France, or, worse still, Siam's new and fast-growing friend – Germany.

The Other Great Powers in the Peninsula

King Chulalongkorn was being bullied by Britain and France. To offset their overbearing dominance, he began to turn to other powers. He appointed a Belgian as a general adviser on foreign policy and an American, Edward Strobel, was employed as his Adviser General. Danes were brought in to train and lead his armed forces and Italians to train his police, but it was the Germans whose influence was growing most rapidly in Siam. Britain became so concerned about other imperial powers nosing around in the Siamese peninsular states that in 1897 it pressured Siam into signing a secret agreement whereby Bangkok promised not to cede or to grant privileges to any other power on the peninsula south of the Isthmus of Kra or on any of its offshore islands without the written consent of Britain. In return, Britain promised to defend Phuket and Siamese sovereignty against any attempted encroachment by another foreign power.

The Kra Canal: France and Japan Nose Around

In 1869 the French engineer Ferdinand De Lesseps, fresh from his success building the Suez Canal, came up with the idea of cutting one through the Isthmus of Kra, from Ranong to Chumporn – the narrowest part of the peninsula. The British were concerned that this would open up the central peninsula to French influence and commerce, and, more importantly, that it would seriously diminish the economic and strategic importance of Singapore and the other Straits Settlements colonies. As one British Foreign Office official wrote, "Whoever holds the peninsula commands the route to the Far East … It is difficult to imagine any event which could be more disastrous to British interests in the Far East than that a foreign power should secure a position on the Bay of Bengal between Tenasserim and the Straits Settlement."[753]

Stiff British resistance eventually prevented the attempt to build the Kra Canal. The ambitious De Lesseps then disappeared off to attempt to dig the much grander Panama Canal but went bust, failed miserably and then died. But Singapore repeatedly tried to use the threat of a Kra canal to try to convince London to annex the whole peninsula, or at least the tin areas of the central peninsula. The idea was resuscitated in the early 1890s and again in the 1930s, when Singapore newspapers reported breathlessly that the Japanese had approached Bangkok with an offer to build the canal. Despite several such alleged attempts, this Kra canal project was always foiled by British pressure on Siam. This Kra Canal idea is still occasionally bandied about by some of the more sensationalist Thai politicians today.

Russia's Failed Attempt to Make Phuket Island a Naval Colony

By the late 19th century Russia had become a Pacific Ocean power, but had a major problem moving its navy from west to east. The Russian navy usually sailed south via the Black Sea, the Suez Canal, the Straits of Malacca then north to Vladivostok. But the fleet needed secure naval and coaling stations on the route.

During his 1897 European tour, King Chulalongkorn visited Tsar Nicholas II in St Petersburg and it was reported in the British Straits newspapers that they had discussed a Russian lease for a coaling station and settlement on Phuket Island. Several Russian cruisers did visit Phuket and in 1889 they were reported (to the British Foreign Office) to be regularly mooring in Phuket and making "general enquiries."[754] It was also reported that the Russian ambassador in Bangkok had made several visits to the king's palace and and rumors got into the British press that a long-term agreement was being drafted to lease Phuket to the Russians.

30.5 King Chulalongkorn cozying up to Tsar Nicholas II of Russia. In 1889 it was rumored that Bangkok had granted Russia a long-term lease to use Phuket as a naval base. The British pressured Siam to cancel the deal and in return promised to protect the independence of Siam and Phuket from other colonial powers.

The British, knowing from their own experience with Penang and Singapore that a "long-term lease" was likely to turn into a full-blown naval base and then colony, had no wish to see this "coaling station" right in the middle of their sphere of influence. One alarmist memo from Singapore to the Foreign Office in London in 1889 declared that Russia's plan "was to make Tongkah (Phuket town) her headquarters, as long as possible whilst she preyed upon British commerce."[755] Spurred on by Forward Party pressure, London, along with the French and Japanese, applied extreme pressure on Bangkok to stop the project and Siam was forced to back out of the deal.

German Peninsular Hopes Held at Bay

Germany, which had only formed as a country in 1871, was late to the colonial table and most of the good stuff was already gone. So this powerful newcomer had to scrape around collecting the crumbs ignored by the earlier European colonial powers – the parched deserts of Namibia, the butt-end of New Guinea, the small river valley of Togo, a few minuscule Pacific islands and the like. By the 1890s, as the new strong man of Europe, Germany was desperate to establish its imperial place in the sun, by force if necessary, and Siam was one of the few un-colonized gems left. So Berlin began to focus its attention there.

Siam was happy to use Germany to offset Anglo-French bullying and in 1886 King Chulalongkorn established a Siamese embassy in Berlin. Soon more than 30 German advisers were working with the Siamese government in banking, finance, and other fields. German capital and advisers were engaged to build the telegraph and postal system and much of the new railway system. Some of King Chulalongkorn's many sons became the first foreigners ever to be accepted into the German Imperial Military Academy. German advisers joined the Siamese military and soon Germany, not Britain, was supplying the Siamese army most of its weapons. The efficient Germans also took over much of Siam's trade from Britain and by 1901, of 576 ships that came to Siam that year, 272 or 53 percent were German, while only 24 percent were British. [756]

In 1890 a British Foreign Office memorandum from Singapore to London alarmingly reported that Germany was "secretly negotiating with Siam to obtain Phuket for a coaling station."[757] The British applied heavy pressure on Bangkok to stop this move. Germany then offered the Siamese cheap capital to build the peninsular railway from Bangkok to Singapore under German management. The British again aggressively objected and strongly pressed Siam to refuse the offer. In 1900, it was reported by the Singapore press that the Germans had struck a deal with the sultan of Keddah to lease Langkawi Island as a coaling station and port. The sultan, when questioned by British journalists, did admit to dealing with the German company Bahn Mayer and C°. Another large German company, Deutsche Uversec Gesellschaft, also applied for a mining concession on Langkawi and was also turned down, again due to British pressure. Prince Damrong, the king's half-brother, was forced to write to the Germans that "it is unnecessary to say what danger it will be to grant such concession especially to a German company, which may have political power at its back."[758]

Britain's Final Peninsular Land Grab

British investors from the Straits Settlements still wanted to get access to mineral-rich Monton Phuket and southern Siam. The Siamese court, however, remained rightfully paranoid about British designs and stonewalled most British commercial requests. In a dispatch to London, the British Chargé d'Affairs in Bangkok voiced British frustration: "The Siamese government seems reluctant to grant even reasonable concessions to any British subjects preferring possibly to keep the Malay states closed to foreign enterprise."[759] Britain, he suggested, had to be more forceful to "break down the barriers of Siamese exclusion and obstruction."[760] These calls for commercial access into southern Siam, plus the attempts by Russia, Germany and the other Great Powers to get a foothold in Phuket and the peninsula, made the Forward Partyists in Singapore particularly animated. During the official visit by King Chulalongkorn to Singapore in 1902, and without London's consent, Governor Swettenham privately buttonholed the young King Chulalongkorn to try to persuade him to cede to Britain Phuket Island, Langkawi and all other Siamese islands south of the Isthmus of Kra. Chulalongkorn refused and the arrogant Swettenham wrote most huffily to the British Colonial Secretary: "He wants all the advantage of British support without any concession from him."[761] The British Foreign Office which was against Swettenham's scheme reprimanded him, claiming his actions had been "of very doubtful expediency."[762]

The Forward Party in Malaya realized that only strategic arguments would have any hope of moving London to consider further annexation on the peninsula. Some of the more disaffected Malay leaders, such as the sultan of Patani, also realized this and threatened that if Britain did not protect them against Siam, they would be forced to apply to other powers for protection, such as Germany. The Forward Party now used this strategic argument, along with the same old commercial arguments, to influence London so that in 1909, with war in Europe clearly brewing, London finally agreed to let Singapore enter into formal negotiations to annex Siam's peninsular territories. In these negotiations Henry Strobel, the American adviser to King Chulalongkorn, recommended to him that he give up the Malay states "to relieve [Siam] of this source of weakness, danger and annoyance which had caused her more difficulty than benefit."[763] Another of the king's advisers recommended the same, comparing the situation with a sick patient agreeing to have his legs amputated to save the body.

King Chulalongkorn eventually agreed to give up his rights over Terengganu, Kelantan, Perlis and Keddah, in return the British agreed to give up extraterritoriality as they perceived Siamese law was now working along modern Western lines (by this time many of Siam's judges were in fact British). They agreed to give a low-interest loan of four million pounds for a peninsular railway if all the construction work went to British firms. They also recognized Thai rule over Monton Phuket and the four provinces that formerly made up the kingdom of Patani. So in late 1909 an agreement was signed between Siam and Britain which settled the Siamese-Malay border at its current position. This left the hapless sultan of Keddah to lament that "My country and my people have been sold as one sells a bullock!"[764]

The French followed this British example and gave up their extraterritoriality in exchange for Siam giving them their tributary Cambodian provinces of Battambang and Siem Reap. Thus, by 1910, Siam in effect had been forced to give away most of its former tributary states where few actual Thais lived to keep the Thai parts of Siam independent. David Wyatt, a leading scholar of Thai history, wrote, in somewhat more Marxist terms, that the more powerful Thais and Sino-Thais "purchased their independence … at the expense of the Lao, Cambodians and Malays, who found themselves transferred to European colonial control."[765]

Siam had lost almost half the territory it had ruled only 60 years earlier when Rama III had died. It was now left a smaller, more centrally controlled and more Thai and Chinese run state. As for Phuket, despite the several attempted moves to take or colonize the island over the centuries by the Dutch, French, British, Russians and Germans, the little island, with its rich tin deposits and rather strategic position, somewhat enigmatically still remained a part of the Kingdom of Siam.

31

Inhuman Industry and Breaking Heads

1800 TO 1910

The Chinese, it has been said, have followed the Thai peoples south "like their own shadows."[766] The Thai people originated in what is now China, so physically and culturally the two peoples have always been closely connected and have assimilated easily.

Chinese Confucianism dictated that people should stay at home near their ancestors, as did Chinese law, which for most periods until the later 18th century outlawed emigration. One Ching Dynasty law, for example, read, "All officers of government, soldiers and private citizens who clandestinely proceed to sea to trade or who remove to foreign lands … shall consequently suffer death by being beheaded."[767] This was a fairly strong disincentive to go, unless one was desperate. But there were plenty of desperate people in the overpopulated southern coastal provinces of China, subject to droughts, floods, famines, wars and oppression. So despite the draconian laws, many still went to the "Nan Yang" (South Seas). As one 18th century Chinese wrote:

> "The Fukien [Hokkien] and Kwangtung [Cantonese] people, treating life lightly, go overseas, face the risk of inclement weather and great waves, they disregard the threat of shipwreck and do not care about the dangers involved. The reason they do this is that their native country is densely populated and the land scarce."[768]

Most of the Chinese who came to the Malay Peninsula or Siam over the years were reluctant emigrants compelled to go abroad for economic or political reasons. They were predominantly poor, single men who usually took a wife once they had arrived. As John Crawfurd, the EIC emissary to Siam in 1822, noted, "The Chinese resort to Siam unaccompanied by their families. They soon intermarry with the Siamese, there being no scruples against this on either side. They even adopt the Buddhist religion."[769] Karl Gutzlaff, an early Protestant missionary in Siam in the 1830s and the first person to translate the Bible into Thai, wrote that the Chinese,

> "When they enter into matrimonial alliance with the latter [Siamese], they become Siamese in every respect … Within two or three generations all the distinguishing marks of the Chinese dwindle away and a nation which adheres to its national customs so obstinately becomes wholly changed to Siamese … one

reason is that Chinamen here take Siamese, Burman, Laos and other country women for wives whose prejudices are even stronger than those of the Chinese themselves."[770]

Thus, while first-generation Chinese tended to preserve their Chinese ways, within three generations, their offspring usually ended up assimilated as Siamese.

Chinese Emigrants in the Peninsula and Phuket

The Malays, however, usually regarded the Chinese rather as a separate race. Chen Lun Ch'iung, who traveled in the Malay states of Siam in the late 18th century, noted that although "the common people are most licentious, women are prohibited from marrying Chinese. Those of whom fornicate with Malays and are discovered are seized and imprisoned."[771] Some Chinese immigrants, of course, were already Muslim and others, with their chameleon-like ability to integrate, converted to Islam, were circumcised and married local lasses, giving rise to Phuket's and the peninsula's distinctive local "Peranakan" culture which blends Chinese and Malay traditions.

The Chinese were generally viewed as good subjects in the peninsula, not only because of what one British Straits Settlements administrator describes as their "inhuman industry and talent for business,"[772] but also because they usually integrated well and, thanks to their outcast status, brought little political baggage with them. They were generally passive migrants, not interested in converting or spreading new ideas among the natives and they made little attempt to interfere with native political systems, social customs or religious beliefs. Most of these poor sinkeah [coolie] migrants came to the peninsula to try to amass sufficient wealth to remit money home and hoped to return to their family and ancestors in China a richer man. Many found little more than oppression, squalid living conditions and a nameless grave in the epidemic-infested, lawless peninsula or its pirate-ridden seas. Almost all worked hard and the more entrepreneurial took risks or got lucky and did prosper, some most handsomely. John Crawfurd felt that the Chinese were "the most active and valuable agents in developing the resources of the peninsula"[773] whilst Sir Frank Swettenham, the later Straits Settlements governor, noted, "Their energy and enterprise have made the Malay states what they are today, it is impossible to overestimate the importance of their share in the development of the peninsular states."[774]

Since the mid-19th century, the same can also be said of the Chinese on Phuket. The Malays and Thais on the peninsula had traditionally lived off the bounty of the land and generally avoided hard work or anything that might make them rich, believing that it would probably only be stolen from them by their avaricious overlords. Or, as one bombastic 19th century British official remarked somewhat less sympathetically, "They were the most incorrigible loafers on the face of the earth."[775] The poor Chinese immigrants, on the other hand, had neither land nor capital on their arrival in the peninsula and so, for them, "Lack of access to capital or land for farming meant hard work and self employment in petty trade was the only avenue for upward mobility, or for accumulating capital in a liquid form to take home."[776] When Lt. James Low visited Phuket and Phang Nga in 1824 he noted:

> "The Chinese … are exempted from the duty imposed on every Siamese of serving the state when called on, either in the capacity of soldiers, artisans or day labourers. They are left at more liberty to enjoy what their industry produces. The reason is obvious. The Chinese are a more intelligent, ingenious and laborious race than the Siamese, to whom they have the art to render themselves absolutely necessary, … We may likewise suppose that the Siamese would not like to irritate a class of men who are so numerous in all their towns."[777]

Life in the peninsular states of Siam, with their despotic and unpredictable rulers, was hard for these gutsy Chinese immigrants who, unlike the Europeans, received no support from the government of their mother country. They often suffered from jealousy and oppression. One British naval captain visiting Siam's southwest provinces in the 1830s noted, "The insolent contumely they endured at the hands of the Malays struck me very much. The natives when ill-treated, chattered like a nest of rooks. Not so the Chinese, they bore it with cringing and shrinking, one could see though, by the twinkling of their little glittering eyes, that they only abided their time, waiting to bite the heel that bruised them."[778]

Gutzlav, the somewhat bigoted Protestant missionary, felt that, in Siam, "The Chinese cringe before their oppressors and pay a heavy tax for being exempted from military and corvée services by labouring from morning to night to feed their insolent and haughty tyrants, who think it beneath their dignity to earn their bread by their own efforts."[779] Lt. Low admired their ability to prosper despite the oppression, intrigues and wars in the central peninsula. "Unwilling as they may be to turn rulers, where nothing could be obtained, or be put in competition with their mercantile gains, they do not seem to be at all averse to intrigue with one, or even with both sides, so that whatever the result, their interests may continue unaffected … The real leaning in such a case will be to the stronger party, although the weaker will be cajoled by promises and aided by supplies of arms, the sale of which, at high profits, they can easily effect."[780]

The Boom Period in Chinese Emigration, 1860-1910

In 1727 the Chinese government rescinded the law condemning emigrants to be executed. This sparked the first major boom in Chinese emigration, which caused the governor of Fujian province in China at the time to lament the lifting of this ban, saying, "In the fifth year of the reign of Yung Cheng this interdict was removed and there has been, from that time, a movement of traders … abroad as unceasing as the welling of a spring."[781] Rescinding the law also meant that former emigrants were free to return home. However, the more prosperous emigrants often elected not to return because, as one contemporary wrote,

> "If they return with wealth enough to live upon, they are liable to the vexatious extortions of needy relatives, sharpers and police, who have a handle for their

fleecing whip in the old law against leaving the country. Although this clause has been neutralised by subsequent acts and is not in force, the power of public opinion is still against going."[782]

In Fujian there was a general saying about such emigrants, "Out of every ten who go abroad, three die, six remain and only one comes home."[783]

The establishment of Penang and the other British Straits Settlements ports with their free trade and liberal economic policies attracted thousands of these emigrant Chinese. L. A. Mills, a 19th century Penang resident, noted that the Chinese thrived on the lack of restrictions in these British colonies and were generally "Indifferent to who ruled them, so long as their businesses were not interfered with. They regarded the British as inexplicable philanthropists, who, for some quite undiscoverable motive, took all the burdens of administration off their shoulders and left them at full liberty to make as much money as they choose."[784] As early as 1794 Sir Francis Light, the first governor of Penang, wrote, "The Chinese constitute the most valuable part of our inhabitants ... they are the only people of the East from whom a revenue may be raised without extraordinary efforts of government."[785] They were good at raising this revenue mainly because of their general penchant for sin. Unlike the Malays and Siamese, for whom chewing copious amounts of betel, until their teeth turned irretrievably red, was often their sole addiction, the Chinese were most enthusiastic in their pursuit of gambling, drinking, whoring and drugs. All of these sins provided handsome tax revenues, and they were usually paid for in cash, not in wearisome part-shares of agricultural produce as the Malays and Siamese often paid.

After the Second Opium War in China (1858-1860), the USA and European powers grabbed control of China's best ports and they allowed the Chinese residents of these free "treaty ports" "the inalienable right of free migration ... for the purposes of curiosity, trade or permanent residence." So for the next 50 years there were almost no barriers to the Chinese either leaving China or arriving on the peninsula and the numbers of immigrants to both Penang and Phuket soared during this period. Coolie and emigration agencies established themselves in the Chinese free ports and throughout southern China. These emigration agents tempted people with alluring stories of the quick fortunes to be made by pointing to new houses in the villages being paid for by remittances from émigrés in the Nan Yang, America or Europe. These agents usually got a dollar-a-head commission for finding new emigrants.

Many of the poorest emigrants to the peninsula had their passage prepaid for them by mine or plantation owners and arrived already indentured for several years' work. One 19th century British steamship captain, plying between China and Singapore, noted that his most common cargo was "coolies and Chinamen themselves." These coolies were often treated as barely human and traveling conditions were often frightful. There are stories of them being locked in the stifling heat in dark, airless and overcrowded holds or being nailed in under hatches during violent storms, as depicted in Joseph Conrad's novel Typhoon. Conrad worked on such coolie transport steamers during the later 19th century. In one passage of Typhoon he illustrates the utter disdain the European captain has for his cargo of Chinamen in the hold,

> "[During the height of a wild typhoon storm] Jukes lost his footing and began to flounder. "I was thinking of our passengers."
>
> "Passengers?" wondered the Captain, gravely. "What passengers?"
>
> "Why, the Chinamen, sir," explained Jukes.
>
> "The Chinamen! Why don't you speak plainly? Couldn't tell what you meant. Never heard a lot of coolies spoken of as passengers before. Passengers, indeed! What's come to you?"[786]

Warrington Smyth, a British superintendent of mines working for the Siamese government in Phuket and southwest Siam in the late 19th century, traveled in 1893 on the Phuket-based coastal steamer the Cornelia that ran between the mining centers of Phuket, Takuapa and Ranong with cargo and passengers. He tells us that the small ship was "doing the work of two vessels. Crowded with people, there was literally no sitting room on her decks, there must have been three hundred native passengers on board and anything in the shape of panic would have been disastrous. The boats only had room for perhaps fifty, but they could never have been cleared anyway."[787] In addition to contending with the overcrowded conditions and running the risk of being raided by pirates, William Brown, the British captain of another similar Phuket-based coastal steamer, commented, he had to use sea charts for the Siamese west coast that "were laughably inaccurate" and appeared to be carried "chiefly for the purpose of amusing the more knowledgeable passengers."[788]

Kongsis and Triads

These Chinese pouring into the Straits Settlements were from different provinces, clans and tribes – Hokkien, Teochiew, Cantonese, Hakka and Hainanese – all speaking different languages. They established their own kin organizations called Kongsi, which erected shrines, set up a help association with attached lodging houses, to assist anyone newly arrived from the same clan back in China. The large majority of the Chinese coming to Penang and Phuket were Hokkien from Fujian Province, whose clan organizations, such as the Tan Kongsi, were established in both Penang and Phuket by successful earlier émigrés.

The Chinese also brought their triads, which usually cut across kinship, clan and race lines. Triads also served as workers' unions for the coolies, providing protection and assistance to members and sorting out disputes within the diverse but autonomous Chinese communities in Phuket and Penang. While kongsis were generally benevolent, triads could also be malevolent. Professor Kenneth Landon in his book on the Chinese in Thailand notes, "Competition and jealousy set group against group and the Chinese often killed one another without regard to the laws of the land."[789] L. A. Mills, in Penang at the end of the 19th century, mentions a "peculiar form of protest indulged in by the Straits Chinese, when they wished to obtain redress for grievances, if for example a law were passed which they did not understand, or of which they disapproved, they would close their shops and take to breaking one another's heads."[790] He also adds, however, that they generally kept this fighting amongst themselves. "Europeans were very rarely molested" and that "apart from their triads and gambling, the Chinese were a remarkably law abiding race and easy to control."[791]

The biggest triads in Penang and southern Siam were the Ghee Hin and the Ho Seng, both of which accepted most Chinese, whatever their origins. In Phuket, however, a more or less exclusively Hokkien triad, the Kian Teck or Putaogong, became the most powerful and by the time of the big Chinese riots in southern Siam in 1876 was said to have some 20,000 members in Phuket, Penang and the surrounding provinces. This triad was controlled predominantly by the Hokkien Tan family towkays (bosses) of Phuket and was run on more hereditary lines than other triads. For example, if someone was banned, so were all his offspring, which tended to engender fierce clan loyalty.

31.1 An early photograph of massed Chinese coolies, digging, like a swarm of worker ants, in Kathu in the 1890s.

Triads were particularly powerful in the relatively lawless tin mining camps and especially in remote or outlying districts. In 1838 Stamford Raffles tells of one of his assistants visiting a remote mining camp where "Hundreds of Chinese, armed to the teeth, awaited him on the bank … wherever the Chinese went they took their secret societies with them. These indeed were practically the only social organisation they had … The influx of Chinese was so great, that it was beyond the capacity of the Malays to keep order and the Chinese, free from any control … began faction fights among themselves."[792] Often, the worst characters evicted or chased from China ended up in the Siamese tin mines. Warrington Smyth describes one remote inland tin mine on the way to Nakorn.

"The Chinese miners were the wildest Chinamen we had ever met and had mostly been imported direct by junks from the interior of Kwantung, Kwangsi and Hainan... They were in the habit of capturing and holding local folks up to ransom … it is ridiculous that the local people should allow such things but the Chinese coolies are money-makers and therefore protected by the officials and sixty wild beasts from Kwantung are an awkward crowd for a few Siamese country folk to deal with unaided."[793]

In 1893 he noted this same lack of law and order in the more remote mining town of Takuapa north of Phuket:

"All the usual symptoms of inefficient government existed – unsatisfied litigants, unsettled claims and untried prisoners. The police, who numbered 24 all told, were underpaid and overworked. They were ill-clad, disgracefully housed and worse armed. Scattered in twos or three about the province, they were so outnumbered by the coolies, of whom there were probably eight thousand … that they were practically useless for purposes of keeping order."[794]

Serious Chinese riots erupted quite frequently. As early as 1730, there was a major riot by the Chinese in Ayutthaya. In 1854 triad riots in Singapore went on for many days and left over 400 Chinese dead on the hot streets. In the central peninsula, there were murderous Chinese riots in Langsuan near Chumporn in 1848, in Penang in 1867 and in Ranong and Phuket in 1876.

31.2. A boat heading upriver into the interior of the peninsula in the late 18th century, rivers were often the only ways into the primordial and thickly jungled interior.

The Coolie's Life

In 1820 the population of Chinese in Penang was 17,000. By 1860 it had risen to more than 70,000. Many of these new "sinkeah" (coolie) arrivals moved on to the less developed tin fields of southern Siam. Some were funded by relatives, or benefactors from their Kongsi, some were already indentured to mine owners in Phuket and some came under their own steam. One British captain in 1857 described seeing a boatload of Chinese prospectors about to head up a river into the interior jungles.

"Because the river was the only highway through the jungle, the main road into the heart of that empty country ... they were loaded with sacks of rice, jars of coconut oil, tobacco, gambier, spirits and opium in chests. They had hoes, axes and other tools and baskets for carrying earth. They took weapons for their protection – muskets, gunpowder, knives and spears. Each man had his personal bundle or box containing his spare clothes and his few other possessions in the world."[795]

Hans Morgenthaler, a mining geologist in southern Siam in the early 20th century, tells us of "Chinese and Siamese mining people who came to my office with specimens of ore, telling fabulous stories of immense treasures lying somewhere deep in the forest. I was the man who had to get there and see whether they were justified or only empty dreams. ... [He would go out with] ... a company of forest men, six or seven hunters with muzzle loaders from the days of the Portuguese emigrants."[796]

In Phuket the early methods of mining involved a minimum of overheads. The coolies would be paid no wages but would receive a share of the profits, if any, or they would rent the mining land for a fixed royalty or tribute payable to the concessionaire or tax farmer. Many prospected further into the jungles of Kathu, Chaofa and Thalang for new and hidden ore bodies which they could work illegally.

When an ore body was discovered, the jungle would be cleared, bamboo and atap sleeping huts would be built and dams or other arrangements for water catchment for sluicing would be created. The overburden was then dug away until the "wash dirt" or tin-bearing stratum was exposed. The coolies, dressed in their "pha-tai-seng" – rough black or blue cotton work clothes – would then, in the words of Warrington Smyth, the mining engineer, "dig at these alluvial paddocks with as much intelligence as that [with] which Buffaloes plough the soil."[797] The tin-bearing earth was carried out of the pit by coolies carrying two wicker baskets of earth, one on either end of a pole over the shoulder. They worked all day in the stifling heat, climbing up and down the pit wall or using ladders formed from cutting steps into a tree trunk wedged against the side of the pit. This wash dirt would then be emptied into the top of wooden water-sluice chutes. These were fitted with many small cross-ridges and gunny bags, allowing the heavier tin to separate out and get caught as the earth was washed downhill. It was backbreaking work, done mainly in the rainy season when water for sluicing was more plentiful, but the water caused the additional problem of flooding in the pits. To solve this, huge wooden waterwheels were built and powered by coolies who would spend their days, like human hamsters, endlessly climbing the steps of treadmills to keep the wheel turning, baling out the mine pit and often supplying water to the sluices.

Death lay in these unused and flooded test bore and other surrounding pits, whose still waters bred the larvae of the mosquitoes that spread malaria, dengue fever and Chikungunya – all potentially lethal sicknesses, generally known as "jungle fevers", of which neither the cause nor the cure was known until the late 1890s. These attacks of "jungle fevers" were always worst at newly opened mines when the test pits were dug and then left open to flood. These mosquito-borne and other tropical diseases killed roughly 20-25 percent of all miners opening new mines and in some cases as much as 90 percent. But still, these hardy Chinese kept coming, chopping back the jungle and digging, impelled like lemurs by their longing for wealth. The historian J. M. Gullick, for example, tells us of the opening up of one interior jungle mine at Ampang in Malaya. "Each day several more went down with fever, lay trembling in a delirium for a day or two then died. Within a month all but eighteen of the eighty seven pioneers of Ampang were dead … [but soon] …one hundred and fifty more men came up river to take the places and live on the supplies of those who were dead."[798]

These mining camps and towns were extremely unsanitary. The British mines inspector Warrington Smyth described some of the mining towns of southwest Siam such as Taptieng near Trang which he called "a filthy place, as all Chinese towns are."[799] And he says of another, "as its inhabitants were chiefly Chinese, everything was consequently filthy." The Protestant missionary Gutzlav in Siam also noted, "The Chinese delight to live in wretchedness and filth."[800] These filthy conditions and the lack of any real medical facilities in Phuket added to the high death rates from disease and infection amongst the Chinese miners.

At night these exhausted coolies would go back to their huts, bathe off the mud in collected rainwater or local rivers and don their sre-ton, or white T-shirt. While swatting at the evening mosquitoes, they would cook and eat some rice and vegetables, maybe with fish or pork, or the meat from any animals they might have been lucky enough to have caught and killed that day – like tigers, wild boar, bears, deer, monitor lizards, civet cats, snakes, birds, frogs, insect grubs, etc. The Chinese have a saying that any animal can be eaten if "its back points to heaven." The coolies' main joy in the evening would be to get out a bottle of warm, nasty, arrack or stoke up a pipeful of marijuana or opium and smoke and drink themselves into a relaxed stupor for a few hours before falling asleep, often with the tropical rain dripping on them during the night through the flimsy atap roofs of their huts.

The Growth of Phuket Town and Get Ho (Kathu)

In 1849 the mayor of the new mining center of Phuket Town was Phra Phuket Kaew. He was succeeded in the 1850s by his son Phra Thut, who initially proved to be a good administrator and worked hard at marketing and attracting more and more Chinese to the island. Many he carried on his own steamship, the Phaya Phuket. Under Phra Thut, Phuket Town grew very rapidly so that by 1861 the king upgraded Phuket Town to the same status as Thalang. In recognition of his good works, in 1870 Phra Thut was given the title of Phaya Wichitsongkran and made governor of the island. He was of Indian descent, either from an old Chola family or from the prosperous local Afghan trading community who were based in Bangkhli, Phang Nga. These traders were known as 'Gabu' people by the locals in Phuket, a name said to be derived from the Afghan city, Kabul.

In that same year (1870) the Bangkok newspaper proprietor, the American Rev. Dr. R.B. Bradley, visited Phuket Town and tells us his version of its fast development.

"The Chinese soon flocked in numbers to Phuket, P'ra Palat furnished them with funds to commence work and the place prospered and grew apace … and now what was a paddy field is covered with brick houses and numerous population … most of the buildings have been built by the raja [governor]. The revenues are farmed out the same as in Bangkok. Tongkah Bay is the port of Poket. A good road leads to the town which is 1.5 miles distant from the harbour master's office and that is about two miles from the junk anchorage. The population of Phuket [town] consists of 25,000 Chinese, 300 Siamese, 200 Siamo-Malays, 200 British subjects and 200 Indians, Malays and other Europeans … The Chinese are divided into different factions and are continually at variance with each other. These men during the south-west monsoon [the rainy season] find plenty of employment at the tin mines but during the northeast monsoon numbers of them are idle, being out of employment owing to the scarcity of water for washing the tin … why this province should be rent by factions where there is room enough to spare for 25,000 in Salang is beyond my comprehension. Gambling predominates more than in Bangkok and is the principle cause of so much trouble in the island."[801]

These Chinese immigrants would arrive in Phuket town on the larger junks, trading ships and the twice-weekly mail, cargo and passenger steamships that sailed the west coast between Singapore, Penang, Phuket, Takuapa, Ranong, Mergui and Rangoon. They would moor in at Tongkah Harbor (Sapan Hin Bay off Phuket Town). Phuket Town itself was about one and half miles up a river through the mangroves of Sapan Hin. This river, called Klong Bang Yai, today passes through town as just a large cement storm water drain but it was previously a substantial river navigable by junks, prahus and river boats before it was gradually silted up by extensive mine works. Charles Kynnersley, who would later become the governor of Penang, visited Phuket in 1901 and then 1903, and noted this rapid silting-up process. In 1903 he wrote: "The harbor continues to silt up and undoubtedly the mining works have made matters worse. Where I landed last time is now a mud-flat which I hear is going to be mined."[802]

31.3 *The elegant new Phuket Town waterfront on the Klong Bang Yai River in the late 19th century: This was where most new Chinese immigrants to Phuket landed.*

These coolies, mail and supplies would be unloaded from the sea-going vessels in Tongkah Harbor onto smaller boats which would bring them up the river to the main pier in town where the Tavorn Hotel stands today. There they would be met by relatives who had already arrived, existing kongsi members or people looking to hire new laborers or pick up pre-organized indentured workers. The Siamese police would also be waiting, mainly to collect the one-baht per head immigration tax on each imported Chinese arrival. Ernest Young, an American reporter in Siam at that time, explains. "The receipt given was a small piece of bees' wax. This was in the form of a seal to be worn on the wrist fastened by a piece of string. There is nothing that a Siamese policeman so much enjoys as leading some unfortunate Chinaman to pay the tax should the seal be lost."[803]

These laborers, food and supplies would then be distributed in Phuket town and its surrounding mines or paddled or poled further up river to Get Ho village in the growing mining area of Kathu. However as the mines of Kathu used all the water available the river became less navigable and people had to travel by a dirt track. In 1903 Charles Kynnersley visited Get Ho and had to travel the "six miles there" there by this road. He travelled "in a Java pony trap (a stylish two-man carriage) through open grass country with scrub on which buffaloes were grazing." The road, he tells us, was "too awful for words, big stones ruts and holes. It is certainly the worst road I have ever attempted to drive over ... we got out and walked. The jolting was frightful. ... There is a great deal of traffic on it, a stream of mining coolies, a good many buffalo carts."[804]

Get Ho was a dirty, bustling frontier mining town of coolies, traders, tin buyers, smelters, tool sellers, gamblers, food stalls, mine equipment, food, arrack and opium shops and prostitutes, often working in the back of the same bamboo, atap or wooden shops. A few Siamese police or soldiers were there to try to ensure the local tax farmer and the governor was getting their fair cut of the business. By 1903 legal and law and order matters were run,

13.4. Siamese street stores in the late 19th century.

as elsewhere in Phuket, by government appointed ampurs who, Kynnersley tells us, were "a sort of district officer ... they get low salaries and are often corrupt" though he sympathetically noted that with so much wealth being pulled out of the ground around them "it cannot be wondered at that they supplement their salary."[805] Kynnersley visited the huge new mines in Kathu and noted that "The whole country seems full of tin." He later took tea with "a Chinese toukay" (a wealthy mine owner) who told him the road from Phuket Town used to be "in a much worse state", but mused Kynnersley, "this I think is impossible." He chose to return to Phuket Town not by the road but down the "river or creek in a small dug out hauled by eight Siamese."[806]

These Chinese towkays (wealthy mine and business owners) often ran most of the auxiliary businesses in the camps and towns – shops, gambling and opium dens – paying the tax farmer, triad bosses or local governor for the privilege. Usually, the more coolies a mine owner employed, the greater was his income. It is estimated that many coolies spent more than half their wages on opium. In this way, Phuket mine owners could keep their mines running, even if prices slumped below the production costs of the more technologically advanced British Malayan mines. Wages were almost the entire cost of production and were far lower in Siam than in Malaya. The mine owner got most of the wages back from his coolies by selling them all their requirements, especially the important ones of gambling, prostitutes and opium.

31.5 Cherngtalay main street: a typical Phuket Chinese mining town in the late 19th century.

The Later 19th Century Peninsular Tin Market Boom

During the second half of the 19th century, there was a huge upsurge in demand for tin from Phuket. The island's tin had previously been used mainly in China in religious ceremonies – when hammered paper-thin, tin burns brightly. In India and the West it was used in making bronze, gun metal (bronze and zinc) for maritime cannons, pewter and also as speculum for mirrors.

During the Napoleonic Wars non-corrosive tin was first used in cans for keeping military rations and this use soon spread and cans became popular for food storage among the general public in America, Europe, Britain and its colonies. The main demand for tin grew with the Industrial Revolution when it started being extensively used for tin plating, a technique for coating steel or iron with non-corrosive tin to prevent rusting. Tin plating was used for cooking utensils, ships, trains and railway lines, roofing material, bridges, nails, oil drums – indeed, for just about any steel or iron that was exposed to the elements. Tin plate output in Europe increased by 700 percent between 1825 and 1875. The greatest boom in demand for Phuket's tin, however, started after 1853 when Britain abolished the high import tariffs that had previously protected its tin mines in Cornwall. Tin imports to Britain from the cheaper peninsula increased over 2,000 percent from 4,000 tons in 1850 to 85,000 tons in 1870.

"Province-Eating" Governors

By the early 1870s this huge increase in demand for Phuket's tin led to an equally huge increase in mining activity on the island and hence the arrival of many more new Chinese laborers. This massive rise in Phuket's Chinese population was a boon for the governor, Phaya Witchitsongkran. He made a great deal of money from these coolies, many of whom he not only transported to and from the island on his own steamer, but also employed as cheap indentured workers in his mines. Warrington Smyth, the British mines inspector in Phuket, estimated that "taking all the farms and taxes into consideration, the government took forty per cent of the earnings of every coolie in the place."[807] Little of this revenue taken by the governor and his tax farmers was ever put back into the community. In Siam, this process was common and was referred to as a governor "eating the province."

This lack of reinvestment in any infrastructure in Phuket was a sore point with the Chinese mine owners and entrepreneurs. Commander Giffard, skipper of a British naval vessel in Phuket, ostensibly on piracy patrol, but actually monitoring the place for unrest and possible British annexation, wrote to the Foreign Office of the dissatisfaction of the Phuket mine owners, many of whom, though Chinese, were also British citizens of Penang. "The government levies a tax on carts and never repairs the roads or does anything for them at all and … the Chinese mine owners have to keep the roads in repair themselves."[808]

31.6 Elephants hauling mining machinery – unlike Malaya, Phuket and the rest of Southern Siam suffered from a severe lack of infrastructure and investment by the local governors or Bangkok.

The mine owners also complained about the lack of reservoirs and other water catchment facilities for mining and washing tin in the dry season, which often forced work to stop for months. Hans Morgethaler, an Austrian geologist working at the turn of the 19th century, decried southern Siam's lack of infrastructure. "In striking contrast with the Federated Malay States where English influence has brought western ideas of strait roads into the remotest valleys and villages to fetch tin ore, there are still no roads in southern Siam. The trifling inland traffic is maintained by means of narrow jungle paths, by coolies, boats and elephants … the whole country is covered with dense virgin forest … the haunt of wild beasts."[809]

The Tax Farm Wars

Phaya Wichitsongkran paid only 17,000 baht a year to Bangkok for his tax farm rights over Phuket Island and, moreover, he was usually late with his payments. A wealthy Singaporean Chinese, Tan Kim Ching, saw an opportunity in this. Tan Kim was a scion of a wealthy Hokkien family from Malacca, who already had many business interests in Siam such as sugar mills, shipping and the opium tax farm for all the southeastern Siamese provinces. A few years before, as a British citizen, he had been made the governor of Kraburi as a sweetener to the British when they had complained about the French plan to build a canal there across the Kra Isthmus. In 1872, this Tan Kim tossed a cat amongst the pigeons by putting in a greatly improved bid to Bangkok to buy out all the tax farm concessions in the southwest. Where the tax farm of Ranong had been worth 4,700 baht a year to the crown, he offered 160,000; for Phuket he offered 360,000 baht annually and so on. He also informed Bangkok of how much money Phaya Wichitsongkran and his Na Nakorn family relatives in the region had been withholding and highlighted the governor's lack of reinvestment into the island's infrastructure.

Bangkok turned down Tan Kim's prodigal offer, partly because when he was governor of Kraburi, he also had "eaten the province" and had reinvested almost nothing. He was also a British citizen and therefore could not be trusted not to run off to the British with his province, but probably the main reason for Bangkok's refusal was that he would then have controlled all the opium farms for all of southern Siam. And this was too strategic a franchise. Any disruption in the opium supply was a sure way to set the coolies to "breaking each other's heads" again.

On one visit to Takuapa, for example, Warrington Smyth illustrates the importance of having a regular opium supply. The local Phuket steamship Setthi sank while bringing supplies from Phuket – mainly rice and opium. This caused extreme angst among the wealthy Takuapa towkays. Very soon, Warrington Smyth tells us, "the coolie class was becoming clamourous and restive and we were invaded by a crowd of anxious inquirers."[810] To avert a riot, a message was urgently sent to Phuket requesting that the Siamese navy gunboat based in Phuket be rapidly dispatched to Takuapa with more opium "which everyone seemed to consider more essential to the maintenance of order than even rice."[811]

Instead of accepting Tan's offer, therefore, Bangkok left the tax farms with the existing governors but ordered them to pay significantly more. Phaya Witchitsongkran was also ordered to pay back his long overdue debt to the government. As a result, as Cushman tells us, "the governors of Ranong, Takuapa, Phang Nga and Phuket, while liable for these onerous new payments, were faced with the necessity of increasing production, spending less on provincial improvements, or keeping less of the intake for themselves, with the last option being the least attractive."[812] Phaya Wichitsongkran attempted to earn the extra money he needed by bringing in more coolies and increasing their entry tax by 500 percent, from 1 baht to 6 baht. He imposed increases of a similar magnitude in other tariffs and cut civil expenditures even further.

The "Angyee" Chinese Riots of 1876

This extra tax burden on the Chinese mine owners and coolies happened to coincide with a fall in the world tin price in the mid-1870s. With the mines so overtaxed, several became unprofitable and the mine owners laid off many workers or simply stopped paying their wages. These Chinese mine owners, as we have seen, were often also the office bearers of the local triads, known as "Angyee" in Siam. The Chinese, who now vastly outnumbered the Siamese police and natives in Phuket, became increasingly aggressive towards the government and demanded a tax reduction. A letter in the Thai national archives from the period shows that the Siamese Department of Defense foresaw trouble, warning that "Phaya Phuket is not able to follow through on governing, he cannot gain the respect of the Chinese … The Chinese often offend and insult the governor of Phuket. It recommended that more troops and weapons be sent to Phuket."[813]

The Chinese miners in Ranong encountered similar problems. It is said that the coolies in Ranong were already so tightly squeezed that they referred to the town as "a great pit, easy to fall into but impossible to get out [of]."[814] In 1876 these frustrated Ranong coolies started rioting and a Thai source tells us that in that year some "oppressed" miners, "primarily from China … rose up against the governor, other officials and mine operators."[815] It appears that some 600 miners, allegedly Hakkas from the Gee Hin triad, though other sources say they were Hokkien from the Kian Teck, went on a rampage. They killed some Siamese army guards at the Burmese border and 21 people in the town, including government officials and other Chinese miners. The town was then ransacked and the outlying areas were also attacked and pillaged. Most locals resorted to their time-honored response and fled off into the jungle. Things eventually calmed down when the Siamese naval gunboat the Murathavissawat, with a detachment of Siamese marines, arrived from Phuket.

Some of these Ranong rioters fleeing from potential punishment then went down to Phuket to seek support from the more numerous Hokkien Kien Teck triad members there. The military commissioner of Phuket at the time, Chum Bunnag, ordered a second Siamese gunboat to Phuket. When it arrived, some of the Siamese sailors, allegedly drunk, came ashore and got into a fight with some Chinese miners. The local British police chief of Phuket at the time, a Captain Webber, arrived with his men and arrested two of the Chinese miners. Soon around 300 choleric coolies gathered at the Phuket Town police station to demand the release of their two compatriots. The duo were set free in an attempt to calm the angry mob, but the Chinese, with their blood now up, started attacking government offices and, by that evening, the riot had escalated to the point that some 2,000 coolies had joined in and were burning and looting all over Phuket Town. Some say over a hundred people were killed in these riots – mostly the victims of Chinese infighting – and most of the locals fled, many heading south with their valuables to the safety of Wat Chalong. Phaya Wichitsongkran's mansion in town was attacked and ransacked and the governor himself had had to flee off the island to Kao Te See in Phang Nga.

31.7 Siamese armed police in Phuket town in the late 19th century. Southwest Siam was notably lawless because the often fractious and better-armed Chinese immigrants usually hopelessly outnumbered the police.

Chum Bunnag, the military commissioner, eventually came to Phuket Town to meet the Chinese clan leaders there. They had three main demands:

1   The government must suspend the heavy taxation, until the tin price rose.

2   The government must allow them to grow marijuana and export it for extra income.

3   The government must grant an amnesty to the rioters.[816]

Chum Bunnag agreed to these terms and promised to "improve living conditions to benefit the local people and ensure peace and prosperity for all."[817] The local Chinese leaders were either not convinced by the commissioner's promises, or had no real control over the situation, as the riots and lawlessness went on for another month. Many more people, mainly Chinese, were killed and many of the remaining businesses and some homes in town were sacked and looted. The province was said, in one Siamese report, to be "lost to the government." This was of grave concern to Bangkok, not least because the government knew that such disorder could give the British a good pretext to move in and take over Phuket – Britain had just used the mining wars in Pahang in Malaysia as an excuse to advance their power into that state.

The military commissioner, Chum Bunnag, ordered more troops up from Keddah and from the southern division military headquarters at Nakorn Sri Thammarat. When these extra troops arrived, the fighting and rioting were suppressed. The head monk of Wat Chalong – Luang Pho Chaem – brokered a fragile peace. He had sheltered many of the terrified residents of the island and on one occasion had managed to hold off a cantankerous mob of Chinese coolies who wanted to attack the refugees in Wat Chalong to get at their riches and loot. He is are held in the greatest esteem by the people of Phuket today.

All through 1876, however, rioting continued in sporadic outbreaks. Bangkok acceded to all the concessions demanded by the local Chinese towkays. They also gave sweeteners to some of the leading triad bosses, such as Tan Jao, Tan Gaik Tham's son, who was the leader of the Hokkien triad. He was given a royal title and awarded the lucrative monopoly for the distribution of opium in Phuket. In 1878, after the governor of Krabi was suspiciously assassinated, Tan Jao was also allowed to operate the Krabi province tax farm. An amnesty was also granted because, as one Siamese lord in Bangkok noted, "If the government

31.8 The remains of Phraya Wichitsongkran's large and well-fortified residence and law court complex in Tharua today. He moved there from Phuket Town for his own protection after Phuket's deadly Chinese riots of 1876. It also held barracks for his many private guards and armed police.

wished to prosecute the rioters it would be difficult since they are so many in numbers. If the government became too forceful they may threaten another riot."[818] This restrained and conciliatory reaction, plus Siam's beefed-up military presence, eventually restored order in Phuket. But this came at a cost, as Chum Bunnag later wrote: "Henceforward, since the Thai government has no power to punish Chinese people, the Chinese are the most powerful people in the kingdom ... please consider this carefully."[819]

Phaya Wichitsongkran eventually came back to Phuket but decided not to live among the Chinese any longer. He built a new fortified house in Tharua, further from the massed Chinese and nearer to his boat in Tharua Harbor, in effect living rather as the earlier European traders had lived – near an escape route to his boat. The remains of his great fortified house in Tharua, dating to the late 1870s, is one of Phuket's oldest extant buildings and is a public park and historical site today.

The Angyee riots of 1876 marked a turning point in the political power on the island, with power moving from the older hereditary Na Nakorn and other Siamese lordly families to the now richer and more numerous Chinese. This process was tempered and helped by later judicious intermarriages between the two groups.

Life in Phuket Town at the end of the 19th Century

By around 1890 Chinese immigration into Phuket had peaked, with the Chinese population on the island probably reaching nearly 50,000 and dwarfing the Thai and Malay population of perhaps 1,000-2,000. (As there was never an official census at this time, the population of Phuket can only be estimated from other sources: for example a British Foreign Office memorandum in June 1885 estimated the number of Chinese on the island at 45,000 compared to only 1,000 Thais.)[820] The island, and particularly Phuket Town, therefore, had become almost entirely Chinese.

Tin mining remained the primary raison d'etre for Phuket Town's economic existence. Charles Kynnersley on his 1903 visit tells us, "The site of the present town is all tin land … The mines absorb all labor. Cultivation does not seem to be encouraged, no one cares to plant so long as mining pays so much better … Rice, fruit and provisions of all kind are imported. Fruit and vegetables come from Penang … Everybody is hard at work making money at the mines." He tells us there was even "a new mine parallel to the principal shop street." Land clearing for new mines was going on all around the town: "jungle fires are still frequent and there is no timber to speak of near Toungkah … the principal road to the landing place has also been diverted to allow a mine to be opened. … Borings are being taken by the Government Offices and if tin is found the site will be sold and new Offices built elsewhere. Everything is sacrificed to the mines."[821]

The Shop Houses

As these mines generated huge profits for the dominant Tan clan families and the more successful new Chinese immigrants. Shops, offices and houses which had previously been mainly just one story shacks made from atap and wood were replaced by more substantial, often two story shop-houses built of timber planks and bricks and mortar with clay tile roofs. These early shop houses were much more rustic than the ornate ones that can still be seen today. They were made with thick walls to keep the interior cool. The best examples of these early shop-houses can still be seen in old Takuapa town, one of the last places where this historic architecture remains in southern Siam.

The more ornate shop-houses one sees in Phuket City today were mainly built in the first quarter of the 20th century. Some of the first of these type of shop houses were built on Dibuk Road by the Tan clan towkay Tan Engkee, who took the Thai name Wisetnukoonkij and became the biggest shop-house landlord in town. He used a Penang architect to design them in a style now often referred to today as "Sino-Portuguese". However this is a bit of a common misnomer. 'Sino-European' is closer to the truth, or even 'Sino-British', since this form of regimented shop-house was actually designed in 1819 by Stamford Raffles, a man from Hampshire in England, when he established Singapore. He based property taxes on the width of the shop frontage, so these shop-houses are invariably narrow, usually only five meters wide, but very long, often with an open courtyard inside. Raffles also decreed that a covered public walkway be built along the front of the ground floors of the shop, so that people could walk along the street without exposure to the tropical sun and rain. Unfortunately, unlike the French colonial city planners, he neglected to enforce the planting of trees. This omission left the enclosed streets of Phuket Town, like those of the other Straits Settlements towns, almost like furnaces in the summer, exposed all day to the baking tropical sun. In 1890, when King Chulalongkorn visited Phuket Town on his tour of the south, observers counted 685 shop-houses in town, 318 built of brick and 367 of wood. [822]

31.9 Thalang Road in 1903 at the height of Phuket Town's early construction boom.

Babas and Nyonyas

The local-born, often mixed-blood offspring of the Chinese towkays in Phuket became known as Babas (male) or Nyonyas (women) and together as "Peranakan", or local-born Chinese. To this day they still uphold and thrive on their distinctive culture, dress and food. Their daughters and sons were usually married to relatives, often just outside the limit of incest taboos. Others married into powerful Siamese or Malay families in the region, giving these nouveau-riche Chinese more influence and the local Siamese and Malay families more access to money. These wealthier Phuket-born "Baba" families looked down on what they called the "one mat one pillow crowd" – the poor Chinese-born coolies arriving off the boats. They tried, as they still tend to do today, to keep marriage among their own kind, just as the old Chinese saying goes, "The dragon marries the dragon. The phoenix marries the phoenix. The hunchback marries the hunchback."

By the early 20th century these wealthy Chinese in Phuket Town began to build offices and ornate shrines, temples and some larger Penang or 'Straits-style' houses just outside town. Several of these can still be seen today dotted around in Phuket City, which has now expanded around them. The wealthy also helped the community to build Chinese schools, hospitals and halfway houses (homes for the destitute). But let's not paint too romantic a picture here. Most houses around Phuket Town at the time were still simple, rather shoddy, shacks of wood with thatched or corrugated tin roofs. The town was, by all accounts, hot, filthy, squalid and unsanitary, with no proper water supply, unpaved roads that regularly flooded or became mud baths in the rainy season and little in the way of garbage removal or proper sanitation and drainage. The nostrils of any visitor would have been assailed by a congregation of foul and pungent smells – garbage, frying tofu, un-refrigerated meat markets, rotting seafood waste, open sewers, buffalo dung, shops with fish drying in the sun and shrimp paste manufacturing and the like. The Penang Gazette referred to Phuket Town in the last years of the 19th century as "a most rotten and unhealthy place … a collection of Chinese huts and hovels."[823] Kynnersley on his 1901 visit said that "the place swarmed with pigs."[824] Warrington Smyth, visiting the Chinese town of Takuapa, regales us with its insalubriousness and stench, and then he notes, "for filth and mismanagement this place ran Phuket very fine."[825]

Sin and Distractions

The main entertainment for these traders and the mine coolies after sweating out in the mines all day was gambling. Sir Francis Light, when governor of Penang, had noted, "The Chinese are excessively fond of gaming, there is no restraining them from it. This invariably leads them into many distresses and frequently ends in ruin."[826] During his visit to Kathu in 1903 Kynnersley described Get Ho town as "a long street where hundreds of coolies were assembled and the Gambling Farm was densely packed. Only Chinese are allowed to gamble not the Siamese."[827] The Chinese also smoked copious amounts of opium. In 1869, for example, 109. 5 chests of opium – about seven tons – were officially imported into Phuket. At least double that amount would probably have been smuggled in undeclared, to avoid the onerous taxes of up to 20 percent on sales and another 11 percent on cooking it. That represents an intake of well over one kilogram of opium for every man on the island that year.

A highlight for a miner would have been his occasional trip to one of the comparatively high-class brothels in Soi Romanee (allegedly named after a famous Rumanian Mamasan who worked there) for a night of arrack, opium, sex and gambling. Dr. Landon, a 19th century writer about the Straits Chinese, noted that in Penang, "Of late years many [Chinese] women have come chiefly as prostitutes who are bought by brothel keepers to carry on their trade here. The writer knows no instance of a respectable [Chinese] woman emigrating with their husband."[828] Many brothels in Penang and some in Phuket were run by Japanese women. Though the majority of the prostitutes were Chinese, there were also Japanese and Siamese girls and even some Europeans. In Penang and Singapore, the press was regularly outraged when white women, usually Eastern European or Russian, were discovered in Chinese brothels. "It is quite disgraceful," puffed the Malay Mail on one such occasion. Several European prostitutes were deported from Penang for working in such Chinese brothels.

One suspects some of them may have made their way north to less priggish – but also affluent – Phuket to ply their lucrative trade. As one Chinese writer tells us, prostitution was always quite accepted by the Chinese.

"Although always classed as a vice, prostitution was tacitly approved of by traditional Chinese society ... merchants and government officials transacted much of their business and scholars wrote some of their best lines of poetry in whore houses. If prostitution was ill-regarded by traditional mores the basic reason was the economic ruin of the wayward son and not any intrinsic moral abhorrence."[829]

31.12 Chinese opium smokers.

Figures for the incidence of venereal diseases in 19th century Phuket do not seem to exist. But if the figures from nearby Penang are anything to go by, such diseases were rife. In 1898 a commission in Penang investigating venereal disease in prostitutes found more than 80 percent infected. Dr T. C. Mugliston, the Principal Civil Medical Officer of Penang, had the onerous task of examining over 3,000 prostitutes, which he describes as a "dreadful business." He reported that most of these girls still had to service customers despite some "very bad" infections. "She has no say in the matter, she is the brothel keeper's property ... they have no protection in that way, they are at the mercy of the brothel keepers ... [which meant] ... an enormous increase in their suffering generally."[830] In Penang, legislation against such activities was passed (the Contagious Diseases Ordinance), but it appears that there were no such laws in Phuket. Dr. Mugliston estimated that over 50 percent of Chinese men in Penang had some form of venereal disease and, more notably, over 80 percent of the single European men were infected. But the business, as always, continued relentlessly. Mr. Evans, the government protector of the Chinese in Penang, complained, "The well to do and highly respected Chinese residents do not think it at all derogatory to themselves to own brothels and to build houses on their properties as brothels … they are glad to make money out of it."[831]

There were also more sublime diversions – such as kite flying and troupes of entertainers from China touring the peninsula with acrobats, comedies and opera troupes whose actresses were noted for making extra money as escorts to the local towkays, who would take them out after performances to show them how rich they were. Temporary theaters and street opera houses, known as "wayang", would be erected in Kathu, Phuket Town and Cherngtalay; these were bamboo structures with atap roofs. In 1863, one German traveler in southern Siam, Adolf Bastian, records seeing one of these operas. "The first Chinese play I ever witnessed … and most certainly the last I should ever wish to see, for methinks a continuation of such noise for a succession of nights would render me unfit for anything but Hanwell and Bedlam (two British lunatic asylums) excepted."[832]

The Vegetarian Festival

A commonly related story is that one of these opera troupes introduced the vegetarian festival to Phuket – somewhere between 1830 and 1890 (the exact date is unclear). The opera troupe had set up in Kathu to entertain mine workers and their families, but the filthy conditions in the Chinese mine camp meant that epidemics, particularly cholera, were common. As one Phuket historian tells it, "While the Chinese troupe was in Phuket, an epidemic broke out and many people died. The Chinese performers also became ill … They realised it was the ninth month of the Chinese lunar calendar and they had not fasted or paid homage to the nine Emperor Gods as they did in China."[833] We are told that one of their members returned to Fujian to perform a ceremony to invite the emperor gods to Phuket and brought back an urn containing an incense stick that had been kept alight since the ceremony in China. Starting on the full moon of the ninth night of the ninth moon, the opera troupe started eating only vegetables and erected a Ko Teng pole – for the gods to come and go by – and started performing self-purification rituals. And, lo and behold, the epidemic stopped and everybody lived happily ever after. Since then people in Phuket have celebrated this festival. For a long time the festival had only a small following, but since the 1970s, with the growth of tourism and the greater prosperity of the locals, the festival has become more popular and is now the most conspicuous Chinese festival in southern Thailand.

Part 6

The 20th Century

32

The Efficacious Khaws

1820 TO 1914

Khaw Soo Cheng was born around 1797 into a peasant family in Lungxi district, Fujian province, in China. He was apparently also a member of the Heaven and Earth Triad at roughly the same time as Tan Gaik Tam who, as we have seen, went on to become one of Phuket's first towkays (see Chapter 27). Like Tan, Khaw Soo Cheng also fled the crackdown against the triad by the Qing Dynasty police in 1822 by taking a junk to Penang, where he arrived almost penniless, aged 25.

He first found work as a laborer then mustered some savings and bought some oranges, which the Chinese in Penang were just beginning to farm. He peddled these around town from a wicker basket. Gradually his fruit-selling business expanded and by 1827, with some capital, he moved north to Takuapa in Siam. There, as a handsome and ambitious young fellow, he won the support of a local businesswoman, Thao Thepsunthorn, who we are told was "a lady who possessed considerable capital for doing business in Takuapa."[834] She appears to have been the daughter of a wealthy Hokkien man from Penang, who had sent her to be a wife of a member of the region's ruling Na Nakorn family. She advanced Soo Cheng some capital and he acquired a small boat, went back to Penang and bought sundry trade items – candles, mining tools, soap, sewing materials, crockery, clothes and the like – and then braved the seas and the local pirates to sail back north to trade these items in the isolated mining camps and towns along the remote Siamese west coast. In Phuket, Soo Cheng appears to have used his old triad acquaintance, Tan Gaik Tam, as his distribution agent. With this trading business going well, Soo Cheng became prosperous enough to marry a Sino-Thai girl in Penang, whom he brought to Takuapa and they started a family.

Having won the trust of Lady Thepsunthorn and, through her, members of the Na Nakorn family in the area, Soo Cheng, now in his mid-thirties, resolved to move into the tin business. He set his eyes upon Ranong. In the 1830s Ranong was a remote, lawless backwater, surrounded by towering jungled hills, "more like a forest than a town." The boat carrying the provincial tax receipts to the capital, for example, was so frequently robbed by pirates that the people charged with fetching these government revenues "did not dare proceed to Ranong to make the necessary collections … officials were urged not to travel alone but to join with the officials of Trang and the other west coast ports to bring their tax receipts together in an armed escort up to Bangkok."[835] Tin in Ranong was being mined in a desultory fashion at the time and Soo Cheng used his

Na Nakorn connections to obtain the rights over some new mining areas. He moved his family there and was again most successful. By 1844, aged 47, he was appointed the tax farmer for Ranong and given the Siamese lordly title of Luang Rattaasethi by the viceroy of Nakorn.

As Soo Cheng grew steadily richer, he took several more wives around the region and sired nine children. His daughters were judiciously married off – one into the local Na Nakorn family, one into the powerful Bunnag family of Bangkok, which controlled the Ministry for the South and another to a wealthy Penang Chinese merchant, no doubt to assist him in raising capital for his business ventures. He also arranged strategic marriages for his sons, such as into the now well-established and influential Tan family in Phuket. He gave each son parts of his growing business empire to oversee. One ran his shipping and trade business and another oversaw the tax farm and public works for Ranong. Like other Chinese in Siam, he invested his excess wealth in the more secure Penang property market and banks and sent another son there to look after these investments.

32.1 Members of the Na Ranong family at the family gravesite in Ranong. Khaw Sim Bee can be seen standing in the back row, third from the left.

As Ranong's tax farmer, Khaw Soo Cheng increased the provincial revenues and submitted his tax payments on time. In 1854, due to his good works and his strategic family connections, he was appointed the governor of Ranong province. Unlike most other regional governors, Khaw Soo Cheng actually worked at and spent some of the tax income on improving the infrastructure of the province. He built roads, a jail and courthouse and drafted and applied mining laws. In 1862 his success was crowned when King Mongkut bestowed on him the lordly title of Phraya Na Ranong (Baron of Ranong) for his good work in turning "the forest" into a prosperous commercial center.

In 1882 Khaw Soo Cheng died in Ranong (his vast Chinese family grave can still be seen today beside the road on the way to the Club Andaman Casino pier). To hold his diverse family and businesses empire together, he created a trust in Penang and put all his business interests into it. His will stipulated that, to benefit from the trust, his relatives must come together every three years in Ranong to pay their respects at the family grave. In this way the various wings of the family stayed in touch and the Khaw lineage remained bound together economically and socially. Such a requirement was common among these Chinese émigrés, with children from several wives, to preserve the cohesiveness of their families and their businesses. The ancestral grave made Ranong the new spiritual center for this diverse émigré Hokkien family in Siam, in much the same way as the bigger Chinese families in Phuket, such as the Tans, Gans and Yaps, also revolve around their ancestral graves on the island. The Tanthai family, for example, has its large family grave on the left of the road going from Central Festival shopping complex to Kathu. This grave still keeps this extended Sino-Thai family together, despite its members living in places as far apart as Phuket, London, Texas, Bangkok and Bangladesh today.

The Khaw Family Rises to Regional Power

In 1876, after the miners riots occurred in Ranong, Khaw Soo Cheng had stepped down as governor and his eldest son, Khaw Sim Cheng, replaced him. However Sim Cheng was killed the following year on a trip to China when the boat he was traveling on was attacked and taken by pirates. Soo Cheng's next eldest son, Khaw Sim Kong, then became the new governor and proved a most able administrator. Warrington Smyth, who visited Ranong in 1893, felt that the Khaws' "enlightened rule" had "from a fishing village, made the place into an important mining centre. Landing stages, smelting houses, first class roads and charming bungalows sprang into being in the pretty semicircle of hills … A regular system of mining regulations was established, an efficient police force was created and justice meted out to all."[836] Prince Damrong, the king's half-brother, wrote of Sim Kong that, "as collector of royalties … he promoted business activity, created prosperity and thereby increased the government's income."[837] For this good work and for having stabilized this remote area on the border with British Burma – wanted at the time by France (for its planned canal) and by the British (to prevent it) – Khaw Sim Kong was promoted to be the governor of the more important province of Chumporn.

Bangkok remained worried by pressure from the British Straits Settlements Forward Party to annex southwestern Siam on the grounds that the region was "maladministered". The Forward Party mouthpiece, the Siam Free Press newspaper, for example, wrote at the time, "we are very near the day when Great Britain will refuse to tolerate the present state of affairs in the Siamese States of the peninsula."[838] Bangkok therefore knew it was under pressure to encourage the development, stability and prosperity in southwestern Siam. The Khaw family was well placed in this regard. Its members had good connections in Penang, allowing them to allay British concerns and to attract investment from the wealthy Penang Chinese (who were officially British citizens). They were also culturally equipped to minister to the requirements of the region's Chinese, who now formed the majority in most of the revenue-earning centers. They had proved their ability to improve a province; they paid their taxes on time and, as a Siamese lordly dynasty, they had taken the "Oath of the Waters" to the king; also, their intermarriage with the Bunnag family, which ran the Ministry of the South, gave them powerful backers in the capital.

In 1882, the youngest of the Khaw sons, Khaw Sim Bee, who had married into the powerful Na Nakorn family of the former Viceroy Noi, was appointed governor of Kraburi (north of Ranong). Another son, Khaw Sim Tek, was appointed governor of Langsuan (north of Chaiya). Warrington Smyth, who met Khaw Sim Tek 15 years later, tells us that this son had degenerated into an indolent ladies' man:

> "All the young actresses in Langsuan were his wives ... he exercised practically no control over the Chinamen who carry on the government of the province under him ... Eighteen years of the steamy climate of Langsuan is perhaps not conducive to energy of any sort and the rajah's real or professed ignorance of everything in his province astonished me, much accustomed as I am to evasion."[839]

Enterprising Khaw Sim Bee

The youngest son, Khaw Sim Bee, was made of far more enterprising stuff. Weighing over 90 kilos but standing less than 1.5 meters tall, he was a plump, stumpy little man. There is a frequently reproduced photo of him taken in 1900, his chest plastered with government service medals pinned to his governor's uniform. He did not always dress so formally. William Brown, the captain of one of the Khaw family steamships in Phuket, recalled that one day:

> "A strange object came up the gangway, something that made me rub my eyes and look again – Sim Bee in a plus four suit of a devastating check pattern and with his pig tail done up in a red ribbon ... By Jove he was proud of those clothes. He strutted around on deck while the Malay and Chinese seamen goggled. He had seen a catalogue picture of this suit and considered it just right for his build."[840]

Khaw Sim Bee was an intelligent and astute man of enormous ability, described as "a complex and mercurial personality who could shift in a moment from humorous affability to stern dignity."[841] Warrington Smyth describes a lunch he had with Khaw Sim Bee at a Chinese planter's house near Trang one day, where they were served some "messy concoctions" of Chinese pork. Warrington Smyth notes that he had "lived too long not to have a horror of pig"[842] and was therefore

> "constrained to depend on the only clean dishes before us, boiled rice and pineapple shavings ... it amused the kind hearted old rajah and never shall I forget the scorn and wonder with which he shouted, 'What! Not eat pork!' as he dived into the dishes spread before him. ... Another horror at these entertainments is the neat Brandy of a fiery nature of which one is always pressed to partake during the hottest hours of the most sweltering days."[843]

Khaw Sim Bee had been educated in China and spoke five Chinese dialects, a valuable asset in dealing with the region's diverse Chinese mine workers. He also spoke English, Siamese and Malay and proved to be an outstanding governor. When King Chulalongkorn made his southern tour, he was "most pleased" by the reforms Sim Bee had implemented in Kraburi and rewarded him by appointing him as governor of the much more important province of Trang.

32.3, 32.3 Two pictures of Khaw Sim Bee: one in his official High Commissioner's uniform and one with his son in his fancy new golf attire.

Once again Khaw Sim Bee's governorship proved outstanding. Warrington Smyth tells us that the "dacoity" or banditry, which had once been particularly bad in Trang, "practically disappeared … ten miles of road had been completed, six large wells had been sunk, a gaol, a courthouse and a landing pier had been built and hundreds of acres of padi had been cleared and drained"… [no other governor] … can equal him in energy, popularity or good nature."[844] While he was governor of Trang, on his own initiative, Khaw Sim Bee went to Sumatra and obtained rubber tree seeds and was the first person to promote rubber plantations in Siam. Under his governorship, Trang became the southern banner province for King Chulalongkorn's economic reforms and modernization.

In Phuket, after the Angyee riots of 1876, Bangkok soon replaced Phraya Wichitsongkran as governor, appointing in his place Phraya Tipkosa, a Sino-Thai from Bangkok of quasi-royal lineage. He was very loyal to the crown and therefore not likely to go "running to the foreigners"[845] and, for example, sell Phuket Island to them. Although Phraya Tipkosa was half-Chinese, Warrington Smyth noted that he was "imbued with a profound hatred of the Chinaman … and very anxious to see the last of him."[846]

Phraya Tipkosa, like most other Siamese governors, started "eating" the province and reinvesting little.

In 1896 Siam's provincial government structure was reformed and Phuket town was made the center of Monton Phuket, a new super-province that included all the surrounding west coast provinces from Kraburi and Ranong in the north to Trang in the south. Bangkok now also insisted on collecting taxes directly, no longer via local tax farmers. As the unfortunate man who attempted to take away the lucrative tax farms from the governing Na Nakorn and Khaw families in the region, Phraya Tipkosa soon earned the enmity of both, along with that of the Tan clan and the other Chinese towkays in Phuket. These powerful local families worked together and soon had Phraya Tipkosa removed. In his place, because of his good governorship of Trang, Khaw Sim Bee was promoted to be the new high commissioner of the super-province of Monton Phuket in 1900 and to do so he was also given the lordly title of Phraya Rassada.

Phraya Rassada: Public Office, Private Business

When Phraya Rassada (Khaw Sim Bee) took over as high commissioner of Monton Phuket, the Khaw family empire was already extensive, with several large commercial tin concessions in Ranong and Takuapa and control of the tin smelting in most provinces. They also owned the Koe Guan shipping company in Penang, whose steamers ran up the west coast from Penang to Rangoon, stopping at most of the smaller ports and giving them a monopoly over the movement of tin ore, coolies and trade items. Most lucratively, they also retained the opium monopoly over all the western seaboard states, despite Bangkok's recent ruling against tax farms. It seems that Prince Damrong and the Bunnags wanted to ensure the Khaws' loyalty to Siam and kept them sweet by allowing them to keep their lucrative monopolies. That way there was less chance that the Khaws might collude with Britain – with its fairer rules and markets – to give or sell the remote but tin-lucrative province of Monton Phuket to the British.

Penang was much closer than distant Bangkok. It had also rapidly become one of the most modern and progressive towns in Asia. Adjarn Pranee Sakulpipatana, former assistant history professor at Phuket's Rajabhat University, tells us that for the Chinese of Phuket, "Penang in those days was like our nearest London."[847] Penang provided banks and financial security for

32.4 The Phuket based, Khaw family steamer "Damrong Rat".

their savings; it had mechanisms for raising capital and offered all the latest fashions, cosmetics and medicines from Europe. The Khaws, like other prosperous Chinese in the region, built splendid colonial mansions in Penang and spent much of their time there. It was, after all, only an overnight cruise away on their own steamers. The first class cabin passengers would dine with the Danish and British captains in their elegant tropical white uniforms. Pracha Tanthawanit of the Tan clan, whose father, Chin Satanpitak, was the local ticketing agent for the Khaws' Phuket-based steamer Tong Ho, explained that "The ship housed eight passenger rooms on its third deck … the Western food served on board for first class passengers was delicious."[848]

Phraya Rassada also bought a grand colonial mansion in the old Northam Road in Georgetown, Penang (originally Scotia House) which he renamed "Chakrabong House" and which the Penang Gazette described as one "that could scarcely be surpassed in Penang … standing on the brink of the sea, with its verandahs opening on the lovely view of the harbour and purple heights of Keddah beyond … backed by the dark green of palms and flanked with tennis courts … The dining and drawing rooms are large enough for huge gatherings and the latter might easily accommodate four or five sets of lancers."[849] There he threw sumptuous parties for the European and Chinese élite of Penang, the financiers, businessmen and miners who all wanted to be on good terms with him to win mining, logging and business concessions in the promising province of Monton Phuket.

32.5 Phuket Town in 1905.

The Development of Phuket Town

After taking power in Phuket, wily Phraya Rassada was quick to rally the other predominantly Hokkien Chinese towkay élite business families around him. In the first decade of the 20th century most of Phuket's mines were still controlled by Tan clan families such as the Tanthai and Tanthawanit families. For example, the two Tanthai brothers, Tan Pek Kiet and Tan Pek Huat, operated more than 64 mines in the area employing thousands of coolies and both had received lesser Siamese lordly titles – Luang Kachon and Luang Armaskhon. The Tan and Khaw family forefathers, as we have seen, were old associates and the families were already intermarried. Phraya Rassada recruited most of the island's Hokkien towkays into an advisory council and also made a corps of special bureaucrats to accommodate other important families. He also married some of his own children into the Tan families of Phuket, such as the Tandavesa family. The patriarch of this family received the Siamese noble title of Luang Amnatnararak for his community work such as building a hospital and the Saengtham shrine in Phang Nga Road.

32.6 An Island of opportunity: Koi Somboon, A Hokkien Chinese towkay in Phuket's first car in 1902. He originally started off in Phuket with a small confectionery shop and ended up as a wealthy mine owner.

In the 16 years of his governance following his appointment in 1900, Phraya Rassada and the Tan families, supported by a healthy cash flow from a rapidly recovering tin price, turned Phuket into a flourishing provincial town. Paved roads with drains were built and running water and some sanitation arranged. The first Chinese school, the Xin Min School, opened in 1910 and later became the Hua Bun School. In 1913 a specifically Hokkien school was opened. Phraya Rassada imposed a tax of 10 satang per sack on rice and sugar to raise money and Tan Siew, the mayor of Phuket town, with the Siamese lordly title of Phraya Chan, also donated land to build the Song Tek School on Debuk Road. Similarly, the Poey Eng Chinese school in Cherngtalay was built with money from the local Chinese mining towkays there. Money was raised for a beggar settlement. A "guaranteed station" (quarantine home) next to the harbor was built in 1911 to inspect immigrant coolies for communicable diseases. In 1899 there had been another serious outbreak of the plague in the southwestern provinces and all Phuket had to be quarantined for two months, with resulting damage to the local economy. After another bad outbreak of tuberculosis on the island, a hospital was built on the site of the old Phuket Thai Hua School. In 1906 Phraya Rassada raised funds to start the Vachira Hospital and brought in a British doctor.

Phraya Rassada was also not averse to striking side deals with foreign investors to improve the town. Under Phraya Rassada, concessions granted to foreign companies often meant the applicant agreeing to some donation for social work or civil infrastructure and it was during his governorship that most of Phuket City's historic buildings were built.

Until 1907 there were no international banking facilities in Phuket. That year he invited the Standard Chartered Bank from Penang to build a branch on Phuket Road on the condition that they also build a police station opposite it, partly for the bank's own protection, but also for that of the town. This Talad Yai police station, with its clock tower, still stands at the junction with Phang Nga Road opposite the old Standard Chartered Bank building. Similarly, when an Italian consortium applied for a mining licence in Kathu, Phraya Rassada agreed they could have it if they built a cinema – and so the Charlermto Movie House was built. Its ornate stucco exterior can still be seen on the corner of Djibuk and Yaowarat roads opposite the Lok Tien Restaurant today.

32.7 Government officials in 1909 at the 'Sala Klang' in Phuket Town, the new government administration center for "Monton' Phuket, (greater province Phuket), which at the time covered all of Siam's Southwestern provinces except Keddah..

The beautiful Sala Klang, or provincial hall, designed by an Italian architect, was built between 1907 and 1913 and more recently starred as the US Embassy in Roland Joffe's Oscar winning movie The Killing Fields. Other notable buildings included the governor's mansion, the tin mines department building, the old provincial court building, the prison and the colonial villa that today houses the Baan Klung Jinda Restaurant, which was built as the residence for the provincial treasurer. The island's first ice factory was also built and the first electricity was introduced. Several elegant colonial mansions were built by wealthy locals, mainly Tan family tin barons, in this boom period. The huge mansion at 98 Krabi Road was built by Tan Ma Siang, who had previously been awarded the Siamese lordly title of Phra Pitak Chinpracha and was the founder of the influential Tanthawanit family on Phuket. Another Tan towkay, Tan Peck Huat (who had also received the Siamese title of Luang Aramsak) built the handsome villa that now houses the Thai Airways office on Ranong Road.

Outside Phuket town a British man, Henry G. Scott, ran the Mines Department of Monton Phuket. Henry Scott may even have been a descendant of the James Scott who had lived in and tried to take over Phuket in the 18th century. [850] Henry Scott eventually married into the Hongsyok family, a leading Tan clan family in Phuket and both he and Phraya Rassada ensured the regional tin goose kept laying its golden eggs by creating better administration, roads and transport facilities to the mines. The arrival of Standard Chartered Bank in 1907 also helped the growth of the mining industry by helping to mon-

32.8 A Classic towkay's mansion. This house is now demolished, but in 1908 it sat just outside Phuket Town (on the site of Satri Phuket School today) on luxurious lawns overlooking the Klong Ban Yai with To Sae Hill behind it. Several such mansions still exist round Phuket City today.

etize the local economy – which previously operated on a barter system, mainly of agricultural produce and tin. The availability of commercial loans at fair prices allowed the tin miners credit facilities and enabled enterprising locals to start new businesses. Previously the only sources of credit were loans either from wealthy benefactors or kin members, which had centralized much business and power in the hands of the dominant Tan family, or from Indian "chettiar" money lenders in Phuket town, who generally charged such usurious rates that few but the desperate would take them.

A telegraph system to Phuket had been started in the mid-1880s but was never completed. Warrington Smyth tells us of the state of the unfinished telegraph line in Phang Nga in 1894:

> "We followed the clearing made some years ago by the order of the Siamese Government for the telegraph which was to have connected the whole of the peninsula with Bangkok … The clearing was made at great expense through all the provinces … through swamp and forest and posts put up throughout … the materials were purchased and were taken to the various points and there left. The fatal lack of decision, which has cost Siam so much, intervened once more. The wires, insulators and all the gear lie rusting, or are being slowly stolen all up and down the country. Wild elephants now amuse themselves butting down the posts while the country cries out for communications." [851]

Mr. Charles Kynnersley, the British government agent from Penang who visited Phuket town in 1901, noted, "We did not ask to telegraph anywhere as we had been told that the telegraph posts and wires which run along the new road lead nowhere." [852] Phraya Rassada got the telegraph line fixed up within Monton Phuket. He also used his own steamer service to improve the mail service – at a profit to himself, naturally. So, within a few years of his appointment, even the anti-Siamese Penang Gazette had to admit that Phuket town had been changed from a "rotten and unhealthy place … [to] … a place holding out attractions for capital and enterprise."[853]

In 1909 Crown Prince Vajiravudh, the future Rama VI, visited Phuket. After seeing the new villas, the rows of new white or pastel colored shop-houses, the new cinema, the new brewery, the new ice factory, the many rickshaws and horse-carriages and even the four motor cars on Phuket's roads at the time, he commented that "apart from Bangkok, there were no other places more highly developed in Siam than Phuket."[854]

32.9 Thalang Road, Phuket's main street in 1908: on the left is the former Standard Chartered Bank with its new clock tower (then with no clock), on the right is the old police station and in the foreground the newly built bridge over Klong Bang Yai, all paid for by the bank.

British Economic Competition and the Straits Tin Smelting Co

Phraya Rassada was also happily predisposed to use his public office for personal gain and he created advantageous monopolies to preclude most competition. Mining concessions were often conditional not only on side-donations for the public good, but also on a personal stake for Phraya Rassada himself. He used his position to ensure that the Khaw fleet of steamers virtually monopolized much of the carrying trade on the southwest Siamese coast. The Khaw family steamer "Amboyna", for example, had a monopoly on the route from Ranong and Takuapa to Phuket and back, a route its British captain Brown called "a picturesque run, far off the beaten track of all other shipping."[855] In 1913 the frustrated British vice-consul in Tenasserim, Burma, had complained that in southwest Siam, "The shortage of shipping is a matter of some inconvenience to those ports, as freights are extremely high owing to the lack of competition."[856]

By 1907 British complaints that Phraya Rassada was deliberately passing legislation to keep British businesses off his turf reached a crescendo. Jan Westenguard, the later American adviser to the Siamese government, was sent south to look into these complaints and to study "the administration ... with a view to the Future of Monton Phuket." He warned Bangkok of the frustration the Phuket administration's actions were causing the British in the Straits Settlements. The British consul general to Siam also officially complained that "No enterprise [in Phuket] will ever get a fair chance so long as [the island] is run by the present high commissioner who has his finger in every pie and by himself or his family levies tolls on everything."[857]

A good example of this conflict is the case of the Straits Tin Smelting Co Ltd. On a visit to Australia a British resident from Singapore saw a new smelting method in the iron industry that he felt was more efficient and economical than that he had seen used by the Chinese and he felt it could be adapted for tin. Some Singapore-based investors took up his idea and Straits Tin Smelting Co Ltd was formed. The company obtained a loan from the Chartered Bank of India, Australia & China and built a smelter, brought in an Australian expert to operate it and was also given credit to buy up ore from the Chinese tin miners for cash. The company overcame the existing monopolies and opposition from triads in the tin fields of Malaya and won the confidence of the Chinese miners because, with more efficient smelting, they could afford to pay more for the ore, and to pay in cash not in a part-share of the smelted tin. Within a few years, by 1900, Straits Tin had captured almost 50 percent of the Malayan ore smelting market.

In 1902, Straits Tin approached Bangkok to obtain an ore-buying license in Monton Phuket, stating that the company could help Siam's tin mining industry by offering better prices for ore than their Chinese competitors whose smelting process was more primitive. The existing smelting in Monton Phuket was a cozy monopoly between the Khaws and the Tans, who put pressure on the local miners to use their smelters. Khaw family ships brought the ore from other provinces, and from the mines of Phuket the ore was taken to Tongkah down river on small flat bed boats or by buffalo cart for smelting.

The Phuket smelters still used an inefficient old Chinese process, whereby tin ore was placed between layers of charcoal in a large clay cauldron; a fire was lit inside and forced by manual bellows to create sufficient heat to melt the tin. It then dripped out of a hole in the bottom into an ingot mould. This method used a lot of charcoal and separated only 60 percent or so of the tin in the ore. The smelter took a hefty 17 percent royalty (one slab in six), which Warrington Smyth, the mines inspector, felt was too high and was one cause behind the poor showing of the local industry.

In Bangkok, Prince Damrong, the Minister for the Interior and the king's half-brother, despite being a strong advocate of the policy of "Siam for the Siamese", was also well aware of the growing chorus of calls by the British Straits Settlements Forward Party for the annexation of Phuket. He was also aware that although Siam's tin deposits were much greater and of higher quality than those of the British Malay states her tin output was much smaller. In 1900 for example, Siam produced 3,900 tons of ore, whilst the

Map 11
Main Tin Deposits in Phuket

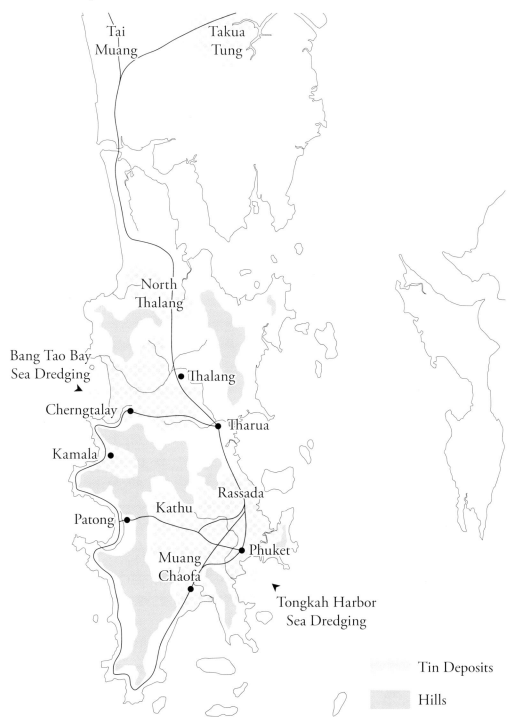

Tai
Muang

Takua
Tung

North
Thalang

Bang Tao Bay
Sea Dredging

Thalang

Cherngtalay

Tharua

Kamala

Rassada

Kathu

Patong

Muang
Chaofa

Phuket

Tongkah Harbor
Sea Dredging

Tin Deposits

Hills

British Malay states produced 42,444 tons. Damrong knew the reason for this was superior technology, capital investment, freer markets and better legislation. Damrong reluctantly granted a license to Straits Tin but with the impossible Thai-style compromise proviso that the new business "should not be prejudicial to Siamese subjects engaged in similar forms of trade."[858]

32.10 A primitive high bamboo sluice in Kathu for separating tin ore with water, by 1900 Phuket's tin production was lagging far behind Malaya's due to its lack of infrastructure and investment in technology.

Straits Tin sent an Englishman, Frank Adam, to Phuket to manage the ore buying. The island was still a very lawless place, with insufficient police. Robbery was rife, as were vice, fights and murders between Chinese gamblers, tin speculators, triads and drunks. According to Mr. Brown, Phraya Rassada's steamer captain in Phuket, the unpopular Mr. Adam, had to set up his home and office as "a veritable fortress with six foot Sikhs manning the palisades."[859]

The Khaw-Tan-dominated administration made life extremely difficult for these more efficient foreigners – just as some of the still-corrupt petty local government administrators in Phuket continue to happily do to foreign investors today. We are told that, for this foreign company, "Local property leases were refused, the Phuket Treasury was uncooperative about currency transactions and the rules for conducting business were constantly amended to suit the whims of local administrators."[860] After suffering such "local vexations" for three years, which denied the company any profit in Phuket, C. McArthur, the Straits Tin managing director in Singapore, who had spent some time in Phuket, wrote to the shareholders, "Our business has not made the progress we had hoped for and lately, has suffered some serious setbacks." This, he explained most succinctly, was not due to a lack of ore to buy but simply because "The present game in Tongkah seems to be one in which ... a select circle of well informed and powerful Chinese figure as the players ... and in which we and our customers figure as the ball."[861]

Such blatant obstructionism from the entrenched Hokkien élite and Phuket's corrupt local officials led another frustrated British administrator in Penang to write, "Things will never be right [in Monton Phuket] until the present high commissioner is removed."[862] More seriously, Charles Kynnersley, the governor of Penang, was prompted to write a forceful letter to Bangkok stating clearly that "unless the Siamese government takes action and adopts a progressive policy in regard to Phuket ... the British Government will insist that the country be opened up, either by Siam, or if she be unwilling, then by Great Britain herself."[863]

Despite the bureaucratic obstacles, the higher prices paid in cash by Straits Tin (and possibly a stern word in Phraya Rassada's ear by Prince Damrong) resulted in many Chinese miners finding ways to sell their ore to Straits Tin. Over the next decade the company's business in Phuket thrived. Between 1904, when Straits Tin came to Phuket, and 1914 Phuket's production of smelted ingot fell but it's production of tin ore increased over 1,000 percent.

All this ore, of course, meant that more ships were needed, both to bring more coolies to dig it and to transport the tin ore to the new Straits Tin smelter in Butterworth near Penang. In Malaya, Straits Tin had already set up a subsidiary company, Straits Steamship Cº Ltd. for this purpose. With some more British imperial pressure applied to Bangkok, Straits Steamship was also eventually allowed to open a shipping service between Penang and Phuket, undercutting the high and monopolistic rates of the Khaws' Koe Guan shipping service. Despite further interference from the local administrators, the economics of the situation, backed by strong British government pressure, meant the new cheaper Straits Steamship service became a success and the Penang papers celebrated this breaking of the "monopoly" of "the wealthy Khaw Sim Bee ... who has much power as a Siamese official."[864]

The Hokkien Response

The Khaws and the Tans realized the danger to themselves of this advance of British capital, technology and business into Phuket's economy. However, being Hokkiens – who can almost always outwit a simple white man in business – they quickly adapted. The Khaws formed a joint venture with another wealthy Hokkien in Penang who owned Beng Kee Shipping Cº They then went to the Penang capital market for funds and in 1907 registered their joint venture, Eastern Shipping Cº , as the ninth joint stock "sterling company" established in Penang. The offering raised £1.4 million and with these funds they used an Australian shipbroker in Penang to buy four new steamers from Union Steamship Cº of New Zealand. Eastern Shipping deliberately set its prices below those of Straits Steamship, expanded its services to China and soon became Penang's biggest shipping company. And the Hokkiens were not yet finished with the

British. To take on Straits Tin the Khaws established their new smelting company, Eastern Smelting C⁰ , in Penang. The Penang Gazette noted: "Our Chinese friends … have grasped the fact that although human labour is very cheap, it is not so cheap as when assisted by modern western contrivances and inventions in machinery … That they have now come to recognise this, with regard to the tin industry, may be regarded as a sign of the times."[865]

Their new effort to raise capital for this venture fell a bit short and the Khaws reluctantly had to use the still opulent cash flow from their Siamese opium farm, which was referred to as "a veritable money tree"[866] – and which, oddly enough, Phraya Rassada had never actually canceled, despite Bangkok's instructions to do so. They also used the cash from the family's insurance business, Khean Guan Insurance C⁰ , which was the insurance company used by most of the local government and mining companies in Monton Phuket. With this capital Eastern Smelting built the first modern-style smelter near Phuket town and also started buying tin ore for cash.

The Great Dredgers of Phuket

The indefatigable Phraya Rassada also decided to try to apply "modern western contrivances" to the mining of the tin. When Eastern Shipping had bought its New Zealand ships it used a shipbroker in Penang called Captain Edward T. ("Teddy") Miles, a 57-year-old Australian. He had come to Penang after an eventful career as a ship's master, a salvager and the Minister of Mines and Railways in the Australian state of Tasmania. Phraya Rassada informed Teddy Miles that he had a tin property in Phuket that he wanted "worked by modern European methods" and Miles visited Phuket to review the property. In New Zealand's gold fields a new type of giant, floating, steam-driven bucket-dredger was being used and Miles thought this equipment might also work for tin. He felt it would be easier to use this dredger to mine offshore, for instance in the shallow bay of Tongkah Harbor, where the seabed was known to be full of alluvial tin washed down from Kathu. In 1906, Phraya Rassada arranged a license for Miles to dredge in Tongkah Harbor. Miles registered Tongkah Harbour Tin Dredging C⁰ in Hobart, Tasmania and raised capital in New Zealand from public subscriptions. Most of the shares, however, were reserved for "Eastern shareholders", these being, of course, the Khaw family and the other Hokkiens in Phuket and Penang. Having raised the necessary funds, Miles ordered his first bucket-dredger to be built in the Clyde shipyards in Scotland. It was shipped to Penang in parts, bolted together there and then towed to Phuket by steam tug.

At first things went badly. There was too much muddy overburden in the bay and bad ore separation by the dredger. However, working with his indefatigable Hokkien mechanics, Miles had the dredger modified and from 1908 on it began to work well, producing tin more efficiently than any other mine in Phuket because "One dredge with 12 foot buckets could dig and treat … as much ore as 2000 coolies could during the same time."[867] Tongkah Harbour C⁰ had initially invested £17,500 in the dredger, but it then cost only four pence to mine a cubic meter of soil, three times cheaper than using Chinese coolies. This new mechanical dredging technology signaled the end of the era of mass coolie labor in Phuket and mass Chinese immigration to the island.

By 1911, five years after it started, Tongkah Harbour C⁰ had five huge dredgers working and accounted for 25 percent of all of Siam's output of ore. Other companies soon began to acquire dredgers and the Department of Mines records that ore output from dredging on Phuket almost quadrupled between 1910 and 1918, from 1,250 tons to a massive 4,110 tons, representing 46 percent of all the tin ore produced in Siam.[868] These dredgers were brought to work on inland mines too as they circumvented the problem of mines flooding in the rainy season. Now, the mines were allowed to flood so that the huge dredgers could float and the water was used to wash the ore on board in huge spinning canister sieves, or by great syringe jets so work could go on year-round even in the dry season.

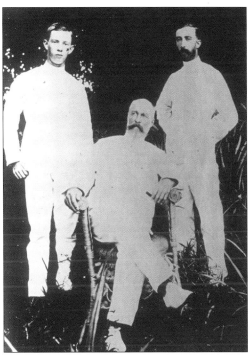

32.11 The Tasmanian Edward Miles and his two sons in Phuket. "Teddy" Miles helped Phraya Rassada buy and operate the first huge floating tin-dredge in Phuket in 1906.

A Danish visitor in 1926 described how one of these dredgers worked, "A dredge passes through the river bed, the stuff that is brought up is squirted over by a syringe so that the tin ore, which is heaviest, is left behind whilst the sand and gravel flows out with the water. In this way a lake is dug, tin taken up at one end of the lake and the other end filled with mud and rubbish. Everyday the artificial lake moves bit by bit."[869]

For almost 80 years these leviathan dredgers, housed in massive corrugated-tin structures gradually churned up, consumed and spat out vast tracts of the island's valley floors, leaving the regurgitated land in their wake looking like a lunar or desert landscape. The huge flooded craters they dug became the mobile lakes on which they traveled around. Digging the earth in front of them and excreting it behind them, these dredgers and their lakes slowly moved across the landscapes of Kathu, Thalang, Chalong, Rassada, Chaofa, Kamala, Bang Tao Bay and Phuket town. After the Second World War, as the richest deposits were consumed and became less economical, the great dredgers gradually disappeared. Tongkah Harbour's last working tin dredger, in Phang Nga, was taken out of operation in 2001. Today Tongkah Harbour C⁰. is still listed on the Malaysian and Bangkok stock exchanges and still has its head office in Phuket City but now concentrates on mining gold in central northern Thailand.

32.12 A huge tin-dredger in Thalang floating on its mobile lake and chewing its way across Phuket's landscape.

Bushes and scrub have reclaimed the masticated land left by these great dredgers. The many small lakes that still litter Phuket's valley floors are the remnants of these flooded open-pit mines. Many of these lakes that surrounded Phuket town in the 1960s and 1970s have now been filled in with the city's expansion. Phuket's Bangkok Hospital and the Chatuchak weekend market in Phuket town, for example, both sit on the filled-in sites of old dredge mines. Today most of the island's golf courses are built on former open-pit tin mines. These flooded tin-mine lakes also served the next mad rush of greedy immigrants who arrived on Phuket at the start of the 21st century – the foreign property developers. They, too, have used these lakes as oases around which to construct their fancy housing developments and resorts.

33

The Golden Years

1914 TO 1942

Assassination of the High Commissioner

It was a hot, cloudless day in early February 1913. The new pier in Trang stood exposed to the relentless glare of the midday sun. The sweltering heat smothered everything like a blanket, alleviated only occasionally by the thin breeze blowing in from the Andaman Sea. A group of top local officials, predominantly Hokkien Chinese, and all dressed obediently in the new Western uniforms prescribed by King Chulalongkorn, some with umbrellas against the sun, stood on the exposed, baking pier. From under the shade of their thatched stalls the local food hawkers watched them with some anticipation, one of whom was making these hot officials' ordeal worse with the odious reek of frying tofu.

They were gathered for the arrival of the Siamese government steamer Damrong Raat. On board was Phraya Rassada (Khaw Sim Bee), the high commissioner of Monton Phuket, who was stopping at Trang on his way home to Phuket from Satun. Loitering at the back of this group of officials was Ma Chan, a fairly handsome Chinese man in his early fifties. According to various accounts, Ma Chan was a pleasant and reasonable man who worked as the hospital dresser in the new Trang hospital, which, like the new pier, had also been built by Khaw Sim Bee when he was previously the governor of Trang.

The Damrong Raat appeared, painted a spiffy white and spewing a rather heavy smoke into the almost cloudless sky. Its propellers noisily churned the sea as it maneuvered alongside the pier. The uniformed crew, also dressed in spiffy white, secured the ship to the pier with sisal ropes as thick as pythons. The timber-and-rope gangway was then fed across to the pier and the stumpy little high commissioner, followed by his Hokkien nephew, Khaw Joo Keat, the new governor of Trang, descended across it triumphantly to meet the waiting officials. Ma Chan the hospital dresser moved from the back of the crowd through the officials until he stood right beside the little high commissioner. Then he pulled out a revolver and shot him.

Khaw Sim Bee had instinctively turned away as he saw the pistol being aimed and the bullet passed through his arm into his torso and lodged in his back. He stumbled and fell on to the wooden planks of the pier. In the brief, astonished silence after the sudden shot, Khaw Joo Keat, the new Trang governor, and his relative, was the first to react, bending down towards his fallen uncle. As he did so, Ma Chan shot him as well. The bullet hit him in the spine, severing it and came to rest in his stomach.

Ah Hooi, another Hokkien relative and triad member, to whom Khaw Sim Bee had recently given the Trang opium farm, lurched forward in an attempt to grab the pistol from Ma Chan. But the hospital dresser dodged backwards, lifting the pistol until it was pointed nearly point- blank at Ah Hooi's face and barked at him to back off. There was a fitful standoff until Ah Hooi backed away cautiously. Ma Chan aimed his pistol threateningly at the other frightened officials, who gave him space. He then slowly backed off the pier, turned abruptly and walked back towards town. Some of the crowd guardedly followed him. When Ma Chan reached town, he went into the airy new post office building, sat down rather dejectedly and waited for the local police to come and arrest him.

On the pier, Khaw Joo Keat, the new Trang governor, died fairly quickly. Khaw Sim Bee, the high commissioner, remained alive, lying in an expanding pool of blood. He was gingerly loaded back on to his steamer, which immediately set sail for the best hospital in the region, back in Penang. Khaw Sim Bee was still alive when he reached Penang, but fell into a coma in the hospital after the bullet was removed. Almost a month later he died, "being", according to the Penang Gazette, "unable to rally from the shock."[870]

The newspaper headline labeled the incident the "Trang Outrage" and there was much speculation over the motives for the assassination. Some Trang officials explained that Ma Chan had a very young and particularly beautiful wife in Phuket who two weeks earlier, had apparently boarded the government steamer in Phuket alone to go to visit her husband in Trang. Khaw Joo Keat, the Trang governor, reportedly on the same boat, noticed this beautiful young girl traveling alone and "unprotected" and apparently asked the captain to put her back ashore as he feared there might be improper gossip. It was said that she was then put back on the pier in Phuket and that Ma Chan became incensed when he found out why his wife did not arrive on the steamer. He had then apparently asked the Trang governor for leave from the hospital in order to accompany his wife from Phuket, but was refused. He even cabled Phraya Rassada himself, but received no answer. Thus, according to the Penang Gazette, Phraya Rassada had been shot "by this miscreant who fancied he had a grievance against him,"[871] and his cousin, the Trang governor, was "shot by accident, getting in the way of the bullet."

At the trial, however, Ma Chan himself told a quite different story. He claimed that Phraya Rassada had been on that steamer and tried to have sex with his wife and when she refused he became angry and put her ashore on a remote island. Somprasong Phuwadol, a Thai historian who is very knowledgeable about this period, believes that Phraya Rassada was probably not on the same steamer as the young wife. However there was much gossip at the time that, in addition to his big appetite for wealth, little Phraya Rassada also had a big appetite for women. The British Foreign Office hinted at this in a memo in 1913, "One hears varying estimates of the high commissioner as a man, as a polygamous Chinese with less reason for restraint than most men."[872] There was also loose gossip in Phuket at the time that the alluring young Mrs. Chan was indeed seeing one of the wealthy Khaw family, if not Phraya Rassada himself.

During the court hearing it was also alleged that Ma Chan might have been "encouraged" in the assassination by some Bangkok officials who had embezzled provincial revenues and feared the disclosure of their misdeeds. In 1913, for example, Monton Phuket raised over four million baht in revenues for Bangkok, but was allocated just 100,000 baht by Bangkok for spending on infrastructure. Jan Westenguard, the American adviser to the Siamese government had earlier warned his boss, Lord Devawongse, that he had detected rising frustration on the part of Phraya Rassada. "The high commissioner would like to spend money on improvements but he is apparently tied down by Bangkok."[873] Fitzmaurice, the British consul in Bangkok, also did not discount the possibility of more sinister motives behind the assassination.

"Though the motive for the attack seems to have been a personal one, there is no doubt that both Phraya Rassada and his nephew were far from popular with the Siamese officials of the province ... These two Chinese officials have hitherto had no difficulty in maintaining an almost despotic power over the Siamese officials in their districts and this forceful character ... is doubtless the chief cause of their unpopularity among the Siamese."[874]

Whatever the real motive may have been, Ma Chan, who reportedly maintained a cheerful demeanor during the whole trial process, apart from one occasion when he tried to slit his own wrists, was duly executed by having his head chopped off with a sword. Phraya Rassada and his nephew were given fine state funerals and interred in the large family grave in Ranong. Despite grumbling so much about him during his life, the British in Penang had also respected Phraya Rassada, as one colonial office agent noted, "I have no doubt about his energy and ability, he has done more for Trang and Phuket as High Commissioner than any of his predecessors."[875]

The new high commissioner of Monton Phuket appointed by Bangkok was Phraya Surindaracha, a former military officer from a good Siamese family and educated in England. He had previously worked closely with the British on the boundary commission to delineate the border between Siam, Burma and Malaya. He was said by the British press in Penang to be a man of "pleasant manners ... the best type of modern military officer in Siam"[876] and a complete contrast with his "half trader, half autocrat" predecessor.

Modernization Continues under Rama VI

King Chulalongkorn died in 1910 and his son, Prince Vajiravudh, ascended the throne as Rama VI. Educated in England, at Sandhurst Military Academy and Oxford University he was a modernist and quite pro-western. He continued the westernizing reforms of his father, promoting education for all and the creation of many more schools and universities and promoting the institutions of the Boy Scouts and Girl Guides. Rama VI was also a most slick and modish Western dresser who continued to push Western-style dress on to the Thais, Chinese and Muslims. Many of the wealthier Chinese in Phuket adopted western style clothes and their wives changed their hairstyles from the traditional Thai short en brosse and Chinese pigtail styles to Western styles. They also started dressing in modern Western styles such as two-piece skirt suits. Rama VI also promoted Western recreations such as Western-style music, dancing and art, the reading of books, football and recreational swimming and picnics at the beach.

33.1 Chinese men in Phuket in 1928 posing in the new Western dress style promoted by kings Rama V and Rama VI.

With the concept of nation states rather than kingdoms becoming more widely accepted in Europe, Rama VI began to promote the concept of a Thai nation instead of the former, more feudal kingdom of Siam. This was by its nature pro-Thai and therefore anti-Chinese and anti-Malay and he is seen today as the Father of Thai Nationalism. In 1913 he enacted the first law decreeing that all Siamese must have Thai names and those who didn't – like most of the Phuket Chinese and Malays – must adopt one. As a royal favor, he granted names to well-to-do Chinese families. It was from this time that the Chinese in Phuket and some Malays were given or took Thai names. Several of the Tan families in Phuket received names from the king. Tan Jin Ghuan, for example, was given the surname Hongsyok (heavenly bird). Tan Kay Giew became the first Tantawit; Tan Tua Choa was the first Ekwanit and Tan Eng Kee became the first Udonsap.

Rama VI also promoted better public health measures. In 1914, for example, he passed a compulsory vaccination law and one American journalist in Siam at the time wrote, "So ready are most people to be vaccinated, that they are sometimes exploited by quacks and swindlers. During one smallpox scare a bogus doctor vaccinated the entire population of three villages with Nestlé's tinned milk at two baht a head."[877]

The king also attempted to abolish all gambling houses. Gambling was at its most prolific in those places with the highest concentrations of Chinese, namely Bangkok and Phuket. Phuket during the coolie days was crammed with gambling houses and shacks where one could gamble on just about anything. These gambling houses were the source of so much fighting and financial ruin, so many suicides, robberies and murders, that the king wanted them closed. But not wanting to forgo the considerable tax revenue they produced, the king supplanted gambling with a national lottery. This lottery has become the biggest legal form of gambling in Thailand. It is also probably the only institution in modern Thailand that still makes Phuket's people revert to their pre-Buddhist animistic beliefs as they rub trees or tortoise bellies or analyze phone and invoice numbers searching for any supernatural omen that might permit them to divine what the next winning national lottery number may be.

33.2 A sales vehicle and crowd in prosperous and growing Phuket Town in the early 20th century.

Love-Struck Folly

Ernest Young, an American who traveled around Thailand at the end of the 19th century, explains how this early national lottery worked.

> "The government farms out the monopoly and gains considerable revenue from it ... The lottery farmer chooses everyday one out of thirty four characters of the [Thai] alphabet as the lucky one for that day ... The gambler goes to one of the many writers of lottery tickets and names a number ... the writer inscribes the number upon a sheet with the name and address of the purchaser ... it is the policy of the local lottery farmer to have his agents scattered all over the city."[878]

He then recounts the story of one rather love-struck gambling farmer who

"lost a considerable sum of money through his own indiscretion. He had obtained a new wife of great beauty of whom he was passionately fond. One day she asked him what letter he had chosen for the winning one. 'Why do you wish to know?' said he. Woman-like, she replied, 'Oh, I merely asked you out of curiosity. ' 'Well,' said the infatuated adorer, 'promise me that you will on no account reveal it to any single person you may meet. Remember if people were to know what letter I had chosen I should lose a tremendous sum of money. ' The favorite answered, 'I promise not to tell,' so he gave her the letter and faithful to her promise, she kept the secret. But she did go to one of the town writers and staked all the money she had on what she knew was to be the lucky character. The writer knew who she was and jokingly asked her why she had chosen that particular letter. She answered that she had simply selected it as anyone else might have done in order to try her luck. Several people standing by heard the conversation and learning that the chief had been to see her the day before in her own quarters, they thought it extremely probable that she was in possession of a better knowledge of that day's winning number than themselves. They all promptly followed her example, with the result that her confiding spouse lost several thousand dollars on the day's transactions. He at once accused her of betraying his trust and, although she desperately pleaded her innocence, he sold her within a few days to gratify his want of revenge, or perhaps simply to recoup himself in part for the losses he had sustained as the result of his own folly."[879]

Thailand in the First World War

In 1914, war broke out in Europe. Being a former Sandhurst man, Rama VI favored the Allies, but with no real reason to join the war, he declared neutrality. Siam watched on, possibly with a smidgen of Schadenfreude, as the bullying colonial powers dissipated their military might in the wretched mud of Flanders. Siam, the only neutral power in Asia, became a center for some Casablanca-type espionage – spies meeting in smoke-filled tea shops, lights twinkling from lonely shores and German agents helping Indian nationalists to undertake seditious deeds against the Raj.

In 1917, when the USA entered the war against the central powers, President Woodrow Wilson called on all neutral countries to do the same. Now that it seemed the Allies would win, Siam joined the USA in declaring war on Germany and the Austro-Hungarian and Ottoman empires, mainly to gain favorable treatment in postwar dealings with the Allies. Forty German ships in the East had taken shelter in the neutral ports of Siam, three of them in Phuket. These were immediately seized by the Siamese military before their crews could scuttle them. These ships were then divided among Britain, France and Japan as supply ships and Siam, which had actually captured them, was given only two. The 14 German companies working in Siam were also taken over and more than 250 German, Austrian and a few Turkish civilians living in Siam at the time were arrested and confined to the German Club in Bangkok. Just when they were resigned to having to play billiards and drink gin and tonics and schnapps for the rest of the war, the British complained that the Siamese were being far too nice to them, and the prisoners were all later interned in civilian POW camps in India. The British were of course most enthusiastic to take this opportunity to remove their successful German commercial rivals from Siam completely.

When it declared war, Siam had a standing army of just ten divisions of 2,000 men each. The German Minister of Foreign Affairs reportedly raised his eyebrows quizzically when he heard that "the tiny Thai army should come to fight with their teachers – the Germans!"[880] The British proposed that Siam could assist by sending men to work with the donkey caravans, transporting supplies in the Mesopotamian campaign, but the Siamese felt this was far too demeaning. Instead, Siam offered to send a force of 1,200 doctors, nurses, orderlies, truck drivers and 20 Thai pilots to the Western Front. The only hiccup was that none of the 20 "pilots" could actually fly a plane. This Thai expeditionary force arrived in Europe 1918 and by the time the pilots had been trained in England, the war finished. The doctors and nurses, however, were noted for their caring ways and Allied Forces wounded must have found them a sight gentler than some of the strapping northern lasses working in the military hospitals. The truck drivers were renowned as the most heroic, winning accolades for their derring-do under heavy shellfire at the front.

Siam's participation in the war on the side of the winners did, as hoped, result in benefits. The Siamese government was allowed to take over the railways Germany had built and, shortly after the war, led by Germany and America, most of the European powers began to renegotiate their commercial treaties with Siam, to the advantage of the Siamese.

The influenza pandemic of 1918-19, which killed as many as 50 million people worldwide – many more than the war itself – also hit Phuket badly and exposed the lack of proper medical facilities on the island. The Vachira Hospital in Phuket town was rebuilt and expanded after the epidemic with money donated by the Na Ranong (Khaw) family. The old hospital site on Komarapat Road was prone to flooding in the rainy season. In addition, as so many people had died there during the influenza epidemic, many Siamese and Chinese were scared to go there because of the many ghosts. A new site was chosen on Yaowarat Road and a new building, with less ghosts, was built in 1920.

Phuket in the Roaring Twenties and Thirties

Under the new governor Phraya Surindaracha Phuket continued to thrive during the 1920s as both the tin price and the island's tin output soared. Phraya Surindaracha, like his assassinated predecessor Phraya Rassada, was a progressive man who encouraged development. Several more fine buildings were constructed in Phuket town. In 1932, the children of Tan Chin Nguan (Luang Anuphas), who established the Hongsyok family, built the fine mansion opposite the Bangkok Bank on Thepkrasattri Road. Public and civic works were paid for by donations from the wealthy Chinese tin families.

Chinese and some also progressive Thai women began to wear their hair in a Western bob and some dressed in modish Western clothes as well as the more traditional but flamboyant "baju panjang" and "cheongsams". The wealthy Baba Chinese towkays threw lavish weddings and parties where their extravagantly dressed Nonya wives created foods from the different cultures that have helped make Phuket a melting pot of the world's culinary delights. Adjarn Pranee Sakulpipatana, former assistant history professor at Phuket's Rajabhat University, explains that local Phuket Nonya culture always revolved around food. "But," she adds, "We have strict rules. We can only eat in certain types of weather. If it's raining, we are allowed to get together to eat, as we can't go out. If it's not raining, we are allowed to celebrate by going out to eat. So we only eat when it's raining or not."[881]

33.3 One of the island's new cars at the coast beside Chalong pier near to where Kam Eng seafood restaurant sits today.

The red light street, Soi Romanee, did a roaring trade. People in Phuket town continued to smoke opium until it was made illegal (in 1958), and this time the ban was actually enforced. Singing halls and dance halls, some with taxi dancers, opened up with the latest trends in music. Two more cinemas opened in town and more motorcars were imported by the wealthy. The island's first golf course opened at Surin Beach. The United Club, in the elegant town hall building with its tennis courts and the Miners Club in Saphan Hin, with its traditional men's bar, became the haunts for the predominantly British, Australian and Dutch mine company managers and other expatriates on the island. Phuket also earned a name for itself amongst expatriates in Bangkok and Penang as a cracking good place for a spot of elephant-back hunting for boar, deer and especially tigers. One of the most notable landmarks of this affluent era, the stylish On On Hotel on Phang Nga Road was opened in 1929. This hotel, though rather dog-eared now, recently flirted with fame again as Leonardo De Caprio's backpacker hotel in the movie "The Beach".

Telephones lines were strung and the old post office in town was built in 1923. By 1922, some 57 miles of laterite and earth roads had been built on the island to reach the new mining areas from town.[882] The thick covering of jungle was cut back and new roads of compacted earth or stones were laid as new areas were cleared for agriculture, orchards or rubber trees. New vehicles started appearing – in town numerous rickshaws pulled by out-of-work coolies, bicycles and more motorcars and motorbikes.

33.4 The new Post Office built in 1923. We can see that the Klong Bang Yai River still flowed wide and deep in front of it even at that time.

The New Peninsular Railway
In 1923, the new railway line from Bangkok to Penang opened. There was still no real road on the mainland opposite Phuket – only the rail line to the port in Trang a steamer ride away – but Bangkok was now accessible in just a few days' travel. Hans Morgenthaler, the Austrian geologist, made this train trip in the early years of the railway. The trains traveled "three times a week," moving through the jungle "with a frequent long drawn whistle for the benefit of the buffaloes which have a predilection for getting on the rails … Herds of wild elephants have their abode close to the railway line. … The dog of a barefooted station master was carried off by a tiger" and "with the exception of the few paddy fields around the villages … the whole country is covered with dense virgin forest."[883]

In 1914 Don Muang airport opened in Bangkok and by 1930 the first regular seaplane with mail, and a few passengers, started to fly to Phuket. The first island airstrip was built in Ban Manik and then a new airport was built on the present site in north Phuket, running from east to west to benefit from the seasonal monsoon winds.

33.5 *The first Phuket provincial government plane in 1928 on Phuket's first airfield, which was originally in Manik before moving to its present position.*

Ebbe Kornerup and the Loyal Danes

In the 1920s, in the reign of Rama VI, several popular international authors began to visit Siam and write about its exotic pleasures. Somerset Maugham in his book The Gentleman in the Parlour, for example, wrote of meeting "miss pretty girl", a masseuse in a Bangkok Turkish bath whose calling card noted how she could give a "gentle massage" that would "put you in dreamland with perfume soap, latest gramophone music, …you come now! Miss pretty girl want you."[884] Such hedonistic publicity began to spread, for the first time, Siam's renown as a bit of an exotic Eden for more adventurous and sybaritic recreational travellers. Ebbe Kornerup, a reputedly gay Dane, was one of these early tourists and also a writer. "Siam is the newest holiday land … one of the most interesting countries in Asia; self government has made the nation original; you can tell you are travelling among a free people."[885]

In 1926 Kornerup travelled on the newly built peninsular railway which had been driven through the jungles of southwestern Siam, "one of the most beautiful regions of Siam. On both sides of the railway line mighty forests grow wild over mountainous country, great trees of enormous height have gleaming white trunks, magnificent palm trees lift up their luxuriant heads … this is the true primeval forest. If the railway did not exist the forest would be just as it was ten thousand years ago."[886] He tells us the country-side was "uninhabited with only a few stations, no people, no rice fields. ... here dwell the Tapir and the rhinoceros in the hot undergrowth, elephant, dwarf deer, wild boar and in the clearings buffalo; gibbons in the trees, monkeys and more monkeys, many colored screaming birds."[887] On one bicycle excursion he recalls that, "suddenly we saw something black dash across the road, it panted, a yellow eye flashed – a black panther had crossed our path as swiftly as a flung stone. There was a gentle rustling and all was again still."[888]

He reached Monton Phuket or, as he called it, the "tin country of Siam" where "Tin was found and dug up since the morning of time."[889] Like most travelers at that time he dis-embarked from his railcar at the railhead at Kantung port near Trang where "the Siam Navigation Company's fine ships link southern Siam with Bangkok and Singapore by a weekly service to the islands of Puket and Penang."[890] In Kantung he stayed "at a second rate Chinese hotel, the only one there was." He then set off "on a little steamer on our way to the island [Phuket]. It was lively on board, Siamese, Chinese, Malays and Euro-peans all travelling together. The ship had a list and looked as though she might turn turtle any moment."[891] They sailed past "an archipelago of rocky islets. Strange solitary rocks of fantastic shapes which rose perpendicularly out of the sea ... It was like sailing through a prehistoric country from one of the earlier periods of the globe."[892]

He claims that Phuket was:

"the richest tin country in the world and was known as long as two thousand years ago to the Indians who worked the mines at that time; later the Portuguese took their turn, until at last the Chinese discovered them; and to this day it is Chinese coolies who dig up the tin for Chinese, Australian or English compa-nies. In the harbor itself on the other hand an Australian company mines by machinery [Tongkah Harbour Ltd] pumping water over the slime brought up and separating the tin, bringing up millions of ticals worth of tin every year."

He tells us that mining was going on all over the island:

"all the alluvial tracts between the hills have in the process of time been ploughed through for tin ... in one of the Chinese mines the veins of the tin lie thirty feet below the surface, the shafts were open and dug in terraces, The stuff brought out was rinsed in running water, washed clean ... the tin was collected in sacks and carted away. Foremen wearing big straw hats sat on the slopes and kept watch." The [Chinese] workmen's huts were miserable, unclean bamboo pigsties, stinking of opium."[893]

"It is tin that has made Puket world-famous ... Puket was formerly a very noto-rious [meaning 'disreputable' in the 1920s] spot, up to the time when Governor Phya Rassada came to the island and laid roads and planted trees ... Then Gov-ernor Phya Surindaraja arrived and trod in Rassada's footsteps and the island changed out of all recognition. From being a desolate place overgrown with elephant grass, where you had to pay for drinking water and bought your betel, coconut, fruit, or eggs at exorbitant prices, Puket has now become a garden, an Eden, through the medium of policy, roads, trees, aqueducts and schools alone. Palm trees wave in the fresh sea breeze. The houses are well kept. There are Gardens all over the island. Coconut and betel, which used to be imported, are now exported to Penang. Everything is entirely changed."[894]

"At its northern point a strait cuts Phuket off from the mainland which is very near. The sea is Blue. Small ships put out. People work busily ... Opposite on the mainland a forest road leads to Ranong. On this road lies Takua Pah."[895] Kornerup tells us that the East Asiatic Cº owned a rich tin mine at Pong, by Takuapa, which was worked by a giant dredger "bought in the United States, sent over in parts, and assembled on a temporary slip. Water conducted through heavy pipes down from a mountain stream two thousand feet above ... is able to drive the electrical apparatus which drives the machinery."[896]

33.6 In the 1930s new roads were cut through some of the jungles and hills of Monton Phuket to places that were previously only accessible on foot or by horse, elephant or boat.

The East Asiatic Cº was started in Bangkok in 1897 by H. N. Andersen, the Danish owner of the Bangkok Oriental Hotel. By 1908 it owned Siam Steam Navigation Cº , the company operating the weekly peninsular steamer service from Bangkok via Singapore up to Penang, Krabi, Phuket, Ranong and Rangoon. During the later 19th century the Danes were regarded with relative trust by Siam, mainly because of their apparent lack of colonial ambition and also their proven loyalty. Danish mercenary officers distinguished themselves in leading Siamese armies in their northern campaigns. Danish officers were used to establish the modern Siamese navy and police force. In Phuket Danes had been posted as the early police chiefs, and Fritz Haurowitz, a Danish harbor master, had developed much of the island's new harbor facilities. Haurowitz, a keen recreational sailor himself, drowned in 1914 when his yacht sank while sailing to Trang, where he was buried. In 1926 the Danish run East Asiatic C° , in addition to mining rights, also held a massive logging concession right across the jungled peninsula from Takuapa on the west coast to Bandon on the east. Within this vast uninhabited tract, Kornerup tells us,

> "Gigantic 'mai yang' trees rise in the primeval forest, the tree attains a height of two hundred feet and is between nine and twelve feet thick at the height of a man … hundreds of Elephants and buffaloes work, and the saw mills … are kept very busy where the 'mai yang' are cut up to be shipped away into the world. These enterprises the company has set on foot here have opened up this out of the way region."[897]

Back on Phuket, Kornerup tells us that despite the huge influx of Chinese, the fields on Phuket were still mainly worked by Thais who believed: "'Let others be tradesmen and shopkeepers, we are free, we till our ground. Let the Chinaman kowtow to any man who spends two satangs in his shop if he likes; that is his affair. Nor are we slave-drivers in the mines like the Chinese, who keep dog-kennels for their labourers. ' … So civilized is the Siamese in his ideas and dealings. He has the mind of a carefree bird and puts nothing by for a rainy day."[898]

Kornerup tells us that the main road on the island (probably Thepkasatri Road from the Saracen Bridge to Phuket City today) "runs through rampatan, coconut and rubber plantations and through villages in a beautiful country of forests and hills . . . there is really something garden-like about Phuket, something luxuriant, something captivating. Wealth pours out of the earth, green and sappy. It is a pleasant place to live, firm red roads, rolled lawns, government buildings built of stone, things are moving here as in few other places in Siam."[899]

During the 1930s, after Kornerup's visit, the tin price increased further and even more mines were opened and even more local Chinese, British, Australian and Dutch firms entered the mining business. In this period the huge Muang Chaofa tin field was opened up and dredged. In 1914 there were only six dredgers on Phuket. By 1921 just before Kornerup visited there were 13, and by 1940, the peak year for tin mining production in Phuket, there were 45 dredgers working for over 30 separate

33.7 *Phuket Miners bringing their increasingly valuable tin yields to the buyer's storehouse in the 1930s.*

Chinese, British, Australian and Dutch companies. In that year they produced a record haul of 44,551 tons of tin ore that year, making Phuket Island the biggest tin producer in the world at the time.

The increased mechanization, with the use of water jets and dredgers in the tin mining industry, meant that thousands of Chinese coolies were displaced. Many left the island, returned home or moved elsewhere and many stayed on and set up new businesses and shops in Phuket's prosperous and growing new towns. As Chinese immigration became more difficult in the 1940s more and more Thais and Malays from elsewhere in Siam began to arrive in Phuket. Some found work in mining and associated businesses, some fished, made small farms or cooked in the markets to help feed the island's growing population. Many more however busily set about cutting back the thick forests to make way for the island's new boom industry – rubber.

33.8 A tin mine on the wide river that used to flow from Cherngtalay to Bang Tao Beach in the late 1930s, (now another storm water drain), with the familiar profile of the Cherngtalay hills behind.

34

The Seeds from
Mr. Wickham's Shoes

1895 TO 2000

A Brief History of Rubber

Rubber trees were introduced to Phuket in the early years of the 20th century. In the 100 years since then, rubber has consistently been either the island's largest or second-largest export earner after tin or tourism.

Rubber trees are not native to Phuket; they originated in the Amazon rainforest where Portuguese colonists and adventurers first came across them and their pliant and sticky white sap in 1525. Around 1770, an English inventor discovered it could be used to rub out slate pencil marks, hence its English name. Demand, though, was tiny. All the world's rubber trees grew wild. Then in 1823, a Scotsman, Charles Macintosh, invented a technique for laminating fabric with rubber to create waterproof garments, such as raincoats and boots. Then, in 1839, Charles Goodyear, an American, discovered a process called vulcanization, which made rubber harder and able to withstand heat. Vulcanized rubber began to be used for flexible pipes, hoses, shoes and as solid bicycle tires. The rubber band was patented in 1845 and in 1888 John Boyd Dunlop, another Scot, made a pneumatic tire for his bicycle. Fifteen years later, the Frenchman Claude Michelin did the same for his car and since then rubber has been used in ever more applications.

Henry Wickham

As the entire world's supply of latex came from inaccessible wild trees in the Amazon, the price of rubber shot up several hundred percent with these inventions in the late 19th century. Brazil did not allow any plantations, as it preferred to encourage Brazilian tappers to move into the Amazon to assist in its territorial claims there against Peru and Bolivia. Brazil was highly protective of its rubber monopoly but in 1875 an Englishman, Henry Wickham, smuggled some rubber seeds out. The romantic story goes that he hid them in the heels of his shoes, but given that a rubber seed is roughly the size of a large grape, and that he brought out some 70,000 seeds, he must have worn a

34.1 Sir Henry Wickham

suspiciously colossal pair of shoes as he walked past the Brazilian port guards. However he did it, he got the seeds out – a feat that earned him a knighthood in England and great opprobrium in Brazil.

These kidnapped seeds were delivered to the greenhouses of the Royal Botanic Gardens in Kew, London where only 2,800 of the 70,000 seeds germinated. Some of these saplings were then sent to the botanical gardens in Ceylon and Singapore as their climates more closely matched that of the Amazon. Of the 22 saplings that reached Singapore only nine survived, but these nine saplings have now propagated most of the millions and millions of rubber trees that cover much of Phuket as well as large swathes of tropical Southeast Asia today.

Rubber Ridley

These 22 aspiring saplings arrived in Singapore a week or so before a short 32-year-old Englishman, prematurely bald and supporting an improbably huge black moustache. His name was Nicholas Henry Ridley and he had come to take up the post of director of the botanical gardens in Singapore and Penang. Ridley immediately saw the potential of rubber and developed a tremendous enthusiasm for its commercial value. He soon became known in Straits society as "Rubber Ridley" or "Mad Ridley", as he carried his beloved rubber seeds to social occasions and gave them to all and sundry with exhortations that they go out and plant them. Most planters in Malaya at the time grew coffee and gambier (a tree that produced an astringent used in tanning) and were not impressed with this

34.2 Nicholas "Rubber" Riddley who in his 30s nurtured nine rubber tree saplings in the Singapore botanical gardens in the 1880s which have now multiplied into the millions of rubber trees that cover much of Phuket and Southeast Asia

new tree which did not produce a yield for six years. Undaunted, Ridley battled on. He created plantations in the 1890s in Singapore, which came to maturity just before the turn of the century. Then, between the years 1900 and 1910, the price of rubber jumped by more than 400 percent. There was a sudden rush for this new crop and by 1916, rubber had surpassed tin as Malaya's chief export earner. "Mad Ridley" was proven right.

Rubber Farming in Southern Siam

The first rubber trees to arrive in Siam were brought by the ever-enterprising Khaw Sim Bee when he was the governor of Trang. With his usual astuteness, he went to Sumatra in 1901 and purchased a few dozen seeds and then forced people in Trang to cultivate them on just 36 rai of land. He then persuaded the government to change the law to allow farmers to cut back the jungle, plant rubber on the cleared land and then own it. As the rubber price relentlessly rose in the early 20th century, the Chinese in Phuket started burning and cutting back the jungle and "stately trees" that had shrouded the island's interior. The felled timber was sold and most of the wildlife it had sheltered, since time immemorial, was eaten. All over the island, forested land began to be claimed to plant rubber trees or to be sold off as the next prospective tin mine.

In 1910, rubber reached an historic high price of nearly £850 per ton and that year just 15 tons were produced on the whole Malay Peninsula. By 1935, annual production had leapt to 900 tons – just as the price collapsed in the Great Depression. But the uses for rubber continued to increase until it was used in almost everything mechanical, electrical or automotive, and, after oil and steel it had probably become the third most important commodity required to run an economy, or an army. For example, each US Sherman tank in World War II required half a ton of rubber. Therefore, when Japan suddenly invaded and occupied most of the rubber-growing areas of Southeast Asia during the war, the USA and Europe had to scramble desperately to find substitutes. The Allied secret project to mass-produce synthetic rubber was ranked second in importance only to the "Manhattan project" to produce the atomic bomb. Synthetic rubber for a variety of uses was created in just two years, and companies such as Du Pont, Shell, Bayer, BASF and Dow all invested heavily in synthetic rubber production.

After the creation of Thailand in 1939, the new country's pro-Thai laws hindered the entry of large Western firms into the rubber business, unlike in the earlier tin industry. Foreign firms could not buy land and could lease only 800 acres for 30 years. Other problems facing the rubber industry at this time were the shortage of free labor and the fact that the infrastructure was less developed than those of colonial Malaya, Indochina or Sumatra. The rubber industry in Phuket, therefore, remained mainly in the hands of local smallholders and was rather evenly shared out amongst Chinese, Thais and Muslims.

The production cycle generally follows a regular pattern. A rubber tree takes about six years to reach maturity, when tapping can begin; in the meantime, pineapples are usually planted between the rows of trees to bring a temporary income. A rubber tree has a productive life of around 30 years, after which it is cut, the wood sold and new trees and new pineapples are planted.

The post-war world market for natural rubber continued to expand, and a new all-time high price was reached in 1951. In these rubber boom years, more and more of Phuket's jungle was frantically cut away and replanted with rubber trees, three meters by five meters apart, giving a stroboscopic effect as one drives by these plantations. Rubber planters' huts and villages cropped up all over the island and indeed all over southern Siam. New roads were created to previously inaccessible places. One Thai writer noted,

"All over, new roads are built and towns have come to life in the rubber centres."[900] In 1926, Ebbe Kornerup, the Danish visitor, was impressed with how the lucrative new industries of rubber and logging had caused the jungled lands to be opened.

"Southern Siam has now been opened up by roads and railways … One rubber plantation succeeds another …The old towns that a few years ago lay sound asleep surrounded by all possible romance have suddenly put forth new shoots and flowers. An entirely new tradition of wheels, motors and machinery has been created. The country is unrecognizable."[901]

In 1960, for the first time, rubber became Thailand's largest export earner, overtaking even rice. So those few small seeds from Mr. Wickham's shoes have utterly transformed the appearance and the ancient ecosystem of Phuket, an island on almost exactly the opposite side of the world from their original Amazonian home. No longer is Phuket island hidden by a spectral blanket of "impregnable jungle full of tigers wild elephants and rhinoceros"[902] as earlier visitors described the place. No longer is the region a thinly peopled and jungled "wilderness"[903] as King Mongkut described it in 1855.

Thai government figures today claim that natural forest now covers only 26 percent of Phuket Island and rubber covers almost 60 percent. But these official figures seem incorrect. Today the hiker or rambler in Phuket's hills and national parks sees that much of this so-called "natural" and protected forest is also illegally interplanted with these ubiquitous and lucrative rubber trees. This on-going process of reforestation with rubber is still continuing deeper into the national parks and higher up in Phuket's mountain forests today.

35

From Siam to Thailand

1930 TO 1942

Rama VI died in 1925 and was succeeded by his younger brother, 32-year-old Prajadhipok, as Rama VII.

At this time, it was still entirely royals or royal favorites who ran the Siamese government. Previously, the only channels for social advancement for an ambitious Thai commoner had been through loyalty to the king or possibly the monkhood. It was not through business success, as almost all business in Siam was run by the Chinese or Indians, not the Thais or Malays. During the early years of the 20th century, however, the legal profession, medicine and the army became new avenues of social advancement for Thai commoners. The modernizing army, in particular, was much more of a meritocracy than society at large and a diligent commoner could rise up through the ranks.

By the early 1930s a middle class, mainly comprising Sino-Thai families, was beginning to form in Siam. These were educated people who were not beholden to the royal government for their position. Some of their children were being sent abroad to be educated and came back with the latest trendy Western ideas of nationalism, democracy, republicanism and socialism. A public opinion was also becoming identifiable, led by the many newspapers in English, Chinese and Thai. Some intellectuals even began writing trenchant anti-monarchist articles complaining that Siam was absolutist, corrupt, backward and that the people needed some constitutional means of expressing their opinion – a Parliament or House of Representatives. Under Siam's historically formidable lèse majesté laws several of these dissenters were imprisoned for their efforts and some executed.

Rama VII was slow to respond to these growing public calls for constitutionalism; he was more concerned with repairing the national coffers which had been depleted during the reign of his more spendthrift older brother. His budget fixing measures included cutting military spending and introducing a salaries tax, both of which hit the middle class and army officers, further fueling the growing fire of discontent amongst these groups. These economic problems were compounded by the onset of the Great Depression in the 1930s. Although Rama VII acknowledged this rising chorus of calls for a representative body, his budgetary worries meant he felt it inappropriate to enlarge his government at that time – but he waited too long.

The 1932 Revolution

In early June 1932, Rama VII retired as usual to the royal seaside resort of Hua Hin to escape Bangkok's summer heat. At 7 a.m. the next day, while he was playing golf on his private golf course, a messenger arrived to inform him that the previous night revolutionaries had invaded and taken over his palace in Bangkok and were holding over 40 high-ranking officials hostage. These were mainly other royals, who ran the government, the police and the military. The revolutionaries had support from segments of the army, who were out controlling the streets of Bangkok.

This revolution was not like those that had preceded it, which had generally been palace coups amongst the royals, with some killing others and then usurping power. This time the revolutionaries, calling themselves the People's Party, included some 100 ambitious commoners from the middle and upper ranks of the army and navy, many of whom had been educated in Europe, plus a number of left-leaning civilian intellectuals such as Pridi Phanomyong, a socialist lawyer who had studied in Paris and taught at Chulalongkorn University. They issued a strongly worded manifesto condemning the royal government and ordered the king to return to the capital to reign under a constitution to be drawn up by the People's Party. If he declined, they would appoint another more liberal royal as king and if any retribution were attempted "the princes held in pawn will suffer in consequence."[904] The king, who was faced in effect with a fait accompli, wrote back: "For the sake of peace, in order to save useless bloodshed … and because I have already considered making this change myself, I am willing to cooperate in the establishment of a constitution under which I am willing to serve."[905]

By midday the revolution was complete. Siam's absolute monarchy, stretching back almost 700 years, had ended. Over the coming months, a constitution was drafted and Siam's first elections were planned. But infighting soon began in the People's Party. The more leftist civilian faction headed by the lawyer Pridi made increasingly extreme socialist proposals, such as nationalizing all rice-growing land. This put them at odds with the more conservative military faction, who staged another semi-coup and forced out Pridi and his leftist supporters.

Then, in 1933, reactionary royalist forces under Prince Bovoradej mounted an armed counter-revolt against the new government and there was fighting around Bangkok. This counter-rebellion soon collapsed and a 42-year-old army officer, Lieutenant Colonel Plaek Phibulsongram, now known to Thais simply as Phibun, came out on top of the victorious People's Party. The king, soon discerned the sort of man Phibun was and, claiming he required eye surgery, sailed away to England. There on March 2, 1935 he abdicated, stating that he would rather resign from the throne than turn his power over to "any individual or any group to use in an autocratic manner without heeding the voice of the people."[906] The Privy Council in Thailand decided that the next king in line was a 10-year-old boy, Ananda Mahidol, who was at the time living and attending school in Switzerland. With this new king Rama VIII being conveniently young and far away, Siam fell squarely under the imperious and more republican control of Phibun and his ruling military clique.

Phibun in Power

Phibun came from a family of durian farmers near Bangkok who had sent him to military academy. His good performance had won him a scholarship to study in France and Germany, after which he joined the army general staff as a major. Phibun believed in reform through strong government, much as Hitler, Mussolini and particularly Kemal Atatürk in Turkey were doing at the time. Some have called Phibun and his cronies fascists, some saw him as a pro-Thai social reformer but many others saw him simply as an egotistical, self-serving opportunist. Colonel Phraya Ritthi Akhaney, one of the original leaders of the revolution, was certainly one of those who were distinctly un-enamored with Phibun, as he noted: "Throughout his entire life, this man has displayed not a jot of sincerity, honesty or adherence [to any principles]."[907]

35.1. *The Thai nationalist field marshal Plaek Phibulsongram (Phibun) who killed off heterogeneous Siam and enforced a more homogenous Thailand.*

Phibun soon set about establishing his absolute authority over the government of Siam. Dissenting journalists were arrested, as were Phibun's opponents in the party, the army and further afield. In his first month in power, Phibun had 40 members of the royal family arrested. Eighteen were executed and the remainder were exiled to isolated penal colonies set up on remote Ko Tao and also on Taratao Island, south of Phuket. Phibun expanded funding for the army, giving his loyal officers better salaries, better equipment and better opportunities for handsome kickbacks.

One of Phibun's top advisers was the Minister of Propaganda, Luang Wichitwathakan (known as Wichit), an even more Thai ultra-nationalist ideologue, whom the British ambassador to Siam described as "the Thai Dr. Goebbels". [908] Luang Wichit introduced state control and censorship of radio and newspapers and attempted to develop a cult of personality around Phibun, whose portrait and sayings were posted everywhere. It was also declared illegal to display pictures of any former king. The constitution was changed so that more than half the newly formed national assembly was appointed by Phibun's cabinet and the law was then changed to allow Phibun to stay in power indefinitely. By 1940, Col. Phibun had so consolidated his control over the government and military that the British Foreign Office observed, "The prime minister is a virtual dictator ... his word is law with the cabinet."[909]

The Creation of Thailand and the Enforcement of "Thainess"

Phibun believed that Siam's feudal and royalist values had to be forcefully uprooted and cast aside to make the country a modern state. On June 24, 1939, after being prime minister just six months, he and Wichit killed off Siam (Prathet Syam), the old feudal, multi-ethnic and multi-religious kingdom, and in its place created Thailand (Prathet Thai), a modernist, nationalistic, authoritarian and rather xenophobic state. As Phibun explained, "We are of the Thai race, but our country is named Siam … If the great number of immigrants settling in this country continues we might not be able to distinguish whether Siam is the Thais, Chinese or other people's country."[910]

Phibun and his clique decided that everyone in the new Thailand must become Thai. There was no room in Phibun's new Thailand for separate communities of Chinese, Malays, Mons, Khmers, Muslims, Europeans, or Indians as there had been in Siam. The Thai Colonel Luang Saranuprabhandi composed a new national anthem with the stirring nationalist lyrics still used today; "Thailand is the unity of Thai blood and body. The whole country belongs to the Thai people… etc."

The old Siamese flag – a white elephant on a red background – had been changed in 1917 by Rama VI because, the story goes, he was upset that it was too often, in error, hung upside down. He therefore created the less complicated "Trairong" or tricolor Thai flag of today, which conveniently looks the same even if it's hung the wrong way up. Respect for this new flag and the practice of flag-waving were enforced by Phibun. All citizens were required to drop everything and stand to attention twice each day while the Thai flag was raised and lowered and the national anthem played. Military conscription was stepped up and national military values were pushed on to the Thai youth via the Yuwachon, a copy of Germany's Hitler Youth movement. It was also decreed that every citizen, whatever his or her origins, must take a Thai name and speak only Thai.

Borrowing from Hitler's aggressive, but successful, pan-Germanic "Grossdeutschland" ideology, the concept of a "Maha Prathet" (a greater T'ai empire) was also promoted with a view to reuniting all T'ai peoples (i.e. the Shans in British Burma and the Lao in French Indochina) under one glorious Thai-led T'ai super state headed by Phibun himself, now with the rank of General. Nationalist literature was promoted by the military clique, such as the book Prawatisat Sakon (universal history), written, funnily enough, by the propaganda minister Luang Wichit himself, in which, after examining the world's major civilizations, he proved unquestionably that the Thai race is one of the greatest ever in world history.

Also under Luang Wichit, a particularly Orwellian government department was created – the Bureau of Mind Culture. This bureau was to create what Phibun called "new national traditions" in order to make the people in his new state more civilized ("araya"). Phibun, Wichit and their clique then set about inventing and enforcing how they believed a Thai in the new modern state of Thailand should behave. As Phibun told the cabinet, "If the people remain poor in culture and exhibit ignorance about hygiene, health, clothing and rational ways of thinking, our country can never claim to be civilised."[911]

From 1939 on, the Bureau of Mind Culture brought out a series of Ratthaniyom (cultural state decrees); these were new laws defining how the people of this new country of Thailand should live and act and how they should dress. No Siamese, Chinese, Malay or any religious or national clothing was allowed. Everyone should henceforth wear Western clothing. Women should wear three-quarter-length skirts, blouses, bobby socks, shoes and gloves. Men had to dress, essentially, like Humphrey Bogart and both sexes must wear hats when they went out. Many women and men took offence at this personal intrusion and were arrested, fined or even imprisoned for still wearing their traditional clothing, not wearing the correct clothing or for going bare-headed. Grandiose slogans were pasted up everywhere, such as "Wearing a hat will enable Thailand to achieve great nation status."[912] Specifically punishable dress offences mentioned in the Ratthaniyom decrees included the wearing of sarongs, the wearing of underwear or "garments fit for sleeping" in public (presumably aimed against Chinese shopkeepers) and wearing shorts in public. Women in the country working in rice fields could no longer go topless as had previously been normal and convenient.

Other Ratthaniyom clauses decreed that Thai citizens were no longer allowed to spit, chew betel or aggressively push into queues – or more specifically, as Ratthaniyom Article 4 put it: "No forceful acquisition of space such as on buses, ticket windows or at cinema entrances."[913] Another Ratthaniyom decree also banned, "bathing on public roads."[914] There was also a total ban on sitting on pavements; the Ratthaniyom specifically warned that this most seditious behavior made the whole nation look physically weak. Everyone also had to eat with

35.2 A Thai poster from Phibun's era showing unacceptable old Siamese ethnic dress styles and the new Thai dress style people were coerced to wear.

knives and forks, not with their hands or chopsticks and, when eating, they must sit at a table on chairs and not on the floor as was traditional. Everybody, it was most sternly decreed, must clap their hands after political speeches and music shows. Another, somewhat more intrusive law, decreed that all men must kiss their wives before leaving for work and on returning home. Failure to do so risked a fine or imprisonment if one partner chose to report the other to the police. This campaign, by Phibun's Mind Culture Bureau, which began as one of persuasion, soon became one of coercion and compulsion. Several of these Rattihaniyom articles are still observed, including two edicts that now make up unique and enduring Thai traits today. The first decreed that people must greet each other by making a wai and saying "sawadee" to each other every day. The second decreed, on pain of punishment or a fine, that both Thai men and women must also say "thank you", with the honorific Kha (female), or Khrap (male), after everything they said.

Phibun's government also successfully undertook many less frivolous social advancement programs, such as expanding education and attempting to build a national road network. A state social welfare department was established to look after hygiene, housing, mental and physical needs, employment and nourishment. Beggars and orphans were banned from the streets and would be taken care of by government institutions. The Thai military was built up with modern weapons and training, particularly from Britain and Phibun's two new friends, America and Japan. Changes had already been made to the national administration to increase Bangkok's control over the southern provinces. In 1933 Monton Phuket, the wealthy super-province covering most of southwest Thailand run from Phuket Town was abolished. Phuket Province was reduced to just cover the island and Phang Nga, Trang, Krabi and Renong got their own provincial administrations run by governors and officials appointed by Bangkok.

Squeezing the Chinese

As we have seen in earlier chapters, until the 20th century, the Chinese who had come to Siam were mainly single men who had later interbred with local girls. Dr. Virginia Thompson tells us that, "when a Chinese married a Siamese woman, the wife – not the husband – became head of the family and controlled its property and cash."[915] In this way they integrated with Siamese society. The British consul to Bangkok, Sir Josiah Crosby, wrote that, in 1904, "children of mixed race born of such unions were brought up as Siamese, regarding Siam as their home and merging readily with the population around them."[916]

In the early 20th century, however, increasing numbers of Chinese women began to arrive in Siam. The nationalist war in China, the collapse of the silk industry in the south and a British policy encouraging Chinese women to migrate to the Malay Peninsula, as a presumed steadying influence on the bad habits of single Chinese men, meant that thousands of Chinese women began to arrive in the peninsula, Phuket and Bangkok. These women were highly valued by Chinese men in Siam: "The price of the bride, or 'milk money' as it was called, was from 50-200 [baht] for a Thai peasant girl, from 100-300 for a Sino-Thai girl and from 300-500 for a Chinese girl."[917]

With more Chinese women around, Chinese men started integrating less with Thais, they raised their children as Chinese and the Chinese started becoming a more separate society – and the one that controlled most of the business in Siam, had powerful secret societies, took the jobs of Thais and paid less in tax than the Thais. This all led to increasing Thai animosity against them. In 1910, not long before his death, Rama V had amended the tax rules so that Chinese who previously had to pay no tax now had to pay the same tax as the Siamese. This had caused huge Chinese riots and Chinese shops and businesses closed in protest, the economy ground to halt and it became apparent just how much of a stranglehold the Chinese really had over Siam's economy.

Shortly after these Chinese riots and strikes, a pamphlet was widely circulated, entitled "The Jews of the East". It was written by an anonymous author called "Asavabhahu" and was widely believed to be the pen name of Rama VI himself. In it, the author virulently attacked the Chinese, claiming they had little loyalty to Siam, that they avoided their civic duties as citizens, had ominous secret societies and regarded the Siamese as barbarians who existed only to be robbed or cheated. The pamphleteer wrote that the Chinese drew off all the money in the economy and remitted it to China and were

> "willing to undergo any sort of privation for the sake of money … anyone who has watched Chinese coolies eat cannot but feel a sense of revulsion, since it seems that the food they eat would hardly attract the curs who roam the streets … As for living it is amazing that so many persons can squeeze themselves into a space so small no other race could breathe in it. It is not surprising that the Chinese can therefore manage to corner all the available work for themselves."[918]

These articles set out the main Siamese gripes against the Chinese, although, as Victor Purcell, a historian of the Chinese in Siam points out, the writer "ignored the fact that without the Chinese there would have been little wealth to draw off."[919]

Resurrecting this anti-Chinese sentiment under the slogan "Thailand for the Thais", Luang Wichit launched a Hitlerite public campaign vilifying the Chinese and instituting pro-Thai policies that essentially allowed Phibun's clique a freer hand to take lucrative businesses away from the Chinese and allocate them to themselves and their military and police cronies. The Thai government, for reasons of pride and national security, also formed state corporations and nationalized many sectors of the economy which were at that time dominated by Chinese and other foreigners, such as salt, tobacco, vehicle hire, shipping and oil importation. Several licenses were given out in the 1930s and early 1940s to Thais to start banks, another business previously dominated by foreigners.

A signboard act was passed, heavily taxing any signs written in Chinese. Chinese were also prohibited from working in strategic occupations or strategic areas of the country. Strategic occupations, reserved only for Thais, included working in government, banking, the police and the armed forces. Other trades classified as strategic were somewhat more obscure – bricklayers and barbers – though one can see some sense in the latter; a Thai government official, busy purloining Chinese businesses, would probably feel rather uncomfortable having a Chinaman holding a sharp razor so close to his throat in the morning.

Phuket's Chinese in Stormy Seas

In Phuket, after the introduction of more mechanized mining techniques around the turn of the century, the Chinese population had started to decline from its high of around 50,000. By the 1920s there were probably fewer than 25,000 Chinese on Phuket, more and more of whom were now mixed-race Peranakan (local-born) mestizo Sino-Thais. As these Peranakan mixed Sino-Thais families effectively ran the local government and as the island was a smaller, more relaxed place than Bangkok, the Thai and

Chinese communities in Phuket generally got along less acrimoniously than in Bangkok. Nevertheless the highly lucrative bird's nest concessions in Phang Nga were taken from the existing wealthy local Phuket Chinese concessionaires by the new Thai military government officials, who handily classified the islands off Phuket where the nests were collected as "strategic areas."

When Phibun took power, there were some 259 Chinese schools in Siam and the majority of these, including most in Phuket, were either closed by the new regime or were reduced to teaching no more than two hours a week in Chinese. One Chinese elder in Phuket recalled how, in the old Thai Hua Chinese school on Krabi Road in Phuket City, a lookout was posted to watch for the local schools inspector (a Chinese himself). The Chinese pupils were drilled so that, if the inspector was seen approaching, they would run out the back, hide their Chinese books and return to the classroom with Thai books. The Thai Chronicle newspaper reported in August 1939:

35.3 *The Chinese couple Mr Chengtek and Mrs Daeng Ekaslip, in their living room in Phuket Town during the Phibun era. Like many other Chinese they had already taken Thai names.*

"By the middle of August more than thirty Chinese schools and ten of the eleven Chinese newspapers had been closed, numbers of Chinese had been deported, hundreds were being called in for the Tong [secret society] probes. Raids on Chinese schools, newspaper plants and homes were becoming a daily occurrence, several prominent Chinese were put in jail for remitting too much money back to China and the entire Chinese community was in an uproar."920

In Phuket, to circumvent these restrictions, the local Chinese started to send their children to Chinese boarding schools in Penang instead, but the Thai government also tried to close this loophole by decreeing that the parents of any child of school age who left Siam would be liable to a hefty 500 baht tax on each departure. The richer Chinese and Peranakan families in Phuket, however, could handle this, and most well-to-do Phuket Chinese and Peranakan families continued to send their children to schools in Penang, as some still do today.

In 1940, the number of new Chinese allowed to enter Thailand was cut from 10,000 a year to just 200 and another new law made it compulsory for anyone born in Thailand to take Thai nationality, not that of their father, as before. A new revenue code taxed the commercial class – that is, the Chinese – very heavily, and the alien registration fee doubled. By 1938, in the face of these measures, immigration had reversed and more Chinese were leaving Siam than arriving. The net result was that those Chinese who elected to stay in Thailand were forced to sidestep this battery of anti-Chinese laws by taking up Thai citizenship and Thai names, speaking Thai and acting like Thai. Pranee

Sakulpipatana, an elder Phuket Sino-Thai, sums up the outcome, namely that, after Phibun, the Chinese majority in Phuket "all ended up with Chinese blood, Indian names (as most Thai names have an Indian origin) and Thai nationality." She recalls her Chinese grandfather in Phuket town, during Phibun's second term in office, putting down his morning paper and cursing Luang Wichit (who was himself believed to be either half or 100 percent Chinese). He then solemnly warned the family, "We Chinese are in stormy waters, we need to be keep our heads down and be especially vigilant of our ship."[921]

The other way for the Chinese to buy economic shelter from this storm was by inviting high-ranking Thai members of the government and armed forces to take a share in their businesses. Phibun and his military and government clique, in essence, weaned the Chinese off working with, or for, the old royal ruling élite and on to working with his new military élite.

Laws were also passed decreeing that no foreigners could control land or any "strategic" business in Thailand. Phibun made this principle clear in a speech in 1938, stating that "foreigners … should not be allowed to take all kinds of jobs from the owners of the country."[922] Under Phibun's tenure, the process was begun that forced foreign companies to take in majority Thai shareholders or suffer discriminatory rules against them; these rules are still in force today.

Squeezing the Muslims and Indians

It was not just the Chinese who were targeted. The Muslims, Malays and Indians were also pressured to give up their traditional clothes and headdresses, adopt the new Thai rules of dress and behavior and change their names, religion and culture to conform with the official strictures.

It is estimated there were between 30,000 and 60,000 Indians – Hindus, Sikhs and Muslims – in the country at the time,[923] mainly living in Bangkok, but with quite a few in Phuket who had come up from Malaya with British companies to work as supervisors, technicians or security guards in the mines. Many of these Indians started their own trading, textile-importing or money-lending businesses and established communities in Phuket. In 1939, for example, the first Sikh Gurdwara (temple) was built in Phuket town. These Indians were often disliked by the Thais, partly because they were usually harder working and better businessmen, but also because many were involved in usury and charged high interest rates that the Thais often could not repay.

Wichit's nationalistic propaganda painted the Indians in an especially negative fashion, as dark-skinned, selfish money-grubbers who did not assimilate culturally and repatriated their profits to India, to which they would eventually return. Most of the Indians, however, being just as shrewd as the Chinese, also sidestepped the slew of new racist laws and learned Thai, took on Thai nationality, integrated and where possible assimilated.

Islam and Islamic laws concerning marriage and divorce were also banned. The Malays, however, particularly in southeast Thailand, simply refused to comply. This brought on some heavy oppression from the unchecked Thai army and police. A British journalist from Malaya, who was in the south of Thailand at the time, reported:

"The Siamese officials are trying their best to put the Islamic religion out of existence in the state by forcing the Malays to believe in Buddhism. They order the Malays to pay homage to or worship Buddhist idols ... they must wear European hats in place of their turbans, while women must put on western skirts or gowns. People failing to obey are punished."[924]

Any minorities in Thailand who refused to follow Phibun's dictatorial edicts were treated very heavy-handedly. The Thai historian, Kobkua Suwannathat-Pian, tells us: "Not being Buddhist was considered a social stigma and discriminatory measures were employed against those who refused to embrace the national religion ... no jobs in government, firings, police harassment, fines, jail and economic harassment."[925]

With the birth of Thailand, despite the fact that historically the Malays and Indians had been on the peninsula and Phuket Island over a thousand years longer than the Thais, they started being referred to as "Khaek", a rather derogatory word meaning "guest" or "outsider". Through such forceful laws, methods and propaganda, in just a few years, Phibun succeeded in creating the new country of Thailand out of old Siam and changing the look and feel of the country so that it became a more modern nationalist Thai state.

Many Thais, however, disagreed with Phibun and his clique, believing that their actions were, at best, not well intentioned. The Thai Colonel Phraya Rith-Akahany, one of the original anti-royal revolutionary ringleaders in 1932, wrote:

"I cannot believe, even now, that one man alone could be the cause of all that happened to the Thai way of life and habits ... I think that this one man must have had inept friends ... for such inept friends would always have let him have his way ... during my involvement with the National Council for Culture, it greatly saddened me to see that in a critical time the country was clearly in the hands of those who harboured dishonesty in their hearts and were ... untrue to their friends."[926]

Today some of the more liberal (and also a few of the more reactionary) Thai academics still call for the abolition of Thailand as it now is and the reinstatement of traditional Siam.

36

"The Losing Side Will Be Our Enemy"

1935 TO 1943

Japan and Thailand Become Bedfellows

In 1932, at the time of the Thai revolution, Britain and France were still predominant in most aspects of Thailand's economic and foreign policy. Phibun, however, turned towards increasingly powerful and ambitious Japan as a potential partner for his further aggrandizement. Japanese business penetration and immigration into Thailand grew rapidly under his rule. By the late 1930s cheap Japanese products such as cotton textiles, matches, bicycles and toys had begun flooding the Thai market. Japanese banks opened branches and Japanese companies started offering funding and bidding to construct new roads, new harbors, an oil refinery and even the proposed Kra Isthmus canal project. By 1939, Japanese ships were carrying the biggest share of Thailand's trade and Japan overtook both Britain and America in supplying arms to Thailand's military and was also sending pilots and engineers as trainers and advisers.

In return, when Japan invaded Manchuria in 1937, Phibun's Thailand was one of only a few states in the League of Nations to support Japan. Nevertheless, the League voted to put an embargo on Japan for its aggressive belligerence in China. This embargo was supported by the Western powers and all their Asian colonies. This meant Japanese industry was now denied the commodities and raw materials they previously obtained from the Western nations' colonies in Southeast Asia. So they turned towards friendly Thailand which was the only Asian market into which Japan could still expand and also one of a very few which could still supply Japan (and through it her Axis partners Germany and Italy) with rice and of course tin and rubber which had become critical to these countries' military machines.

Assisted by Phibun's most pro-Japanese minister, Wanit Pananom, Japanese companies started buying up much of Thailand's commodities – rice, sugar, rubber, wood and tin – and selling basic manufactured goods, such as toys, textiles, chinaware and military equipment, to Thailand in exchange. Japanese companies also started buying up land in southern Thailand to establish rubber plantations. In 1938 Mitsubishi Mining Company was granted rights to start tin mining in Surathani district and also applied for mining rights in Phuket. Japanese agents came to Phuket and attempted to buy up as much of the island's tin and rubber production as they could get their hands on. In 1941 Japan made a bid to buy the whole of Thailand's tin and rubber production for the year, but the Allies pressured Phibun to resist this and in reality it was too hard to arrange.

Okura Tokuji was one of these Japanese tin buyers. He was posted to Thailand by the Mitsubishi Shoji Company in 1941:

> "[I had] orders to buy all I could and get it to Japan as fast as I could. There was no ore to be had in Bangkok so I left for Phuket, cash in hand, to do my buying … back then there weren't any banks in southern Thailand and because I would have to deal with Chinese, who for the most part did business in cash and to expedite the buying, I took baht with me wrapped in a cloth Bundle … On the train south … I'd be asking for trouble if I slept with it placed beside me, so I tied it to my leg and went to sleep. In the south there were quantities of ore available, I'd pay the money and have load after load shipped … In this way I was able to get a goodly amount of ore shipped off to Japan by the time the war broke out."[927]

By the late 1930s, with Japan and Germany becoming increasingly militaristic and belligerent, the dark shadow of war began to loom over Europe and Asia. As early as 1935, British Intelligence first heard of a secret Japanese plan to pass through Thailand to attack British Malaya, Singapore, Burma and the oil-and-commodity-rich Dutch East Indies. Japan wanted Phibun's cooperation for this, whilst Britain also wanted his cooperation to help defend Malaya. The Great Powers became acutely aware of

36.1 Thailand's military prepares for war.

Thailand's strategic position as the center of Southeast Asia and the ever-opportunistic Phibun, seeing an advantage in this situation, played up to all sides, seeking maximum benefit for himself, his cronies and Thailand. Officially Phibun's public line was that Thailand would stay neutral. "Neutrality is the best policy for us … if we are friendly to all, who will be hostile to us? Conversely were we to become hostile to others who would be good to us?"[928]

The Thai/Indochina War of 1941

In late 1939 war broke out in Europe and by June 1940 France had fallen to Hitler's Blitzkrieg. In French Indochina a new pro-Axis French Vichy government took over. In September 1940 a large Japanese force advanced from their war in China into Vietnam to close the Haiphong to Yunnan railway that was being used to supply the Chinese forces. When the Franco-Vietnamese Vichy forces attempted to stop this Japanese intrusion they were badly defeated. On the back of this defeat the Vietnamese communist rebels then started a general armed uprising. Seeing this weakness in French Indochina, whose meager military forces were spread thinly and were under severe pressure, the ever-opportunistic Phibun decided to formally request from Hanoi an immediate correction of the Thai-Indochina border and the return of those lands that had earlier been forcibly grabbed from Siam by France. The Vichy French rejected this request. So, in November 1940, to the accompaniment of jingoistic propaganda in the Thai press such as the largest circulation and very nationalist Thai Rasdr and then anti-French rallies in Bangkok, 60,000 Thai soldiers advanced into Cambodia and Laos, supported by 134 new Mitsubishi and Vickers tanks from Japan and Britain plus 140 aircraft from the USA and Japan and even some Japanese pilots. The Thai forces made good gains in Laos but were held in Cambodia.

The small Thai navy moved its ships down to the southeast Thai islands of Ko Chang and Ko Mok off the French Indochina (now Cambodian) border. However the older but bigger and stronger Vichy French Indochina fleet found them there and attacked at 6. 20 a. m. on January 17, 1941. By 9. 20 a. m. – just three hours later, at no cost to the Vichy French – all of Thailand's expeditionary naval force, indeed almost its whole navy, was sunk.

On land, the two armies became deadlocked. Phibun had to request help from his new friend Japan, which brought a powerful naval squadron south to stand off Vung Tao in Vietnam and then strongly pressured Vichy Indochina to accede to a peace agreement with Thailand. Vichy Indochina was in no position to resist Japan and had to agree. Under Japan's "mediation", some of Siam's "lost territories" west of the Mekong were returned to Thailand. This was probably General Phibun's finest hour, winning him acclaim from many Thais. In recognition of his own brilliance, Phibun had the Victory Monument built in Bangkok and promoted himself to Field Marshal.

Captain Torigoe Shinichi, the Japanese Special Liaison Officer with Thailand at the time, reported back to Tokyo that in return for this Japanese help Field Marshal Phibun had re-confirmed his secret agreement with Japan that if they chose to attack Malaya he "would permit the passage of troops through south Thailand and would provide provisions and other resources."[929] Phibun had also apparently agreed that Thailand's newly established national bank would extend war loans to Japan.

Duplicitous Phibun

Japan soon moved its troops and planes into bases in Indochina along the Thai border and was now within striking distance of British Malaya. By late 1941 it appeared increasingly likely to the Allies that Japan was going to launch an attack on Malaya and it was now the turn of the British in Malaya to become paranoid. Malaya was desperately short of men, planes and ships and Britain, stretched by the war in Europe, could send little help, reinforcements or new materiel. Britain now urgently needed Thailand's co-operation to try to defend Malaya. However Japan also needed Thailand's cooperation to attack it. But neither the British nor the Japanese trusted the word of the duplicitous, self-serving Phibun or trusted what he might actually do if the Japanese did invade

Thailand. The British ambassador to Thailand, Sir Josiah Crosby, prophesied that "it will always be their [Thai politicians'] instinctive policy to side with the stronger party. They will sit on the fence as long as they can and not leave it until they feel sure they have spotted the winner."[930]

The British in Malaya began to draw up plans for a potential preemptive invasion of southern Thailand. One was called Operation Etonian, which was to be a full invasion as far north as Chumporn and Ranong, including taking Phuket Island with its airport, port and tin resources. Under this plan, British Malaya would be directly linked to British Burma. The second option was Operation Matador, a scaled-down invasion to capture the rail and road junction of Hat Yai and the port, airstrip and railhead at Songkla and deny access to these facilities by any Japanese invaders. The strategic importance of these positions was that they were located on the flattest area of the peninsula where forces could be deployed most rapidly from one coast to another. Further south Malaysia is divided by high central mountains ranges making such deployments harder and much slower. From Bangkok, however, Sir Josiah Crosby argued vehemently against either move, believing such a preemptive strike would make the Thais regard Britain as the enemy.

To the Allies Phibun openly implied that he would be willing to fight with them against Japan. In 1940 he signed a mutual non-aggression pact with Britain, promising not to assist any third party in a war against Malaya and also using the occasion to ask Britain for loans and deliveries of planes and tanks. Just afterwards, however, Phibun also made a "secret proviso" with Japan: if they would ensure the return of those Malay states that Siam had lost to Britain in 1909 he "indicated … his intention to go with Japan if it declared war on Britain."[931]

It does appear that by not disclosing his intentions, the opportunist Phibun probably felt he could still milk the situation to get the best deals from both his important new suitors – the Allies and Japan. In November 1941, for example, Britain did send Thailand some limited field artillery, ammunition and aviation fuel. Phibun officially rejected this paltry offer and demanded planes and tanks, as he was getting from Japan. His capricious actions led the British ambassador in Bangkok to write disparagingly to London that Phibun was as "unstable as water", motivated by extreme vanity, and that under his nationalist cabinet "Thailand is behaving nowadays like a prostitute ready to sell herself to the highest bidder."[932]

To the Thai public Field Marshal Phibun spoke most heroically, declaring that Thailand would remain neutral. If necessary, he defiantly promised to undertake a scorched-earth policy within Thailand to deny provisions to any invader and he stirringly exhorted the people to resist any aggressor. "We must be determined to defend our neutrality … I implore you, my fellow countrymen, to sacrifice even your lives for the neutrality and safety of our nation."[933] In late 1941, the Thai Assembly then passed a law making it the legal duty of all Thais to resist to the death any foreign aggressor on their soil. Refusal to do so would be punished by death! – not really leaving the people a great choice in the matter. [934] It is better, propaganda minister Wichit declared heroically on radio broadcasts, "to die as freemen than to live as slaves."[935]

In early 1942 Phibun's opportunist intentions were fleetingly divulged, much as ambassador Crosby had foretold, when he reportedly asked his chief-of-staff, "Which side do you think will be defeated in this war? That side is our enemy."[936] Phibun formally announced to his cabinet on November 28, 1941 that if war came, "It was better to side with [Japan] because Thailand would suffer less and, if Japan were victorious, Thailand could get back its lost territories."[937] On December 2, 1941, just a few days before the Pacific War started, Phibun sent an order to all his military commanders "to be in preparedness to repulse the Japanese if they invaded."[938] Yet the very next day, December 3, the Japanese military attaché in Bangkok, Col. Hiroshi, reported to Tokyo that Phibun had just confirmed to him "that he would overlook any Japanese military operations south of Prachup Kiri Khan Province",[939] meaning that he was going to allow the Japanese to freely enter and pass through the south of Thailand to attack Malaya.

These three totally contradictory declared positions – Phibun's speeches to the Thai public ordering them to resist any invader to the death, his agreement to side with Britain and his agreement to side with Japan and to let them pass through Thailand unmolested – were utterly incompatible. On the very eve of war, it still remained unclear to the Japanese, the Allies and even his own cabinet which course the duplicitous, self-serving Phibun might actually choose.

Phuket Prepares for War

In Phuket, the war in Europe meant that the tin and rubber markets were badly affected by a lack of shipping, and production fell drastically as there was a severe shortage of fuel oil and electricity for the mines. In 1939, when Italy joined the war on the German side, two unarmed Italian cargo ships, the Sumatra and the Volpi, were in the Bay of Bengal in British-controlled waters. Rather than be captured, these ships had made for Phuket as the nearest neutral port. The crews then scuttled the two ships in what is now the deep sea port at Ao Makam and the Italian sailors stayed on Phuket, essentially on holiday, while the war raged in Europe. Being Italians, they soon worked their charms on the local girls and to this day their descendents still form a small Thai-Italian sub-population on Phuket.

British plans were made for evacuating the roughly 250 Allied personnel living in Phuket, mainly Australian and British, but also a few Dutch and Indian mining engineers, managers and their families. Major Warren Parsons, a retired Australian military officer who had come to Phuket in 1932 to work for Tongkah Harbour Mining Cᵒ , was appointed the Allied coordinator for the defense and evacuation of Phuket's foreign personnel. From Singapore and Penang, weapons and radios were smuggled into Phuket on Tongkah Harbour Cᵒ ships disguised as mining equipment or hidden in oil drums, and were secretly held at the Tongkah Harbour compound at Saphan Hin to be distributed to the Allied foreigners if the Japanese invaded. Maj. Parsons made arrangements that, in the event of a Japanese invasion, the farangs were to gather at Saphan Hin in Phuket town and a Tongkah Harbour boat would take them to the north of the island to the airstrip where British aircraft would fly up from Malaya to evacuate them.

The local Chinese started to move some of their valuable assets out of Phuket down to Penang, as did the Standard Chartered Bank. Or they simply hid them or buried them in the forests, as they had done in the old days. The Chinese were well aware of the maltreatment of Chinese and the atrocities the Japanese were committing against them in their war in China. Many wealthy Phuket Chinese had been big buyers of Chinese war bonds to support their homeland in the war against Japan. Some of the richer Chinese fled to Penang or prepared hiding places and refuges for themselves in more humble houses in the country, living like plantation workers in the forest. The Muslims on Phuket tended not to take sides and for the most part continued with their fishing, farming and businesses.

The governor of Phuket at the time was Captain Luang Teanprasitsarn, a former military officer. He instructed the Thai soldiers, police and Yuwachon (youth) brigades that if Thailand was invaded, they should immediately secure the strategic points on the island – the radio towers, the telegraph line, government offices, the port and the airfield – and be ready to defend them to the death.

Meanwhile, many new Japanese residents and visitors had begun appearing in Phuket and all over the central peninsula. Ostensibly they were there only as tourists, businessmen, tin buyers, dentists or toy salesmen, but as Seni Pramoj, the later Thai prime minister recalls, "It was an open secret among the Thai people that nearly all of these strangers from the north were engaged in espionage."[940] The Japanese in Phuket were also secretly smuggling in arms and military uniforms with instructions that, when the Japanese invasion of the peninsula started, they were to don their uniforms and order or coerce the Thais, depending on their reaction to the

36.2. War atrocities: Japanese troops using live Chinese prisoners for bayonet practice. Phuket's Chinese, were well aware of the atrocities the Japanese were inflicting on Chinese in all the lands they were occupying.

invasion, to let them take control of the island's strategic points – particularly the airfield – and hold them till the arrival of the Japanese army.

So, for the historian looking back, it would appear that, if war did come, with the Thais, the Allies and the Japanese on Phuket all intent on immediately taking control of the airfield, this was probably where the action was going to be.

37

Saved by the Bombs

1942 TO 1945

In early December 1941 an American reconnaissance plane observed that over 50 Japa-nese war and transport ships had gathered at Cam Ranh Bay in Vietnam. Was this the expected Japanese invasion fleet? Was it bound for Siam, British Malaya or the Phil-ippines? A tropical storm then formed over the South China Sea covering the region in cloud. By December 5 when partial visibility returned, the huge fleet had moved.

Allied planes from Singapore, Malaya and the Philippines frantically took off into the stormy and ominous skies to locate this missing fleet. At 9:00 a.m. on December 7, one of these reconnaissance planes – a British Catalina piloted by a young Australian, Patrick Bedell and seven British crew members from the Malayan Volunteer Air Force – was searching in blustery weather over the South China Sea when five Japanese Na-kajima Ki-27 fighters came out of the cloud behind them in an attacking pass, guns blazing, and riddling the slower-moving Catalina with bullets. The Catalina exploded in midair. The plane's wreckage and its young crew plummeted to their deaths in the choppy, grey South China Sea far below before any radio message could be sent.

Unbeknownst to the Catalina crew they had been almost over the missing Japanese fleet. Flying officer Bedell and his crew were shot down some 17 hours before the Japa-nese air strike on Pearl Harbor and were probably the first Allied casualties of the coming Pacific War, which would claim millions more lives over the next three years. The stormy weather and low cloud cover meant the Japanese invasion fleet was still not located for the rest of the day.

Japan Invades

That night the stormy weather had reached southeast Thailand. At 11:40 p.m. two Thai policemen patrolling the Samila beach road in Songkla thought they saw, about a kilo-meter out to sea, what looked like the dark silhouettes of several ships with their lights suspiciously off. On board one of these 20 ships was Colonel Tsuji of Yamashita's crack 25th Army, battle hardened from years in the China campaign. His troops were to be the first to go ashore. Col. Tsuji recounts the scene:

> "Our large transport ship was rolling heavily … When the boats were lowered into the water, the engineers, with the agility of monkeys, climbed into them. Soon, nearly a hundred landing craft were floating beside the transports, tossing up and down on the waves like the leaves of a tree in the wind. With poles, the

engineers desperately kept them from bumping the sides of the transports. In the dim moonlight the loading of the boats somehow proved easier than had been thought possible. Soon the signal appeared 'Commence transshipment'."[941]

The landing craft headed to the shore in the darkness and landed near Samila beach. Japanese infantrymen poured out and ran ashore at a low crouch into the casuarina trees lining the beach. Some local members of the Thai civil defense units, imbued with Field Marshal Phibun's recent fiery radio speeches, had just been alerted by the police and had fetched some guns. They began to appear on the beach road ready to fight off these invaders. In 2005, 75-year-old Saman Mahanpan from Songkla, who witnessed the invasion as a 12-year-old boy, described the scene. "The first thing the Japanese did was to climb up the telephone poles to cut the wires. Some folk shot at them. The Japanese were brave … one fell but another soon took his place. They didn't care about being shot."[942]

Cutting the phone lines was important because that landing in the wee hours in Songkla was the first landing that day of a vast Japanese attack, not only on Thailand, but all around the Asia Pacific region. The huge Japanese invasion fleet had split up in the Gulf of Thailand and other landings were taking place or just about to take place at Patani, Nakorn Sri Thammarat, Surathani, Chumporn, Prachup Kiri Khan and Kota Baru in Malaya. In addition, all along the Cambodian frontier that night, thousands of troops from Japan's crack Imperial Guard crossed into Thailand heading for Bangkok. A few hours later (due to the international dateline it was on December 7) the American naval and airbases of Pearl Harbor and then Clark and Subic in the Philippines would be attacked and Japan would also bomb Singapore, Hong Kong and even invade the bleak, wintry Aleutian Islands off Alaska.

In the afternoon of December 7, just before this invasion, Field Marshal Phibun had left Bangkok, rather suspiciously, telling almost no one. He headed out to somewhere near Aranyapathet on an "inspection tour" of the eastern province. That evening, just after he had left, the Japanese presented the Thai government with an ultimatum – they were going to invade Thailand that night. They gave the Thais three choices:

1 Fight them and be at war.
2 Join them to fight the British.
3 Simply do not resist and let them pass into Malaya.

No one but Phibun could make such a momentous decision, as Colonel Tamura Hiroshi, the Japanese military attaché to Thailand at the time, had informed his superiors in Japan, "Phibun definitely had control of Thailand's government."[943] The cabinet eventually contacted Phibun and a plane was sent off to get him. He refused the plane and instead he elected to return by car, a trip that took several hours so that he did not arrive back in Bangkok till 7:30 a.m. the next morning, December 8, after the invasion had started and Thai army and militia were already fighting and resisting the Japanese. Phibun called an urgent cabinet meeting and just after 11:00 a.m. a decision was made – the Japanese would not be resisted. Phibun then made a public radio announcement to

Map 12
The Japanese Invasion of the Peninsula 7th to 8th December 1941

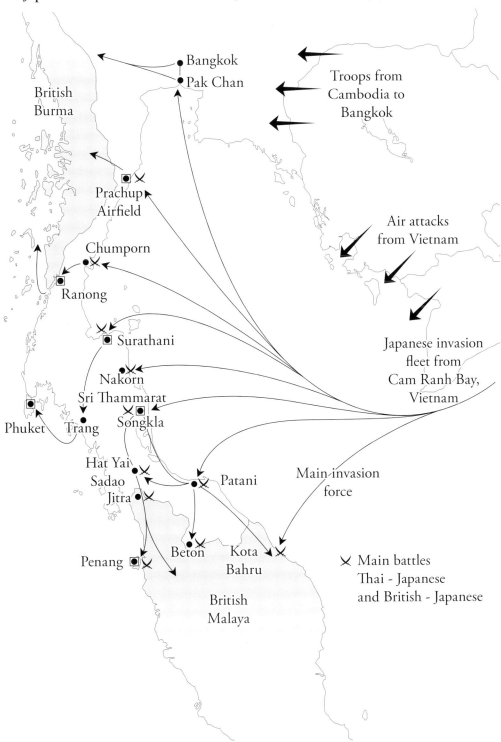

Bangkok
Pak Chan

Troops from
Cambodia to
Bangkok

British
Burma

Prachup
Airfield

Air attacks
from Vietnam

Chumporn

Ranong

Japanese invasion
fleet from
Cam Ranh Bay,
Vietnam

Surathani

Nakorn
Sri Thammarat

Songkla

Phuket

Trang

Main invasion
force

Hat Yai
Sadao
Jitra

Patani

Penang

Beton

Kota
Bahru

✗ Main battles
Thai - Japanese
and British - Japanese

British
Malaya

the country at 11:55 a.m., explaining the Thai cabinet decision to order a ceasefire and to let the Japanese pass. This he said was "deemed the best course to follow in the interests of the country under such circumstances. From now on please rest assured that Japan is Thailand's friend." [944]

Orders were immediately sent out to the Thai field commanders to cease resistance. But for hundreds of Japanese and Thai soldiers, police, airmen, schoolboys and militiamen who died that morning, Phibun's ceasefire announcement came too late.

Southern Thai Resistance Battles: Songkla

Earlier that morning, at around 2:45 a.m. in Songkla, with no other instructions than the field marshal's recent militaristic exhortations to resist any invaders to the death, the Thai people were prepared to fight. Men such as 30-year-old Captain Dejd Tulawa-nthana of the 13th Artillery Battalion in Songkla who recalled: "After being woken by the alarm I quickly got dressed and grabbed my field glasses and pistol … before I sped away to report to my barracks … I told Private Bua [his batman] that all my belongings in my compartment were his if I died."

Colonel Tsuji, a Japanese spy chief, in his later testimony said that the plan was that there was to have been no resistance in Songkla, as the Japanese consul there, who was also the town's dentist, had already paid off the local Thai police and army chiefs. According to Tsuji, the plan was that crack Japanese troops were to have been supplied with Thai police uniforms and some local dance hall girls. They were then to drive south to try to cross the Malayan border in the early hours, waving Union Jacks and with the dance hall girls acting provocatively to distract the British Indian border guards. The Thai police had allegedly taken the Japanese money but had still resisted.

The outnumbered Thai forces defending Songkla town were soon encircled and by-passed. The Japanese moved straight on and captured the local airfield before four pre-arranged squadrons of Japanese Zero fighters flew in from Vietnam to base themselves there. Eyewitness accounts at the time claim some 15 Japanese and 23 Thais were killed in the fighting. The bulk of the Japanese troops concentrated on rapidly off-loading materiel, while others headed off quickly by truck and commandeered local buses and a train going towards Hat Yai and the Malayan border.

Southern Thai Resistance Battles: Hat Yai

These Japanese forces leaving Songkla by rail and bus encountered stern resistance at the Hat Yai rail junction where the Thai army and locals had blocked the road and railway with road construction vehicles. Fierce close-range fighting started as the first Japanese troops arrived by bus at around 4:00 a.m. The Thai troops, who were increasingly outnumbered as more Japanese troops arrived in Hat Yai, retreated slowly, but they still prevented the Japanese forces from advancing for several hours until around midday when they received Phibun's instructions ordering them to cease resistance. Some 20 Thais soldiers died in the action near Hat Yai and many more were wounded.

Southern Thai Resistance Battles: Surathani

The Japanese landed unopposed near Surathani in the darkness and marched into town in heavy rain. There was desultory street fighting for several hours against armed Thai police and civilians until the order came for the Thais to lay down their arms. From Surathani, Japanese troops crossed by rail to the Trang railhead and from there about 400 came north by boat to occupy Phuket.

Southern Thai Resistance Battles: Chumporn

Twelve ships disembarked the crack Japanese 143rd Infantry Battalion on the beaches near Chumporn. As they approached the town they encountered resistance from Thai armed police units and schoolboys of the local Yuwachon (youth) brigades roused from their beds. Under heavy fire and outnumbered these police and school children stubbornly held their ground and succeeded in preventing the Japanese infantry from entering the town until the ceasefire instructions arrived after midday. The Japanese then entered the town, boarded trucks and crossed over the peninsula by road to Ranong and the British Burma border. Seventeen brave Thai schoolboys and police died in the fighting in Chumporn that morning.

Southern Thai Resistance Battles: Prachup Kiri Khan

This town saw one of the most heroic Thai defenses take place. The first Japanese troops had landed in the darkness at around 3:00 a.m. and advanced into the sleeping town. A Japanese soldier approached the local police station with a note demanding the town's surrender. A Thai police sentry challenged him and a scuffle ensued in which the Thai sentry bayoneted the Japanese. The Japanese troops immediately opened fire, killing the sentry and firing into the wooden police quarters where over 20 Thai police were sleeping. The startled policemen inside, partially dressed, grabbed guns and fired back. Then a grenade exploded inside the wooden station and Japanese troops burst in and shot most of the defenders.

The Prachup airfield at the north end of beautiful sweeping Manao Bay, the base of the Fifth Wing of the Royal Thai Air Force, was attacked by the main Japanese force but they were kept at bay by vicious fire from two Thai machine guns posts, one set up on the airbase tennis court. Some of the young Thai pilots in Prachup had got up early that morning to go night fishing further along the beach. On seeing the Japanese assault craft they ran back to their airbase and under heavy fire they ran across the runway near the beach to reach their six old bi-wing, two-manned, fighter planes. One pilot was shot dead running to his aircraft. The undercarriage of another plane was shot away while trying to take off and crashed. Three planes did take off and swooped back to attack the Japanese ships in the bay, but Japanese anti-aircraft gunners soon shot down all three slow-moving planes, killing their young pilots and gunners.

Before he could start his plane engine the young pilot of the last Thai aircraft was shot in his cockpit by some Japanese troops who were advancing up the runway from the beach. His rear gunner turned his machine gun against the advancing Japanese, killing several and scattering the rest. He continued to hold them at bay until his machine gun's ammunition ran out, when he leapt from the plane and escaped into the long grass by the runway unhurt.

By the early light of dawn, the Thais had probably killed over a hundred Japanese attackers, but were overrun. The Thai defenders retreated into the forested hill and long grass next to the airfield and airbase and stubbornly kept fighting through the morning until nearly midday, when a civilian car adorned with a white flag, a Thai flag and a Japanese flag, appeared on the airstrip with the Thai provincial secretary, who ordered the defenders to cease firing as Phibun had declared these Japanese were their "friends". Of just under 100 Thai troops defending the airfield, 38 were killed and 28 wounded in the seven-hour battle. All the pilots and many police were also killed. Thai eyewitnesses estimated that over 200 Japanese were killed and some 300 wounded. The Japanese military officially admitted to 115 dead, but they had an interest in underplaying the casualties – they were supposedly being welcomed to Thailand to liberate their Asian brothers. Local eyewitnesses said that the many Japanese bodies littering the airfield "were collected that afternoon and dumped into a large pit and quickly cremated with gasoline in a ceremony that evening."[945]

Southern Thai Resistance Battles: Patani

A Japanese force landed at around 3:00 a.m. in heavy rain in the flat muddy estuary of the Patani River. Seventy-six men from the nearby Thai 42nd Battalion, under the command of Major Ingkay, were alerted and rushed to the scene by truck. They set up a Browning machine gun on the truck and strafed the Japanese infantry coming ashore in the exposed muddy estuary, killing many – possibly over a hundred – before a Japanese grenade was thrown into the truck which killed the gunner and destroyed the machine gun. Close-range firefights then continued on the road into town for several hours. At one point the Japanese made a bayonet charge and fought hand to hand. Major Ingkay was hit by a machine gun blast and although badly wounded he continued fighting and directing the battle. When the Japanese infantry reached Patani town, armed police, civilian volunteers and Yuwachon schoolboys prevented them from crossing the bridge over the Patani River. Five brave schoolboys died holding the bridge. By late morning a telegram came from Bangkok ordering all fighting to cease. The Japanese commandeered all the Thai military and civilian trucks in town and immediately set off for the Malayan border. Major Ingkay died of his wounds, as did over 40 of his men. Local Thai witnesses later claimed that nearly 200 Japanese invaders had been killed. [946]

Southern Thai Resistance Battles: Nakorn Sri Thammarat

Probably the nastiest fighting took place that stormy morning round Camp Vajiravudh, the headquarters of the Thai Sixth Army Division. The Japanese had started landing at about 3:00 a.m. at Tha Pae and Japanese infantry columns carrying Thai flags headed inland. Major General Luang Senanarong, the Thai camp commander, sent out patrols into the rainy night and before the first light of dawn the fighting started. The Thais from the military camp used their two Bofors guns on the base to start bombarding the Japanese landing area. But a heavy and accurate return barrage from the Japanese warships offshore knocked out the Thai guns and killed several of the Thai artillerymen.

Nasty close-quarters fighting took place in the early dawn rain and mud in amongst the swamps, canals and mangroves on either side of the Tha Pae Road. Thai machine gun crews in the marshes held out under intense Japanese fire from just a few meters away; those who died were quickly replaced. One truckload of Thai infantry got bogged down within range of a Japanese heavy machine gun which raked the truck, killing many. A Japanese column was mowed down while crossing a wooden bridge by two already-wounded Thai soldiers who had dragged their Madsen heavy machine gun into some nearby reeds. At around 8:00 a.m. the Thais counter-attacked in force and drove the Japanese backwards, but the Japanese advanced again and dead bodies began to litter the elevated Tha Pae Road.

Before midday, General Luang received a telegram from Bangkok instructing him to stop fighting. But amongst the isolated pockets of troops in the swamps, fighting continued till the late afternoon. The following day, after sending his troops to collect the bloodied and muddied corpses of his many dead men and officers from the swamps around the camp, General Luang received a personal telex from Field Marshal Phibun: "Have been informed of your actions. Am exceedingly grateful. Let them pass through. Am extremely sorry for the damage and losses."[947] General Luang apparently ripped up the telex and threw it on the ground in disgust.

Capitulation and the Japanese Advance

Seni Pramoj, the pro-Allied Thai ambassador to the USA at the time, later said, "The capitulation was brought about by Phibun and 'a small clique of four Quislings in the Thai cabinet'."[948] Cynical historians today believe that Phibun had already agreed to work with the Japanese and knew they were coming. They say he had gone away the night before so as to allow limited resistance to occur. This would make it look to his people and the Allies as if his hand had been forced. Going away was probably Phibun's best way off the very sharp horns of the dilemma upon which he had sat himself with his totally contradictory prewar statements. It was in fact a very Thai, opaque, solution. Phibun explained as much to his cabinet, according to the minutes of their emergency meeting the very next morning: "We'll say we made an effort to fight, that finally the Japanese came and asked to negotiate … to continue to fight would be a waste of lives and property. Therefore we were willing to compromise with them and finally we'll ask that the people continue to support their government."[949]

The Thai naval captain, Thian Kengradomying, in the cabinet agreed, "We have done the best thing, we have fought them up to now … it was good you came a little late, if the prime minster had returned too quickly that would have caused trouble too."[950] Khun Wichit his information minister also agreed, saying to Phibun, "About the People, I think they'll accept whatever way the government decides to go because they don't know that much."[951]

In retrospect, capitulation surely was Phibun's best option. To fight Japan would have been suicidal. As Phibun had said to his cabinet just before the invasion, "If we fight and Great Britain does not come to our assistance the country will be in total ruin, the People's Party will lose its credibility ... and we will probably be dead."[952] In fairness to Phibun, he had asked for but received very little military help from Britain or the USA. Crosby, the British ambassador in Bangkok, reported that just before the invasion Phibun had come to see him with a "very oily and conciliatory"[953] manner and had requested British arms and military advisers. But Britain, already stretched in Malaya, had none to give. Churchill in return had only sent a note promising Phibun that "If you are attacked defend yourself, we shall regard an attack on you as an attack on ourselves and we shall come to your aid with the utmost of our power."[954] According to Crosby Phibun had received this answer "badly and with suspicion."

But even the pro-Phibun Crosby was shocked at his rapid capitulation after his brave talk and fiery exhortations. "It would have been better," wrote Ambassador Crosby later, "not to have boasted."[955] Direck Chayanam, the ever urbane Thai foreign minister, replied to Crosby's statement in the usual disarming Thai way. "We had to bluff, we also knew we couldn't fight, but we talked the way we did to try to keep that tiger from coming in."[956]

Phibun's decision to capitulate did, however, spare the people of Thailand and Phuket, particularly the Chinese, from the cruelties, massacres and destruction that befell so many other surrounding countries under Japanese occupation. In 1945, after the war, Alec Adams, Britain's consul general in Bangkok, declared philosophically, "The fault of Phibun was to have been pro-Siamese."[957] The Thai leaders had, it seems, "bent with the wind" yet again.

The rapid succession of Japanese victories in the region over the next few weeks was breathtaking. By December 10, in just four days of intensive bombing, they had destroyed most British air power in the central peninsula. That day off Kelantan, they also sank the only two capital British battleships in the region, the Prince of Wales and the Repulse, with the loss of over 840 men. Churchill later wrote after receiving news of their destruction by Japanese dive bombers: "In all the war I never received a more direct shock ... There were now no British or American ships in the Indian or Pacific Oceans except the American survivors of Pearl Harbor who were hastening back to California. Over all this vast expanse of water Japan was supreme and we were everywhere weak and naked."[958]

A week later, on December 17, the Japanese took Penang, where their troops looted, tortured, raped and massacred thousands of Chinese. The same later happened in Kuala Lumpur, Singapore and other Chinese towns in Malaya. By the end of December, Hong Kong had fallen and America had lost the Philippines. In January 1942 Kuala Lumpur fell. In February and March Singapore, the Andaman Islands, Rangoon and

Java were all overrun. The swaggering white men, after throwing their weight around in the region for over a century, had been most ingloriously hoofed out of Southeast Asia in just a few months. No Allied forces now remained within two thousand kilometers of Phuket, or Thailand, and Japan appeared unstoppable.

With this whirlwind of Japanese successes and possibly to revive the morale of his now rather crestfallen military, the ever-opportunistic Phibun "bent with the wind" yet again. Believing Japan would be the victor Phibun got his cabinet to declare war on the Allies. The historian Kobkua Suwannathat-Pian writes, "It appeared, in Phibun's calculations, that a total commitment to Japan would not only be beneficial to the country and the People's Party but also bring personal glory to himself … and his place in history would be assured."[959] Many Thais disagreed with this declaration of war and some ministers such as the anti-Japanese Pridi Banomyong, Phibun's main opponent within his cabinet, refused to sign the declaration.

The Americans also reportedly refused to accept Thailand's declaration of war, claiming it was done under the heel of Japanese oppression and therefore "thought it better to ignore the matter." Washington pressed London to do the same. The British, however, disagreed, noting that the war declaration had won majority support in both the Thai cabinet and Thai National Assembly and that Thailand and its army were already actively assisting the Japanese in both Malaya and Burma. Richard Law, the British Under Secretary for Foreign Affairs, replied to the US request: "I remain unconvinced … to maintain the fiction that the Thais are a jolly, friendly little people … will irritate further a public opinion which is already highly irritable about the Far East."[960] Britain therefore accepted the Thai declaration of war and replied by sending planes from Burma to bomb the docks and the king's palace in Bangkok.

The War in Phuket

On the morning of the Japanese invasion, the allied European civilians (farangs) on Phuket urgently made their way, as planned, to the airstrip or the Tongkah Harbour Cº ship in Phuket Town which was already loaded with arms, provisions and radios. The ship headed up to the Phuket airfield under the leadership of Major Warren Parsons, the Australian manager of Tongkah Harbour Cº. He spoke Thai, Malay and Hokkien. This group of around 120 armed British, Australian and Dutch expats and their families reached the airfield before the Thai police had secured it. They set up a perimeter defense and then waited as planned for planes to fly up from Malaya to evacuate them. However, due to the heavy Japanese air cover over all northern Malaya and the extensive bombing of all the airfields there no planes were available. The evacuees were informed by radio that they would now have to wait for a ship instead.

Soon, two truckloads of Thai armed police arrived from Phuket town. The farangs, however, refused to give up their defensive position round the airfield as they were ordered. A tense standoff ensued. As Thailand was still officially neutral the Thai police officer, faced with these resolute and well-armed farangs, several of whom he probably knew, artfully decided his best course of action was to return to Phuket town to get further instructions. The governor of Phuket, a friend of Warren Parsons, advised the police not to fight the farangs as Thailand was not at war with the Allies.

Meanwhile, after Phibun's capitulation and ceasefire order that morning, the Japanese "tourists" and "toy salesmen" who had previously gathered in Phuket donned their military uniforms and appeared before the governor demanding he give them control of the island's strategic points until the arrival of Japanese troops. But he simply refused.

Many Chinese and other residents moved out of Phuket town to their pre-arranged hiding places. A large group went to the Thepabutra forest, north of Chalong, where some families stayed for most of the war, clearing the area for new rubber plantations and acting like poor peasants.

The farangs at the airport waited anxiously, not knowing whether the invading Japanese forces would reach Phuket before their rescue ship. The late Prasit Chinakorn, a Phuket historian who was alive during this period, wrote that on the third day of waiting, a British submarine appeared off Mai Kao Beach (near the airport) and the farang evacuees were rowed out to it in wooden boats and taken back to Malaya. However, Rachan Karnchanawanit, a close post-war friend of Major Warren Parsons, is assured it was a British ship not a submarine that came to get them.[961] As Khun Rachan notes, 120 or more farangs could not have fitted into a submarine and Malaya officially had no submarines at the time and even if it had, it would surely have had better uses for them.

Whatever the form of transport, the farangs of Phuket got away to Malaya. Some were captured when Singapore fell a month later and some made it to India and fought against the Japanese in Burma. These included Major Warren Parsons. He returned to Phuket after the war and was later appointed the island's Australian and British honorary consul. He lived in Phuket until 1957, when he retired to his farm in Victoria, Australia with his wife; he died there peacefully in the 1970s.

Two days after the farangs had been evacuated some 400 Japanese troops arrived from Trang to occupy Phuket. They set up three camps, one near Phuket town (at the site of the current bus station on Phang Nga Road), one near the airfield (the site of the current airport today) and the third in Sapam Bay near a reserve airstrip. The main airfield was improved and Japanese planes arrived and used Phuket as a reconnaissance and attack base for Andaman Sea and Bay of Bengal operations. The biggest Japanese military bases and airfields nearby were at Ranong and Surathani. The Japanese improved the road from Phuket to Ranong and they also built the first trans-peninsular railway from Chumporn over to Ranong as a quick way to move materiel west to the Indian Ocean and Burma war theaters before they completed the main "Death Railway" to the west via Kanchanaburi and the River Kwai.

Older locals in Phuket who lived through the war years say that the Japanese troops in Phuket generally behaved themselves well enough. As Thailand was officially Japan's only ally in Asia the troops were ordered not to mistreat or upset the locals. Consequently there was almost no violence towards the Chinese residents, unlike that in the Sook Ching massacres in Singapore and Malaya. One local mining engineer, Sakul Na Nakorn, who lived in Phuket throughout the war years, explained that unless someone was caught actively resisting the Japanese or spying – and only a handful were – the Phuket people were generally unmolested by the Japanese during the war years.

37.1 Farang members of The Miners' Club in Phuket Town just before WWII. When Japan invaded Thailand these armed British, Australian and Dutchmen and their families established a defensive position at the Phuket airfield to wait until they could be evacuated to Malaya.

One of the handful who were tortured was Than Khuon Lertpokaraksa (Lert) of the Hongsyok family. Lert was a former immigrant Chinese coolie who had originally bought a boat to transport people in Phuket harbor. He made good and invested in the first motorboat to take passengers across the Pak Pra channel between Phuket and the mainland. He was invited to drive the boat for Rama VII when he visited Phuket in 1928. In the years before the war Lert had become a trusted friend of Warren Parsons when they had worked on the Tongkah Harbour tin dredgers together. Before he left Phuket, Parsons handed over to Lert all the important British consular and mining documents to keep until his hoped-for return. Khun Lert reportedly buried them in a sealed jerry can. The Japanese, however, got word that Khun Lert knew where these British documents were. He was arrested, interrogated and beaten for three days. "The Japanese could not find it and they pounded and beat me hard, but I never gave away its hiding place."[962]

Lert received his reward after the war in the early 1950s when a subsidiary company belonging to Anglo Oriental Tin and Tongkah Harbour Co called Rang Eng Tin was being closed. Rang Eng owned 9,000 rai of tin-rich land in Rassada in Phuket and

Warren Parsons pushed the joint-venture directors to sell the mines cheaply to Khun Lert. "My farang bosses were very satisfied and some of them sold their mines to me,"[963] explained Lert in an interview in 1966. This deal made him one of Phuket's more prosperous residents. He later married into the old local Na Ranong (Khaw) family and he and his son were the first of the local Chinese tin mining families on Phuket to decide to diversify away from tin mining and into the hotel business; he opened the Pearl Hotel in Phuket town in the 1970s. Khun Lert passed away in 1971 but his family still controls the Pearl Hotel in town, the trendy new Indigo Pearl Resort in Nai Yang Beach plus a lot of land and other businesses on Phuket.

The main impacts of the war for most people of Phuket were severe shortages, economic hardship and insecurity. The Japanese demanded that all tin and rubber be sold to them at pre-arranged prices. These low purchase prices, plus the lack of gasoline and shipping, resulted in tin production falling to just 4 percent of its pre-war 1940 peak. There was also much tin smuggling to sell at a better price on the black market and one Phuket resident, Tan Jin Lai, set up an illegal smelter making much smaller ingots just for this purpose. With little for people to do, the Chinese soon turned to gambling and established casinos in houses in Phuket town and gambling took off again in a big way. Many people ran up huge debts and to pay them off, some people reportedly had to give away their children as workers, or daughters as "mui tsai" (little sisters), to the wealthy and moneylenders just as in the old days.

As there was still no road from Bangkok to Phuket most goods were carried to and from the island by ship from the railhead at Trang. In 1941-43 the British navy was chased out of the Indian Ocean and even had to move its main eastern naval base from Ceylon to Kenya. But by 1944 with the Japanese navy more occupied in the Pacific the British navy became ascendant again in the Andaman Sea and started attacking and sinking many local Thai and Japanese ships traveling to and from Phuket.

In 1944 the youngest submarine captain in the Royal Navy, 21-year-old Captain Tony Troup, brought his submarine Strongbow from Ceylon to patrol around Phuket and Penang. He torpedoed the 800-ton Japanese coaster Toso Maru as it was leaving Phuket harbor. He also recorded sinking nine local junks, a tug and two cargo lighters between Phuket and Penang. In 1944 a Japanese naval destroyer and cargo ship leaving Phuket were sunk by British planes off Ko Kradan Island to the south of Phuket. Also in 1944 SS Petaling, a former Straits Steamship Cº vessel used for carrying tin ore, captured and used by the Japanese for cargo supply to Phuket, was torpedoed by a British submarine in full sight of shore off Nai Harn Bay. The crew escaped and floated in with the current before being picked up off Kata Noi Beach. Another locally owned cargo steamship, the Tong Ho, was also torpedoed and sunk in 1944.

So by late 1944, with the British Navy effectively controlling the Andaman Sea again, and faced with numerous Japanese sea mines planted around Phuket, local boat captains stopped even attempting the risky trip to Trang. This was despite being able to charge huge mark-ups on any goods they brought back to Phuket. Phuket's residents had to become self-sufficient in food. They started using coconut oil instead of gasoline for their vehicles, mining machinery and lighting. And occupied Phuket became a place of oil lamps, early sleepers and sturdy walkers.

37.2 The Phuket supply ship Thong Ho was sunk by a British submarine off Phuket in 1944.

Thai Disaffection and Resistance

Being part of Japan's "Greater East Asia Co-prosperity Sphere" soon palled for most Thais, as the relationship quickly became one of typical colonial exploitation, with Japanese policy being to force Thailand to sell its primary produce – rubber, tin, rice, etc. – at low prices and in turn to buy Japanese manufactured goods at higher prices. Japan also forced Thailand to give it large loans, cleaning out the Thai treasury and collapsing the baht. In addition Japan made its promised delivery of the "lost territories" in the Malay Peninsula conditional on Thai cooperation with its demands. In March 1943 the New York Times – naturally somewhat biased against Japan – reported that Thailand "is afflicted with an economic crisis, inflation and a shortage of commodities. The Japanese who flattered that land into becoming an ally now treat her peoples as slaves."[964] The Thai historian Rong Syamananda says, "In fairness to the Japanese, one could say that they hardly interfered with the daily life of Thai people. However as economic conditions deteriorated they became more and more disliked."[965] This ill will increased with the gradual strangulation of the Thai economy. Seni Pramoj, the pro-Allied Thai ambassador to America, later noted that while Phibun's government officially referred to the Japanese as "maha mit" meaning "great friend", most Thais took to pronouncing it as "mah mit", meaning "dog of a friend".[966] Pramoj also predicted, after Japan's invasion of Thailand and Phibun's alliance with the Japanese, that the Thais would soon resist or revolt as it was "not in the nature of Thais to submit meekly and willingly to foreign domination."[967]

And he was right. By early 1943 one US wartime intelligence report explained, "Thai resentment has found expression in the spontaneous formation of small groups of noncollaborationists ... these groups gradually made contact and set up an underground organization."⁹⁶⁸ At first, this resistance was on a small scale. In Phuket, for example, one old Chinese local, who was a teenager during the war, told of sneaking out on to the Phuket airfield at night to throw broken glass and sharp debris on to the runway to damage the tires of the Japanese aircraft. Another popular pursuit was to jump on to the slow-moving trains loaded with supplies for Malaya or Burma and throw off the goods. In this way, the perpetrators provided for their local villages, denied supplies to the Japanese and made a good profit all at the same time.

Some examples of course were more extreme, such as the gutsy Chinese stationmaster in Bangkok who stole a train and four carriages fully laden with tanks and other Japanese war material and drove the whole train off the rails on a bridge and into the Chao Phraya River. He jumped clear and survived, but was later captured and beheaded by the Japanese. In the south of Thailand, the "Saha Samakhom Totan Yipun" (South Thai Anti-Japanese Alliance) was organized. This mainly Chinese organization ran local guerrilla activities, attacked isolated Japanese vehicles, outposts or lone Japanese soldiers. Locals also tell of preparing food for the Japanese troops using poisonous plants or copious amounts of khee lek and makham kaek leaves, which are both severe laxatives. Others stole and stockpiled gasoline, weapons, arms and even military vehicles in readiness for a general uprising.

By late 1943 many Thais, illegally listening in to Allied radio broadcasts, noticed that the tide of the war was turning against Japan. Pridi Phanomyong, the pro-Allied former prime minister who had been ousted by Phibun ten years before, began secretly to organize the Seri Thai, or Free Thai resistance army. This group started by saving downed Allied airmen from capture, providing intelligence and arranging local resistance. Faced with this growing disaffection, the Japanese pushed Field Marshal Phibun to introduce martial law in Thailand, but this move just increased resistance and more calls for Phibun to resign.

By 1944 the Japanese, under military pressure everywhere, were too short of men to occupy Thailand in a hostile manner, so the best they could do was to try to shore up support for Phibun by, at last, transferring to Thailand the "lost" Malay states. Despite Phibun's propaganda about this great victory, it was already too late; people could see that he had backed the wrong horse. There were three attempts on Phibun's life in short succession and in July 1944 he was voted out of office by the Thai National Assembly. With most of his followers abandoning him and without real Japanese support, he resigned and was replaced by Khuang Abhaiwongse, an urbane centrist, who sided with Pridi and his pro-Allied Seri Thai resistance. The smooth Khuang was chosen to dissemble to the Japanese, while Pridi concentrated on organizing the resistance and making contact with the Allies and the overseas Seri Thai, which consisted mainly of Thai students and Thai embassy staff members who had been abroad when the war broke out.

Agent Infiltration and the Balmoral Base

The Japanese never had more than about 50,000 troops in the whole of Thailand, which made it difficult for them to control or secure the country. Seri Thai agents trained abroad began to be landed by submarine and Catalina planes at night on the remote coasts north and south of Phuket. They then began to make contact with and coordinate the local resistance. In late 1944, a joint SOG (Special Operations Group) and Seri Thai operational base named Balmoral was secretly established on Chan Island just off the coast of the Japanese naval base at Victoria Point and Ranong. This base reported on Japanese coastal shipping movements and was used for transshipping information and weapons. At one point, 14 agents – American, British and Thai – were based on the island and Catalina seaplanes regularly shuttled between there and India. The governor of nearby Ranong, who was also a member of the Seri Thai, arranged for the local Customs inspection vessel to carry men and materiel between the island and the mainland.

In early 1945, a Thai agent called Watana Ratchani and two Chinese were flown in from Ceylon with orders to go to Phuket and coordinate with local resistance on a plan being hatched by the British in India to invade Phuket. The agents were to be dropped by Catalina at Balmoral. To get the men to Phuket, the island's operatives invited some local fishermen to the island to have a bit of a drinking party. When the Catalina arrived that night from India, the fishermen even helped unload supplies from the plane. But to preserve secrecy, these hapless fishermen were then held up at gunpoint and loaded back on the plane and taken back to India, where they spent the rest of the war in a British internment camp. Their boat was then used to take the agents to Phuket. A British operative, who later visited the fishermen at their internment camp, reported that their leader, Ma Hem, a "thirty three year old fisherman of Malayan ethnicity, complained of homesickness, illness and beatings at the hands of the camp guards."[969]

Ma Hem and his colleagues were not alone in being kidnapped. As a lead-in to this planned Allied invasion of Phuket, many other local fishermen were captured for intelligence purposes, such as the 19 Muslim fishermen from Phuket who were captured at sea by the British submarine HMS Clyde in early 1945. They also spent months in an internment camp in India before being repatriated at the war's end. In operation "Durian II" two Thais and two Sino-Thais from Ko Muk (who had been captured earlier when a British submarine had sunk their boat off Trang) were trained in India as British SOG (Special Operations Group) operatives. In November 1944 they were landed by submarine on Ko Kradan Island south of Phuket with over a ton of guns and radio equipment to be distributed to the Seri Thai resistance forces forming in the southwest. However they were seen by some local fishermen and captured by the Thai police who then refused to hand them over to the Japanese and kept them in Thai custody in Bangkok till the end of the war. [970]

The secret Balmoral camp on Chan Island was eventually compromised when a patrolling Japanese plane spotted a parachute entangled in some trees that had been left by an airdropped operative. The Japanese sent an investigative expedition to the island the next day, but the Allied operatives had been alerted and had secretly moved to another island during the night and were soon spirited away by a nearby British submarine.

The Raid on the Italian Ships in Ao Makam

In late 1944, the British received intelligence reports that the Japanese, now critically short of ships, had re-floated the two Italian ships that had been scuttled in Ao Makam Bay in Phuket at the beginning of the war and were about to sail them to Singapore to refit them as troop transports. The British decided to go in and blow them up.

The submarine HMS Trenchant crossed from Ceylon and moored off Ko Dok Mai Island. Strapped to the Trenchant were two undersea "Chariots" – modified motor torpedoes steered by two-man frogman crews. That night, four British naval frogmen mounted on the two Chariots left the submarine and approached the Italian ships underwater to fix huge explosive charges to their hulls. One of the mines would not attach, so one of the divers, Stewart Brown, daringly climbed aboard the ship carrying the mine after the timer had been set. He was later awarded the Distinguished Service Medal for his bravery. He rushed back to his Chariot and the four men then hurriedly attempted to get back to the open sea and the Trenchant, but the breathing apparatus on one of the Chariots broke down; two of the men had to come up and travel on the surface out of the guarded harbor. They were just clear of the harbor at 5:30 a.m. when the explosives went off, blowing great holes in the two Italian ships' hulls and re-sinking them. In the ensuing confusion, all four divers made it back to the submarine. Worried that a Japanese destroyer was nearby, the submarine captain ordered the Chariots to be dumped, the divers were taken aboard and the Trenchant made good its escape.

These two discarded Chariots have been located on the sea floor near Ko Dok Mai, but the British government – which still officially owns them – refuses to allow them to be salvaged. This was the last time these underwater Chariots were used in the war. The British navy prohibited their use after the Japanese high command sent a specific warning notice to the British that anyone captured using them in the future "would lose both eyes and their testicles."[971]

Operation Priest and War Crimes

Operation Priest was the name given to the overall Allied plan to re-invade Malaya. It was under the command of Lord Louis Mountbatten, based in Ceylon. His staff decided the best place to start this re-invasion would be Phuket Island. Their reasons were that the Japanese would most likely be expecting the invasion further south in Malaya, the Japanese had fewer than 400 men garrisoned on Phuket at the time, there were good beaches for an amphibious landing and help could be expected from the local Chinese and burgeoning Thai resistance on the island. Also, as Allied air and sea power was already dominant, it would be hard for the Japanese to mount a seaborne counter-attack and Phuket's harbors and airfields could then be used as a forward base for air attacks and bombing raids to cut communications, supply and rail links to isolate the Japanese further south in Malaya before the main re-invasion landing at Port Dickson.

In the spring of 1945, a British SOG team of seven operatives, led by a Major Maxwell, was sent to Phuket to reconnoiter beach elevations and Japanese defenses and to coordinate with the local resistance. These men were dropped by submarine at night off Mai Kao beach and paddled ashore in canvas kayaks. Unfortunately for them, the moon was bright that night and they were spotted by a Japanese sentry. Japanese troops were rushed from the airfield garrison to the beach and a firefight erupted. One SOG operative was killed and one more, Sergeant-Major Smith was wounded so badly he could not move. Major Maxwell ordered the other men to split up and flee to try to surrender to the more sympathetic Thai police. Under the bilateral agreement between Thailand and Japan, the Japanese army in Thailand only had jurisdiction over any prisoners they took themselves, while the Thais had jurisdiction over any prisoners they caught. The Thais were notably more lenient with their POWs, even, in some cases in Bangkok, allowing them to join Thai officers to go out drinking and womanizing at night. Four of the SOG operatives gave themselves up to the Thai police and were held until the end of the war. [972]

Smith and Maxwell, who had stayed with him, were captured by Japanese soldiers and after several days of beatings and interrogations in Phuket had disclosed nothing. They were later taken to a Kempetai (Secret Police) prison in Singapore and were again interrogated and tortured. In his diary, one of the interrogating Japanese officers, Major Ikoda, wrote: "We tried to get information out of them but in vain." Faced with their obstinate silence, Major Ikoda eventually took them outside, as well as a young British pilot called Tomlinson recently shot down near Port Dickson in Malaya. Major Ikoda noted in his diary, "Showing him the way of beheading, I beheaded F. O. Tomlinson and ordered Lt. Kajiki to behead Major Maxwell and Sgt. Major Smith."[973] During a war crimes trial after the war in Singapore, Major Ikoda and Lieutenant Kajiki were charged with these beheadings and several others. The day before the trial started, they confessed to beheading 18 Allied soldiers and, so as not to discredit their superiors, they later both committed suicide, performing "Hara Kiri" (ritual samurai suicide) with their prison-issue pewter cutlery.

The Sinking of the Haguro

On May 16, 1945, the Japanese heavy cruiser Haguro, with Vice Admiral Shintaro Hashimoto and 1,200 crew and soldiers on board, left Penang and was heading north past Phuket to re-supply the Japanese forces in the Andaman Islands. The Japanese destroyer Kamikaze accompanied her. In stormy weather late that afternoon to the northwest of Phuket the Haguro encountered a squadron of five British torpedo destroyers under the command of the rather macho-named Captain Manley Power. The two Japanese ships attempted to make a run back to the protection of the Japanese naval base in Penang. The engagement began at dusk and throughout a stormy night of heavy squalls, high seas and vivid lightning storms, the ships fought it out in a dramatic high-speed chase (almost 50 knots). The Haguro, firing as she went, was slowed when a torpedo from the destroyer HMS Saumarez hit her. She was then hit again by a second torpedo from HMS Vigilant and sank later that night, bow first, some 55 kilometers short of Penang. The destroyer Kamikaze escaped. Fewer than 300 survivors were pulled from the choppy seas the next morning. Over 900 Japanese sailors perished, including Vice Admiral Hashimoto. This was the last Anglo-Japanese naval battle of the war and the only time that destroyers alone sank a heavy cruiser.[974]

Operation Roger: The Allied Invasion of Phuket

Meanwhile, the plans for the invasion of Phuket were finalized. The operation was given the code name "Roger" by some wag on Lord Mountbatten's staff in Trincomalee, who presumably, like most British at first, read the name of Phuket phonetically. (In English slang at the time, to "rodger" meant to have sexual intercourse.) Two Ceylon-based Seri Thai operatives, Wattana Chitwari and Phitsadet Ratcahni,[975] were landed near Phuket by submarine and made arrangements for more Seri Thai and SOG operatives to go ahead to Phuket and link up with the local resistance there to direct bombing and naval fire and incite an uprising and generally cause mayhem. This was to be followed by an invasion by the British 3 Commando Brigade and two divisions of the 23rd Indian Infantry Brigade – fresh from their victory over the Japanese at Imphal in Burma – and the Nigerian 81st West Africa Division which had been fighting in Arakan, Burma.

British reconnaissance planes were sent over to Phuket from Ceylon to get aerial photos of the Japanese defenses on Phuket. Flight Lieutenant Laurie Jones, aged 22, piloted one of these planes; he recalls approaching low at night at "300 feet, flying over a dark and glassy sea." As the day dawned they approached Phuket

> "but at a low level we were confused by the maze of islands ... our first run took us down Sapam Bay past the Jap airfield and the anti-aircraft Batteries, but all was quiet. At the end of this run we did a steep turn away and dived to water level behind a row of rough hills that jutted out into the straits. Turning back on track we climbed to 1,000 feet that put us roughly level with the heavy coastal and antiaircraft gun emplacements in the hills commanding the beach and our flight path. The concentration of spot on flying and nervous tension had me sweating, but we were past the guns before the Japs reacted ... [On their next fly past] ... we swept low over a large timber factory and then found ourselves straddling a road filled with long marching columns of Japanese infantry about 20 feet below ... We did sustain some damage to the port fin rudder and tail plane from their small caliber fire. We dropped down to 50 feet until out of radar range and then headed home."[976]

The date for the invasion of Phuket was set for August 14, 1945 and, because this was during the southwest monsoon when big surf hits the western beaches, the landings were planned for Rawai and Chalong beaches on the more sheltered east coast.

The Assault on Phuket by Force 63

The first phase of the operation was "softening up". In July a British fleet code-named "Force 63" was sent to Phuket to launch air attacks on strategic points in the region and clear the heavily mined seas around the island. This was called "Operation Livery". The fleet consisted of two aircraft carriers, HMS Ameer and HMS Empress, the battleship HMS Nelson, the heavy cruiser HMS Sussex, three destroyers and five minesweepers. They arrived off the south of Phuket on the night of July 23, 1945 and Ko Racha was occupied as a forward base. The fleet sat off Cape Phromthep.

The next day continual sorties by British Hellcat fighter-bombers of 808 Squadron took off from the two carriers to bomb targets in the region, airfields, ports, the peninsular railway, etc. The minesweepers started mine clearing operations in the southern approaches to Phuket. After some mines were swept and exploded at 6.15 that evening the minesweeper HMS Squirrel struck one mine, setting off a huge explosion that killed seven of her crew. A press photographer on one of the other fleet ships caught this explosion on camera. The

37.3 The British Royal Navy minesweeper HMS Squirrel Photographed as it hit a mine and sunk off Cape Phromthep whilst mine-clearing prior to the planned allied invasion of Phuket.

Squirrel's bow began to sink forward and the fire spread all over the ship. The remaining crew leapt into the sea and rescue boats from HMS Vestal came to their aid. One of the Squirrel's survivors, Frank Owen, says that her propellers were still running but now they were up at the surface and, "In my inflated lifebelt I was helpless against the pull of the screw." He screamed for help, and on the verge of meeting "a messy end in the ships propeller … I caught the tip of the blade of an extended Paddle." He was pulled to safety by the rescue whaler from the Vestal. "I still wake in a cold sweat,"[977] he recalled decades later. That night the burnt-out hulk of the Squirrel was fired upon by the fleet destroyer HMS Rotherham to scuttle it.

The remaining four minesweepers cleared many mines over the next few days, sometimes working so close in shore that "the enemy could be seen, but they dared not give away the position of their batteries that they guard by poor camouflage. The Nelson was the reason … she would have blown any resistance to hell. Radar aerials were clearly visible, small ack ack guns too, many little machine gun nests had been spotted."[978] When some minesweepers were fired upon the next day, the Nelson and the heavy cruiser HMS Sussex did open up for a while with their 8-inch guns blasting the Japanese and Thai installations and fortified positions on Cape Phromthep.

Over the next three days the Hellcat fighter-bombers from the two carriers flew more than 150 sorties and, amongst other damage, reportedly destroyed more than 30 Japanese aircraft at the Phuket, Surathani and Ranong airstrips. One Hellcat bomber was shot down by anti-aircraft fire over Chalong and one Phuket resident recalled seeing the plane "crash violently into a nearby building and explode."[979] On July 25, the Hellcats attacked the wooden piers at the ports at Makham Bay, Phuket town and Tharua. One elder Tharua local recalled that they missed and "their bombs landed harmlessly in the surrounding mangroves."[980] They did, however, hit one Phuket-owned ship in Sapam and one of two Japanese ships off Phuket town at the time. The other Japanese ship tried to make a run for it, but was repeatedly attacked by the Hellcats and apparently sank just south of Ko Lon in Chalong Bay. George Coyne, an 18-year-old English sailor on HMS Sussex at the time, recalls: "A Jap ship was sunk leaving about 20 survivors in the water. One of our ships, at great risk to themselves stopped to rescue them. Without exception they refused help and so they all drowned. What fanaticism!"[981]

The Hellcats also bombed the Japanese and Thai army auxiliary bases in Chalong, hitting an armory and setting off a mighty explosion. At Rawai and Chalong beaches and Ha Yaek village (the site of the current Chalong roundabout), the Japanese had set up trenches, sandbags and machine gun emplacements against potential landings. These were bombed, as well as Wat Chalong because the British were informed that Japanese troops had taken refuge there. The only person killed in the Wat Chalong bombing was the pregnant Thai wife of the janitor, and one monk lost a foot to shrapnel.

37.4. US built British Navy 'Hellcat' fighter-bombers returning to the aircraft carrier HMS Ameer sitting off Phuket. These planes flew five days of continual bombing sorties against targets on Phuket and the surrounding region to "soften them up" before the planned allied invasion of Phuket in August 1945.

Kamikazes at Cape Phromthep

On day three, the British fleet came under attack from Japanese bombers, which did little damage. Then came the Kamikaze attacks. The first happened in the afternoon of July 26 when a single Mitsubishi Ki-51 Sonia dive-bomber flew high over Cape Phromthep then dived at the carrier HMS Ameer. The fleet's massed gunners hit the plane in its descent, the pilot lost control and the plane exploded in the sea a hundred yards from the Ameer. Then at dusk as another of Phuket's technicolor tropical sunsets was receding into the west, three more Japanese planes appeared very low over Cape Phromthep. The Japanese troops on the cape reportedly cheered up at these brave young pilots passing low overhead on their flight to death.

The three planes dipped down over the cape and came in just above sea level. Peter Connold a crewman on the minesweeper HMS Vestal recalls: "All at once hell was let loose. Every ship opened up with their anti-aircraft guns, it was bedlam." The evening sky was filled with a violent cacophony of tracer fire and anti-aircraft explosions from the fleet's gunners. The lead Japanese plane headed directly for the big cruiser HMS Sussex. Bright lines of tracer bullets from the fleet's anti-aircraft guns converged on it and "at last – not ten yards from her starboard side – she blew up in a mass of yellow flame and smoke. What was left ricocheted against the starboard quarter then dropped into the water."[982] The armored hull of the Sussex was only slightly damaged.

The cones of tracer fire then zeroed in on the second plane, also heading for HMS Sussex, but as Connold on the Vestal then describes, this plane was also hit:

"a puff of smoke a brilliant flame then it went out, the plane banked over, missed the ship and continued on making an arc. At first she seemed to go in the direction of Plucky, would it dive on her? No, she'll miss that one. On it came to our port, it flattened out and with our hearts in our mouths we saw she was going to crash on us. With fanatical determination it came, all yellow and green, a brand new plane. Undercarriage down and the pilot's head just above the fuselage. Our guns blazed. Will she hit us? Yes, of all the ships there we were the target. On it came nearer and nearer and then Boom!!"[983]

A huge fireball explosion engulfed the vessel. After the blast Connold recalls the man in front of him "covered in the blackness of the blast, blood oozed out from many wounds, his head arms legs and chest were peppered with splinters … I saw the engine and boiler room casualties brought past, some burnt out of all recognition."[984]

37.5. and 37.6. The British heavy cruiser HMS Sussex and a close up of the damage inflicted by a ka-mikaze plane which hit the water 10 yards short of her, exploded and bounced into her causing limited damage. The planes silhouette can be seen imprinted on her heavy armor-plated side.

The third Kamikaze had also headed for HMS Sussex and held its course through the intense anti-aircraft fire until it was hit and crashed into the sea short of her target. The center of HMS Vestal was a blazing crater and she later sank. 18 men died in the explosion. The survivors and wounded were rescued and put on the battleship Nelson. Two more sailors died from their wounds that night as Connold recalls: "we went on deck to the service and watched the two small bundles of two young lads, both 19 years … dropped into the black shining sea to be swallowed up by its depth … there was no sleep for us that night nor the next, planes attacked the next day but were shot down."[985]

HMS Vestal was the last British ship sunk in WWII and the Kamikaze attacks off Phuket were the last in the Indian Ocean. In 2004 HMS Vestal was located by divers from a Phuket recrational dive company. She lies 72 meters down on a sandy bottom covered in snagged local fishing nets and is now used as a site for more adventurous deep-water recreational deep-dive trips.

The Force 63 fleet then returned to Trincomalee in Ceylon to refit and repair in preparation for the full invasion of Phuket to be launched two weeks later on August 15. Young George Coyne on HMS Sussex recalls, "After returning to Ceylon and being repaired, we were sent to join a huge armada forming in the Indian Ocean ready to attack the Malayan Peninsula. We were all very apprehensive and scared."[986]

37.7 The minesweeper HMS Vestal: sunk by a kamikaze attack from Phuket airfield in July 1945 with the loss of 18 men. She was the last Royal Navy ship sunk in WWII and probably the last allied ship sunk by a kamikaze attack.

On August 10, the fleet and troops for the invasion of Phuket left from Ceylon and Rangoon to the Andaman Islands to meet up. A further 20 Seri Thai agents and 10 radio operators were infiltrated into Phuket and surrounding towns such as Takuapa. A forward observation team of British SOG commandos landed on Laem Sing beach at night and were met by local Sino-Thai resistance operatives.[987] On the Andaman Islands the Indian, African and British troops boarded the invasion ships.

Saved by the Bombs

Meanwhile in Japan just four days earlier on August 6, "Little Boy", the first atomic bomb, had obliterated Hiroshima. On August 9 "Fat Man", the second bomb obliterated Nagasaki. The next day, August 10, as the Allied invasion fleet in the Andaman Islands was ready and about to set sail against Phuket, Japan surrendered. Coyne on the Sussex recalls; "We were told of the A bombs and that the Japs had surrendered. There was much celebration and relief onboard … thank god for the bombs, we should get home safely now."[988]

Phuket Island and its people, most of whom had had no idea they were about to be invaded in just two days' time, were saved at the last gasp from the death, destruction and horrors of war by those two diabolical bombs

38

Tin to Tourists

1945 TO 2010

The Japanese Surrender on Phuket

In early September 1945, less than a month after the Japanese surrender, a British Dakota carrying passengers and mail from newly liberated Singapore to Rangoon was struggling through heavy rainy season turbulence up the west coast of the central peninsula. In grim consternation the 18 passengers aboard were staring out of their portholes at the cloud and electric storm surrounding them when suddenly the labored drone of the portside engine stuttered and then chak-chaked to a stop. The pilot, Englishman Frank Savage from Burnley, explains, "It couldn't have happened at a worse time, the weather was foul ... We were over hilly country and the only airstrip I could make for, on Phuket, was 120 miles away."[989]

Allied occupation troops had not yet reached Phuket and the armed Japanese garrison was still there. How might they react to a British plane landing? "No one had landed there before," the pilot recalls.

> "We eventually got over Phuket, but found no strip. I was sweating because my one good engine was getting so hot I didn't think she would make it ... then we found the strip and although it was short, I got her down which surprised me more than anyone ... We were soon surrounded by natives, fortunately, one passenger could make himself understood. The first thing we wanted to know was, 'Are their any Japanese here?' Their answer was, 'yes, about a hundred'."[990]

A few minutes later, a military truck with armed Japanese troops in the back drove out on to the wet airstrip and squelched to a halt near the plane. Frank Savage recalls:

> "One could speak English and introduced his commanding officer, who tried to shake hands with me. I ignored his hand and tried to look stern though my knees were shaking a bit as I didn't know what their attitude was going to be ... I decided to take the offensive and asked how many men he had, where they were, etc. ... and ended up by ordering them to go back to their camp and stay there until the British Navy came for them in two days' time – a story I made up on the spur of the moment. ... This they proceeded to do and we saw no more of them ... Next, the local district commissioner rolled up in a car. He was delighted to see us and couldn't do enough for us. We were, he told us, the first English plane to land since the war started and he wanted us to disarm the Japanese right away ...

the next Tuesday one of our own aircraft came and took us off, leaving a ground crew to repair the engine … [During our stay] the governor of the island made us welcome … every night some of us went to town thirty miles away and dined with the governor, the local prince, or some of the managers of the tin mines. We had all the fruit we wanted, bananas, pineapples, coconuts and lots of eggs, all given by enthusiastic villagers."[991]

38.1 Phuket's airport in the early 1950s.

The British and Indian occupation/liberation troops did not arrive in Phuket for another three weeks. When they did, the Japanese troops were peacefully disarmed. Phuket local residents alive at the time say that just before the British forces arrived the Japanese dumped most of their vehicles, weapons, anti-aircraft guns and heavy equipment into the sea in Pak Pra (just to the west of the present Sarasin Bridge). As there were no reports of major atrocities or war crimes on Phuket, the Japanese there were shipped off to Singapore and then repatriated to Japan. Given the horrors of the last years of the war for many Japanese soldiers and the general amiability of most local people, Phuket must have been considered a fortunate posting and it is unlikely many of the Japanese had felt much like rocking the boat. Within a few months of the war's end most Japanese troops in Thailand had been rounded up, but a few fought on. In fact, the longest-fighting Japanese after the war appear to be two young Japanese soldiers who remained hidden in the jungles of southern Thailand. They soon joined a band of communist rebels and kept fighting the British Malayan and Thai troops from their jungle hideouts along the southern border until finally surrendering in 1990 when both men were over 70 years old.

The Chinese in Phuket generally welcomed the Allied victory and British post-war occupation as they felt they might now be rid of the ill treatment they had received at the hands of Phibun's government and no doubt also because they felt their tin mining and rubber businesses could now make money again. Some Thais however, were not so happy. In Bangkok, where Chinese and Thai mutual animosity was more manifest than in more laid-back Phuket, matters came to a head when many Chinese started celebrating the Allied victory over Thailand publicly in the streets. This was not well taken by certain more nationalist Thais and scuffles broke out. The Thai police fired on these Chinese revelers and set off major riots and a week of armed clashes in Bangkok between the Thai police and Nationalist elements and militant Chinese groups. In these clashes 27 people died and over 180 were wounded.[992] The Thais were also disgruntled that the British occupation army consisted mainly (65 percent) of Indian troops. Under Phibun the Thais had been taught to look down on Indians and anyone from any neighboring Asian countries that had been either ruled by Siam previously or colonized by Europeans. Therefore with little political correctness, the Thai military liaison officer in Washington, Colonel Khap Khunchon, declared that America should put a stop to this "humiliating" British move as it was creating "great friction … since the Thai army is very hostile to Indians … even American negroes would be preferable."[993]

War Reparations and Britain's Last Grab for Phuket

Immediately after the Japanese surrender, the new pro-Western government of Khuang and Pridi conveniently rescinded the Thai government's declarations of war against the Allies and also immediately returned to Britain and France the "lost territories" Phibun had annexed during the war. The pro-Allied Pridi, who had helped start and run the Seri Thai resistance movement, was therefore allowed to remain in power. Despite recognizing the modest contribution of the Seri Thai resistance, Britain still insisted on treating Thailand as a defeated enemy country and expected significant war reparations. These were both for the cost of the war and for all the British businesses, machinery and property the Thai government and military had "confiscated" from British firms in Thailand after declaring war on the Allies. British business and colonial interests in Malaya saw this situation as yet another opportunity to get their hands on Phuket and its lucrative tin deposits. This time they were backed by British military and political opinion. Lord Denning, Lord Mountbatten's political consultant, openly called for British annexation of the whole Malay Peninsula and its islands as far north as Prachup Kiri Khan both for strategic reasons and "as a punishment for going to war with Great Britain."[994] In London Sir Anthony Eden also called for this annexation and Leo Amery, the Secretary of State for India, waxed lyrical in Parliament about the prospect of linking the British colonies of Burma and Malaya, right down the peninsula.

The Americans, the new post-war power, took a rather jaundiced view of Britain's annexation plans. The USA was now worried about the communist threat in Asia and wanted Thai support, and also wanted to reduce British influence in Thailand to advance its own. Therefore the State Department was dead set against this British plan that "favored a free Thailand, but greatly reduced geographically and in particular … [joining] … peninsular Thailand with Malaya and Burma thus putting all the rubber and tin areas into the hands of British businessmen."[995] Dilworth Brinton, a US military operative in Bangkok, summed up American opinion on the annexation proposal: "The British drive American jeeps and fly American planes but treat us like we are trespassers on their sacred soil."[996] With Britain economically and militarily exhausted after the war and in need of massive aid from the USA, London had no option but to bow to Washington's will and had to back off. Britain also urgently needed to feed her war-torn and starving Asian colonies, so instead of Phuket, Britain agreed to accept a Thai offer of one and a half million tons of rice as "compensation". (The Thais, backed by the US government, insisted this could not be called "reparations".) So little Phuket was once again saved by external events from this, the last attempted European colonial grab for the lucrative island. As it was the Thai government eventually weaseled its way out of delivering much of the promised rice by claiming that as the rice belonged to private farmers it was not theirs to give away and they had little money to buy it. These negotiations marked the end of some 150 years of British bullying and imperium over the economic and political evolution of Phuket and the surrounding region.

Post-War Phuket

By October 1946 the British and Indian occupation forces had pulled out of Thailand, leaving behind a few British technical advisers. During the war the Japanese had built a road from Phuket to their main base at Ranong. Now, for the first time, it was possible to drive a car in two days the whole way from Phuket to Bangkok via Ranong. A small, open car ferry started operating across the Pak Pra channel until the first Sarasin Bridge was built in 1967. Thai Airways began a regular passenger flight from Bangkok to Phuket in 1947, which suddenly made the island just a few hours' travel from downtown Bangkok.

38.2 The old Pak Pra ferry, which operated until the Saracen Bridge was built in 1967 linking the island by road to the rest of Thailand.

The increased post-war price of tin and particularly rubber brought renewed prosperity to Phuket. Many of the British and Australian companies and nationals came back to

Phuket, the tin dredgers were put back to work and the United Club and the Miners Club re-opened their doors. The mining companies as they resumed operations now began to employ mainly Thais as laborers as Chinese immigrants were now prohibited from entering Thailand.

Khun Rachan Karnchanawanit, a well-born Thai, was studying at Stanford University, California, when the war broke out. He worked with Seri Thai in the USA during the war. After the war, he returned to Thailand and was sent by the Thai government to Phuket to negotiate reparations for the British and Australian companies that had lost much of their equipment and assets. Khun Rachan was later hired as managing director of Tongkah Harbour Mining Cº based in Saphan Hin in Phuket town. He recalls that Phuket town was still a comparatively isolated, dirty and run-down place in the 1950s and 1960s without the distractions or sophistication of Bangkok. But it was a nice posting for recreation. He kept a yacht, which he recalls he was still able to sail up the Klong Bang Yai into Phuket town as far as the old Tavorn Hotel, where he and the crew could have sundowners.

38.3 Post-war prsoperity in Phuket. Mr Kawee Ekasilapa and his bride Monta enjoy the Thai "Ram Wong" dance at their wedding in 1955.

As Khun Rachan spoke excellent English, he was also given responsibility for the farang cemetery that lies near the Catholic Church that was built in Phuket in 1958. He recalls one incident in the early 1960s when a flatbed truck pulled up outside his office. Tied upright to a chair on the back of the truck was a dead Scottish mining engineer who had had a heart attack while working on a Kamra Tin Cº dredge in Kamala. The local workers were informed they should take the corpse to Phuket town for Khun Rachan to deal with. The only way to travel from Kamala to Phuket in those days was by boat or to undertake a long drive on the unpaved, rutted road via Cherngtalay and Tharua. So when the dead engineer eventually reached Khun Rachan in town, rigor mortis had set in, with the corpse fixed in a seated position, which caused some awkward issues when it came to fitting him into a coffin. When asked why the workers had tied the dead man to a chair on the back of a flatbed truck, the urbane Khun Rachan, in his most dignified Thai way, replied, "I'm afraid you would have to ask them that."[997]

Demand for rubber picked up again after the war and the widespread jungle clearance for rubber plantations continued, which further opened up and drastically altered the appearance of Phuket. Land was still very cheap and the wealthy Chinese mining families were able to acquire plenty of it at very little cost. Most of the animals previously so abundant in Phuket's jungles were hunted and chased from their habitat; Today there are no wild deer, elephants, antelope, black panthers, sun bears, rhinoceros, porcupines or tigers on the island. Phuket's last recorded wild tiger was shot in Kamala in 1974. It lived in the forest in the high hills behind Kamala and had come down nine times and carried off goats from a pen very near the old Kamala school and the local parents were becoming nervous for their children's safety so some local villagers hunted it down and shot it. [998]

38.4 A tiger shot in 1965 just outside Cherngtalay by local police Lt. Col. Toksakan Thawan. Phuket's last recorded tiger shooting was in 1974 in Kamala Village, but reports of tiger sightings in the hills above Kamala continued until the early 1990s.

Post-War Politics

Back in 1935, when the deposed Rama VII had died, a nine-year-old royal Thai boy living in Switzerland, Ananda Mahidol, was chosen as Rama VIII, his successor. When Rama VIII completed his studies in Europe in late 1945, he was aged 20 and, with the war over and the anti-royalist Phibun now gone, he returned to Thailand to much joyous celebration from the Thai people. Then in June 1946, just a few months later, this new young king was found shot in the head in his palace bedroom under suspicious circumstances. Amongst a melée of conspiracy theories, two palace courtiers were found guilty of the murder and executed. The crown was then offered to the murdered king's younger brother, Bhumipol Adulyadet, then a 19-year-old, also studying in Europe. He agreed to become the new king and after his studies in France in 1950 he bravely followed in his murdered brother's footsteps and returned to Thailand to huge popular acclaim to be crowned Rama IX. He still sits on the Thai throne today, 61 years later, and is loved by his people for his good works in office and his role in uniting the kingdom and serving as a source of stability and moderation during some trying political years in Asia in the post-war era.

After his ousting in July 1944, Field Marshal Phibun was imprisoned, charged with war crimes and faced the death sentence. In the court after the war despite plenty of evidence against him, he was released as Thai public opinion was predominantly sympathetic towards him for saving Thailand from the worst ravages of war. Then in 1947, again with the backing of the military, Phibun staged another coup and the leftist prime minister, Pridi, was forced to flee into exile in France. Phibun retook the reins of a military government and had several of his rivals and opponents killed off or eliminated extrajudicially. Although the Western powers regarded Phibun as a rather odious character, America, worried by the communist threat in Asia, preferred him to the more socialist Pridi. With the USA now clearly the new world power, the chameleon-like Phibun "bent with the winds" yet again and now turned to the former adversary to be his new defender and protector. The Thai historian Manich Jumsai recalls meeting Phibun at that time, just before he left to attend a UNESCO meeting. He claims that when he asked Phibun what policy stance he held, Phibun replied unashamedly that he would "observe what the Americans did and vote with them."[999] This simple policy stance however effectively ensured that US anti-communist aid poured into Thailand, particularly extensive military aid, which made Phibun's military supporters and cronies very happy and rich.

Phibun resurrected many of his old Thai nationalist policies. With China now communist, he labeled the Chinese in Thailand potential communist fifth columnists and stopped any Chinese immigration completely. He again set about closing the Chinese schools. Faced with this renewed racist pressure from successive post-war nationalist military governments the Chinese in Thailand all gradually assimilated and became Thai. The historian David Wyatt wrote that, for the Chinese, "Their ladder to success in the Thailand of the 1960s and 1970s, a time of rapid economic growth, consisted of a Thai education, Thai surnames, Thai language and intermarriage with Thai families ... This benefited the better Thai families who got access to wealth and the Chinese who got access to political acceptance."[1000] Today one hardly sees Chinese writing or signs or hears Chinese spoken on Phuket, an island that was almost 90 percent populated by Chinese born in China just two generations ago. Today it is only Chinese religious beliefs, their temples, graves and festivals that have been allowed to survive unhindered. The wall-hung red "San Jao Ji" prayer shelves with their joss sticks and offerings now hang like badges identifying the numerous (former) Chinese shops, businesses, houses and families that still predominate in Phuket City and the older towns on the island.

Phibun's new military government tried again to coerce the Muslims and Malays to become Buddhist and Thai and to substitute Thai law for their Islamic laws. Islamic schooling was forbidden and strongly repressed. This provoked disturbances and many southern Malay leaders were arrested. In April 1948, large-scale Muslim resistance broke out yet again in Patani and the Malay-speaking south. Bangkok put down these rebellions with brutal military force, including using the air force to bomb Muslim villages. The Thai military government's forceful actions further fed the communist and Islamic rebel causes in the far and mid-south during the 1960s, 1970s and 1980s, including in Phang Nga and Surathani provinces. It is said that one of the reasons for the construction in 1982 of the large Rachaprapat Dam between Phuket and Surathani, in addition to water storage, was to flood the cave systems of Khao Sok, which were used as a base by such rebels. Today, the southeastern Thai provinces, formerly the ancient kingdoms of Langasuka and Patani, still remain violent and mutinous against Thai rule. A resurgence of armed uprising began in 2004, and since then over 4,000 people have been killed and they are still being shot, blown up, burnt and decapitated each year by Muslim and Malay insurgents, rebels, independence fighters, gangsters and by the heavy-handed Thai military and armed police who still struggle to control this ever-rebellious southern ward.

38.3 Yaowarat Road, Phuket town in 1951.

In 1957, Field Marshal Phibun himself was overthrown and chased into exile in Japan by a military coup led by his defense minister, General Sarit Thanarat and his associate Thanom Kittikachorn. These two men and their very self-serving military government and cronies then ran the country until 1973 when they were evicted by a violent student-led popular pro-democracy uprising. During this period, as long as the Thai military government did more or less what America wanted, Thailand was backed politically and financially by the USA with few embarrassing questions asked, despite the egregious corruption in the Thai administrations. When Field Marshal Sarit died in 1963, for example, he was found to have over US $600 million in his bank accounts after receiving a government salary of less than half a million baht a year. He also maintained some 50 girlfriends or "mia noi" (minor wives) around the country who soon appeared out of the woodwork after his death clamoring to claim a share of his ill-gotten loot.

Sarit and Thanom were both Thai-educated traditional conservatives and royalists and their regimes resurrected and promoted the prestige of the Thai king after Phibun's egocentric and anti-monarchical years. Their strong-arm regimes, combined with the caring and greatly respected character of the current king, Rama IX, provided the country with a stability and cohesion during the turbulent 1960s and 1970s in Southeast Asia. The communist threat in Indochina and Thailand's position as the front-line Western domino meant that the USA strongly supported the country through this period. America pumped up the Thai economy by building roads, airfields, schools and military bases. In some years the USA poured more money into the Thai military budget alone than the country's entire tax income, which was handy, as how the military budget was spent remained a military secret, sequestered from the prying eyes of pesky journalists – as it still partially is today.

During this period the number of Thai people on Phuket increased greatly as the Thai population as a whole more than tripled from around 15 million in 1945 to over 50 million by 1985. Many Thais moved from surrounding regions to Phuket, which was relatively prosperous from tin and rubber, to find work. The Chinese and Muslims, previously in the majority on Phuket, continued to assimilate, intermarry and also become more Thai. The whole population was also imbued daily at school and afterwards with the need to respect their new country of Thailand, the anthem, the flag and the king, so that by the 1980s, most of Phuket's previously racially diverse residents began to feel they were now Thai people and Phuket Island was an integral part of the kingdom of Thailand.

Both the king and the successive military governments encouraged self-sufficiency and widespread education. In 1932, when the military first took over, Thailand had fewer than 1.2 million people who had finished school. Today the figure is closer to 40 million. They also better integrated the country and its economy by building up its national road network and promoted and guided first agriculture and then industrial development which helped the Thai economy – and its numerous Chinese businessmen – to make Thailand's economy one of the, if not the, fastest growing in the world since the Second World War.

The Demise of Tin Mining

Union Carbide of the USA built a modern tin-smelting factory at Ao Makham near the deep-water port in 1965. But by the late 1970s the tin industry, Phuket's traditional breadwinner, began to flounder. Phuket's tin yields began to fall as the island's better and more easily mined ore bodies ran out at the same time as cheaper sources of supply opened up in Bolivia, Brazil, Indonesia, Peru, China and Russia. In the late 1970s and 1980s, the dredgers and mines in Phuket started shutting down, a process accelerated by a slump in the world price of tin in the 1980s. The Standard Chartered Bank, which originally came to Phuket to service the tin market and had helped to create a cash economy on the island, closed its doors in 1974. By the 1980s local entrepreneurs, seeing the writing on the wall for tin, also saw the rising potential for tourism. But these two industries were somewhat incompatible and the government sided with the proponents of tourism. Taxes on tin were increased to 24 percent, which eventually drove even Tongkah Harbour C° , the grand old dame of Phuket's tin-mining glory days, to close its last regional tin-dredging operations in Phang Nga in 2005. It now mines for gold in central and northern Thailand.

38.6 A dredger on the klong that empties into Bang Tao Bay between the Sunwing Hotel and Bliss Beach club site. Such dredgers worked in Bang Tao Bay until the late 1980s.

A Tantalum Tantrum

The 1970s, however, did see a new rising global demand for a by-product of Phuket's tin called tantalum. This is used in electronics, nuclear missiles and medical equipment. The rich tantalum content of the soil had never been processed in Phuket and most of the slag (old mined ore) left over from decades of tin mining remained replete with this expensive new metal. In the mid-1980s some local entrepreneurs moved to build a tantalum smelter to reap new profits from the old slag piles and the government and Thai banks stepped in to assist the project. The year 1986, however, saw the deadly gas leak at the Union Carbide plant in India and then the nuclear plant meltdown at Chernobyl in Russia. Rumors soon spread amongst the Phuket population that the new tantalum processor was potentially dangerous to Phuket's air and environment and many local residents decided they did not want the smelter built on the island. But the developers, government and banks pushed on regardless. So, in a classic old-style Phuket rebellion, a crowd of thousands of local residents and activists attacked the smelter, burnt it down and went on a rampage in Phuket town, burning police cars and smashing the banks that had funded the plant and also setting fire to the Merlin Hotel, where the people behind the project stayed. The army had to be called in to restore order, but the protest, as usual, worked. The government agreed that the smelter should be built at the Map Ta Phut industrial zone on the eastern seaboard, where, incidentally, cancer rates are now the highest in Thailand.

This incident, along with so many other invasions and blockades of government buildings over the years, such as a takeover of the island's international airport by political protesters in 2009, show that – as through most of its history – the apparently laid-back, smiling local people of Phuket still remain very independent-minded, refractory and truculent. Phuket locals still regularly disregard rulings and laws from Bangkok and enforce their will locally by rioting and blockading police stations, government offices, hotels or other workplaces to get redress for perceived ills. Disputes in both business and love on the island are still, almost weekly, resolved by the simple expedient of having one's opponent shot dead by a relatively inexpensive hit-man.

Laws made in Bangkok are applied lightly. For example, despite a law made in 1996 that motorcycle helmets must be worn on pain of a fine or imprisonment, a 2010 police night study on Phuket showed that less than 25 percent of motorcyclists on Phuket ever bother to wear them. The global trend towards increasing government intervention into people's lives now happening in much of the world is resisted by the people of Phuket, who prefer a more human, free and easy lifestyle. And so apparently do the millions of visitors from all over the world who spend billions of dollars each year to come to the island to holiday or live. The island's enduring independent and free character will no doubt remain as long the island stays under the control of the Thais – the "free people".

The Growth of Tourism
By 1968 over 50,000 US troops were stationed in Thailand to support the war in Vietnam. Numerous hotels, bars and other facilities opened to serve them. The dress code reforms that had been introduced by the later Chakri kings and more strictly enforced by Field Marshal Phibun had succeeded in changing Thai girls from the short-haired, black-toothed, red-ochre-mouthed, betel-chewing, unisex-clothed beings of the past, into attractive and shapely young women dressed in modern Western clothes. Under their new make-up and Western fashion clothes however, these Thai girls still maintained their traditionally freer views on sexuality and chastity and also their traditional role as market dealers and money earners. It was, therefore, not surprising that large numbers of girls started moving into the cities or to work in hotels and bars near the US bases to provide comfort services to these thousands of moneyed US troops and sailors.

At the same time, coming out of the same former unisex-dressing culture of Thailand and its more free sexual attitudes, where Thai Buddhism traditionally never regarded same-sex eroticism or sodomy as a sin, some homosexual Thai men also began to dress as women to try to make some money from these horny foreigners too. These transvestite or trans-gender "katoeys", or "Lady-boys", first started appearing in the late 1960s night spots of Udonthani and Bangkok. They have since become a common and accepted feature of Thailand's accommodating culture. Over the last two decades, with tourist numbers soaring in Phuket, these katoeys have made the fast nightlife world of Patong one of their main national centers, and from this Phuket has also recently evolved into a leading world center for sex-change operations.

Due to this extensive US presence in the 1960s and 1970s, Thai people of all levels also became more exposed to Westerners' ways and needs and a tourism infrastructure of roads, airports, hotels, bars and sex-services was in place already as global tourism and air travel became cheaper and more mass market. During the early 1970s, many young backpackers began traveling through Asia and passing overland up or down the Malay Peninsula. Word spread amongst them about idyllic Phuket Island

38.7 Surin Beach in the early 1970s looking out from what was the edge of Phuket's first nine-hole golf course and clubhouse (now Surin park) built by Phraya Rassada in 1912.

and particularly a beach called Patong (banana tree forest) – a laid-back place with an all-weather white sand beach surrounded by palms and tropical hills where beer, sex, seafood, marijuana, massages and magic mushroom omelets were cheap and available.

Patong in the 1970s still consisted of just one rustic Thai village (near Wat Patong) and one Muslim fishing village a bit nearer the beach. The rest was an empty pastoral scene of coconut palms, fruit trees, water buffalo pasture, swamp land and rice fields. Until the first dirt trail was cut over the hill from Phuket town in 1947, Patong was only accessible by boat or by a difficult trek over the thick, jungled hills from Kathu through tiger country. With the coming of backpackers in the 1970s, thatched rental bungalows began to appear on Patong and other west coast beaches, charging as little as 10 baht a night. Then a few restaurants and bars appeared. The current sealed road over the hill was only completed in 1976 and electricity first arrived in Patong only in 1979.

In 1976 Phuket airport became international and during the 1980s visitor numbers to the island began to rise rapidly. Phuket's accommodation moved more up-market in the late 1980s with the construction of more salubrious brand-name beach hotels such as Club Med in Kata, Holiday Inn in Patong, the Phuket Yacht Club in Nai Harn, the Meridien in Karon, the Chedi and Amanpuri in Surin and the Laguna Resort, built on old tin mine lands in Bangtao. The Yacht Haven and Boat Lagoon marinas, several golf courses and a myriad of diving businesses opened in the early 1990s, promoting yachting, boating, golf and scuba diving.

Since the mid 1990s, the pace of hotel development became frantic. In 1995 there were less than 8,000 hotel rooms on Phuket; today there are well over 50,000 official rooms and probably almost as many unregistered rooms and thousands more apartments and villas that are rented out each year. This massive growth in tourists and visitors has given rise to a hectic kaleidoscope of new restaurants, bars, discotheques, shopping centers, bike rentals, massage parlors, tour operators, taxis, supermarkets etc. In Patong in 1980, prime land could still be bought for less than 50,000 baht a rai. Today 30 years later it sells for up to 80 million baht per rai, a 1,500-fold increase, or an average long-term appreciation over this period of around 50% per year, every year.

38.8 Looking north on Patong Beach in 1980. No hotels, restaurants and apartments blocks were built on the shore and hillsides yet.

Phuket now receives almost six million visitors annually and this number continues to rise. That is an average of over 16,000 visitors a day. The island's tourist industry is now making vast profits for the whole country. But, just as in the tin-mining industry boom days, Phuket still gets a relatively raw deal from Bangkok which collects much of this income and redistributes these revenues to each provinces based on politics and the officially registered population not based on how many people actually live there or the income revenue that province produces. Last year, in 2011, for example, Phuket's budget allocation from the central government was the 72nd smallest of 76 provinces despite the fact that Phuket is high in the top ten income earning provinces for the Thai government most years.

The official registered population for government budget purposes over the last decade was only 313,835. In reality during that period there was around two to three times that many people living on the island most days. These are mainly Thais from, and registered in, other provinces who now live and work in Phuket. There are tens of thousands of laborers from neighboring countries who now do the dirty jobs Phuket people no longer want nor need to do. These people are often illegally on the island and not counted. Then there are the tens of thousands of foreign tourists and long-term foreign residents none of whom were counted either.

Slightly more realistically, the latest preliminary figures just released from the most recent 2010 census taken on Phuket show the official population of Phuket as 525,000, of which 115,881, (21%) are foreigners, 67,000 of whom are laborers and low-paid workers from Burma, Lao and Cambodia. But this new census is still way short of the mark, as even the census taking department head has admitted in interviews. For example, much of this latest census was voluntary and people were simply expected to know about it and download forms from the Internet and send them in. In reality most people did not do this and no census takers ever visited their house. The thousands of tourists each day on Phuket are not counted and thousands of Burmese and Lao workers are illegally employed on Phuket so both they and their employers avoid having them counted. Therefore a more realistic guess at the actual number of people on Phuket most days at the present time (in 2012) must be well over one million people and growing.

This chronic problem of insufficient funds redistributed by Bangkok to Phuket means that Phuket's Police force remains too small and inadequately funded, government hospitals and schools are underequipped and undersupplied, and the road system is always under pressure. Bangkok's refusal to devolve much direct fiscal power to Phuket province also means that most of the generally ambitious local Phuket government proposed projects to improve the island such as road widening, a convention center, more piped water, putting electric wires underground, making it a special economic zone, etc. Usually require permission from a myriad of different government departments in Bangkok who are often slow to respond or politically motivated or simply corrupt.

Despite these handicaps the local government and utility providers on Phuket do deserve credit for managing to develop the island's infrastructure, its electric and water supply, roads, garbage disposal, street cleaning, drainage, airport capability, etc. at a pace fast enough to almost keep up with the breakneck pace of private sector development on the island over the past two decades and rapid growth in population and vehicle numbers.

The 21st Century Property Boom

After the Asian financial crisis of 1997, the Thai baht's traditional peg to the US dollar (of 25 baht to the dollar) collapsed. The baht fell to a low of 58 baht to the US dollar, making Phuket, for foreigners at least, suddenly around half the price it had been. This new price attractiveness, plus the infrastructure already developed on Phuket for foreign tourists, gave rise to a new industry on the island – residential housing development for foreigners. Starting almost entirely after the 1998 baht crash, and continuing until today (2012), over 10,000 villas and apartments, mainly for foreign owners, have popped up like acne all over the island at an average rate of well over 50 new villas or apartments per month during the first decade of the 21st century. This intense property boom sucked a tsunami of foreign money into Phuket in a short period, flooding the island with cash and driving up land prices everywhere. Even outlying parts of the island have experienced the same increase in the capital value of property – of over 1,000 percent over the last decade – that has been seen in Patong.

This housing development boom simultaneously spawned a massive range of new support businesses all over the island – architects, lawyers, banks, accountants, brokers, project managers, construction companies, building materials suppliers, swimming pool companies, furniture shops, antiques dealers, car sales premises, landscaping services, property management companies, etc. Unlike tourism, which can be a fickle business, Phuket's new property development business is a more permanent industry that can be viewed almost in agricultural terms. The vast new crops of villas that are sprouting up so quickly all over the island are now permanent features, rather like the rubber trees planted early last century. These foreign owned villas and apartments are now harvested annually by a wide range of local service providers: of home repairs, pool maintenance, estate management, accounting services, security, gardeners, maids, etc. (and thieves), who ensure that like the rubber trees, they provide a regular annual cash crop to the island.

38.9 A villa at Samsara, one of thousands of luxury villas built and bought mainly by foreigners which attracted a new tsunami of investment cash and prosperity to the islands property market in the first decade of the 21st century.

Phuket City and Phuket's People Today

After its first growth spurt and glory days under Phraya Rassada in the early 20th century (see Chapter 32), Phuket town benefited later from post-war rubber and tin prosperity in the 1950s, 1960s and 1970s. However, despite its increasing wealth it has in many ways kept its rough and ready, Chinese mining-town character, replete with corruption, vice, shootings, prostitution and even slavery. In 1984, for example, after a fire in one cheap brothel hidden at the back of a local food shop in town, the charred remains of five young girls were found still chained to their beds in rooms with locked iron doors. The police chief confirmed they had been Isan girls lured south and held as captive slave prostitutes. The brothel owner, a well-known local man, admitted to the crime and was fined a mere 4,000 baht, which even then was a most paltry sum.[1001]

Today, much of the wealth being generated by Phuket's booming tourism, land sales and development industry is still ultimately cornered by the old élite Sino-Thai families of Phuket Town who own much of the island's land plus many hotels and import agencies for alcohol, soft drinks, cars, building materials, etc. Phuket town is now nearly 200 years old, and as its residents grow richer and more respectable, the Sino-Thai community there now have a saying "If someone is rich, please don't ask how they got their money, if someone is poor, please don't ask why".

In 2004 Phuket town was given official city status. The city has also seen huge increases in the value of its real estate over the last few years. Today many of Phuket city's leading residents are still local-born Phuketian who no longer see China as their ancestral home as their great-grandparents and some grandparents did. They have now become Thais and Phuket is their new ancestral home. Phuket city's old Sino-European buildings and shop-houses, many of which had been left to decay slowly in the tropical rain and sun are now more respected by the affluent locals for their heritage, cultural and economic value and are now being restored by locals and foreigners. Old Phuket town is now being promoted by the local Peranakans to gain UNESCO world heritage status like Georgetown on neighboring Penang Island.

Phuket's Muslims Today

The Muslims of Phuket today, as we have seen, come from many different heritages – Malay, Tamil, Arab, Pakistani, Indian, Javanese and Persian – but since Phibun's reforms, they are now generally all known as Thai Muslims. Since the Second World War, the comparative affluence of Phuket also attracted many more Malays and Muslims, mainly fishermen and their families, from other places on the coast such as Krabi, Ko Lanta and Langkawi in Malaysia. In Phuket, they settled to fish or grew rubber, established fruit orchards and opened small businesses. Today a majority work in the tourism and hotel industry. Muslims make up over 30 percent of Phuket's population, there are over 50 mosques on the island and most Muslims usually live in the vicinity of these mosques. Almost all Phuket's Muslims are Sunnis and speak Thai, unlike the more recalcitrant Malay Muslims in Thailand's thorny southeast, who still continue to speak their native Jawi or Bahasa Malay.

Phuket's Muslims have also benefited handsomely from the recent property price boom, which has been particularly marked for coastal and beachfront land. This is because, as we have seen, the Muslims traditionally lived nearer the coast, while the Thais traditionally lived inland for security and because the land was better for agriculture. Beachfront land was previously only second-class land, on which coconut tree plantations gave a poor yield or a few goats grazed. However, with the tourism boom, many Muslims have become multi-millionaires by selling their now premium beachfront land to foreign property developers. Unless one knows the local village gossip, however, it is not always very apparent which of the local Muslims are super-rich millionaires and which are dirt poor, as they usually continue to dress and live humbly in their traditional way in their community regardless of how wealthy they are.

Phuket remains a place of great religious tolerance. There are few other places in the world like Phuket city, where one can find a Catholic church, a Muslim mosque, a Thai wat and a Chinese temple all on the same street and never any religious animosity between them. Given this tolerant religious backdrop and the balmy climate of the island,

Phuket's Muslims are on the whole a relaxed and liberal group. Many have married with Buddhists and farrangs, and in this way they continue to forge Phuket's age old, mixed blood melting pot character.

Phuket's Indians Today

During the administrations of Phibun and succeeding nationalistic military governments, the Indians in Thailand, like the Chinese, were pressured to assimilate, speak Thai and take up Thai nationality. With the recent tourism boom many more immigrants from the subcontinent have arrived – Indians, Pakistanis and Nepalese – mainly to work in their traditional business of textiles and tailoring shops, where they have both connections and the advantage over most Thais of speaking better English, enabling them to sell more easily to tourists. The island's small Sikh community has been particularly successful in post-war Phuket, having expanded the range of businesses in which Sikhs have traditionally engaged, such as usury and textiles, to include property, shops, restaurants and hotels and they are now one of Phuket's more affluent communities.

Phuket's Farangs Today

As we have seen, in the 20 years between 1990 to 2010, as better international travel, communication, housing and recreation facilities were developed on Phuket, an influx of somewhere between 30-50,000 international expats arrived to live on the island. They either work, run businesses, are retired or simply use the island as a pleasant global base in an increasingly cyber-connected world. These foreign expats originate mainly from Europe and most are British, French, Dutch, Swiss and Germans, but also from the rest of the world, particularly Australia, America, Russia, Korea and Japan.

This growing farang community on Phuket, (and in all Thailand), still remains completely disenfranchised because Bangkok still chooses to adhere to many of the old nationalistic laws born from the insecurity of the Phibun era 70 years ago. A majority of these new farang immigrants on Phuket today have married Thai spouses, are raising families, living, working, investing, and paying taxes in Phuket, in some cases for over 30 years. Despite this they are still strictly denied any right to vote, own land or certain businesses or have any real political representation or power. This lack of political power, plus the fact that farangs are perceived by many locals as automatically rich, unfortunately makes them an easy target for some of the more unscrupulous and corrupt locals and government officials on Phuket who use the ill-defined or poorly-enforced Thai laws to line their own pockets at the foreigners expense. There remains a common trend for populist Thai officials in Bangkok and Phuket to blame foreigners, often irrationally, for many of the ills of their own society.

Some of these new farang residents do sometimes behave rather arrogantly, make little effort to learn Thai and put little back into the community. However as a whole, this growing and generally entrepreneurial new international community, which now makes up almost 10% of Phuket's population does punch well above its weight in contributing to both the island's economy and society. Not just through their many investments, businesses and spending but also via the several farang-funded charities that have been established on the island, also new farang-built and operated international schools that are open to all and new international sports facilities such as Thanyapura (built by a German), or the new cricket ground (built by a former British consul on Phuket). Even new spiritual facilities have been established on this most religiously tolerant island such as the new, gold-domed, Russian-funded, Orthodox Church in Thalang or the new Kuwaiti-funded Mosque in Patong.

38.11 Luk Kreung; the authors two daughters of mixed Thai, Chinese and Scottish descent on summer holiday in Europe. Phuket's rapidly expanding new generation of Luk Kreung are an amazingly cosmopolitan, culturally diverse and well travelled group of youngsters and the modern embodiment of the millenia-old tradition of eastern and western cultures meeting and synthesizing on Phuket's balmy shores.

Into the Future

Most of this new community of international expat immigrants arrived as single men. And, much like the many Indian, Arab, Portuguese and Chinese immigrants in the past, many have now married or interbred with Thai women and are raising 'luk kreung' ('half-children') - as the mixed-blood children of Thais and farangs are known in Thai. These children qualify for Thai citizenship from their mothers' side and likely will have full political rights in the country. This new phase of widespread Thai-farang interbreeding on Phuket is still mainly in its first generation. As we have seen from the history of Phuket it takes about two to three generations for the visitors and existing islanders to mutually absorb the best of each other's cultures and assimilate. In the future these numerous luk kreung now being born on Phuket should therefore ensure that the island will continue to develop into an ever more cosmopolitan, and hopefully, a more considerate and less corrupt society.

Although he is in sprightly good health for his age, Sakul Na Nakorn is nearly 90 years old. He is a local Sino-Thai man of good heritage, the result of a union between Ligor's old Thai-Malay Na Nakorn family and a successful Phuket Hokkien Chinese mining family. In his youth in the late 1930s, during Phibun's clampdown on Chinese schools, Sakul was, like many of his peers, sent to study in a British school in Penang. He became a British-qualified mining engineer and after the Second World War he worked with British and Australian mining companies in Phuket. He is another example of the ancient tradition of eastern and western culture meeting and merging on Phuket. He has seen many changes on the island during his long and colorful life and when asked his feelings about the recent rapid development on the island he replied cheerfully; "This is Phuket. We adopt what's good and we reject what's bad. That's what the people of this island have been doing for thousands of years".

Bibliography

Abbreviations:

BEFEO	Bulletin de L'Ecole Française d'Extrême Orient
CUP	Cambridge University Press
EUP	Eastern Universities Press
FO	Foreign Office Historical Records
HKJO	Hong Kong Journals online see: http://sunzi1.lib.hku.hk/hkjo/
IAHA	International Association of Historians of Asia
JBBRAS	Journal of the Burmese Branch Royal Asiatic Society
JBRS	Journal of the Burma Research Society
JMBRAS	Journal of the Malayan Branch Royal Asiatic Society
JRAS	Journal of the Royal Asiatic Society
JRGS	Journal of the Royal Geographical Society
JSBRAS	Journal of the Singapore Branch Royal Asiatic Society
JSEAH	Journal of South East Asian History
JSEAS	Journal of South East Asian Studies
JSS	Journal of the Siam Society
MASJ	Modern Asian Studies Journal
MJHPSS	Malaysian Journal of History, Politics and Strategic Studies
OUP	Oxford University Press
SEA	South East Asia
SOAS	School of Oriental and African Studies
SST	Singapore Straits Times

Ahmat S: Balastier, First American Consul in Singapore 1833-1852, 1966, JMBRAS, Vol. 39

Alatas SH: The Myth of the Lazy Native, 1977, Cass & Co, London

Albuquerque A: Commentarios do Affonso Alboquerque, 1557, Hakluyt Society, London

Aldrich R: The Key to the South, 1993, OUP, Oxford

Anandale N: The Siamese Malay States, 1900, Scottish Geographical Journal, Vol. 16

Andaya BW and Andaya LY: A History of Malaysia, 1982, Palgrave, Basingstoke

Anderson J: English Intercourse with Siam in the 17th century,1889, Kegan Paul and Co. , London

Anderson J: Descriptive Sketch of the Tin Countries, 1962, JMBRAS, Vol. 35(4)

Anderson J: Political and Commercial Considerations Relative to The Malayan Peninsula, 1824, W. Cox, London

Aung Thwin: The problem of Ceylonese-Burmese relations in the 12th century, 1976, JSS, Vol 64, No 1

Bacon G: Siam Land of the White Elephant, 1893, New York, reprinted 2000, Orchid Press, Bangkok

Baker C, Na Pombejra D, Van der Kraan A and Wyatt DK: Van Vliet's Siam, 2005, Silkworm Books, Chiang Mai

Bangkok Post: Chronicle of Thailand, Headline news since 1946, 2010, Bangkok Post editions, Didier Millet (ed), Bangkok

Barbosa, D: An account of the countries bordering the Indian Ocean, 1518, Vols 1 and 2, reprinted 2002, Longworth

Basset DK: The New Cambridge History of India, 1989, Vols 2-5, CUP

Basset DK: The British in SEA in 17th and 18th centuries, 1990, Paper no. 18, S. E. A Studies, Hull University

Bastin J: A Historical Sketch of Penang in 1794, 1959, JMBRAS, Vol. 32(1)

Bastin J and Winks RW: Malaysia Selected Historical Writings, 1966, OUP, Kuala Lumpur

Beekman D: A voyage to and from the island of Borneo, 1718, Warner and Bartley, London

BBC: WW2 People's War. An archive of World War Two memories, available at: www.bbc.co.uk/

ww2peopleswar/stories/

Begbie PJ: The Malayan Peninsula, 1834, reprinted 1967, OUP, Kuala Lumpur

Benedict R: Thai Culture and Behaviour, 1952, S. E A. Program Data paper No. 96, Cornell University

Birch De Gray W: The Commentaries of the Great Afonso D'alboquerque, 1875, Hakluyt Society, Vol. 2

Blackburn TR: The Defeat of Ava – The First Anglo Burmese War 1824-26, 2009, APH Publishing, New Delhi

Blagden CO: Report of Governor Balthazar Bort on Malacca 1665-1677, 1927, JMBRAS, Vol. 5(1)

Blankwaart W: Notes upon the relations between Holland and Siam, 1926, JSS, Vol. 20(3)

Bock C: Temples and Elephants: A Journey Through Upper Siam and Lao, 1884, London, reprinted 1986, OUP, Kuala Lumpur

Bonney R: Francis Light and Penang, 1965, JMBRAS, Vol. 38(1)

Bowie KA: Slavery in nineteenth century Northern Thailand, 2006, Kyoto Review of SEA

Bowrey T: A Geographical Account of Countries Around the Bay of Bengal 1669-1679, 1679, reprinted 1905, reprinted 1993, Delhi

Bowring J: The Kingdom and the People of Siam, Vols 1 and 2, 1857, JW Parker, London, 1857, reprinted 1989, OUP, Kuala Lumpur

Boxer CR: The Portuguese Seaborne Empire 1415-1825, 1969, Hutchinson, London

Boxer CR: The Dutch Seaborne Empire 1600-1800, 1977, Hutchinson, London

Braddell R: Notes on Ancient Times in Malaya, 1947, JMBRAS, Vol. 20, reprinted as A Study of ancient times in the Malay Peninsula, 1980, MBRAS, Kuala Lumpur

Breazeale K: From Japan to Arabia; Ayutthaya's Maritime Relations with Asia, 1999, The Foundation for the Promotion of Social Sciences and Humanities Textbooks Project, Bangkok

Breazeale K: The Memoirs of Pierre Poivre; The Thai Port of Mergui in 1745, 2009, JSS, Vol. 97

Briggs LP: The Appearance and Usage of the terms 'Tai, Thai, Siamese, and Lao', Journal of the American Oriental Society, No. 69, April 1949

Brown RJ: Chinese Business Enterprise, Vol. 1, 1996, Taylor & Francis

Bruce J: The Annals of the Honorable East-India Company, 1810, Black, Perry and Kingsbury, London

Bruce R: King Mongkut and His Treaty With Britain, 1969, Journal of the Royal Asiatic Society, Hong Kong, Vol. 9

Bruguiere B: Description of Siam in 1829, translated K Breazeale and M Smithies, 2008, JSS, Vol. 96

Buchanan K: The Southeast Asian World: An Introductory Essay, 1968, Anchor Books, Doubleday, New York

Bulley A: Free Mariner: John Adolphus Pope in the East Indies 1786-1821, 1992, British Association for Cemeteries in South Asia, London

Bunnang T: The Provincial Administration of Siam 1892-1915, 1976, OUP, Kuala Lumpur

Burney H: The Burney Papers, Records of the Relations Between Siam and Foreign Countries, 16 vols, 1915, Vajiranana National Library, Bangkok

Burton RF: The Thousand and One Nights, 1885, London

Busch N: Thailand: An Introduction to Modern Siam, 1959, Van Nostrand, Princeton, NJ

Cady JF: South East Asia: Its Historical Development, 1964, McGraw-Hill, NY

Cambridge History of South East Asia: Vol. 1, Part 1, From Early Times to 1500, 1999, CUP, Cambridge

Cambridge History of South East Asia: Vol. 1, Part 2, 1500-1800, 1999, CUP, Cambridge

Chakrabongse C: Lords of Life: The Paternal Monarchy of Bangkok 1782-1932, 1960, Taplinger, New York

Chandran MJ: The Contest For Siam 1889-1902: A Study in Diplomatic Rivalry, 1977, Penerbit Universiti, Kuala Lumpur

Chou Ta Kwan [Zhou Daguan]: The Customs of Cambodia, 1902, translated P Pelliot, reprinted 1993, The Siam Society, Bangkok. (See also Tchou Ta Kwan 1902 and Zhou Daguan 2007)

Chin YF: Chinese Female Immigration to Malaya, 1980, in MA Hassan and HS Rahman (eds), The Eighth Conference, IAHA: selected papers

Chinakorn P: A History of Thalang and Phuket (in Thai), 2001, Phuket

Chutintaranond S: Cakravartin Ideology 1538-1854, 1988, JSEAS (Special Burma Issue)

Chutintaranond S: The Image of the Burmese Enemy in Thai Perceptions and Historical Writings, 1992, JSS, Vol. 80(1)

Chutintaranond S and Than Tun: On Both Sides of the Tenasserim range: A history of Siamese Burmese relations, 1995, Asian Studies Monographs No: 050, Chulalongkorn University, Bangkok

Clodd HP:Malaya's First British Pioneer – The Life of Sir Francis Light, 1948, Luzac and Co. , London

Coedes G: The Empire of the South Sea, 1944, JSS Vol. 35(2)

Coedes G: The Indianised States of Southeast Asia, 1968, University of Hawaii Press, Honolulu

Cogan H (trans): The Voyage and Adventures of Fernand Mendez Pinto, 1969, Dawsons, London

Cohen E: The Chinese Vegetarian Festival in Phuket, 2001, White Lotus, Bangkok

Collis M: Siamese White, 1936, Faber & Faber, reprinted 1986 DD Books, Bangkok

Conrad, J: Typhoon, 1902, Putnam, New York

Correa G: The Three Voyages of Vasco da Gamma and His Viceroyalty, 1869, Hakluyt Society, London

Crawfurd J: History of the Indian Archipeligo, Vols 1-3, 1820, Archibald Constable and Co. , Edinburgh

Crawfurd J: The Crawfurd Papers, 1821, reprinted 1915, Vajiranana National Library Thailand

Crawfurd J: Journal of An Embassy to Siam and Cochin China, 1822, reprinted (DK Wyatt, ed) 1967, OUP, Kuala Lumpur

Curzon G: The Siamese Boundary Question, 1893, The Nineteenth Century Journal, No. 197, July 1983, London

Cushman J: Chinese Kinship, Marriage Strategies, and Social Mobility, Proceedings of the International Conference on Thai Studies, Vol. 1, Australian National University, Canberra, July 3-6, 1987

Cushman J: Family and State: The Formation of a Sino Thai Tin Mining Dynasty, 1991, OUP, Singapore

Cushman D: The Royal Chronicles of Ayutthaya, A Synoptic Translation (ed DK Wyatt), 2006, Siam Society, Bangkok

Cushman J and Milner AC: Eighteenth and Nineteenth Century Chinese Accounts of the Malay Peninsula, 1979, JMBRAS, Vol. 52(1)

Da Gama V: Journal of The First Voyage, 1898, edited by Ravenstein, Hakluyt Society, London

Dalton W: Phaulkon the Adventurer, 1862, Beaten, London

Dampier W: A New Voyage Round The World, Vols 1 and 2, 1697, reprinted 1927, Argonaut Press, London

Damrong R: The History of Renong, 1928, Bangkok

Damrong R: The Introduction of Western Culture in Siam, 1959, JSS, Vol. VII

Damrong, Prince Rajanubhab: Phra Raja Phongsawadan Krung Rattanakosin Rajakan [The Royal Annals of Bangkok, King Rama II], 1983, Khuru Sabha, Bangkok

Damrong R: Our Wars With The Burmese 1539-1767, 2001, White Lotus Press, Bangkok

De Barros J: Segunda Décadas da Ásia &c. , 1553, Germão Galherde, Lisbon

De Bourges J: Relation du Voyage de Mgr. l'Evéque de Beryte, vicaire apostolique du Royaume de la Cochinchine 1666, Denys Bechet, Paris

De Campos J: Early Portuguese Accounts of Thailand, 1940, JSS, Vol. 32(1)

De Choisey A: Journal of a Voyage to Siam 1685-1686, translated by M Smithies 1993, OUP, Kuala Lumpur

De Coutre, J: Aziatische Omzwervingen: Het Leven van Jaques de Coutre, 1988, unpublished manuscript, English translation by Philippe Annez

De Lionne A: Journal de Voyage au Siam de l'Abbe de Lionne, 1687, reprinted 2001, Eglises D'Asie, Paris

De Morga: History of the Philippine Islands, 1609, reprinted 1971, Hakluyt Society

Deller LV: The World of Tin, 1963, OUP, Kuala Lumpur

Devahuti D: India and Ancient Malaya, 1965, Eastern Universities Press, Singapore

Dhiravegin L: Siam and Colonialism 1855-1909, 1973, Thai Wattana Panich Co. , Bangkok

Dubbs H: A Roman City in Ancient China, 1957, The China Society, London

Earl GW: The Eastern Seas, 1837, Allen London 1971, OUP, Kuala Lumpur

Farrington A: Low's Mission to Southern Siam, 1824, reprinted 2007, White Lotus Press, Bangkok

Ferguson D: Captain Benjamin Wood's Expedition of 1596, 1903, JRGS, reprinted Loeb Classical Library, No. 231, 1984, Harvard University Press

Fielding K: The Settlement of Penang: By James Scott, 1955, JMBRAS, Vol 28, No 1, 37-51

Flood C (Trans): The Dynastic Chronicles, Bangkok Era, The Fourth Reign 1851-1868, Vol. 1, 1965, Tokyo

Flood T: Japan's Relations with Thailand 1928-1941, PhD dissertation, 1967, University of Washington, USA

Floris P: His Voyage to the East Indies in the Globe 1615-1611, reprinted 2002, White Lotus Press, Bangkok

Forrest T: A Voyage From Calcutta to the Merguei Archipelago, 1792, J. Robson, London

Fortescue JW: History of the British Army, Vol. 6, 1815-1838, 1923, London

Furnival JS: Samuel White – Port Officer of Mergui, Burma Research Society, Vol. 7, December 1917

Galvano A:Discoveries of the World, 1862, Hakluyt Society, London

Geocities: Thailand in World War II: see http://www. geocities. com/thailandwwii

Gerini GE: A Historical Retrospect of Junkceylon Island, 1905, JSS

Gervaise N: The Natural and Political History of the Kingdom of Siam, 1688, reprinted 1998, White Lotus Press, Bangkok

Gesick L: In the Land of Lady White Blood, 1995, SEA Program, Cornell University

Giles HF: A Critical Analysis of Van Vliet's Historical Account, 1938, JSS, Parts 1-5, Vol. 30(2) and 30(3)

Glover I: Early Trade Between India and Southeast Asia, 1989, Paper No. 16, SEA Studies, University of Hull

Grimes A: The Journey of Fa-Hsien from Ceylon to Canton, 1941, JMBRAS, Vol. 19(1)

Guehler U: The Travels of Ludovico di Varthema and His Visit to Siam, 1959, JSS, Vol. 7

Gullick JM: The Story of Early Kuala Lumpur, 1956, D. Moore, Singapore

Gullick JM: They Came to Malaysia – a Traveler's Anthology, 1995, OUP, Kuala Lumpur

Hall DGE: Henry Burney, A Political Biography, 1974, OUP, Kuala Lumpur

Hall, DGE: A History of South East Asia, 1987, Palgrave Macmillan, New York

Hall KR: Maritime Trade and State Development in Early Southeast Asia, 1985, University of Hawaii Press

Hamilton A: A New Account of the East Indies, Edinburgh, 1727, reprinted 1930, Argonaut Press, London

Hamilton A: A Scottish Sea Captain in South East Asia 1689-1723, 1997, edited by M. Smithies, Silkworm Books, Chiang Mai

Haseman JB: The Thai Resistance Movement During World War II, 2002, Silkworm Books, Chiang Mai

Havelock H: Memoirs of the Three Campaigns Undertaken by Sir Archibald Campbell in Ava, 1828, Serampore, India

Herbert T:Some Years Travels Into Diverse Parts of Asia and Africa, 1638, Hakluyt Society, London

Hummel CL and Phawandon P: Geology and Mineral Deposits of the Phuket Mining District South Thailand, 1967, Dept. of Mineral Resources, Bangkok

Hunter C: The Adventures of a Naval Officer, 1905, Digby Long & Co. , London

Hussain Z: The silent minority: Indians in Thailand, 1992, Chulongkorn University, Bangkok.

Hutchinson EW: 1688: The Revolution in Siam (Father de Beze), reprinted 1968, White Lotus Press, Bangkok

Hutchinson EW: Adventurers in Siam in the 17th century, 1985, DD Books, Bangkok (reprinted from JRAS, 1940)

Hyam R: Empire and Sexuality, 1991, Manchester University Press, Manchester

I Tsing: A Record of the Buddhist Religion: 671-695, 1896, translated by J. Takakusu, New Delhi, AES, 2005

Ibn Al Faqih: Concise Book of Countries, 903, MS 5229, Ridawiya Library, Frankfurt

Ibrahim IM: The Ship of Sulaiman, translated by J. O'Kane, 1972, Routledge & Kegan Paul, London

James H: Trade, Culture and Society in Thailand Before 1200, 2003, JSS, Vol. 91

James L: Raj, The Making and Unmaking of British India, 1997, St Martin's Press/Griffin, New York

Jayanama D: Siam and World War II, English edition by JG Keyes, Social Science Assoc. of Thailand Press

Jeshrun C: The Anglo French Declaration of January 1896 and The Independence of Siam, 1970, JSS, Vol. 58(2)

Jeshrun C: The Contest for Siam 1899-1902, 1977, Penerbit Universiti, Kuala Lumpur

Jumsai M: History of Thai German Relations, 1978, Chalermnit, Bangkok

Jumsai M: Popular History of Siam, 2000, Chalermnit, Bangkok

Kaempfer E: A Description of the Kingdom of Siam, 1690, reprinted 1987, White Orchid Press, Bangkok

Kasetsiri C: The Rise of Ayudhaya, A History of Siam in the Fourteenth and Fifteenth Centuries, 1976, OUP, Kuala Lumpur

Keay J: The Honourable Company, 1993, Harper Collins, London

Keay, J: The Spice Route, 2006, John Murray, London

Keppel H: The Expedition to Borneo of HMS Dido, 1846, reprinted 1991, OUP, Singapore

Khan GM: A History of Keddah, 1958, Premier Press, Penang

Khor NJK and Khoo KS: The Penang Po Leung, Monograph 37, 2004, MBRAS, Kuala Lumpur

Kim KK: The History of South East, South and East Asia, Essays, 1977, OUP, Kuala Lumpur

Kleinen J and Osseweijer M: Pirates, Ports and Coasts in Asia, 2010, ISEAS Publishing, Singapore

Koening, DR: Journal of a Voyage From India to Siam and Malacca in 1779, 1894, JSBRAS

Kornerup E: Friendly Siam: Thailand in the 1920s, 1928, Putnam, New York (translated M Guiterman), reprinted 1999, White Lotus Press, Bangkok

Kynnersley CW: Notes of visits to Phuket, Ghirbee and Trang, 1904, JSBRAS, Vol 42

Landon KP: The Chinese in Thailand, 1941, OUP, London

Launay A:Histoire de la Mission de Siam 1662-1811, 1920, Documents Historiques, Vol. 2, Paris

Le Blanc M: The History of Siam, Vols 1 and 2, 1692, Horace Molin, Lyons, reprinted 2003, Silkworm Books, Chiang Mai

Lee KH and Tan CB: The Chinese in Malaysia, 2000, OUP, Kuala Lumpur

Legge J: A Record of Buddhist Kingdoms (account by Fa Hsien 399-414), 1886, reprinted 1965, Paragon, London

Leider P: Tilling The Lord's Vineyard and Defending Portuguese Interests, 2002, JSS, Vol. 90(1) and 90(2)

Lewis D: Jan Compagnie in the Straits of Malacca 1641-1795, 1995, Ohio University, Athens, Ohio

Liang Shu (or) The Book of Liang: edited by Yao Silian, 635, reprinted Sun Yat Sen University, Kaoshing, Taiwan

Light, F: A letter from Captain Light to Lord Cornwallis dated 20th June 1788, 1938, JMBRAS, Vol 16, No 1 (communicated to the MBRAS by CE Wurtzburg)

Lockhard C: Societies, Networks and Transitions: A Global History to 1500, 1998 Houghton Mifflin, Boston

Logan JR: The Journal of the Indian Archipelago, 1849, Bodleian Library, Oxford

Loofs H: Problems of Continuity in Buddhism, 1973, paper for the London Colloquy on early SEA, SOAS, London

Loubère S de La: The Kingdom of Siam, 1693, reprinted 1986, OUP, Singapore

Luce GH: The early Siam in Burma's History, 1958, JSS,Vol 46

Luce GH: The Geography of Burma under the Pagan Dynasty, 1959, JBRS, Vol 42

Luce GH: Old Burma – Early Pagan, 1971, JBRS, Vol 54

Lukas H: Christoph Carl Fernberger: The First Austrian in Patani and Ayudhya, 2007, Siam Society Lecture

Mabbet IW: Truth, Myth and Politics in Ancient India, 1971, Thompson Press, New Delhi

Mahmud N: British Policy towards Thailand during the Second World War, 1993 MJHPSS, Vol. 21, 83-124

Ma Huan: The Overall Survey of the Ocean Shores, translated J. Mills, 1970, Hakluyt Society, reprinted 1997, White Lotus Press, Bangkok

Majumdar RC: Ancient Indian Colonies in the Far East, Vol. 2, 1937, Asoke Kumar Majumdar, Dacca

Manarungsan S: Economic Development of Thailand 1850 -1950, 1989, University of Groningen, Holland

Marks T: The British Acquisition of Siamese Malaya (1896-1909), 1997, White Lotus Press, Bangkok

Marrison GE: The Siamese Wars with Malacca During the Reign of Muzaffar Shah, 1949, JMBRAS, Vol. 22(1)

Martin J: A History of the Diplomatic Relations Between Siam and the USA 1833-1929, 1948, PhD dissertation, Fletcher School of Law and Diplomacy, 2 vols

Maugham S: The Gentleman in the Parlour. A Record of a Journey from Rangoon to Haiphong, 1930, Heinemann, reprinted 2001, Vintage Classics, London

Miller H: The Story of Malaya, 1965, Faber & Faber, London

Mills JA: The Swinging Pendulum – A Study of Southern Tenasserim, 1997, JSS, Vol. 85

Mills JV: Two Dutch Portuguese Sea Fights, 1938, JMBRAS,Vol. 38(1)

Mills JV: Arab and Chinese Navigators in Malaysian Waters A. D. 1500, 1974, JMBRAS, Vol. 47(2)

Mills LA: British Malaya 1824-1867, reprinted 1966, OUP, Kuala Lumpur

Milton G: Nathaniel's Nutmeg, 1999, Hodder and Stoughton, London

Ming SL: References to SEA (translated by Wade), Asia Research Institute, Singapore, http://www. epress. nus. edu. sg/msl/

Moorhead FJ: A History of Malaya and Her Neighbours, Vol. 1, 1957, London

Moreland WH: Peter Floris, His Voyages to the East Indies, 1934, Hakluyt Society, London

Morgenthaler H: Matahari: Impressions of the Siamese Malayan Jungle, 1921, reprinted 1994 as Impressions of the Siamese-Malayan Jungle, White Lotus Press, Bangkok

Morson I: Four Hundred Years, the British and the Thais, 1993a, A Nai Suk's Edition, Bangkok

Morson I: The Connection Phuket, Penang and Adelaide, 1993b, Siam Society, Bangkok

Mouhot H: Travels in Siam 1858-1860, 1864, John Murray, reprinted 1986, White Lotus Press, Bangkok

Munro-Hay S: Nakhon Sri Thammarat: The Archeology, History and Legends, 2004, White Lotus Press, Bangkok

Murashima E: The Thai Japanese Alliance and the Chinese of Thailand (translated) in PH Kratoska (ed), Southeast Asian Minorities in the Wartime Japanese Empire, 2002, Routledge, New York

Na Pombera D: A Political History of Siam Under the Prasathong Dynasty 1629-1688, 1984, PhD thesis, London University

Na Pombejra D: Court Company and Campong, the VOC in Ayutthaya, 1992, Amarin Printing, Bangkok

Na Pombejra D: Towards a History of 17th Century Phuket, in S Chutintaranond and C Baker, Recalling Local Pasts: Autonomous History in South East Asia, 2002, Washington University, Seattle

Neale FA: Narrative of a Residence in Siam, 1852, reprinted 1986, White Lotus Press, Bangkok

Newbold TJ: A Political and Statistical Account of the British Settlements in the Straits of Malacca, 1839, J. Murray, reprinted 2008, Kessinger Publishing, Montana

O'Neill HS: The Natural and Political History of the Kingdom of Siam, 1928, Siam Observer Press, Bangkok

Osborn S: The Blockade of Keddah in 1838, 1857, reprinted 1987, OUP, Singapore

Osbourne M: Southeast Asia, An Introductory History, 1997, Silkworm Books, Chiang Mai

Owen N: Death and Disease in South East Asia, 1987, OUP, New York

Owen R: The Pirate Wind: Tales of the Sea-robbers of Malaysia, 1986, OUP, Singapore

Owens F: The Fall of Singapore, 2002, Penguin, London

Pallegoix JB: Description of the Thai Kingdom or Siam, 1854, reprinted 2000, White Lotus Press, Bangkok

Parker EH: History of the Churches of India, Burma and Siam, 1893a, China Review, Vol. 20(6)

Parker EH: The Coast of Tenasserim, 1893b, China Review, Vol. 20(4)

Parkin TG and Pomeroy AJ: Roman Social History, 2007, London

Parry JH: Europe and a Wider World, 1949, Hutchinson, London

Pearn B: An Introduction to the History of South East Asia, 1963, Longmans, Malaysia

Phuketscape: Magazine published by Old Phuket Town Foundation, Phuket City

Pinto Fernao M: Peregrinação: 1614 - The Travels of Mendez Pinto, translated by R. Catz, 1989, University of Chicago Press, Chicago

Pires T: The Suma Oriental: 1515, translated by A. Cortesao, reprinted 1990, Laurier Books, Ottawa

Pluvier J: South East Asia from Colonialism to Independence, 1974, OUP, Kuala Lumpur

Polo, Marco: The Travels, translated by R. Latham, 1958, Penguin Classics, Middlesex

Pramoj S: Thailand and Japan, 1943, Far Eastern Survey, 12(21), 204-208, Institute of Pacific Relations

Purcell V: The Chinese in South East Asia, London, 1951, reprinted 1965, OUP, London

Purcell V: The Chinese in Modern Malaya, 1956, D. Moore, Singapore

Raschke M: New Studies in Roman Commerce with the East, 1978, Aufstieg und Niedergang der römischen Welt im Spiegel der neueren Forschung II 9(2) (De Gruyter): 604-1361

Reid A: Female Roles in Precolonial Southeast Asia, 1988, MASJ, Vol. 22

Reid A: Southeast Asia in the Age of Commerce 1450-1680, Vol. 1, The Lands Below the Winds, 1988, Vol. 2, Expansion and Crisis, 1995, Yale University Press, New Haven, Connecticut

Reid A: Charting the Shape of Early Modern South East Asia, 2000, ISEAS

Reid A and Brewster J: Slavery, Bondage and Dependency in South East Asia, 1983, St Martin's Press, New York

Reynolds B: Thailand's Secret War, 2004, CUP, Cambridge

Roberts E: Embassy to the Eastern Courts of Cochin-China, China and Muscat, 1832-34, 1837, Harper and Brothers, New York, reprinted Scholarly Resources, New York

Rockhill, WW: Notes on relations and trade of China with the eastern archipelago and the coasts of the Indian Ocean during the fourteenth century, 1915, T'oung Pao, Vol 16: 236-271.

Ross JD: Sixty Years Life and Adventures in the Far East, 1911, Hutchinson, London

Rubin AP: The International Personality of the Malay Peninsula, 1974, Penerbit Universiti, Malaysia

Sakulpipatana P and Khoo SN: A Symposium on the Phuket-Penang Relationship, 2008, Thai Peranakan Association, Phuket

Sangermano F: A Description of the Burmese Empire, 1969, Augustus M Kelley, New York

Sardeasi DR: Southeast Asia Past and Present, 5th edn, 2009, Westview Press, Colorado

Sastri N: The Cholas, 1955, University of Madras, Madras

Satheun S: The Political life of Col. Phraya Ritthi Akhany a tiger soldier of the 1932 revolution, 1972, Wacharin Publications, Bangkok

Scammell GV: Indigenous Assistance in the Establishment of Portuguese Power, 1980, MASJ, Vol. 14(1)

Sejarah Melayu: The Malay Annals, translation by C. Brown, reprinted 1970, OUP, Kuala Lumpur

Sheehan JJ: Seventeenth Century Visitors to the Malay Peninsula, 1934, JMBRAS, Vol. 12(2)

Sherwin-White AN: Pliny, the Man and his Letters, 1989, CUP, Cambridge

Simmonds EHS: The Thalang Letters 1773-94, 1963, SOAS Bulletin, Vol. 26(3)

Simmonds EHS: Francis Light and the Ladies of Thalang, 1965, JMBRAS, Vol. 38(2)

Singhal DP: India and World Civilization, Vol 1, 1972, Rupa & Co. , New Delhi

Sirisena WM: Sri Lanka and South East Asia: Political, Religious and Cultural Relations, 1978, Sri Lanka University Press, Colombo

Skinner GW: Chinese Society in Siam, 1957, Cornell University Press, New York

Skinner C: The Interrogation of Zeya Suriya Kyaw 1809-1810, 1984, JSS, Vol. 72(1) and 72(2)

Skinner C: The Battle For Junk Ceylon, the Syair Sultan Maulana, 1985, Foris Publications, Dordrecht, Holland

Smith AH: Chinese Characteristics, 1894, Eastbridge, New York

Smith G: The Dutch in Seventeenth Century Thailand, 1974, De Kalb, Northern Illinois University Press

Smith M: A Physician at the Court of Siam, 1947, Country Life Ltd. , London, reprinted 1982, White Lotus, Bangkok

Smith VG: Princes, Nobles and Traders, 1980, Contributions to Asian Studies, Vol. XV

Smithies M: Jacques de Bourges and Siam, 1993, JSS, Vol. 81(2)

Smithies M: Descriptions of Old Siam, 1996, OUP, Kuala Lumpur

Smithies M: The Siam of Mendez Pinto's Travels, 1997, JSS, Vol. 85(1) and (2)

Smithies, M: A Resounding Failure: Martin and the French in Siam, 1998, Silkworm Books, Chiang Mai

Smithies M: Three Military Accounts of the 1688 Revolution in Siam, 2002, Orchid Press, Bangkok

Smithies M and Bressan L: Siam and the Vatican in the 17th Century, 2001, River Books, Bangkok

Smyth, HW: Five Years in Siam 1891-1896, 1994, White Lotus, Bangkok

Songprasert P: The Development of Chinese Capital in Southern Siam, 1868-1932, 1986, PhD thesis, Monash University, Melbourne

Srisudravarna S: The Real Face of Thai Sakdina Today, 1987, in C Reynolds (ed), Thai Radical Discourse, Cornell University, Ithaca, New York

Standage T: An Edible History of Humanity, 2005, Walker and Co. , New York

Stavorinus JS: Voyages to the East Indies, 1798, reprinted 1969, Damsons, London

Stevenson EL: Claudius Ptolemy: The Geography, 1932 (N. Y. Public Library) reprinted 1991, Dover, New York

Stifel LD: Rubber and the Economy of Southern Siam, 1971, JSS, Vol. 59(2)

Stone H: From Malacca to Malaya 1400-1965, 1966, G Harrap & Co. , London

Sujit Pornchai, Opinions on Thalang's History, 1985, Phuket, unpublished paper presented to History of Thalang Seminar

Suphasophon S: The Political Life of Col. Rithakkanay (in Thai), 1971, Wacharin Publishing, Bangkok

Suwannathat-Pian K: Thai Malay Relations from the 17th to the 20th Century, 1988, OUP, New York

Suwannathat-Pian K: Thailand's Durable Premier, 1995, OUP, Kuala Lumpur

Suyama T: Pang Societies and the Economy of Chinese Immigrants in Southeast Asia, in Papers on Malayan History, in KG Tregonning, ed, 1962, JSEAH, Singapore

Swan W: Japan's Economic Relations with Thailand 1875-1942, 2009, White Lotus Press, Bangkok

Swettenham FA: British Malaya: An Account of the Origin and Progress of British Influence, 1907, G Allen and Unwin, London

Swettenham FA: Footprints in Malaysia, 1942, Hutchinson, London

Syamanda R: A History of Thailand, 1972, reprinted 1988, Chulalongkorn University and Thai Watana Panich Co. , Ltd.

Tachard G:A Relation of the Voyage to Siam, 1688, reprinted 1981, White Orchid Press, Bangkok

Tarling N: The Fall of Imperial Britain in South East Asia, 1993, OUP, Singapore

Tarling N: Imperialism in South East Asia: A Fleeting Passing Phase, 2001, Routledge, London

Tate DJM: The Making of Modern South East Asia, 1979, OUP, Kuala Lumpur

Tawney CH: The Katha Sarit sagara; or, Ocean of the Streams of Story, 1880, reprinted 1993, Munshiram Manocharlal, New Delhi

Tchou Ta Kuan [Zhou Daguan]: Memoires Sur les Costumes de Cambodge, 1902, Trans: P Pelliot, BEFEO, Vol II, No 2. (See also Chou Ta Kwan 1902 and Zhou Daguan 2007)

Teixeira P: The Travels of Pedro Teixeira, 1902, Hakluyt Society, London

Templar J: The Private Letters of James Brooke, 1853, Richard Bentley, London

Thamsook N: The Anglo-Siamese negotiations 1900-1909, 1966, PhD thesis, London University, London

Thaitakoo D: Phuket Urban Conservation Versus Tourism, 1994, in M Askew, WS Logan and C Long (eds), Cultural Identity and Urban Change in South East Asia, Deakin University Press, Geelong, Australia

Thompson PA: Lotus Land: Being an Account of the Country and People of Southern Siam, 1906, T Werner Laurie, London

Thompson V: Thailand the new Siam, 1941, Macmillan and Co. , New York

Tregonning KG: Straits Tin – A Brief Account of the First Seventy Five Years, 1963, JMBRAS, Vol. 36(1)

Tsuji M: Singapore, The Japanese Version, 1960, Ure Smith, Sydney

Turner J: Spice, 2005, Vintage Books, Random House, New York

Turpin F: History of the Kingdom of Siam, 1771, reprint 2010, Applewood Books, Mass.

UKCIA. org: Marijuana – the First 12,000 Years, see: http://www. ukcia. org/research/abel/5. php

Van der Cruysse D: Siam and the West, 2002, Silkworm Books, Chiang Mai

Van Linschoten JH: His Discourse of Voyages into the East and West Indies, 1598, John Wolfe, London

Van Nijenrode C: Account of the Situation in the Kingdom of Siam, 1621, reprinted Historical Society of Utrecht, 27, 1871

Van Vliet J: Historical Account of Siam in the 17th Century, 1647, translated by WH Mundie, 1904, JSS, Vol. 30(2)

Vartema L: The Travels of Ludovico Varthema, 1863, Hakluyt Society, London

Vella WF: Siam under Rama III, 1957, Locust Valley, New York

Wade G: Southeast Asia in the Ming Shi-luan, Asia Research Institute, see http://epress. nus. edu. sg/msl/entry/768

Wales HG Quaritch: The Making of Greater India, 1951, Bernard Quaritch, London

Wales HG Quaritch: The Malay Peninsula in Hindu Times, 1976, Bernard Quaritch, London

Walters OW: The Fall of Srivijaya in Malay History, 1974, Cornell University Press, Ithaca, New York

Wang, G: The Nanhai Trade, 1958, JMBRAS, Vol. 2(2)

Warren JF: The Sulu Zone 1768-1898, 1985, New Day, Quezon City

Wheatley P: A Curious Feature on Early Maps of Malaya, 1954, Imago Mundi, Vol. 11

Wheatley P: The Malay Peninsula as Known to the Chinese in the 3rd Century, 1955, JMBRAS, Vol. 28(1)

Wheatley P: Geographical Notes on Some Commodities Involved in Sung Maritime Trade, 1959, JMBRAS, Vol. 32

Wheatley P: The Golden Khersonese, 1961, reprinted 1966, University of Malaya Press, Kuala Lumpur

Wheatley P: Impressions of the Malay Peninsula in Ancient Times, 1964, EUP, Singapore

Wild A: The East India Company, Trade and Conquest from 1600, 1999, Harper Collins, London

Wilkinson RJ: Early Indian Influence in Malaysia, 1935, JMBRAS, Vol. 13(2)

Winstedt R: A History of Malaya, 1935, Luzac and Co. , London, reprinted 1935, JMBRAS, Singapore

Winstedt R: Notes on the History of Keddah, 1936, JMBRAS, Vol. 14(3)

Winstedt R: Malaya and Its History, 1948, Hutchinson and Co. , London

Wright J: God's Soldiers, A History of the Jesuits, 2004, Doubleday, New York

Wurms S: Atlas of Intercultural Communication in the Pacific and Asia, 1996, de Gruyter, Berlin

Wurtzburg CE: see Light F

Wyatt DK: The Politics of Reform in Thailand, 1969, Yale University Press, New Haven, Connecticut

Wyatt DK: The Crystal Sands: The Chronicles of Nagara Sri Dharmaraja, 1975, Ithaca, New York

Wyatt DK: Thailand – A Short History, 1982, Yale University Press, New Haven, Connecticut

Wyatt DK: Mainland Powers in the Malay Peninsula, in DK Wyatt, Studies in Thai History, 1999, University of Washington Press, Seattle

Wyatt DK: Siam In Mind, 2002, Silkworm Books, Chiang Mai

Yahaya AB: South of Ayudhya: International Rivalries in the Malayan Waters A. D. 1611-1641, 2002, History Department Publication, National University of Malaysia

Yip HH: The Development of the Tin Mining Industry of Malaya, 1969, University of Malaya Press, Kuala Lumpur

Young E: The Kingdom of the Yellow Robe, 1898, Constable, reprinted 1983, OUP, Australia

Yule H: Cathay and the Way Thither (4 vols), 1866, Cambridge Library – Hakluyt first series, reprinted 2010, CUP, Cambridge

Zhou Daguan: A Record of Cambodia: The Land and Its People, translated, with an introduction and notes, by Peter Harris, 2007, Silkworm Books, Chiang Mai. (See also Chou Ta Kwan 1902 and Tchou Ta Kwan 1902)

End Notes

Notes to Chapter 1

1   Cited in Wheatley, 1964, 14
2   Pomchai Sujit, 1985, 227 – cited in Chinakorn, 2001
3   Burke, 1905, 184 – cited in Gerini, 1905, appendix
4   Sheehan, 1934, JM-BRAS Vol. 12, 104
5   Cited in Gerini, 1905, 36
6   Forrest, 1792, 29-36 – cited in Gerini, 1905, 61-75

Notes to Chapter 2

7   Rig Veda, Book 1. 56, 2 (see: www.sacred-texts.com/hin/rigvedarv01057. htm)
8   Khan, 1958 and Logan, 1849
9   Logan, 1849, 3-12
10 Khan, 1958, 9-12
11 Ibid
12 Wheatley, 1964, 32
13 Op cit, 32 or see Tawney, 1880
14 Singhal, 1972, 25.
15 Bradell, 1947, 15, 24
16 Tchou Ta Kuan,1902 (see also Zhou Daguan 2007)
17 Turner, 2004, 57, The Lay of the Anklet
18 Bradell, 1947, 13
19 Yule, 2010, Vol. 1, 18
20 Stevenson, 1932, book 7, 158
21 Pliny the Elder, Natural History, 12, 84 – cited in Parkin and Pomeroy, 2007, 289
22 Raschke, 1978, 605

Notes to Chapter 3

23 Legge, 1886, 42-43 – cited in Wheatley, 1961, 38
24 Wheatley, 1964, 79
25 Wheatley, 1964, 42
26 Gerini, 1905, 137
27 Boullay – cited in Smithies, 1995, 60
28 Reid, 1995, 57
29 Smithies, 1993, 115
30 Reid, 1995, 115
31 Van der Cruysse, 2002, 143
32 Smithies, 1993, 116
33 Smithies, 1995, 63
34 Van der Cruysse, 2002, 142
35 Wheatley, 1954

Notes to Chapter 4

36 Liang Shu, ch. 54, 6, cited in Purcell 1951
37 Coedes, 1968, 42
38 Coedes, 1944, 62
39 Devahuti, 1965, 19
40 Wales, 1951, 22
41 Wheatley, 1961, 22
42 Op cit, 18
43 Munro-Hay, 2004, 27
44 Ibid
45 Op cit, 28
46 Coedes, 1944, 63
47 Wheatley, 1961, 217
48 Op cit, 218
49 Wheatley 1961, 219
50 Burton, 1885
51 Ibid
52 Ibid

Notes to Chapter 5

53 Wilkinson, 1935, 8
54 Wheatley, 1961, 298
55 Winstedt, 1935, 37
56 I Tsing, 1896 – see the Takakusu translation, 2005
57 Ibid
58 Wheatley, 1961, 292
59 Coedes, 1944, 68
60 Op cit, 65
61 Coedes, 1944, 65
62 Ibid
63 Ibn Al Faqih, 903, 1
64 Chinakorn, 2001, 32
65 Ibid
66 Wheatley, 1964, 89-92
67 Ibid
68 See Luce 1958, 1959 and 1971, for further information
69 See Wyatt 1975 and 1999 for further information and, for a Sri Lankan and a Burmese view on this period, see Aung Thwin 1976 and Sirisena 1978 respectively
70 Hall, 1987, 169

Notes to Chapter 6

71 Wheatley, 1961, 61
72 Farrington, 2007, 29
73 Personal communica-tion, T. Bikul, director of National History Museum of Nakorn Sri Thammarat
74 Munro-Hay, 2004, 67
75 Op cit, 68

Notes to Chapter 7

76   Zhou Daguan, 2007
77 Jumsai, 2000, 102. See Zhou Daguan 2007 for the

most recent translation

78 Kasetsiri, 1976
79 Wade, Ming Shi Luan, Book 325

Notes to Chapter 8

87 Bowring, 1857, 46
88 Van der Cruysse, 2002, 412
89 Swettenham – cited in Braddell, 1947,19
90 Hall, 1974, 55
91 Suwannathat-Pian, 1988, 11
92 Forrest, 1792, 29-36
93 Cushman and Milner, 1979, 16
94 Mouhot, 1864
95 Breazeale, 2009, 183
96 Wheatley, 1961, 217
97 Van Nijenrode, 1621, 279-318
98 Farrington, 2007, 25
99 Pinto, 1614
100 De La Loubère, 1693, 91
101 Coen, 1615 – cited in Reid, 1988, 122
102 Earl, 1837, 141
103 Ibrahim, 1688, 90 – cited in Reid, 1988, 123
104 Hall, 1974, 55
105 Mabbet, 1971, 54
106 Artieda, 1573 – cited in Reid, 1988, 125
107 De La Loubère, 1693, 90
108 Matelief, 1608 – cited in Reid, 1988, 122
109 Anderson, 1826, 275 – cited in Reid, 1988, 124
110 Pires, 1515 – cited in Reid, 1988,125
111 Hwang Chung, 1537, 128 – cited in Reid, 1988, 129
112 De Morga, 1609, 274
113 Bowring, 1857, 191 – cited in Bowie, 2006, 4
114 Alabaster, 1890, 447 – cited in Bowie, 2006, 12
115 Ibrahim, 1972, 131
116 Galvão, 1544, 126 – cited in Reid, 1988
117 Bowring, 1857, 193
118 Bock, 1884 – cited in Bowie, 2006, 4
119 Pallegoix, 1854, 118

80 Rockhill, 1915
81 Polo, trans Latham, 1958, 25
82 Pires, 1515, trans Cortesao
83 Marrison, 1949, 61

120 Bastin and Winks, 1966, 225
121 Mouhot, 1864 – cited in Bacon, 1893, 238
122 Galvão, 1544, 89 – cited in Reid, 1988, 146
123 Pires, 1515, 267 – cited in Reid, 1988, 147
124 De Morga 1609, 275
125 Ibn Majid, 1492 – cited in Reid, 1988, 155
126 Ma Huan, 1997
127 Earl, 1837,169
128 Hamilton, 1727, 96
129 Purcell, 1951, 14
130 Tchou Ta Kuan, 1902, Vol. II, 2 (see also Zhou Daguan 2007 for a more recent translation)
131 Pinto, 1614
132 Raffles, 1815, 318 – cited in Reid, 1988, 148
133 Sejarah Melayu, 1612, 78
134 Reid, 1988, 153
135 Ibid
136 Fernberger, 1624 – see Bangkokpattaya. blogspot. com/2009/prostitution-in-thailand-historical. html
137 Morgenthaler, 1921, 102
138 Hamilton – cited in James, 1997, 211
139 Ma Huan, 1433, 104
140 Reid, 1988, 150
141 Pires, 1515 – cited in Reid, 1988, 102
142 Herbert, 1638
143 Gervaise – cited in Smithies, 1995, 38
144 Ibid
145 Neale, 1852, 153
146 Roberts, 1837
147 Pallegoix, 1854, 73
148 Guehler, 1959, 18
149 Beckman, 1718, 41
150 Reid, 1988, 155
151 Gervaise, 1688, 25

84 Op cit, 63
85 Ibid
86 Sejarah Melayu, 1970, Chapter 8-1

152 Van Neck, 1604, 225 – cited in Reid, 1988
153 Roberts, 1837
154 Wolseley, 1858 – cited in James, 1997, 221
155 Scott, 1606, 176 – cited in Reid, 1988,156
156 Reid, 1988, 156
157 Na Pombejra, 1992, 55
158 Ibn Majid, 1462, 206 – cited Reid 1988, 155
159 Ibrahim, 1688,136 – cited in Reid 1988
160 Na Pombejra, 1992, 28
161 Young, 1898, 124
162 Albuquerque, 1557, 61
163 Pallegoix, 1854, 224
164 Reid, 1988,165
165 Bacon, 1893, 247-8
166 Gervaise, 1688, 45-47
167 Reid, 1988, 139
168 De La Loubère, 1693, 87
169 Cushman and Milner, 1979, 18
170 Breazeale, 2009, 182
171 Anderson, 1824, Appendix, 54
172 Van der Cruysse, 2002, 235
173 Reid, 1988, 141
174 Van der Cruysse, 2002, 26
175 Op cit, 32
176 Anderson, 1889,106
177 Op cit, 31
178 Van der Cruysse, 2002, 450
179 Thompson, 1906, 284-7
180 Cited in Bacon, 1893, 237
181 Op cit, 242
182 Ibrahim, 1972, 157
183 Breazeale, 2009, 183
184 Young, 1898, 150
185 Pallegoix, 1854, 123
186 Swettenham, 1942, 17-18
187 De La Loubère, 1693
188 Pallegoix, 1854, 110-111
189 Gervaise, 1688, 24
190 Breazeale, 2009, 181
191 Pallegoix, 1854, 103-104

192 De Bourges, 1666, 146
193 Thompson – cited in Alatas, 1977
194 Morgenthaler, 1921,100
195 Bowring, 1857, 467
196 Srisudravarna, 1987, 54
197 Breazeale, 2009, 186

Notes to Chapter 9

208 Parry, 1949, 36
209 Turner, 2005, 108
210 Op cit, 195
211 Flaubert, 1856 – cited in Turner, 2005, 227
212 Op cit, 100
213 Da Gama, 1898, 77
214 Op cit, 87
215 Turner, 2005, 22
216 Da Gama, 1898, 77
217 Correa, 1869, 312
218 Ibid
219 Op cit, 331
220 Standage, 2005, 92
221 Correa, 1869, 311
222 Guehler, 1959, 18

Notes to Chapter 10

249 Pinto, 1614, 31-34

Notes to Chapter 11

251 Fitch – cited in Gerini, 1905, 35
252 Winstedt, 1935, 100
253 Ibid
254 Op cit, 101
255 Gerini, 1905, 36
256 Winstedt, 1935, 100
257 Op cit, 102
258 Hakluyt, see: www.columbia.edu/itc/mealac/pritchettoogenerallinks/kerr/vol07chap09sect06.html
259 Ferguson, 1903, 330

Notes to Chapter 12

282 See www. ukcia. org/research/abel/5. php
283 Bowrey,1679 – cited in Na Pombejra, 2002
284 Op cit, 92
285 Op cit, 94
286 Op cit, 92
287 Ibid
288 Op cit, 96

198 Op cit, 196
199 Koenig – cited in Gerini, 1905, 50
200 Op cit, 51
201 Bowrey, 1905, 248
202 Ibid
203 Koenig – cited in

223 Sejarah Melayu – cited in Reid, 2000, 162
224 Pires, 1515, 256
225 Winstedt, 1935, 69
226 Albuquerque, 1557, Vol. 3, 127
227 Ibid
228 Galvano (Galvão), 1862, 113
229 Ibid
230 Op cit, 112
231 Pires, 1515, 106
232 Op cit, 107
233 Scammell, 1980, 143
234 Winstedt, 1935, 79
235 Barbosa, 1518, Vol. II, 109
236 Pires, 1515, 109

250 Pinto, 1614, 40-45

260 Winstedt, 1935, 102
261 Van Linschoten, 1598, 102-103.
262 Van Linschoten, 1598, cited in Yahaya, 2002, 95
263 Van Linschoten,1598, 104
264 Munro-Hay, 2004,137
265 Van der Cruysse, 2002, 34
266 Winstedt, 1948, 49
267 Munro-Hay, 2004, 361
268 Lewis, 1995, 15
269 Ibid
270 Stone, 1966, 55

289 Op cit, 93
290 Op cit, 95
291 Gerini, 1905, 45
292 Ibrahim, 1972, 68
293 Cushman and Milner, 1979, 33
294 Ibid
295 Na Pombejra 1992, 123
296 Winstedt, 1935, 85

Gerini, 1905, 50
204 Forrest, 1792 – cited in Smithies, 1995, 108
205 Suwannathat-Pian, 1988, 39
206 Srisudravarna, 1987, 54
207 Suwannathat-Pian, 1988, 104

237 Ibid
238 Ibid
239 Smithies, 1997, 66
240 Pinto, 1614, 146
241 Kleinen and Ossweijer, 2010, 21
242 Pinto, 1614
243 Pinto, 1614, 31, Munro-Hay, 2004, 131
244 Hyam, 1991
245 Scammell, 1980, 148
246 Leider, 2002, 43
247 Manrique – cited in Leider, 2002, 44
248 Ibid

271 Ibid
272 Morson, 1993a, 23
273 Winstedt, 1935, 105
274 Anderson, 1889, 50
275 Winstedt, 1935, 87
276 Reid, 1988, 156
277 Blankwaart, 1926, 8
278 Anderson, 1889, 74
279 Hutchinson, 1985, 33
280 Op cit, 34
281 Tarling, 2001, 37

297 Op cit, 79
298 Anderson, 1824, 53
299 Op cit, 54
300 Cushman and Milner, 1979, 19 and 33
301 Crawford, 1822, 452
302 Na Pombejra, 2002, 93
303 Ibrahim, 1972, 95
304 Van Vliet, 1647, 35

305 Op cit, 37
306 Op cit, 38
307 Op cit, 43
308 Op cit, 44
309 Op cit, 43
310 Op cit, 45

311 Op cit, 46
312 Op cit, 48
313 Ibid
314 Op cit, 49
315 Ibid
316 Ibid

317 Munro-Hay, 2004, 147
318 Op cit, 161
319 Op cit, 367
320 Na Pombejra, 2002, 128
321 Smithies, 1998, 20

Notes to Chapter 13

322 Stone, 1966, 65
323 Smith, 1980, 12
324 Lewis, 1995, 23
325 Blagden, 1927, 125
326 Stone, 1966, 61
327 Dampier, 1697, Vol. 2, 88
328 Light, 1938, 119
329 Stone, 1966, 65,
330 Munro-Hay, 2004, 148
331 Wild, 1999, 132
332 Boxer, 1977
333 Wild, 1999
334 Munro-Hay, 2004, 358

335 Op cit, 150
336 Sayamanda, 1972, 73
337 Na Pombejra, 2002, 109
338 Op cit, 105
339 Munro-Hay, 2004, 149
340 Op cit, 369
341 Na Pombejra, 2002, 110
342 Winstedt, 1948, 131
343 Na Pombejra, 2002, 110
344 Ibid
345 Ibid
346 Op cit, 111
347 Ibid

348 Ibid
349 Op cit, 112
350 Ibid
351 Ibid
352 Op cit, 117
353 Munro-Hay, 2004, 165
354 Na Pombejra, 2002, 111
355 Ibid
356 Light , 1938, , 119
357 Osborn, 1857, 87-88
358 Lewis, 1995, 125
359 Boxer, 1977, 84

Notes to Chapter 14

360 All quoted material in
   this chapter comes from

Bowrey, 1679 – cited in Na
Pombejra, 1992, 115-18

Notes to Chapter 15

361 Breazeale, 1999, 107
362 Smithies, 1993, 121
363 Van der Cruysse, 2002, 131
364 Op cit, 138 and146
365 Baudiment, 1934, 27 – cited
   in Smithies, 2002, 31
366 Smithies, 2002, 104
367 Gerini, 1905, 40
368 Na Pombejra, 2002, 120
369 Smithies, 1998, 20
370 Ibid
371 Op cit, 23
372 Op cit, 26
373 Na Pombejra, 2002, 12
374 De La Loubère – cited in
   Munro-Hay, 2004, 265
375 Gerini, 1905, 41
376 Na Pombejra, 2002, 94

377 De Choisey, 1993, 98
378 Hutchinson, 1985, 156
379 Smithies, 1998, 39
380 Ibid
381 Op cit, 57
382 Ibid
383 Ibid
384 De Lionne, 1687 – cited
   in Hutchinson, 1985, 166
385 De Lionne, 1687, 91
386 Le Blanc, 1692, 84-87
387 Smithies, 1998, 131
388 Op cit,102
389 Op cit, 82
390 Op cit, 83
391 Ibid
392 Le Blanc, 1692, 148
393 Op cit, 149

394 Ibid
395 Smithies, 1998, 35
396 Le Blanc, 1692, 150
397 Op cit, 151
398 Ibid
399 Op cit, 152
400 Van der Cruysse, 2002, 463
401 Smithies, 1998, 114
402 Op cit, 119
403 Hutchinson, 1985, 182
404 Smithies, 1998, 118
405 Ibid
406 Op cit, 119
407 Ibid
408 Na Pombejra, 2002, 122
409 Hutchinson, 1985, 190

Notes to Chapter 16

410 Van der Cruysse, 2002,
   473
411 Smithies, 1998,118
412 Munro-Hay, 2004, 161
413 Gerini, 1905, 131
414 Op cit, 132
415 Breazeale, 2009, 192 and

   194
416 Purcell, 1956, 3
417 Basset, 1990, 43
418 Breazeale, 2009, 92
419 Hamilton, 1997, 46
420 Op cit, 47
421 Op cit, 43

422 Op cit, 52
423 Breazeale, 2009, 180
424 Op cit, 182-3
425 Op cit, 187
426 Op cit, 195
427 Op cit, 192
428 Anderson, 1824, 63

429 Begbie,1834, 436
430 Breazeale, 2009, 188
431 Op cit, 185
432 Gerini, 1905, 61

433 Op cit, 69
434 Op cit, 68
435 Hamilton, 1997, 173-179
436 Ibid

437 Ibid
438 Ibid
439 Ibid

Notes to Chapter 17

440 Milton, 1999, 116-119
441 Ibid
442 Ibid
443 Forrest, 1792 – cited in
    Gerini, 1905, 63
444 Anderson, 1824, Appendix
    53
445 Farrington, 2007, 50
446 Gerini, 1905, 49-50
447 Bastin, 1959, 11
448 Wheatley, 1961, 226
449 Bowrey, 1993, 268
450 Gullick, 1995, 119
451 Light, 1938, 120
452 Keppel, 1991, Vol. 1, 192-

201
453 Warren, 1985, 158
454 Keppel, 1991, Vol. 1, 196
455 Mills, 1966, 253
456 Ross, 1911, 26-33
457 Ibid
458 Warren, 1985, 239
459 Ibid
460 Ibid
461 Gerini, 1905, 54
462 Warren, 1985, 240
463 Ibid
464 Ibid
465 Op cit, 241
466 Ibid

467 Op cit, 241-242
468 Op cit, 241
469 Hunter, 1905, 60
470 Warren, 1985, 250
471 Mills, 1966, 252
472 Farrington, 2007, 63
473 Op cit, 45
474 Op cit, 45-46
475 Mills, 1966, 257
476 Op cit, 266
477 Op cit, 275
478 Templar, 1853, Vol. 2, 110
479 Suwannathat-Pian, 1988,
    99
480 Mills, 1966, 277

Notes to Chapter 18

481 Turpin 1771, 168 cited
    in Chutintaranond and
    Than Tun, 1995, 7
482 Jumsai, 2000, 352
483 Simmonds, 1963, 1
484 Anderson, 1824, Ap-
    pendix 68
485 Gerini, 1905, 55

486 Anderson, 1824, Ap-
    pendix 63
487 Ibid
488 Gerini, 1905, 132
489 Ibid
490 Clodd, 1948, 25
491 Ibid
492 Morson, 1993, 24 and

text of a Malay display
note at the Penang
History Museum
493 Gerini, 1905, 56
494 Launay, 1920, 301
495 Jumsai, 2000, 400
496 Op cit, 405

Notes to Chapter 19

497 Simmonds, 1965, 217
498 Simmonds, 1963, 604
499 Gerini, 1905, 64
500 Ibid
501 This is the version of this
    story as told in the annual
    heroines re-enactment play

staged at the Phuket History
Park in Thalang, Phuket
502 Simmonds, 1963, 602
503 Op cit, 598
504 Anderson, 1824, 129
505 Gerini, 1905, 73
506 Simmonds, 1963, 600

507 Op cit, 598
508 Op cit, 608
509 Op cit, 602
510 Op cit, 603
511 Ibid

Notes to Chapter 20

512 Simmonds, 1963, 596
513 Gerini, 1905, 49
514 Op cit, 52
515 Bulley, 1992, 107
516 Fielding, 1955, 39
517 Anderson, 1824, Ap-
    pendix 50
518 Gerini 1905, 63
519 Ibid
520 Monkton – cited in
    Morson, 1993, 24
521 Simmonds, 1963, 612

522 Clodd, 1948, 31
523 Simmonds, 1963, 594
524 Gerini 1905, 184
525 Anderson, 1824, Ap-
    pendix 53
526 Simmonds, 1965, 222
527 Op cit, 226
528 Ibid
529 Op cit, 225
530 Op cit, 222
531 Ibid
532 Anderson, 1824, Ap-

pendix 50
533 Ibid
534 Op cit, 21
535 Op cit, 58-60
536 Ibid
537 Op cit, 58
538 Op cit, 66
539 Clodd, 1948, 31
540 Simmonds, 1963, 600
541 Anderson, 1824, Ap-
    pendix 69-70
542 Op cit, 59-60

543 Clodd, 1948, 29
544 Light letters – cited in Morson, 1993, 24
545 Op cit, 25-26
546 Anderson, 1824, 64
547 Gerini, 1905, 69
548 Anderson, 1824, 131
549 Anderson, 1824, Appendix 60, "Letter from Scott"
550 Op cit, Appendix 61
551 Ibid
552 Op cit, 64-65
553 Op cit, 59

554 Gerini, 1905, 53
555 Simmonds, 1965, 215
556 Simmonds, 1963, 594
557 Ibid, 607
558 Clodd, 1948, 31-32
559 Anderson, 1824, 129
560 Ibid
561 Anderson, 1962, 133
562 Simmonds, 1965, 597
563 Op cit, 598
564 Simmonds, 1963, 601
565 Op cit
566 Op cit, 601

567 Ibid
568 Clodd, 1948, 39
569 Simmonds, 1963, 605
570 Ibid
571 Op cit, 606
572 Ibid
573 Op cit, 604
574 Op cit, 608
575 Morson, 1993, 113
576 Ibid
577 Skinner, 1984, 91
578 Ibid

Notes to Chapter 21

579 Gerini, 1905, 169

580 Op cit, 135

581 Ibid

Notes to Chapter 22

582 Sangermano, 1969, 62
583 Op cit, 93
584 Skinner, 1984, 66
585 Op cit, 65
586 Op cit, 67
587 Ibid
588 Ibid
589 Op cit, 68
590 Gerini, 1905, 87
591 Skinner, 1984, 68
592 Ibid
593 Op cit, 10
594 Skinner, 1985, 135
595 Jumsai, 2000, 441
596 Op cit, 442

597 Fortescue, 1923, 289 – cited in Skinner, 1985, 13
598 Havelock, 1828, 73 – cited in Skinner, 1985, 13
599 Skinner, 1985, 71
600 Skinner, 1984, 70
601 Skinner, 1985, 103
602 Op cit, 105-113
603 Ibid
604 Skinner, 1984, 91
605 Skinner, 1985, 131-135
606 Ibid
607 Op cit, 129
608 Jumsai, 2000, 442
609 Skinner, 1984, 68

610 Parker, 1893a, 12
611 Skinner, 1985, 137
612 Op cit, 137 and 147
613 Op cit
614 Op cit, 189
615 Op cit, 139
616 Op cit, 159
617 Op cit, 69
618 Op cit, 163
619 Op cit, 187- 202
620 Op cit, 205
621 Skinner,1984, 71
622 Ibid
623 Op cit, 72

Notes to Chapter 23

624 Skinner, 1985, 241-244
625 Winstedt, 1935, 170
626 Farrington, 2007, 7 and 30
627 Hall, 1974, 22
628 Gerini, 1905, 96-97

629 Suwannathat-Pi-an, 1988, 113
630 Op cit, 81
631 Begbie, 1834, 105
632 Anderson, 1824,

8-9 and 16-17
633 Osborn, 1857, 190-193
634 Anderson, 1824, 9
635 Op cit, 6-7

Notes to Chapter 24

636 Anderson, 1824, 132-133
637 Mills, 1966, 159
638 Op cit, 156
639 Rubin, 1974, Chapters 8 and 11
640 Op cit, Chapters 8 and 12
641 Crawfurd, 1821, 23-24
642 Mills, 1966, 160
643 Crawfurd, 1822, 8
644 Op cit, 9
Notes to Chapter 25
645 Farrington, 2007, 81

646 Rubin, 1974, Chapters 8 and 20
647 Farrington, 2007, 90
648 Op cit, 25
649 Op cit, 26
650 Op cit, 60
651 Op cit, 11
652 Op cit, 31
653 Op cit, 54
654 Op cit, 55
655 Op cit, 54
656 Ibid

657 Ibid
658 Op cit, 27
659 Op cit, 28
660 Op cit, 28 and 29
661 Op cit, 32
662 Op cit, 30
663 Op cit, 31
664 Op cit, 32
665 Ibid, 32
666 Op cit, 37
667 Op cit, 36
668 Op cit, 37

669 Anderson, 1824, 137
670 Farrington, 2007, 42

Notes to Chapter 26

674 Burney, 1915, Vol. 2, 23
675 Low – cited in Munro-Hay, 2004, 204
676 Hall, 1974, 65
677 Burney, 1915, Vol. 2, 24
678 Crawford,1822, 418
679 Hall, 1974 151
680 Op cit, 26
681 Burney,1915,Vol. 2, 20
682 Hall,1974, 40
683 Bowie, 2006, 21-22

Notes to Chapter 27

702 See Thalang History Museum display, Phuket
703 Farrington, 2007, 42
704 Op cit, 35
705 Cushman and

Notes to Chapter 28

707 Gerini, 1905, 108-109
708 Op cit, 110
709 Op cit, 113

Notes to Chapter 29

714 Tarling, 2001, 49
715 Bruce, 1969, 3
716 Vella, 1957, 139
717 Brooke to Palmerston: FO 69/1, Oct. 5, 1850, FO Records
718 Roberts – cited in Martin, 1948, 22
719 Dhiravegin, 1973, 11
720 Wyatt, 1982, 165 (quoting from The Royal Chronicles of Ayutthaya – see Cushman 2006 for the

Notes to Chapter 30

737 Miller, 1965, 82
738 Dhiravegin, 1973, 22
739 Op cit, 17
740 Curzon, 1893, 53
741 Op cit, 50
742 Jeshrun, 1970, 110
743 Op cit, 111
744 Op cit, 117
745 Curzon, 1893, 54
746 Op cit, 53

671 Op cit, 49
672 Op cit, 104

684 Op cit, 22
685 Burney, 1915, Vol. 1, 200
686 Op cit, Vol. 1, 54
687 Hall, 1974, 43
688 Suwannathat-Pian, 1988, 87
689 Hall, 1974, 81
690 Burney, 1915, Vol. 1, 170
691 Op cit, Vol. 2, 65
692 Hall, 1974, 52
693 Burney,1915, Vol. 1, 92
694 The Burney Treaty,

Milner, 1979, 33
706 For further information contact Mr. Beattie who is now part of the Tan family and has con-

710 Op cit, 113-115
711 Osborn, 1857, 218-220
712 Munro-Hay, 2004, 217

definitive synoptic translation of the Chronicles)
721 Phraklang to Brooke: FO 69/3, April 23, 1851, FO Records
722 Tarling, 1993, 98-99
723 Bowring, 1857, 243
724 Tarling, 1993, 177
725 Op cit, 188
726 King Chulalongkorn to Prince Damrong, 1903 – cited in Suwannathat-Pian 1988, 90

747 Jeshrun, 1970, 119,
748 Op cit, 2 (Jan. 8, 1996)
749 Op cit, 16
750 Aldrich, 1993, 77
751 Swettenham,1907, 328
752 Ibid
753 Cushman, 1991, 44
754 Op cit, 46
755 Ibid
756 Marks, 2007, 29-30

673 Op cit, 84

Article 10, in Burney, 1915, Appendix
695 Hall, 1974, 57
696 Burney, 1915, Vol. 2, 71-72
697 Hall, 1974, 63
698 Burney, 1915, Vol. 1, 100
699 Op cit, Vol. 1, 99
700 Op cit, Vol. 2, 74
701 Ibid

ducted his own private research on the family: A.beatie@gws.edu.au

713 Quoted in Suwannathat-Pian, 1988, 87

727 Bowring, 1857, 226
728 Tarling, 1993, 176
729 Ibid
730 Van der Cruysse, 2002, 27
731 Jumsai, 2000, 484
732 Op cit, 499
733 Wyatt, 1969, 256
734 Jumsai, 2000, 514
735 Op cit, 489
736 Smith – cited in Dhiravegin, 1973, 24

757 Cushman, 1991, 46
758 Marks 1997, 26
759 Ibid
760 Op cit, 38
761 Ibid
762 Cushman, 1991, 47
763 Suwannathat-Pian, 1988, 108
764 Thamsook, 1966, 252
765 Wyatt, 1982, 192

Notes to Chapter 31

766 Landon, 1941, 1
767 Purcell, 1951, 26
768 Cushman and
   Milner, 1979, 41
769 Purcell, 1951, 94
770 Op cit, 99
771 Cushman and
   Milner, 1979, 19
772 Mills, 1966, 238
773 Newbold, 1839, 8
774 Swettenham, 1907, 232
775 Mills, 1966, 236
776 Smith, 1894, 165
777 Farrington, 2007, 50
778 Purcell, 1951, 97-98
779 Op cit, 100
780 Op cit, 94
781 Op cit, 27
782 Op cit, 29
783 Suyama, 1962, 193
784 Mills, 1966, 251
785 Bastin and Winks,
   1966, 173
786 Conrad, 1902
787 Smyth, 1994, 24
788 Cushman, 1991, 2

789 Purcell, 1951, 114
790 Mills, 1966, 240
791 Op cit, 247
792 Bastin and Winks,
   1966, 176
793 Smyth, 1994, 131
794 Op cit, 19
795 Purcell, 1951, 112
796 Morgenthaler,
   1921, 15 and 50
797 Smyth, 1994, 29
798 Gullick, 1956, 12-15
799 Smyth, 1994, 11
800 Purcell, 1951, 97
801 Gerini, 1905, 169-170
802 Kynnersley, 1904, 8
803 Young, 1898, 64
804 Kynnersley, 1904, 8
805 Op cit, 9
806 Ibid
807 Cushman, 1991, 38
808 Op cit, 34
809 Morgenthaler, 1921, 13
810 Cushman, 1991, 61
811 Smyth, 1994, 21
812 Cushman, 1991, 38

813 Phuketscape, Vol 2,
   Oct. 2008, 72
814 Cushman, 1991, 38
815 Op cit, 39
816 Phuketscape, Vol 2,
   Oct. 2008, 74
817 Cushman, 1991, 41
818 Phuketscape, Vol 2,
   Oct. 2008, 74
819 Op cit, 75
820 FO 422/12/8, Satow,
   June 20, 1885, cited in
   Cushman, 1991, 49
821 Kynnersley, 1904, 8
822 Thaitakoo, 1994, 139
823 Cushman, 1991, 69
824 Kynnersley, 1904, 8
825 Smyth, 1994, 19
826 Purcell, 1951, 244
827 Kynnersley, 1904, 9
828 Chin, 1980, 259
829 Op cit, 360
830 Khor and Khoo, 2004, 47
831 Op cit, 48
832 Purcell, 1951, 100
833 Cohen, 2001, 51

Notes to Chapter 32

834 Cushman, 1991, 11
835 Damrong, 1928, 19
836 Smyth, 1994, 27
837 Prince Damrong, quoted
   in Cushman, 1991, 31
838 Marks, 1997, 15
839 Smyth, 1994, 62-63
840 Cushman, 1991, 15
841 Ibid
842 Smyth, 1994, 12
843 Ibid
844 Op cit, 8-9
845 Cushman, 1991, 48
846 Op cit, 49
847 As told to the author by
   Assistant Professor Pranee

Sakulpipatana of Rachap-
rapat University, Phuket
848 Sakulpipatana and
   Khoo, 2008, 23
849 Cushman, 1991, 58
850 Further research remains
   to be done on the subject
   of James Scott's wives,
   children and descendants in
   both Phuket and Penang
851 Smyth, 1994, 18
852 Kynnersley, 1904
853 Penang Gazette, Jan
   17, 1903 – cited in
   Cushman, 1991, 69
854 Thaitakoo, 1994, 139

855 Cushman, 1991, 59
856 Op cit, 47
857 Op cit, 61
858 Op cit, 62
859 Ibid, 62
860 Ibid
861 Ibid
862 Ibid
863 Op cit, 47
864 Op cit, 63
865 Op cit, 84
866 Op cit, 80
867 Yip, 1969, 134
868 Manarungsan,
   1989, 149-154
869 Kornerup, 1928, 200

Notes to Chapter 33

870 Cushman, 1991, 91
871 Ibid
872 Ibid
873 Op cit, 92
874 Op cit, 92-93
875 Op cit, 89

876 Op cit, 94
877 Benedict, 1952, 12
878 Young, 1898, 156
879 Op cit, 157-158
880 Jumsai, 1978, 70
881 Personal communica-

tion to the author by
Pranee Sakulpipatana,
Phuket town, 2009
882 Manarungsan, 1989, 153
883 Morgenthaler, 1921, 13
884 Somerset Maugham,

see chulie. word-press. com/2008/08/10/maugham-miss-pretty-girl-cabbages-condoms

885 Kornerup, 1928, v
886 Op cit,158
887 Op cit, 158 and 132

888 Op cit, 181
889 Op cit, 159
890 Op cit,133
891 Op cit, 200
892 Op cit, 201
893 Op cit, 202
894 Op cit, 202 and 203

895 Op cit, 203
896 Op cit ,204
897 Ibid
898 Op cit, 203
899 Op cit, 204

Notes to Chapter 34

900 Manarungsan, 1989, 110
901 Kornerup, 1928, 132-133

902 Na Pombejra, 2002, 94
903 Bowring, 1857, 46

Notes to Chapter 35

904 Syamanda, 1972, 163
905 Op cit, 164
906 Translated from Satheun, 1971, 38
907 Suwannathat-Pian 1995, 1
908 Aldrich, 1993, 178
909 Suwannathat-Pian, 1995, 18
910 Op cit, 113
911 Op cit, 102

912 Op cit, 119
913 Op cit, 115
914 Ibid
915 Thompson, 1941, 114
916 Purcell, 1951
917 Op cit, 124
918 Op cit, 121
919 Op cit, 123
920 Op cit, 137
921 As recalled by Pranee

Sakulpipitana, former Assistant History Professor at Rajapat University, Phuket

922 Suwannathat-Pian, 1995, 146
923 Hussain , 1992, 7
924 Op cit, 133
925 Op cit, 130
926 Op cit, 102

Notes to Chapter 36

927 Swan, 2009, 113
928 Suwannathat-Pian, 1995, 247
929 Swan, 2009, 120
930 Crosby to FO, June 10, 1938, F668, cited in Mahmud, 1993, 84
931 Flood, 1967, 681-682
932 Crosby to FO, Septem-

ber 8,1939, F10320, cited in Mahmud, 1993, 85
933 Suwannathat-Pian, 1995, 247
934 The Act to preserve the duties of Thai people in times of hostilities BE 2482 (1941), cited in Mahmud, 1993, 118

935 Op cit, 97
936 Suwannathat-Pian, 1995, 263
937 Swan, 2009, 149
938 Op cit, 150
939 Ibid
940 Pramoj, 1943

Notes to Chapter 37

941 Tsuji, 1967, Chapter 1
942 See Geocities, "Thailand in the Second World War", Songkla page
943 Swan, 2009, 156
944 Murashima, 2002, 196
945 Op cit, see Prachuap Kiri Khan page
946 Op cit, see Patani page
947 Op cit, see Nakorn page
948 Pramoj, 1943, 3
949 Minutes of cabinet meeting cited in Swan, 2009, 290
950 Ibid
951 Op cit, 278
952 Suwannathat-Pian, 1995, 231
953 Aldrich, 1993, 341

954 Swan, 2009, 151
955 Op cit 299
956 Op cit, 289
957 Aldrich, 1993, 368
958 Owens, 2002, 68
959 Suwannathat-Pian, 1995, 263
960 Aldrich, 1993, 364
961 As told to the author by Khun Rachan Karnchanawit, former managing director of Tongkah Harbour Co. Ltd.
962 Phuketscape magazine, Vol. 2, March-May 2008, 41
963 Ibid
964 Quoted in Pramoj, 1943, 1
965 Syamanda, 1972, 173

966 Pramoj, 1943, 3
967 Op cit, 8
968 Haseman, 2002, 39
969 Reynolds, 2004 , 298
970 Op cit, 263
971 Phuket Gazette, July 15-21, 2006, 27
972 BBC, "WW2 People's War. An archive of World War Two memories", article by Ron Bowey, Article A4438703: www. bbc. co. uk/ww2peopleswar/stories/32/a4438703. shtml
973 See Fleet Air Arm Officers Association website at www. fleetairarmoa. org/pages/images_pages/page26.

htm, "Suicide of Japanese officers at Rengam"

974 See Wikipedia website, "Battle of the Malacca Straits"
975 Haseman, 2002, 118
976 AD LIB, magazine of No. 160 Squadron, quoting from Jones's account in J. M. Turner, The RAAF at War, see www. rquirk. com/no18. htm
977 See "The Loss of HMS Squirrel", p. 1, see http://www. deep-blue-divers. de/images_de/ spezial/squirrel. pdf
978 Op cit, 3
979 Chinakorn, 2001, 35 (in Thai)

980 Op cit, 35
981 BBC, "WW2 People's War. An archive of World War Two memories", article by George Coyne, "Aboard HMS Sussex (1945)", Article A1171432, see www. bbc. co. uk/ww2peopleswar/ stories/32/a1171432. shtml
982 See "The Loss of HMS Squirrel", p. 3, see http://www. deep-blue-divers. de/images_de/ spezial/squirrel. pdf
983 Ibid
984 Ibid
985 Op cit, 5
986 BBC, "WW2 People's War. An archive of World War Two memories", article by

George Coyne, "Aboard HMS Sussex (1945)", Article A1171432, see www. bbc. co. uk/ww2peopleswar/ stories/32/a1171432. shtml
987 As told to the authors friend in 1999 by a then elderly Chinese Phuket resident who said he was amongst those who met the British commandos at Laem Sing beach
988 BBC, "WW2 People's War. An archive of World War Two memories", article by George Coyne, "Aboard HMS Sussex (1945)", Article A1171432, see www. bbc. co. uk/ww2peopleswar/ stories/32/a1171432. shtml

Notes to Chapter 38

989 BBC, "WW2 People's War. An archive of World War Two memories", article by Frank Savage, Article A3839754 – see www. bbc. co. uk/ww2peopleswar/ stories/54/a3839754. shtml
990 Ibid
991 Ibid
992 Reynolds, 2004, 381
993 Op cit, 387

994 Op cit, 368
995 Aldrich, 1993, 372
996 Reynolds, 2004, 402
997 As told to the author in 2008 by Rachan Karn-chanawit, former managing director of Tongkah Harbour Co. Ltd.
998 As told to the author by villagers in Kamala in 2001, relatives of the man

who shot the tiger and who is now deceased
999 Jumsai, 2000, 600
1000 Wyatt, 1982, 281
1001 Bangkok Post, January 30, 1984
1002 Sukul Na Nakorn in a private conversation with the author, 2009